FRONTIER AND OVERSEAS EXPEDITIONS FROM INDIA.

FRONTIER AND OVERSEAS EXPEDITIONS FROM INDIA

COMPILED IN THE INTELLIGENCE BRANCH

DIVISION OF THE CHIEF OF THE STAFF
ARMY HEAD QUARTERS

INDIA

VOL. III

BALUCHISTAN AND THE
FIRST AFGHAN WAR

The Naval & Military Press Ltd

Reproduced by kind permission of the Central Library,
Royal Military Academy, Sandhurst

Published by
The Naval & Military Press Ltd
Unit 10, Ridgewood Industrial Park,
Uckfield, East Sussex,
TN22 5QE England
Tel: +44 (0) 1825 749494
Fax: +44 (0) 1825 765701
www.naval-military-press.com
© The Naval & Military Press Ltd 2006

In reprinting in facsimile from the original, any imperfections are inevitably reproduced and the quality may fall short of modern type and cartographic standards.

Printed and bound by Antony Rowe Ltd, Eastbourne

NOTE.

A SHORT narrative of the First Afghan War has been added to this volume, as the main portion of the British Army invading Afghanistan during that war passed through Baluchistan, and the histories of the two countries at that period are thus closely connected.

CONTENTS.

PART I.

BALUCHISTAN.

CHAPTER I.

INTRODUCTORY AND GEOGRAPHICAL.

Introductory—Origin of name Baluchistan—Derajat—British Baluchistan—Baluchistan Agency Territories—Dera Ismail Khan—Dera Ghazi Khan—Administration of Native States—The forward policy—Independent tribes—Boundaries—Scenery—Physical features—Mountain ranges—Sulimans—Toba Kakar—Khojak and other passes—Central Brahui range—Kirthar and Pab ranges—Makran—Kharan—Chagai—Rivers—Lakes—Coast line—Rainfall—Climate—Communications . . *Page.* 1—12

CHAPTER II.

HISTORY AND ETHNOGRAPHY.

Early history—Rise of the Brahuis—Sikhs arrive in Derajat, 1819—Treaty between Ranjit Singh and Shah Shuja—Tripartite Treaty, 1838—Edwardes in Derajat—Derajat affairs during Sikh War—Annexation 1849—Indigenous races—Distribution—Boundaries of Pathan and Baluch—Male population—Pathans—Kakars—Tarins—Panis—Other Pathan tribes—Origin of Baluchis and Brahuis—Baluchis—Baluch migration—Mani groups of Baluchis—Baluchis in Dera Ghazi and Dera Ismail Khan—Sulimans occupied by Baluchis—Brahui invasion—Brahuis—Sarawan—Jhalawan—Language—Education—Character of Pathan and Baluch—Result of British occupation—Appendix A: Showing genealogically main divisions, locality, etc., of Afghans in Baluchistan—Appendix B: Genealogical Tree showing connection of various Baluch Tribes . . . . 13—32

CHAPTER III.

KALAT.

Early history—Tribal service—Formation of Kalat State—Muhabbat Khan—Acquisition of Kachi—Nasir Khan I—Kalat constitution—Kalat in Nasir Khan's time—Mehrab Khan—Early intercourse with Kalat—Siege of Kalat—Subsequent affairs—Unrest in Kalat—Rebels sieze Kalat—Capture of Lieutenant Loveday—General Nott

VOL. III.

occupies Kalat—Action at Dadar—Murder of Lieutenant Loveday—Action at Kotra—Native account of the action—Colonel Stacy, special envoy to Kalat—Treaty with Kalat, 1841—Tribal affairs, 1840-41—John Jacob in Upper Sind—Methods of administration—Early arrangements on Sind Frontier—John Jacob and Kalat affairs—Treaty with Kalat, 1854—British Agent deputed to Kalat—Death of Nasir Khan II—Accession of Khudadad—Rebellious chief—Marris submit to the Khan—The Khan visits Makran—Khudadad deposed and reinstated—Sir Robert Sandeman—State of the Baluch Frontier, 1866—Harrand raid, 1867—The Sandeman system—The Mithankot conference—Frontier affairs, 1871-75 . . . . *Page.* 33—60

CHAPTER IV.

THE OCCUPATION OF QUETTA.

Sandeman's First Mission, 1875—Sandeman's Second Mission, 1876—Mastung Durbar—Treaty with Kalat, 1876—Quetta chosen as cantonment for escort—Sandeman appointed Agent, Governor-General, Baluchistan—Quetta occupied, 1877—Fanatical outrage—Conference with Pathan tribes, 1878—Affair at Haramzai—Our policy and its results—Extracts from the District Gazetteer—Acquisition of land—Soldiers' park and club . . . . 61—69

CHAPTER V.

EASTERN BALUCH TRIBES.

Gurchanis—Mazaris—Marris—Bugtis—Khosas—Legharis—Khetrans—First Expedition—Billamore's hill campaign, 1839—Kahan occupied by Captain Brown—Destruction of Lieutenant Clark's detachment—Nafussak Pass—Captain Brown surrenders Kahan—Bugtis' fatal raid, 1847—Raid on the Kasmor Post in 1849—Affairs subsequent to annexation of the Punjab—Raid by Marris and Gurchanis on the Asni plain, 1857—Raid on Harrand in 1867—Conduct of the Marris and Bugtis subsequent to 1871 . . . . . . 71—101

CHAPTER VI.

KASRANIS AND BOZDARS.

Expedition in 1853—1853-57—Bozdars—Expedition against the Bozdars in 1857—Terms of submission—Conduct of the tribes from 1861 to 1863—Lieutenant Grey kidnapped by Kasranis—Kasranis blockaded, 1863—Subsequent conduct of the tribes—Appendix A: Composition of force employed against Kasranis in April 1853—Appendix B: Composition of force employed against Bozdars in March 1857 . . 103—134.

CHAPTER VII.

THE BALUCHISTAN AGENCY.

Sibi and Pishin occupied—Treaty of Gandamak, 1879—The Baluchistan Agency—Events after the Treaty of Gandamak—Murder of Captain

CONTENTS. iii

Showers—Attack on Lieutenant Fuller's Camp—Panizai affairs—Achakzai affairs—Early history—Arambi Glen—Major Keene's moveable column—Unrest, 1880—General Baker's Expedition, 1880—Railway detachment escort attacked—Attack on Mal—Marris defeated by Major Douglas—Marri Expedition, 1880—Kahan reached—Submission of Marris—Settlement with Marris, 1881—Shorawak affairs—Affair at Sayyid Baz, 1879—Shorawak occupied, 1880—Shorawak evacuated, 1881—Southern Afghan Field Force evacuates Baluchistan, 1881—Thal Chotiali Field Force, 1878—Chari mountain—Affair at Baghao—Vitakri cantonment—Bozdar Field Force—Baluchistan subsequent to the Second Afghan War—Quetta leased, 1882—Tribal levies—Troops of Native States—Las Bela forces—Kharan forces—Khojak tunnel—Chaman—Las Bela, 1892—Death of Sir Robert Sandeman—Khudadad Khan deposed—Las Bela, 1896—Sarawan troubles, 1897—Jafir Khan—Arms traffic from Persian Gulf, 1907—Appendix A: Distribution of Quetta Division, 1881—Appendix B: Camel Transport in Baluchistan *Page.* 135—165

CHAPTER VIII.

SHIRANI AND USTARANA TRIBES.

Shiranis—Ustaranas—Expedition against the Shiranis in 1853—Conduct of Shiranis from 1853 to 1882—Blockade of the Shiranis in 1883—Survey Expedition to the Takht-i-Suliman mountain in 1883—Troops with the expedition—Affair near Pezai springs—Appendix: Composition of Shirani Expeditionary Force, 1853 . . . . 167—187

CHAPTER IX.

ZHOB AND BORI.

Zhob district—Jogizai family—Shah Jehan—Zhob Valley Expedition, 1884—Affair near Ali Khel—Destruction of forts and villages—Settlement with Zhobwals—Survey work—Withdrawal of expedition—Medical—Transport—Bori and Zhob Affairs, 1885-90—Loralai occupied—Gumbaz—Submission of Shah Jahan—Dost Muhammad and Banghal Khan—Mina Bazar—Apozai—Zhobis under British protection—The Gumal Pass—Shiranis troublesome—Fort Sandeman and Mir Ali Khel—Expedition against the Khidarzai Shiranis—The Zhob Field Force . . . . 189—210

CHAPTER X.

ZHOB AND SHIRANI AFFAIRS.

The Zhob Field Force—Affair at Draz and Zam—Domandi and Drazand occupied—Submission of the Khidarzais—Namar Kalan occupied—Ascent of the Takht-i-Suliman—Termination of the operations—Zhob affairs subsequent to 1890—Afghans in Zhob—Dost Muhammad and Bengal Khan—Shiranis—Mahsud Wazir Blockade—Administration of Zhob . . . . 211—239

CHAPTER XI.

MAKRAN.

History—Azad Khan—Sandeman's visit, 1884—Result of settlement—Second visit—Affairs in Kej—The Gichki Sirdars—The Khan visits Makran—The Khan's troops are introduced into Makran—The seeds of rebellion remain—Nazim Diwan Udho Das—Events that led to the expedition of 1898—Captain Burn's camp attacked—Despatch of troops to Makran—Loyalty of Sirdars—Arrival at Urmara—Concentration of troops at Karachi—Pasni chosen as base—The march from Pasni—Action of Gokh-Prusht—Demolition of Turbat and Charbuk forts—Expedition to Bolida—Demolition of Chib and Khushk forts—Expedition to Mand—Difficulties of transport—The Durbar—The last of the rebels—Return of the expedition—The Tump detachment—Pardon to rebel Sardars—Subsequent history of Makran—Muhammad Umar Khan—Border depredations—Tour of the Political Agent, 1891—Irafshan and Bampusht—Sib and Dizak—The Persian Sirtip's Army—The Sirtip—Bairam Khan—Operations in Makran, 1901-02—Capture of Nodiz Fort—Makran Levy . . . . *Page.* 241—237

PART II.

The First Afghan War.

CHRONOLOGICAL TABLE OF EVENTS.

CHAPTER XII.

AFGHANISTAN—THE COUNTRY AND PEOPLE.

Geographical position—Mountains—Rivers—Climate—Kabul—The Kabul-Peshawar road—The Khaibar Pass—Kabul to Ghazni—Ghazni to Kandahar—Kandahar—Herat—The people—Duranis—Ghilzais—Non-Afghan tribes—Nomad tribes—Early history—Invaders of India—The Durani Empire—Western designs on India . . . . 271—284

CHAPTER XIII.

BURNES' MISSION TO KABUL.

Burnes' mission to Kabul—Travels in Afghanistan—Despatch of the mission—Kandahar politics—Friendly disposition of the Amir—Viktevitch—Amir seeks mediation of England with Ranjit Singh—Departure of British and Russian missions from Kabul—Russian ascendancy—Siege of Herat—Arrival of Simonich—British action—Russian intrigues—Policy of the Indian Government—Macnaghten's mission to Lahore—The Tripartite Treaty—Military preparations—Political arrangements . . . . 285—302

CONTENTS.

CHAPTER XIV.

OCCUPATION OF AFGHANISTAN.

Assembling of the Army of the Indus—Line of march—The Sind Amirs—March of the Bengal Division—Surrender of Karachi—Arrival at Shikarpur—The Bolan Pass—Arrival at Quetta—Burnes' mission to Kalat—The Shah's and Bombay columns—Flight of the Kandahar Sirdars—Arrival at Kandahar—Herat after the siege—Dost Muhammad's difficulties—Capture of Ghazni—Dost Muhammad's opposition—Arrival at Kabul—Military problems—Arrival of Prince Timur—The garrison of Afghanistan—Departure of the troops—The outlook—Honours for the campaign—Contemporary politics—Russian designs—Macnaghten's anxieties—Internal affairs of Afghanistan—Expedition against the Ghilzais—Baluchistan . . . . 305—324

CHAPTER XV.

MILITARY OPERATIONS.

Operations round Bamian—Escape of Dost Muhammad from Bokhara—Turkistan—Attack on Bajgah—Engagement with Dost Muhammad at Bamian—Attack on Julgah—Anxiety at Kabul—Encounter with the Dost at Parwandarrah—Surrender of Dost Muhammad—Risings of the Duranis and Ghilzais—The British officials at Kandahar—The withdrawal of the mission from Herat—Aktar Khan—The Ghilzais—Action near Kalat-i-Ghilzai—Wymer's action at Assiyai—Ilmi—Akbar Khan's fight at the Helmund—Another action with Akbar Khan—Chambers' expedition against the Ghilzais—Expedition to Tarin and Dehrawat—Capture of Akram Khan—Situation at Kabul—The cantonment—The Political aspect—Attack on Monteith at Butkhak—Affair in the Khurd-Kabul—March to Gandamak . . . . 325—341

CHAPTER XVI.

THE OUTBREAK OF INSURRECTION.

Storm warnings—Murder of Burnes—Military measures—The rebellion spreads—The outposts—Capture of Muhammad Sharif's fort—Supplies—Political developments—Shelton comes into cantonments—Affair at the Rickabashi fort—Fight on the Bahmaru Hills—The disaster at Charikar—Macnaghten's recommendations—Second fight on the Bahmaru Hills—Akbar Khan's return—Distress of the garrison—Abandonment of Muhammad Sharif's fort—News from Jalalabad—Discussion of the treaty—Evacuation of the Bala Hissar—Preparations to leave Kabul—Murder of Macnaghten—The capitulation . . . . 343—367

CHAPTER XVII.
THE RETREAT FROM KABUL.

Sale's Brigade—Rear-guard action—Plan of defence—First fight at Jalalabad—Second engagement—News of the Kabul disaster—Orders for evacuation—Progress of the defences—Dr. Brydon's arrival—The retreat from Kabul . . . . 369—383

CHAPTER XVIII.
THE AVENGING ARMY.

Efforts at retrieval—The despatch of reinforcements—Brigadier Wild at Peshawar—Ali Masjid—Inadequacy of the force—The defence of Jalalabad—Situation at Jalalabad—The earthquake—The blockade—The forcing of the Khaibar—Arrival at Jamrud—Arrangements for the march—Action in the Khaibar—Occupation of Ali Masjid—Arrival at Jalalabad—Action at Jalalabad . . . . 385—402

CHAPTER XIX.
KANDAHAR.

Last days of Shah Shuja—The British prisoners—Death of Shah Shuja—Shah Shuja—Affairs at Kandahar—Massacre at Saiyidabad—Maclaren's brigade—Concentration at Kandahar—Mutiny of Janbay—Action on the Arghandab—Situation at Kandahar—Orders for evacuation—Action near Kandahar—Attack on Kandahar—Wymer's action near Kandahar—Capitulation of Ghazni . . . . 403—416

CHAPTER XX.
POLLOCK'S ADVANCE.

The question of withdrawal from Kandahar—Failure of England's column—Co-operation of Wymer with England—Government policy—Rawlinson's views—Pollock at Jalalabad—Affairs at Kabul—Akbar Khan captures the Bala Hissar—The advance from Jalalabad—Transport—Actions in the Shinwari valley—The prisoners—Action near Gandamak—Action of the Jagdalak Pass—March of the second division—Action of Tazin . . . . 417—435

CHAPTER XXI.
FINAL OPERATIONS.

The advance from Kandahar—Defence of Kalat-i-Ghilzai—Actions near Kandahar—Evacuation of Kandahar—Cavalry action—Action near Ghoyen—Action at Ghazni—Somnath gates—Action at Saiyidabad—Re-occupation of Kabul—Action at Istalif—The return march—Effect of the victories—Action of the Haft Kotal—M'Caskill's division—Rawlinson's review of Afghan affairs—Arrival at Ferozepore—Appendix I: Bengal and Bombay Armies—Appendix II: Composition of Force which returned from Kabul—Appendix III: Note on Defensive Works in Jalalabad.—Chronological Table of Events . . . 437—466

LIST OF MAPS.

General map of Baluchistan	In pocket.
The Bozdar country	,,
The Marri country	,,
The Shirani country	,,
General Map of Afghanistan	,,
Plan of Ghazni	To face page 314
Plan of Kabul	,, ,, 336

The General Map of Afghanistan, which is not yet ready, will be sent to all recipients of the book on publication.

PART I.

BALUCHISTAN.

BALUCHISTAN.

CHAPTER I.

INTRODUCTORY AND GEORGRAPHICAL.

Introductory. This volume deals with the country now known as Baluchistan and the Suliman Hills between that province and the Derajat.

The Gomal marks the northern boundary of the region, the Derajat and Sind the eastern, Persia and Afghanistan lie to the west of it, and on the south is the Arabian Sea.

Origin of name Baluchistan. The Baluchis have given their name to Baluchistan, but in reality that area contains comparatively few of the race. There are only 80,000 Baluchis in the country, whereas the census of the Sind and Punjab shows 950,000 in those provinces. The Brahuis are the most numerous people in Baluchistan, numbering 300,000; next come the Pathans with 200,000, and then the Baluchis.

Derajat. Derajat means the "country of camps," and was so called by the Sikhs after the "deras" of Ismail, Fath, and Ghazi Khan.

Military expeditions in this area have been few, and we have principally to deal with the history of the acquisition of a territory considerably larger than the British Isles,[1] and inhabited by several distinct races, speaking different languages—by means other than conquest. Certain districts were obtained by treaty, others taken over at the request of the inhabitants, and some are leased from the Khan of Kalat.

---

[1] Baluchistan and the Sulimans south of the Gomal have an approximate area of 135,000 square miles.

Baluchistan may be divided into British Baluchistan and the Baluchistan Agency (both administered by the Agent to the Governor-General).

British Baluchistan includes the territory ceded by the treaty of Gandamak in 1879, and formally declared part of British India in 1887.

British Baluchistan.

It comprises Sibi, Duki, Pishin, Shorarud, and Chaman—an area of 9,403 square miles. Also the "Administered Areas" of Thal, Chagai, and Loralai (except Duki)—an area of 36,401 square miles, and the territories leased from the Khan of Kalat, including Quetta, the Bolan, Nushki, and Nasirabad. From these territories the British authorities collect revenue.

The Baluchistan Agency includes the Native States of Kalat and Las Bela—79,382 square miles—and the "Tribal Area" of the Marris, Bugtis, and tribes east of the railway—an area of 7,129 square miles.

Baluchistan Agency Territories.

The administration of the Suliman Hill country east of Baluchistan is in the hands of the Punjab and North-West Frontier Province Governments. The Dera Ismail Khan district of the latter includes the semi-independent area of the Shiranis, whose affairs are administered by the Kulachi sub-division of the district.

Dera Ismail Khan.

The hill country south of this is included in the Dera Ghazi Khan district of the Punjab, and the tribal affairs are in the hands of the Deputy Commissioner of Dera Ghazi Khan.

Dera Ghazi Khan.

As regards Native States, Kalat is [1] now largely controlled by the Political Agent, whose services are lent by the British Government. A native official is lent to assist in the affairs of the Jhalawan country; he resides at Khuzdar. Makran is under the control of a Kalat official, known as the Nazim. The rest of the country is divided into *niabats*, administered by Kalat officials. Las Bela and Kharan have become practically independent of the Khan and are not subject to his interference. The chiefs of these States deal direct with the Political Agent, Kalat, whose headquarters are at Mastung.

Administration of Native States.

---

[1] 1907.

There was, until recently, a special political Agent for Southern Baluchistan and Las Bela. Now, however, the direct British influence in the State is exercised by the Wazir, an official appointed with the joint approval of the British authorities and the Jam of Las Bela.

The conquest of Sind in 1843 and annexation of the Punjab in 1849 advanced our North-West Frontier across the Indus to the hills bordering Afghanistan and Kalat. In this connection one feature is distinctly noticeable. Prior to the Tripartite Treaty of 1838 the district of Harrand Dajal—including the Gurchanis, Mazaris, and certain Marris—was claimed by the Khan of Kalat By that treaty Britain adjudicated this territory to the Sikhs. Ranjit Singh, however, never established his authority over it, and in 1849 we renounced our claim, and fixed our border so as to exclude those tribes. They thus became independent, owning allegiance neither to Sind, the Punjab, nor Kalat.

The Forward Policy.

Independent tribes.

North of Sibi and Peshin the Pathan tribes of Bori and Zhob were also to all intents and purposes independent, and the Baluch tribes of the Suliman were entirely so. It will be shown in this volume how this independent territory, as well as Kalat and certain Afghan districts, have gradually come under British control, the outcome of what is known as the "Forward Policy."

Lord Roberts explained in his memorable speech in 1898 that this "Forward Policy" is the policy of endeavouring to extend our influence over, and establish law and order in, that part of the Border where anarchy, murder, and robbery up to the present time have reigned supreme. Some forty years ago the "policy of non-interference" with the tribes, so long as they did not trouble us, may have been wise and prudent—though selfish, and not altogether worthy of a great civilising Power. During that time circumstances have completely changed, and what was wise and prudent then is most unwise and imprudent now. At that time Russia's nearest outpost was one thousand miles away; her presence in Asia was unheeded by, if not unknown to, the people of India; and we had no powerful reason for anxiety as to whether the two hundred thousand warriors on our Border would fight for us or against us.

To-day Russia is our near neighbour; her every movement is watched with the keenest interest from Peshawar to Cape Comorin; and the chance of her being able to attack us is discussed in every bazar in India.

For the defence of India it is evident that we must have command of the most important of the roads which run through the mountains on our frontier, and, to use a favourite expression of the Duke of Wellington, "we must be able to see the other side of the hill." Unless we know for certain what is going on there, it will be impossible to prevent an enemy from making use of the passes, and debouching on the plains of India when and where he pleases. Roads and railways cannot be made through a hostile country, and we should do all in our power to enter into closer relations with the tribes through whose lands the roads and railways would have to run.

In support of this statement Lord Roberts says:—

"Throughout the unusual frontier excitement of 1897 not a shot was fired in Baluchistan, which is under our control, and where our boundary has become practically coterminous with Afghanistan. . . . . . I trust you will not be persuaded to believe that the tribesmen—in the event of a foreign invasion—would fight for us, if left to themselves.

Why should they? They would have nothing to fear from us, and nothing to gain by siding with us, for we should have nothing to offer them in return. On the contrary, they would probably be induced to fight against us by the prestige which an advancing army always carries with it, and by promises—which would be freely given—that they should share in the plunder of the riches of India."

Boundaries. The eastern boundaries of this area have been arrived at by decisions of the Government of India for administrative purposes, and the reader is referred to the map. In 1887 it was decided that the Baluch tribes resident in the hills, who had sections of the tribe in the Derajat, should be administered by the Punjab Government. The Bozdars, although entirely resident in the hills, were also placed under Punjab administration, as their dealings were closer with the Derajat than with the Pathan tribes on their western border. All the other Baluch tribes of Baluchistan were included in the Baluchistan Agency.

With regard to other tribes on this border the Khetrans were included in Baluchistan, and the Shiranis were divided; the Bargha or Highland Shiranis going to Baluchistan; the Largha or Lowland Shiranis remaining under the jurisdiction of the Punjab.

The northern and western boundaries, however, were not so easily determined. The northern boundary gradually advanced from 1843, when it was that of Upper Sind, until 1881, when it was the northern limits of Pishin. By the acquisition of Zhob, it became coterminous with Afghanistan, and necessitated the Baluch-Afghan Boundary Commission of 1895-96, when Captain McMahon[1] brought to a successful conclusion the demarcation of the Durand Line from the Gomal to Koh-i-Malik-Siah.

Koh-i-Malik-Siah is the so-called tri-junction of British India, Afghanistan, and Persia. Southwards from this point to Kuhak a boundary line between Baluchistan and Persia was proposed by Sir Thomas Holdich in 1896, in consultation with a Persian Commissioner, but has not yet been demarcated. South of Kuhak to Gwattar Bay the Perso-Baluch boundary was settled by the Goldsmid Mission in 1871.

The country generally is barren, hill and vale alternating with stony plain. Thin lines of cultivation along the water-courses, and occasional tree-clad mountains alone relieve the monotony of this inhospitable land, which Sir Charles Napier described as "the place where God threw the rubbish when he made the world." There are, however, within the mountains narrow glens whose rippling water-courses are fringed in early summer by the brilliant green of carefully terraced fields. Rows of willows, with festoons of vines, border the clear water, and good crops of various kinds are raised.

Scenery.

The whole country is, as a rule, mountainous. From the west the mountains run in an easterly direction, gradually curving northwards, and, on approaching Sind, north and south.

Physical features.

The country slopes gradually from the Arabian Sea and Kharan to the elevated plateau which extends from Kalat to Hindubagh.[2] In this plateau are valleys varying in elevation from 4,500 to 7,000 feet, and mountains which reach 11,000 feet. From this tableland

---
[1] Now (1907) Sir Henry McMahon, Agent to the Governor-General in Baluchistan.
[2] Known locally as Khurasan.

the hills have again an eastern strike towards Zhob, and then diverge into two branches running north and south, descending southwards to Sibi and the Punjab Plains, and rising northwards to the Takht-i-Suliman.

There are, further, two level strips o country— as Bela and Kachi. These are both triangular in form, their apexes northwards bounded east and west by rugged hills. The people of each of these level strips differ in language from their highland neighbours and —if not actually of a different race—are a mongrel people.

Mountain Ranges. Sulimans. The Suliman range extends from the Gomal to the Indus south of Dera Ghazi Khan. It separates Baluchistan from the Punjab. In the north it attains a height of 11,000 feet, and slopes gradually until it is lost in the plains in the south. In the south vegetation is scarce; the higher slopes on the northern hills are covered with pines; in the central portion the wild olive abounds.

The narrow gorges which cross the range at right angles form its most remarkable feature. These clefts form the roadways between Baluchistan and the Punjab. The principal routes are through the Ghat, Zao, Chuhaikhel Dhana, Sakhi Sarwar, and Chachar passes.

There are two "hill stations" in the Sulimans—Shinghar, thirty miles north-west of Fort Sandeman, and Fort Munro, distant sixty miles from Dera Ghazi Khan.

Toba Kakar. The Toba Kakar range in Zhob and Pishin forms the boundary between Baluchistan and Afghanistan, and is the watershed between the Indus and Helmand basins. This range is an offshoot of the Safed Koh, and rises in three parallel ridges from the Gomal 5,000 feet in a south-westerly direction to the peaks of Sakir (10,000), Kand (10,500), and Nigand (9,500) in the centre. Thence it descends westwards to Chaman where it takes a sharp turn southwards and continues as the Khwaja Amran to opposite Shorawak, where it is known as the Sarlat Range. Eventually after a course of 300 miles it merges into the centre Makran Range.

The country between the Gomal and Kand Peak, drained by the Kundar and Zhob rivers, is known as Kakar Khorasan. West of the Kand Peak is the Toba Plateau. The winter in these wind-swept uplands is most severe, and they are usually deserted during that season. Wood and cultivation are scarce. The country

is covered with a low shrub called southernwood, which can be used for fuel, and camel-grazing for the hill camel. The Sind camels, it was found in the Afghan Wars, could not digest the herbage of this country.

Several passes cross the Khwaja Amran from Baluchistan to Afghanistan. The principal are the Bogra, Khojak, Roghani, and Gwazha Passes. The Khojak Pass is now a high road, and the Gwazha is practicable for all arms, or could be quickly made so.]

Khojak and other Passes.

The Central Brahui Range occupies the whole of the country between the Pishin, Lora, and Zhob rivers on the north and the Mula on the south. Between the Mula and Quetta the hills run north and south North of Quetta the strike changes to east and south-east to meet the Sulimans. The highest peaks in this range are Zarghun (11,738 feet), Takatu (11,375 feet) and Chiltan, all near Quetta—and Khalifat (11,440 feet) at the north-east end of the range near Ziarat (8,400 feet) the summer head-quarters of the Baluchistan Agency.

Central Brahui Range.

The North-Western Railway traverses the Bolan and Harnai Passes, the Chaman extension following the Pishin Valley from Bostan. In the south, the Mula Pass connects Baluchistan and Makran with Sind. This range in parts is comparatively well clothed with vegetation, especially the Ziarat, Zarghun, and Harboi mountains.

At its southern extremity the Central Brahui Range breaks up and is continued southwards by the Kirthar and Pab Ranges to the sea coast. A branch known as the Garr Hills leads off to the west and then turns southwards, dividing Jhalawan from Kharan and Makran. These mountains are all more or less barren.

Kirthar and Pab Ranges.

From this short description of the mountain system of Baluchistan, it is apparent that except in the southern Makran route an invasion of India by land south of the Gumal would have to traverse a gigantic gridiron of parallel mountain ranges, at right angles to the advance, and parallel to the Indian Frontier. These ranges, combined with the barren nature of the country, constitute a series of obstacles of great difficulty.

Makran. Makran, the area of which is about 26,500 square miles, lies between the sea and the Siahan mountain range. East of it is Las Bela, and Persia lies to the west. Most of the country is mountainous. The mountains run east and west in three parallel ranges—the Coast, Central, and Siahan ranges. These mountains gradually increase in height from the sea coast until, in the Siahan range, an elevation of 7,000 feet is reached. Within these hills lie the cultivated valleys and areas of Kulanch, Dasht, Nigwar, Kej, and Panjgur. The Kej valley—well watered and fertile—forms a natural highway between India and Persia.

Kharan. North of the Siahan Mountain Range extends the plain country of Kharan, mostly desert, but containing some cultivated areas at the foot of the hills. The country, the area of which is 14,200 square miles, slopes from an elevation of 2,500 feet on the east, where it touches on Jhalawan, to 1,600 feet on the west or Persian frontier. It is roughly quadrilateral in shape, and is separated from Chagai by the Ras Koh Hills. The Ras Koh Range (highest peak 10,000 feet) is 140 miles in length and is practically barren. Ibex abound on it. The winter in Kharan is cold, the heat in summer great during the day time. The nights, even in July and August, are cool. Rain falls in small quantities during January and February. Good grazing is often to be had in the spring.

Chagai. North of Kharan across the Ras Koh Hills lies the Chagai Division of the Baluchistan Agency. In this district is included the country known as Western Sinjrani, a tract of pebbly plains and sand hills which is probably the most uninviting region in Baluchistan. The area of the district is roughly 16,500 square miles and the estimated population some 11,000. The people live an entirely pastoral existence. The Sistan Trade Route runs through this district from railhead at Nushki to Koh-i-Malik-Siah, where the British, Afghan, and Persian boundaries meet.

The districts of Zhob, Bori, Sibi, and Pishin are dealt with more fully in the chapters relating to the expeditions in those regions.

Rivers. There are no large rivers in this country, carrying a permanent flow of water. As a rule the beds contain, at most, a shallow stream. After

heavy rains the rivers become raging torrents which subside as quickly as they rise. The largest river in the country is the Hingal in Makran. The north-eastern part of Baluchistan is drained by the Zhob and Gomal on the east, and Pishin and Lora on the west. Further south the Nari receives the drainage of the Loralai and Sibi districts, and passes through Kachi.

The Jhalawan country is drained by the Mulla, Hub, and Purali.

In Makran the Dasht river carries off the drainage to the south and the Rukh Shan, which joins the Mashkel, that to the north.[1]

The water of all these rivers except in times of heavy flood is absorbed in irrigation.

Lakes. There are no lakes of importance. The Hamun-i-Mashkel and Hamun-i-Lora only fill after heavy floods, and the same may be said of the salt marshes or "Kaps" in Makran.

Coast Line. The coast line of Baluchistan is 472 miles in length. The whole coast is barren, presenting a succession of arid clay plains intersected with water-courses. The chief ports are Sonmiani, Pasni, and Gwadar—all mere roadsteads where large ships must lie a long way from the shore.

Rainfall. Baluchistan and the Sulimans lie outside the monsoon area, and the rainfall is very variable and scanty. Shahrig, which has the largest rainfall, only boasts $11\frac{3}{4}$ inches per annum. In the highlands the greatest rainfall (including snow) is in winter, derived from the shallow storms advancing from the Persian plateau.[2] The plains and lower hills, including Zhob, receive most of their rain in the summer, July being the wettest month.

Climate. The climate in Baluchistan is one of extremes. In Makran, the Arabian Sea Coast, and Kachi the fiercest heat is experienced; while in the Kalat and Pishin highland districts the winters are most severe. The Zhob and eastern border enjoy a somewhat more equable climate. In the Quetta, Pishin, Kalat, and Bolan districts rain

---

[1] Universal Gazetteer, 1903.

[2] The approach of these storms can be so well timed that 48 hours' notice of a impending snowfall is generally received in Quetta.

and snow may be expected from December to March. The summer months throughout the whole country are practically dry. Curiously enough, a larger rainfall is experienced in the summer months in the Harnai and Zhob valleys than in the winter—the exact opposite to the conditions prevalent in all other parts of the province.

Quetta had formerly a bad reputation as regards climate. This, however, was chiefly due to the fact that the troops were camped on the low ground, now the civil lines, which was then undrained. Since the formation of the cantonment the health of the station has steadily improved, and most people find the climate excellent. Chills, however, are very common in a climate where the variation in temperature during twenty-four hours is so great—in spring and autumn as much as 70°.

This liability to chill is particularly trying to those who arrive in Quetta already suffering from malaria, as exemplified in the following instance:—

A certain regiment had suffered severely from malarial fever in the Ghorpari Barracks at Poona in 1879. They had benefited greatly by a short stay in Hyderabad, Sind, after which they were marched through the Bolan at the hottest time of the year. In the pass they lost sixteen men from sunstroke, but were otherwise healthy until they reached Gulistan. Here the nights were very cold compared to the days, the water was not good, and the clothing was insufficient for constitutions saturated with malaria. Diarrhœa broke out in the regiment, which continued its march to Southern Afghanistan and was encamped in the Arghandab Valley. The hardships of service and climate told on the men, already enfeebled. Diarrhœa merged into dysentery, and between the 1st October and 15th December forty-nine men were carried off, fifty invalided to India, and the sick report showed 138 men in hospital out of a total of 556.

As against this, the "bill of health" was excellent in the march down the Bolan in 1881 when the troops had become inured to the climate and had learnt to avoid chills.

Communications.

A glance at the communications in Baluchistan will be interesting, and make it easier to understand the geography of the region. All the roads follow the watered and cultivated valleys as far as possible.

Of the railway little need be said. The map makes the route clear. The Maskaf-Bolan section from Sibi to Quetta follows those passes on a high level above the river beds; the ruling gradient between Mach and the upper end of the Bolan is 1 in 25—one of the steepest in the world. At Spezand the new line to Nushki branches off to the south. Beyond Quetta—at Bostan—the alternative route from Sibi by the Harnai Valley is met; it is not quite so steep a gradient as the Bolan route. From Bostan the railway runs through the Pishin Valley to Chaman, piercing the Khojak Range by a tunnel 2¾ miles long. The line from Killa Abdulla to Chaman is double. After leaving the tunnel at Spinwana the railway descends some 2,000 feet into the Kunchai plain, where the terminus at Chaman is on level ground.

The main roads are from Sibi to Quetta *viâ* the Bolan—a metalled cart road 95½ miles long, with a rise from 495 feet to 5,500 feet. Thence to Chaman, over the Khojak Pass, is a similarly good cart road 79 miles long: from it, at Yaru Karez and Saranan metalled roads lead to Pishin. From Pishin the great frontier road runs to Dera Ghazi Khan, 294 miles.

The other main roads are from Quetta *viâ* Gandak, Harnai, and Loralai to Fort Sandeman: this is a metalled road from Harnai to Fort Sandeman. From Pishin to Sibi there is a road in rear of Takatu mountain by the Harnai Pass, fit for pack animals. A good unmetalled road has been recently constructed from Fort Sandeman to Dera Ismail Khan, 115 miles through the Chuhar Khel Dhana *viâ* Draban.

Southwards from Quetta the only metalled road is that to Kalat, 88 miles. From Kalat caravan routes lead to Sind, Makran, and Kharan.

The Sistan trade route starts at Nushki and traverses the practically desert country of Chagai, 376 miles, to Robat on the frontier at Koh-i-Malik-Siah. Wells have been dug along the entire route. It is essentially a caravan road, the camel being the sole means of transport in the district.

The main highways running through Makran parallel to the sea coast are clearly shown in the map. They are camel tracks and the marches from water to water are usually long.

In concluding this chapter on geography it may be well to repeat that the country is generally one of sultry deserts, barren

plains, or rugged mountains. Armies can only move along certain well defined routes. Even in one of the best of these, the Sakhi Sarwar Pass, the Emperor Babar found that his cavalry were starving and was obliged to turn off from Bori to Ghazni.

CHAPTER II.

HISTORY AND ETHNOGRAPHY.

Early History, 327 B. C.

ALL the early Western invasions of India,[1] prior to that of Alexander, are believed to have come through Makran. The latter's return from India led him through the same country, while a second division under Crateros traversed the Mula Pass, and probably sent a detachment through Quetta and Peshin. Nearchus sailed from Tatta with the fleet and, passing Karachi and Sonmiani, followed the coast line up the Persian Gulf. The accounts of the early historians of Alexander's retreat point to the fact that the geography and climatic conditions of the country traversed by his armies, and the coast line followed by his fleet have undergone little if any change, and Colonel Holdich deduces[2] the fact that the Arabs were masters of the country in those days, and many of the descriptions of the people and their habits tally with the conditions found to-day.

In 635 A.D. Rai Chach, the Hindu ruler of Sind, had conquered Makran, and appears to have extended his conquests northwards towards the Helmund. His rule, however, was short, as Omar, the first Arab invader after the Hijra, reached Makran in 643 A.D.

It is unnecessary to describe the various invasions in detail, but that of Muhammad Kasim, sixth Khalif, is interesting from a military point of view.

712.

In 712 A.D. he passed through Makran from end to end with a force of 6,000 cavalry, 6,000 camel sowars, 3,000 infantry, and a large train.[3]

Thenceforward for several centuries Makran remained a great commercial highway. Ruins of large towns along its main route

---

[1] (1) Semiramis, 23rd century B. C. (2) Sesostris. (3) Cyrus, 538 B.C. (4) Darius.
[2] "Notes on Makran."—*Holdich.*
[3] His siege train for the capture of Naringkot (modern Hyderabad), however, came round to the Indus by sea.

testify to its having been the connecting passage between east and west, the "open sesame of India." These cities were well known throughout the Arabic world, and quoted by Arabian writers.

In the early part of the 11th century Baluchistan fell into the hands of the Ghaznivids from whom it passed to the Ghorids. In 1219 we find it included in the dominion of Sultan Muhammad Khan of Khwarizm (Khiva).

In 1223 came Chengiz Khan's Mongol hordes, whose raids have burned deep into the memory of Baluchistan. From Makran to the Gomal the Mongol (locally known as Mughal), and his atrocities are still a byeword in every household.

Henceforward the history of Baluchistan is intimately connected with Kandahar, whose rulers generally exercised suzerainty over the whole of Baluchistan. The fourteenth and fifteenth centuries are most important in Baluch history. During this period the Baluchis spread over Kalat and Kachi into the Punjab, and the wars between Mir Chakar Rind and Gwahram Lashari, celebrated in Baluch folklore, took place.

In 1485 A.D. the Arghuns from Kandahar invaded Kachi by way of the Bolan Pass.

<small>Rise of the Brahuis.</small> About this same time the Brahuis were gaining power, and established themselves in the neighbourhood of Kalat.

From 1556 to 1595 the country was under the Safavid dynasty, after which it fell into the hands of the Mughal Emperors of Delhi. In 1638 the Persians once more asserted their authority over Baluchistan.

In 1708 the Ghilzai power became paramount in Baluchistan, followed in turn by that of Nadir Shah and Ahmed Shah Durani.

Thenceforward until 1879 the north-eastern portion of the country remained under the actual or nominal suzerainty of the Sadozais and Barakzais, the south-western portion being consolidated into the Kalat confederacy.

<small>Sikhs arrive in Derajat, 1819.</small> In 1819 Ranjit Singh invaded the Derajat, and forced the Afghan Governor to evacuate Dera Ghazi Khan.

In 1827 the Nawab of Bhawalpur, on behalf of the Sikhs, from whom he farmed the Dera Ghazi Khan district, seized the Harrand Dajal territory from the Khan of Kalat.

General Ventura, in Sikh employ, succeeded the Nawab of Bhawalpur as Governor of the Derajat in 1830. He was succeeded in 1832 by the able Diwan Sawan Mal, who held office until 1844. During the period of the Sikh occupation the Baluch border tribes were perpetually in revolt. Mazaris, Gurchanis, Khetrans, and Bozdars all gave trouble. The Sikh scheme was to play one tribe off against another. They were not successful, however. The country was entirely lawless, and the Sikhs lived shut up in forts. Revenue was only collected with the aid of a large force, or not at all.

In 1833 Shah Shuja, the ex-monarch of Kabul, who was living as a British pensioner at Ludhiana, resolved to make another effort to recover his kingdom. In order to obtain the assistance of Ranjit Singh, he made a treaty with him in 1834 by which, in return for active assistance, he renounced all claim to the countries bordering on the Indus. Ranjit Singh thus gained the Dera Ismail and Dera Ghazi districts, provided Shah Shuja proved successful. The Shah's expedition was a failure, and he fled to Kalat for refuge. Here he was well treated by Mehrab Khan, and given safe conduct to the Indus, whence he again returned to his asylum in Ludhiana.

Treaty between Ranjit Singh and Shah Shuja.

In 1838, however, the British Government, suspicious of the intentions of the Russian and Persian Governments, made Shah Shuja their tool for establishing British influence in Kabul.

In order to obtain the friendship of the Sikhs in their efforts to place Shah Shuja on the throne of Kabul, the British Government in 1838, at Lahore, ratified the treaty of 1834 between the Shah and the Maharajah.

Tripartite Treaty, 1838.

By this treaty Shah Shuja renounced his claim to all jurisdiction over the province of Harrand Dajal, at that time still nominally in the Kalat Khanate.

The British Government also made him renounce all rights to tribute from Sind, which was to become a sovereign state of the Sind Mirs, allowing him, however, certain arrears. This paved the way for the permanent occupation of Sind, shortly afterwards, by Sir Charles Napier.

Soon after Ranjit Singh's death in 1839, no one having been found fit to fill the place of that astute ruler, the whole of this part of the country fell into a state of anarchy. The Kalat Sardars, instigated, it is said, by the Khan, raided Harrand Dajal in retaliation for the conduct of the Sikh Government, and in their endeavour to recover the stolen province, all became anarchy and confusion throughout the Dera Ghazi Khan district. During the First Afghan War certain portions of Kalat territory and Pishin were occupied by the British troops in charge of the line of communications. After the conquest of Sind in 1843 the British frontier became coterminous with Kalat territory, bordering the Baluch tribes on the north and the Brahuis proper on the west.

In 1844 Diwan Sawan Mal was succeeded by his son Mulraj, whose defiance of Sikh authority caused the outbreak at Multan.

Sir Herbert Edwardes was then in the Upper Derajat, his services having been lent to the Sikh Durbar with a view to effecting a settlement in that district. In 1848 came the news of Mulraj's rebellion, and the murder of Anderson and Vans Agnew at Multan. The British Resident in Lahore ordered Edwardes to seize the Upper Derajat and endeavour to win over the Lower.

Edwardes in Derajat.

Having collected a large force from his own Multanis, and the tribes, Baluch and Pathan, Edwardes marched south. He first advanced on the Sikh fort at Mangrotha, which surrendered. He then moved towards Dera Ghazi Khan which, however, had already fallen to Van Cortland (an officer in the Sikh service) who had also collected some Baluch levies. Harrand, the only remaining Sikh fortress, also fell. The united forces of Edwardes and Van Cortland then crossed the Indus, defeated Mulraj at Kaneri and Saddozam, and proceeded to aid General Whish in the reduction of Multan.

Derajat Affairs during Sikh War.

On the annexation of the Punjab in 1849 the Derajat was occupied, and two thousand of Edwardes' Irregulars were taken into the service of the Government as Border Police. The faithful sardars received pensions.

Britain thus became in 1849 heir to a district where the frontier was a haphazard one, roughly defined by the Sikhs but a few years before. The contiguous tribes had, in most cases, sections living within the

Annexation, 1849.

British Border. They were as follows, starting from the north :—

(a) *Pathan Tribes.*

1. Shiranis—Entirely outside the Border.
2. Ustaranis—Partly within the Border.

Various Trans-Border Tribes.

(b) *Baluch Tribes.*

3. Kasranis—Partly within the Border.
4. Bozdars—Entirely outside the Border.
5. Khosas—Partly inside the Border.
6. Legharis—Partly inside the Border.
7. Gurchanis—Partly inside the Border.
8. Mazaris—Partly inside the Border.

Besides these, there were the Marris, Bugtis, and Khetrans, the two former Baluch, the latter a mixed tribe, who, though not exactly on the frontier, raided into our territory and were important factors in both Sind and Punjab frontier affairs.

In 1879 the Second Afghan War took place, when certain provinces of Baluchistan were acquired by Great Britain.

Between 1880 and 1890 practical British influence was established over the whole region treated of in this volume.

The principal indigenous tribes in this region are the Pathans, Baluchis, and Brahuis. Besides these, there are a few scattered elements such as the Khetrans; the Jats, cultivators of the plains; and Dehwars, cultivators of the highlands.

Indigenous races.

The Pathans occupy the north-eastern portion of the country, all of which is directly administered by the Baluchistan Agency.

Distribution.

To the south of them, in the warmer parts of the province, are the Baluchis of the Marri, Bugti, Dumki, Umrani, and Kaheri countries, and the Kachi plain. In the highlands we have the Brahuis, stretching through Chagai on the north, to meet the Baluchis of Western Sinjrani. South and westwards, the Brahui marches with the Las Bela State, and the Baluchis of Makran. The small piece of Kachi occupied by the Brahuis is the only non-mountainous part of their country: it was obtained from the

Kalhora dynasty of Sind in 1740 in compensation for the death of the Khan of Kalat in a battle with the Sindians.[1]

In the Sulimans are the Baluch tribes extending north as far as Vihoa, after which Pathan tribes are met with.

Boundaries of Pathan and Baluch.

As a rough guide, a line drawn from Vihoa to Thal Chotiali, thence to Sibi, and prolonged *viâ* Quetta to the Gwazha Pass may be taken to mark the northern boundary of the Baluch (and Brahui). North of that line are the Pathans.

Male population.

The male population of the various tribes and districts will now be given. It is noteworthy that throughout this country the female population is usually from four to six per cent. less than the male—as is usually the case in hilly and barren countries. Males capable of bearing arms may generally be taken as one-fifth of the male population.

District or tribe		Male population.
Quetta and Pishin { Pathans 78 per cent. Brahuis 8 per cent. }		68,000
Loralai		38,000
Zhob		39,000
Chagai		11,000
Bolan		15,000
Sibi		40,000
Marris		11,000
Bugtis		10,000
Kalat—Sarawan	36,000	
Jhalawan	115,000	
Kachi	34,000	308,000
Makran	35,000	
Kharan	88,000	
Las Bela		29,000
Baluchistan, total		569,000
Punjab administered area of the Sulimans (estimated)		8,000
Grand total		577,000 males.

[1] The great Nadir Shah was the adjudicator of this compensation.

A peculiar interest attaches to the Pathans in this area in that the Zhob and Suliman district is by common Afghan tradition considered to be the cradle of their race. Thence they are supposed by some authorities to have spread north as far as Dir and Swat, and southwards and westwards to Sibi, Pishin, Shorawak, and Kandahar. As Baluchistan is not really named after the majority of its inhabitants, so Afghanistan contains not more than half of the Afghan race, the remainder, under the name of Pathan, reside on the Indian side of the Durand line.

The most numerous and important indigenous Pathan tribes in Baluchistan are the Kakars (105,000), Tarins (37,000), Panis (20,000), and Shiranis (7,500).

Afghan genealogies, whatever be their value, all commence with Qais Abdur Rashid, alleged to be the thirty-seventh in descent from Malik Talut (King Saul). His home was, according to many traditions, in the tract immediately to the west of the Takht-i-Suliman, known to the Afghans as Khurasan, and to us as Kakar Khurasan. From the three sons of Qais Abdur Rashid, Ghurghusht, Saraban, and Baitan, sprang the various Pathan tribes.[1]

The Kakars, who number over 100,000 souls, are to be found principally in the Zhob, Quetta-Pishin, and Loralai districts. By far the most important section is the Sanzar Khel who number 64,000 persons. Next in importance come the Snatia, Targhara, and Sargar sections. The most important group of the Sanzar Khel is the Jogizai, the most influential family in Zhob. The majority of the Snatias are to be found in Pishin. A section of them hold the Hanna valley near Quetta.

The Tarins, who number 37,000 souls, are second only to the Kakars in numerical strength, and have acquired further importance from their connection with the rulers of Afghanistan—the Sadozais and Barakzais. More than half of the Tarins belong to the Bor Tarin or Abdal section, almost the whole of whom again are Achakzais. The other two sections are known as Spin Tarin and Tor Tarin.[2]

---

[1] *Vide* appendix A. to this chapter.
[2] The Tarins are descended from three brothers—Bor Tarin, Tor Tarin, and Spin Tarin. Bor Tarin was also known as Abdul by which name that section of the Tarin is often known.

The Achakzais will be dealt with fully in Chapter VII.

The Spin Tarins have migrated from Pishin, and live almost entirely in the Shahrig and Duki Tahsils.

The Tor Tarins, who are twice as numerous as the Spin Tarins, are almost equally distributed in the districts of Quetta-Pishin and Loralai.

Although ethnically connected, the three sections of the Tarins might be classed as separate tribes. They have no dealings with one another.

Of the twenty thousand Panis resident in Baluchistan some four thousand are to be found in the Sibi and Loralai districts, the remainder in Zhob. Included in the Panis are the Musa Khel who inhabit the Tahsil of that name in Zhob.

Panis.

The Mando Khel section of the Panis reside in the neighbourhood of Fort Sandeman, and should really be classed as Kakars.

The Panis of Sibi include the important sections of Barozais and Khajaks. The former administered Sibi on behalf of the Afghans during their rule.

There is no cohesion between the Musa Khels, Panis of Sibi, and Panis of Zhob.

Other Pathan tribes.

The other Pathan tribes in this area are of no great importance.

Regarding them, the reader is referred to the genealogical table of Pathans—Appendix A to this chapter.

The Shiranis and Ustaranas are treated of in Chapter VIII.

The origin of the Baluchis and Brahuis is a much vexed question. Both claim an Arab origin and to have come from Aleppo in Northern Arabia. A Persian origin is, however, most commonly assigned to the Baluch race, and a Turkish or Kurdish origin to the Brahuis.

Origin of Baluchis and Brahuis.

The Makran Baluch has very probably an Arab strain, and there is every reason to believe that intercourse between the coast of that country and Arabia existed many centuries before the Arab invasion of Sind, which traversed Makran in 643 A.D.

For a discussion of the theories regarding the origin of these races the reader is referred to the "Census of India," 1901 (Baluchistan), the Imperial Gazetteer, 1905, and "The Baluch Race"

HISTORY AND ETHNOGRAPHY.

by Dames. Both races are now thoroughly mixed, and language cannot be taken as proof of origin.

The names of the races also have given rise to much controversy.

Baluch is said by some authorities to mean "wanderer," and Braho to be a corrupt form of Ibrahim, and Brahui to mean descendants of Braho. Another theory connects Brahui, which is also called Barohi with Ba, and Rohi meaning "people of the hills." The fact that "Uch" means desert might point to Baluch, meaning "people of the desert," and Barohi or Brahui, meaning people of the mountains—certainly a fair description of the races.

Baluchis. The Baluchis, wherever they may have come from originally, have now to a large extent left Baluchistan and moved into the Punjab and Sind.

There are roughly 80,000 of the race in Baluchistan as against 950,000 in the Punjab and Sind.

The important Baluch tribes in Baluchistan are the Marris, Bugtis, Buledis, Dumkis, Magassis, and Rinds.

The Bozdars, Gurchanis, Legharis, Lunds, and Kasranis are generally regarded as offshoots of larger tribes which are to be found in the Punjab.

Unlike the Brahuis, the Baluchis never appear to have coalesced into a homogeneous nation. Although several of their tribes joined the Brahui confederacy from time to time, they appear to have generally broken away from it again. Two of them, however, the Rinds and Magassis, still maintain their connection with the Brahuis.

A description of the important Baluch tribes will be found in the various chapters treating of our dealings with them. The genealogical tree given in Appendix B to this chapter is interesting if not authentic. It is deduced from Baluch traditions.

Baluch Immigration. The following is a short account of the Baluchis and their wanderings, as traced from the various authorities.

The name Baluch is mentioned in the Shahnama by Firdaosi as being that of a people who formed part of the army of the great Cyrus. This is, however, mythical, and the first mention of the Baluch on which credence can be placed—in the poem above mentioned—shows the Baluch attacked by Naushirwan and afterwards

forming part of his army. At this time they appear to have been resident in Kirman, about 550 A.D., where the Arabs found them in their invasion of that country in 636. It is noteworthy that the province of Kirman at that time bordered Makran. For the next 600 years the history of the Baluch is practically untraceable. There were some Baluchis in Sistan during the period, and later they arrived in Makran. There were probably two movements of the Baluch race during this period, each corresponding with an inroad of northern invaders which greatly affected this part of Asia. The abandonment of Kirman and the settlement in Sistan and Western Makran corresponded with the Seljak invasion. The second migration into Eastern Makran and Sind corresponded with the invasions of Chengiz Khan.

From the arrival in Makran Baluch legends begin, and we hear of their marching under one chief, Mir Jalal Khan, to fight the Arabs of the coast. This Mir Jalal Khan had four sons and one daughter, who gave their names to the various Baluch tribes—*vide* Appendix B to this chapter. Doubtless the invaders mingled with the Jats and Arabs then living in Makran.

At the end of the twelfth century a body of Baluchis entered Sind and allied themselves with some of the local tribes. During the thirteenth century the Baluchis were employed against his enemies by Doda IV, the Somra ruler of Sind.

At the end of the thirteenth century the Somra rule in Sind gave way to the Samma dynasty. A section of the Somras, headed by their chief Doda, took refuge with the Baluchis, and were gradually assimilated under the name of Dodai Baluch. The Gurchanis, now the principle tribe of Dodai origin, are not looked upon as pure Baluchis.

Longworth Dames described the Baluch nation as divided into the following groups in the fifteeeth century, on the eve of the invasion of India :—

Main Groups of Baluchis.

(1) the five main bodies of undoubted Baluch descent, *viz.*, Rind, Lashari, Hot, Korai, Jatai ;
(2) the groups afterwards formed in Makran, *viz.*,—Buledhis, Ghazanis, and Umaranis ;
(3) the Dodais ; and
(4) the servile tribes.

Since then the Gichkis in Makran and Jakranis in Sind seem to have been assimilated in comparatively recent times.

Nothing more is heard of the Baluchis until the middle of the fifteenth century when we again find them raiding in Northern Sind. Here also the forward move of the Baluchis takes place at a time of general unrest. The invasion of India by Temur then occupied men's minds. The Tuglak monarchy of Delhi disappeared, and a succession of feeble rulers allowed the Lodi Afghans to seize the sovereignty, and opened a tempting prospect to needy adventurers from across the border. Gradually the Baluchis worked up along the line of hills, keeping to the west of the Indus, and pushing the Pathan tribes north and west.[1]

About the year 1450 A.D., we hear of the ruler of Multan granting land across the Indus to Sohrab, a Baluch Chief of the Dodai tribe, in return for aid in quieting the Trans-Indus districts. Sohrab's son at this time founded Dera Ismail Khan, and another member of the same Baluch tribe founded Dera Ghazi Khan shortly afterwards. Gradually these towns became the capitals of practically independent districts, Dera Ghazi Khan becoming comparatively important under its Mirani rulers.

Baluchis in Dera Ghazi Khan and Dera Ismail, 1450—1500 A.D.

The movement of the Rinds under Mir Chakur to the Punjab at this time is doubtless connected with the invasion of Kachi by the Arghuns in 1485 A.D.

According to Baluch legends, the Rinds under Mir Chakur enlisted the aid of the Turks (Arghuns) against the Lasharis under Gwahram. Accounts are given of many years of fighting culminating in the wholesale departure of the Rinds to the Punjab.[2] On arriving in the Derajat the Rinds found the Dodai Baluchis settled on the right bank of the Indus, and proceeded to Multan, whose ruler gave them lands. The Baluch migration into the Southern Punjab continued, and gradually they held most of the Multan district. When the Arghuns—after taking Sind from the Sammas in 1520—attacked Multan, they were opposed by an army composed mostly of Baluchis.

---

[1] A movement of the Pathans into the richer districts of Afghanistan is perhaps the reason of the Baluchis establishing themselves in the Sulimans. Such a movement did occur consequent on the depopulation of Southern Afghanistan by the raids of the Mongols.

[2] The headquarters of the Rinds now remaining in Baluchistan is at Shoran in Kachi.

In 1526 Babar arrived in India. With him, attracted by the tales of wealth and plunder, came hordes of Baluchis from Sind and Makran. All the Baluch tribes now occupying the Dera Ghazi Khan frontier trace their settlement to this period. At this time, too, they appear to have spread over the Southern and Western Punjab. Holding the Suliman Hills, the Baluchis gradually overran the plains on the right bank of the Indus.

Sulimans occupied by Baluchis, 1526—1550.

Before this great national migration of the Baluchis they appear to have been in possession of the Kalat Highlands.

There is a common belief that a Hindu tribe called Sewa was in possession of Kalat at the time, and called in the assistance of the Brahuis against the Baluchis.

Brahui Invasion.

Where the Brahuis came from is, as already mentioned, a much disputed question. It is noteworthy that the Arghuns, a Mughal family claiming descent from Chengiz Khan, were very active at this time. The Rinds invited their assistance, and lost their territory to them. Why may not the same state of affairs have existed in Kalat? Be that as it may, however, the migration of great numbers of the Baluchis gave the Brahuis their chance. They extended down the highlands of Sarawan and Jhalawan, driving a wedge between the Baluchis of Makran and the Sulimans, and gradually establishing authority over those of the former country.

The Brahuis—whatever their origin—gradually constituted a semi-military organisation. Consequently homogeneity of race was by no means necessary for its formation.

Brahuis.

Hughes Butler[1] states that Khudadad Khan, the ex-Khan of Kalat, gave him the following classification of the principal tribes :—

    a. Real Brahuis tracing their origin to Aleppo—Kambranis, Mirwanis, Gurgnaris, and Kalandaris.[2]

    b. Rind Baluch—Bangulzai, Langav, Lehri—who, the ex-Khan says, were earlier inhabitants than the Brahuis.

---

[1] Census Report, Baluchistan, 1901.

[2] A branch of which is the Ahmadzai, the ruling family.

c. Afghans or Pathans—Raisanis, Shahwanis, and Sarparras.

d. Persians—Kurds and Mamasanis.

e. Jats[1]—Bizanjo, Mengal, Sajdi, and Zehri. The chief of the Zehri is, however, said to be an Afghan.

f. Aboriginal Tribes—Muhammad Shahi and Nichari, who were in the country before the Rinds arrived.

This classification by the ex-Khan is extremely interesting, as the sequence given by him tallies exactly with the waves of migration which have passed over the country.

Sarawan. The two main divisions of the Brahuis are the Sarawan or Highlanders and Jhalawan or Lowlanders.

The principal sections of the Sarawan are the Lehris (5,400), Bangalzais (9,000), Kurds (3,100), Shahwanis (6,300), Muhammad Shahis (2,800), Raisanis (2,400), and Sarparras (900). All these tribes are cultivators or flock-owners. In addition to these tribes are the Langavs (17,000), an agricultural people, who cultivate the Valley of Manguchar.

The Raisanis are the most influential section of the Sarawan, their chief being also the Sarawan Sardar.

Sarawan. Most of the Sarawan tribes leave the mountains in winter, and make their way to Kachi, where they live in blanket tents or mat huts, and assist in cultivation.

Numbers of horses are bred in the district, and Manguchar donkeys are renowned throughout Baluchistan.

Jhalawan. The Jhalawan tribes comprise the Zehris (49,000), Mengal (69,000), Muhammad Hasni (53,000), and Bizanjan (14,000), besides many smaller sections. The ruling Sardar of Jhalawan belongs to the Zarakzai clan of the Zehri tribe. The population is almost entirely Brahui with, here and there, a sprinkling of Baluchis.

Agriculture and flock-owning are the only occupations of the people, who live for the most part in blanket tents or mat huts.

In winter all the tent-living inhabitants migrate to Kachi and Sind, where they engage in cutting the crops, returning to the

---

[1] Scythian origin. The Scythian invasion reached Baluchistan in 120 B.C.

highlands in spring. The Jhalawan country is not so well cultivated as the Sarawan.

In the Pab Range camel breeding is extensively carried on, principally baggage camels. Horses are much less plentiful in Jhalawan than in Sarawan.

A study of the numbers of the Jhalawan and Sarawan given above will show that they offer a fair field for recruiting for the local Baluch and Baluchistan regiments.

The Pathans of Baluchistan and the Sulimans speak the soft Pushtu spoken in Kandahar. In the Marri and Bugti country, and in Kachi, as well as in the Southern Sulimans, Baluchi is the principal language. In these districts, however, a small portion of the population speak the agricultural Jatki. In Makran and Kharan the Baluchi dialect is the language usually spoken. Las Bela has for its language Lasi—a corrupt form of Sindhi—and, on the seacoast, Makrani-Baluchi. The Khetrans speak a distinct dialect akin to Western Punjabi. Brahui is the principal language of Sarawan, Jhalawan, and Chagai; but Baluchi is also spoken in these districts.

Language.

A discussion of the various languages would be outside the scope of this volume. Baluchi and Pushtu present no great difficulty as to origin, but in the Brahui language the student is confronted with a philological problem which has been much disputed. Baluchi is for various reasons more popular than Brahui. In the first place Baluchi is simpler, and those who speak Brahui as their mother tongue, frequently learn Baluchi or Pushtu when living near tribes speaking those languages. But other tribes and Europeans experience great difficulty in acquiring a knowledge of Brahui.

Brahui again has a very small vocabulary, and consequently Baluchi, with its elastic substratum of Persian, is being rapidly adopted to meet the new requirements of civilization. A third and potent cause of the extended use of Baluchi is the fact that the Khan of Kalat and Sarawan Sirdars marry into Baluch tribes. Hence the rising generation in the ruling houses is more conversant with Baluchi than Brahui, as the mothers always give their language to the race.

The Brahui language may be due to early intermarriage of the Brahuis with women of the aboriginal (Sewa) tribes whom they

displaced. For it is remarkable to find in Baluchistan a Dravidian tongue surrounded on all sides by Aryan languages; the nearest country where it is again met being the Gond Hills of Central India.[1]

Education. Education is carefully fostered in the territories directly administered by the Baluchistan Agency, but in Kalat and tribal territories it is almost entirely neglected. A few chiefs and influential families employ *mullas* to teach their sons. Las Bela is an exception, and has a school which is fairly well attended. At Mastung a school has now been opened, intercourse with Quetta having impressed on the Brahuis of that district the need of education.

Character of Pathan and Baluch. The character and habits of the Pathan and Baluchis have been fully dealt with in the preface to Volume I of this series, to which the reader is referred.

The Pathans of this district differ but little in character and habits from those dealt with in Volumes I and II.

Having, however, been for many centuries in touch with the strong governments of Persia, Kandahar, and Delhi, they are somewhat less rude than the tribes to the north. Moreover, their country and that of the Baluchis and Brahuis is infinitely less difficult. Again, they have no back door so long as there is a strong Afghan Government in their rear.

Mere detachments have penetrated to the very heart of the Marri country. It requires a *corps d'armée* to enter the Tirah Hills with a prospect of success.

In character the Baluch and Brahui are fairly similar, and both are, on the whole, chivalrous and true.

When Walpole Clarke was killed near Kahan the Marris themselves sent us word how bravely he had died and how many of their own number had fallen to his sabre. Of their own free-will they erected a monument over his grave; and, when Captain Brown surrendered at Kahan in 1840, they not only strictly kept to the terms of their agreement, but treated our troops with honour and even kindness.

---

[1] If Brahui is Dravidian.

Lieutenant Loveday is the only officer who has ever suffered violence at the hands of a Baluch or Brahui except in case of open strife. His case was exceptional. In addition to being personally disliked by the people, he was the official instrument of an unpopular policy, which the British Government afterwards saw fit to change.

Previous to British occupation Baluchistan, as has already been stated in Chapter I, was largely occupied by tribes more or less independent. The State of Kalat was, of course, an exception.

<small>Result of British occupation.</small>

In taking over the Derajat from the Sikhs we succeeded to an inheritance of anarchy, the result of their mismanagement.

The whole country was studded with forts, each the head-quarters of a robber chief. The revenue was collected by an army—or not at all. Similarly in Sind the border was a happy hunting ground for Marris and Bugtis. With the introduction of English rule a change was at once apparent, and the border became tranquil in comparison with its former condition. However, expeditions were necessary to show the border tribes the strength of the British Government, and the folly of resisting it by force of arms.

The lesson once taught, no effort was spared to encourage friendly feelings and show the trans-frontier people that all the British Government insisted upon was the peace of its border. This ensured, they were as free to come and go for trade or other purposes as our own people. Gradually all these tribes, as well as the Pathan tribes of Zhob and Bori, have come under British influence to their own great advantage, as well as securing peace on our borders.

Among these small and badly organised frontier tribes—

"Independence means bloodshed, desolation, risk, and danger in every shape and form, and in the interests of peace and civilisation it is absolutely essential that the turbulent tribes, should be brought under some paramount power. The only title to independence they have is that of the pirate or highway robber, having cut themselves adrift from all wholesome governing authority, thereby obtaining a license to cut throats, and murder and plunder their neighbours.

There is a natural instinct in the minds of these men that this spurious independence is not permanent, and it is only the evil-doers, who make plunder and bloodshed pay, who resist being brought again under a sovereign power. If the Amir or the Khan of Kalat claim tribes as their own, they

should admit and act up to their responsibilities and keep them in order. If they are under no rule, the sooner they are brought under one the better it will be for themselves and all concerned.

The chiefs and men of position, who possess landed property and a share in the country, look on the state of affairs as unwholesome, and regard the intervention which restores the country to a healthy condition with gratitude. Nothing has done more mischief than the encouragement of the theory that these tribes are independent, or tends so much to keep them outside the pale of civilisation." [1]

This was written in 1884. The Marris and Bugtis, who were particularly referred to, have now acquired a *healthy* independence, and are a strength instead of a weakness to our frontier.

---

[1] The Forward Policy.—(*R. I. Bruce.*)

I

AFGHA

1. DESCENDANTS OF SARABAN, SON OF QAIS ABDUL RASHID.

DESCENDED FROM SHARF-UD-DIN alias SHARKHABUN, SON OF SARABAN.

DESCENDED FROM KHAIR-UD-DIN alias KHARSHABUN, SON OF SARABAN.

Tarin					Shirani	Miani or Mianai	Barech	Urmar	Kansi	Kand	Jamand or Zamand
Abdal or Bor Tarin			Spin Tarin	Tor Tarin	Jhat Tarin						

Abdal or Bor Tarin sub-divisions:
- Popalzai
  - Sadozai
- Barakzai
  - Khwa Alizai
  - Achakzai
  - Budezai
  - Nurzai
    - Sultanzai
    - Odhi Alizai
    - Mir Alizai
    - Nasratzai
    - Malizai
    - Hamidzai
    - Ashezai

Spin Tarin sub-divisions:
- Alwani
- Marpani
- Laviani
- Ilu-wani
- Nemani
- Wanechi
- Zaam

Tor Tarin sub-divisions:
- Abubakar
- Alizai
- Makhyar
- Makhianni
- Nurzai
- Saigi

Shirani sub-divisions:
- Babar
- Chuhurkhel
- Harooni
- Hasankhel
- Kapip
- Machai
- Obokhel

Miani sub-divisions:
- Zmarai
- Jalar
- Tatri (with the Luni)
- Siloch (with the Hasni section of Khetrans)
- Bilifur (with, besides they are known locally as Ghattal)
- Ikawani (with Khidrani clan of Marris)

Barech: No sub-divisions were recorded.

Urmar: No sub-divisions.

Kansi sub-divisions:
- Achakzai
- Ahmad Khanzai
- Akazai
- Budiezai
- Ghanzzai
- Gulzai
- Khaltar
- Khwajzai
- Mirzai
- Sammungli
- Shahmani
- Shokh
- Smali

Kand: No sub-divisions.

Jamand or Zamand: No sub-divisions.

Notes (Jamand or Zamand column): A few families of the Zamand or Jamand tribe, now called Muhammadzai, are to be found in Pishin and there are also said to be some among the Dehwars of Mastung.

Notes (Kand column): The progenitor of the Yusafzais and Mandars of Peshawar, Swat, etc. The only descendants of Kand in Baluchistan are to be found among the Dewars of Kalat.

Notes (Kansi column): The Kansis held the fort of Shal-Kot (Quetta) under the Durrani dynasty, and were continually at feud with the Kakars and Brahuis.

Notes (Urmar column): None of Urmar's descendants are to be found in Baluchistan. They are living in the Peshawar district.

Notes (Barech column): ...

Notes (Miani column): Mianai is not known or recognised as a tribal name in Baluchistan, but a few Mianis are to be found with the Marris. Outside Baluchistan the use of Miani as a tribal patronymic is said to be common.

Notes (Shirani column): The Babars, who live near Fort Sandeman, appear to be practically independent of the main body of the tribe who live on the Frontier. The Shiranis have given their name to one of the main clans among the Marris, the Loharani-Shirani, and have also spread to Shorawak.

Notes (Jhat Tarin column): The Jhar Tarins are now not recognisable as a separate tribe. It is thought that the Jharkhels among the Dehwars and the Zarakzais among the Zohri Brahuis are the remnants of this group.

Notes (Tor Tarin column): The Tor Tarins in Pishin and Loralai are independent of one another in tribal matters. The Makhianis are an affiliated group.

Notes (Spin Tarin column): The Wanechis are locally known as Marraui and are probably an affiliated group.

Notes (Abdal or Bor Tarin column): The Raisanis have supplied the nucleus of the chief Sarawan tribe among the Brahuis.

Notes (Barakzai column): Though classed on an equal footing in Provincial Table No. 2, laterals, the Barakzais constitute an older group, of which the Badezais, Khwa Alizais, and Achakzais are branches. The Nurzais served under the Muhammadzais, the present ruling dynasty of Kabul, the Muhammadzais, are collaterals of the Achakzais. The Achakzais in Baluchistan constitute almost the entire population of the Chaman sub-division of Quetta-Pishin. Only three representatives of the Alizais are to be found in Baluchistan.

Notes (Popalzai column): The Popalzais and Sadozais are now generally considered collaterals, though the Sadozais are in reality the younger branch. The Popalzais in Baluchistan are principally refugees and Government servants. Most of the Sadozais have now made their homes in the Punjab. Those in Baluchistan are chiefly Government servants. Ahmad Shah Abdali, the founder of the Afghan State, was a Sadozai.

Habitat (Jamand column): The Pishin Tahsil of the Quetta-Pishin district and Mastung.

Habitat (Kand): Kalat.

Habitat (Kansi): Quetta, Tahsil of the Quetta-Pishin district.
Chagai, Quetta-Pishin, and Zhob, a few also in Kalat.
Also to be found in Shorawak and the Helmand valley.

Habitat (Urmar): ...

Habitat (Barech): Duki and Barkhan in Loralai, Musskhel in Zhob.

Habitat (Miani): Fort Sandeman Tahsil, Zhob district. Branches are also to be found in the Marri country and in Shorawak.

Habitat (Shirani): Mastung in the Sarawan country and Zohri in the Jhalawan country of the Kalat State.

Habitat (Jhat Tarin): The Abubakr, Malikyar, Nurzai, and Saigi live in Quetta-Pishin. The rest in Loralai.

Habitat (Tor Tarin): Sanjawi and Duki Tahsils and a few in Kalat.

Habitat (Spin Tarin): Quetta-Pishin and Kalat.

Habitat (Abdal/Barakzai): Quetta-Pishin.

Vol. III.

(31)

2. DESCENDANTS OF GHURGHUSHT, SON OF QAIS ABDUR RASHID.

DANI.									BABI.	MANDO.
Kakar.					Pani.	Naghar.	Dawi.			
Targhara.	Sargara.	Sanzarkhel.	Sanatia.	Siani.	Jantai. Khajak. Dehpal. Lawnr. Alikhel. Safi. Marghazan. Isot. Barozai (descended from Sanzi). Musakhel.	Khuldai. Hotakzai.	Hunnar. Dumar.	Nuszai.		Mandokhel.
Sur. Sulemankhel. Barakzai. Ahmad Khel. Abbas Khel.	Atozai. Bahlolzai. Daozai. Haronzai. Mandazai. Mirjanzai. Malezai. Barakhel. Abdullazai. Utmankhel. Alizai. Uliazai. Shamozai. Nissi. Sanakhel. Tarnankhel. Taimani.	Hindi. Kibzai. Arabkhel. Niakhel. Prezun. Isakhel. Brahimzai. Shamozai. Basai.	Panozai. Sarangzai. Mahtarzai. Mallazzai.		A few Dawis can be localised among the Kakars and also among the Panis.		There are a few Nahars among the Marris, and also among the Khetrans.	In former days this tribe was engaged in the carrying of trade and Kalat to Sonmiani. Afterwards a few settled in Kalat, but they have now moved to Quetta.	There were two Mandos, one the son of Ghurghusht, and the other son of Pani. In the census records all the Mandokhels have been classed under "Pani." Whether any descendants of Mando, son of Pani, exist is not known, the Zhob Mandokhels are admittedly the descendants of Mando, son of Ghurghusht.	
Though a well recognised clan of the Kakars, the Targharas probably consist of affiliated groups, as the names of the sections Barakzai, Sulemankhel, and Sur, etc., indicate.	The Sargaras of Hindu Bagh and those of Quetta-Pishin have now no political connection with one another.	The most numerous and important clan of the Kakars. They hold nearly the whole of the Zhob valley. The classification of the Sanzarkhel in Provincial Table No. 2 is very faulty. The Dumars, though sharing good and ill with the Sanzarkhel are descended from Dawi, brother of Kakar. The Taimani clan lives in Afghanistan, whilst the twelfth brother, whose name is unknown, became a Hindu. Some of his descendants are said to be living in Sind.		There are a few Sianrs in the Toba-Kakari in the Pishin Tahsil, but they were apparently not enumerated by their own name as they are not to be found in Provincial Table No. 2.	The groups above in the column for distribution include all those who have been identified and classed under Panis. The Panis have been shown as a separate tribe in Provincial Table No. 2. The other sons of Pani were Marghazni, Yusaf, Qasim, Umar, Manda, Shorn, Jadum, and Kakazai, but groups with these patronymics have not been found in Baluchistan. Possibly the Umarzais now shown among the Khajaks may be descendants of Umar, and the Sodis are probably descended from Shodi, son of Shorn. Among the other clans shown as Panis in Provincial Table No. 2, the Abdulhais, Beguns, Kurk, Luni, Mandokhels of Zhob, Mushi, Miri, Pirozi, and Usmani are not united to the Panis by kinship.		Hassan, an adopted son of Dawi, was the son of a Khujandi Sadozai, and his descendants were hence vulgarly called Khudai, i. e., Khujendis. Now affiliated with the Kakars. Vide also note on Zakhpels, col. 10. There is a clan among the Dumars called Umarzai, which is possibly identifiable with the descendants of Humar.			
Toba Kakari and Barshor in the Pishin Tahsil of the Quetta-Pishin district. A few in Loralai and Zhob.	Quetta-Pishin and the Hindu Bagh Tahsil in Zhob.	Quetta-Pishin Tahsil in Zhob.	Shahrig Tahsil, and Hindu Bagh Tahsil.	Toba Kakari in the Pishin Tahsil.	Musakhel Tahsil in Zhob and Sibi Tahsil.	Kila Saifulla, Bori and Fort Sandeman Tahsil in Zhob, and Quetta-Pishin. There are also a few in Loralai.	The Khurdis live in the Musakhel Tahsil of the Zhob district. Quetta-Pishin, Loralai, and Zhob.	Quetta-Pishin and Kalat.	Fort Sandeman and Hindu Bagh Tahsils of the Zhob district.	

APPENDIX A.

Showing genealogically the main natural divisions, locality, etc., of the Afghans in Baluchistan.

SERIAL No.	NATIONALITY OR RACE.	EPONEMOUS ANCESTORS.			LOCAL TRIBAL DISTRIBUTION SHOWING CHIEF SUB-DIVISIONS.		NOTES.	PRESENT LOCATION IN BALUCHISTAN.	REMARKS.
1	2	3	4	5	6	7	8	9	10
3		3. DESCENDANTS OF BAITAN, SON OF QAIS ABDUR RASHID.	DIRECT DESCENDANTS OF BAITAN, SON OF QAIS ABDUR RASHID.	Gajen, or Kajen.	Not represented in Baluchistan.				Indigenous groups whose origin is doubtful are the Zakhpel, Khudar, Lamar, and Neknamzai. The Zakhpels are associated with the Dumars in Sanjawi and Bori. They claim to be Saiyids, but their assertion is unsupported and they are probably of Ghilzai origin. The Khudars and Neknamzais have been enumerated with the Isots of the Musakhel Tahsil. Nothing is known of the origin of the Khudars. The Neknamzais are possibly the descendants of a Davi saint who was called Neknam. The Lamars have been enumerated as Kakars, but are looked upon as aliens.
				Warshapun.					
				Ismail.					
			DESCENDANTS OF BIBI MATO, DAUGHTER OF BAITAN, AND SHAH HUSSEN GHORI.	Ibrahim, surnamed Loedi (Lodhi).	Descendants of Sianai, son of Ibrahim Lodhi. Mahpal.		A few non-indigenous Lohanas, Niazis, and Lodhis are to be found in Baluchistan, and some of the Surs have been affiliated with the Targhara clan of the Kakars.		
					Lohanai.	Marwat.			
					Sur.				
					Prangai.				
					Dotanai.				
					Niazai.				
				Ghalzai.	Khoroti.		The only clans unrepresented in Baluchistan at the time of the 1901 census were the Alikhel and Akakhel. Most of those enumerated in Baluchistan are merely nomads and have their homes in Afghanistan, but some of the Sulimankhel seldom leave the confines of the Zhob district.	Zhob, Quetta-Pishin, and Loralai.	
					Nasir.				
					Tokhe.				
					Hotak.				
					Tarakai.				
					Andar.				
					Sahak.				
					Akakhel.				
					Alikhel.				
					Sulimankhel.				

APPENDIX B.

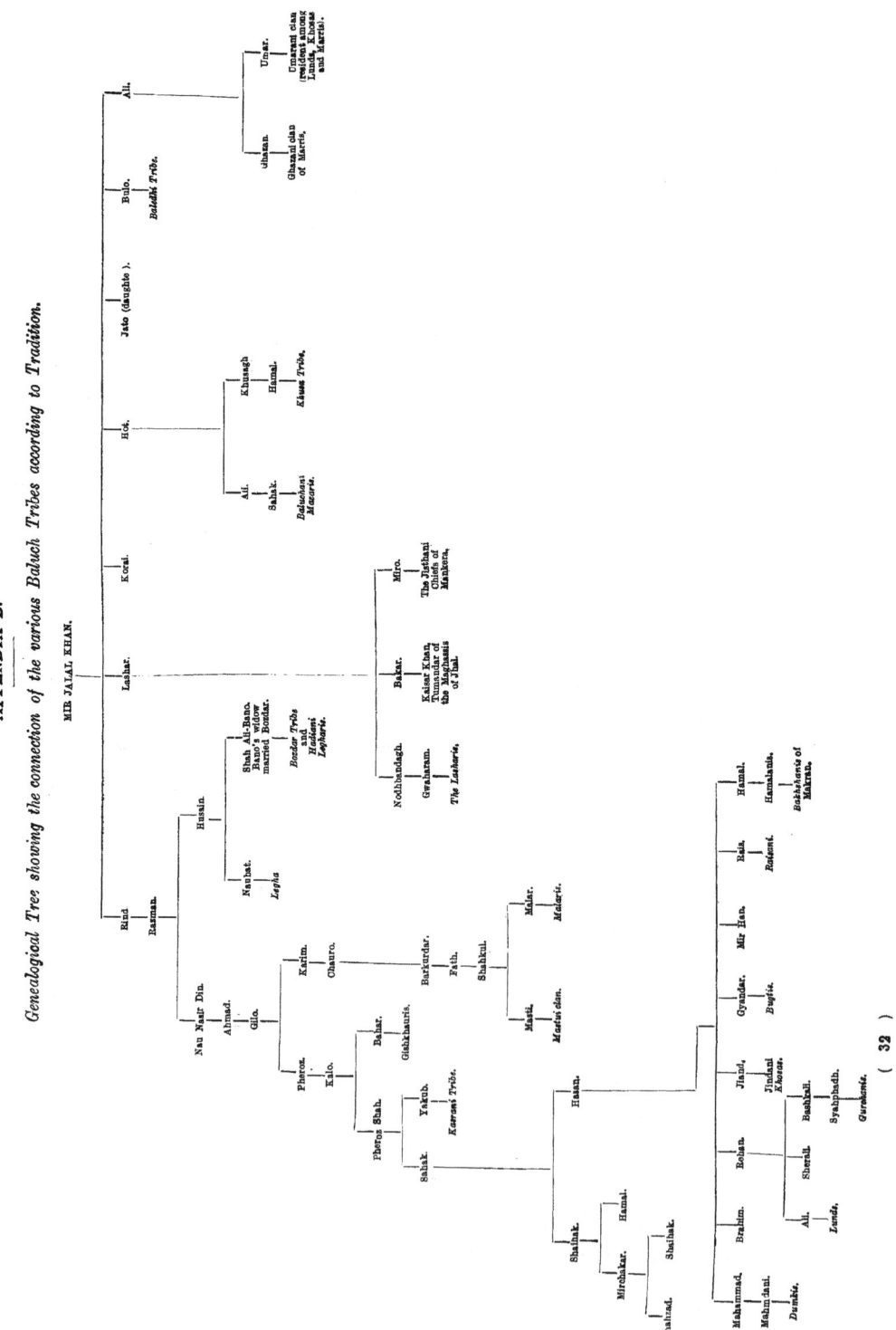

Genealogical Tree showing the connection of the various Baluch Tribes according to Tradition.

MIR JALAL KHAN.

- Rind
  - Rasman
    - Nau Nasir Din
      - Ahmad
      - Gulo
      - Karim
        - Chauro
      - Pheroz
        - Pheroz Shah
          - Yakub — *Kaurani Tribe.*
          - Kalo
          - Bahar — *Gishkhauris.*
        - Sahak
          - Shahak
            - Mirchakar
              - Shahzad
            - Hamal
            - Shahak
          - Hasan
            - Brahim
              - Ali — *Lunda.*
              - Sherik
                - Bashful
                - Syahphadh — *Gurchanis.*
            - Bohan
              - Jiand — *Jindani Khosas.*
            - Gyandar — *Bugtis.*
            - Mir Han
            - Bais — *Rodenis.*
            - Hamal — *Hamalanis, Bakhsharis of Makran.*
            - Mahammad
            - Mahmduni
            - Dumki
        - Barkurdar
          - Fath
          - Shahkul
            - Masti — *Masivi clan.*
            - Malar — *Maderis.*
    - Nasibat — *Legha*
    - Hussin
      - Shah Ali-Bano, Bano's widow married Bozdar. *Bozdar Tribe and Hadiani Legharis.*
  - Nothbandagh
  - Gwaharam — *The Lasharis.*
  - Bakar
    - Kaisar Khan, Tumandar of the Magbassis of Jhal.
  - Miro — The Jisthani Chiefs of Mankera.
- Lashar
- Korai
- Hot
  - Ali
  - Sahak — *Baluchani Mauris.*
  - Khusagh
  - Hamal — *Khosa Tribe.*
- Jato (daughter)
- Bulo — *Baledhi Tribe.*
- Ali
  - Umar — Umarani clan (resident among Lunds, Khosas and Marris).
  - Jhaan — Ghazni clan of Marris.

Vol. III.

(32)

CHAPTER III.

KALAT AFFAIRS.

Early History.

THE authentic history of Kalat begins with the reign of the Brahui Khan Mir Ahmed I, about 1650. Prior to this, what little is known has been roughly sketched in Chapter II.

This Mir Ahmed is said to have been the twelfth descendant in the direct line from Mir Ibrahim the first Khan, who, according to some authorities, gave his name, in the corrupt form of Braho for Ibrahim, to the governing class of Brahuis.

At that time Kalat was a very small and uninfluential State.

Tribal service.

The Khans, therefore, gradually engaged the assistance of the chiefs of their kindred tribes in the neighbourhood by giving them fiefs in Kalat. In return for these fiefs they were bound to furnish troops, in certain specified cases and numbers, for the aid of the Khan.

This is highly significant, as although primarily entirely independent in their own territories, these chiefs became, doubtless, as regards these fiefs, quasi-feudal vassals of the Khan.

By means of the troops so raised, the territories of the Khan were extended by conquest, such conquests being on behalf of the Khan only, and not for the affiliated tribes.

Here it may be noted that until the reign of Nasir II no other force beyond this tribal one was at the disposal of the Khans. That prince first raised a standing army, with the money granted by the British Government for the upkeep of tribal levies on the trade routes.

Formation of Kalat State.

Thus bound together, and finding mutual cohesion essential against their powerful neighbours, Persia, Afghanistan, and Sind, the petty state of Kalat, the independent Baluch and Brahui tribes, and their joint conquests gradually became amalgamated into one federal

State under the authority of the Khan. The conditions of this arrangement, however, secured to the confederate chiefs practical self-government in their own previously independent territory.

In the first half of the eighteenth century the ruler of Kalat was one Muhabbat Khan. This ruler was the great aggrandiser of his line. Adroitly joining Nadir Shah in his conquests in India, Muhabbat Khan obtained from him Kach, Gandava, and other lowland districts formerly appertaining to Sind.

Muhabbat Khan.

In these newly acquired districts Muhabbat Khan assigned fiefs to the Tribal Sardars, but established his own Naibs or Lieutenants to govern them, their headquarters being at Gandava, a walled town of some importance, well situated on the Nari River.

Acquisition of Kachi.

At a later period, however (1731), Muhabbat Khan incurred the displeasure of Ahmad Shah Durani, ruler at Kabul, and was by him removed from the Khanship in favour of Nasir Khan I. His brother Nasir Khan held the reins of government during the greater part of the latter half of the eighteenth century. He was the great organiser of his race, and consolidated the power of his family.

Nasir Khan I. the Great.

To his laws reference is made to-day. Tradition and the accounts of early travellers such as Pottinger and Masson attribute to Nasir Khan the regular systematising of the various customs which immediate exigencies had, from time to time, called into existence during the reigns of his predecessors. To him were due rules regulating commerce, the administration of justice, and treatment of Hindus and other foreigners and travellers. In the time of Nasir Khan I there were two great provinces, Sarawan and Jhalawan, meaning "highland" and "lowland." Over these Sardarships, or Supreme Chiefships, had been established. These Sardarships were hereditary in the families of Raisani for the Sarawan and Zehri for the Jhalawan.

Kalat Constitution.

These Sardars possessed an important authority in affairs of State, though apparently rather consultative than executive. They occupied chairs in durbar, the Sarawan on the right, the

Jhalawan on the left, of the Khan. They were admitted to all deliberations generally affecting the State.

Another curious arrangement was the hereditary office of Wazir or Prime Minister in a family which, although converted to Muhammadanism, was of Hindu origin. Breaking through this rule of appointing the hereditary Wazir probably cost Mehrab Khan his life in 1839.

It appears that, save as controlled by the consultative functions of the two Supreme Chiefs and the Wazir, the power of the Khan as regards external matters was supreme and absolute. He could make peace or war on behalf of the State.

He could call out any or all of the tribal levies, and use them for war or the maintenance of order. He could make treaties binding on the State; but if damaged thereby, any particular chief could claim compensation. One point in this connection is not clear. Doubtless, the petty chiefs had some share even in the decision of external matters, but it is not known whether they gave their opinions directly or through the two Supreme Chiefs as their representatives. As regards internal authority, the Khan had apparently power to a certain extent to make general laws for the whole State. The administration of those laws, however, was not his affair, subject to the reservation that a sentence of death required his confirmation. He was the final arbitrator in disputes between chiefs, especially in regard to boundary questions.

Within Kalat itself, and the conquered and annexed territories, the Khan ruled directly through his Naibs or Lieutenants.

The chiefs were elected by the elders of the tribes, their election being subject to confirmation[1] by the Khan. This confirmation once given, the chiefs were only bound to obey the Khan in external matters, to submit to his orders when appeals were made to him, to require his confirmation to death sentences, and furnish their quota of troops when called upon. On the other hand, the Khans were elected by the chiefs, the choice having to be made, however, from members of the Ahmedzai family.

The chiefs jealously guarded the important agreement by which the Khan was prohibited from having any armed force other than the tribal levies.

---

[1] This confirmation early became a matter of form.

From this it will be seen that the Kalat confederacy was founded by a *voluntary* federation. There was but one *feudal* element in the constitution, namely, tribal service of troops in return for fiefs granted to certain of the chiefs by the Khan, out of their own personal estate. This matter is important as furnishing, subsequently, a bone of contention between the Sind and Punjab Governments, and leading to different policies being adopted for many years by them towards certain Baluch tribes.

The proof of this "federal" idea came into prominence in 1869. In that year the grievances of the chiefs were enquired into by the Sind authorities, whose principal demand was that all engagements with the British Government should be made not by the Khan personally, but by him as the head of the Confederation.

The chiefs themselves were merely the elective heads of free communities made up of sub-divisions of tribes, beneath which again were villages; each with its own elected head. The higher the authority the more usual was the selection from one family, which gradually became hereditarily that from which the headman or chief was elected.

We have many examples in history of a similar conditions of things in the early constitution of States which afterwards became absolute monarchies. This is generally due to the gradually increasing power and wealth of the sovereign, his ability to keep a standing army, and, in consequence, to suppress rebellion.

We shall find later that the British subsidy to the Khan of Kalat enabled him to pay a standing army, by the aid of which his ambitions led him into armed conflict with the greater number of his confederated chiefs.

However, although morally supported by the Sind Government in considering himself a sovereign and the chiefs his vassals, he failed to effect his object, and had finally, in 1876, to invite the British Government to settle affairs between himself and his Sardars.

In the time of Nasir Khan the territory of the Kalat State was bounded on the north by the Afghan Provinces of Pishin and Sibi and the tribal territory of the Kakar and Tarin Pathans. Sind bounded it

Kalat in Nasir Khan's time.

on the east, but the Kalat province of Harrand Dajal[1] reached north of Sind to the Indus through the Marri and Bugti countries which were tributary to Nasir Khan. Persia and the sea were its western and southern boundaries. Makran and Kharan had been added to Kalat by conquest, Las Bela by treaty.

Before the time of Nasir Khan I, Las Bela was an independent State, inhabited, as now, by a mongrel Sindi-Rajput race. Nasir Khan determined to annex it, and made the then Jam,[2] Mian Khan, his tributary. To cement the friendship of Mian Khan he gave him his daughter in marriage.

Thus the State of Kalat was consolidated under the government of Nasir Khan "The Great," who made himself not only the political head, but also the spiritual leader of the confederation. Assuming the rôle of a religious enthusiast he was, before his death, esteemed the holiest man in Baluchistan, an example of his acumen in dealing with a wild uneducated people.

Mehrab Khan.

Nasir Khan "The Great" was succeeded by his son Mahmud Khan, an indolent debauchee, who was in turn followed by Mehrab Khan his son.

During the reigns of these two chiefs the power and influence of the Khan rapidly declined. Travellers such as Pottinger in 1810, Conolly in 1830, and Haji Abdul Nabi in 1838, tell us that the very slightest bonds kept the confederacy together. Tribute to Kalat was the exception, but military service against a common foe was still recognised. In the days of Mehrab Khan the feudal army of the Khanate, when called into the field, was composed of the two great families of Sarawan and Jhalawan. The Sarawan formed the right wing of the army, the Jhalawan the left.

The Marri, Bugti, and Gurchani clans were included in the Sarawans, and in those days they not only rendered feudal service to the State, but paid tribute to the Khan.

A regular organisation existed, the memory of which is still dearly cherished by the chiefs, and rendered the Kalat State capable of holding her own against all comers, except the British.

---

[1] Harrand Dajal was given to Nasir Khan by Timur Shah in return for assistance rendered by the former against the Mahrattas.

[2] Local name for ruler—a corrupt form of Cham learnt from the Tartar invaders of India.

The first official intercourse between the British Government and Kalat was in 1838. In that year Lieutenant Leech was deputed to the Khan to arrange terms for the passage of British troops through his territory on their way to Kandahar. His abortive mission, and the subsequent theft of the treaty from Sir Alexander Burnes, are episodes in the history of the First Afghan War. Briefly, the circumstances were these. Mehrab Khan, grandson of the Great Nasir Khan, had removed the hereditary Wazir of Kalat from office, and replaced him with a creature of his own. The son of the deposed Wazir was Mulla Muhammad Hasan. The latter harboured revenge against the Khan for the disgrace to his family, and his opportunity occurred when Mehrab Khan, himself repenting his breach of the constitutional custom, appointed him to the hereditary office.

Early intercourse with Kalat.

Throughout the negotiations between the Khan and the British Government, Mulla Muhammad Hasan laboured to breed fear on one side and distrust on the other. When in spite of his machinations Sir Alexander Burnes brought matters to a satisfactory conclusion, the Wazir caused him to be robbed of the treaty shortly after he had left Kalat.

During their march towards Kandahar, the British troops were much harassed by the tribesmen in Kachi and the Bolan, and supplies were unobtainable. This state of affairs, Mulla Muhammad Hassan informed the British authorities, was due to the direct instigation of the Khan. Too late, papers were discovered in Kalat proving the entire innocence of Mehrab Khan. He paid the penalty with his life in the capture of Kalat by General Willshire, an act described by Malleson as "more than a grave error, a crime."

In consequence of the reported hostility of the Khan of Kalat throughout the British advance to Kandahar, General Willshire (afterwards Sir Thomas Willshire), commanding the Bombay Column, on its return to India, was ordered to proceed to Kalat from Quetta to depose Mehrab Khan.

Siege of Kalat.

Owing to the want of public carriage, and the limited quantity of Commissariat supplies at Quetta, as well as the reported want of forage and water on the road to Kalat, General Willshire

despatched to Gandava the whole of his cavalry and most of his artillery.

With him to Kalat he took the troops detailed in the margin. Only perfectly fit men were taken and consequently the regiments mustered only some 300 each.

<blockquote>
Two guns, Bombay Horse Artillery.
Four guns, Shah's Artillery.
H. M's 2nd Foot.
H. M's 17th Foot.
31st Bengal Native Infantry.
Bombay Engineer Detachment.
Two Squadrons, Irregular Horse.
</blockquote>

The force numbered 65 officers, 12 native officers, and 1,184 of other ranks on the 13th November 1839, the date on which Kalat was taken, exclusive of two squadrons of the Shah's (Bengal) Irregular Horse, who were left in charge of the baggage during the action.

The troops marched from Quetta on the 4th November 1839. The first seven marches, with one halt, *viâ* Mastung, were without incident. Contrary to expectation water and forage were found to be so abundant, and the road so good, that the whole force might have proceeded to Kalat without difficulty.

On the 11th November, when the column was two marches distant from Kalat, a letter of defiance was received from Mehrab Khan, directing the immediate halt of the British troops pending negotiations, and stating his intention of moving out from Kalat with all his troops to meet the British force.

The force at command of the Khan was estimated at 2,000 fighting men, with five guns. Reinforcements under his son were daily expected from Nushki. General Willshire proceeded next day to Girani, a village eight miles from Kalat, hoping that Mehrab Khan would advance and not shut himself up in the fortress.

During the march to Girani some desultory skirmishing took place between reconnoitring parties of the Irregular Horse and the advanced Kalati scouts. The conduct of the Irregular Horse was so unsatisfactory that they were left as a baggage guard on the following day.

The night of the 12th and 13th November was spent under arms, and every precaution was taken against a possible night attack by the Khan's force, or the reinforcements from Nushki expected in the rear. The night passed quietly however, and the march was resumed on the 13th.

After proceeding about a mile, a body of Baluch Horse appeared on the right of the column. Perceiving that the British force was without cavalry, they became very bold, and for six miles kept up a running fight with the advanced guard, the 17th Foot, under Major Pennycuick, galloping up close to the column and discharging their matchlocks from horseback.

Having marched seven miles, the British column surmounted a small range of hills from which the town and fortress of Kalat, about a mile distant, came into view.

Of the Kalat position Sir James Outram, who was with General Willshire as aide-de-camp, thus writes :—

> It was truly an imposing sight. Some small hills in front were crowned with masses of soldiers, and the towering citadel which frowned above them in their rear was completely clustered over with human beings, chiefly ladies of the harem, who had assembled to witness the discomfiture of the Feringhees, and the prowess of their lords, all of whom, with the Khan at their head, had previously marched out to the heights, where they awaited us in battle array.

As the British column topped the ridge, they came under fire of five guns posted on the hills north of Kalat. The guns were badly served, however, and inflicted no loss.

Seeing that determined resistance was to be expected, General Willshire here halted the troops to give the baggage time to close up. This was parked and committed to the charge of the Irregular Horse. Meanwhile, Captain Peak, Chief Engineer, was sent forward to reconnoitre. It was discovered that three heights to the north-west of the fort were strongly held with infantry, five guns being in position. The whole hostile front was protected by small parapet walls, turning each hill top into a redoubt. During this delay two companies were sent to clear some gardens on the left of the British position.

The following plan of assault was then communicated by the General :—

> Under cover of the artillery, the three redoubts on the heights are first to be carried, four companies of each regiment being told off for this duty, each regiment having a redoubt assigned to it.
>
> Two companies are to advance through the gardens on our left.
>
> The remaining ten companies will be held in reserve.

The object of this attack on the redoubts was twofold. In the first place the British camp was commanded by artillery fire from them, and, in the second, from these heights the British artillery could shell Kalat.

The storming columns were led by their commanding officers, Major Carruthers of the Queen's, Lieutenant-Colonel Croker of Her Majesty's 17th Foot, and Major Western of the 31st Bengal Native Infantry. The whole was under the command and direction of Brigadier Baumgardt. The reserve under General Willshire moved in support, formed in three columns.

Brigadier Stevenson, commanding the artillery, moved his guns forward into range, and quickly developed a destructive fire on the hostile infantry and guns. Meanwhile the attacking columns advanced steadily, and began to ascend the heights. They soon came under the fire of the enemy's guns which caused some loss, but did not delay the advance.

The enemy, meanwhile, were suffering severely from our artillery, and, before the attacking columns reached their respective summits, evacuated their position, endeavouring to take their guns with them.

General Willshire, observing this, ordered the attacking column of the Queen's, which was nearest the north gate of the fort, to break off down the hill, pursue the enemy, and, if possible, enter the fort with them; but, at all costs, to prevent the guns being taken into the fortress. Captain Outram, who carried these orders to the Queen's, reached that column before it arrived at the redoubt C. The column rushed down the hill, but arrived too late to enter the fort with the enemy, who, however, abandoned their guns outside the gate.

This detachment then took up a position under cover of some ruins, marked E on the map.

General Willshire then despatched orders to the companies at G under Major Pennycuick to advance, and take up a position as near the Kandahar gate as possible.

They took cover behind a wall at H within fifty yards of the gate.

In taking up these positions at G and H the chief losses of the day occurred, the troops so engaged being exposed to an exceedingly hot and well-directed fire from the walls.

The guns had meanwhile been dragged up on to the heights evacuated by the enemy, which were now occupied by our troops. Four of the guns, from the point B B, were to play on the towers commanding the gateway, whilst the other two were ordered down to D for the purpose of battering the gate itself. From the point D the two guns opened upon the gate, and a few rounds were sufficient to throw down one half of it. Instantly, the parties at E and H dashed into the gateway, led by Major Pennycuick. They were closely followed by the remainder of the storming parties which had been moved up in readiness.

These advances were much harassed by the enemy from the walls, a heavy matchlock fire being sustained until our troops had entered the fortress, when the Baluchis slowly retired to the citadel, disputing every inch of ground.

The reserve was now brought up to the Northern Gate, and General Willshire determined to take steps to prevent the escape of the enemy by the Southern Gate. For this purpose the troops detailed in the margin were despatched round the western side of the fortress to seize the heights under which the southern angle is situated. Major Western, 31st Bengal Native Infantry, was in command of the whole detachment and Captain Darby of the Company of the 17th.

<small>1 Company, 17th Foot.
2 Companies, 31st Bengal Native Infantry.</small>

Two companies of the 17th were sent round the eastern face of the fortress under Major Dithon, accompanied by 2 guns of the Shah's Artillery under Lieutenant Creed.

Major Western's detachment found the heights at K lightly held. He stormed the position, and had the good fortune to enter the Southern Gate with the fugitives. Here he was joined by Major Dithon, and the two detachments having united proceeded to fight their way up to the citadel, against which the northern attacking force had not yet made any impression. The two guns which had accompanied Major Dithon took up a position at N and quickly effected a breach in the citadel. More troops were sent from the reserve to co-operate, and in a few moments the British standards waved over the highest towers of Kalat.

A desperate resistance was made by the Chief, Mehrab Khan, who fell, sword in hand, with most of his principal nobles at the entrance to the citadel. Desultory firing was kept up for some

time from detached buildings difficult of access, and it was not until late in the afternoon that those who survived were induced to surrender on a promise of their lives being spared.

Sir James Outram who was present says :—

The soldiers displayed much greater forbearance than they usually do on such occasions. Quarter was never refused by them when craved by cries of 'Aman,' 'Aman,' and before nightfall nearly two thousand prisoners had been removed from the fort unharmed.

Four hundred of the garrison are computed to have fallen in this affair, including the Khan and many of the principal Baluch chieftains, every person of note having been either slain or captured. From prisoners it was afterwards ascertained that Mehrab Khan had endeavoured to escape by the Southern Gate, but, finding that our troops had occupied it, he returned to the citadel where he was found among the slain.

Considering the small number of our troops—of whom not more than one-half were actually engaged—our losses were heavy. The killed numbered thirty-two, including Lieutenant Gravatt of the Queen's, and wounded one hundred and seven, among them eight officers. The Queen's lost most severely, having sixty-nine of all ranks killed and wounded : the 17th Foot had thirty-three, and the 31st Bengal Native Infantry twenty-two casualties. The artillery had three men wounded, and the Engineers and Irregular Horse one each.

Before the attack on Kalat, Mehrab Khan sent his son (afterwards Mir Nasir Khan II) in the charge of Darogah Gul Muhammad to Nushki. Lieutenant Loveday pursued him to that place, and the young prince proceeded to Panjgur, and thence to Kharan, where he was well received by Azad Khan Naushirwani. Meanwhile the British authorities placed Shah Nawaz on the throne of Kalat. Shah Nawaz belonged to another branch of the ruling family of Kalat, and had been a pretender to the throne in the time of Mehrab Khan, by whom he had been imprisoned. He managed to escape and accompanied Shah Shuja on his march from India to Kandahar. Before his death, Mehrab Khan reproached Shah Shuja for befriending Shah Nawaz, reminding him of the hospitality he had received at Kalat when a fugitive in 1834.

Shah Nawaz asked General Willshire to leave a British officer at Kalat. Accordingly Lieutenant Loveday was appointed British Agent with the Khan. Unfortunately, Nawaz Khan was disliked by all classes in Baluchistan.

Lieutenant Loveday.

Moreover, as by right of conquest, the British Government disposed of a portion of the country, annexing parts of Sarawan, Kachi, and Gandava to the Kabul Power, under the administration of British officers. On completion of these arrangements General Willshire marched towards Sind *viâ* the Mulla Pass.

Departure of British Force.

Unrest among the tribesmen became at once apparent on the departure of the British force, and the chiefs were enraged at the partition of their country.

Unrest in Kalat.

Lieutenant Loveday made himself unpopular with the Brahui Chiefs. Among other things he farmed the revenues of Mastung to his *munshi*, whose oppressive measures caused the Sarawan Chief to rebel against Shah Nawaz. Early in 1840 Muhammad Khan Shawani headed the revolt and recalled Mehrab Khan's son from Kharan with intent to place him on the throne of Kalat. Azad Khan himself escorted the young prince from Kharan to Mastung, which immediately fell into the power of the rebels. The rebels then made an unsuccessful attempt to take Quetta. They were, however, allowed to assemble at Mastung, unmolested by the British garrison at Quetta. Thence they proceeded, some 2,000 strong, to attack Kalat.

Shah Nawaz stood a siege for a few days, assisted by Lieutenant Loveday and Mr. Masson, the traveller, with the escort of 40 sepoys. After repulsing a few attacks, the Khan surrendered the town and was permitted to depart to Sind. Most of the Political Agent's escort were put to the sword, and Lieutenant Loveday and Mr. Masson were made prisoners. The insurgents once more returned to Mastung, and despatched Mr. Masson with letters of negoiation to Captain Bean, Political Agent at Quetta. Though under obligation to return, Mr. Masson was detained a prisoner by Captain Bean who apparently, connected him with the disturbances in

Rebels seize Kalat.

Capture of Lieutenant Loveday.

Kalat. This erroneous assumption prolonged the rebellion, and probably cost Lieutenant Loveday his life, as we afterwards acceded to all the requests of Mir Nasir Khan's party. At this juncture General Nott's Brigade arrived at Quetta *en route* to Kandahar, and he received orders to re-occupy Kalat. Having obtained information of the intended move, the rebels marched to Kachi, taking with them Lieutenant Loveday. General Nott found Kalat deserted on 3rd November and re-occupied it with a small garrison.

<small>General Nott occupies Kalat.</small>

Finding that Dadur was held by a weak garrison, the rebels attacked it on November 1st, but were repulsed by Captain Watkins.

On November 3rd Major Boscawen collected a small force from the troops on the lines of communication and marched to the relief of Dadur. An action took place outside that post in which the Baluchis were signally defeated, and fled to the hills.

<small>Action of Dadur.</small>

During the flight from the field Lieutenant Loveday, tied on camel, was left alone with his jailor Kaissu. The latter acknowledged at his trial that he had killed Lieutenant Loveday on his own initiative as he found that, otherwise, he would be rescued by the pursuing British troops. Apparently he discussed the necessity of this dastardly deed with the unfortunate officer, for he naively remarked at his trial that, at the request of his prisoner, he endeavoured to obtain the Khan's sanction to the murder, and that having failed to find the Khan he determined to act on his own responsibility. He was executed after trial at the Agency Camp in Quetta.

<small>Murder of Lieutenant Loveday.</small>

After their defeat at Dadur, the rebels marched southwards and took up a position in the hills near Kotra where they remained until the battle of Kotra on November 30th.

<small>Action at Kotra.</small>

During this interval Nasir Khan opened negotiations with Mr. Ross-Bell, the Agent to the Governor-General in Upper Sind. The published account of this affair at Kotra in Field Army Orders by Major-General Brooks commanding the Forces in Upper Sind, dated December 6th, 1840, is to this effect:—

The Major-General having received authentic intelligence that Nasir Khan with the garrison of Kalat, about 4,000 men, had

encamped in a strong position in the hills within eight miles of Kotra, and that reinforcements to the extent of many thousands were on the road from Thull to join them, directed Lieut.-Colonel Marshall with troops as per margin to proceed to attack the Khan in his position. The despatch reached Lieut.-Colonel Marshall on November the 30th.

2 Guns, under Lieutenant Pruen.
2nd Bombay Grenadiers, under Captain Boyd.
21st Bombay Native Infantry, under Captain Ennis.
25th Bombay Native Infantry, under Captain Teasdale.
60 Irregular Horse, under Lieutenant Smith.

On December the 1st that officer with 900 bayonets, Native Infantry, 60 Irregular Horse, and 2 guns delivered his attack. The enemy were completely surprised. Nasir Khan with two followers escaped on foot at the first alarm, but his chiefs and followers made a long and desperate defence, and it was not until four of the principal chiefs and upwards of 500 men lay dead on the field, and nearly the whole of the force had been put to flight, that the enemy's chief commander, Mir Bohir, with his son, six other chiefs, and 132 of their bravest followers surrendered as prisoners. The whole of the enemy's baggage and a large quantity of arms fell into the hands of the British in this " brilliant achievement."

There is, however, another side to this affair. In future relations with the British authorities pending the final instalment of Nasir Khan a year later, the Brahuis and Baluchis showed the greatest distrust of British sincerity, and perpetually cited the affair of Kotra as a breach of faith.

Native account of the action.

Colonel Stacy states that he was informed on all sides by the chiefs that they were in daily intercourse with the British authorities and Lieut.-Colonel Marshall, when they were treacherously attacked. Darogha Gul Muhammad stated to Colonel Stacy that the Khan's envoys were actually in Colonel Marshall's camp when the attack was made, adding " it is not the custom to send proposals of peace and friendship in the evening, and next morning make an attack. Who shall say how many men were killed, wounded, and taken; how much property was seized; what was the extent of our misfortunes."

In December 1840, Colonel Stacy, commanding the 43rd Bengal Native Infantry, was appointed specially to proceed to Kalat to open up negotiations with the young Khan who

Colonel Stacy, Special Envoy to Kalat.

was still in Kachi, and endeavour to induce him to disband his army, and wait upon Mr. Bell, the Agent to the Governor-General in Upper Sind.

Colonel Stacy proceeded forthwith to the Brahui Chiefs accompanied by a few attendants but without escort of any kind. Thus from the start he gained their confidence, and the chiefs made themselves responsible for his safety. His courteous treatment of the Khan and his chiefs, a great contrast to what they had hitherto received from the British representatives, gained for him a great personal influence over them, and to this was largely due the success of his mission. In July Nasir Khan entered Kalat as the guest of the British Government, and on the 6th October 1841, was installed as Khan of Kalat by Sir James Outram, who had succeeded Mr. Ross-Bell as Agent of Upper Sind and Baluchistan.

Nasir Khan installed Khan of Kalat.

The provinces shorn from the Kalat State after the capture of the capital in 1839 were restored, and a treaty was drawn up between that State and British India. The terms were as follows:—

1. While recognising the Khan's vassalage to Shah Shuja (afterwards annulled), the reigning chief at Kalat should always be ruled by the British Resident.

Kalat Treaty, 1841.

2. British troops might occupy any position in Kalat territory in any force.

3. The Khan's foreign relationships must be absolutely at the discretion of the British Government.

4. The British Government guaranteed the Khan his dominions, and undertook to assist him in preserving order.

While these affairs were happening at Kalat the tribes on the east of the Bolan had also been dealt with. The Marris and Bugtis had been taught a lesson by the force under Major Billamore which passed successfully through their hills in 1839, defeating the Bugtis in two engagements, and paying a visit to Kahan, the Marri capital. These events are elsewhere related in detail.

Tribal affairs, 1840-41.

After the treaty with the Khan, however, the safety of the Bolan Pass had to be arranged for, and agreements were arranged between the British Government and the Kakars, Marris, and Bugtis at Mastung and Lehri. The Marris and Bugtis acknowledged the supremacy of the Khan, as did the Dumkis and Jakranis

Kachi. These treaties were arranged by Sir James Outram and Colonel Stacy. During the years 1841 and 1842 the convoys through the Bolan were protected by the Sind Horse under Captain John Jacob.

When the troops returned from Afghanistan in 1842 all the frontier troops were withdrawn to Sind. After the conquest of Sind, however, in 1843, the frontier was again occupied. In the interim the Dumkis and Jakranis had become much emboldened, and the Khan lost all control over them. In consequence Sir Charles Napier proceeded against them in 1845 with 7,000 men. In this campaign the Marris aided the British troops, having been won over by Captain John Jacob. The result of this expedition was that the Dumkis and Jakranis were transported to Sind where they were given land, thus ceasing to belong to the Kalat State. Kachi now became the raiding ground of the Bugtis. An account of their raids and gradual pacification will be found elsewhere.

On the 9th January 1847, John Jacob arrived on the Upper Sind Frontier. His work and the doughty deeds of his Sind Frontier Force pertain more to the history of Sind than of Baluchistan. But as his expeditions were made against the Baluch tribes, his work being at first the pacification of the Baluch border, and later the establishment of the authority of the Khan of Kalat, a short résumé may be of interest.

In February 1848, John Jacob was appointed to sole political power on the Upper Sind Frontier, Military Commandant of the Frontier Force, and authorised to arrange with the Khan of Kalat all questions relating to matters between the two Governments and to tribes, beyond the frontier, subject to the Khan.

<small>John Jacob in Upper Sind.</small>

The system introduced and the principles followed by Jacob cannot be better stated than in his own words, as given in a rough memorandum drawn up by him in August 1854. They were entirely offensive measures.

Extract from a rough memorandum by Major J. Jacob on Sind Frontier Proceedings since 1846, dated 9th August 1854.

Entirely offensive measures on the part of the troops, the possibility of attack by the marauders never being contemplated.

No defensive works whatever allowed anywhere : existing ones destroyed or abandoned : the troops always freely exposed, and obstacles to rapid movement removed as much as possible : the people protected.

No distinction permitted between plundering and killing by private persons—whether friend or foe. Robbery and murder treated as equally criminal, whether the victim be a British subject or not, the plea of family blood feud or retaliation, in such cases, considered as an aggravating circumstance—proving the most deliberate malice aforethought.

No private person allowed to bear arms, or possess them, without written permission.

The highest moral ground always taken in all dealings with the predatory tribes, treating them always as of an inferior nature so long as they persist in their misdeeds : as mere vulgar, criminal, and disreputable persons with whom it is a disgrace for right-minded people to have any dealings ; and whom all good men must, as a matter of course, look on as objects of pity, not of dread—with hatred, perhaps, but never with fear.

As perfect information as possible of all movements, or intended movements, of the plundering tribes residing beyond our border. Such information acted on with the greatest activity, our knowledge of the nature and habits of the Baluchi robbers being sufficient to enable us in almost every single instance to judge correctly of their probable proceedings, and effectually to check and counteract them at a distance from the British boundary.

The feeling instilled into every soldier employed being that he was altogether of a superior nature to the robber—a good man against a criminal, the plunderers being always considered not as enemies, but as malefactors.

The strictest justice always acted on, and no success, or want of success, or any other circumstance whatever allowed to influence the terms offered to, or the treatment of offenders—whether whole tribes or individuals. Violence, robbery, bloodshed held as equally disreputable in all men ; the abandonment of such practices and the adoption of peaceful and industrious habits being considered as most honourable, and encouraged in every way.

A few words will sum up the whole system :—

At first, put down all violence with the strong hand. Then, your force being known, felt, and respected, endeavour to excite men's better natures, till all men, seeing that your object is good, and of the greatest general benefit to the community, join heart and hand to aid in putting down or preventing violence. This is the essence of the whole business. The working of true principles is now apparent here in almost total absence of open physical force.

When we came to the Sind Frontier in 1847, the people had no idea of any power but violence. The proceedings of the British authorities tended to confirm this state of feeling.

When the men of Kachi plundered in Sind, the only remedy applied was to recommend the Sindis to plunder in Kachi. Both parties then were equally guiltless or equally criminal; no idea of moral superiority was thought of. Such being the case, it was absolutely necessary in the first instance to have recourse to violent measures, to show the predatory tribes, that we possessed, in far greater degree than themselves, the only power which they respected more brute force. Our first year on the border (1847) was one of enormous bodily labour. We had literally to lie down to rest with our boots and swords on for many months together. We crushed the robbers by main force, and proved far superior to them, even in activity. And it may be well to observe that at this time only one regiment of the Sind Horse was on the frontier.

When our frontier was in a disturbed state, I had my posts close to the hills, esteeming this arrangement to be an advantage. Since quiet has been established, I have withdrawn them, save as respects some Baluchi Guides. Having by the use of force made ourselves feared and respected, we were able to apply better means, and to appeal to higher motives than fear. This I had in view from the very first. The barbarians now feel (which they could not even imagine before) that strength, courage, and activity may be possessed in the highest degree by those also influenced by gentle and benevolent motives.

Under the influence of this growing feeling, the character of the border plunderers has been changed; whole tribes, within and without our border, amounting to more than 20,000 souls, have totally abandoned their former predatory habits, and taken to peaceable pursuits. Our Jakranis and Dumkis—formerly the wildest of the border raiders—are now the most honest, industrious people in all Sind. The Bugtis are practically settled down.

Every man of the Sind Irregular Horse is looked on and treated as a friend by all the country folk. In truth the moral power of their bold and kindly bearing and proceeding has spread far and wide through the country, and effected what no mere force would have done.

Even the Marris who have not felt our physical force much, are fast coming under this influence, and are beginning to feel themselves disreputable.

This somewhat lengthy description of Jacob's methods is interesting in a work on Frontier matters. To maintain proper and wholesome influence over the wild spirits to be met with on our Indian frontiers, firmness and consistency are necessary, combined with kind and just treatment. The tribes must

Methods of administration.

be taught to know and feel that the administration is working for the public good, but that implicit obedience must be yielded. That the British officers are their best friends, to be respected and not thought lightly of. Palliative measures are not only ephemeral, but generally lead to greater complications, and are always regarded as an exhibition of weakness. Win the confidence of these people by proofs of superiority *in all respects*, by showing a keen and thorough interest in their concerns, and a determination to be obeyed, and force has seldom to be resorted to.

Previous to the arrival of Jacob in Upper Sind, the frontier had been held for five years by a brigade consisting of a native cavalry regiment, a field battery, a camel corps 500 strong, and two native infantry regiments.[1] The headquarters were at Shikarpur, and various posts were established along the frontier. Anarchy, however, prevailed. Depredations by the border tribes were of daily occurrence, and the outposts were confined to their entrenchments.

Early arrangements on Sind Frontier.

Major Jacob saw that the previous want of success was largely due to the absence of trust between the officers and tribes generally.

The officers who had to serve on the frontier disliked the locality and the work. The climate was bad, and the accommodation of a wretched description.

Jacob's position was peculiar. He made the frontier his home and let the people know it. He built a large house, laid out an estate and endeavoured to establish a school of officers who would be trained to fill the different positions in regular gradation; officers who would become well acquainted with the people and their circumstances, and have a thorough interest in their work. This system was at first adhered to, but gradually was changed to provide appointments for senior officers from other parts of India.

Jacob's methods.

In 1851, having entire charge of all Sind frontier matters, military and civil, Jacob turned his attention towards Kalat. Nasir Khan II at this time was almost at open feud with his chiefs. His Wazir, Muhammad Hasan, had stirred up ill-feeling between the Khan

Jacob and Kalat affairs.

---

[1] Mostly Bengal troops

and his nobles for his personal aggrandisement. He was only removed from his office when Jacob proved to the Khan in 1853 that he was actually plotting to depose him and assume the Khanship. At this time, 1851, the Khan was powerless and at the mercy of his chiefs. The northern tribes, particularly the Marris, had thrown off all allegiance and raided everywhere; claims for redress against them on behalf of British subjects met with evasive answers from Kalat.

In 1854, in view of the possibility of war between Britain and Russia, it was determined to strengthen the power of the Kalat State.

Treaty with Kalat, 1854.

Accordingly a meeting took place at Jacobabad early in that year, at which the Khan's authority was recognised south of Kalat to the Arabian Sea, and west of Sind to Persia, including Las Bela. In May of the same year, at Mastung, a treaty was drawn up between the Khan and the British Government, the text of which is here given.

From this time to 1856 the Khan set about reducing his rebellious Sardars, and raised a few regular troops, mostly ex-soldiers of the Indian Army.

The Kalat Treaty of 1854.

Article 1.—The Treaty concluded by Major Outram between the British Government and Mir Nasir Khan, Chief of Kalat, on the 6th November 1841 is hereby annulled.

Article 2.—There shall be perpetual friendship between the British Government and Mir Nasir Khan, Chief of Kalat, his heirs, and successors.

Article 3.—Mir Nasir Khan binds himself, his heirs, and successors, to oppose to the utmost all the enemies of the British Government; in all cases to act in subordinate co-operation with that Government, and to enter into no negotiation with other States without its consent; the usual friendly correspondence with neighbours being continued as before.

Article 4.—Should it be deemed necessary to station British troops in any part of the territory of Kalat, they shall occupy such positions as may be thought advisable by the British authorities.

Article 5.—Mir Nasir Khan binds himself, his heirs, and successors to prevent all plundering or other outrage by his subjects within or near British territory; to protect the passage of merchants to and fro between the British dominions and Afghanistan, whether by way of Sind or by the seaport of Sonmiani or other seaports of Makran; and to permit no exactions to be made

beyond an equitable duty to be fixed by the British Government and Mir Nasir Khan, the amount to be shewn in the schedule annexed to this Treaty.

Article 6.—To aid Mir Nasir Khan, his heirs, and successors in the fulfilment of these obligations, and on condition of a faithful performance of them year by year, the British Government binds itself to pay to Mir Nasir Khan, his heirs, and successors an annual subsidy of half a lakh (50,000) of Company's Rupees.

Article 7.—If during any year the conditions above mentioned shall not be faithfully performed by the said Mir Nasir Khan, his heirs, or successors, then the annual subsidy of Rs. 50,000 will not be paid by the British Government.

British Agent deputed to Kalat.
Death of Nasir Khan II.

In 1856 Major (afterwards Sir Henry) Green was deputed a British Agent to Kalat, chiefly to supervise the expenditure of the Khan's subsidy. He left shortly afterwards, however, to proceed on the Persian campaign. During his absence Nasir Khan II died in 1857, his death being due, some said, to poison administered by the Darogha, Gul Muhammad, who feared he was losing control over the affairs of State.

Accession of Khudadad.

The chiefs elected Khudadad Khan, half brother of Nasir Khan, as their head. He was only 16 years of age, and passed at once into the power of the Darogha. The latter forthwith embroiled the young Khan with his chiefs by opening fire on them from the walls of Kalat. They were encamped there having arrived, headed by the Jam of Las Bela, to demand redress of the wrongs they considered they had been labouring under during the last years of Nasir Khan's reign. On this the chiefs at once fled, and collecting their followers, rose in rebellion. Lieutenant Macaulay, who was deputed to Kalat at this time, says, however,

Rebellious Chiefs.

that the majority of the chiefs even then sought nothing beyond the removal of their grievances, chief among which was the fact that the Khan had surrounded himself with evil advisers and paid a small standing army with the British subsidy, which they had expected to share in keeping open the passes.

Azad Khan Naushirwani, Chief of Kharan, however, who shortly afterwards assumed the lead of the movement, had more

ambitious views. Sir Bartle Frere and General John Jacob attempted to arrange matters amicably but failed, the chiefs having been led by Darogha Gul Muhammad to distrust the sincerity of the British Government. At this juncture Khudadad dismissed Gul Muhammad, and appointed as his Wazir Shahgassi Wali Muhammad, who served him faithfully throughout. Meanwhile the insurrection spread, and Azad Khan Naushirwani put forward Fateh Khan, another member of the ruling family, as a claimant to the throne.

Sir Henry Green, having returned to Kalat, endeavoured, at the request of the Khan, to arrange matters with the chiefs, and for a time induced them to return to their allegiance. He also prevailed on them to drive away Azad Khan and his protégé, who both fled to Kandahar, and to quell a revolt which occurred in Makran. Shortly after this, however, the chiefs again became estranged from the Khan.

In 1858, Azad Khan having appealed to the Amir, an Afghan envoy arrived at Kalat and threatened the Khan with Dost Muhammad's displeasure if he violated the country of Kharan, which he claimed to be tributary to Afghanistan. Sir Henry Green, however, ridiculed the idea of Kharan belonging to the Kabul ruler, and the envoy left Kalat.

In 1859 Sir Henry Green induced the Khan to undertake a campaign against the Marris. The Khan was present in person, and the Marris submitted to him.

Marris submit to the Khan

In 1860 the Khan undertook an armed progress through Makran, during which he received the submission of the Gichki Chiefs. Two months sufficed to pacify the country; all forts were destroyed; and the chiefs of Kej and Panjgur tendered their allegiance.

The Khan visits Makran.

At this time also the Jam of Las Bela, who had been in revolt, came to terms with the Khan.

In the years 1859 and 1860 the British Government allowed the Khan an extra Rs. 50,000 as an incentive to keep order in his State, and as a reward for the efforts he was then making. The history of the next few years is one of anarchy and rebellion. In 1862 the Khan chose to put a deliberate insult on Taj Muhammad, the Jhalawan Sardar, by refusing to fulfil a marriage agreement

into which he had entered with that chief. In 1863 a general rebellion of the chiefs took place. The Khan was attacked and wounded, during a conference, by his cousin Sherdil Khan, and was forced to fly to Sind. He was followed by the British Agent, Colonel Malcolm Green.

<small>Khudadad deposed and reinstated.</small>

Sherdil Khan was elected Khan, but was murdered by the commander of his mercenary guard within a few months of his accession. Khudadad Khan was then replaced on the throne in 1864, the Jam of Las Bela alone dissenting.

Within a year of Khudadad's recall to the throne, the standard of revolt was again raised by Taj Muhammad, the Jhalawan Chief. He was defeated, however, and imprisoned in Kalat, where he died two years later.

In July of the same year the Jam of Las Bela and Nur Din the Mengal Chief, assisted by Azad Khan Naushirwani, raised a revolt. They were defeated by the Wazir Wali Muhammad. The two former were kept for some time in arrest at Kalat. Azad Khan fled to Kandahar. Things did not improve much, and in 1869 the Political Agent of the Upper Sind frontier, Colonel Phayre, gave an audience to representatives of the chiefs at Jacobabad. Their grievances may be summarised in the one fact that the Khan had exceeded his rights as the mere head of a *confederacy*.

Nothing came of this assemblage, and a month later the Jam and Nur Din, the Mengal Chief, were again in revolt. The Wazir again defeated them, and the Jam fled to Sind to the protection of the British Government: he was shortly afterwards removed to the Deccan; Nur Din fled to Kandahar.

As this brings us to the arrival of Sir Robert Sandeman on the scene, it will be necessary to turn for a short time to the Punjab frontier and trace events up to the period of the occupation of Quetta.

In 1866 Sir Robert (then Captain) Sandeman was appointed Deputy Commissioner of Dera Ghazi Khan.

<small>Sir Robert Sandeman.</small>

In those days the state of affairs on the Dera Ghazi Khan frontier was similar to that existing to-day on the border of most of the Punjab Frontier districts.

State of the Baluch Frontier, 1866.

The country outside our own territory was a *terra incognita*. A British Officer's life was not safe a few miles inside the hills; no friendly relations were maintained with the hill tribes; and on the principle of *omne ignotum pro magnifico* the fighting strength of the tribes was immensely exaggerated. The Marris and Bugtis were the terror of the country side, and were only kept in comparative order by the fear of our military strength, represented by the three regiments of Scinde Horse maintained at Jacobabad, with their numerous outposts along the foot of the Bugti Hills, and the Punjab Frontier Force.

Trade through the passes had practically ceased. Long strings of caravans used to assemble at Shikarpur waiting for safe conducts which never came, and the whole Sind Border had been kept for years in a more or less disturbed condition.

It is clear, therefore, that the two burning questions of the time, when Sandeman arrived in Dera Ghazi Khan, were the best methods by which to control the Marris and Bugtis, and the policy most likely to introduce peace into Kalat.

On these questions the young Deputy Commissioner soon formed decided opinions. He very shortly had an opportunity of dealing with the tribes on the occurrence of the Harrand Raid, described elsewhere.

Harrand Raid, 1867.

After this raid, Sandeman applied to the Sind authorities to obtain redress from the Khan of Kalat for the loss sustained by British subjects at the hands of his tribesmen. The reply of Sir Henry Green the Political Superintendent, Upper Sind Frontier, is given *verbatim* :—

With regard to the raid, the Marris—being Baluchis—are certainly nominally subject to the Khan of Kalat, and are held by him under the same control as the Afridis of the hills surrounding the Peshawar Valley are by the ruler of Kabul. Any complaint to the Khan of Kalat would be about of as much use as the Commissioner of Peshawar's bringing to the notice of the Amir the conduct of the said Afridis.

Sir Henry Green then acknowledged that the Punjab officers must trust to their military posts to keep the tribes in order.

On receipt of Sir Henry Green's letter the Punjab Government determined to deal direct with the Kalat tribesmen on its frontier.

Sandeman threw himself into the work with characteristic promptitude. He assembled a tribal conference at Mithankot which the Marri Chief was obliged to attend, owing to the fact that Sandeman held several of his tribesmen prisoners captured at Harrand. The conference was thoroughly successful. The cis-frontier and trans-frontier chiefs laid their grievances before Sandeman. Feuds were amicably settled, and a small levy of the trans-border tribesmen, principally Marris, was taken into our pay and service. The money for this was obtained by farming a salt tax on the Border. This was the commencement of Sir Robert Sandeman's system of tribal service. It proved completely successful, and thenceforward the peace of the Southern Punjab Frontier was secured.

The Sandeman system. Of Sir Robert Sandeman's methods Lord Curzon wrote:—

The system adopted by Sir Robert Sandeman consisted in reconciling conflicting local interests under the common *aegis* of Great Britain; in employing the tribes as custodians of the highways, and guardians of the peace in their own territories; in paying them for what they did well (and, conversely, in fining them for transgression), in encouraging commerce and traffic by the lightening or abolition of tolls, and the security of means of communication; in the protection, rather than diminution, of tribal and clan independence, subject only to the overlordship of the British " Raj "; in a word, in a policy, not of spasmodic and retributive interference, but of steady and unfaltering conciliation.

This is not by any means a new principle. Edwardes advocated it very strongly after the Sikh Wars. In his own words—"A newly conquered population, to be pacified, must be employed." Lord Dalhousie threw open the ranks of the native army to all the people of the Punjab without distinction. Thus he prevented the disbanded Sikh army, some eighty thousand men, from returning to their homes, to which they had for years been remitting money, to be an additional burden on the land.

All the great conquerors of all times have recognised the necessity of employing the military population of their conquests. It is far easier than to destroy them; their fidelity is secured at the outset by severing them from their old associations. When Hannibal prepared to invade Italy, Carthage poured her Africans into Spain,

and defended Africa with Spaniards. In India the British have often pacified countries by employing the indigenous tribes to hold them; for example, the Bhil Corps in Khandesh, the Mair Corps, the Sylhet Local Infantry, and many others. Burning a village will never pacify a tribe; but entertain some of their number, and the whole are satisfied. Employer and employed gain respect.

One can readily imagine the hopelessness of, for example, the Marris when suddenly deprived of the possibilities of plunder and given no other means of making a livelihood. Their country consists, for the most part, of rugged hills destitute of water or verdure—an ideal robber stronghold, but impossible agricultural country. A strong tribe like the Marris could have chosen better land, had they intended to live peaceably. Now they are forced to live peaceably, and not permitted to start that peaceful existence by one final campaign to acquire a country suited to that form of life. Hence the necessity of giving such tribes service,[1] and endeavouring to improve their status generally.

The unsatisfactory state of affairs in Kalat at this time, and particularly with regard to the Marris, has been already referred to.

In September 1870, the Amir of Afghanistan brought to the notice of the British Government the bad treatment of the Sarawan Chief, Mulla Muhammad, by the Khan of Kalat. This brought Kalat affairs generally into prominence, and the Viceroy ordered a conference to be held of the Sind and Punjab officials to discuss the means best suited to deal with the circumstances.

The Mithankot Conference, 1871.

The conference took place at Mithankot in February 1871. There were present:—Sir H. Durand, Lieut.-Governor of the Punjab; Sir William Merewether, Commissioner in Sind; General Keyes, Commanding the Punjab Frontier Force; Colonel Phayre, Political Superintendent, Upper Sind Frontier; Colonel Graham, Commissioner of the Derajat; and Captain Sandeman, Deputy Commissioner of Dera Ghazi Khan.

At this conference it was decided that the dual control of the various tribes on the border should cease, and their affairs were placed

---

[1] The land question now (1907) is a difficulty in the Marri country. Their country, under present conditions, is unsuitable for agriculture and other peaceful pursuits.

in the hands of the Political Superintendent, Upper Sind Frontier, in subordination to whom, as regards the affairs of Kalat tribesmen, was the Deputy Commissioner of Dera Ghazi Khan.

Further, it was decided to give tribal service to the Marris and Bugtis to the extent of Rs. 32,000 per annum, to ensure the tranquillity of Sind, the Punjab, and Kalat borders.

The tribal service, however, was not immediately put in force by the Commissioner in Sind. Intertribal frays ensued, and the Marris looted caravans in the Bolan Pass.

Frontier affairs went from bad to worse. Colonel Phayre and Sandeman looked upon the Marris and Bugtis as practically independent of the Khan of Kalat, and held that the Kalat Sardars in their rebellion against the Khan were " more sinned against than sinning." The Commissioner in Sind held diametrically opposite views.

Frontier Affairs 1871—75.

In 1871 and 1872 the whole of Kachi was captured by the rebels. Khudadad Khan, despairing of success, requested the Commissioner in Sind, Sir William Merewether, to arrange an agreement between himself and his chiefs. This Sir William Merewether endeavoured to do in a conference at Jacobabad, but he pleased no one. He would not support the Khan with troops, nor acknowledge the rights of the chiefs to a share in the Khan's councils. For a time things were more settled, but in 1873 the state of Kalat was such that the Political Agent, Major Harrison, was withdrawn, and the Khan's subsidy suspended. From 1872 to 1875 our relations with Kalat continued to grow worse, and more and more detrimental to British interests. Outrage followed outrage; the Bolan was closed; and no redress could be obtained.

1872 to 1875.

The state of affairs was so unsatisfactory that Sir William Merewether recommended armed intervention in the Marri country and the deposition of the ruler of Kalat.

The British Government, however, determined to make another effort in the cause of peace by sending Major Sandeman into the Marri Hills, under the orders of the Commissioner in Sind. His *régime* on the Derajat border had been so successful that he was deputed to the Marris with a view to effect, if possible, a settlement of the troubles on our immediate frontier, and to provide for the

safety of the Bolan route. He was further instructed, should those measures prove successful, to inform the Khan that the British Government would be willing to re-establish affairs on the old friendly footing with the Kalat State, provided he expressed regret for what had occurred, and guaranteed future good behaviour, and the safety of trade through his country.

Prior to this in 1873 Major Sandeman had opened up relations with the Marri Chief, Gazzan Khan, and had prevailed upon him to visit the Political Superintendent, Colonel Loch, at Jacobabad.

CHAPTER IV.

THE OCCUPATION OF QUETTA.

ON the 18th November 1875, Sandeman left Dera Ghazi Khan for a tour in the Marri country. He was accompanied by an escort of one troop, 1st Punjab Cavalry, and 150 rifles, 4th Sikhs, under Captain Wylie, and by a large number of Baluch chiefs with a numerous following. *En route* he was joined by several Marri Sardars and by the Bugti and Khetran chiefs. On arriving at Kahan, the Marri capital, he was welcomed by Gazzan Khan, the Chief. Thence he proceeded to Sibi where he was joined by the Sarawan chiefs, including Mulla Muhammad Raisani. Thence, at the request of the Khan of Kalat's deputy in Kuchi, he proceeded to Dadur. From Dadur he marched up the Bolan to Quetta and from there, at the Khan's request, to Kalat.

[margin note: Sandeman's First Mission, 1875.]

Sandeman's methods of dealing with the tribesmen are thus described by Sir Hugh Barnes:—

> It was a useful lesson in frontier tribal management to watch Sir Robert Sandeman in Durbar surrounded by an eager, noisy crowd of Baluch notables, encouraging, threatening, and persuading in fluent Hindustani; never losing his temper, patient to hear all that was urged in reason, but his putting foot down at once on all extravagant claims; making the best terms he could for the Government, while recognising the legitimate claims of the chiefs to fair and generous treatment, and, finally, clinching the bargain by stirring appeals to the loyalty and public feelings of the Sardars.

The results of this first mission of Sir Robert Sandeman to Kalat were briefly as follows:—

Although the Khan would not make peace with the tribes without reference to the British Government as to the policy to be pursued, still he sent submissive letters to the Viceroy and Lieutenant-Governor asking permission to represent his views. The Marri and Brahui Sardars agreed to peace on certain terms

and professed a desire to protect trade. The Marri Chief agreed to prevent raids in Kachi.

The Government of India, commenting on the mission, after remarking that it had been "by no means unsuccessful," added that "it proved, if it did nothing more, that the advent of a British Officer as a mediator was most welcome to the Kalat Chiefs, Major Sandeman having been received by all parties in a spirit of marked friendliness and respect."

During this first mission to Kalat, there was great friction between Sir W. Merewether, Commissioner in Sind, and Sandeman. The former indeed, at one time, sent Sandeman peremptory orders to return to the Punjab. In consequence, the Government of India placed Kalat affairs in the hands of the Commissioner of the Derajat Division, Colonel Munro.

In 1876 Government determined to continue the policy of mediation between the Khan and his chiefs.

His Excellency in Council now desires that it should be clearly understood that the political jurisdiction of the Commissioner of the Derajat Division (Colonel Munro) extends through the whole length of the Kalat frontier from Harrand to the sea. In short, the Government of India, having full confidence in Colonel Munro and Major Sandeman, desire that the latter be allowed, under the Commissioner's orders, full opportunity of effecting, under the most favourable circumstances, a settlement of Kalat affairs.

Several communications passed between the Indian Government and the Khan, with the result that Sandeman was deputed to arbitrate between him and his chiefs, and place affairs on a satisfactory footing.

Sandeman's Second Mission, 1876.

Accordingly Sandeman proceeded on his second mission to Kalat, escorted by detachments of the Sind and Punjab Frontier Forces, including 2 guns of the Jacobabad Mountain Battery, under command of Captain Wylie, 1st Punjab Cavalry. A start was made from Jacobabad early in April 1876.

As soon as the mission left Jacobabad hostilities in Kalat were suspended, in anticipation of Sandeman's arrival at Quetta. Large caravans were allowed to follow the mission unmolested up the Bolan; the Brahui and Baluch Sardars co-operating for their protection. At Quetta on the 24th April arrangements were

made with Sandeman, by the various tribes on the route, to foster trade in the Bolan.

On the 14th July 1876, a grand durbar of the Khan and all the chiefs took place at Mastung.

Mastung Durbar.

The claims of the Khan, and grievances of the chiefs were presented to Sir Robert Sandeman. This durbar and settlement has been described as the " Magna Charta " of the Kalat Confederacy.

Many of the chiefs declared to Sir Robert that the best solution of the difficulty would be for the British Government to depose the Khan, and openly assume the sovereignty of the whole Khanate, an arrangement, however, never contemplated by the British Government.

The result of the conference was that all disputes between the chiefs and the Khan were arranged, except as regards the Marris, the former submitting to the Khan, and the latter restoring to them their ancient rights and privileges. Satisfactory arrangements were made for keeping open the trade routes, responsibility being fixed on certain chiefs and tribes.

A settlement having been arrived at between the Khan of Kalat and his chiefs, the British mission was free to return to India, and preparations were made for a movement down the Bolan.

The Khan and chiefs, however, heard with dismay Sandeman's proposal to withdraw from Kalat. His personal influence, and the dignity lent to the conference by the presence of his escort, had alone led to the happy issue of the durbar.

After deliberation, the Government of India determined to retain Sandeman in Kalat territory,

Treaty with Kalat, 1876.

and a formal treaty was concluded with the Khan and his chiefs before the end of the same year— 1876.

The terms of that of 1854 were re-affirmed, whereby the Khan agreed to oppose the enemies of Great Britain; and act in subordinate co-operation with that Power, and abstain from any negotiations with other foreign States. By the 4th and 5th Articles of the new treaty, a British Agent was to be established at the court of the Khan, whose arbitration in disputes between the Khan and his Sardars was to be considered final.

By the 6th Article, British troops were to be stationed in Kalat territory. Provision was also made for the construction of railways and telegraphs.

The 8th Article stipulated for freedom of trade, and the 9th arranged for an annual subsidy to the Khan of Rs. 1,00,000 (£6,500), and an additional sum of £1,400 for the establishment of certain posts and the development of trade routes.

Terms were also arranged by which the ex-Jam of Las Bela, Mir Khan, was released and replaced as Jam of that State on his acknowledging the suzerainty of the Khan.

As regards the Marris and Bugtis, former transactions had so conclusively proved the inability of the Khan of Kalat to keep them in order that it was decided to deal with them independently.

The tribal service already granted to them was continued, and they were encouraged to take additional service under the British Government.

Quetta chosen as cantonment for escort. Quetta was chosen for the location of the troops of the Agent's escort on account of its strong military position, almost unassailable if occupied by well armed troops. Further, it controls the trade routes from Kandahar to Kalat and the Bolan Pass; also the routes *viâ* the Kakar Hills to Zhob, Bori, Thal Chotiali, and the Punjab. Mitri was also garrisoned, but the Bolan Pass was entirely handed over to the tribes, in order to interest them in the protection of trade.

The garrison of Quetta was to be :—

1 Mountain Battery
1 Regiment Infantry
1 Squadron Cavalry

{ In addition to 300 men of the 4th Sikhs already there as escort (under Captain Scott).

and that of Mitri at—

1 Mountain Battery.
1 Regiment of Cavalry.
1 Wing, Native Infantry.

Mitri was, however, found too hot for occupation in summer, and the force was withdrawn to Jacobabad, leaving a line of detachments to watch the hills.

An interesting point to notice here is a letter by Jacob in 1854 regarding a possible war with Russia. He writes:—

Quetta should be occupied with a well-found British force. There should be a good road from that place through the Bolan to Dadur, and thence through Kachi to the British frontier to connect with the roads in Sind. The road from Dadur to the sea must, eventually, be a railway.

He dwelt on the superiority of the Bolan Pass over the Khyber as a trade or army route from Herat and Central Asia, and hence the necessity of holding its debouchure on Afghanistan.

His idea assumed shape in 1856 at the time of the Persian campaign in which he took part. He writes:—

I hold a decided opinion that the expedition is a great error. It appears to me that we could command success by another far more easy and certain mode of proceeding.

He referred to the subjugation of Baluchistan, to be so successfully carried out by Sir Robert Sandeman.

John Jacob then proposed to Lord Canning to lease Quetta from Kalat and place 5,000 British and Indian troops in it. He worked out a scheme containing all the necessary details. It received the earnest consideration of the Government of the day, but was finally negatived by Lord Canning—chiefly on the question of the supposed difficulty of supply.

Thus—twenty years before its actual occupation—Jacob saw the advantage of the Quetta position, dominating the two most important trade and army routes from Central Asia to India, and effectually flanking the others to north and south.

Sandeman appointed A. G. G., Baluchistan.

On the occasion of the Khan's visit to Delhi in January 1877, the Government of India finally decided that "the charge of the Political relations of the British Government with the Kalat State and its dependencies should be vested in Major R. G. Sandeman, C.S.I., under the designation of "Agent to the Governor-General for Baluchistan."

A very important point then decided was that, "for the escort of the Agent to the Governor-General, it was arranged that any requisition from that officer for 160 infantry, 50 cavalry, and 2 mountain guns should be complied with, without his being compelled

to furnish the particulars required under the existing Army Regulations." This greatly strengthened Sandeman's hand in a country where prompt action was so necessary in dealing with the people.

Early in 1887 troops were marched up to Quetta, and building operations were commenced on houses for the Political and Military Officers and huts for the troops. The Quetta Fort—known as the Miri—was retained in possession of the Khan's troops. At this time the Khan's regular army consisted of 3,500 mercenary troops with 30 guns and 500 cavalry.

Quetta occupied, 1877.

On the 26th July 1877, a fanatical outbreak occurred which led to our occupation of the Miri. Three local Kakar Pathans attacked Lieutenants Hewson and Kunhardt, both of the Royal Engineers, who were inspecting building operations at the Residency. The former was killed and the latter wounded. A Sikh of the 4th (now 54th) Sikhs rushed up and saved Lieutenant Kunhardt's life, but lost his own. Captain Scott, who was drilling his men near by, then rushed up, followed by some of his men. He killed two of the murderers with a bayonet (having seized a rifle with fixed bayonet from one of his men), but was wounded by the third.[1] His men, however, arriving at this moment, killed his assailant. The cause of this raid was the imprisonment of certain influential Bazai Pathans for the wanton destruction of some Government camels. These Bazais had been imprisoned in the Miri, and there the raid had been planned. In consequence, Mr. R. I. Bruce, the Political Agent, determined to seize the fort, which was effected by Captain Charles, commanding the troops at Quetta, without opposition. Since then it has remained in British possession and is now the Arsenal of Quetta; the Khan's troops evacuated the Quetta valley for ever.

Fanatical outrage.

In view of imminent hostilities with Afghanistan, in October 1878, the Kakar Pathan tribes inhabiting the neighbouring country, and the Dumars on the Bolan, were invited to a conference at Quetta. Service was given to the headmen to the extent of Rs. 4,940 in return for promised assistance in case of an outbreak of hostilities. A very important point in the negotiations was that the trans-border

Conference with Pathan Tribes, 1875.

---

[1] Captain Scott was awarded the Victoria Cross.

Kakars, especially those of the Lora Valley in Pishin, were guaranteed from injury hereafter when peace should be concluded with the Amir. This was absolutely necessary, as the reprisals by Dost Muhammad on those of his subjects who had remained even neutral during the First Afghan War had not been forgotten.

In October 1878, relations with Afghanistan were very strained and news was received that a number of Afghan Horse had collected at Haramzai, a Kalat village, two miles outside the border of Pishin, and distant fourteen miles from Quetta, on which it was their avowed intention to make a sudden raid. Next day at daybreak Haramzai was surrounded by 300 infantry, 150 cavalry, and 4 guns, under command of Colonel Morgan commanding the Quetta Garrison. Sandeman had lost no time; he was himself present and summoned the headmen to submit. There were 310 horses in the village, which Sandeman removed, and one Saiyid Kharan, said to be the head of the movement, was made a prisoner.

Affairs at Haramzai.

Underlying our dealings with Kalat at this time there was, doubtless, an ulterior motive. We wished to exclude Afghan influence from Baluchistan, to substitute our own, and to obtain a point of vantage for operating from the political or military side as might be required on Southern Afghanistan. It was with this dual object that British troops were stationed in Quetta.

Own policy and its results.

After events proved the value of these transactions. The possession of Quetta, the opening of the Bolan Pass, and our friendly relations with the Khan of Kalat were of inestimable benefit to the British Government during the Second Afghan War. In this connection Sir George Pomeroy Colley's views may be quoted—written shortly before the advance from Quetta into Afghanistan in the Second Afghan War. Writing on the whole policy adopted during 1875-77 he says:—

We believed that an opportunity had presented itself of substituting a friendly, peaceful, and prosperous rule for the utter anarchy and devastation that had prevailed in Baluchistan for nearly twenty years, and at the same time of securing a position of enormous value strategically for the defence of our southern border. Militarily speaking, Quetta covers five hundred miles of our Trans-Indus Frontier from Dera Ghazi Khan to the sea. The policy of the measure has been much disputed. Of its practical results, however, I can

personally speak. During the three years preceding Sandeman's mission hardly a month passed without some raid on our borders, and the Bolan Pass was absolutely closed. During the two years following, there had not been a single raid of any sort or kind. The Bolan Pass is perfectly safe, and has been traversed by thousands of caravans. The tableland of Baluchistan, which could then barely support Sandeman's small garrison of one thousand men, is now able to furnish several months' supplies for the force of ten thousand now being collected there. Were matters now in Baluchistan as they were when Lord Lytton came out to India, so far from being prepared to-morrow to commence our advance from Quetta, into Afghanistan, we should still be collecting in the plains of Kachi, and preparing for the difficult operation of forcing the Bolan Pass. I may add that not only have the Baluch Sirdars enthusiastically supported Sandeman in all our complications with the Amir, but that the Khan of Kalat has placed all his supplies at our disposal, and that even the more distant ruler of Las Bela has offered his army for service in Afghanistan if necessary.[1]

Quetta.

Extracts from the District Gazetteer.

Quetta, which lies at the northern end of the valley of that name, has an elevation of 5,500 feet above sea-level. The town lies beneath the slopes of Murdar, the mountain which bounds the Quetta valley on the east. To the north closing in the valley, are the long straight ridge of Zargun and the peaks of Takatu. On the west is Chiltun. Through the gap thus left in the north-west corner of the valley at Baleli the road and railway pass into the Kuchlak valley, which again leads to Pishin.

Quetta consists of the native town in the south-east, the civil lines on the south-west, and the cantonment on the north, the first two being separated from the last by the Habib Nala known to Europeans as "The Thames."

Acquisition of land.

The land on which Quetta has been built was bought by Government between 1878 and 1883. The total area purchased was 3,754 acres, of which 3,496 were in cantonments and 258 acres in the civil town. The total amount paid for both the land and water supply was Rs. 2,54,848, out of which Rs. 2,15,201 were for the cantonment lands and Rs. 39,647 for the civil town. A large

---

[1] Life of Sir George Pomeroy Colley by Sir William F. Butler, K. C. B.

portion of the cantonment consisted of waste stony land of little value, while the whole of the land in the civil station was valuable.

Since then the cantonments have been largely extended, and now cover an area of fourteen square miles.

Prior to the British occupation, the only trees in Quetta were a few ancient mulberries, still to be seen in the Residency garden. Now the whole of the civil lines and the lower portion of the cantonments have good gardens and fine avenues of trees. The cantonment, however, has spread up the slopes of Murdar whence the soil has been washed to form the fertile valley below, and as a whole is stony and dusty. The Staff College has recently been built above the cantonments near the entrance to the Hanna Pass. Mud is the building material of Quetta. The officers' quarters are owned by Government. The idea of a Soldiers' Park and Club was initiated by Lieutenant-General H. L. Smith-Dorrien, C.B., D.S.O., on his arrival in Quetta in 1903. It was commenced by voluntary labour from the troops. The grounds are terraced and provide various playing fields and gardens. From the latter—mostly fruit gardens—a good income is expected. In the park, which covers sixty-seven acres, stands the club house which comprises supper, billiard, reading, and recreation rooms.

Soldiers' Park and Club.

CHAPTER V.

EASTERN BALUCHISTAN TRIBES.

THIS chapter deals with the Baluch tribes east of Kalat territory comprising Bugtis, Marris, Mazaris, Gurchanis, Khosas, and Legharis, together with the mixed tribe of Khetrans. All were practically independent prior to the establishment of British authority. The Khan of Kalat claimed the allegiance of the Bugtis and Marris, but failed to establish it.

The *Gurchanis* own the Mari and Dragal hills, the Sham plain and half the Phailawar plain beyond our frontier, and are also located in the Dera Ghazi Khan district in the neighbourhood of Harrand. Beyond the border they are bounded on the north by the Legharis and the Khetrans, on the west by the Marris, and on the south by the Bugtis and Mazaris.

Gurchanis.

They are divided into eleven clans, of which the chief are the *Durkani, Shekhani, Lashari, Petafi, Jiskani,* and *Sabzani*. The last four are true Baluchis; the remainder are said to be descended from Gorish (from whom they derive their name), a grandson of Raja Bhimsen, of Hyderabad, who was adopted by the Baluchis, and married among them. He is said to have accompanied Humayun to Delhi, and on his return to have collected a Baluch following, and ejected the Pathan holders from the present Gurchani territory.

The whole of the Durkani, and about half of the Lashari, clans live beyond our border, and are independent, the remainder of the tribe, being located in British territory. The Gurchanis number some 5,000 all told.

In 1848, when Mulraj, the Governor of Multan, rebelled, Lieutenant H. B. Edwardes arrived in the Dera Ghazi Khan district on his way to Multan, and sent a summons to Ghulam Haidar Khan, the Gurchani Chief, to attend him. Ghulam Haidar Khan came with 200 horsemen, and was with Lieutenant Edwardes until Dera Ghazi Khan was taken. The Gurchani Chief was then sent with

Lieutenant Young against Harrand, but he afterwards again joined Lieutenant Edwardes before Multan, where he remained until the siege was over. After the conclusion of the war he was made a *jemadar* of horse, ten *ba'girs* in the militia were given to him, and he was presented with a *khila'* of Rs. 1,000 for his services. For the first years after the annexation, the Gurchanis had an exceedingly bad reputation as robbers and raiders and their border was always disturbed.

The *Mazaris* are a Baluch tribe occupying the extreme south of the Dera Ghazi Khan district, their western boundary being the hills, and their eastern the river. Rojhan is their head-quarters. They formerly occupied the hill country to the west now held by the Bugtis, but, obtaining grants of land in the lowlands, gradually shifted eastward towards the river.

Mazaris.

The tribe is divided into four clans—*Rustamani, Masidani, Balachani,* and *Sargani,* of which the first two are the most numerous although the chief is a Balachani. The majority of the tribe reside in British territory, where they own a large number of villages, only a few families being located beyond our border. In independent territory they have the Gurchanis on the north and the Bugtis on the west. For some years after the annexation, the Mazaris had perhaps the worst reputation of any tribe on this border. Elphinstone, in his *History of India*, mentions them as famous for their piracies on the Indus, their robberies on the highway, and their depredations into the country of all their neighbours. They have, however, now settled down peaceably as cultivators of the soil. Their total population is now calculated at 5,500 persons, of whom less than 160 reside in the hills.

Mazaris.

The *Marris* are a Baluch tribe of Rind origin, inhabiting the hills to the west of the Gurchanis. They are bounded on the north-east by the Khetrans, on the east by the Gurchanis, on the south by the Bugtis, on the west by the plains of Kachi, and on the north by the Bori Pathans. They are the most powerful and the most troublesome of all the Baluch tribes.

Marris.

They are divided into four clans—the *Ghazani, Loharani, Mazarani,* and *Bijarani* ; of which the Mazarani live beyond

Sibi and the Bolan, and are almost independent of the rest of the tribe. The country inhabited by this tribe is for the most part barren hill, but it contains some extensive valleys and fertile spots. There are two main rivers, which rise to the east of the Marri country and flow westward, emerging into the plains of Kachi at Tali and Lehri respectively.

The Marris are rich in cattle of all kinds, and have a good many horses. Their habits were formerly altogether predatory, and they plundered their neighbours on all sides. There is considerable traffic now through their hills, and the roads of late years have been much improved.

The drainage of the Marri country runs east and west, between very abrupt, impracticable hills, and the communications in this direction are comparatively easy, while those from north to south are very difficult. The whole country was, however, traversed by our troops with artillery in 1880. Cultivation is very [scanty, and is only found near Kahan and on the banks of the streams; the rest of the country has a barren, desolate appearance, and produces nothing. No supplies could be reckoned on in these hills. Grass would probably be found after rain; wood would be scarce everywhere, and water only found at certain spots, which it would always be necessary to ascertain beforehand.

The Marris are inveterate robbers. Their hand is against every man, and every man's hand is against them. They lead a nomadic life, and have no villages except a few mud forts, and, with the exception of those members of the tribe who live about Mandai, depend very little on agriculture. They are able, at the shortest notice, to leave any particular tract and move off their herds and encampments twenty miles. Their nominal allegiance to the Khan of Kalat did not prevent them from committing constant raids into his territories. The Marris are now under the management of the Baluchistan Agency. They number 11,000 persons.

Bugtis.

The *Bugtis*, like the Marris, are a Baluch tribe of Rind origin, occupying the angle between the frontiers of the Punjab and Upper Sind. They are bounded on the north by the Marris, on the east by the Mazaris, on the south by British territory (Sind), and on the west by Kachi.

The Bugtis are divided into six clans—*Kaheja, Nuthani Musuri, Kalpur, Phong* and *Shambani,* or *Kiazai*. The Bugti

country is chiefly rugged and barren, but contains much good pasture-land and some fertile valleys. The regular occupation to the tribe was, till lately, plundering, carried on systematically and on a large scale. Every man of the tribe was a robber. The Khan of Kalat claimed sovereignty over them, but they paid revenue to no one, and, protected by their rocky fastnesses, maintained a stormy independence, usually at war with the Marris, and perpetually plundering their neighbours.

The wealth of the people consists in cattle, which they bring down for sale to British territory. They carry on a direct trade with Rojhan, Rajanpur, and Harrand in the Punjab, and with Kashmor and Jacobabad in Sind. In return for their cattle and wood they take cloth, salt, *gur*, sugar, and grain; a few of their traders get cloth, etc., at Multan and Jhang. Although the tribe is not dependent on British territory for subsistence or food, a blockade would put them to great inconvenience. When their trade is stopped, they are indirectly dependent either on Kalat or on the Marris and Khetrans. A large number of Bugtis now occupy land in British territory. They are, like the Marris, under the political management of the Governor-General's Agent in Baluchistan. They number 10,000 persons.

Khosas. The *Khosas* are a Baluch tribe occupying territory within and beyond our border, having the Kasranis on the north, the Legharis on the south, and the Bozdars on the west. Their territory in the plains extends from the foot of the hills nearly across to the river Indus. They do not occupy all the land within these bounds, but are scattered about in patches. A certain number of this tribe are settled in Bahawalpur, and they also hold extensive lands in Sind, which were granted to them by Humayun in return for military services.

The Khosas are divided into six clans, of which the Babelani and the Isani are the most important. They are true Rinds, and were formerly one of the most powerful and influential tribes on this border. They are very independent of their chief, and are among the bravest of the Baluchis. Many have done good service in the ranks of the British army. Their internal disputes have, however, reduced them to political insignificance, although their industrious habits make them one of the wealthiest tribes on this border.

The Khosas live almost wholly in the plains, and only the Halatis and the Jajelas—sections of the Isani clan—live beyond the border. The lands of the tribe depend entirely on the water in the mountain streams, with that collected in the different ponds, and on occasional rain, for irrigation; and in seasons of drought the tribe deserts its own for other lands nearer to Dera Ghazi Khan. Some of the tribe are graziers, and have numerous flocks. Occasionally feuds break out between the Khosas and their neighbours, the Bozdars and the Legharis; but they are friendly with the Khetrans. In 1848, when the Multan war broke out, Kaora Khan, the chief of this tribe, besieged and took Dera Ghazi Khan from the Sikhs, and handed it over to Lieutenant H. B. Edwardes. He accompanied that officer, with about 300 of his clansmen, to the siege of Multan, and behaved splendidly throughout. The Khosas are a large tribe numbering 24,000 souls, but only about 1,000 reside in the hills.[1]

Legharis. The *Legharis* are located on our border to the south of the Khosas, extending as far as the Gurchani limits, and are bounded on the west by the Khetrans. They are a Baluch tribe of pure Rind origin, and are divided into four sections, the *Hadiani, Aliani, Boglani,* and *Haibatani,* of which the first inhabit the hills beyond our border and the others are located within our territory. The Hadianis are nomadic, and inveterate thieves. They are wild and difficult to manage. The chief of the Leghari tribe belongs to the Aliani clan. The famous shrine of Sakhi Sarwar is within the Leghari limits. Their principal passes are the Sakhi Sarwar, Choti, and Kura.

Legharis-Khetrans. The Leghari and Khetran Chief's families have been for many years connected by marriage; for which reason, among others, the Leghari Chief possesses great influence with the Khetran tribe.

During the Sikh rule, the Legharis were greatly favoured by Sawan Mal as a counterpoise to the Khosas and Gurchanis, and

---

[1] General Pollock wrote of the Khosas in 1859: "It is rare to find a Khosa who has not been in prison for cattle stealing or deserved to be. A Khosa who has not committed a murder, debauched his neighbour's wife, or destroyed his neighbour's landmark is a decidedly creditable specimen; if, in addition, he be out of debt, he is a perfect marvel.

consequently, when the rebellion broke out in 1848, they were arrayed against the British, and amongst the warmest supporters of Mulraj until, finding his the losing side, they deserted him.

The Legharis number about 20,000, of whom some 2,000 are resident in the hills.

Khetrans. The *Khetrans* are a mixed tribe, living beyond the Legharis. They are bounded on the north by the Luni Pathans, on the east by the Legharis and Gurchanis, and on the south by the Marris. Their original settlement was at Vihoa, in the country of the Kasranis, where many of them still live and hold land between the Kasranis and the river. But the Emperor Akbar drove out the main body, and they took refuge in the hills where they are now located. They are not pure Baluch, and are held by many to be Pathans, with whom they in some cases intermarry. But they resemble Baluchis in features, habits, and general appearance; the names of their subdivisions, moreover, have the Baluch termination, *ani*. They speak a language of their own, akin to Sindi and the Jatki dialect of the southern Punjab. They are divided into four clans, *Gangura, Dariwal, Hasani,* and *Nahar.* [1]

The Khetrans are anything but a warlike tribe. They are all engaged in the cultivation of the soil; and the peculiar features of their country, which is a succession of large valleys lying between parallel ranges of hills, the soil of which is most fertile, render their occupation remunerative, and make them one of the wealthiest tribes on the frontier. Grain is generally much cheaper with the Khetrans than in British territory: the consequence is that the neighbouring tribes buy from them; and hence, although they sometimes have quarrels with them, they cannot afford to keep them up long. The valleys in the Khetran country are dotted over with small mud forts, each the centre of a tract of cultivation; and wheat crops cover the surrounding country.

---

[1] The *Hasanis* and *Nahars* are the remnants of old Baluchi clans which have now ceased to exist as distinct tribes. The Hasanis were destroyed by perpetual wars with the Marris in the beginning of the last century. In the map accompanying Pottinger's *Travels in Baluchistan* (1816) they are shown as occupying the northern part of the country now held by the Marris and their ruined forts are still found there. The Nahars formerly occupied the country about Harrand, but having quarrelled with Ghazi Khan and the subsequent governors of Dera Ghazi Khan, they were at length defeated, and took refuge with the Khetrans where they have now settled down.

Khetrans.

The climate is considered good, being moderately hot and cold. In the spring and autumn a considerable amount of rain falls, which insures an ample supply of water for cultivation. Several streams run through the Khetran country, most of which unite to form the Kaha, which issues from the mountains at Harrand.

They are not a plundering tribe, but are receivers of property stolen in British territory; and at one time, when there was a great deal of raiding going on, it was found that stolen camels were selling at Barkhan, or Haji Kot, their principal town, for Rs. 10 a head. They also afford protection to absconded criminals and others, whom they are glad to allow to fight and plunder for them. But the enforcement of pass responsibility on the Dera Ghazi Khan frontier has tended to modify their conduct in these respects, and they are now fairly well behaved. They have little or no intercourse with Sind, and the only raid they ever engaged in on that frontier was in conjunction with the Bugtis and Marris in the attack on Kasmor in April, 1849.

The Khetrans, as already mentioned, are closely connected with the Legharis, and they are also friendly with the Bugtis, but their relations with the Marris, Bozdars, Musa Khel, and Luni Pathans are not so good. They carry on a large trade with British territory by the Sakhi Sarwar and Choti passes, and this, combined with the fact that the country is completely open to the operations of troops, renders the coercion of the Khetrans an easy matter.

Our relations with this tribe have been, since 1887, carried on through the Governor-General's Agent in Baluchistan, the tribal country being located in the Sibi Division.

The total population of the Khetrans is 14,000 souls—including 2,000 resident in Thal Chotiali.

The first occasion on which the British Government came into contact with any of the tribes treated of in this chapter was in 1839 when operations were undertaken against the Marri and Bugti tribes to punish them for their predatory attacks on the British lines of communications.

In 1839, after Sir John Keane's Army had passed through the Bolan Pass, these attacks became so dangerous and frequent that steps had to be taken to put a stop to them.

The first attempt to bring the tribes to order is noteworthy only as an instance of what troops must suffer in Upper Sind during the summer. On his advance from Sukkur, Sir John Keane had left behind at that place about 150 European troops, men chosen from every regiment of the army, Royal and Company's. Needless to say, they were the refuse of the army—the weedy, the sick, the disorderly, the discontented.

It was decided to send an expedition against the Jakranis and Dumkis in June 1839. John Jacob, then a lieutenant of artillery, was given command of the troops above mentioned, and ordered to form a battery of artillery for service against the tribes in Kachi.

First Expedition.

With forty men and Lieutenant Corry of H. M.'s 17th Regiment, Jacob marched from Sukkur for Shikarpur on the 3rd June —the guns being sent by water. Jacob himself says :—

The season was one of intense heat which has never since been equalled; the thermometer in the hospital shed at Shikarpur commonly stood at 130°, and on several days reached the astonishing height of 140°,—one memorable day it touched 143°. Duststorms like a blast from a furnace were common, sometimes accompanied (in Kachi) by the simoon—a poisonous wind, which is equally destructive to animal and vegetable life.

Such was the climate in which British soldiers were for the first time to proceed against the wild tribes of Eastern Baluchistan.

Beyond Shikarpur the expedition never went. Though the detachment marched at night and was never directly exposed to the sun, the heat was too great for human nature to bear. It is three very short marches from Sukkur to Shikarpur. The detachment of two officers and forty men crawled into Shikarpur the third day minus Lieutenant Corry and fifteen men, all struck dead by the heat. No treatment appeared to have the smallest effect in checking this mortality.

The authorities recognised the impossibility of proceeding with the expedition until the summer heat had abated, and operations were postponed until October. In that month a detachment of the 1st Bombay Grenadiers, one company, 5th Bombay Native Infantry, two howitzers, a small detail of artillery, and some Sappers and Miners, was sent under the command of Major T. R. Billamore to punish the offending tribes and render the

Billamore's Hill Campaign, 1839.

road safe for the passage of convoys. This force marched from Sukkur *via* Shikarpur to Pulaji (*see* Map) on the 20th of October 1839, and it was intended first to punish the Dumkis and Jakranis[1] in the plains. They, however, fled to the Bugti Hills under their leader Bejar Khan, abandoning all their villages.

As an example of the Baluch character the following incident is, perhaps, worth relating:—

During the earlier part of Billamore's "Hill Campagin," October, 1839, against the Dumkis and Jakranis, the British force after a long day's unsuccessful pursuit of the elusive hillmen arrived, weary and disgusted, one evening at Uch springs.

Scarcely, however, had the horses had time to drink, when, as if by magic, suddenly appeared, not half a mile off, opposite to an opening in the hills, two noted Baluch Chiefs[2] and a hundred Baluch horse, drawn up in regular line, as if to charge the British detachment. Instantly the men were in their saddles, and, riding in, formed line against the enemy so fairly opposed to them. Janee and his men drew their swords and advanced with a shout. Valiant deeds appeared to be about to take place. The ground seemed ideal for a "gentle passage of arms," a soft green meadow stretching between the combatants. Suddenly every horse of the British detachment sunk into the earth, some planted over girth and saddle flaps, all in hopeless confusion. The Baluchis had played a huge practical joke. They had lured their enemies into an extensive quicksand. Their shouts of provocation were exchanged for peals of laughter.

One officer, however, John Jacob, being splendidly mounted struggled out on the farther side. Alone, on his now utterly jaded animal, he advanced against the Baluchis. Though Jacob was absolutely at his mercy, Janee generously returned, at speed, into the hills.

The campaign which followed is a striking example of what British officers can accomplish when thrown on their own resources. The country was a *terra incognita*. The scanty information derived

---

[1] The *Dumkis* and *Jakranis* inhabit the eastern part of Kachi. They were formerly most active and formidable marauders, but are now peaceful and well-behaved. The Dumkis now occupy the land about Lehri, and the Jakranis cultivate the ground near Shahpur. After Major-General Sir Charles Napier's campaign in 1845, a large number of these tribes were removed to Sind.

[2] Janee and Rahmut.

from native sources showed nothing procurable save water and fuel—and but little of either. Nevertheless with a hastily arranged commissariat the force advanced from Pulaji into the Bugti hills. As the British troops approached the stronghold of Dera, the Bugtis seemed at first submissive and friendly; but the smallness of the force tempted them to hostilities, and they attacked Major Billamore with their whole strength. They were twice signally defeated with great loss; their chief, Bibrak, was captured and sent a prisoner to Sind; the town of Dera was taken and plundered, and great loss inflicted on the tribe generally. After punishing the Bugtis, the force proceeded against Kahan, the Marri capital, arriving before it on the 29th December 1839.[1]

The Marris deserted Kahan, and retired with all their families and property to the northern part of their country, and a detachment of 100 men of the 1st Bombay Grenadiers was left to garrison it, under Ensign E. T. Peacocke. They once assembled in full force to oppose us, but, being outmanœuvred, changed their minds and did not venture to engage in a struggle. They offered some slight opposition to the work of making the road over the Naffusak Pass (*see* Map), but did not seriously obstruct the troops marching through their country. The British force left the hills in February 1840, and in the month of April a detachment was sent, under Captain L. Brown, 5th Bombay Infantry, to occupy Kahan permanently.

This detachment assembled at Pulaji on the 8th of April 1840, and consisted of 300 bayonets, 5th Bombay Native Infantry, under Ensign W. W. Taylor; two 12-pounder howitzers, under Lieutenant D. Erskine; and 50 Sind Horse under Lieutenant W. H. Clarke; besides 50 Pathan mounted levies. It was to convey 600 camels with four months' supplies to Kahan, and Lieutenant Clarke was then to return with 80 infantry and 50 horse to escort supplies for another four months. Owing to delays of the Commissariat Department, the detachment did not start until the 2nd May.

Kahan occupied by Captain Brown.

On the 20th April Lieutenant Clarke made a raid into the hills against a party of Kalpur Bugtis, who had been engaged in plundering excursions. The attempt failed, owing to the treachery of the

---

[1] For an interesting account of Billamore's "Hill Campaign," see "General John Jacob," Chapter III, by G. I. Shand.

guide, and the detachment, which consisted of 50 Scinde Horse and 100 Baluch levies, suffered terribly from heat and want of water when crossing the desert on their return to Pulaji. The Baluch levies alone left twenty-five men behind them, of whom three died.

On the 27th April Captain Brown was ordered to send back the guns and go on without them, but, hearing of the intention of the Marris to oppose him at the Naffusak Pass, he took one gun.

On the 2nd May he started, leaving behind one gun and the Pathan mounted levies, whom he did not trust; he could, however, march but slowly; the thermometer ranged to 116°, and the gun kept them back.

On the 8th the force reached the Sartaf pass, about seven miles from the Naffusak.[1] The road up the pass was very steep, and the gun was dragged up by the men. Here the Marris first showed themselves, but did not offer opposition.

On the 10th the detachment crowned the Naffusak Pass. The convoy took twelve hours going up the pass, which is only a quarter of a mile in length. They were attacked by the Marris, but beat them off.

On the 11th the force descended into the Kahan plain, and the Marris, seizing the summit of the pass at once, kept up a fire at a respectful distance. Kahan was found deserted, and was occupied without opposition. On the 16th Lieutenant Clarke started for Pulaji with 160 bayonets, 5th Bombay Infantry, and 50 sabres, Scinde Horse. Having surmounted the first hill, he sent back 80 of the infantry and proceeded with the cavalry, and the remaining 80 bayonets, and 700 unladen camels (100 having been captured from the Marris a few days previously). On seeing the last of the camels over the hill, Subadar Bagu Jadao, the native officer in command of the detachment left behind, returned. Half-way down the hill they fell into an ambush of 2,000 Marris, and, though the men fought gallantly, the whole party was cut up, only one doolie-bearer escaping.

Destruction of Lieutenant Clarke's detachment.

Captain Brown was thus left with 140 bayonets and one gun to defend the fort, which had 900 yards of wall.

---

[1] *See* Map.

Lieutenant Clarke, meanwhile, had made his way to the Sartaf Pass, thirteen miles from Kahan, where he found the Marris assembled in large numbers on the crest. After placing his convoy to the best advantage, he advanced to drive them off with 30 bayonets, but the task was too great; there were 2,000 of the enemy against him, with the command of ground in their favour, and so, after fighting nobly for two hours, and expending his last cartridge, the whole of the infantry were cut up with the exception of twelve men. The cavalry escaped to Pulaji, and all the camels were captured. The Marris lost 300 killed.[1]

On hearing of this disaster, Captain Brown quickly set to work to put the fort in a state of defence. On the 4th of June he received an express to say that no reinforcements could be sent him, but that Captain J. D. D. Bean, the Political Agent at Quetta, had been asked to send some Kakars to his assistance. This was not of much use, however, for these very Kakars soon after attacked Captain Bean himself.[2]

The Marris constantly hovered about, coming down on any helpless grass-cutters or followers who strayed too far; but they never attempted an assault. Bad water and food, and hard work soon began to tell on the men, and on the 14th July Captain Brown records that 90 out of his 140 men were unable to put on their belts owing to ulcers.

He then commenced putting all his camp followers through a course of drill. The Marris continued their respectful blockade, stationing small picquets all round out of range, till about the 10th August, when they became more energetic, upon which Lieutenant Erskine dropped a shell in the middle of them, killing and wounding fifteen. On this day, the garrison managed to capture three hundred sheep and fifty-seven goats, which were grazing too near the fort.

On the 12th of August, 1840, a detachment, consisting of 464 bayonets, 1st and 2nd Bombay Grenadiers,[3] a detail of 34 gunners, and three 12-pounder howitzers, marched for Kahan, under Major T Clibborn.

---

[1] Lieutenant Clarke, 1st Bombay Grenadiers, commanded the Irregular Horse in Billamore's campaign, and performed many deeds of personal valour.

[2] On June 23rd, 1840, a force of 800 Panizais, under a leader by name Gafur, attacked Quetta. They were driven off in about three hours, leaving 22 dead on the field. The British loss was 3 wounded.

Now 101st and 102nd Grenadiers.

It had been intended to send a detachment of Her Majesty's 40th Regiment, but for some reason this was countermanded. The force had charge of 12,000 camels and 600 bullocks. At Pulaji it was increased by 200 sabres, Poona Horse and Scinde Horse, under Lieutenants W. Loch and G. Malcolm, respectively. The detachment entered the hills on the 24th, and reached the foot of the Sartaf Pass in five marches. It took fourteen hours to get the convoy and guns up this pass, and the troops suffered much from the burning heat of an August sun. The night was passed on the tableland on the summit, with no water nearer than the foot of the pass. The men had little rest, as the picquets were much harassed during the night. At 2 A.M., on the 31st August, the march was continued to the Naffusak Pass (*see* Map). The road was very bad, and it was 10 A.M. before the foot of the defile was reached. The crest was seen to be crowded with the enemy. The troops were wearied and exhausted, and the heat was fearfully oppressive. A letter from Captain Brown in Kahan on the 27th reported that abundance of rain had fallen, and that no doubt a sufficiency of water would be found at the encamping ground below the Naffusak Pass. It was found, however, on arrival that there was no water,

Naffusak Pass.

and the supply with the troops was exhausted. In these circumstances it was evident that the whole force must perish from thirst, unless the pass of Naffusak was carried. Beyond, water was said to be procurable, and the fort of Kahan was distant only about six miles. Major Clibborn waited anxiously till half-past one for the rear-guard. At 2 A.M. the dispositions for attacking the pass were concluded, and the storming party moved up the steep face of the mountain. The road had been destroyed by the enemy, and breastworks constructed at different points. These were surmounted, and the crest almost gained, when the enemy opened a tremendous fire, and rushed down with a wild shout, sword in hand, on the advancing troops. Hundreds poured over the ridges of the mountain, and, leaping into the midst of the men, bore all before them. The attack of the Marris was carried out with such gallantry and impetuosity that it was not until they arrived almost at the muzzles of the guns that their advance was checked. Here, being exposed to a brisk infantry fire, and to the fire of the howitzers, which were pouring grape into them, they were repulsed with

great slaughter, dispersing in all directions, and numbers falling in the flight. The loss on the mountain side was now found to have been very severe; nearly half the storming party had fallen, including their gallant commander, Captain C. B. Raitt, 1st Bombay Grenadiers, and three other officers.

The enemy had been repulsed, and most of their influential men were lying dead around; but the pass remained in their possession, and their numbers were still very great. To follow up such a success was impossible; the heat was intense, and the sufferings of the men and cattle from exhaustion and thirst were dreadful. The men grew clamorous for drink, and the cries of the wounded and dying for water were increasing. The few bottles of beer among the officers' baggage, given to allay the wants of the greatest sufferers, gave rise to scenes of frenzy and despair. Men of all castes rushed and struggled for them. The scene was agonizing to behold. Parties were sent to search for water; and, on receiving a report that there was some in a ravine at some little distance, all the *pakhal* camels and the *bhisties* were ordered there, under the escort of the Irregular Horse, and were accompanied by the artillery horses which were too exhausted to be fit for any work. The evening was spent in collecting and bringing off the wounded, and about sunset it was reported that no water had been found, and that the whole party sent for it had been surrounded in a ravine, the greater part cut to pieces, and the horses carried off. To add to the difficulties of the situation, most of the camelmen and doolie-bearers had absconded after the action. In order to save the remainder of the troops and followers, no course remained but to make a rapid retreat to the water at Sartaf, abandoning the guns and stores, and the garrison of Kahan.

Accordingly, at 11 o'clock, having spiked the guns, the detachment moved off, the wounded men being carried on the few camels that it was possible to take with them. Nearly everything else was abandoned—guns, stores, camp equipage, etc., as there was no means of removing them. The top of the Sartaf Pass was reached, fortunately, without opposition. Here all discipline was at an end; the men, rushing down the hill, leaped into the pools of water like mad men. The rear-guard was attacked by a large body of the enemy, and the slaughter among the camp followers was immense. As soon as the men could be got from the water, they were formed

into square, as the enemy were reported on all sides, and daybreak was awaited. When daylight broke it was found that the detachment was without food, and nothing remained but to make a forced march to Pulaji, distant more than fifty miles. The sufferings of all on this march from the intense heat is not to be described.

Captain A. C. Heighington, 1st Bombay Grenadiers, died the day after the force reached Pulaji, from the effects of the sun and fatigue, and many of the men died on the march. Major Clibborn's exertions were untiring, and his courage and self-possession through these trying scenes were most conspicuous and were the admiration of all. In his official despatch he deservedly noticed the gallant bravery of Lieutenant W. Loch of the Poona Irregular Horse, and Lieutenant G. Malcolm of the Sind Horse. The officers killed in the disastrous attack on the pass were Captain C. B. Raitt, Lieutenant R. R. Moore, Jemadar Jurakin Singh, 1st Grenadiers; and Lieutenant H. Franklin, Ensign A. Williams, and Subadar Guru Bakhsh, 2nd Grenadiers; and of the non-commissioned officers and men, 179 were killed and 92 wounded, out of a force of about 650 men.

Referring to this affair Jacob says:—

Thus Major Clibborn gained a signal victory over, and with tremendous loss to, the Marri tribe; then appalled by the fearful heat and want of water, unfortunately his victory was followed up by all the consequences which usually attend on a disastrous defeat.

In the meantime the gallant little detachment at Kahan remained in suspense; they had witnessed the attack on the pass, but it was not for seven days that they had the slightest idea that any disaster had happened. They thought that Clibborn, finding the Naffusak too strong, had gone round by the Dera route.

On the 7th of September the truth was known and Captain Brown accordingly began to make preparations for the worst. On the 17th a letter reached him from the Brigade-Major at Sukkur, informing him of the disaster, and leaving him to his "own resources, it being impossible to send any further relief."

Captain Brown surrenders Kahan.

The number of sick, and the weakly state of the rest of the detachment, gave little chance of escape by a night march. Still Captain Brown put the best face on the matter, and, making a calculation, found they could hold out until the 15th

October on quarter rations and the gun bullocks; he, therefore, decided on holding out unless he got honourable terms.

On the 22nd a messenger came from Doda, the Marri Chief, to say that if Captain Brown would leave his fort, he was willing to make terms. To this he received answer that his fort would be given back to him on condition that he would give security for the safe arrival of the detachment in the plains. These terms were agreed to, and on the 28th September the garrison left the fort, taking with them their guns. It is unnecessary to describe the details of that return march; suffice it so to say that, after overcoming great difficulties and enduring much suffering, the little band arrived at Pulaji on the 1st October, emaciated, ragged, hungry, and destitute, yet bringing with them their gun and their honour. The Baluchis kept to the terms of their treaty, showing honour and even kindness to the garrison.

From the date of Captain Brown's leaving the Marri hills there was little communication between the British Government and this tribe until Major-General Sir Charles Napier's expedition against the Bugtis in 1845. It was then an object of great importance to cut off the retreat of the latter tribe to the north, and Sir Charles Napier, in a characteristic letter to Captain J. Jacob, then in political charge of the frontier of Upper Sind, asked him to undertake to gain over the Marris. Captain Jacob sent messengers who found that the Marri Chief with all his people had deserted Kahan, and had retreated to the next valley on the north, and consequently there was considerable difficulty in gaining them round. However, the chiefs were at last persuaded to wait on Captain Jacob at Lehri, and having explained the wishes of the Major-General, he induced them to visit him at Dera and give the necessary co-operation. This they did effectually and thus closed two lines of retreat to the Bugtis. Sir Charles Napier treated the chiefs with favour, and gave them handsome presents.

To turn now to the operations against the Bugtis. At the beginning of 1845, provoked by repeated acts of lawlessness on the part of the Dumkis, Jakranis, and Bugtis, Major-General Sir Charles Napier, G.C.B., commanding in Sind, determined to undertake a campaign, with a view to exterminating or capturing them all. The force assembled consisted of four 9-pounder guns, nine

howitzers, three mortars, and a siege train of twenty-one pieces; 2,000 cavalry,[1] and 2,500 infantry,[2] besides the forces of Amir Ali Morad and other auxiliaries, amounting to 2,000 men and 10 guns. The plan of operations was to drive the enemy into the hills in front of Pulaji, Uch, and Shahpur, and then advance from Sind by Zarani, and, while the enemy was engaged in front, to send a force from the left to cut them off from the Marris.

Before entering the Bugti hills, Sir Charles Napier issued a proclamation to the neighbouring tribes, stating that his object was to punish the Dumki, Jakrani, and Bugti robbers, who had hitherto plundered, unchecked, in British territory. On the night of the 15th of January 1845, an advanced column under Captain Jacob surrounded the village of Shahpur, and captured sixty-two Baluchis, three men being killed and three wounded on our side.

At the same time a force was detached to Uch, to cut off the retreat of the Bugtis; this force came on the enemy in position, 700 strong, under Daria Khan, the Jakrani Chief, and immediately charged and dispersed them, capturing 3,000 head of cattle. In the meantime the levies had occupied Pulaji, the enemy retreating eastwards to the hills. A magazine was formed at Shahpur, where supplies for fourteen days were collected.

A column was now ordered to advance from Pulaji on Bugti Dera, a distance of seven marches; and at the same time the Major-General, with a second column, advanced by the passes to the south of Dera. The enemy, however, alarmed by the movement in their rear, did not wait to meet our troops, but abandoned their position and escaped to the east. On the 30th January the force from Pulaji reached Dera, which was occupied without opposition, and the following day Sir Charles Napier opened communication with this column.

The enemy having thus escaped to the east, the Major-General halted and sent foraging parties to scour the country and bring in cattle. These were more or less successful; but the enemy now commenced to harass the communications, the post was twice intercepted, sixty camels were carried off and several followers

---

[1] 9th Bengal Cavalry—Scinde Horse (now 35th) Bundelkhand Legion.
[2] 2nd Bengal European Regiment—4th Bombay Infantry (now 104th Rifles), 64th Bengal Infantry.

murdered, and, a panic arising among the camelmen, they deserted with five hundred camels from Shahpur.

Intelligence was now received that the confederate chieftains, having ensconced themselves in a fastness only twenty miles distant, were starving, and the next day a message was received to say that their leader, Bijar Khan, the Dumki Chief, wished to surrender. To this the Major-General replied: "Let the Khan lay down his arms at my feet, and be prepared to emigrate with his followers to a district which I will point out on the left bank of the Indus, and he shall be pardoned. If he refuses these terms he shall be pursued to the death."

On the 5th February a patrol discovered and killed several armed hillmen between the passes. But famine now menaced the army, owing to the difficulty in getting camels, and Sir Charles Napier detached the Sind Camel Corps,[1] which formed part of the force, to fetch food from Shahpur. In one night, after a march of fifty miles, they reached Shahpur, and, having loaded their camels with forty-five thousand pounds of flour, they regained camp on the morning of the 8th, having taken but two days and three nights for the whole expedition.

On the very day this supply came, another message was received to say that not Bijar Khan only, but all the chiefs, were ready to surrender; but the following day a treacherous attack was made on the post, and several men of the escort were killed. Another attack was made on a small reconnoitring party, which was, however, repulsed with a loss to the enemy.

Negotiations having failed, orders were given for active operations to be resumed, and the right of the force moved forward to within a short distance of the Mazari frontier, the extreme left being at Dera. At the same time the Mazaris were warned against giving the Bugtis assistance. Fortunately, the latter, just before the commencement of the campaign, had plundered some hill Mazaris, and that, combined with the Major-General's warnings, induced them to send in several chiefs with three hundred followers as hostages for their good behaviour.

On the 18th news was brought in that the enemy's camp was at a place on the Mazari frontier, about twenty miles distant, and it was

---

[1] Transferred to the Bengal Presidency in 1849, and now the 59th Scinde Rifles.

accordingly determined to surprise them. For this purpose the troops marched on the 19th, but, by an accident, the enemy discovered this intention, and fled from their position. A large quantity of grain and a hundred and fifty loads of baggage were, however, captured. The extreme fatigue of the troops, who had been twenty-two hours under arms, prevented any attempt to pursue the enemy.

The Bugtis and their allies had now retreated to the north-east corner of the Bugti country, to the Khetran frontier; but they were refused an asylum in the Khetran and Sikh territories, and were delivered over to the British operations. At last they took refuge in Traki, a natural fortress to the north-east of Dera, where they were surrounded by the British troops, and preparations were made to storm their fastness. On the 4th March, however, Bijar Khan, Dumki; Islam Khan, Bugti; and Daria Khan, Jakrani, the principal chiefs of the enemy, came in to make their submission. They demanded terms, and were told that these were—submissions transportation from their hills, and settlement in the plains.

To these the chiefs would not agree; so the Major-General sent a number of small columns to scour the interior. Two brother. of Bijar Khan were captured on the 7th, but the chief himself eluded our troops till the 9th, when he surrendered, and was transported to Sind. Islam Khan, Bugti, escaped to the Khetrans. The campaign, after fifty-four days of incessant exertion, having thus been brought to a conclusion, the force left the hills on the 15th March, and returned to Shikarpur, where it was broken up.

These operations against the Bugtis do not seem, however, to have had much effect, for, on the 8th August 1846, the Collector of Shikarpur issued the following proclamation:—

Know all men living in the British territories of Sind, that it has become necessary to make arrangements for keeping off the Bugtis and other mountain robbers, and putting a stop to their robberies. Therefore, it is hereby ordered, that whoever will seize any of the Bugti mountaineers, and deliver them to the British horsemen, shall receive a reward of Rs. 10 for each man of the mountaineers so seized and delivered up.

That there was some reason for this proclamation was soon shown, for on the 10th December 1846, the Bugtis assembled a force of some 1,500 armed men, mostly on foot, and marched into

Sind; they passed through the British outposts to within fifteen miles of Shikarpur, remained twenty-four hours in British territory, secured every head of cattle in the country round, and returned to their hills, seventy-five miles, with all their booty—15,000 head—in safety. They conducted their proceedings with the greatest coolness and system, bringing with them, besides the armed force, nearly 500 unarmed followers to drive the cattle. This inroad was thought to be in too great force for the detachments at the outposts to attempt any resistance. Timely information reached the Shahpur post, but no troops moved out from it against the invading Bugtis. A regiment of cavalry and 200 bayonets were sent from Shikarpur to repel the invaders. The cavalry came on them at Hudi, some forty-five miles from Shikarpur, their unarmed attendants meanwhile continuing to drive the cattle towards the hills. However, the British troops being ignorant of the ground, and thinking the robbers too strong to be attacked, returned to Shikarpur without attempting anything further. The Bugtis ultimately reached their hills with all their prey, and without the loss of a man.

Major Jacob was now ordered up to the frontier from Hyderabad with the Scinde Irregular Horse, and from the date of his arrival a new era commenced.

Bugtis' fatal raid, 1847.

The Bugtis found that their master had come on the scene. Raids, however, did not cease at once, and several were committed during 1847, and on the 1st October of that year occurred the famous raid in which Lieutenant W. L. Merewether, Scinde Irregular Horse, killed nearly 600 marauders.

In this affair, a large body of Bugtis having entered the plain and attacked some villages, Lieutenant Merewether, with a party of the Scinde Horse—133 of all ranks—started in pursuit from Shahpur at 1-30 A.M. on the 1st October. He came up with the enemy soon after daybreak. Lieutenant Merewether's account of this affair is interesting:—

I was informed by a local Baluch guide that he heard loud shouting and much noise in the direction of Koonree. My detachment was marching in column of troops; I wheeled them into line and proceeded in the direction of Koonree; when near the jungle about that place, I saw the nemy formed in a deep and long line to my left. They were making a

side movement towards the jungle. I therefore passed rapidly along their front so as to head them away from the jungle in the plain. By this time they had halted in some rough broken ground with sand hillocks and bushes, but probably fancying from my galloping along their front that I did not mean to attack them, they left their vantage ground and rushed forward to attack me with much firing, loud shouts, and howls. This at once gave me all I wished for, namely, a fair field.

Immediately I changed front to the left and charged. The charge was made steadily, rapidly, and with irresistible effect. The Bugti had formed a solid mass to receive us, but were overthrown at the first onset with terrible loss. They then moved off towards the hills—distant some three miles—in disorder, but shouldering together as closely as they could. We continued our attacks, killing numbers, until on re-crossing the Teemanee river they made another short stand. They were again broken up and driven into the open plain. The effect of our little carbines, used in one hand at close quarters, was quite terrible to behold. Every shot appeared to kill or disable an enemy, who were often by reason of the bushes and broken ground enabled to keep just out of swords' reach. They were now approaching the low hills when Ressaidar Shaikh Ali, very judiciously getting some men in advance, cut them off from their place of refuge. They then turned back towards Koonree.

Their numbers were now getting small. Repeated offers of quarter were made to them, but they obstinately continued to fight until the destruction was so great that of their original 700 only some 120 remained fighting, of whom many were wounded. They were then induced to throw down their arms, and surrender. Not a single footman escaped death or capture. Two horsemen alone escaped.[1] From prisoners I learnt that the force was 700 strong including 25 horsemen.

Our own loss was only 9 killed and wounded. Nine horses were killed and ten wounded.

The whole tribe, broken and disheartened, fled for refuge to the Khetrans. The Bugti Chief, Islam Khan, was married to a sister of Mir Haji, the Khetran Chief. These two tribes then united, and attacked the Marris, and at first had some success, but the Marris eventually defeated the Bugtis with trifling loss to themselves, but with a loss of 500 to their opponents.

Notwithstanding these losses, the Bugtis endeavoured to make one more effort in Sind, but without success. Still the chief did not surrender, and, to bring matters to a crisis, Major Jacob gave

---

[1] Subsequent reports from native sources showed a considerably larger number.

out that he was going to Dera in person to seize Islam Khan. When this intelligence reached that chief, he came into British territory and gave himself up, and he and a number of the tribe, who also made their submission, were located in British territory. Islam Khan, however, shortly after decamped with his family, and returned to the hills.

In spite of the severe lessons they had received, this border continued to be harassed by parties of Bugtis.

With the Marris we had had little communication after 1845, and although they carried on their depredations without check over Kachi, as far south as Kanda, yet they took care to avoid encroaching on British territory until 1849, when, becoming bold by long impunity, and instigated by the golden promises of Diwan Mulraj of Multan, they commenced predatory incursions into British territory, and on the 7th April of that year joined the Bugtis and the Khetrans in an attack on the Kasmor post.

The detachment of the Scinde Irregular Horse (40 sabres) at that place had been relieved by a similar party. The relieved party under command of Naib-Risaldar Karam Ali Khan, marched from Kasmor towards Kumbi about two o'clock on the morning of the 7th April, and had only departed about one hour, when the party at Kasmor, which had not yet gone into the lines, but was encamped outside, was surrounded and attacked on all sides. A duffadar going his rounds first fell in with the enemy and was killed. The hillmen, immensely outnumbering the men of the Scinde Horse, rushed in among the horses, and a desperate hand-to-hand conflict ensued, which ended in the enemy being beaten off with some loss, leaving many of their number dead on the ground. On our side the Scinde Horse had one duffadar and three sowars killed, and four sowars severely wounded, and the Baluch Guides had two sowars killed. When the attack commenced on the party at Kasmor, Naib-Risaldar Karam Ali Khan was about four miles distant on the road to Kumbi; but, hearing the firing in the direction of Kasmor, he galloped back with his party towards that place, and, as he approached, he came on a body of 300 or 400 horsemen, driving off 1,000 camels. He at once charged and dispersed them with severe loss, and then, following them up for a considerable distance, recovered and brought back the whole of the plunder. He then returned to Kasmor.

The attacking party, it was afterwards ascertained, had assembled in Bugti territory, and consisted of about 500 men of the Bugti, Marri, and Khetran tribes. Their loss was forty killed, more than that number wounded, and a great number of their mares killed, wounded, and taken. The party was led by Mir Haji, the Khetran Chief, and others.

This attack on the Kasmor post was merely a blind for a more serious attempt to the westward, some 1,500 Marris having, at the same time, entered the plain country by the Lehri river. Owing to the activity of the troops on the frontier, this threatened raid led to nothing.

After the attack on Kasmor, two other raids were made by the Bugtis during the year 1849, but in both of these the camels carried off were recovered, although the raiders escaped.

On the 24th December, 1850, a party of Bugtis carried off a number of camels from the jungle near Kand Kot. Durga Singh, the native officer of the Kand Kot detachment of Scinde Horse, started in pursuit, and, after a ride of sixty miles, arrived, with only three men, in the face of the robbers, who numbered one hundred. Notwithstanding, this officer gallantly charged and killed a great number, losing, however, his own life and that of two of his troopers. The place of his death is pointed out still with unfeigned admiration by the Baluchis, and is known as *Durga Kushta.*

Affairs subsequent to annexation of the Punjab.

After the annexation, the Mazaris and Gurchanis gave much trouble on our border, and up to 1853 armed parties of the former continued to carry on their plundering expeditions in British territory. About this time an Assistant Commissioner was appointed to Mithankot, and thenceforward the reclamation of the Mazaris commenced; so that those once inveterate plunderers are now peaceable and useful subjects. During the troubled times of the Mutiny the chief of this tribe showed his loyalty by doing good service for the Government.

The Gurchanis, however, after the Mazaris had settled down into peaceful subjects, continued turbulent. The sections of the tribe which gave most trouble were the Petafis and Lasharis. They were inveterate thieves, and their highway robberies in Harrand, Dajal, and Fazilpur became notorious. The Lasharis lived

mostly in the hills, but they used to come down to graze their flocks along the border, and had connections and accomplices in the plains. They also aided the Marris on several occasions in raiding on the Punjab frontier.

In January 1852, a severe shock of earthquake occurred at Kahan. One side of the fort wall was thrown down, the remainder much shattered, and the greater number of the houses inside were overthrown, burying beneath the ruins many men, women, and children, with some cattle, and a great deal of property.

At the same time another even more fearful calamity overtook a portion of the tribe living with their cattle in a large cave some little distance to the northward. The hill in which the cave was, was violently shaken and fell, burying nearly every living being at that time within it. The road by Naffusak to Kahan was completely closed by the hill falling and filling up the pass; two hundred and sixty Musalmans, including women and children, were killed, and upwards of eighty Hindus, with a large quantity of cattle.

On the 11th December, 1852, a large body of Marris, said to have been the whole assembled tribe, horse and foot, suddenly issued from the hills and attacked the town of Pulaji, occupied by Kaihiris, a small Baluch tribe friendly to the British. The Marris killed forty, chiefly unarmed cultivators and herdsmen, and wounded many more, without apparently suffering any loss themselves. They then carried off all the cattle from the country round, and returned to their hills. This raid was committed with the connivance and assistance of some of the principal Kalat Sardars, headed by the Wazir, Muhammad Hassan. Major Jacob accordingly wrote a strong remonstrance to the Khan of Kalat.

On the 3rd April 1853, a party of Mari marauders carried off some cattle from near Kasmor. Risaldar Shekh Karim, of the Sind Horse, in command of the post, went in pursuit, and came on the enemy, eighty horse and eighty foot, the latter strongly posted on the hill. The troops at once attacked them, though they only numbered thirty-two sabres. After a hard fight the enemy fled. The loss of the Sind Horse was one native officer, seven sowars, and nine horses killed, and two men wounded. A great many of the enemy were killed, but in the darkness of the night the number could not be ascertained.

On the 18th May 1853, 180 Marris and Lasharis attacked a small detachment of the 4th Punjab Cavalry on the Dera Ghazi Khan border, and cut up six grass cutters and five of the escort.

After this the Marris carried on their depredations chiefly in Kachi, and avoided making attacks on Sind territory, although their raids on the Punjab frontier did not altogether cease. They were also engaged in a war with the Bugtis, which was carried on with varying fortunes.

From 1854 to 1857 the Gurchanis continued to give much trouble, and in the latter year a party acted as guides to a large body of Marris in a formidable attack on the Punjab frontier. This raid was made on the 17th August by 220 horsemen. The marauders, on emerging from the hills, divided into two parties, one taking the road towards Drigi, and carrying off all the cattle they could lay hands on, the other scouring the plain in front of Muhammadpur and Fatehpur, and collecting all the herds they could find; the parties then united on the plain opposite Fatehpur, and made for the hills. In the meantime, Bijar Khan, the Drishak[1] Chief and commandant of Asni, who with about 60 horse and foot was patrolling in that direction, heard from a villager that the Marris were making for the hills with their booty. The chief immediately sent notice to the neighbouring posts, and being reinforced by 56 horse and foot, he proceeded to attack the enemy; but the latter were more than double the number of our levies, who were ultimately defeated with great slaughter, the marauders making good their retreat with immense booty. In this engagement, the chief, Bijar Khan, his eldest son, and twenty-six of the party were killed, besides several wounded, the loss being chiefly among the Drishak tribe, who rallied round their chief, and fell fighting by his side; of the twenty-six killed, twenty-four were Drishaks, the other two being Bugtis. The loss of property was estimated at Rs. 6,000.

The success of this raid was principally due to the absence of all regular troops from the Rajanpur frontier, owing to the 1st Punjab Cavalry having been withdrawn for service in Hindustan.

---

[1] A Baluch tribe of the Dera Ghazi Khan district whose head-quarters are Asni. The tribe, however, is much scattered in the district.

On the 28th March 1858, a party of 40 police and levies following up some stolen cattle into the hills, were attacked by a party of 100 Marris, and defeated with some loss.

In addition to their raids on the Dera Ghazi Khan frontier, the Marris continued their inroads into Kachi, and their conduct in that direction became so intolerable, that, in 1858-59, Khudadad Khan, the young Khan of Kalat, on the advice of Brigadier-General J. Jacob, C. B., the Political Superintendent, Upper Sind Frontier, collected the whole forces of the Khanate to punish them. Just at this time Brigadier-General Jacob died, and was succeeded by Major W. H. R. Green, who accompanied the expedition with an escort consisting of a squadron of the Scinde Irregular Horse, under Major Malcolm S. Green.

The forces of the Khan assembled at Bhag on the 21st January 1859, to the number of 4,000 horse and 4,000 foot, and marched on the following day. Dera was reached on the 3rd February, and Kahan was occupied without opposition on the 7th. The fort was destroyed, and the force halted to await the arrival of a convoy of provisions from Kachi. This convoy arrived on the 23rd, and on the following day the force moved to the north, in which direction the Marris had retreated.

On the 28th the Marri Chief came into camp with a number of his followers, and tendered his submission to the Khan of Kalat, and begged for mercy for his tribe. Negotiations were accordingly opened with the Marris, who professed their willingness to accede to any terms offered, to acknowledge the Khan as their lawful prince, and to give hostages for future good behaviour.

To this arrangement Major W. H. R. Green was most averse, for though there was little doubt that the tribe had met with most severe punishment, their fields and forts having been destroyed, their supplies of grain and 1,800 head of cattle captured, yet his knowledge of their innate love of plunder made him fear that if some very severe example was not made of them when within the Khan's grasp, they would soon return to their old habits. However, His Highness considered they had been sufficiently punished, and the same opinion appeared to prevail among many of the other Chiefs. As the Khan had been the principal sufferer by the Marri depredations, Major Green considered that it would not be proper to force further hostilities. He, therefore, informed the Khan that

he was at liberty to act as he pleased, but that he would be held strictly responsible for any depredations made by this tribe on British territory at any future time.

Accordingly, having taken hostages for the future good conduct of the tribe, the force again marched for Kachi by the difficult Chakar Pass, and re-entered the plains on the 14th March.

One result of this expedition was to prove to the Marris how even their most inaccessible strongholds can be entered and destroyed. Since the disaster which befell the detachment of British troops under Major T. Clibborn in 1840, the Marris had regarded themselves as invincible. This campaign completely destroyed their prestige.

One of the guns lost by Major Clibborn in 1840 was recovered during the expedition, and was sent to Jacobabad.

After the raid on the Asni plain in August 1857, already narrated, the Lashari clan of the Gurchanis, who had acted as guides to the Marris on that occasion, absconded to the hills, and the greater part joined the Marris, with whom they continued to raid in the plains. At last, in March 1858, Captain F. R. Pollock, Deputy Commissioner of Dera Ghazi Khan, with the consent of Government, determined, under cloak of an expedition by the Survey Department to the Mari Hill, just beyond our border, to surprise some Lashari villages in the vicinity. The attempt was not, however, successful, as the Lasharis, having obtained intelligence of the intention, moved off to the mouth of a small pass within our territory, sending at the same time a party to follow and annoy the surveyors.

It appears, however, that the spot to which the Lasharis had removed was within a convenient distance of the Shambani Bugtis and Mazaris, and these tribes—thinking the opportunity a good one to punish their common foe and enrich themselves—made an attack on them, and carried off 2,000 cattle. In this affair seven Lasharis and two Bugtis were killed. The conduct of the Mazaris and Bugtis was undoubtedly reprehensible, but there were several circumstances of an extenuating character, and it was well known that we desired to punish the Lasharis.

The first attempt to reclaim the Lasharis was made in 1860, and although the process was slow, a change for the better gradually took place.

After the expedition against the Marris in 1859, there was a long respite from raids till February 1862, when several raids were committed on the Punjab border and on the Bugtis in their hills The conduct of the latter with regard to the British, from 1852 to 1861, was most exemplary, but in that year, owing to internal dissensions, the tribe became disorganised, and raids were again commenced on the Sind Frontier. The offenders belonged chiefly to the Kalpur and Musuri clans.

On the 26th January 1867, occurred the great raid on Harrand by 1,200 Marris, Bugtis, and Khetrans, under the leadership of a noted freebooter, Ghulam Husain, Musuri Bugti. Timely information of the intended raid was conveyed to Major W. H. Paget, commanding at Rajanpur, by the Bugti Chief. On the morning of the 26th the hillmen came out of a pass, about ten miles north of Harrand, and their horsemen at once swept round to try and collect the cattle, but met with little success, as these had been driven off to the rear on receipt of warning of the intended raid. The footmen had, in the meantime, fired some of the hamlets, and the whole then retired towards the hills.

The news of the raid immediately spread, and the Gurchanis, numbering some 350 horse and foot, assembled under their *tumandar*, Ghulam Haidar Khan. The detachment of the 5th Punjab Cavalry,[1] from Harrand, numbering 27 sabres, under Jemadar Imam Khan, turned out most promptly. The burning of the hamlets showed the outposts the position of the raiders, and no time was lost in arriving on the scene of action. The force overtook the enemy, who had formed a line close to the hills. The ground was very bad for cavalry, and Ghulam Haidar Khan wished to wait for reinforcements. The native officer, however, insisted that he must advance, as the enemy would get into the hills and the cavalry would be unable to act. Accordingly, the 5th Punjab Cavalry detachment, followed by Ghulam Haidar Khan and the mounted Gurchanis, broke into a trot. The sight of the cavalry thus advancing was too much for the raiders; they moved forward for a short distance, then wavered, and all attempts of Ghulam Husain to rally them being futile, fled as soon as the cavalry got within carbine range. They were followed by the Gurchani footmen

---

[1] Now 25th Cavalry (Frontier Force).

up the hillside, and the pursuit was continued towards the Dragal mountain, under which a body of twenty-three Marris and twelve Musuri Bugtis were surrounded, and the latter, refusing to surrender, were killed. The enemy's loss in this affair was two hundred and fifty-eight killed (ninety-three Bugtis, seventy Marris, and ninety-five Khetrans and Pathans) and twenty-four prisoners. Among the killed were Ghulam Husain and several noted criminals. The loss on our side was one duffadar, two sowars, and about fifty Gurchanis wounded.

For his gallant conduct on this occasion, Jemadar Iman Khan received the Order of Merit. As a reward for his services, the grants which had previously been confiscated were restored to Ghulam Haidar Khan, and also the privilege of collecting his share in kind.

After this raid the Marris and the Bugtis refrained from molesting the Punjab frontier, although the former continued to carry on depredations in Kachi and in the Bolan Pass. In 1871, after consultation between the Punjab and Sind authorities at Mithankot,[1] arrangements were made for the better management of these tribes. Allowances were granted to them to induce them to desist from raiding on the British border in return for tribal service. The system of policy towards these tribes on the Sind and Punjab frontiers was at the same time made uniform, and since then their management has been much simplified. The attitude of both the Marris and the Bugtis, instead of being one of continued hostility, became friendly, and their chiefs showed a readiness to assist the British officers entrusted with the management of this border.

But, although they respected British territory, their inter-tribal feuds continued. In 1873 the Marris raided in Kalat territory, and in December of that year they made an attack, headed by their chief in person, on the Khetrans, quite close to the British border in front of Dera Ghazi Khan. The Khetrans lost seven killed, and a number of cattle and sheep were carried off. The Marris had two men killed. In January 1874, they made a similar attack on the Musa Khel Pathans, sixteen of whom were killed, the loss of the Marris being only two. In this case also a large amount of booty was carried off. In the beginning of 1874 the Commissioner

---

[1] See page 58.

of Sind proposed that the Marris should be punished by a blockade, and, in the event of that failing, by a punitive expedition. This course, however, was not sanctioned by the Government, and it was decided to settle matters, if possible, without resorting to coercive measures.

In the meantime fresh complications occurred. The Bugti tribe, aided by some Marris, committed a serious outrage in Sind territory, and carried off some 2,000 head of cattle. The effect of this raid was to embroil the two tribes directly with the British Government; whereas previous to this occurrence there was no complaint against the Bugtis, and the culpability of the Marris consisted in the contumacious attitude assumed by the chief and tribe towards their superior, the Khan of Kalat.

There is little doubt that the cause of the Marris assuming this line of conduct was the facility of playing off the Sind and Punjab authorities one against the other. Comparatively tractable to the latter, they had justly rendered themselves obnoxious to the former by violating openly and repeatedly their nominal subjection to the Khan of Kalat. The Government therefore determined to deal directly with the tribe in future so as to render it impossible for them to evade their responsibilities. Eventually, a satisfactory settlement was effected, both with the Marris and Bugtis.

At the beginning of 1877 the Lashari section of the Gurchani tribe showed a tendency to revert to their old marauding habits, but measures were taken with much success to recover property stolen by them, and to prevent a recurrence of such misdeeds. In 1880 the Durkanis, one of the hill sections of the Gurchanis, gave some trouble by their lawless behaviour. They became involved in a feud with the Khetrans, and were joined by a few of their brethren from British territory. In December 1880, this feud had so spread as to threaten the whole border. The matter was taken up by the local British authorities, who, in January 1881, succeeded in patching up a peace between the two tribes at Harrand. The Durkanis, however, in March violated their agreement, and committed a serious raid on the Khetrans. For this offence a blockade was imposed, and shortly afterwards they made their submission, and the blockade was removed on the 29th July 1881. They, however, did not cease to make reprisals, and

plunder their neighbours in the hills beyond the border. The main reason for their restlessness was the reduced condition of this clan, many of whose members were in poor and straitened circumstances. A grant of land was made to the Durkani headmen, on condition of its being cultivated by their clansmen, in order to induce them to take to more settled habits. The Lasharis, the other hill section of the Gurchanis, have behaved fairly well since then.

The Gurchani *tumandar*, Sardar Ghulam Haidar Khan, who had been the chief of the tribe since the annexation, died on the 23rd March 1884. His son, Jalal Khan, succeeded him.

A feud broke out in 1889 between the Durkanis and the Hodiani section of the Legharis, and the former were blockaded for some time.

CHAPTER VI.

KASRANIS AND BOZDARS.

OF the Kasranis, about one-third reside now (1907) in the hills beyond the border, and are all under the political jurisdiction of the Deputy Commissioner of Dera Ghazi Khan. The northern boundary of their territory is the Kaora Nala, which marks the dividing line on the Sulimans between Pathan and Baluch, the Kasranis being the most northerly Baluch tribe.

The tribe is poor and the number of men in the hills capable of bearing arms is probably less than 500.

The total population of the tribe is some 5,000.

EXPEDITION AGAINST THE KASRANIS, BY A FORCE UNDER BRIGADIER J. S. HODGSON, IN APRIL 1853.

Expedition in 1853.

When the Multan outbreak took place in 1848, and Lieutenant H. B. Edwardes took the field against Diwan Mulraj, Mita Khan, the Kasran Chief, took possession of the fort of Mangrotha, and ejected the *Diwan's* deputy. He then quietly waited to see how events would turn out, prepared to act his part accordingly. When he saw the scale turning in favour of the British Government, he offered his services to Lieutenant Edwardes.

On annexation, he was confirmed in the grants he had enjoyed under former rulers of the Punjab, which he seems to have done little to deserve; for he winked at raids and petty robberies by the hill portion of his tribe, and by his neighbours, the Bozdars.

The conduct of the Kasranis after the annexation continued to be most unsatisfactory; the country round Dera Fateh Khan was continually harassed by them, and many hundred head of stolen cattle were conveyed through their passes into the interior.

At last the conduct of the tribe became so bad that, early in 1852, Major J. Nicholson,[1] the Deputy Commissioner of Dera Ismail

---
[1] General Nicholson of Mutiny fame.

Khan, suggested that the Kasranis in the plains should be held responsible for the good conduct of their brethren in the hills.

Shortly after this, in March 1852, the Kasranis signalised themselves by a most audacious attack on Dera Fateh Khan. One of their chiefs, Yusaf Khan, held a village in British territory. From this village a subordinate (a fiscal *employé*) disappeared under suspicious circumstances. Yusaf Khan was summoned to answer, but did not appear. His brother was, however, found and sent in to the civil officer, when, in trying to escape from custody, he fell from a wall, and received injuries from which he died. Yusaf Khan then organised an expedition against Dera Fateh Khan, about twenty miles from the hills—a measure which had been once before adopted in the Sikh time—and, on the evening of the 16th of March 1852, about 300 Kasrani foot, with 40 horse, started from the Kaora Pass, and marching between the posts of Gurwali and Vihoa, arrived at Dera Fateh Khan at early dawn on the 17th. The force at the *thana* consisted of 14 horse and 19 foot, but it was not strong enough to offer much opposition; and the Kasranis plundered such portion of the *bazar* as was not under fire from the *thana*, and then retired, with the loss of three killed and one prisoner, but carrying off most of the cattle of the village. Our loss was five killed and three wounded, and in addition three horses were killed and five wounded.

The Kasranis in their retreat took a more southerly direction than in their advance, making for the road between Vihoa and Thata; to both of which posts, the most northerly of the Dera Ghazi Khan district, news of the attack had been sent by the *Thanadar*, who was following up the Kasranis, and collecting as many of the people of the country as he could as he went along. About seven miles south of Vihoa he was joined by the cavalry detachments from these outposts, when the force altogether mustered two native officers and forty-three sabres of the 4th Punjab Cavalry[1] and thirty-nine horse and sixty foot of the levies.

The Kasranis had taken up a strong position behind an embankment, where they were out of fire. The *Thanadar* wanted to attack with the foot levies first, but the cavalry native officer determined to charge at once, which was done in a most gallant manner, although the attack was repulsed with the loss of one native officer

---

[1] Afterwards disbanded.

and three sowars killed, and six sowars wounded, besides three horses killed and nine wounded.

The enemy, it was believed, had many casualties, but they made good their retreat with their booty, except four *baniahs* they were carrying off for ransom to the hills, who managed to escape in the *mêlée*.

In the month of April following, the Kasranis assembled and threatened British territory, but a force from Dera Ismail Khan, consisting of the 5th Punjab Cavalry and Sind Camel Corps, moved down during the night to Vihoa, where it was joined by a detachment of the 4th Punjab Cavalry and 200 men of the Police Battalion from Dera Ghazi Khan, and the enemy then dispersed.

The tribe, however, continued their depredations, and a blockade was accordingly imposed on the hill Kasranis.

Mita Khan, the chief, did not join in the attack upon Dera Fateh Khan, because he had too much at stake in the plains to commit himself openly against the Government; but he did not exert his influence to avert it, and he sent no intimation of the gathering or intentions of his tribe to any of our frontier officers or posts.

On being taxed by Major Nicholson with his culpable neglect, he attempted to deny that he possessed any influence among his tribe, or knew anything of their intentions; but on it being recalled to his recollection that he had shown his influence a few years before by laying siege to Dera Fateh Khan at the head of his tribe, and being told that he must either be with or against the Government openly, he changed his tone, and next day, as an earnest of his intentions, sent in two men he had had seized, and promised to capture more.

Major Nicholson considered the infliction of summary punishment on the Kasranis desirable; but he thought the chastisement of such a poor hill tribe, thinly scattered over a very rugged country, and without anything deserving the name of a village, extremely difficult.

In the meantime he considered that the posts of Vihoa and Thata should be increased to 50 cavalry each with a sufficient number of foot to enable the whole of the cavalry to take the field in an emergency; that a post should be established at Daulatwala of the same strength; and that at least 100 infantry should be left at Dera Fateh Khan, to reassure the people, who were much alarmed, and

inclined to forsake their homes for some place of greater security. Until Yusaf Khan was captured or killed, or heavy retribution inflicted on the Kasrani tribe, he did not consider it safe to relax these precautionary measures.

In the spring of 1853, owing to Major Nicholson's representations, on the return of the expeditionary force from the Shirani hills, the opportunity was taken to chastise the Kasranis. Accordingly, a force (*see* Appendix A), consisting of 495 of all ranks, under the command of Brigadier J. S. Hodgson, commanding the Punjab Irregular Force, and accompanied by Major J. Nicholson, marched from Pehur towards the Bati pass (thirteen miles) at 10 P.M., on the night of the 11th of April 1853. The column reached the mouth of the pass at daybreak the next morning, and found the enemy (who had evidently received intelligence of the approach of the troops) in position behind breastworks on the hills on both sides of the pass.

<small>Detachment, 4th Punjab Cava'ry.
1st Punjab Infantry.
6th Police Battalion.</small>

These hills were ascended and the breastworks taken by two companies, 1st Punjab Infantry,[1] under Lieutenant C. P. Keyes, and two companies under Lieutenant E. J. Travers, whilst the remainder of the force advanced up the pass for about a mile, when the village of Bati, the head-quarters of the tribe, was reached; it was defended by a very high stockade erected on the crest of a precipitous ridge above the village, the fire from which swept the gorge. As the right flankers had difficulty in enfilading this position, it was carried by a rush of the light company of the 6th Police Battalion and some twenty men of the 1st Punjab Infantry, under Lieutenant Keyes, supported by the remainder of the 6th Police Battalion. Bati consisted of some eighty or ninety well and substantially built houses, and it was, with two other hamlets, completely destroyed, with the exception of the mosque and the houses of a *malik* and his son, who had held aloof from the misconduct of the tribe.

The enemy had not time to remove their property, of which a great quantity was destroyed; some of the Kasrani flocks were captured by the skirmishers and two *zamburaks*,[2] which the Kasranis had captured from Sawan Mal,[3] with a number of matchlocks, were

---

[1] Now 55th Coke's Rifles.
[2] Small field guns used in the Sikh Army.
[3] Sikh Deputy in the Derajat previous to our occupation.

also taken. The troops then retired in the same formation as they had advanced, and reached the mouth of the pass at 10 A.M., the enemy ineffectually trying to harass the retirement. There was no water between Pehur and the hills, and the force had therefore to march back to its encampment at Pehur where it arrived at 2 P.M.; the main body having marched thirty-four miles, whilst the skirmishers had marched some forty miles in all.

Whilst the troops were employed in the pass, the police and levies had destroyed the encampments of those portions of the tribe in the plain who were known to have joined the enemy as the troops approached, but two encampments in the neighbourhood, the inhabitants of which remained peaceably in their homes, were not molested. The 4th Punjab Cavalry, under Captain G. O. Jacob, had patrolled between the Bati Pass and Vihoa during the operations. Our loss amounted to one killed and ten wounded; that of the enemy was not known; they acknowledged to have had five killed and wounded. The Indian medal, with a clasp for the "North-West Frontier" was granted in 1869 to all survivors of the troops engaged in these operations.

After this expedition, raids for the most part ceased, and before the end of the year (1853), the chief of the plain Kasranis, Mita Khan, who had previously been lukewarm, and who, when called to account, had urged that he could not be responsible for the control of his hill neighbours unless the lost rights of retaliation were restored to him, engaged to guard the passes of the Kasrani hills, seven in number. He had formerly enjoyed perquisites and privileges under Sikh rule, worth about Rs. 500 per annum. These had been continued since the annexation. He was now to receive Rs. 500 more in cash from the British Government in return for the responsibility undertaken.

1853—57.

This arrangement was so far successful, that the authorities were enabled in 1854 to remove the prohibition against hill Kasranis entering British territory. Soon after, Yusaf Khan died, and his son was subsequently pardoned, and permitted to return to his village.

In the operations against the Bozdars in 1857, Mita Khan, with some of his tribe, were employed with the levies.

Bozdars. The Baluchi tribe of Bozdars is, for the most part, resident in the hills. At first, after the annexation of the Derajat in 1849, this tribe was guilty of many marauding expeditions into the plains. Their chief, however, was subsidised with a small assignment of land revenue inside the British border, which rendered the tribe amenable for some time. This assignment was resumed at the time of the expedition in 1857, but re-granted shortly afterwards.

The tribe is entirely under the political jurisdiction of the Deputy Commissioner of Dera Ghazi Khan. The Bozdars have ceased to give trouble, and serve readily in the Baluch Levy Corps at Dera Ghazi and Fort Munro. A relative of the Bozdar Chief has recently (1906) been given a direct commission in the 127th Baluchis, and an experiment is now being made in that regiment to enlist the men of this tribe in the regular army. Living entirely in the hills, the Bozdars are not big men. They are, however, like all Baluchis—possessed of great endurance. They are of Rind extraction and are said to be an offshoot of the Legharis.

They are divided into the *Dulani, Ladwani, Ghulamani, Chakrani, Sihani, Shawani, Jalalani Jafrani,* and *Rustamani* clans. They fight with the matchlock rather than with the sword.[1] They are more civilised than most of the trans-frontier tribes, and are of all the Baluchis the strictest Muhammadans. They are great graziers, and their name is said to be derived from the Persian *buz*, a goat, as they were formerly famous for the immense number of sheep and goats which they possessed. The hill Bozdars number 5,000 souls. According to the last census, there are about 3,000 Bozdars in British territory; these live in scattered villages about Rajanpur and among the Legharis, and have no connection with the parent tribe.

The Bozdar country is entirely mountainous, being formed of the outer spurs of the Suliman range. The main spurs run down from the parent range with a direction generally easterly, and instead of sinking gradually into the plains, they split into successive ridges, running north and south, connected with each other by a distinct watershed, but having the appearance from the plains of forming three separate ranges. These curious parallel and knife-edged

---

[1] Unlike other Baluchis.

spurs are divided from each other by the main drainage lines of the country, which run east and west. These are called the Drug, Lundi, Saunra, Sori, and Vidor passes, of which only the Lundi extends beyond and to the west of the third range. The main ravines have generally more or less water in them, but the lesser ones seldom or never, except after rain. There is another peculiarity in the Bozdar hills, which, however, is common to the whole border from Sind to Bannu, namely, the narrow defiles called *tokhs*, running north and south between what may be described as enormous walls, so precipitously do the hills rise on either side. By these *tokhs* there is communication from the northernmost to the southernmost point of the Bozdar country, and it would be quite possible for a marauding band of northern Bozdars to go by them and raid in the southernmost part of the Khosa country without entering the plains at all in coming and going; but though continuous, the route is by no means direct, as the road follows the ravines, though preserving a general direction north and south.

The greater portion of the tribe are situated between the first and second ranges; the Ghulamani section inhabit the Majvel valley, north of, and contiguous to, the Khetran country. The road between the Majvel and the main valley is through a very narrow pass called Saunra.

The language, dress, and food of the Bozdars are the same as of other Baluch tribes. Owing to their strictness with regard to their religious observances, a large number of priests and *Saiyids* reside in their lands, and consequently a few mosques, built of mud or thatch, are to be seen here and there. They are, however, by no means fanatical, nor do they seem to have any distaste for British rule. The Bozdars are constantly at feud with their northern neighbours, the Ustaranas, and also with the Khetrans on their south.

In former times the Bozdars had always a turbulent character; and being so powerful, and living in such close proximity to the border, previous Governments found it politic to bestow a yearly allowance on the chiefs, in order to give them a certain hold over the tribe. Thus it appears, as far back as the reign of Akbar, they received an allowance of eighty *maunds* of grain per annum. Under the Sikh rule, they repeatedly carried fire and sword into the Dera

Ghazi Khan district. The Sikh ruler, Sawan Mal of Multan, in vain endeavoured to repel them by force. Finally he built a fort at Mangrotha and granted an allowance to the Bozdar Chief, in return for which the chief agreed to guard the passes through his country. The Sikhs, however, were unable to enforce these conditions.

Bozdar Expeditions.

Expedition against the Bozdars, by a force under Brigadier N. B. Chamberlain, in March 1857.

After the annexation of the Punjab, the allowances which had been made to the Bozdar Chief by the Sikhs were continued by the British Government; but, by way of evading the conditions, he arranged that his followers should plunder in places distant as well as near, and should carry their booty into the hills by passes other than their own. In 1850 they committed one raid on Umarkot, below Mithankot, far away to the south, the marauders being chiefly mounted; and another on the Khosa village of Yaru, to the north of Dera Ghazi Khan. Towards the close of the same year a party of 120 raiders attacked Vidor, a place of some importance on the frontier opposite Dera Ghazi Khan, but were stoutly resisted by the villagers. In 1852 a party of ninety Bozdars, having lifted the camels of the Bulani village, were pursued by a detachment, 4th Punjab Cavalry, from the Mangrotha post, when the camels were recovered, the detachment having one horse killed by the fire from the hills.

In 1853 there were three forays by the tribe. Two of these incursions were successful as regards spoil, but no life was lost; in the third, however, though well mounted, they were pursued for many miles by a detachment, 4th Punjab Cavalry,[1] and forced to disgorge their booty at the mouth of the Mangrotha pass. In 1853 it became necessary to prohibit any hill Bozdar from visiting the plains under pain of imprisonment if seized. At the beginning of 1854, the Bozdar Chief was confirmed in the grant of his old allowances, amounting to Rs. 4,332 per annum, and the proceeds of some rent free lands, amounted to Rs. 2,000 more, when he renewed his engagements to prevent plundering. For a

---

[1] Since disbanded.

time these pledges were kept. One of the Bozdar Chiefs visited the camp of the Chief Commissioner in the winter of 1854. During 1854 no raids were reported; but unfortunately during 1855, the Bozdars returned to their bad habits, several raids occurred, villages were plundered, and a large number of minor thefts were committed—no less than seventy-four in six months. In order partially to reimburse the sufferers a sum of Rs. 2,500 was deducted from the allowances of the chief. Many robbers and murderers, refugees from British territory, were also sheltered in the Bozdar hills. The Bozdars crowned their misdeeds of 1855 by a serious raid on the village of Kaleri, on the 1st December, carrying off spoil, chiefly cattle, valued at Rs. 1,200 and murdering one man. The marauders were 200 strong. All the chiefs were then summoned, under safe conduct, to answer for the misconduct of their tribe, and to offer such explanations as they could.

But nothing satisfactory appears to have come of this, and in March 1856, the Governor-General sanctioned the discontinuance of the cash allowance of Rs. 4,332 to the tribe, who were to be warned that on the occurrence of any further raids or forays their rent-free lands would also be confiscated and a rigorous embargo laid on them.

Up to the middle of 1856 no serious outrage was committed by the Bozdars, although there were cases of cattle-stealing, highway robbery, etc., but in June of that year the outposts had to be reinforced, as it was reported that the Bozdars were collecting for an attack on Mangrotha, and from that time up to the close of the year they made eleven forays into British territory, generally in large parties of from 20 to 200 men. Most of these were attended with bloodshed; numerous others were planned, but were baffled by the outposts. On two occasions (in the month of December) the detachments of the 2nd Punjab Cavalry and 4th Punjab Infantry had skirmishes with the Bozdars on the hills near the border; in the latter of these (on the 27th of December) the enemy were driven from four different positions, which they successively occupied, our loss being one sepoy killed and two sowars wounded.

At the beginning of January 1857, the whole of the 2nd Punjab Cavalry[1] was moved to the frontier. On the 17th January a

---

[1] Now 22nd Cavalry, Frontier Force.

reconnoitring party of one non-commissioned officer and eight sowars of that regiment was surrounded by a party of 150 Bozdars, and lost two men in cutting their way through the enemy.

The Chief Commissioner, Sir John Lawrence, now strongly urged that an expedition should be sent against them, as the only effectual way of putting a stop to the harassing annoyances to which the villages and posts were exposed. The Commissioner of Leiah, Lieutenant-Colonel D. Ross, had represented "that the Bozdars carried on these forays in the vain hope that they would lead to the restoration of the money payment, which they had forfeited through their own misconduct, and that it was evident they would not cease to give trouble until a force was sent to chastise them, when the destruction of their crops would reduce them to great straits, and bring about a state of things which the mere interdiction of their intercourse with the plains had failed to effect." Sanction for the despatch of an expedition was therefore accorded in February 1857, and the confiscation of all the rent-free lands of the Bozdars was ordered.

The spring was considered the best time for punishing the tribe, when the crops were ripening. Accordingly, on the 5th March 1857, the troops (see Appendix), forming the expeditionary force, were assembled at Taunsa,[1] under Brigadier N. B. Chamberlain.

No. 1 Punjab Light Field Battery	4 field guns.
No. 2 Punjab Light Field Battery	4 mountain guns.
No. 3 Punjab Light Field Battery	4 ,, ,,
2nd and 3rd Punjab Cavalry	113 sabres.
Sappers and Miners	58 bayonets.
1st Sikh Infantry	443 ,,
3rd Sikh Infantry	445 ,,
1st Punjab Infantry	471 ,,
2nd Punjab Infantry	476 ,,
4th Punjab Infantry	484 ,,

Captain F. R. Pollock, Deputy Commissioner of Dera Ghazi Khan, was to accompany the force as Political Officer.

Eight hundred levies were also collected, at Brigadier Chamberlain's request, from the district, to be used as guides and to keep open communications with the plains, and as foraging parties to search for the grain and cattle which the enemy, it was reported, had hidden, or driven off to the higher hills.

Arrangements were made by the district officer for supplies for ten days for man and beast. Four days' supplies were to be

---

[1] See Map I in pocket.

carried regimentally, and six days' supplies for the whole force by the civil authorities. Sick and weakly men were to be left behind at Mangrotha as the troops advanced; three *doolies* with all the *dandies* and *kahars*[1] and also *kajawahs*[2] to accompany the force. All superfluous baggage, camp followers, and animals were to be left at Taunsa. Officers were to be restricted to one tent each, and one mess tent per regiment. The whole of the bullock ammunition boxes attached to regiments were to be carried on mules and pack ponies.

There were three main passes by which the Bozdar country might be entered from the plains, termed by the Baluchis, *nais*, channels cut through the hills, at right angles to the strata, by the mountain torrents. They are usually dry, except after rain.

These passes were:—

1st. The *Vihoa*, in front of the village and military post of that name.
2nd. The *Sangarh*, opposite Taunsa, and immediately in front of the fort of Mangrotha.
3rd. The *Mahoi*, twelve miles to the south of the Sangarh, and in front of the Mahoi outpost.

The first mentioned was not only circuitous, but was reported to be impracticable for guns; and, in addition to the disadvantage of its passing through the lands of other tribes, it entered the Bozdar country at one corner near the Drug Valley, from which access to other parts was very difficult.

The second was the principal entrance, and the only one in ordinary use. It was practicable for wheeled carriages, and it was stated that after the portion of the defile known as the Khan Band was passed, the more open and cultivated lands were at once entered upon, whence there was access to every part of the Bozdar country.

The third pass was difficult in the extreme, if not impracticable when defended; at one place the path skirted a precipice commanded from above, along which a single horse had to be led with care.

In these circumstances, the Sangarh Pass was in every way best suited for the troops to enter by. The strong places where the enemy were likely to make a stand were reported to be—first

---

[1] Ambulance bearers and hospital followers.
[2] Rough camel panniers.

at the mouth of the Drug Nai or *nala*, where it was said a strong breastwork of stones had been erected; and, secondly, at the Khan Band, about twelve miles from the mouth of the Sangarh Pass, which, it was anticipated, would be the enemy's main position. It was here that, in an attempt to force the passage in front, Sawan Mal, in the time of the Sikhs, had met with considerable loss.

As no real advantage was to be gained by making a false attack by the Mahoi Pass, the Brigadier thought it best to let it become generally known beforehand that he intended to enter by the Sangarh defile; for, whilst it could make no difference as to the result of our attack whether there were a few more or less of the enemy, there was no doubt that the value of success would be greatly enhanced by encountering the tribe on its own ground and thus not admitting of any excuse being afterwards made by the Bozdars to explain away defeat. The example upon all the neighbouring tribes would be also much more beneficial.

Having strengthened the frontier posts considerably, and provided for the safety of Dera Ghazi Khan, so as to give confidence to the people during the absence of the troops, Brigadier Chamberlain marched from Taunsa on the evening of the 6th March and after proceeding across the plain for seven miles, reached the mouth of the Sangarh Pass at daybreak. A few Bodzars were seen on the heights but no attempt at opposition was made, and the shots fired were evidently only intended as signals to announce the arrival of the force.

The march was continued up the stony bed of the Sangarh Nai (which was the only road) for about four miles, when a convenient place for encamping (Dedachi Kach) was reached, and the force halted for the day.

Towards noon a party of the enemy made some show of driving in one of the picquets, but on its being supported by Captain G. W. G. Green, commanding the 2nd Punjab Infantry,[1] they retired. One sepoy was severely wounded.

In the afternoon a reconnaissance of the Khan Band (*see* sketch) and the approaches to it was made by Brigadier Chamberlain, with a force consisting of 300 men of the 3rd Sikh Infantry[2] and 1st

---
[1] Now 56th Punjabi Rifles.
[2] Now 53rd Sikhs.

Punjab Infantry.[1] About eight miles from its mouth the Sangarh Nai was joined by the Drug Nai, which flowed from a small valley of that name some twenty miles to the north-west, in the Bozdar country. From this point of junction to its opening out at the Haranbore Kach, a distance of about three miles and a half, the Sangarh Pass presented a formidable defile. Thence to the point where the Sangarh Nai turned at right angles to the west, it was bounded on either side by scarped hills of considerable height, which completely commanded the road, a matchlock fired from one hill reaching to the foot of the other. Beyond this again the hills had to be passed at right angles to their strata, when, instead of having one range on either side to deal with, a series of precipitous spurs, rising one after another in close succession, had to be crossed, which completely commanded the road below.

It was to this particular portion of the defile that the term Khan Band was generally applied, though, strictly speaking, the name applied only to that one spot across which a mound of stones and earth had at some former period been raised to add to the natural defences, or hold water for agricultural purposes.

On arriving at the point where the defile turned to the west, a view of the Khan Band was obtained, and the enemy were seen clustered on every ridge and pinnacle commanding the defile. The position was so strong that to carry it in front would be a very doubtful operation, and one certainly not to be accomplished except at a large sacrifice of life; but it was possible to turn the position by its left, and Brigadier Chamberlain therefore determined upon attacking the Khan Band from that side, after assuring himself, both by conversation with the guides and by observation, of the practicability of the hills from the Drug Nala. During the reconnaissance a duffadar of the mounted police was killed, and one man of the 1st Punjab Infantry wounded. By sunset the Brigadier returned to camp, and the night passed undisturbed.

At daybreak on the 7th March, the force continued its advance up the Sangarh Nala, and by 7 A.M. halted in front of the enemy's position. Some delay occurred in making arrangements for the protection of the baggage and camp followers, and, this being accomplished, the troops moved to the attack.

---

[1] Now 55th Coke's Rifles.

The plan of attack was as follows:—The 4th Punjab Infantry,[1] under Captain A. T. Wilde, was to ascend (by its northern spur) the hill which commanded the Sangarh Nala from the west, covered by the fire of the four field guns of No. 1 Punjab Light Field Battery and the four mountain guns of No. 3 Punjab Light Field Battery. The 1st Punjab Infantry, under Major J. Coke, with the four mountain guns of No. 2 Battery, to advance up the Drug Nai, in the hope of finding a practicable spur by which to ascend the heights south of the *nala*, in support of the 4th Punjab Infantry, and to acquire possession of those heights, for this was indispensable to success.

The 3rd Sikh Infantry and the 2nd Punjab Infantry were placed in support at the junction of the two *nalas*, whilst a portion of the 1st Sikh Infantry,[2] under Major G. Gordon, was sent to crown the hill which closed in the Sangarh Nai to its east, with instructions to move along its summit so as to keep parallel with the 4th Punjab Infantry.

The enemy on the left of his position had failed to occupy the spurs to the north side of the Drug Nai, and this was turned to immediate account by parties of Major Coke's men, who occupied them as they advanced.

Becoming alive, however, to the object we had in view, the Bozdars lost no time in strengthening their left flank, and numbers at once crossed the Drug Nai and took up a strong position on its northern side. A hill on the southern side of the *nala* was also strongly held by the enemy, whilst the *nala* itself between these positions was closed by a breastwork. The fire the Bozdars were thus able to bring to bear from three sides was more than Major Coke could hope successfully to oppose, more especially as the hills were knife-edged, with the faces next the *nala* a steep wall, and the Brigadier therefore supported Major Coke with the 2nd Punjab Infantry, under Captain G. W. G. Green, and withdrew Lieutenant Mecham's four guns from Captain Wilde, sending them to Major Coke's assistance.

On the arrival of this support, the 1st and 2nd Punjab Infantry, well aided by the fire of the eight mountain guns (against which the enemy stood their ground most determinedly), at once attacked

---

[1] Now 57th Wilde's Rifles.
[2] Now 51st Sikhs.

the position on the left of the Drug Nala, Captain Green advancing against the right, and Major Coke against the left, of the position. The gallantry displayed by officers and men of both regiments was the admiration of all. In this attack almost the whole of our casualties took place, and the Bozdars suffered most. Major Coke received a severe wound in the shoulder, although he continued to exercise his command throughout the day. His native adjutant, Mir Jaffir, was wounded at his side, and received another bullet through his shield and clothes.

The Bozdars, on being driven from this position, crossed to the southern side of the Drug Nala, followed by the 2nd Punjab Infantry and a portion of the 1st Punjab Infantry. The remainder of the latter regiment, with the mountain guns, had to move up the bed of the stream, as the hills were too precipitous to admit of the guns being taken up.

Whilst these events were passing on our right, Captain Wilde's regiment had gradually ascended, and carried the enemy's position on the left bank of the Sangarh near its junction with the Drug. This had been done with little loss, under cover of the artillery, and Captain Wilde then pressed along the ridge of the hill overlooking the Sangarh Nai, his advance being greatly facilitated by Lieutenant J. R. Sladen's field guns.

Major G. Gordon, with the 1st Sikh Infantry, had been enabled in the meanwhile to crown the heights on the east of the Sangarh Nala without loss, as the few Bozdars who had at the outset occupied this range fell back without offering any opposition.

The heights on both banks of the Sangarh having thus been seized, the guns of No. 1 Punjab Light Field Battery, with the 3rd Sikh Infantry and the detachment of cavalry, were enabled to advance up the bed of the *nala* without opposition; and the artillery, taking up successive positions, covered Captain Wilde's advance along the left bank. As these troops reached the point where the defile turned to the west, it became evident from the movements of the enemy, who were holding the Khand Band, as well as from the sound of firing on their left rear, that the Bozdars were giving way, and that the time had come to threaten the Khan Band in front.

Whilst Lieutenant J. R. Sladen plied the enemy with shell, Captain R. Renny, with a company of the 3rd Sikh Infantry, carried the nearest ridge with a loss of only three men wounded, and Captain J. P. W. Campbell, with two companies, moved on their next breastwork. But by this time portions of the 1st and 2nd Punjab Infantry, which had ascended from the Drug Nala, were crossing the hills in pursuit of the Bozdars they had defeated; the Khan Band was thus threatened from the rear, and the flight became general. To add to the enemy's embarrassment, the detachment of cavalry under Captain S. J. Browne was ordered to dash through the defile, and after reaching the more open ground, to go on as far as the nature of the country permitted. Success was now complete, and arrangements were made for pitching the camp at Haranbore Kach, at the western entrance of the Khand Band defile.

Major J. Coke was the only British officer wounded in this affair; five men killed and three native officers and forty-five men wounded (*see* Appendix D). The Bozdars, whose numbers were estimated at 1,700 men, lost from twenty to thirty killed, and from fifty to seventy wounded. Their chiefs afterwards admitted that they had no doubt of their ability to hold the pass against us. As our troops were advancing they had called to Brigadier Chamberlain from the hills, asking, in a jeering manner, why we did not come on; and so far from expecting that their position would be turned from the Drug Nai, the Bozdars stated that it had been arranged that the body of men which had been in position on the right of that *nala* was to have attacked the rear of the column whilst the head of it was engaged at the Khan Band.

Nor was this self-reliance to be wondered at, for they had seen General Ventura and Jemadar Khusial Singh, with a large Sikh army, retire before this stronghold, and they claimed to have killed, on another occasion, 1,200 of Diwan Sawan Mal's soldiers, and plundered his baggage.

The conduct of the troops, Brigadier Chamberlain stated, had been excellent; they exhibited the highest spirit, and well maintained the reputation of our arms. The services of Major J. Coke, Lieutenant W. H. Lumsden, and Assistant Surgeon J. R. Jackson, of the 1st Punjab Infantry, and of Captain G. W. G. Green, Lieutenants T. Frankland, W. P. Fisher, and Assistant

Surgeon W. F. Clark, of the 2nd Punjab Infantry, together with the native officers of both these regiments, called, Brigadier Chamberlain said, for special mention, and he recommended them to the favourable notice of Government.

The Brigadier added that the artillery which supported Major Coke's attack had earned distinction; and he brought to notice the services of Lieutenants G. Maister and R. Mecham, commanding Nos. 2 and 3 Punjab Light Field Batteries, and the officers and men employed with the mountain guns.

On the march of the force from Taunsa, the levies had been left at Mangrotha in charge of the reserve supplies, for it was an object not to employ them in concert with the troops before our ability to chastise the Bozdars without any other assistance had been shown to all, and they were now ordered forward; and to Mita Khan and his Kasranis was assigned the task of occupying the Khan Band, and keeping open the communications with the plains.

After the troops had emerged from the Khan Band, it became evident, from the ruggedness of the country, that there was little chance of hemming in the tribe, or capturing their cattle, without greater numbers; and, in communication with the Deputy Commissioner, arrangements were made by Brigadier Chamberlain, during the evening of the 7th, to invite the Ustarana tribe to come down and plunder their enemies on the north, whilst the force closed in upon them from the south.

The invitation was accepted with alacrity, and a portion of the tribe, entering by the Drug Valley, had commenced to plunder and lay waste, when they were stopped and ordered to return home, in consequence of the submission of the Bozdars.

During the 8th the troops halted, to admit of the wounded being sent to Mangrotha.

A detachment, consisting of the 2nd Punjab Cavalry and the 3rd Sikh Infantry, was employed during the day in reconnoitring the Sangarh Nai as far as Bharti, and its course was marked by the smoke of the huts and stacks of forage. The country was found abandoned, and only a few Bozdars were seen on the summit of the hills, apparently occupied with watching the movements of the troops.

During the 9th the force halted, awaiting the return of the ambulance party from Mangrotha, which arrived in the evening. On this day a reconnoitring party was employed in penetrating the country, and doing as much injury as possible.

On the 10th the force marched to Bharti, distant about six miles. It was one of the principal places of the Bozdars, and presented luxuriant vegetation, and with its clumps of date trees resembled the scenery in the neighbourhood of Dera Ghazi Khan. The road, as heretofore, was up the stony bed of the Sangarh Nai, but during the march five or six cultivated spots were passed. The house of Naorang Khan, the chief of one section of the tribe, on the summit of a hill near Bharti, was destroyed.

Reconnoitring and other parties were always accompanied by some of the levies, who exhibited great skill in discovering concealed property. When our sepoys failed to find anything a Baluch ally would follow up the track of a man's or woman's feet, and speedily return with plunder which had been hidden in the hurry of flight.

During the 11th and 12th the force had to halt to enable supplies to be brought up, for it was not considered prudent to enter further into the hills without having ten days' supplies in camp. On both days the country in advance, both to the right and left, was patrolled by reconnoitring parties, and everything was destroyed. The column of smoke which rose over a circumference of some miles must have been a distressing spectacle to the Bozdars; but to have spared their crops and property would have been to neutralize the object of the expedition, and to withold the punishment most likely to have a lasting impression.

Of all the frontier tribes none were less deserving of consideration, for plunder and murder had been their avocation for years past, and, but for our military posts, the country in their front must have been abandoned. Nor did they confine their raids to the plains, for they plundered all their neighbours, and it may truly be said that their hand was against every man, and every man's hand against them.

The secret of their success in plundering was attributable to the inaccessibility of their country, for nature had made it equally unapproachable on all four sides. Within, it was found

to be a network of hills and ravines, unassailable except by disciplined bodies. The Bozdars had ample cultivation, were rich in flocks, and well-to-do, and had, therefore, the less excuse for living on their neighbours.

On the 13th the force continued its march up the Sangarh Nai for about ten miles, and encamped in a well-cultivated hollow at the entrance of the Saunra Pass. Just before descending into the cultivation, a few horsemen and footmen were seen, but they disappeared in the defile as the force approached. On this day's march the enemy sustained much loss in the destruction of numbers of their hamlets and stock, and as they belonged to the section of the tribe most given to plundering on our border, there was the greater reason for not sparing anything.

The Saunra Pass, or, more properly speaking, defile, is to the Bozdars on the west what the Khan Band is on the east. One section—the Ghulamani—possesses lands to the west of the defile; and the tribe claim the country up to the hills which separate them from the Luni Pathans on the west, and the Khetrans on the south-west; but when at feud with these tribes, and obliged to act on the defensive, they retire, and hold the Saunra Pass, thereby closing the only entrance from the west.

Brigadier Chamberlain had expected, from all that the guides had stated, to find this defile difficult, for the natives had always pronounced it impracticable for artillery, and had adverted to its strength and the necessity for holding it if the force went beyond it into the Ghulamani lands. But, although he had looked for a strong position, it far exceeded his anticipations; indeed, he said that he had never yet seen in Afghanistan anything to be compared with it, for it might be pronounced impregnable from the west, and, according to the reports of trustworthy persons, was not to be turned on the north nearer than by the Vihoa Pass, thirty miles off, or on the south nearer than by the Vidor Pass, distant forty-five miles. From the east side it was difficult but practicable, and the Bozdars, having failed at the Khan Band, appeared to have thought it was useless to defend it. Its inaccessibility from the west arose from the mountain being scarped on that side, presenting at its summit a precipice several hundred feet in height, which scarp was said to run north and south as far as the Vihoa and Vidor Passes.

In the days of the Mughals, this road was used for keeping open the communications between the Southern Punjab and Kandahar; and when Shah Shuja was defeated by Dost Muhammad Khan at the latter place, a remnant of his followers returned by this route.

Late on the evening of the 13th two Bozdars came into camp, stating that they had been sent by the chiefs, who wished to come in and sue for terms, and begging that the work of destruction might be stayed. The chiefs were ordered, in reply, to present themselves in camp the next day, when our demands upon the tribe would be made known; but if they failed to attend within the prescribed time, hostilities and the work of destruction would recommence; in the meantime the force would halt, and cease to cut their crops and burn their property. On the following evening, Naorang Khan and Ashak Muhammad Khan, the two chiefs of the tribe, made their appearance; but it was too late to transact business, and the meeting was deferred until the next morning.

At a *darbar* held on the following day, the reasons for our invasion, and the terms demanded were publicly made known. These terms were—

Terms of submission.

1st. Compensation at the rate of Rs. 125 for the life of every ma killed or wounded in British territory during the previous year.

2nd. Restitution of, or compensation for, all cattle killed, or stolen, or injured, or property carried off or destroyed during the previous year, the restitution or compensation to be completed within two months.

3rd. The immediate expulsion of all refugee criminals. Not to afford an asylum to refugees from British territory, or to harbour thieves or bad characters of any tribe; nor to allow anyone to pass through their country, to plunder or commit acts of violence; nor to permit stolen cattle or property of any kind to be taken through their passes.

4th. To pay a fine of 200 sheep in consideration of the remainder of the crops being spared, with 100 additional sheep from the Ghulamani Bozdars, whose country beyond the Saunra Pass had escaped injury. The sheep were to be given to the troops.

5th. To give approved hostages, for twelve months, as security for good conduct, and to have a *vakil* always at the Mangrotha *tehsil*.

A ready assent was given to every demand, and the demeanour of the Bozdars was thoroughly subdued. Doubtless more might have been demanded, and would have been acceded to, but it seemed to the Brigadier and Deputy Commissioner that the future peace of the frontier was more likely to be secured by dealing leniently with them, and it was hoped that, having now felt our ability to punish, the Bozdars, like the Shiranis and Kasranis, would become peaceable neighbours. Had they not given in, they would in all probability have suffered considerable loss in cattle, for the Ustaranas had closed in upon them, and they could only have escaped by finding refuge among the Pathan tribes further west.

After the affair at the Khan Band, a detachment, detailed in the margin, under Lieutenant G. A. P. Younghusband, 5th Punjab Cavalry,[1] had proceeded from Mangrotha up the Mahoi Pass, destroying the cultivation there without opposition, and orders were now sent to the officer commanding at Mangrotha to stop all further punitive operations.

2nd Punjab Cavalry, 17 sabres.
3rd Punjab Cavalry, 28 ,,
5th Punjab Cavalry, 29 ,,
4th Punjab Infantry, 66 baoynets.

On the 16th the force commenced to retrace its steps, a portion returning by the road by which it had advanced, the remainder by the Lundi Nai. Both columns united on the 17th at Haranbore Kach.

From the 18th to the 21st the troops halted, the sheep not having been brought in, for the Brigadier felt that it was both just and necessary to exact the fulfilment of this stipulation before relieving the tribe of our presence. The reason assigned by the chiefs for the delay was the distance the flocks had been driven to avoid capture—an excuse Brigadier Chamberlain did not think reasonable, and which was overcome as soon as the Bozdars understood the alternative, and saw their crops decreasing; for though they were not wantonly destroyed, it was necessary to feed the cattle.

The required number of sheep having been completed on the afternoon of the 21st, the force returned through the Khan Band on the 22nd, and having encamped at Dedachi Kach, re-entered the plains the following morning, after an absence of seventeen days.

The Indian medal, with a clasp for the "North-West Frontier," was granted in 1869 to all survivors of the troops engaged in these operations.

---
[1] Now 25th Cavalry.

The Bozdars evidently profited by the lesson they had received in 1857, and their conduct subsequent to the expedition showed a marked improvement.

Conduct of the tribes from 1861 to 1863.

In January 1861, the Khetrans, Isots, Ustaranas, and Jafars,[1] attacked their stronghold, the Khan Band, on the western side, and drove them from their fastness. Their women and children took refuge in the plains, bringing their cattle with them. Captain C. J. Godby, commanding the 4th Punjab Cavalry, was at Mangrotha at the time. Taking the detachment from the post with him, he at once rode to the mouth of the pass, and met messengers from the Khetrans, who professed that they had no intention of following the Bozdars into British territory, but that, having sufficiently punished the tribe, their camp would break up. The Isots, Ustaranas, and Jafars accordingly returned home at once. The Khetrans imprudently determined to return by the shortest route past the Mahoi Pass, and encamped for the night. An old Bozdar woman watched them, and gave information to the Chief, Ashak Muhammad Khan, pointing out that the Bozdars might easily invest a pass beyond Mahoi through which the Khetrans would have to pass, and so obtain their revenge. The advice was taken. Early next morning, when the Khetrans, quite unsuspicious of the trap laid for them, pursued their journey, they fell into the ambuscade, and were routed with great loss, only effecting their escape by rushing into the plains and making the best of their way to the Sakhi Sarwar, and returning home through the Siri Pass.

On the 15th March 1861, the Bozdars, with some Hadianis, etc., raided some flocks belonging to the Nasir *Powindahs* in British territory, and carried off some 12,000 sheep and goats. The Nasirs afterwards retaliated, and a fight took place, in which twenty-four Bozdars and Legharis and twenty-two Nasirs were killed.

In 1862 a party of Bozdars, Legharis, Khosas, etc., carried off a large herd of cattle belonging to the *Powindahs*, which were grazing inside the passes opposite Chaudwan in the Dera Ismail Khan district. The *Powindahs*, before returning, made arrangements with the Ustaranas to attack the Bozdars. The latter retired until a favourable opportunity occurred to make a night attack, in which both the Bozdars and Ustaranas suffered slight loss, but the

---

[1] A small and insignificant tribe living on the north-west of the Bozdar Hills.

Powindahs escaped. The following season the *Powindahs* were informed that they would not be allowed to enter British territory except on condition that they would abstain from all hostilities while within our border. This at once put a stop to the feud.

On the 1st of June 1863, a small party of Bozdars lifted some camels from British territory, but were pursued up the Mahoi Pass by a detachment of cavalry. The detachment, 17 sabres, was attacked on returning by 100 Bozdars; but they charged, and got out in safety.

In 1864 the Government sanctioned the restoration to the Bozdar Chief of the rent-free wells which had been confiscated in 1857; he also received a certain number of *balgirs* in the frontier militia.

In the autumn of 1868 Lieutenant L. J. H. Grey, Deputy Commissioner of Dera Ismail Khan, was carried off into the hills by Kaora Khan, a headman of the Kasranis. Lieutenant Grey had gone down to Tibi by boat to enquire into a criminal case. His escort having been detained by missing the proper channel, Lieutenant Grey found himself practically alone. However, he proceeded to arrest Kaora Khan and made him over to his orderlies. Kaora Khan's followers at once flocked to his rescue, and Lieutenant Grey, in turn, became a prisoner. Kaora Khan then fled to the hills, taking his prisoner with him. He was pursued, but kept Lieutenant Grey in advance, and himself covered the retreat, threatening, if brought to bay, to kill Lieutenant Grey first, and then sell his own life dearly. This threat kept the pursuers at a distance. Meanwhile Mehr Shah, a priest of the Baluchis, had sent to the Bozdars to close the exit from the Kasrani country.

Lieutenant Grey kidnapped by Kasranis.

Fazl Ali Khan, the Chief of the Kasranis (who had succeeded his father, Mita Khan, in 1861), with the principal Kasranis of Mangrotha and that neighbourhood, joined actively in the pursuit. Kaora Khan with his party was at length brought to bay some thirteen miles beyond Bati, where, after prolonged negotiations, he released Lieutenant Grey. During the day that he was in restraint, Lieutenant Grey was hard pressed for terms, but he succeeded in turning the matter off by expressing his conviction

that the Commissioner would ratify no conditions that he made, and Kaora Khan had to content himself with a promise that all the grain then in his house should be sent to him, and as he pressed it, that Government should be informed of his contrition; and, lastly, that if summoned, he should have a safe conduct, or if Government refused, he should be informed.

Meanwhile, on the news of this outrage reaching Dera Ismail Khan, the 1st Punjab Cavalry, under Captain A. Vivian, accompanied by Mr. Beckett, Assistant Commissioner, at once marched towards Vihoa, arriving at Miran, thirty-three miles, by the morning; but before they could get further intelligence was received that Lieutenant Grey had been given up, and except one troop, which was ordered into Tibi, the regiment returned. The 1st Punjab Infantry under Captain F. J. Keen, and the 4th, under Lieutenant-Colonel J. Cockburn-Hood, embarked in boats, and the latter had started before the news of Lieutenant Grey's release arrived.

Lieutenant Grey returned to Dera on the evening of the 13th, and on the 14th he, in company with the Commissioner, Lieutenant-Colonel S. F. Graham, and escorted by a company of infantry, went down in boats to Tibi to take steps for the capture of Kaora Khan. Sultan Muhammad of Vihoa was deputed to induce the chiefs of the neighbouring tribes to refuse him an asylum; and an attempt was made through the Ustaranas to cut off his retreat, but without success. The Commissioner then sent a deputation to induce him to come in. Kaora Khan received the deputation at the head of 100 men. After a long conference, the deputies failed in their object. The Commissioner then summoned the tribes to his assistance. His call was readily responded to. From the north the Ustaranas brought 500 men, and were placed under the Gandapur Chief, Kalu Khan; and there came also 120 Babar horse and foot and 120 Mian Khel;[1] and from the south the Bozdars came 1,000 strong

---

[1] The Mian Khel are a Pathan tribe of the Dera Ismail Khan district. They hold some 260 square miles of plain country between the Gundapur and Babar tribes. The greater number still engage in the trans-Indus trade, and they are said to be the richest of all the *Powindahs*, dealing in the more costly descriptions of merchandise. They are a peaceable people, more civilised than most of the *Powindah* tribes. They seldom take military service, and cultivate but little, leaving the business of agriculture to their Jat tenants.

followed by the Hadianis 700, and Lunds[1] 400. To these forces was entrusted the duty of blockading the hill Kasranis on the north, south, and west. The principal plain Kasranis were also summoned, and ordered to bring in the criminal under the following penalties :—*1st*, forfeiture of allowances for guarding the hill passes ; *2nd*, confiscation of standing crops as a fine ; *3rd*, deportation of the plain chiefs to Dera Ghazi Khan ; *4th*, blockade of the hill portion of the tribe.

Kasranis blockaded, 1863.

The chiefs at once took up their responsibilities, and collecting their clansmen in the plains, entered the hills, and returned in a few days with twenty-two families, including about forty women and children belonging to the rebels.

The Kasranis were again despatched to the hills to bring in Kaora Khan, and with them were associated, as advisers and supporters on the part of Government, a chief of the Khosas with fifty men, and one of the Gurchanis with the same number. They returned after some days, with five of the principal rebels, but with the intelligence that Kaora Khan, his son, and others, escorted by about eighty of the hill Kasranis, had escaped, and sought shelter with the Musa Khel.

To guard against such escape, or to make such shelter more difficult the Commissioner had proclaimed a reward of Rs. 10,000 on the heads of the four principal offenders ; and to provide the means of payment of the reward, of feeding the tribes who had assembled, and of meeting the fines which would be inflicted on the criminals, the moveable property of Kaora Khan, and a few of his chief abettors, had been seized and sold, producing upwards of Rs. 20,000.

Pressure being continued, Painda Khan, the Chief of the Musa Khels, at last brought Kaora Khan into Mangrotha, and delivered him up to Captain R. G. Sandeman on the 27th of October. A *durbar* was then held by the Commissioner, at which

---

[1] The *Lunds* are a Baluch tribe (or rather two tribes) of the Dera Ghazi Khan district. The *Tibi Lunds* occupy a small area in the midst of the Gurchani country. They are a compact, well-organised little tribe. They have always taken an active and loyal part on the side of the British Government, and have never given trouble to the local authorities. The *Sori Lunds* are a small tribe, only lately risen to importance. Their territory divides that of the Khosas into two parts and extends to the bank of the Indus. They are not pure Baluchis.

he thanked the assembled chiefs, and distributed the following rewards :—

			Rs.
To the Bozdars, who brought 1,000 fighting men,			2,500
„ Hadianis, „	700	„	2,000
„ Lunds, „	400	„	1,000
„ Ustaranas, „	500	„	1,000
„ Khosas, „	50	„	700
„ Babars, „	120	„	750
„ Mian Khels, „	120	„	750
„ Isatos „	100	„	300
„ Gurchanis, „	50	„	300
„ Nutakanis,[1] „	50	„	500
„ Gandapurs, „	40	„	200
	3,130		10,000

Subsequent conduct of the tribes.

At the same time *khilats* were bestowed on the chiefs and others who had given assistance. The political expenses of these measures amounted, in round numbers, to Rs. 15,000 ; and this sum, as well as the Rs. 10,000 reward, was charged to the criminals and to the Kasrani tribe generally, the cost of the *khilats* to the Government.

The Bozdars have always been at feud with the Ustaranas, and in 1869 the latter formed an alliance with the Kasranis, and attacked the Bozdars beyond the border. The Chiefs of the Kasranis and Ustaranas were fined, and required to pay the Bozdars compensation, while the Bozdars made amends for the injuries which the Kasranis complained of, and the dispute was thus satisfactorily adjusted.

In October 1871, a party of 100 Baluch marauders, said to be Hadianis, committed a raid on twenty flocks of sheep and herds of cattle grazing within the limits of the Shirani village of Drazand, in independent territory, but belonging to Nasir *Powindahs* encamped

---

[1] The *Nutakanis* are a Baluch tribe of the Dera Ghazi Khan district, holding a compact territory stretching eastward to the Indus and between the Khosas and the Kasranis. The tribe once enjoyed considerable influence and importance, but no longer possesses a political organisation, having been crushed out of tribal existence in the early days of Ranjit Singh's rule. But the event is so recent that tribal coherence and race characteristics are still retained.

within and on the confines of British territory, in the direction of the Gandapur and Babar villages of Zarakni and Chaudwan. Upwards of ten herdsmen were killed by the plunderers before they secured their spoil. On news reaching the Nasirs in their camps, they immediately started in pursuit, and overtaking the raiders forced them to abandon possession of the plundered cattle and sheep.

In 1874 the Bozdars were attacked by their northern neighbours, the Ustaranas, but both parties abstained from molesting British territory.

In December 1875, the Khetrans violated British territory, in a quarrel with the Bozdars. On the evening of the 12th of that month a large detachment of Khetran horsemen emerged by the Sakhi Sarwar Pass and proceeded from Sakhi Sarwar, taking the road along the foot of the nearest range of low hills by Vidor and Matti (Khosa), to the mouth of the Mahoi Pass, which they appear to have reached, by the light of the full moon, about dawn on the 13th. Their object was to take the Bozdars by surprise, and secure as much spoil as possible. In the pass, just beyond the British border, five Ghulamani Bozdars—returning to their hills from Dera Ghazi Khan with ten camels laden with grain—had passed the night; and some Jats from the village of Mahoi, near the outpost of that name, were engaged filling their donkey *massaks*[1] at a well close by. The Ghulamanis, at once perceiving their tribal enemies, managed to slip away into the hills, leaving their laden animals a prey to the Khetrans, who at first stripped the Jats, and were appropriating their animals, when being assured that these Jats were Government subjects, they restored their property, and set them all at liberty, with the remark that the Khetrans were not at enmity with the Government, but with the Bozdars.

Proceeding further into the pass, the Khetran horsemen were seen by some Bozdar cultivators, who retired to their village to give the alarm. Massu Khan, the Bozdar *mukadam*, probably unaware of the strength of the invading force, hastily got together eventeen armed villagers on foot, whom he headed to meet the Khetrans. The small body of Bozdars, finding the Khetran

---

[1] Water-skins.

scattered in various directions, scouring the ravines and side valleys for spoil, made some resistance, at a spot within the Mahoi Pass, about three miles beyond the British boundary. The firing attracted the main body of the Khetrans, who pursued the Bozdars up the slope of a spur protruding into the pass, and cut them down, one by one, without mercy, as they retreated, still fighting, to the crest. Sixteen Bozdars, including their brave leader, Massu Khan, were killed; two only, one of whom was dangerously wounded, escaping to the hamlet.

The Khetrans, having met with so bold a resistance, immediately after their entrance into the pass, resolved to return with their plunder by the same route carrying two dead and three or four wounded men of their tribe with them. They were, however, intercepted on their return by our troops and militia, and compelled to disgorge their spoil, which was restored to the Bozdars, and a fine was realized from them for their violation of British territory.

Shortly after this, during the same month, the Bozdars similarly misbehaved, on a smaller scale, in proceeding surreptitiously, to the number of thirty-five or forty, *viâ* Hajipur, a British village, to surprise a small party of Shambani Bugtis. The latter were grazing their flocks, unauthorizedly, just within the British border on the Rajanpur frontier. Two Bugtis were killed, the Bozdar party returning without casualty to their hills. In consequence of this outrage, the offending section of the Bozdars, the Chakranis, were debarred from entering British territory, and the allowances of the tribe were stopped. On the 30th August 1876, the tribe came in to the district officer, and agreed to the Government demands. They undertook to pay blood-money on the regulated scale for the two Bugtis killed, to surrender unconditionally, within six weeks, a notorious offender named Tangi of the Lashari (Gurchani) tribe, who had for some time obtained shelter in the Bozdar hills, and who had been the guide in the raid against the Bugtis; and finally to make restitution in all cases of theft from British limits then outstanding against them. The blockade against the Chakrani section was then removed. Tangi, the man whose surrender had been promised, was, however, murdered by a Bozdar in the hills, in pursuance of a private quarrel before the promise could be fulfilled.

In 1876 a raid was made by Hadianis on a Khosa village, but the raiders were followed up and full reparation obtained; and in August of that year a settlement of the disputes between the Khosas and Hadianis on the one hand, and the Khetrans and the Hadianis on the other, was effected.

The Bozdars continued to give trouble by carrying off cattle and other property from our border, and the Jalalani and Ladwani sections of the tribe were especially guilty of acts of misconduct and theft. Accordingly, at the end of January 1878, Mr. F. W. R. Fryer, the Deputy Commissioner of Dera Ghazi Khan, accompanied by Mr. C. E. Gladstone, Assistant Commissioner of Rajanpur, visited the Bozdar hills. He was not very successful in obtaining redress for past grievances of British subjects, until he declared a temporary blockade of the tribe during a time of comparative scarcity, which obliged the Bozdars to submit to the terms in addition to restitution of all property stolen, or its value.

In March 1879, the Musa Khel Pathans, who live beyond the Bozdars, made a threatened demonstration against Vihoa at the instigation, it is believed, of the Kasranis. Timely precautions were taken, and the excitement did not lead to any overt act of hostility. On their return, however, the Musa Khel plundered their old enemies the Bozdars, with whom they were angry for having given information of the intended raid.

In December 1880, the Bozdars plundered two large trading caravans beyond the border, in one of which twenty-seven Kakars were killed; in the other, Kakars and Khetrans were the sufferers. In the latter case it was decided that the Khetrans should be compensated for their losses. To enforce this a blockade was imposed on the Bozdars, and in ten days the tribal representatives paid Rs. 2,680, the compensation demanded. The Bozdars gave every assistance, when, on the retirement of the British forces from Kandahar, a column under Brigadier-General Wilkinson marched through their hills, in December 1882, on its way to Dera Ghazi Khan.

During that year also a satisfactory settlement was arrived at with the Bugti tribe, with whom the Bozdars were at feud, on the basis of a mutual renunciation of claims, at a meeting

of the tribal leaders, in conjunction with the Deputy Commissioner of Dera Ghazi Khan and the Assistant Agent of the Governor-General, Baluchistan, under whose management the Bugtis were.

APPENDIX A.

Composition of the force employed against the Kasranis in April 1853.

Brigadier J. S. Hodgson, Commanding.

Staff.

Captain W. R. Prout, Staff Officer.

Infantry.

1st Punjab Infantry, Lieutenant C. P. Keyes, Commanding.
6th Police Battalion, Lieutenant J. W. Younghusband, Commanding.

Political Officer.

Major J. Nicholson, Deputy Commissioner, Dera Ismail Khan.

Detail of Troops.

Corps.	British Officers.	Native Officers.	Non-Commissioned Officers.	Rank and file.	Total.	REMARKS.
Staff	2	..	..	..	2	
Detachment, 4th Punjab Cavalry	..	2	2	30	34	
1st Punjab Infantry	3	7	46	400	456	
6th Police Battalion	1	13	48	400	462	
Total	6	22	96	830	954	

APPENDIX B.

Composition of the force employed against the Bozdars in March 1857.

Brigadier N. B. Chamberlain, Commanding.

Staff.
Captain J. P. W. Campbell, Staff Officer.
Lieutenant J. G. Medley, Bengal Engineers, Field Engineer.

Artillery.
No. 1 Punjab Light Field Battery, Lieutenant J. R. Sladen, Commanding.
No. 2 Punjab Light Field Battery, Lieutenant G. Maister, Commanding.
No. 3 Punjab Light Field Battery, Lieutenant R. Mecham, Commanding.

Cavalry.
Detachment, 2nd Punjab Cavalry, Captain S. J. Browne, Commanding.
Detachment, 3rd Punjab Cavalry, Lieutenant J. Watson, Commanding.

Infantry.
1st Sikh Infantry, Major G. Gordon, Commanding.
3rd Sikh Infantry, Captain R. Renny, Commanding.
1st Punjab Infantry, Major J. Coke, Commanding.
2nd Punjab Infantry, Captain G. W. G. Green, Commanding.
4th Punjab Infantry, Captain A. T. Wilde, Commanding.

Political Officer.
Captain F. R. Pollock, Deputy Commissioner, Dera Ghazi Khan.

Details of Troops.

Corps.	British Officers.	Native Officers.	Non-Commissioned Officers.	Rank and file.	Field Howitzers.	Field Guns.	Mountain Howitzers.	Mountain Guns.	REMARKS.
Staff	3	..	..	..	..	..	..	..	This does not include the detail, 5th Punjab Cavalry, or troops, left at Mangrotha or in the outposts.
No. 1 Punjab Light Field Battery	3	2	12	69	2	2	..	..	
No. 2 ,, ,, ,,	2	1	6	41	..	..	2	2	
No. 3 ,, ,, ,,	2	1	7	40	..	..	2	2	
2nd and 3rd Punjab Cavalry	7	7	12	94	..	..	..	..	
Sappers and Miners	..	2	8	50	..	..	..	..	
1st Sikh Infantry	3	12	65	378	..	..	..	..	
3rd ,, ,,	2	10	60	385	..	..	..	..	
1st Punjab ,,	3	8	50	421	..	..	..	..	
2nd ,, ,,	4	11	48	428	..	..	..	..	
4th ,, ,,	4	10	52	432	..	..	..	..	
Total	33	64	320	2,338	2	2	4	4	

CHAPTER VI.

The Baluchistan Agency.

ON the 21st November, war with Afghanistan was declared. On the 23rd the district of Sibi was occupied by a British detachment. "Much political inconvenience," Lord Lytton observed, "had been caused by the interposition of this small Afghan district in the midst of Baluch territory; and we had, therefore, determined upon its permanent withdrawal from the jurisdiction of Kabul authority."

Sibi and Pishin occupied.

On the 1st December Sir Robert Sandeman accompanied General Biddulph into Pishin and established friendly relations with the inhabitants. The Bombay Column had passed up the Bolan to Quetta unmolested. The people of Pishin welcomed the advent of the British, and the Achakzai tribe—who inhabit the Khwaja Amran Range—offered their services to Sir Robert Sandeman as guardians of the Khojak Pass, making allusion to the posts they had occupied in that pass in 1839-42. This offer was accepted by the Agent to the Governor-General.

During General Stewart's advance to, and occupation of, Kandahar, the Baluch, Brahui, and Kahar tribes on the lines of communication gave no trouble. They were kept well in hand by Sir Robert Sandeman, who had also made suitable arrangements for the civil administration of Sibi and Pishin. These districts were ceded to Britain as "Assigned Districts" by the treaty of Gandamak in May 1879. The meaning of the word "assigned" was that—while being administered by British officers—any excess of revenue over expenditure was to be paid to the ruler of Kabul. After the treaty had been signed, Sir Robert Sandeman announced to the people that they had become British subjects.

Treaty of Gandamak, 1879.

Thus the conclusion of the first period of the Second Afghan War left Great Britain in possession of the districts of Thal Chotiali, Sibi, and Pishin. This, in addition to our occupation of

Quetta, placed us in a strong position covering the flank of the line of communication with the Punjab and Sind, and enabled us to obtain a hold over the Marri and Pathan tribes.

After the treaty of Gandamak the Baluchistan Agency assumed jurisdiction over a large territory. The duties assigned to the Agency were:—

The Baluchistan Agency.

1. Those duties connected with the treaty of 1876.
2. The Administration of the "Assigned Districts."
3. The duties at the court of the Khan of Kalat, including the affairs of South-Western Baluchistan.
4. The administration of the treasury at Quetta.
5. The affairs of the Marri and Bugti tribes.
6. The affairs of Las Bela and the Makran Coast.
7. The control of Baluch Guides, Tribal Levies, and Postal and Telegraph Sowars.

Political Officers were placed in charge of Kachi, Pishin, and Quetta and Sibi. Dr. Duke was deputed to the Khan's court, Mr. Dames in charge of Vitakri and Barkhan, and to Captain Showers was entrusted the line of communications between Jacobabad and Chaman. The last named officer had complete charge of the Baluch Guides.

On the 3rd September 1879 the British envoy, Sir Louis Cavagnari, and his escort were attacked and killed by the mutinous troops of the Amir at Kabul. At first the ill-effects of this affair were not noticeable in Baluchistan, but subsequently a general unrest appeared, intensified when the following winter found Lord Roberts' force shut up in Kabul.

Events after the Treaty of Gandamak.

At this time the Indian Government determined to build a railway line from Sibi to Pishin and Quetta by the Harnai route. Arrangements were made with the tribes along the route to establish posts for the protection of the working parties and carriage of mails, and were completed early in March 1880, at which time work was proceeding in the Nari Gorge.

On the 24th March Captain Showers, escorted by a few Baluh Guides, determined to explore a new road through the Dumar country from Harnai to Quetta. On the way he was ambushed by some Panizai

Murder of Captain Showers.

Kakars and killed. The same tribe then proceeded to attack the camp of a railway survey party under Lieutenant Fuller, R.E., killing several followers and wounding a European Sergeant and three sepoys.

Attack on Lieutenant Fuller's Camp.

The immediate sequel to this attack was rather unfortunate. A *malik* (headman) in British employ proceeded to the spot and placed a few of his men under a jemadar as a guard over what was left of the camp. Captain Humfrey with some men of the 10th Bombay Infantry, who was in the neighbourhood, marched at once to the scene. Seeing some Pathans in charge, he opened fire on them, only discovering they were "friendlies" when two men had been killed and one wounded.

The Panizais, however, were soon "brought to book" by Colonel Durand who, with a force of 80 cavalry and 300 infantry, advanced from Shahrig to the Chapar Mountain. In an engagement on that mountain the Panizais lost a few men and then dispersed. Their head-quarters, the village of Dirgai, was destroyed and their crops were used as fodder.

Panizai affairs.

The Maiwand disaster occurred on the 27th July 1880, and its effect on the tribes was immediate. It was found necessary to stop work on the Harnai Railway, and to withdraw the troops on duty there for service elsewhere. An account of this will be given later, as also of the unrest among the Achakzai tribes round about Toba and the Khojak Pass. Throughout this time the Khan of Kalat remained staunch. Some of his Pathan troops mutinied, and marched off *viâ* Shorawak to join Ayub Khan, besieging Kandahar. He gave active assistance in the provision of camel transport, and offered men and money.

The Achakzai tribe gave some trouble in 1879 and again in 1880. Prior to the occupation of Pishin in 1878, the Achakzai were entirely Afghan subjects, and their affairs before that date are outside the scope of this work. They are a large clan of Duranis inhabiting the western portion of Pishin and the eastern portion of Kandahar. The larger half of the tribe are now British subjects inhabiting principally the Chaman sub-district and Toba. The last census showed 19,000 persons of this tribe in British territory. Their language is Pushtu; their habits are nomadic. Cultivation is on the

Achakzai affairs.

increase amongst the Achakzai. They are a remarkably fine race physically, but are not enlisted in the regular army on account of their reputation as professional thieves. Many of them used to serve in the Baluch regiments before the introduction of "class companies." The present head of the tribe in British territory is Khan Bahadur Haji Ghulam Haidar Khan, who lives in Chaman.

They first came in touch with the British Government during the First Afghan War, when they formed a body of horse for Shah Shuja-ul-Mulk. Though nominally our allies, they were however, entirely hostile to us when opportunity offered.

Early history.

The Achakzai, undoubtedly, formed part of the forces opposed to General England in the two battles of Haikalzai in 1842. Their temporary success in the first, and complete defeat in the second battle form episodes in the history of the First Afghan War.

No further contact with the Achakzai occurred until the Second Afghan War. They early offered their services to keep the Khojak Pass open, their offer being accepted by Sandeman.

When General Stewart advanced to Kandahar, he left in Pishin, to aid Sandeman in preserving order, a moveable column, strength as detailed in the margin. This force furnished several detachments in the district.

Commanding, Major Keene.
2 Mountain Guns.
1st Squadron, 8th Bengal Cavalry.
300 Rifles, 1st Punjab Infantry.

In January 1879, the Achakzais made a successful raid on a commissariat guard in the Arambi Glen near Kala Abdulla. They then attacked Kala Abdulla itself, but were driven off by the garrison of the 1st Punjab Infantry.[1]

Arambi Glen.

News then reached Sir Robert Sandeman that some 2,000 men, mostly Achakzai, with a few discharged Afghan sepoys, had collected in the Gwazha Pass near Gulistan. As this body threatened our line of communications, Major Keene was ordered to use his moveable column to disperse them. Reinforced by Major Crookshank with 100 Gurkhas, he commenced operations by a surprise visit to the Arambi Glen, where he successfully recovered all the stolen Government property and received the submission of several influential

Major Keene's moveable column.

---

[1] Now 55th Coke's Rifles.

Achakzai *maliks* (headmen). These prompt measures ca used the immediate cessation of all hostilities for the time being.

In May 1879, Captain Wylie, Assistant Political Agent, accompanied by the principal Achakzai headmen of the district, made a tour through the Toba Plateau. With him went seven British Officers and a personal escort of 230 rifles, 2nd Sikhs (now 52nd Sikhs), and 30 sabres, Baluch Horse (now 37th Lancers). The troops were well received by all the chiefs, Achakzai and Kakar of Toba, and much good survey work was accomplished by the officers of the escort.

Toba, 1879.

During the expedition a fanatical Kakar suddenly attacked the advanced party of the escort, and wounded two sepoys with his sword before he was shot. The Kakar Chiefs with Captain Wylie were very indignant at this outrage, and were with difficulty dissuaded from attacking the section to which the fanatic belonged. This incident is interesting, as proving that the Muhammadans themselves recognise tribal responsibility for religious maniacs erroneously dignified with the name of *ghazi*.

In 1880, when the British force was besieged in Kandahar by Ayub Khan, the Achakzais again became hostile. They seized the Khojak Pass, and Old Chaman was for several days completely isolated. A British force, however, drove them off the pass and occupied the crest. Nevertheless, skirmishes were of frequent occurrence for several weeks; picquets were fired on by night, and parties and convoys by day.

Unrest, 1880.

After the battle of Kandahar and defeat of Ayub Khan, the Achakzais became perfectly friendly, but their behaviour was not to pass unpunished. In September 1880, Lord Roberts and Sandeman met at Gulistan, where they decided that an expedition should enter Toba and the Achakzai country round the Khwaja Amran Range.

On the 21st September 1880, General Baker marched from Old Chaman along the foot of the Khwaja Amran to the Bogra Pass. He had under his command the following troops:—

General Baker's Expedition, 1880.

3rd Bengal Cavalry, 80 sabres, under Captain G. T. Morris.
No. 2 Mountain Battery under Major G. Swinley.
72nd Highlanders under Major C. M. Stockwell.
2nd Sikhs under Lieut.-Colonel J. J. Boswell.
5th Gurkhas under Lieut.-Colonel A. Fitz Hugh.

The plan of operations was to march *viâ* the Bogra Pass up to the Toba camp there, and proceed to Kala Abdulla by the Arambi Glen.

In order to confine the Achakzai in Toba, the passes on the north and west sides were occupied by the 3rd Bengal Cavalry and detachments of regiments sent to the Arambi Glen from Kala Abdulla, *viz.* :—

Commanding—Colonel Chapman, 8th Bengal Cavalry.

8th Bengal Cavalry, 100 sabres.
1st Madras Light Cavalry, 47 sabres.
Jacob's Horse, 10 sabres.
63rd Foot, 100 Rifles.
3rd Bengal Infantry, 30 rifles.

The Bogra Pass is the most northerly of the practicable passes which debouch from Pishin (Toba) on to the Kunchai Plain. It presents (1907) little difficulty for pack transport and could easily be made practicable for guns. From it issues the stream from which water (500,000 gallons a day) is conveyed in a pipe line to the mobilization camp at Chaman.

Baker's force took the precaution of crowning the heights throughout the passage of this gorge, which is nine miles long, but arrived without incident at the summit, where an extensive plateau is reached, most of which lies at an elevation of from 6,000 to 8,000 feet. The Achakzai had, however, practically deserted their country, and disappeared into Zhob. Few were seen, and these were endeavouring to drive off their flocks.

The Cavalry scoured the country on either side, securing what sheep and cattle remained in the district, and reconnoitring generally. The infantry advanced in a south-easterly direction. A few prisoners were made, being found in possession of property stolen from the British Government. In descending the Arambi Glen from Toba some slight resistance was experienced from some armed Achakzais who fired on the column from the hills overlooking the pass. The flanking parties opened fire on and killed two of these snipers, causing their immediate disappearance. A sepoy of the 2nd Sikhs, however, who strayed from the line of march, was murdered. Parties were sent out in all directions to capture the murderer, but were unsuccessful. As a lesson to the people, all the hamlets and

crops within a five-mile radius of the scene of the outrage were destroyed.

The whole march only lasted four days[1] and Kala Abdulla was reached on the 24th September. From the Achakzais were taken 2,300 sheep and goats, 49 camels, 28 bullocks, 10 donkeys. After using what was required for the brigade, the other animals were handed over to the commissariat at Kala Abdulla. The tribe was, in addition, fined Rs. 600.

Expedition against the Marris by a force under Brigadier-General C. M. MacGregor, C.B., C.S.I., C.I.E., in 1880.

On the outbreak of the Afghan War in 1878, the Marris began to commit petty outrages on the line of communications between Dadar and Lehri; but the tribe as a whole attempted no open hostilities until August 1880.

On the receipt of the news of the disaster at Maiwand on the 27th July 1880, the troops on the line of communications were ordered to concentrate at the points of strategical importance. With this object, the detachments along the line of railway, under construction between Sibi and Harnai, were directed to fall back and concentrate at the former place for the protection of the Bolan communications.[2]

On this portion of the railway there were employed at the end of July some 5,000 or 6,000 *coolies,* guarded by detachments principally drawn from the 23rd Bombay Infantry. At Spin Tangi was a post of 75 men, under Lieutenant F. J. Tobin of that regiment, strengthened to about 100 bayonets by a small detachment which came in from an adjacent station. When it became known that the works were to be abandoned, a panic took place among the labourers; some 3,000 of them poured into Sibi at once, while about 1,800 crowded into Spin Tangi, just as Lieutenant Tobin's detachment, with treasure to the amount of a *lakh* and a

---

[1] This route was followed in 1905 by one side of the Double Staff Ride undertaken by the officers of the Quetta Division under General Smith-Dorrion. Few officers present were aware that they were following the route taken by General Baker, most of the reports issued on the affairs of that time having remained confidential,

[2] This precipitate abandonment of the railway works doubtless afforded foundation for widely spread reports that the military power of Great Britain had received a blow equal to that dealt to it in 1841. The impression grew that we were abandoning our Sibi possessions for ever, and tended further to disturb the Marris who had witnessed our withdrawal from Vitakri at a critical period.

half, started on the 6th August on its retreat to Sibi. The road was very difficult, and the mass of *coolies* greatly hampered the march as well as the defensive power of the little force, which was attacked by large bodies of Marris, who saw a good opportunity for plunder, and it was only by abandoning the treasure that the detachment could make its way to Sibi, with the loss of its baggage and tents, several clerks and *coolies* being killed, and Lieutenant Tobin himself being wounded. This raid was followed up by depredations on the line of communications. An attack on Mal, near Sibi, however, was very promptly dealt with by the troops on the lines of communication. The Marris, having raided the district and carried off 2,000 head of cattle, retired to their hills. They were overtaken on the 28th August 1880, by the force detailed in the margin, and an engagement ensued, in which some forty Marris were killed, or wounded. Most of the stolen property was recovered, and no further raids into British territory occurred.

<small>Railway Detachment Escort attacked.</small>

<small>Attack on Mal.</small>

<small>Major A. B. Douglas, 4th Bengal Native Infantry, Commanding.
50 sabres, Sind Horse.
150 rifles, 3rd and 4th Bengal Native Infantry.</small>

To punish the Marris for these outrages, and to place our political relations with them on a sounder basis, it was decided to offer them the following terms, and, in the event of refusal, to send an expedition into their country:—

<small>Marri Expedition, 1880.</small>

  1st. Restitution of treasure and property plundered.
  2nd. Twenty thousand rupees fine.
  3rd. Blood-money, according to tribal custom, for those killed.
  4th. British troops to march through the Marri country by Kahan to Harrand.
  5th. Approved hostages to be given for future good conduct.

The command of the expedition was entrusted to Brigadier-General C. M. MacGregor, C.B., C.S.I., C.I.E., and a force of 393 sabres and 2,496 bayonets, numbering in all 3,074 of all ranks, was placed at his disposal Of these troops, 11-9th Royal Artillery, the 4th Gurkhas, and one company, 2-60th Rifles, were at Harnai,

<small>11-9th Royal Artillery.
2-60th Rifles.
3rd Punjab Cavalry.
2nd Sikh Infantry.
3rd Sikh Infantry.
4th Gurkha Regiment.
5th Gurkha Regiment.</small>

and the remainder, under Brigadier-General MacGregor, were concentrated at Sibi. The whole force, after uniting, was to proceed in the first instance to Quat-Mandai there to await the result of negotiations which were being carried on by the political authorities with the chiefs of the Marri clan.

By the 13th October the force was concentrated at Babar Kach, and on the following day marched eight miles and a half to Quat-Mandai (*see* Map). Here the country was well watered and fertile, and the standing crops furnished ample forage; the villages had been deserted, but no opposition was met with, although the roads had been flooded by the Marris, who were reported to have been joined by the Luni Pathans, and to have thrown off the authority of their Chief, Mir Ulla Khan, who did not wish to fight. It had been Brigadier-General MacGregor's intention to march straight upon Kahan from Quat-Mandai, but as such a step would have had the effect of driving the Marris to the hills, and putting off all chance of an understanding with them, he now decided to cut in between them and their northern neighbours, the Lunis, and, by heading the Marris themselves in the direction of Kolu, inflict on them one crushing blow, and thus end the campaign.

During the 15th and 16th October the force halted at Quat-Mandai, in order to allow a few days' grace to the Marri Chief. Then, no intimation having been received of the result of the negotiations, the Brigadier-General determined to advance, in accordance with his original orders.

On the 17th the force marched to Dalujal (fourteen miles and a half), leaving at Quat-Mandai the 2nd Sikhs, two guns, 11-9th Royal Artillery, and one squadron, 3rd Punjab Cavalry, under the command of Major W. C. Anderson, of the last-named regiment. On the following day the force marched to Spin Kach, the Spin Tangi being traversed without opposition, which was probably partly due to the movement being unexpected. Owing to the difficulties of the road, the rear-guard did not reach camp until twenty-four hours after the commencement of the march, which was five miles in length. At Spin Kach the troops noted in the margin, under Colonel G. S. Morris, which were destined to form the garrison of Thal-Chotiali, joined Brigadier-General MacGregor's column, and the whole

No. 2, Bombay Mountain Battery, 2 guns.
2nd Bombay Light Cavalry, 129 sabres.
15th Bombay Native Infantry, 309 bayonets.

force marched on the 19th to Kuriak (eight miles), and next day to Kandi (eleven miles).

No opposition was met with, and the road was fairly good, except in a few places where the 3,000 baggage animals had to march in single file, on which account the rear-guard on the 20th took ten hours to cover eleven miles. At 6 A.M. on the 21st, the column marched for Sembar. The pass bearing this name though affording the strongest possible defensible position, was unoccupied by the enemy; the road, however, presented formidable obstacles. At about ten miles from the start, Sembar (which is nothing but a name) was reached.

Here there was scarcely any water, and the force was compelled to push on over another *kotal* (4,000 feet), the road becoming worse and worse. The Brigadier-General halted for some hours near the crest, the advanced guard pressing on down the northern slopes, and finally encamping at about 5 P.M. near a well in the Thal plain, about two miles from its southern edge. Meanwhile, the baggage and rear-guard was much delayed, but, fortunately, the opposition was of the slightest, a few shots only having been fired near the eastern end of the pass. It was not, however, until 10 A.M. on the 22nd that the rear-guard reached the camping ground, having been on the road, and almost without water, for twenty-eight hours. The total distance was twenty miles, and during the march 240 transport animals were lost.

On the following day a detachment of two squadrons of the 2nd Bombay Cavalry, which had been unable to catch up the head-quarters of the regiment before, came through the pass, and found four bodies of camp followers, who had been murdered on the previous day. A few shots were fired at this detachment, and one sowar was wounded.

On the 22nd the column marched to Thal (eight miles and a half) across the plain. The effect of the adoption of this route was now proved to meet the Brigadier-General's expectations, and the Lunis, alarmed for the safety of their own villages, thus directly threatened, broke off their alliance with the Marris, and their headmen came into the British camp at Thal to offer their services against their former allies.

The Brigadier-General was still without any intimation of the results of the negotiations with the Marri Chiefs, and was thus

placed in a false position, being uncertain whether he was entering an enemy's country or not. As, however, any hesitation might have a bad effect, he decided, after halting a day at Thal to fill up his supplies, to push forward into the Marri country. To prevent any mistake, however, he wrote to Mir Ulla Khan, the Chief of the Marris, as well as to Karam Khan of Kolu, the Chief of the Bijarani (the most hostile) section, inviting them to come and hear the terms of the British Government.

On the 25th, leaving all the sick and the surplus transport at Thal, the force marched to Chotiali. From this place two roads lead to Kolu—one by Burg, which was said to be bad and waterless, and the other by Bala Dhaka, somewhat longer, but easier. The route *viâ* Bala Dhaka was selected. From Chotiali it was four marches by this route to Kolu, thence three more to Mamand, and from there four to Kahan, a total of eleven marches. Supplies were, therefore, taken for eleven days. Leaving the troops under Colonel Morris to occupy the posts of Thal and Chotiali the Bengal troops advanced on the 26th to Paniali. Here a final message was sent to Mir Ulla Khan and Karam Khan, to the effect that if they did not come in at once, Kolu, Mamand, and Kahan would be treated as hostile districts. On the 27th the force marched thirteen miles to Baniwali, and the following day continued its march to Bala Dhaka and Gusra (nine miles).

At early dawn on the 29th, two regiments were sent on to seize the Khuba Wanga Pass, leading to the Kolu Valley, with orders to render the road practicable. This was effected by 10 A.M. The pass was found to be very difficult and the baggage took all day to accomplish the march, the rear-guard not reaching camp at Nikra until 10 P.M.

The Marris were now completely headed; there was no longer any fear of their joining the Lunis, or seeking an asylum in the Khetran country, and unless they opposed the column, they must withdraw to the westward. Karam Khan had already deserted his fort in Kolu, and the force marched thither on the 30th. It was at this time reported that one portion of the Marris advocated a general assembly at Sawar, to the west, while others were in favor of concentrating near Kahan, on the south-west. Brigadier-General MacGregor's object was to prevent any tendency to assemble in separate bodies, and as it appeared probable that they would make

their principal stand in the Sawar direction, the Brigadier endeavoured to manœuvre so as to compel them to abandon the Kahan position. This was effected by an announcement that he intended to march direct on Kahan by the Dowla Wanga Pass; the result being that the following day the enemy were reported to be abandoning the Kahan position, and retreating towards the Chakar Tangi and Nili with their flocks, women and children.

On this day (the 30th) Major Anderson was instructed to postpone the destruction of Mandai, which he had been ordered to carry out on the 1st of November.

On the 31st the force advanced through the Dowla Wanga Pass, twelve miles in the direction of Mamand. There were two or three difficult places, and some delay occurred in the pass, so that the rear-guard did not arrive in camp till 6-30 P.M. On this day the Brigadier-General received information that the negotiations with the Marris had been broken off, and that he was at liberty to enforce the terms on the tribe. On the receipt of this message, Brigadier-General MacGregor sent to inform the Marri Chief, Mir Ulla Khan, that if he wished to come in he must do so at once. On the 1st November the force marched sixteen miles to Kui. During the afternoon, Mir Ulla Khan arrived in the British camp, and was informed of the terms which the Government demanded, to which a straightforward answer must be given on the following day at Mamand.

The next day the march was continued to that place, and Mir Ulla Khan and Karam Khan both came into camp. After recapitulating the terms and explaining what he proposed to do in the event of their not being accepted, the Brigadier-General addressed them as follows:—" I have now read to you the orders of Government in regard to the terms which they have been pleased to require from you. I have also told you what I propose to do, and I have now only to say this: you must give me a straight answer—' Yes ' or ' No '—in one hour. You must either fight or obey the orders of Government. For myself I do not care much which you do; my troops will be very glad if you fight. Now go away and settle matters." This short address had the desired effect, and within the hour Mir Ulla Khan and Karam Khan gave their unreserved submission. Brigadier-General MacGregor then demanded three hostages—one from the Ghazani section, one from the Bijaranis, and one on the part of the Chief. He also demanded the immediate

payment of Rs. 50,000, and that Mandai should be held until the rest of the fine was realised. This was agreed to, and the Chiefs consented to accompany the British troops to Kahan. On the 3rd November, leaving Mamand on the left, the force marched three miles to the westward, in order to profit as far as possible by the standing crops.

The Brigadier-General's intention, in the event of the non-submission of the Marris, had been here to divide his force into two columns, one to advance by Safed Tok to Nili (four marches), the other to the Chakar Tangi. At the same time Major Anderson, at Mandai, was to advance towards Nili (where the principal body of the enemy was assembled), and effect a junction with the Lunis and the Thal Chotiali garrison from the north, and thus surround the enemy.

On the 4th of November the column marched by the Ghora Dand to Khanki (seven miles) *en route* to Kahan,

Kahan reached.

and on the 5th the advance was continued to Ghar Daf (fourteen miles), the Chief going on to Kahan, to endeavour to have the fine ready on the arrival of the British troops. Kahan was reached on the 6th of November. About four miles from the capital the Brigadier-General was met by Mir Ulla Khan, Karam Khan, and other leading men of the Marris.

Mir Ulla Khan, acting as spokesman, asked for forgiveness in the name of the tribe in most humble

Submission of Marris.

terms; he promised on their behalf to pay up the rest of the fine, and to fulfil all the other conditions, and as an earnest of their intentions he brought with him Rs. 50,000 in cash and the hostages demanded. The Brigadier-General replied in a few words, and said :—" I am glad you have the sense to see that such a wretched band of robbers as you are cannot cope with the British Government. I accept the money and the hostages as a token of your real submission, and I shall therefore not destroy Kahan."

The troops then advanced and encamped on the west of the town. Kahan lies in a magnificent plain, well watered, well wooded, and highly cultivated. During the day arrangements were made for the return of the expeditionary force to India.

The total fine and compensation was fixed at two *lakhs,* the blood-money at Rs. 60,000, and the hostages were—a brother of

Mir Ulla Khan, on behalf of the *Sardars* of the tribe generally; Karam Khan, as the representative of the Bijarani; and Mir Hazar as that of the Ghazani section. The hostages were taken to Khanpur, and then sent in charge of Lieutenant R. H. Jennings by rail to Sibi.

The force halted near Kahan on the 7th November, but the town was not entered by any of the troops, in deference to the feelings of the inhabitants. On the 8th Brigadier-General MacGregor left Kahan, and marched twenty miles over easy country to Suji Kach, crossing the Marri eastern frontier.

On the 9th November the force marched from Suji Kach to Ketchi Kot (four miles and a half), and on the following day to Chatt, by the Burzen Pass. On the 11th the march was continued to Kalchas, and the next day Bet Bakshah, in British territory, was reached. On arriving at Drigi the force was broken up.

The expedition had thus been brought to a successful issue as regards the submission of the majority of the Marris; but the Mandai Marris had not been adequately dealt with. Consequently on the 6th December following, Major Sir Robert Sandeman, the Governor-General's Agent, Baluchistan, made a requisition on the Brigadier-General in command of the communications for the escort allowed him by Government, viz., 2 mountain guns, 1 troop of cavalry, and 160 bayonets, as he intended to move towards the Marri country.

The troops detailed in the margin were accordingly placed at his disposal, and orders were received for these to be increased by 250 bayonets of the 29th Bombay Native Infantry, the escort being under the command of Colonel O. V. Tanner, of that regiment.

Settlement with Marris, 1881.
11-9th Royal Artillery, 2 guns.
8th Bengal Cavalry, 1 troop.
29th Bombay Native Infantry, 2 companies.

On the 18th December Major Sir R. G. Sandeman marched for Mandai, with the intention of entering the Marri hills for four or five marches, in order to support Sardar Mir Ulla Khan, who was endeavouring to recover from the Mandai Marris their share of the fine. Up to that time he had only succeeded in recovering from them Rs. 25,000, and five cartloads of property looted during the outrage on the 6th August. The escort was to be supported by the garrison of Mandai, now consisting of two mountain guns, one regiment of Bombay Infantry, and a squadron of Madras Cavalry, which had

relieved Major Anderson's detachment after the termination of Brigadier-General MacGregor's operations.

The Mandai Marris were, however, overawed by this display of force and tendered their submission to Sir Robert Sandeman, agreeing to pay in full the whole fine of Rs. 50,000.

On the 6th January, 1881, a final settlement was effected with[1] the whole Marri tribe, by which it was stipulated, among other things, that all roads through the Marri country should remain open to traffic, that in the event of thefts or offences being committed either in British territory or on the trade routes, the Chiefs should be responsible for the restoration of the stolen property or for the production of the actual offenders; that when summoned by the Political Officer the *tumandar* or any of the Chiefs should at once attend; that approved hostages with one risaldar and ten sowars should remain at Sibi; and that the Marri tribe should not wage war or attempt to inflict retribution on any other people or tribe without the permission of the British Government.

Shorawak Affairs.

When the British occupied Pishin, Sandeman was very anxious to include Shorawak in its boundaries. He produced evidence of its having belonged to the Pishin rather than to the Kandahar District, from which it is separated by 70 miles of the Registan Desert. Shorawak is inhabited by a Pathan tribe, the Baraich, and is fairly well cultivated.

In order to obtain information regarding this district, Major Duke was directed in March, 1879, to march from Nushki *via* Shorawak to Pishin. With him as escort went the troops detailed in the margin under command of Major F. Humfrey, Jacob's Rifles.

30 sabres, 1st Punjab Cavalry.
176 Rifles, Jacob's Rifles.

On the 27th March 1879, this force was attacked near Saiyid Buz in Shorawak by a body of 1,600 Baraich. The action lasted from 7-30 A.M. till 2 P.M. and was fought in a blinding dust storm, which blew

Affair at Sayyid Buz, 1879.

---

[1] The Baraich are a Pathan tribe akin to the Tarins. Those living in Baluchistan are to be found principally in Chagai and Western Kalat. They were formerly great wanderers and have left their mark in the Bombay Presidency, the town of Baraich (Broach) being called after them.

in the enemy's face, and helped to conceal the movements and small numbers of the British force.

The action started by the cavalry drawing the enemy to a rapidly entrenched position taken up by Major Humfrey. The enemy attacked the entrenchments, our cavalry clearing off to the right.

Major Humfrey advanced his left and swung it round against the enemy's right which caused them to retire. They were at once charged on the other flank by Major Duke at the head of the detachment of the 1st Punjab Cavalry. The whole of the infantry then left their entrenchments, and charged the retreating enemy of whom ninety were killed, and many wounded.

They were completely defeated, and surrendered to Major Duke next day. The British loss was seven severely and several slightly wounded. Major Humfrey was made Brevet-Lieutenant-Colonel for his success in this affair.

At the meeting of Lord Roberts with Sandeman at Gulistan in September 1880, it was decided to send a small force into Shorawak. The inhabitants had remained quite friendly, and the object of the march was solely to obtain and send to Quetta supplies of grain and forage. Precautions had, of course, to be taken in case of hostility. The troops detailed for this duty were under command of Colonel Robertson, 4th Bengal Infantry. Captain Wylie accompanied the force as political agent.

Shorawak occupied, 1880.

Colonel Robertson, Commanding.

1 Squadron, 1st Madras Light Cavalry.
2 guns, Jacobabad Mountain Battery.
4th Bengal Infantry.

Previous to the march of the force from Gulistan, the Gwazha Pass was closed with dynamite to prevent the passage of any hostile parties, and was only opened when the column was ready to start.

On the 9th October a start was made. No opposition was met with. A camp was formed at Mandozai near Nushki and arrangements were made for the weekly despatch of supplies to Gulistan for a period of one month.

In October of that year, a strong grazing and grass pressing depôt in Shorawak was established in view of the forage difficulty on the line of communications from Sibi to Quetta and

Chaman. There, too, it was proposed to send all sick and weakly transport animals and horses.[1]

The column remained in Shorawak until March 1881, the 4th Bengal Infantry having been relieved by the 5th Bombay Infantry. The British Government then decided to give Shorawak back to the Afghan Province of Kandahar, and the troops at Mandozai marched to Khushdil Khan, the former seat of Afghan Government in Pishin, which was temporarily strengthened so as to overawe the Kakars during the withdrawal of the British force from Kandahar.

Shorawak evacuated, 1881.

On the 23rd May, 1881, Major-General Hume reported from Quetta that the last regiment for India had left Sibi. The Southern Afghanistan Field Force became the Quetta Division[2] and the Second Afghan War was at an end.

Southern Afghan Field Force evacuates Baluchistan, 1881.

Thal-Chotiali Field Force, 1878.

The want of a direct route from the Punjab to Quetta and Pishin became very noticeable during the Second Afghan War. The length and heat of the Sind-Bolan route are apparent.

As early as 1875 the Government of India had endeavoured unsuccessfully to come to an understanding with the Kabul Government regarding the old trade route *viâ* Thal-Chotiali to the Derajat.

As the route is now (1907) a highway in our possession a short description of its course and strategical value will be of interest. Starting from Dera Ghazi Khan the route crosses the Suliman Mountains *viâ* the Sakhi Sarwar Pass and Fort Munro; thence through the Barkhan valley over the Han Pass to Thal. The valley of Vitakri is a continuation of the Barkhan valley which is entered from the Rakni Plain, and troops—if there—would dominate the Khetrans, Marris, Bugtis, and the Tarin Pathan tribes of Thal-Chotiali. The Barkhan Plain, too, is of strategical value, considered as a place where troops could be cantoned in support of garrisons at Quetta and Pishin. Thence direct routes lead to Dera Ismail Khan, Dera Ghazi Khan, Rajanpur, and Jacobabad in one direction, and Quetta, Pishin, and Kandahar in the other. These routes lie, for

---

[1] This proposal was not carried out on account of the determination to restore Kandahar and the province to Abdur Rahman.
[2] For details see Appendix A.

the most part, through an open easy country, and connect the valleys of Khurasan with the plains of Punjab and Sind. In a northerly direction the valleys flank all the passes leading from Afghanistan into the Punjab as far as the Gomal, while to the south they flank the Bolan Pass.

In 1879, when the troops were returning from Kandahar, it was decided to open up this route, and Sir Robert Sandeman was ordered to visit General Sir Donald Stewart at Kandahar and arrange for certain troops to proceed to India by that route. Arrangements for supply and political dealings with the tribes were placed in the hands of the Agent to the Governor-General (Sandeman).

Accordingly, a force was collected, strength as detailed in the margin, at Khushdil Khan, near the modern station of Pishin. General Biddulph was in command with Sir Robert Sandeman as Political Officer.

Composition of Field Force.

1st Column.

Commanding, Major Keene.
4 Mountain guns.
1 Squadron, Jacob's Horse (36th)?
1 Squadron, 8th Bengal Cavalry.
4 Companies, 1st Punjab Infantry.

Approximate strength, 750 men.

2nd Column.

Commanding, Colonel Sale Hill.
15th Hussars.
4 Mountain guns.
32nd Pioneers.
1st Gurkhas.

Approximate strength 1,350 men.

3rd Column.

Commanding, Major-General Nuttal.
2 Mountain guns.
2 Squadrons, 8th Bengal Lancers.
6 Companies, 70th Foot (East Surrey Regiment).
9th Company, Sappers and Miners.

Approximate strength, 870 men.

The force advanced in three columns, marching from Khushdil Khan on March 11th, 21st, and 22nd, respectively. Sir Robert Sandeman accompanied the First Column to arrange for supplies with the local tribes, and prevent opposition to the march. General Biddulph marched with the Second Column. To the First Column, naturally, fell the duty of clearing the way. The force marched unopposed to Spiraragha Pass. Here the Dumar Pathans made a show of opposition, but were persuaded by Sir Robert Sandeman of the peaceful intention of the march. Thence the force marched *viâ* the Chari Mountain where a single fanatic, sword in hand, barred the way

Chari Mountain. declaring that none should pass save over his dead body. Hearing this, the Dumar headmen, who had accompanied the column, advanced on his

position and, throwing their long shawls over him, brought him to the ground; not, however, before he had severely wounded one of them

Next day the Column was fired on by a large body of Dumars. Of this affair Sir Robert Sandeman wrote the following account to Lord Lytton :—

We had proceeded some seven or eight miles further when we approached a series of low hills, which we found occupied by Dumars. I and Major Keene, with a party of Infantry and two guns, at once advanced against the hill, which was pretty strongly held, and sent word to the hillmen not to oppose our advance.

The guns were loaded, the hillmen refused to give way, and a collision appeared inevitable.

At this juncture, to our great astonishment, the Roderick Dhu of the day before, who had attentively listened to the parley, suddenly broke loose from those in charge of him, ascended the hillside rapidly and, on reaching the top, fell upon his fellow clansmen calling out " I have surrendered : who are you to oppose the advance when I have submitted ?"

Curiously enough this caused the tribesmen to submit, and eighty of them were disarmed and brought into camp. A conference with the headmen was then held and arrangements were made for establishing posts along the route traversed to keep open communications. The posts were to be held by the clans in whose country they were established, and pay was given at Rs. 15 for a jemadar and Rs. 8 for each of 15 footmen per mensem. This was fixed as the establishment for each post, of which three were formed. Satisfactory arrangements were made for supplying the columns in rear with grain and forage.

The column then proceeded to Chinjan, Chinali, and Kach. At the Kandil Pass the force was stopped by armed men of the Aghbarg Mountain. These were dispersed by a few shells from the guns, and the troops proceeded through the defile to the Smalan Valley. At Sanjawi, Sir Robert Sandeman held another conference, when arrangements for the establishment of posts was made with the headmen of the tribes who had opposed the column at the Kandil Pass.

At Baghao Major Keene's force was opposed by some 3,500 tribesmen of the Zhob and Bori Valleys under the command of Shah Jahan, Chief of Zhob. The enemy suddenly appeared in front and

Affair at Baghao.

on both flanks and advanced across open ground to attack the column. The guns opened fire and stopped this advance, after which Major Keene advanced and succeeded in putting the whole force to flight with a loss of 200 killed and wounded. Major Keene's loss was three killed and a few wounded. Shah Jahan of Zhob sent in a written submission next day.

There was no further opposition, and the 1st Column proceeded *via* Thal and Chotiali to Vitakri in the Barkhan Plain, where it was joined by the other two columns. These latter columns had taken a slightly different route. They marched down the Bori Valley, where the cantonment of Loralai has since sprung up, and through the Anambar Gap across the Chamalang river to Bala Dhaka and Vitakri. Here also arrived from Multan the force detailed in the margin under Colonel Prendergast. It was to form the garrison of a post to command all the passes leading through the Kakar country into Pishin, and yet be within easy reach of the Indian frontier.

<small>15th Bengal Cavalry.
Detachment, 21st Madras Infantry.
Detachment, 30th Madras Infantry.
Detachment, Bhawalpur Contingent.</small>

Vitakri was found to fulfil these conditions, and there Prendergast's column was established for the hot weather. The site proved very unhealthy, and the cantonment was shortly afterwards abandoned when the force was broken up, part proceeding to Dera Ghazi *via* the Sakhi Sarwar Pass, and part to Mithankot by the Chachar Pass. On the 1st May 1879, General Biddulph reached Multan, and the Thal-Chotiali Field Force ceased to exist.

<small>Vitakri Cantonment.</small>

The results of this march were valuable on account of the geographical information gained and survey work accomplished. It was also important in view of the relations established between the Baluchistan Agency and the Kakar Pathan Tribes.

Bozdar Field Force.

Again, in November and December 1881, advantage was taken of the troops returning from Kandahar to explore new territory on our border, and orders were given to march the body of troops

noted in the margin from the Harnai Valley to Dera Ghazi Khan *viâ* the Bozdar country and Saunra Pass.

Commanding Field Force.

Brigadier-General H. C. Wilkinson.

Troops.
8th Mountain Battery.
4 Companies, 1st Battalion, Manchester Regiment.
1 Squadron, Jacob's Horse.
4th Bombay Rifles (now 104th).
9th Bombay Infantry (now 109th).

General Wilkinson commanded the force, which left Quetta on November 1st and arrived at Thal on the 16th. Here the column struck off to the north-east through unknown country to the Suliman Mountains, arriving at Dera Ghazi Khan *viâ* the Vidor Pass on the 11th December. This route crossed that traversed by General Biddulph in 1879 in the Chamalang Valley. The march had important results in proving the possibility of feeding large numbers of animals in the Chamalang Valley, where grass was found to be abundant. Heliographic communication was opened with India on the 26th November. A signalling station had been established on the mountain of Ekbhai and communication was first established from Dadar Mountain, 46 miles distant. No opposition was met with.

Baluchistan subsequent to the Second Afghan War.

The further history of Baluchistan chiefly relates to administration and organisation. The strategical importance of the western and north-eastern portions of the province were recognised, and expeditions were made to Makran, Bori, and Zhob. The first to Makran was in 1883-84, when Sandeman adjusted the quarrel between the Khan and the Naoshirwanis, the second in 1890-91, when the better administration of Makran was taken up. Later—in 1898 and 1901—disturbances in Makran necessitated military expeditions being despatched to that country, of which an account will be given in chapter XI. The expeditions to the Bori and Zhob Valleys will also be dealt with in separate chapters.

Quetta leased, 1882.

In 1882 arrangements were finally made with the Khan of Kalat by which the Quetta District and valley were rented by the British Government for Rs. 25,000 per annum, and the Bolan taken over for Rs. 30,000. The considerations governing the sums fixed depended on the average incomes derivable from the districts, after the expenses of administration had been deducted.

The next few years saw great developments in Baluchistan; careful division into districts, each with its own political officers;

progress of the railway—a high level road up the Bolan Pass to avoid "wash-outs" by flood, and the establishment of levy posts, etc.

Tribal Levies.
After the close of the Afghan War there were numbers of isolated posts in Baluchistan, garrisoned, for the protection of the country, by regular troops. In 1882 a committee sat to consider this situation, ruinous to the discipline and efficiency of regular troops.

Gradually the posts were made over to tribal levies, and the 1st August 1884 saw the final policing of the country by its own people established. The money for these levies was chiefly found by the disbandment of the Baluch Guides. Raised in 1838 this force, whose duties were those of political bodyguard, professional spies, and Government messengers, had served in Sind until 1877, when it was transferred to the charge of the Agent to the Governor-General in Quetta.

Troops of Native States.
The strength of the forces to be kept up by Native States have been fixed from time to time by the orders of the Agent to the Governor-General. The Khan of Kalat's army at present consists of 300 infantry, 300 cavalry, and 90 gunners. The artillery consists of 29 obsolete pieces, of which nine are serviceable. Most of these troops are stationed at Kalat; detachments are located at Mastung, Khuzdar, and in Kachi. The whole force is entirely irregular and practically devoid of organisation or discipline.

Las Bela Forces.
A force of 104 Punjabi Muhammadan Military Police is maintained at Bela under the orders of the Wazir: they are armed with Snider carbines. The State troops consist of 36 cavalry, 212 infantry, and 5 field guns. Besides these troops, certain levies are maintained under the district officials.

Kharan Forces.
In Kharan 450 men, variously armed, are kept up for the maintenance of order. Of this force 170 men form the garrison of Dehgwar to prevent raids by the Damanis of the Persian border. Raghai and Rakhshan are the other Municipal garrisons. The Chief possesses three muzzle-loading cannons and a mortar. All the tribesmen are liable to military service when called upon.

THE BALUCHISTAN AGENCY.

Khojak Tunnel. In 1887 it was decided to tunnel the Khwaja Amran Range between Kala Abdulla and Old Chaman, and to make the terminus of the railway in the Kunchai Plain at the northern entrance to the Khojak Pass. The terminus was called Chaman, where the military station was established.

Chaman. Chaman lies 79 miles north-west of Quetta, from which place there is a metalled cart road leading over the Khojak Pass. It is 4,400 feet above sea-level and is much hotter in summer than Quetta, although the winter is little less severe. The extremes of heat and cold are due to the great Registan desert which begins a couple of miles west of Chaman and over which the prevailing winds blow.

Troops marched into Chaman on the 1st August 1889, that is to say they pitched their camp on a piece of the desert where it had been decided to build the terminus of the railway. A glance at the map will show that at the Gwazha Pass our boundary leaves the Khwaja Amran Range and curves into the Kunchai Plain, attaining its furthest limit therein three miles west of Chaman: thence it curves back to the hills, joining them north of the Bogra Pass. A stretch of level country is thus enclosed, on which the railway terminus and cantonment have been built. This inclusion of part of the Kunchai Plain within our frontier was a very sore point with the Amir, Abdur Rahman of Afghanistan.

Las Bela. In January 1888, Jam Mir Khan of Las Bela died. The succession was disputed. It will be remembered[1] that his eldest son Jam Ali Khan ruled the state during his father's exile in India. On his father's return Jam Ali Khan fell into disfavour. He found that a younger son of the Jam by another wife, a Delhi lady, whom he had married in exile was being pushed forward as the heir apparent. In consequence, he took up arms against his father, and was first exiled by the British authorities and afterwards detained, practically a prisoner, in Quetta.

As the result of his former bad behaviour, Jam Ali Khan was not looked upon with favour by the Indian Government. Sandeman, however, considering the provocation which produced

---
[1] Chapter III.

Jam Ali's insurrection, and the fact of his being a Brahui on his mother's side, whereas the other claimant for the Jamship was the offspring of a foreigner, decided to allow the succession of the eldest son. In January 1889, Jam Ali Khan was placed on the throne by Sir Robert Sandeman in public durbar.

In 1891 Kamal Khan, the Jam's eldest son, fell out with his father, and fled to Quetta. It was chiefly to settle this dispute that Sandeman proceeded to Las Bela.

On the 16th January 1892, he arrived at Sonmiani, whence he marched to Las Bela escorted by a Company of the 1st Baluchis (now 127th).

Death of Sir Robert Sandeman.

Las Bela was reached on the 22nd, and next day Sir Robert Sandeman was taken ill, and died on the 28th. During his illness the Jam, who attributed his possession of the chiefship to Sandeman's efforts alone, had a service of picked horses along the road to Karachi, 115 miles, to bring out medicines or anything else required. Six months later he erected a handsome dome over his patron's grave. Sir Robert Sandeman's funeral took place on the 1st February, the coffin being carried by men of the 1st Baluchis along a route lined with the Jam's retainers, and followed by all the political officers. Lieutenant W. M. Southey, 1st Baluchis, commanded the firing party: he had marched in from Panjgur that morning.

As a curious instance of Eastern ideas, the following extract from a letter of condolence written by the Khan of Kalat to Lady Sandeman is interesting. After expressing his grief at Sandeman's death, Mir Khudadad Khan wrote:—"The remains of Sir Robert Sandeman should be buried either in his native home or in my dominions; and if the Las Bela Chief objects, I am prepared to send an army forcibly to convey the body to Quetta."

In March 1893, it was decided to depose the Khan of Kalat. Khudadad Khan had caused the death of four persons, whom he accused of treachery, and an attempt on his life.

Khudadad Khan deposed.

The British authorities looked upon this action as murder, and decided to remove the Khan. Khudadad was then at Bagh in Kachi. Two columns were formed. The Middlesex Regiment, 1-24th Baluchistan Infantry, Jacob's Horse, and a mountain battery occupied Kalat, and the treasury was removed.

The other force, commanded by Colonel Aitken, R.A., consisted of the 37th Cavalry, 104th Rifles, and 2 mountain guns. This column proceeded to Belpat on the railway in Kachi, and the Khan was ordered to present himself there before the Agent to the Governor-General. On arrival, he was received by Colonel Browne, the Agent, in a square, three sides of which were troops, and the fourth the railway train. The troops were facing outwards when the Khan arrived. He entered the square, no salute was given, the troops turned "about," and the Khan recognised that he was a prisoner. He was taken by train to Quetta, where he abdicated in favour of his son, the present Khan, Mir Mahmud. Khudadad resided for some time in Loralai, and was in 1904 removed to Pishin.

In January 1896, Jam Ali Khan of Las Bela died, and was succeeded by his son Kamal Khan, the present ruler. This Chief was not given full powers at his succession,[1] a Wazir being appointed by the British authorities to assist him in the government.

Las Bela.

Intrigues at this time were known to be at work in Las Bela, and reports were current of large quantities of arms being imported from Kabul. In consequence the political Agent, Major M. A. Tighe, was ordered to proceed to Las Bela with a strong escort, commanded by Major J. O. Mennie, consisting of 200 rifles, 130th Baluchis, and a troop of the Sind Horse.

A start was made from Karachi on the 24th October 1896, and Las Bela was reached on the 31st. The road followed leads from Karachi to the Hab river and thence 101 miles to Las Bela. On the 2nd November Major Tighe ordered the arrest of two of the Jam's councillors who were known to have been intriguing. On the same day Major Mennie occupied the magazine near the palace. Here he found 100,000 rounds of ball cartridge, a much larger amount than the Jam was authorised to keep. Major Mennie removed this ammunition to his camp which had been pitched some two miles from the city. The next day the Political Agent released several men who had been imprisoned by the Jam. These measures caused some unrest in the town, and Major Tighe considered it would be well to seize the gun ammunition.

---

[1] Since 1902 his powers have been somewhat increased.

Accordingly on the afternoon of the 3rd of November Major Mennie removed all the shells to the escort camp and destroyed three thousand pounds of powder which was found in a magazine about a mile from the city. The Political Agent now discovered that there were many more men under arms than were authorised for the Jam's army and ordered the surplus to be disbanded.

The Political Agent remained at Las Bela till the 24th November, when, with Major Mennie and fifty men of the 130th Baluchis, he proceeded to Kanraj, where a survey party had been fired on in the previous year.

News was received on the 25th of an intended attack on the escort by the Mengals at the Kanraj Kotal. Another 50 men were, in consequence, despatched from Las Bela, and the *kotal* was occupied during the Political Agent's stay at Kanraj. Various disciplinary measures were taken in the district, and the escort returned to Las Bela on the 4th December, where it remained until the 14th March 1897, when it returned to Karachi.

The troubles in Kalat and Makran in 1897 have been ascribed to various causes. One theory was that the wave of fanaticism, which swept over the North-West Frontier in that year, had spread southwards to Baluchistan. This may have helped, indirectly, to cause a state of unrest. There is, however, every reason to believe that the actual trouble was entirely due to internal friction in Kalat. The great Raisani family headed by Mir Mehrulla Khan, uncle of the Sardar, had by a long course of systematic intrigue and oppression contrived to drive one Sardar Alliyar Khan Rustomzai over the border, with most of his tribesmen, the Rustomzai section of the Raisanis. This happened in 1895. In 1896 these Rustomzais returned to Baluchistan and the British authorities determined to restore their rights. This, of course, was regarded by the Raisanis with extreme disfavour.

Sarawan troubles, 1897.

Mir Mehrulla Khan, who had become all powerful among the Sarawans, determined to use all his influence to thwart the authorities. Matters were brought to a climax by the highway robberies of Jafir Khan and his band, who took up their quarters in the hills round Mastung. Orders were given for the arrest of Jafir Khan, and then it became clear that he was backed up by the Sarawan Sardars. Troops were sent out against Jafir, who

had taken up a position across the Quetta-Mastung road. He fled hotly pursued, and escaped to Kandahar.[1]

Jafir Khan.

Jafir Khan was sheltered for some time by the Tarasizai Mengals of Chagai, who also gave some trouble to the parties pursuing the outlaw. For this contumacy, a portion of the troops made a forced march at night on the headquarters of the clan, surprised their village Chandan Khan Bund in the Nushki desert, and carried it after some slight opposition. The chief of the clan was brought into Quetta. In this desert march the newly raised Kalat State Camel Corps (since disbanded) proved most useful, each camel sowar taking an infantryman of the 126th Baluchistan Infantry.

The Sarawan Sardars were promptly ordered to present themselves before the Agent to the Governor-General at Mastung. They refused, under the orders, it afterwards transpired, of Mir Mehrulla Khan and Sardar Yar Muhammad, both Raisanis. These men were immediately seized, and placed in confinement. The Raisani Sardar, Sir Ghaus Baksh, was also called upon to give security for loyal behaviour. These arrests caused much excitement in the country. The telegraph wires in the Bolan and on the Quetta-Kalat line were cut; the Bangalzai, Lehri, and Langon Sardars fled to Afghanistan with several influential members of the Raisani and Kurd clans. In October 1897, the Agent to the Governor-General in Baluchistan visited the Khan at Kalat. Affairs were arranged satisfactorily, the chiefs in confinement were released, and those who had fled returned.

Earlier in the year the Khan of Kalat had visited the Agent to the Governor-General in Quetta to consult him on certain important matters in connection with the settlement of the Makran Sardars, notably Mir Baluch Khan Naoshirwani. After the meeting, the Sardars returned to Makran nominally reconciled.

Arms Traffic from Persian Gulf, 1907.

In 1904 it became known that a considerable traffic in arms was taking place between the Persian Gulf and Afghanistan. The caravans bearing these arms had to traverse Persia or Chagai near the tri-junction at Koh-i-Malik Siah in order to enter

---

[1] The pursuing party, consisting of detachments of native cavalry and infantry from Quetta, was commanded by Major Alban, 126th Baluchistan Infantry.

Afghan territory. The British and Persian authorities determined to take steps to put a stop to this illicit traffic.

Early in 1906 two companies of the 128th Pioneers proceeded to Robat, at the western end of the Nushki trade route, on the border, distant 376 miles from rail-head at Nushki. They were relieved in February 1907, by two companies of the 127th Baluchis under Captain W. O. Grant and Lieutenant J. C. Tate. Having obtained information of the possible passage of an arms caravan through British territory, Captain Grant held the various passes with detachments. On the 2nd May the caravan, consisting of 53 camels, with an armed escort of some 50 Afghans, appeared in the Kacha Pass held by Jemadar Rajwali, and 34 men, 127th Baluch Light Infantry, who had marched 62 miles in 22 hours to reach the position in time. The escort showed fight, and after nine men had been killed and sixteen wounded, the remainder fled, and the whole convoy was captured. The capture comprised 795 good rifles of various modern patterns, and 70,000 rounds of ammunition, besides a few revolvers and pistols.

APPENDIX A.

Composition and Distribution of Quetta Division, May 1881.

Old Chaman	2 guns, 5-8th R. A. No. 3 Company, Bombay Sappers and Miners. 7th Bengal Cavalry, 1 squadron. 3rd Bengal Infantry, 4 companies.
Kala Abdulla Gulistan Khushdil Khan[1]	4 guns, 5-8th R. A. 7th Bengal Cavalry, 2 squadrons. Jacob's Horse, 1 squadron. 63rd Foot, 4 companies. 3rd Bengal Infantry (wing). 9th Bombay Infantry (wing).
Segi and Dinar Karez	Jacob's Horse, detachment. 13th Bombay Infantry, detachment.
Kach	Jacob's Horse, detachment. 4th Bombay Rifles, 6 companies.
Chapar	4th Bombay Rifles, 2 companies.
Sharig Harnai Spin Tangi	Scinde Horse, 1 squadron. Jacobabad Mountain Battery, 2 guns. 24th Bombay Infantry.
Ganda Kin Daf Nari Gorge	Scinde Horse, 1 squadron. Jacobabad Mountain Battery, 2 guns.
Thal Chotiali	Jacobabad Mountain Battery, 2 guns. Scinde Horse, 1 squadron. 15th Bombay Infantry.
Bolan Pass	8th Bombay Infantry, 2 companies. 13th Bombay Infantry, detachment.
Sibi and neighbourhood	Scinde Horse, Head-quarters. 8th Bombay Infantry, 6 companies.

---

[1] The cantonment of Pishin was afterwards built near the old Afghan fortress of Khushdil Khan. Till 1903 a garrison of one native infantry regiment was stationed there. It was never a healthy station, the water being bad, and ceased to be necessary strategically when Loralai and Fort Sandeman were occupied. It lies six miles distant from the railway station of Jam Karez.

Quetta and neighbourhood
- A-4 R. A.
- 15-9 R. A.
- No. 4 company, Bombay Sappers and Miners.
- 13th Hussars.
- Jacob's Horse, Head-quarters.
- 61st Foot.
- 63rd Foot (wing).
- 9th Bombay Infantry (wing).
- 13th Bombay Infantry (wing).

In all an approximate total of 8,000 to 8,500 of all ranks.

APPENDIX B.

Camel Transport in Baluchistan during the 2nd Afghan War.

Early in the Second Afghan War it was recognised that the control of camel transport was very difficult for the Commissariat Department, whose complicated systems were utterly unsuitable for a half wild people.

Sandeman was invited to arrange matters with the tribesmen, and did so with great success. His methods are worthy of note. He insisted on having his own officers, who knew the people and their language, for control, arrangements, and payment. He entirely deprecated attachment to corps.

Four hundred and fifty tons of goods left railhead daily. Payment was made at so much per stage. The camelman at Rindli received a "way bill" from the commissariat official, showing the number of maunds his camel was carrying. At the end of the stage, the official of the same department there signed the "way bill" and took charge of the goods. The camelman forthwith took this receipt to the Political Officer at the post who paid him on the spot. With the prospect of prompt payment at the end of his day's journey, the camelman lost no time on the road, and those in possession of good camels often did double marches.

CHAPTER VIII.

Shirani and Ustarana Tribes.

Shiranis.

THE Shiranis are a tribe of Pathans occupying the principal portion of the mountain known as the Takht-i-Suliman,[1] and the country thence eastward down to the border of the Dera Ismail Khan district. To the north, beyond the Gomal Pass, their neighbours are the Mahsud Wazirs; on the south they march with the Ustaranas and Zmarais;[2] and to the west they are bounded, beyond the watershed of the Takht-i-Suliman, by the Kakars. Between the Takht and our border lie several insignificant ridges, running north and south, in the valleys between which the lowland Shiranis[3] have their villages. Almost all these villages are easily accessible, and within a day's march from one or other of the three chief passes leading into the country, namely, the Zarakni or Shekh Haidar, the Daraban and the Chaudwan. Adjoining each village is a *kach*, or stretch of alluvial soil, irrigated generally by perennial water, and fairly well cultivated. Above the lowland Shiranis are the Bargha Shiranis[4] who occupy the higher slopes of the Takht and the western slopes of the Suliman Range, and lead a pastoral life.

---

[1] The Takht-i-Suliman is held in great reverence, and resorted to as a place of pilgrimage. The shrine is about two miles north of the true Takht or southernmost peak visible from the plains. To approach it the pilgrim has to ascend in one place by the aid of a rope. The legend goes that Solomon visited Hindustan to marry one Balkis, and that, as the happy pair were returning through the air, seated on a throne supported by genii, the weeping bride implored the bridegroom to give her a chance of looking back for a few moments on her beloved land. Solomon assented, and, as they had then very opportunely arrived just over the Takht-i-Suliman, he directed the genii to scoop out a stand for his throne. This was done, and the throne placed upon the stand, and Balkis obtained the glance at the sultry plains below which she so much loved.

It is probable, however, that we must look more to a Hindu than to a Musalman origin for the sanctity of the place. It is noteworthy that, until it became too unsafe, the Takht-i-Suliman was far more visited by Hindus than by Musalmans.

[2] The *Zmarais* are a small and insignificant Pathan tribe. They occupy the whole crest of the Misri Koh (Zmarai ghar) mountain and its western slopes They are not extensive traders in British territory, but at the same time are to a certain extent dependent on this trade for their prosperity.

[3] Largha Shiranis, under Punjab Administration.

[4] Under Zhob Agency.

The Shiranis are divided into three main clans, *viz.*, Chuhar Khel living in the vicinity of the new Zhob Road; the Uba Khel in the country east of the Takht-i-Suliman; the Hasan Khel north of the Uba Khel as far as the Zao. The country of the latter clan really extends to the Shirana Nala, but Wazir raids have caused the northern portion of their territory to be abandoned.

During the summer, the flocks from all three sections are pastured more or less promiscuously on the higher slopes and plateau of the Takht-i-Suliman.

The tribe is divided into those who occupy fixed homesteads and those who are unsettled or nomadic. The former largely outnumber the latter, and may all be regarded as well disposed to the British Government—much more so than their nomadic brethern.

Tribal cohesion among the Shiranis is weak; the different sections have at times endeavoured to escape joint responsibility, with the result that the unruly individuals in the clan have, from time to time, indulged their predatory tastes at the expense of the tribe, and it has repeatedly been necessary to compel the Shiranis to control as a body their individual sections or clansmen.

The Shiranis are generally of middle stature, thin, but hardy and active. They have bold features, high cheek-bones, and their general appearance is wild and manly. Their usual food is bread made of Indian corn and butter. Wheaten bread is only produced at festivals. The flesh principally used is mutton. They eat wild olives fresh from the tree, and dried olives, which they are obliged to boil. They also eat wild pomegranates (though they are very sour and harsh), the seed of the *chalghozah* pine and several sorts of berries which grow wild on their mountains.

The principal employment of the Shiranis is agriculture, which is carried on in the valleys. Some places under the hills produce grain without watering, but all the rest of their lands are irrigated by means of dams thrown across the hill streams. They have two harvests, one of rice, Indian corn, and tobacco. It is sown in summer and reaped in autumn. When it is off the ground, they sow wheat and barley, which is cut in the beginning of summer. Their common stock consists of small, black bullocks. They have a few goats and some donkeys; but no mules, buffaloes, or camels. There are very few horses in the country.

There is a *mulla* in every village, who receives a tithe of the produce of its lands and flocks. A great many of the Shiranis learn to read the *Koran*, although none but *mullas* learn to read Pushtu and none Persian. They are very punctual in their prayers, but apparently have little real devotion.

The Shiranis inhabiting the higher slopes of the mountains live in villages of from twenty to forty houses. They cut out the sites of their houses in the slopes of the hills, so that on three sides the earth forms the lower part of the wall. Each cottage contains but one room, and has only one entrance, which is closed at night with a branch of a thorny tree. Even in winter they have nothing to shut out the cold, but sleep on black carpets round the fire, wrapped up in sheep-skin cloaks. Their forests furnish them with firewood, and their houses are lighted with branches of a particular sort of fir, which burns like a torch. In the valleys bordering on British territory the villages are larger than elsewhere, and Drazand contains a hundred and fifty houses, or more.

Although their chief occupation is agriculture, this tribe carries on an extensive trade in the autumn months in the Dera Ismail Khan district. Numbers of the tribe cultivate land to a considerable extent within British territory, and more than three hundred families are located as cultivators at Musazai, Daraban, and Chaudwan. They are dependent chiefly on their intercourse with British territory for their food supply and cloth goods, in exchange for the produce of their hills.

The Shirani male population, as shown by the census of 1901, is roughly 7,090.

Males in Zhob—3,689—
,, ,, tribal country (Dera Ismail Khan) 2,843.
,, ,, Dera Ismail Khan District 541.

Ustaranas.

The Ustaranas are a Pathan tribe inhabiting the outer hills opposite the extreme south portion of the Dera Ismail Khan district. They are the descendants of one Ustarana, a *Saiyid*, who settled among and married into the Shiranis. They are bounded on the north by the Shiranis, on the south by the Kasranis and Bozdars, and on the west by the Zmarais, Isots, and Musa Khel.

Vol. III.

Until about a century ago the Ustaranas were entirely a pastoral and *Powindah* tribe. But a quarrel with their neighbours, the Musa Khel, put a stop to their annual westward migration, and they were forced to take to agriculture, and subsequently acquired a good deal of the country below the hills. They still own a large tract of hill country, in which most of them live, cultivating land immediately under the hills, and pasturing their flocks beyond the border. Their territory only includes the eastern slopes of the Suliman mountains, the crest of the range being held by the Musa Khel, Isots, and Zmarais.

They are divided into main clans, the Ahmadzai and Gagalzai, and these again into numerous sections. There is a blood-feud of long standing between the Ahmadzais and Gagalzais. The former wear the hair in long ringlets, like the Baluch tribes; the latter wear it short. Their land in the plains is very barren and sandy, and is entirely dependent on rain water for cultivation. Their chief village is Kui Bhara, about three miles beyond the border up the Rammak Pass. It is a fine, well-built village of about 360 houses, and has numerous *chauks* and a few Hindu shops. The Ustaranas are venturesome traders, and take goods to Bengal and Kandahar.

The members of the tribe living beyond British territory are largely engaged in trade, and those within British territory are both agriculturists and traders. Their trade is carried on chiefly with the towns of Chaudwan and Vihoa. This tribe is completely at our mercy, as they own a large tract of country within our territory and their principal villages, though beyond the border, might be destroyed in a day.

The Ustaranas are a fine, manly race; they are quiet and well behaved, and many of them are in our army and police. A few of them are still *Powindahs*. They are all *Suni* Muhammadans. They are constantly at war with their neighbours, the Bozdars, by whom they are much harassed.

On the outbreak of the Sikh Rebellion in 1848, 200 infantry of these Ustaranas, under Fateh Khan, the chief of the Gagalzai clan, followed Lieutenant H. B. Edwardes to Multan. They have always been friendly to us, and have never given any serious trouble. The tribe numbers 2,000 males, of whom 900 live in Shirani territory.

Expedition against the Shiranis by a Force under Brigadier J. S. Hodgson in 1853.

Previous to our annexation of the Punjab, the Shiranis had made themselves the terror of the border. They used to carry off not only cattle, but men and women, whom they never released except for a rich ransom. They once sacked the town of Daraban, although defended by a small Sikh garrison. In 1848 the border was laid waste for miles by their depredations, or deserted through fear of their attacks.

The men of the plains made reprisals, and thus the feud was inflamed. The Shiranis were so much feared that the arable lands skirting the base of the hills were left untilled, and the neighbouring plain villages regularly paid them one-fourth of their produce, to buy off their depredations.

After the annexation, efforts were made by the Deputy Commissioner of Dera Ismail Khan to conciliate them. But from the first they made war on our subjects. In 1849 they attacked a village on the Kulachi border, when one of their leaders was slain.

Again, in 1851, Katal Khan, the Shirani Chief, raided British territory near Daraban. The Shiranis, who had entered the plains during the night, were cut off by a detachment of the 5th Punjab Cavalry and some mounted police, under Jemadar Ghulam Ali Khan. The Shirani Chief and two of his sons and a nephew were slain, and the native officer also lost his life. The third remaining son of Katal Khan after this applied for service in the military police. The application was granted; but the man eventually preferred to remain with his tribe and to plunder in British territory.

In 1852 a large body of Shiranis entered the plains near Daraban and were driven back by a detachment of troops, under Captain R. Fitzgerald, 5th Punjab Cavalry, who was in camp at that place, covering the building of the outposts and the construction of the frontier road. The ground was impracticable for

5th Punjab Cavalry, 84 sabres.
[1] Sind Camel Corps, 73 of all ranks.
Mounted police, a few sabres.

---

[1] The Sind Camel Corps was transferred from the Bombay to the Bengal Presidency in 1849. It consisted at this time, in addition to European officers, of 5 subadars, 5 jemadars, 5 colour-havildars, 25 havildars, 30 naiks, 10 buglers, and 450 sepoys. The camel establishment was 1 jemadar-major, 25 jemadars, 42 duffadars, and 477 sowars. Its designation shortly after this was changed to the Sind Rifle Corps, and it is now the 59th Scinde Rifles.

cavalry. The enemy had seven killed and several wounded. Our loss was one non-commissioned officer of the 5th Punjab Cavalry and one sowar of the mounted police killed.

Besides this attack, the Shiranis made several unsuccessful attempts on Daraban, probably in revenge for the death of Katal Khan.

Major J. Nicholson, who was then Deputy Commissioner of Dera Ismail Khan, wrote in 1853, "the Shiranis have regularly plundered and taken blackmail from this border since it came into our possession."

About the beginning of 1853 the Shiranis attacked and burnt a village of the Dera Ismail Khan district. In February 1853, they again plundered and burnt a village near Daraban. These attacks becoming intolerable, troops were assembled. On the 10th of March a body of Shiranis, aided, it was believed, by the Nasirs (a *Powindah* tribe), numbering 700 foot and 70 horse in all, entered the plains. They were driven back after a long skirmish by the Daraban post, consisting of 35 sabres, 5th Punjab Cavalry,[1] and 47 bayonets of the Sind Camel Corps, under a Native Officer of the 5th Punjab Cavalry, leaving one dead, and having many wounded. Two men of the Sind Camel Corps were wounded.

Owing to their hostile attitude and conduct, a small force was now encamped at Daraban. On the morning of the 14th March intelligence was received that the Shiranis had descended in force into the plains and advanced about two miles from their position in the Drazand Zam to attack a reconnoitring party from the Daraban outpost. Captain F. F. Bruce, Sind Camel Corps, who was commanding at that place, at once marched the troops, detailed in the margin, towards the Drazand Pass, a distance of seven or eight miles. On seeing the approach of this detachment the enemy retreated and took up a strong position some little distance up the pass.

5th Punjab Cavalry, 64 sabres.
Sind Camel Corps (2 British officers, 2 native officers, and 123 bayonets, with their camel establishment).
Mounted police, 5 sabres.

This position was strengthened by a stone breastwork, behind which the greater number were concealed. As the force advanced up the pass, a picquet on the left opened fire, but from too great a

---

[1] Now 25th Cavalry

distance to do any harm. After placing a flanking party on the lower hills Captain Bruce attacked the position. On arriving at the foot of the hill held by the enemy, the breastworks were stormed in gallant style by Ensign C. H. Palliser, Sind Camel Corps, who with his men, dashed up in the most daring manner, carrying all before them, and killing and wounding numbers of the enemy.

Among the killed were three chiefs and Mulla Gundah Khan, whose advice carried much weight among the Shiranis. The enemy was dislodged at the point of the bayonet, leaving five dead within their entrenchment, and fled in confusion over the hills. Their exact strength could not be ascertained, but, from the heavy matchlock fire kept up, their numbers must have been considerable. The detachment returned to Daraban without molestation.

Our loss in this affair was 5 killed and 17 wounded, but owing to the strength of the enemy's position this was to be expected. The enemy's loss was subsequently ascertained to have been seventeen killed and thirty-nine wounded.

After this affair it was resolved to follow the Shiranis into their own hills, and punish them severely. Orders were accordingly issued, and a force of 2,795 of all ranks, under Brigadier J. S. Hodgson, commanding the Punjab Irregular Force, was assembled at Daraban[1] on the morning of the 30th of March. No time was lost in arranging for an immediate advance. The 5th Punjab Cavalry had been sent out to the frontier previously, with orders to patrol day and night in front of the Shirani country, to prevent the enemy having any knowledge of our movements.

No. 2, Punjab Light Field Battery.
Detachment, Garrison Artillery.
5th Punjab Cavalry.
Sind Camel Corps.
Wing, 1st Punjab Infantry.
Wing, 3rd Punjab Infantry.
2nd Police Battalion.
6th Police Battalion.

The cavalry and artillery were to make their own arrangements for the carriage of grain for three days. The supplies for the men of the infantry regiments, etc., were carried under arrangements made by the civil officers, regimental *bazar* establishments being employed for issue. No camp followers except those absolutely necessary were to accompany the column One camel and one servant was allowed for every two officers

---
[1] See map accompanying Chapter XVIII.

The fighting strength of the Shirani tribe was at this time believed to be from four to five thousand men,[1] and it became a matter of serious importance to divide and distract it by threatening several passes at the same time, and occupying the attention of those collected to the southward, while arrangements were made to enter the country by the Shekh Haidar Pass, some twelve miles to the north of the Drazand Zam. This was successfully accomplished by encamping the whole force on the 30th opposite the Drazand Pass, and making demonstrations before it and the Chaudwan Pass, twelve miles to the south, where a body of the enemy had collected to oppose our entrance.

At midnight on the 30th Brigadier Hodgson moved on the Shekh Haidar Pass, leaving the camp standing, under Ensign W. H. Paget, with a detachment of the 5th Punjab Cavalry, and of the 2nd Police Battalion, with guards from the different regiments. The column entered the pass a little after daybreak on the 31st March. The heights on either side of the defile were at once crowned by four companies of the 1st Punjab Infantry, without opposition, and the column then advanced. Wherever the route of the column was commanded by heights, they were immediately crowned by infantry. Adopting these precautions, the force steadily progressed and reached the village of Drazand, unmolested, at 5 P.M. The village was found to be deserted, and was taken possession of, the troops bivouacking in its neighbourhood

Shortly after leaving Drazand heavy rain fell, continuing for five hours, and it was doubtful at one time if the troops could move up the pass on account of the torrent. Great difficulties were encountered, and the whole march, a distance of twenty-five miles, took seventeen hours to accomplish; if the enemy had offered any opposition much loss must have occurred. The absence of opposition can only be accounted for on the supposition that the enemy expected the force to enter by the Drazand or by the Chaudwan Pass, and were thus unprepared to oppose the entrance so much to the north. To conceal our intentions to the last, a demonstration in front of the Drazand Zam had been made at daylight on the 31st.

---

[1] The whole male population is only 7,000, so that the fighting strength was probably not more than 1,500 men.

Drazand was found to be very strong, surrounded by a breastwork, defended by eleven towers, and containing 300 substantial houses, which gave shelter to 1,200 inhabitants.

The following day, the 1st of April, the 3rd Punjab Infantry moved to the Drazand Pass to hold it, and to improve the road for the passage of artillery as well as to open communications with Daraban. At the same time the troops were employed in destroying the Shirani villages within a circumference of eight miles of Drazand, strict injunctions being given to respect women and children and all mosques and shrines.

1st Column.

5th Punjab Cavalry	.. 20 sabres.
Sind Camel Corps ..	.. 100 bayonets.
1st Punjab Infantry	.. 100 ,,
6th Police Battalion	.. 200 ,,

2nd Column.

6th Police Battalion	.. 100 bayonets.

3rd Column.

4th and 5th Punjab Cavalry,	20 sabres.
1st Punjab Infantry	.. 100 bayonets.
6th Police Battalion	.. 100 ,,

The first column under Captain F. F. Bruce, Sind Camel Corps, destroyed the villages of Wazir Kot, Murga, and the hamlets of Landai.

The second column, under Lieutenant J. W. Younghusband, of the Police, demolished the village of Zar Shahr.

The third column, under the command of the Brigadier, destroyed Dag, situated to the south of Drazand.

These detachments rejoined the main column at Drazand before nightfall, when a report was received that the road over the Drazand Pass had been rendered practicable for guns. This, besides opening communications direct with the Daraban post, ensured an easy and safe return for the force.

At 5 A.M. on the 2nd April Brigadier Hodgson proceeded in command of the troops, detailed in the margin, to destroy the villages to the extreme south of the Shirani country and situated

5th Punjab Cavalry	.. 100 sabres.
Sind Camel Corps ..	.. 100 bayonets.
1st Punjab Infantry	.. 300 ,,
6th Police Battalion	.. 410 ,,

to the westward of the Chaudwan Pass. The column arrived on the crest of the ridge, facing Landi, the village and stronghold of Rahmat Khan, a Shirani Chief, about 9 A.M. This was immediately taken possession of by a detachment of the Sind Camel Corps, and set on fire.

Detachments under the command, respectively, of Lieutenants C. P. Keyes and E. J. Travers, 1st Punjab Infantry, and Akbar

Shah, 6th Police Battalion, were directed upon the villages of Spin Tangi, China, and Shekh Mela, which were taken with scarcely any opposition, and entirely destroyed. Small parties of the enemy fired long shots. As the troops retired, they attempted to harass the column, but were held in check by the rearguard, under Lieutenant Keyes, and suffered some loss without inflicting any on the troops. The column arrived at Drazand before nightfall, having marched two and twenty miles during the day.

Simultaneously with these operations, one hundred and fifty men, all of the Babar[1] tribe, and British subjects, under their chiefs Dado and Muhammad Gul, entered the Chaudwan Pass, and, by direction of the Deputy Commissioner, co-operated by destroying the village of Saidal, situated about eight miles within the pass. They bivouacked that night within the Shirani country, and the next morning returned to Chaudwan.

During the 2nd the troops left at Drazand had mined and blown up the towers, and, with the exception of one solitary building (a mosque), had razed the village to the ground. The following day the troops returned to Daraban by the pass of that name, and, although a few of the enemy showed themselves, not a shot was fired.

Although the force had been three days in the enemy's country it returned after having accomplished the object of the expedition without the loss of a single soldier or camp follower. Although the Shiranis had time to drive their herds into the interior before the approach of the troops, and no captures were made, the punishment of the tribe was complete; their country had been overrun, and their principal villages destroyed. The extraordinary absence of all opposition was attributed by Major Nicholson to a jealousy between the northern and southern divisions of the tribe, which prevented combination.

---

[1] The *Babars* are a tribe of Shirani stock, though now quite separate from the Shiranis proper. They are divided into two sections, one living wholly within our border, the other holding the hill country opposite, but on the other side of the Suliman range. The two have now little connection with each other. The Babars of the plain hold some 180 square miles in the Dera Ismail Khan district, Chaudwan being their chief town. They are a civilised tribe, much addicted to commerce, being one of the richest, quietest and most honest tribes of the sub-Suliman plains. They number about 500 men fit for army service, a few of them serve in the cavalry. Their language is Pushtu.

The Indian medal, with a clasp for the "North-West Frontier,"
was granted in 1869 to all survivors of the troops engagd in the operations against the Shiranis under Brigadier J. S. Hodgson.

G. G. O. No. 812 of 1869.

After this expedition, the conduct of the Shiranis occasioned comparatively little trouble and Katal Khan's son Azim became anxious to ingratiate himself with the Government.

Conduct of the Shiranis from 1853 to 1882.

He undertook to prevent any small expeditions being organised in his portion of the tribe, and not to allow any marauders to pass through his country. On one occasion he joined in the pursuit of a party of raiders who had carried off cattle near Chaudwan and assisted in recovering the booty.

The Shirani tribe, however, continued systematically to give shelter to criminal refugees from British territory, and, although professing to be on friendly terms with the Government, allowed these outlaws, together with bad characters of their own tribe, to commit depredations on British territory, and more especially on the Gandapur[1] border.

In the early part of 1873, the Gandapur Chief, Muhammad Guldad Khan, was called upon by the Government to act up to his border responsibilities, and was informed that the Government would look to him for their fulfilment in future. This chief succeeded in bringing such influence to bear on one of the branches of the Shiranis, the Sen Khel, that they went in force and brought back from the Khidarzais, a small but troublesome section of the Uba Khel branch, three Hindus who had been kidnapped from British territory by outlaws and carried off to the Shirani hills.

Efforts were at the same time made to break up the band of outlaws, the leaders of which were principally Gandapurs. These efforts were successful, and the headman of this band surrendered unconditionally to the Deputy Commissioner, and was fined Rs. 3,000. The party opposed to the Gandapur Chief were, however, making secret but strenuous efforts to keep up the old state of

---

[1] The *Gandapurs* are a *Saiyid* tribe of Ustarana stock settled in British territory. They hold the whole of the north-western part of trans-Indus, Dera Ismail Khan, east and south of Tank, comprising an area of 460 square miles abutting on the Suliman range on the west. The town of Kulachi is their head-quarters. They were originally a poor *Powindah* and pastoral tribe, but they now cultivate more extensively than any of the other Dera Ismail Khan tribes. They still engage in the *Powindah* traffic.

Vol. III.

excitement on this border. As members of both the Sen Khel and Uba Khel Shiranis had openly violated British territory, it became necessary to enforce the principle that it is by means of the majority of the tribe that visit the plains that the plundering minority in the hills is controlled by Government. Accordingly, in September, 1874, a large Sen Khel convoy was seized at Kulachi, and fifty-four members of this branch were taken prisoners and lodged in the jail at Dera Ismail Khan. The value of their convoy amounted to Rs. 3,000. At the same time seventeen Uba Khel with their property were seized at Daraban, and lodged in the jail at Dera.

The *jirgas* of the two branches came in at once, and soon came to terms. A fine of Rs. 1,500 was imposed on the Sen Khel for the abduction of a Hindu child from Kulachi, and the Uba Khel were fined Rs. 1,000 for the Daraban crime. Both branches were required to acknowledge their responsibility in future for all crimes committed in British territory by members of their tribe, or by anyone dwelling in their hills. The Uba Khel especially undertook to be responsible for the future good conduct of the Khidarzai section of their branch. This agreement was ratified on the 11th of November 1874, in the presence of the *jirgas* of both branches of the tribe.

In March 1875, the Gandapur Chief, Muhammad Guldad Khan, taking advantage of the confidence reposed in him by the British authorities, to prosecute schemes of his own within the Shirani hills, endeavoured to erect a fort in Shirani territory and annex lands. His misconduct brought down upon his dependents, thus employed, a grievous retaliation and the loss of fifteen lives. The Shiranis in a large body attacked the Gandapur workmen at daybreak on the 22nd of March 1875, and prevented any further prosecution of Muhammad Guldad Khan's unauthorised projects. Severe punishment followed in the deposition of the chief, in pecuniary reparation to the families of the slain from his allowances, and in the suspension of several native officials in Government employ who neglected to report, or secretly connived at, the chief's reckless schemings. In consequence of the unfriendly attitude of the Shiranis in this affair, more especially in not having informed the Deputy Commissioner of the state of things before taking the law into their own hands, the tribe was prohibited from entering British territory. No attempt was made by them to molest

the border in retaliation, and in December 1875, it was considered that the tribe, which had acted under grave provocation, had been sufficiently punished, and they were accordingly re-admitted to friendly relations with Government.

From 1875 to 1882 the behaviour of the Shiranis continued good, and they gave no trouble on our border. Throughout the year 1882, however, their conduct was not so satisfactory. During that year, men belonging to the tribe committed numerous offences against British subjects, principally acts of the normal character of border crime, such as thefts, and robberies of cattle. More serious misdeeds were the murder of a Hindu woman and the mischievous destruction of a water-mill and an irrigation dam. In October 1882, the account for compensation due from the tribe, after deducting the value of the property recovered, amounted to Rs. 2,265. A settlement of the account was demanded in that month; the Sen Khel and Uba Khel met the demand by professions of inability to coerce the offenders, while the Chuhar Khel section refused to send their representatives to confer with the British authorities. The only course was, therefore, to put pressure on the tribe.

Accordingly, a blockade was declared from the 1st of January 1883. Simultaneously the military frontier post of Daraban was slightly strengthened, and the post at Shah Alam, situated half-way between Daraban and the large village of Chaudwan, and hitherto held by border police and militia, was occupied by regular troops. Their exclusion from British territory, and deprivation of trade with the Dera Ismail Khan district, soon began to be felt by the Shiranis, who throughout the six months of the blockade, with few exceptions, refrained from retaliatory incursions, and bore their punishment quietly. The Commissioner had been authorised to accept the submission of the tribe on the basis of payment of the compensation due at the date of submission, and of unreserved acceptance of full and joint tribal responsibility; the compensation payable was the sum due on the date of the imposition of the blockade, and such additional compensation as accrued for offences committed during the time the tribe was excluded from British territory. As the main object of coercive measures was to enforce and signalise tribal responsibility, the Lieutenant-Governor considered that a fine, in

addition to compensation for past offences, was unnecessary, provided the purpose of the blockade was attained.

On the 15th July, 1883, the Shirani *jirga* came into Dera Ismail Khan. They agreed in writing to the following conditions:—

- *1st.* To pay Rs. 2,530-3-0 due on account of compensation for offences committed by the tribe. Any stolen property that could be produced to be handed over in lieu of so much of this sum as represented its value.
- *2nd.* To repair the Chaudwan dam and the water-mill which were burnt and destroyed by the tribe.
- *3rd.* As regards future offences, to restore the property stolen, or to point out the offenders or the property when they came down to the plains, and make them over to Government within three months from the date of the offence.
- *4th.* To expel outlaws who, having committed offences in British territory, sought refuge in the Shirani country.
- *5th.* To accept the principle of joint responsibility in such matters.

The terms were considered to satisfy the requirements of Government; the blockade was raised, and the tribe again admitted into friendly relations.

Survey expedition to the Takht-i-Suliman mountain in 1883.

The desirability of exploring and surveying the Takht-i-Suliman mountain had long been recognised by the British Government, and as far back as 1877 it was recorded that the Governor-General in Council was prepared to sanction its exploration whenever the local authorities might consider that this could be effected without undue risk.

In 1882 the Surveyor-General of India represented to the Punjab Government the desirability of an officer of the Survey Department being permitted to visit this country for the purpose of taking observations, urging that the summit of the peaks of the Takht commanded a view of the country to the west for a very considerable distance up to the hill range in the vicinity of the road from Quetta to Kandahar, and stating that very little was known of the country, which was usually represented in the latest and best maps of Afghanistan as a *terra incognita.*

The Government of the Punjab, in reply, intimated that if the expedition could be undertaken with reasonable safety, it would be

sanctioned; and Major Holdich, in communication with the Deputy Commissioner of Dera Ismail Khan, submitted proposals, approved by the Commissioner of the Derajat, but, owing to the Shirani tribe being then under blockade, it was considered desirable to postpone the expedition until matters were settled with the tribe.

After the submission of the Shiranis, the question of the exploration of the Takht was again considered, and the Lieutenant-Governor strongly recommended that the expedition should be carried out on two conditions—

> 1*st*. That the tribe should give their consent.
> 2*nd*. That they should give hostages for maintaining a quiet attitude while the exploration was being carried out.

Troops with the Expedition.

The Lieutenant-Governor considered that, in order to provide against possible contingencies, a strong body of troops should go with the expedition, an escort from which should accompany the surveyors, a considerable reserve being detained at the foot of the hills. The strength of this force was one mountain battery, 1,500 bayonets, and 100 sabres (if fodder was plentiful). The best time of the year for the expedition was considered to be from the 15th of October to the 15th of November, as there would be less fear of snow than at a later date.

These recommendations and proposals were sanctioned by Government, but it was not until the middle of November that the force was ready to enter the hills. It was decided to adopt the more circuitous route by the Shekh Haidar Pass, in preference to the direct road by the Daraban Zam, and to make the ascent of the Takht-i-Suliman from its western base by a pathway up a spur known as the Pazai path. This route presented only one known difficulty, at a point where the Zao Pass was partially blocked by a great fallen rock. *Powindah* camels surmounted this obstacle annually, and the route was said to be practicable for laden hill camels. The civil authorities had succeeded in making satisfactory arrangements with the Shiranis, who had given hostages, as demanded, for the quiet behaviour of the tribe during the expedition. The only section which had failed to attend when summoned was the Khidarzai.

This troublesome section belongs properly to the Uba Khel branch of the tribe, but they are located among the Chuhar Khel, and are practically more connected with them than with the former.

Of the hostages given (one hundred in number) half were to remain at Daraban and the other half were to be with the expeditionary force.

On the 15th of November the troops to accompany the survey party marched from Dera Ismail Khan and reached Daraban in three marches. On the 18th the force, strength as per margin, under Brigadier-General T. G. Kennedy, C.B., crossed the frontier and encamped at Kot Guldad (see Map No. II in pocket). Mr. S. S. Thorburn, C.S., the Deputy Commissioner of Dera Ismail Khan, was Political Officer and Major T. H. Holdich, Royal Engineers, was in charge of the survey operations. The expedition was equipped with mule transport only, but fifteen days' supplies were carried from Daraban on hill camels[1] hired from *Powindahs* of the Nasir tribe.

No. 4 (Hazara) Mountain Battery.
1st Punjab Cavalry, 42 sabres.
1st Sikh Infantry, 500 bayonets.
4th Punjab Infantry, 500 bayonets.
5th Punjab Infantry, 496 bayonets.

On the 19th the force marched to Gandari Kach, seventeen miles beyond our border at the eastern end of the Zao Pass, in which was the obstruction already referred to. The following day was spent in making the road through the pass, which was found to be more formidable than had been expected. The Dabarra rock appeared at first an almost insurmountable obstacle, but before nightfall the road had been made practicable for mules, but it took the whole of the following day to get the laden camels through; most of them had to be unloaded and reloaded on either side of the rock.[2] On the 22nd the force moved through the defile, which is four miles long, and encamped at its further or western end, and the following day marched fourteen miles to Kach Mazrai. Here it was reported that there would probably be opposition at the Pezai Kotal, and that a body of Shiranis, about 300 in number,

---

[1] These camels were well adapted for this kind of work. Mr. Thorburn says that they went over the bad ground like goats. [2] The difficulty here experienced was due chiefly to the large space (nearly eight feet) required by the camels loaded with uncompressed *bhusa*. For a hill expedition where narrow defiles have to be passed, compressed *bhusa* only should be carried. *Bhusa* is chopped straw of wheat or barley.

composed chiefly of Khidarzais, had assembled to dispute the passage.

On the 24th the column moved to Wazdana, and next day reached the Pezai springs, situated about midway between the plain to the west of the Takht and a *kotal* [1] of the range, at the north end of which is the Kaisarghar, the highest peak of the Takht-i-Suliman range. This *kotal*, over which the road to the Takht lay, was found to be held, and to be a formidable position. The following dispositions were made to dislodge the enemy. A flank attack under Colonel H. C. P. Rice, 1st Sikhs, with 540 bayonets, was ordered to leave camp at 2-30 A. M. on the 26th, to turn the enemy's left, and a front attack, under Colonel C. S. Maclean, C.B., 1st Punjab Cavalry, with 4 guns and 540 bayonets, was to leave camp at 6 A.M. The reserve of both attacks, 160 bayonets, under Major C. K. Mackinnon, 5th Punjab Infantry, was to remain with the Brigadier-General in camp, from which both attacks would be to a great extent visible.

Affair near Pezai springs.

1st Sikh Infantry	.. 180 bayonets
4th Punjab Infantry	.. 180 ,,
5th Punjab Infantry	.. 180 ,,
Hazara Mountain Battery.	
1st Sikh Infantry ..	.. 180 bayonets.
4th Punjab Infantry	.. 180 ,,
5th Punjab Infantry	.. 180 ,,

These operations were carried out on the 26th of November. The turning movement, extending over a circuit of about six miles, was admirably executed by Colonel Rice. The front attack carried the advanced positions of the enemy after slight opposition, and, as their last and almost inaccessible position was reached, Colonel Rice appeared on the heights above and on the left rear of it. The enemy at once abandoned the position and the front attack pushing through it, the *kotal* was taken. The enemy was followed up in different directions by both columns until nothing more could be seen of them, and then Colonel Maclean returned to bivouac at the *kotal*, Colonel Rice retiring to the camp. The only casualties on our side were two men of the 4th Punjab Infantry slightly wounded. The enemy were said to have numbered between 300 and 400, and their loss was estimated at about fifteen killed and wounded, among the former being two Khidarzai Chiefs of note.

From the *kotal* Colonel Maclean with his column was entrusted with the actual escort of the survey operations. The remainder

---

[1] By *Kotal* is generally meant the saddle of a ridge over which a road passes.

of the troops were in reserve in camp at the Pezai springs, and a picquet for the protection of the road was placed half-way between the two positions, and was visible from both.

The height of the camp at Pezai was 5,750 feet, and of the bivouac on the *kotal*, which was three miles distant, 8,600 feet. The ascent was steep, and the last part of it very rough. The upper position was dependent on the camp for its water supply which was sent up on mules.

The mountain known as the Takht-i-Suliman was found to consist of two parallel ridges, running roughly north and south, the southern end of the eastern ridge culminating in a point 11,070 feet high, which is the Takht proper, and the western ridge culminating at its northern end in a point 11,300 feet, known as Kaisarghar. Between these two ridges is the *maidan*, a level tableland about 9,000 feet above the level of the sea. Both this *maidan* and the interior slopes of the ridge are, except where too precipitous, covered with pine forests. As the mountain is of hard limestone formation, the soil is not retentive of moisture, and owing to this, and to a long continued drought, no water could be discovered, which added very greatly to the difficulties of the survey, as all water had to be brought up from the camp at Pezai.

On the 27th a reconnaissance towards the northern peak (the Kaisarghar) was made, and proved the road to be impracticable for mules, so that all requirements for any advance beyond the *kotal* had to be carried by men.

Major Holdich decided that it would be sufficient for the survey party to ascend the northern peak only, as the fixed survey point on the Takht proper was inaccessible, and a good substitute for that point could be found without ascending that peak.

On the 28th November, leaving 100 bayonets to hold the Pezai *kotal*, a detachment of 200 bayonets for the ascent of the northern peak, carrying one day's food and water, and a second party of 200 men, carrying another day's food and water for their comrades, moved out seven miles towards the northern peak and bivouacked there, the carriers returning to camp.

On the 29th the advanced party marched four miles, and then climbing 2,300 feet, crowned the northern peak, and—the survey therefrom completed—returned and bivouacked at its foot.

On the following day this party returned to the camp, Colonel Maclean remaining at the *kotal* to organise a further survey escort for the neighbouring heights from a fresh detachment of 200 bayonets of the 5th Punjab Infantry.

On the 1st of December, the whole of the survey requirements having been satisfied during the day, the troops returned to the camp at Pezai by sunset. During this day reports were received that reinforcements were being sent to the hostile Shiranis by the Kakar and Mandu Khel tribes, and accordingly the 4th Punjab Infantry, under Major A. J. D. Hawes, was detached to meet a convoy of four days' supplies then on its way, with orders to remain at Kach Mazrai until the arrival of the rest of the troops on the following day. By that time it was reported that the reinforcements had dispersed, hearing that the Shiranis themselves were no longer opposing us.

On the 2nd of December the return march was commenced, and on the 6th the frontier was re-crossed. It was necessary for the force to return by the same route as it advanced, to meet the additional supplies which had been sent out, as owing to the advance having been delayed at the Zao Pass, the fifteen days' supplies taken had been exhausted. On the 8th the force arrived at Dera Ismail Khan, and was at once broken up, and thus ended a very successful, but extremely arduous, expedition.

APPENDIX.

Composition of the force employed in the operations against the Shiranis in 1853.

Brigadier J. S. Hodgson commanding.

Staff.

Captain W. R. Prout, Staff Officer.

Artillery.

No. 2 Punjab Light Field Battery, Captain H. Hammond commanding.
Detachment, Garrison Artillery, Lieutenant S. W. Stokes commanding.

Cavalry.

5th Punjab Cavalry, Lieutenant H. Bruce commanding.

Infantry.

Sind Camel Corps, Captain F. F. Bruce commanding.
Wing, 1st Punjab Infantry, Lieutenant C. P. Keyes commanding.
Wing, 3rd Punjab Infantry, Lieutenant B. Henderson commanding.
2nd and 6th Police Battalion, Lieutenant J. W. Younghusband commanding.

Political Officers.

Major J. Nicholson, Deputy Commissioner.
Lieutenant A. L. Busk, Assistant Commissioner.

Detail of troops.

Corps.	British Officers.	Native Officers.	Non-Commissioned Officers.	Rank and file.	Total number of fighting men.	9-pr. guns.	24-pr. howitzers.	REMARKS.
Staff	3	..	..	..	3	..	..	
No. 2 Punjab Light Field Battery	1	2	5	48	56	2	1	
Detachment, Garrison Artillery	..	1	1	12	14	..	..	
5th Punjab Cavalry	1	8	14	98	121	..	..	
Sind Camel Corps	3	6	81	573	663	..	..	
Wing, 1st Punjab Infantry	2	8	47	374	431	..	..	
Wing, 3rd Punjab Infantry	2	7	48	386	443	..	..	
3rd Police Battalion	1	11	40	308	360	..	..	
6th Police Battalion	..	18	70	603	691	..	..	
Brigadier's escort, 4th Punjab Cavalry	..	1	2	10	13	..	..	
Total	13	62	308	2,412	2,795	2	1	

CHAPTER IX.

ZHOB AND BORI.

Zhob District. Zhob, situated in the north-east corner of Baluchistan, has an area of 9,626 square miles. The greater part of the country is mountainous, but it is intersected on the southern side by the Zhob Valley and on the north by the valley of the Kundar and its tributaries.

Jogizai Family. In the middle of the 18th century Ahmad Shah conferred the title of "Ruler of Zhob" on the head of the Jogizai family of Kakars, in which the principal authority has continued up to this day.

There is no organisation among the tribes in Zhob which can be called in any sense military. They are all badly armed, and with the exception of the *maliks*, who own a few Martini or Snider rifles, there is not a rifle among them. The majority are armed with swords and an occasional *jezail* is seen. There has never been any combination amongst the tribes as a whole, partly owing to the vast area of Zhob, and chiefly to there being no man who could rally a sufficiently large number to form a really formidable opposition. History shows how few opposed us when Zhob was first taken over by the British Government, in comparison with the strength of the people as revealed in the last census. This lack of organisation enables us to hold so large a tract of country with so few soldiers. The large trade in rifles, which are smuggled into Afghanistan from the Persian Gulf, has not as yet touched Zhob. It is doubtful whether they could afford to buy such weapons. Certainly ammunition would be the difficulty if they did get rifles, as it is very scarce and, when procured, is used up at once in *shikar*.

Before the British took over the district, the different tribes raided each other continually. But this has practically ceased, and cultivation has increased accordingly. There are, however, certain points to be considered in case we should ever be in

difficulties in Afghanistan or driven back on our own defences. The Kakar does not love the British but puts up with us, as he is powerless to do otherwise, but were he to get an opening by which he could harass us in the time of adversity he would certainly take the opportunity. Roads would become unsafe, convoys looted, and *tahsils* burnt. A powerful invader might use the route from Kandahar or Ghazni through Zhob to turn our defences at Quetta. He would be sure of assistance from the inhabitants.

In the " Military Report on Zhob, 1906 " Colonel Jacob states that the Kakars would make good material for the ranks of the Indian Army. His opinion of the Shiranis and Mando Khel is the poorest.

From the outbreak of the Afghan War in 1878, when the attitude of the Kakars of Zhob first became a matter of any importance to us, to the year 1884, the chief authority over them and over the Kakars of the Bori Valley and the adjoining districts of Kach and Khawas was exercised by the Jogizai Family of Zhob Kakars. The most notable member of this family was Shah Jahan, and in his hands rested almost the whole power, though his cousin, Dost Muhammad, constantly endeavoured to head a separate faction. Shah Jahan, by means of his natural strength of character and reputation as a *fakir* and miracle worker, not only obtained the chief authority over all the numerous sections of the Sanzar Khel Kakars, but succeeded in extending his influence among the Sanatia Kakar tribes, such as the Sarangzais and Panezais, so that he could count on their support in any line of policy he adopted.

1878.

Shah Jahan.

It became known very early in the course of the Afghan War that Shah Jahan was hostile towards the British, and would give trouble on our line of communications when opportunity offered. This was proved by the occasional opposition of small bands of Pathans to the first of the columns ordered to return to India by the Thal Chotiali route in 1879, culminating in the action at Baghao, already described.[1]

1879.

---
[1] See page 153.

The murder of the British envoy at Kabul, however, and the abdication of Yakub Khan gave rise to further excitement among the Kakars, and, early in 1880, Captain Showers, Superintendent of Levies, was murdered on the Uzdapagha Pass, the perpetrators belonging to the Panizai section of Sanatias.[1] Some 200 Pathans also attacked and looted the camp of Lieutenant Fuller.[2] This was followed in the autumn of the same year by an attack on the military post at Kach by Zhobis, Sarangzais, and Panizais, instigated by Shah Jahan, in which they were defeated.

1880.

The termination of the Afghan War brought the district of Thal Chotiali under our rule in accordance with the terms of the Gandamak Treaty with Amir Yakub Khan. But as this part of the country was only separated from the Bori Valley by a low range of hills, Shah Jahan and his Bori friends, the Hamzazais, Utman Khel, Kibzais, etc., found it easy to harass the district by outrages on employés of the Government. A series of these outrages ensued, culminating in the attack upon a large number of coolies employed in building at Duki. It was felt that the frontier could never be safe and the railway and the other works never free from danger until Shah Jahan was finally settled with and hostages taken from him for his and the Boriwals' future good behaviour. The matter was referred to Government and sanction obtained to the despatch of a military expedition into Zhob against Shah Jahan. The news of the proposed advance caused a great sensation amongst the people of Zhob, and several of them contemplated making their submission to Sir Robert Sandeman. Dost Muhammad, who was not on good terms with Shah Jahan, is said to have actually started from his house with this object, but was pursued and brought back by Shah Jahan's orders.

1881-84.

THE ZHOB VALLEY EXPEDITION, 1884.

In April, 1884, orders were issued for the movement of troops into the Zhob Valley. At that time the difficulties of procuring food and carriage in the country through which the troops would have to pass were such that it was decided to postpone the expedition until autumn.

---

[1] See page 136.
[2] See page 137.

On the 4th October, 1884, a force, as per margin, had assembled about Thal Chotiali ready to cross the frontier under command of Brigadier-General Sir O. V. Tanner, K.C.B. Two months' supplies of all kinds had been collected by the Commissariat at Thal Chotiali. An advanced force, composed of one squadron, 1st Bombay Lancers,[1] six companies, 2nd Bombay Native Infantry,[2] two companies, Bombay Sappers and Miners, had marched on the 26th from Thal Chotiali to Smalan, where they halted until the arrival of the head-quarters of the force. One squadron, 10th Bengal Lancers, and the 1st Bengal Infantry moved up to Smalan on the 30th in order to watch the pass leading past Trigunis to Kats and Shah Jahan during the passage of the convoy and baggage train.

ARTILLERY.
9-1st Northern Division, R.A. (Mountain Battery) (Lieutenant-Colonel Graham) .. 6 guns.
No. 1 Mountain Battery (Native) Bombay (Captain Keene) 4 guns.

CAVALRY.
5th Punjab Cavalry, Squadron (Major Carr) .. .. 185 sabres.
10th Bengal Lancers, Squadron (Lieut.-Colonel O. Barnes) 161 „
1st Bombay Lancers, Squadron (Major Heyland).. .. 215 „

INFANTRY.
1st Worcestershire Regiment (29th) (Lt.-Col. Douglas) 325 bayonets
2nd North Staffordshire Regt. (98th) (Colonel Simpson) 550 „
1st North Lancashire Regiment, wing (Lieut.-Colonel North) 358 „
Nos. 4 and 10 Companies, Bengal S. and M. (Captain Collie and Lieutenant Maxwell) .. 207 „
4th Punjab Infantry (Major Hawes) .. .. 700 „
45th Sikhs (Colonel Armstrong) 696 „
1st Bengal N. I. (Lieutenant-Colonel Atkins) .. .. 671 „
2nd Bombay N. I. (Lieutenant-Colonel James) .. .. 551 „
Detachment, 1st Madras Pioneers (Lieutenant-Colonel Eyre) 164 „

TOTAL .. { 10 guns.
561 sabres.
4,220 bayonets.

STAFF.
Major Gaselee, A.Q.M.G.
Captain Walker, D.A.A.G.
Lieutenant Chase, V.C., D.A.Q.M.G.
Brigade-Surgeon Bradshaw, P. M. O.
Major Tomkins, R. E., Commanding Royal Engineer.
Lieut O'Donnel, Intelligence Officer.

On the 5th October the force detailed in the margin, under the command of Lieutenant-Colonel Barnes, 10th Bengal Lancers, was despatched to Anambar with orders to reconnoitre through the Anambar Pass into Bori, and to make the road practicable for the march of troops. This force arrived at Lakhi on the 6th, and on the 7th Lieut.-Colonel Barrow, with

No. 1 Mountain Battery.
1 Squadron, 1st Bombay Lancers.
2 Companies, Bengal Sappers.
4th Punjab Infantry.
1 Squadron, 1st Bombay Lancers.
2nd Bombay Native Infantry.

---
[1] 31st Lancers.
[2] 102nd Grenadiers.

50 sowars, 10th Bengal Lancers, 50 sowars, 1st Bombay Lancers, and 50 rifles, 4th Punjab Infantry, reconnoitred through the Anambar Pass up the right bank of the river, to the villages of Anambar. The infantry had been left to hold the *kotal* while the cavalry proceeded up the valley. The *maliks* of the neighbouring villages went out to meet the cavalry and announced their intention of coming in to pay their respects to the British Government and promised to supply grain and flour. The reconnoitring force returned the same day to Lakhi.

Heliographic communication was established between Duki and Lakhi, and on the 8th, Colonel Barnes, leaving the 2nd Bombay Infantry at Lakhi, marched with the remainder of the advanced force to Anambar.

On the 9th Major Shepherd, 4th Punjab Infantry, made a reconnaissance towards Nalai, and on the same day Major Gaselee, 4th Punjab Infantry, reconnoitred as far as Lahor in the Bori valley. Three hundred loads of grain and flour were sent in from the village of Sanatia.

On the 11th the Brigadier-General arrived at Anambar with—

> 9-1 Royal Artillery.
> 5th Punjab Cavalry.
> 2nd Bo. (Grenadiers) N. I.

The 2nd North Staffordshire Regiment, 45th Sikhs, and detachment of Madras Pioneers had been left at Lakhi.

On the 10th October Sir Robert Sandeman received the whole of the Bori Chiefs in public durbar at the entrance of the Bori Valley. They made full submission, and were informed that they must pay compensation for the losses caused by them and give hostages for the security of the country; on which condition the terms of the proclamation would be extended to them. The only tribes not represented at the durbar were the Musa Khel, Kibzai, and Zhob.

It was now decided before marching into Zhob to form a standing camp in Bori, to protect the Duki cantonment, and prevent any risk of disturbances arising in rear of the expedition. From this camp as a base, flying columns were to be sent against

the refractory tribes. Accordingly on the 12th October the headquarters of the force, with—

>9-1 Royal Artillery,
>1 Squadron, 5th Punjab Cavalry,
>1 Squadron, 1st Bombay Lancers,
>2nd Bombay Native Infantry,
>Nos. 4 and 10 Companies, Bengal Sappers,

marched to Dulai, between which place and Lahor a standing camp had previously been determined on, water being good and supplies procurable.

It had been intended to move on the Kibzai and Musa Khel tribes before marching into Zhob, in order to prevent their joining Shah Jahan and perhaps affording him a place of refuge in their country. Shah Jahan, however, accepted the Government terms, and announced his intention of joining the camp of the Political Officer and making full submission. The Kibzai and Musa Khel tribes were also expected to submit. In consideration of this change in the aspect of affairs, Sir Robert Sandeman gave his concurrence to Brigadier-General Sir O. V. Tanner's proposal of marching direct for the head-quarters of Shah Jahan. The Brigadier-General considered it advisable to reach the main object of the expedition whilst the troops and transport animals were fresh.

On the 15th October the force at Lakhi was moved to Anambar, and the sick and spare ammunition were sent on to camp Dulai. A reconnaissance was made up the Torkhezi and Marai Passes and a post was formed at Sinjawi, on the line of communication with Duki, and garrisoned by a small detachment, 10th Bengal Lancers, and two companies, 1st Bengal Native Infantry.

On the 16th October Lieut.-Colonel Atkins, Commanding 1st Bengal Infantry, was appointed to command the standing camp at Dulai, with—

>9-1 Royal Artillery.
>1 Squadron, 5th Punjab Cavalry.
>1 Squadron, 1st Bombay Lancers.
>2nd Bombay Native Infantry.
>Nos. 4 and 10 Companies, Bengal Sappers.

The head-quarters and remaining troops under Lieut.-Colonel Graham, R.A., marched to Anambar on the 17th.

That evening Sardar Bahi Khan, Sarangzai, a Kakar, who had been sent by Sir Robert Sandeman to bring in Shah Jahan, returned to camp and reported that Shah Jahan was merely endeavouring to gain time to remove his family and had no intention of coming in. Notice was also sent in by the Musa Khel and Kibzais that they had changed their minds and were not coming in. For the time therefore negotiations were at an end.

On the 18th October the Brigadier-General marched with the force as per margin to the entrance of Marai Pass.

1 Troop, 5th Punjab Cavalry.
9-1 Squadron, 1st Bombay Lancers.
9-1 Royal Artillery.
2nd North Staffordshire Regiment.
45th Sikhs.
2nd Bombay Grenadiers.

An advanced force composed of :—

    1 Squadron, 10th Bengal Lancers,
    10th Company, Bengal Sappers,
    4th Punjab Infantry,

under the command of Lieut.-Colonel Barnes, 10th Bengal Lancers, preceded the main body and marched through the pass to Serbara.

The force reached Akhtarzai on the 21st, and on the following day the fort of Shah Jahan, six miles to the north-west, was occupied by a wing of the 4th Punjab Infantry.

During the march all supplies were paid for by the Commissariat and until Ali Khel was reached the people were friendly. On nearing the part of the valley inhabited by Shah Jahan's immediate adherents, a gradual change took place in the behaviour of the people. The hamlets and small forts were almost deserted. Sir Robert Sandeman had an unsatisfactory interview with Maliks Hanif and Haidar. The latter, a personal friend of Shah Jahan, said that the attack on the coolie camp was made under Shah Jahan's orders, and that he was too holy a man even to "salam" to the British. He said that Shahbaz Khan, one of the chiefs of Zhob, was still at Vela, and that if four days were allowed he might perhaps submit. This statement was untrue, as all the forts of the valley were found deserted.

The Political Officer now considered coercive measures necessary, and it was decided to seize flocks and to blow up the towers or small forts of the absent chiefs. Accordingly, a number of

camels, sheep, etc., were brought in by the Baluch Guides and large quantity of wheat was collected.

On the 23rd October a party of the 10th Bengal Lancers, under Lieut.-Colonel Barrow, reconnoitred the country about sixteen miles up the valley, which was found to be well cultivated, with large supplies of wheat and *bhusa* stored for the winter.

A detachment, 1st Bombay Lancers, under Major Heyland, reconnoitred the country across the valley to the hills north of camp and reported having met there about 100 armed men, who seemed anxious to fight.

As the ground occupied by the enemy was unsuited for cavalry, Major Heyland was ordered by heliograph not to engage, but to observe their position and return to camp. Two companies, 4th Punjab Infantry, were withdrawn from Shah Jahan's fort, two companies remaining there under Lieutenant Daniell.

Sir Oriel Tanner, with troops as in the margin, left camp early on the morning of the 24th with the intention of attacking the enemy. The cavalry advanced to reconnoitre, and the whole force halted within a mile of the hills for breakfast.

Affair near Ali Khel.

ARTILLERY.

9-1 Royal Artillery, Screw Battery, under Lieut.-Colonel Graham.

CAVALRY.

Under Lieut.-Colonel Barnes, 10th Bengal Lancers.
5th Punjab Cavalry, 1 troop (Major Carr).
10th Bengal Lancers, 1 troop (Captain Wood).
1st Bombay Lancers, 1 troop (Major Heyland).

INFANTRY.

Under Colonel Armstrong, C.B.
200 rifles, 2nd Battalion, North Staffordshire Regiment (Colonel Simpson).
Half battalion, Bombay Grenadiers, Native Infantry, (Lieut.-Colonel James).
Half battalion, 4th Punjab Infantry (Major Hawes).
Half battalion, 45th Sikhs (Major Walker).
Detachment, 10th Company, Bengal Sappers and Miners (Lieutenant Maxwell).

At 9 A.M. the attack commenced. The 4th Punjab Infantry were to turn the enemy's left, half 9-1 R. A., with half company, native infantry, as escort, being well posted to command the main position.

A troop of cavalry under Major Heyland was detached to the left to cut off the retreat on that side. The remainder of the troops were kept in reserve at the mouth of the pass leading to the position.

The 4th Punjab Infantry, under Major Hawes, swept the hills on the right in dashing style, having several hand-to-hand encounters with the fanatics, of whom they killed a great number.

The two companies under Colonel Simpson engaged the enemy on the left, and the half battery under Captain Cunningham, which had come into action from a commanding position, did great execution on the centre. In two hours the enemy's position was captured, their loss being upwards of fifty killed and some prisoners; our loss was only five wounded. The enemy numbered from four to five hundred, but they were badly armed, having very few fire-arms. The troops returned to camp that evening.

On the 25th—

>1 troop, 5th Punjab Cavalry,
>6 companies, 4th Punjab Infantry,
>2 companies, 2nd Bombay Grenadiers,

were sent to join the two companies of the 4th Punjab Infantry at Kala Shah Jahan.

Destruction of Forts and villages.

The following day the whole force marched to Kala Saifulla Khan the towers of which, as well as of the villages of Shah Jahan and Dost Muhammad, were blown up. On the 29th they marched over a bare open plain to Kazha, which had been previously reconnoitred.

Most of the chiefs and headmen, including Shahbaz Khan, had now tendered their submission to the Political Agent.

A few headmen of the Khoedadzai section of the Saran Kakars in the direction of Hindu Bagh had not submitted, and Colonel Armstrong, C.B., was sent against them with the following force:—

>Troop, 5th Punjab Cavalry.
>Half battery, 9-1 Royal Artillery.
>1 company, 2nd Battalion, North Staffordshire Regiment.
>45th Sikhs.
>Detachment, No. 10 Company, Sappers and Miners.

The force halted the first day within two miles of the deserted village of Chikola, which was destroyed. The *maliks* of Chikola came in that evening.

The following day the cavalry under Major Carr reconnoitred up to the villages of Hindu Bagh, and the surveyors accompanying the force completed the survey of the valley. Mr. Bruce, who

accompanied the force, came to an understanding with the headmen of the villages of that region. The cavalry rejoined the camp that evening, having covered from thirty-six to forty miles, and the force marched back to Kazha on the 1st November, having blown up the fort and burnt the village of Bisharat. At the same time a small force under Major Hawes, 4th Punjab Infantry, had been despatched into the hills to the north of the camp as escort to Lieutenant Wahab, R.E., and Mr. Scott of the Survey Department. Bisharat, son-in-law of Shah Jahan, was captured by the cavalry of this force.

On the 2nd November Sir Robert Sandeman came to a satisfactory settlement with the Zhobwals, and the force proceeded down the valley towards Mina.

Settlement with Zhobwals.

It was at first intended to march down the left bank of the river, but reconnaissances made on the 30th October by the 1st Bombay Lancers as far as Kushnob, about twenty miles east of Kazha, showed this to be impracticable owing to want of supplies and water. It was, therefore, necessary to follow the road through the better cultivated district along the right bank of the river.

A small advanced force under Colonel Barnes preceded the main body to reconnoitre the Badzai Tangi. No hostile gathering was found in that direction.

2 squadrons, Cavalry.
4th Punjab Infantry.

The head-quarters and main column reached Ali Khel on the 5th November. From here the sick were sent under escort to Dulai. It had been the General's intention to send the North Staffordshire Regiment to Dulai, but owing to rumours of hostile gatherings down the valley it was decided to keep them with the force. The advanced force marched through the Badzai Tangi without any opposition and was joined by the main body at Ismailizai on the 8th November.

On the 9th November the Brigadier-General marched to Mina Bazar with—

Survey Work.

Troop, 5th Punjab Cavalry. | ½ battery, 9-1 Royal Artillery.
  „   1st Bombay Lancers. | 4th Sikhs.
2nd Bombay Grenadiers.

The remainder of the force halted at Ismailzai.

The survey of the main Zhob valley from Chari Mehtarzai to Mina being completed, it was not thought advisable to advance further east along the Zhob valley, lest it should lead to complications with tribes outside the present operations. Consequently it was decided to march through the Kibzai and Musa Khel countries, the two columns marching from Mina and Ismailzai, converging again at Tangai. This march was undertaken on the 11th November and on the 12th the whole force advanced through the pass to Kakhao (eleven miles), twenty-seven miles from Ismailzai in Zhob to Kakhao in the Kibzai country. This is by far the best pass into Zhob.

On the 15th November the Brigadier-General proceeded with the following force to Murgha Kibzai, the remainder under Colonel Simpson, 2nd North Staffordshire Regiment, returning to Dulai:—

> 9-1st Northern Division, Royal Artillery—2 guns.
> 10th Bengal Lancers—squadron.
> 5th Punjab Cavalry—troop.
> 2nd Bombay Infantry.
> 4th Punjab Infantry.
> 45th Sikhs.
> 10th Company, Bengal Sappers and Miners.

All the Kibzai headmen having submitted, the column marched to Sahra, Musa Khel Bazar, three marches from Murgha, arriving there on the 16th November. The road led through a difficult pass, which was made practicable, with much labour. The Musa Khel all submitted, and the force marched back to Bori valley in three long marches, passing through a country covered with grass, and arrived at Nulai, near Mekhtar, on the 19th November.

Sir Robert Sandeman now declared the objects of the expedition satisfactorily accomplished, and the following arrangements were made for the withdrawal to British territory of the troops composing it:—

Withdrawal of Expedition.

> (a) The Quetta Garrison:—1st Bombay Lancers, 9-1st (Mountain) Royal Artillery, 2nd North Staffordshire Regiment, 2nd Bombay Native Infantry, to march *via* Sinjawi and Khawas to Quetta.

(b) The 4th Punjab Infantry to return to the Punjab *via* Han Pass and Fort Munro.

(c) Wing Worcestershire Regiment, 1st Bengal Infantry, 45th Sikhs, Nos. 4 and 10 Companies, Bengal Sappers and Miners, Detachment, 1st Madras Pioneers, to march to Sibi; thence by rail.

(d) No. 1 Mountain Battery, 10th Bengal Lancers (squadron), 5th Punjab Cavalry (squadron), to return to garrison Thal Chotiali.

The wing, North Lancashire Regiment, was retained at Thal Chotiali for a time, this being recommended by the Principal Medical Officer as the barracks at Quetta were not completed and it was still unhealthy.

The Brigadier-General, accompanied by Major Gaselee, A.Q. M.G., and Lieutenant Chase, V.C., D.A.Q.M.G., proceeded to Thal Chotiali, and leaving the former officer there to complete arrangements, proceeded to Sibi *via* the Harand Pass, by which road it was proposed to march the troops for Sibi, avoiding the Harnai road as cholera had broken out on that line.

On the 22nd November all arrangements for the withdrawal of the troops were completed. In his final despatch, Brigadier-General Sir O. V. Tanner brought to the notice of Government the admirable conduct of the troops during the expedition. All had had hard marching (though not much fighting), the infantry having covered some 700 miles.

Medical.

There was a good deal of sickness amongst the troops owing to the unhealthiness of the Quetta District during the autumn; this specially affected the 2nd North Staffordshire Regiment and the 45th Sikhs. Of the former regiment fifty men had to be sent back to Quetta on account of their weakly condition after the third march. The Sikhs, having been quartered in Quetta four months before the expedition started, were tainted with the prevalent fever. The 4th Punjab Infantry were also affected by it on their march to Thal Chotiali.

Transport.

The transport used in these operations was of three kinds, *viz*:—

1st.—Army transport pack mules.
2nd.—Government camels.
3rd.—Hired camels.

Class 1.—There were 2,094 mules employed, more than half of which belonged to the Quetta district. The remainder were brought from the Bengal Presidency with regiments. The regimental transport system was employed and worked well. There were twenty deaths among the mules during the operations. During the first six weeks the mules nearly always received full rations, and owing to their capital condition the percentage of sore-backs was almost infinitesimal. During the last fortnight a portion of the force marched about 140 miles in very difficult country. Forage and grain being exceedingly scarce, the mules fell off considerably in condition, and sore-backs began to appear.

Class 2.—Government camels may be sub-divided into two classes, *viz.*, seventeen Quetta transport camels and seventy-seven Government camels, with 4th Punjab Infantry.

The seventeen Quetta camels were all bought in Pishin. They did excellent work throughout. None of them died, and there was only one sore-back.

The seventy-seven Government camels with the 4th Punjab Infantry were all Punjab camels. Twenty-two of them were dead on the date the force broke up, and a number were very sickly. These were a splendid batch of camels when they joined the force, and, in their own country would no doubt have done excellent service. In a cold and mountainous region such as they had to work in, they were useless, as was proved by the high rate of mortality. This confirms the experience gained from the Afghan War, that Punjab and Sind camels are not able to bear the hardship of a campaign in a cold, mountainous country until acclimatised.

The camels of the plains do not know what to eat and what to avoid in a hill country. There were two poisonous plants in the Zhob valley that the hill camels always avoided—one, the wild Oleander bush, and the other a bush with a very small dark green leaf called by the natives of the country *peepul*. The plains camels invariably ate these, and the result was certain death[1].

Class 3.—Hired camels.

---

[1] The 57th Camel Corps marched through the Sulimans from Dera Ghazi Khan to Loralai and back in February 1903, the camels retaining excellent condition throughout. *Bhusa* was provided for them at various places by the political authorities: it was only used when the local grazing was bad. The hill camel will live on the country.

Bori and Zhob Affairs, 1885-1890.

1885. As a result of the Zhob Valley Expedition Shahbaz Khan was nominated as the Sardar and ruler of Zhob. All the leading men, with the exception of the fugitive Shah Jahan and his family, and one or two other *motabirs*, promised to assist him in his work, and to put a stop to further raids on the Thal Chotiali district, and hostages were given to secure this object.

1886. The settlement with the Kakars, besides imposing a heavy fine, included an agreement that the Government of India should be at liberty to occupy the Bori valley, should it be deemed advisable, and the following year, when it was decided that a frontier road should be constructed from Dera Ghazi Khan to Pishin, the Bori valley was occupied, and the cantonment from Duki was moved forward in 1886 to Loralai and a military post stationed at Sinjavi.

Loralai occupied.

Loralai, in the Bori valley, is 4,700 feet above sea level, is distant 154 miles from Quetta by road and 57 from the railway at Harnai, and is named from the Loralai[1] river near which it is built

Gumbaz. Gumbaz, forty miles distant from Loralai, on the borders of Pathan and Baluch, is garrisoned from Loralai. It dominates the Thal Chotiali valley.

Previous to the British occupation of Loralai a private quarrel broke out among the Jogizais which eventually led to the formal submission of Shah Jahan and his family, and to their conversion from enemies into friends of Government. In the month of August, 1885, Shahmar Khan, brother of Shahbaz Khan, who, with Bangal Khan. son of Dost Muhammad, were among the

---

[1] Lora is a common name for river in these parts, and Lai is the name of the tamarisk which abounds in the river beds.

The account of Zhob affairs in the succeeding chapters is from Colonel Jacob's Military Report on Zhob, to which the reader is referred for all information on Zhob matters.

hostages given by the Jogizai Sardars, was sent with Bangal Khan to Sinjavi in connection with a tribal case. Bangal Khan, looking upon Shahmar Khan as the only strong man on the side of Shahbaz Khan, as indeed he was, murdered him during the night and fled to Zhob, intending to murder Shahbaz Khan also and usurp the chief power in Zhob. Fortunately the Duki Native Assistant to the Agent to the Governor-General, Khan Bahadur Hak Nawaz Khan, warned Sardar Shahbaz Khan in time, and Bangal Khan was obliged to flee to the hills north of Zhob. Sardar Shahbaz Khan seized this opportunity to make overtures to Shah Jahan and his son Shingal Khan, who were hostile to Dost Muhammad and Bangal Khan, and shortly afterwards Shingal Khan tendered his submission to the Agent to the Governor-General at Quetta. Shah Jahan himself paid his respects to Sir Robert Sandeman at Sibi and promised to act for the future as a loyal ally of the British Government.

1887.
Submission of Shah Jahan.

In the meantime Dost Muhammad, a dissipated and violent tempered person, collected a band of followers from Zhob and Bori and commenced a life of plunder and outrage. At first Dost Muhammad's attacks were confined chiefly to Zhob, but afterwards, with the assistance of Sultan Muhammad, one of the *maliks* of Mina Bazar, he established himself there, thus being enabled to extend his operations into the Bori valley, and even beyond it. Young men of fanatical spirit, or those who had grievances against their chiefs, left their homes and joined the robber band, and the well disposed people of Zhob were unable to check their unlawful proceedings. The construction of the frontier road through the Bori valley and the consequent influx of Hindustani and Punjabi coolies gave opportunities to the followers of Dost Muhammad, and many outrages were committed. Towards the close of 1887 Dost Muhammad commenced plundering the Mando Khels and tribes in the neighbourhood of Mina Bazar. They appealed to Umar Khan, the chief *malik* of the large Abdullazai section of Kakars and the most influential man in Lower Zhob. He assembled a force, and compelled the Pakhezais of Mina Bazar to turn Dost Muhammad out of that place. Dost Muhammad retired to the hills to the north, where his son Bangal

Dost Muhammad and Bangal Khan.

had remained since his flight. Sultan Muhammad, however, remained in Mina Bazar with his followers, and the outrages in Bori continued, Umar Khan concerning himself only with the protection of his own interests, until Sultan Muhammad, venturing into Murgha, was seized by the Kibzai chiefs and handed over to the authorities at Loralai. Even this did not put a stop to the bad conduct of the Mina Bazar people, and it was determined to punish those guilty and obtain security for good conduct in future.

Accordingly Sir Robert Sandeman, after accompanying the Commander-in-Chief along the new frontier road in 1888, marched, with his escort slightly strengthened, towards Murghab through the Musa Khel country, and thence to Mina Bazar, when all the Abdullazai and Pakherzai *maliks* tendered their submission with the exception of the Chief, Umar Khan, who held aloof. Packing up his goods, Umar Khan fled towards the northern hills, but was pursued by the Political Agent and captured with all his family after an exciting chase. With this capture the success of the Mission was secured.

1888.
Mina Bazar.

While the Agency camp was at Mina Bazar, the Mando Khel Chief, Malik Kanan Khan, came in to pay his respects to Sir Robert Sandeman, and invited him to visit one of their chief villages—Apozai.

Apozai.

The camp accordingly moved to Apozai, about twenty-five miles from Mina Bazar, and halted there for three days, when the country about the Zhob river was explored to within twenty-five miles of its junction with the Gomal river. Sir Robert Sandeman held a *durbar* at Apozai, in which he explained the objects of the Mission and announced the penalty inflicted upon the guilty. This included a fine on sections that had been hostile, which was awarded as compensation, for losses sustained, to sufferers from the raids from Mina Bazar. The Mando Khels here presented a petition to be taken under British protection and offered to pay any revenue which might be decided upon. The objects of the Mission having been attained, Sir Robert Sandeman returned by the Central Zhob route and was met at Gwal Haidarzai, by his old enemy and friend Shah Jahan with all his family. Here Shah Jahan and the leading maliks also presented a petition, praying that, as they were unable to keep peace and maintain order, the British Government might

Zhobis under British protection.

take them under its protection, in return for which they were willing to pay revenue.

This is a good example of the impossibility of turbulent tribes remaining independent on the frontier of a civilized power.

Hitherto our dealings with the Zhobis had been carried out with the sole desire of keeping order on the frontier, but the visit to Apozai convinced the authorities of the great importance of the Zhob valley from a military point of view. It not only turned the whole of the difficult country about the Takht-i-Suliman and dominated the tribes occupying this range and the numerous passes through it to the south, but flanked the great Gomal caravan route to Ghazni and Kandahar. Moreover it was becoming more and more evident that the half-measures hitherto adopted were insufficient to ensure the tranquillity of our frontier.

In the summer of 1889 an old quarrel broke out between two of the most important tribes of Upper Zhob, which, if left to itself, would have led to fresh complications. The Officiating Agent to the Governor-General, Sir H. N. D. Prendergast, marched to the spot, and after considerable trouble the feud was settled.

It was now evident that, without some central authority on the spot to enforce obedience to law, the quarrels of the Zhobis would lead to perpetual disturbances, which must injuriously affect our frontier district and military communications. It was, therefore, decided to occupy Zhob, and at the same time to open the Gomal route, which had so long defied the efforts of the Derajat officials, and render it practicable for communication with Afghanistan.

Up to 1889 knowledge of the Gomal Pass and its communications with Zhob and Afghanistan was incomplete, and rested almost entirely on native sources. It was known that this was the great highway of Afghan traders (*powindahs*) between Central Asia and Hindustan, and its importance as a military line of communication had long been recognised. Lieutenant Broadfoot in 1839 traversed it from Ghazni with a caravan of *powindahs*. In 1878 the Deputy Commissioner of Dera Ismail Khan (Major Macaulay) went some thirty miles up the pass and opened negotiations for its pacification. These were unfortunately closed by the Mahsud raid on Tank in 1879, which led to the Mahsud Waziri Expedition in 1881. In 1883 arrangements were made for the exploration of the pass under

The Gomal pass.

tribal escort; and this was successfully carried out by a native surveyor (Yusaf Sharif) who succeeded in making a good survey up to the junction of the Zhob and Gomal streams, about twenty-four miles beyond our border. At the time of the Zhob Expedition in 1884 it was proposed to make a simultaneous exploration of the Gomal, but this proposal was negatived by Government.

In 1887 the subject was again brought forward, and it was decided to undertake a complete examination of the route, as far as Domandi, the junction of the Kundar and Gomal rivers, in the course of the following cold weather. For reasons not necessary to enter into here (as belonging to the country treated of in Volume II) this expedition was not successful.

Failure of the Gomal Survey Expedition, February 1888.

During the summer of 1889, Sir Robert Sandeman was invited to submit proposals for extending a British protectorate over Zhob and the country between the Gomal and Pishin. The Lieutenant-Governor of the Punjab was at the same time asked to co-operate from the eastern side in the important work of opening up the Gomal Pass. Advantage was taken of the Viceroy's tour on the North-West Frontier in the autumn of 1889 to discuss the whole question with the Commander-in-Chief, the Lieutenant-Governor of the Punjab, and the Governor-General's Agent in Baluchistan. It was decided that Sir Robert Sandeman should proceed, as soon as possible, on a tour through the Zhob valley, and explore the country of the Mando Khel tribe down to the junction of the Zhob and Gomal rivers. It was also determined to use the opportunity to try and come to some arrangement with the Waziri tribe for the opening of the Gomal Pass and to effect a satisfactory settlement with the Shiranis, who live on the Punjab frontier to the south of the Gomal.

The troops named in the margin, under the command of Colonel R. M. Jennings, 6th Bengal Cavalry, were detailed to accompany the Governor-General's Agent as escort. Mr. R. I. Bruce, C.I.E., Deputy Commissioner of Dera Ismail Khan, accompanied Sir Robert Sandeman, as the representative of the Punjab Government, to carry out the negotiations with the Shirani and Wazir tribes.

Sir Robert Sandeman's tour through the Zhob and Gomal valleys, 1889-90.
6th Bengal Cavalry— 470 sabres.
No. 3 (Peshawar) Mountain Battery.
23rd Bengal Infantry, (Pioneers)—500 rifles.

On the 19th December the troops forming the escort started from Loralai. In addition to the military escort a considerable number of levies, chiefly from the Thal Chotiali district, accompanied Sir Robert Sandeman.

Proceeding through Bori in four marches, the expedition reached Murgha on the 22nd, and on the following day entered the Gosha plain, marching some twenty miles to the Kibzai village of Lakaband. Gosha was found to be a high plateau of about the same elevation as Quetta. It possesses a fair supply of water and cultivation, and there are stone-built villages inhabited by Kibzais and Khwastais dotted about the plain and at the foot of the surrounding hills. On the 24th the expedition halted at Lakaband, continuing the march the following day across Gosha to Garda (seventeen miles), the chief village of the Babar tribe. The Babar headmen here came in to pay their respects, and the force on the 26th marched down the Siliaza Nala into Apozai, about eighteen miles. Here Sir Robert Sandeman was met by a deputation of the Mando Khel chiefs and by Umar Khan, the chief of the Abdullazai. At Apozai a darbar was held which was attended by all the principal Zhob *maliks*, and the objects and intentions of the British Government were explained.

Some time was spent here in securing the attendance of the various *jirgas* and making the necessary arrangements with them. After the negotiations had been brought to a successful issue, the *jirgas* of the Mahsuds, Zalli Khel, Dotanis, and the Bargha division[1] of the Shiranis entered into an agreement with Government. Service grants and emoluments were allotted to them, on condition that they should be responsible for the safety of the Gomal Pass, and keep it and the Zhob route open to traffic. The Largha division[2] of the Shiranis, or an influential portion of them, including the Khidarzai section, alone refused to come in and were apparently unfriendly. A party of cavalry under Colonel Jennings, while patrolling in Kapip, were fired on by a band of Khidarzais under a notorious thief, named Ranagul. It was, therefore, decided to leave the Larghawals out of the pacific arrangements, and to conclude a separate

Shiranis troublesome.

---

[1] Highland Shiranis of Baluchistan.
[2] The Largha or lowland Shiranis belong to the Derajat.

settlement with the Bargha division, who were to be made over to the charge of the Political Agent, Zhob, until the whole tribe should be dealt with.

The negotiations with the tribes being completed and the agreements ratified, Sir Robert Sandeman, leaving at Apozai Captain I. MacIvor, Political Agent, with an escort started for the Gomal with the remainder of the troops. The road had been made roughly by the 23rd Pioneers and Wazir labourers, and this facilitated the march of the troops. Kajuri Kach, at the junction of the Zhob and Gumal rivers, was reached on the 25th January 1890, and here a halt of two days was ordered to allow of the road over the Gwaleri kotal being improved. On the 28th January the camp moved to Nili Kach, all the transport, consisting of 400 mules and 643 camels, being safely passed over the *kotal*. A havildar of the 23rd Pioneers was murdered at Kajuri Kach on the morning of the 28th. This was said to have been the work of the Suliman Khel who were hanging about the outskirts of the camp, the havildar having wandered in the dark beyond camp bounds. With this exception the march from Loralai to Tank was accomplished without misadventure. The night at Nili Kach passed without incident, and Sir Robert Sandeman marched the following day into Tank. Here a farewell *durbar* was held, and in consideration of the loyal conduct of the Mahsud Wazir Maliks, Sir Robert Sandeman was authorized to announce the immediate suspension of the tax—which was then being levied as a fine for former bad conduct—on their imports into British territory.

1890.
6th Bengal Cavalry—160 sabres.
No. 3 (Peshawar) Mountain Battery—2 guns.
23rd B.I.(Pioneer)—200 rifles.

After the successful issue of the expedition, the head-quarters of the Political Agent, Zhob, were permanently established at Apozai which was named Fort Sandeman, and arrangements were made for the location there of a small force. Orders were also given for posts, garrisoned by local levies, to be established to protect the road, and for a military post to be built at Mir Ali Khel to link Fort Sandeman with the Gomal. Fort Sandeman is distant 169 miles from the railway at Harnai. It lies 4,500 feet above sea level. It is entirely dependent for water on a piped supply from Kapip, nine miles off. It is the head-quarters of the Zhob Levy,

Fort Sandeman and Mir Ali Khel.

an efficient force of 626 cavalry and 631 infantry which supplies various detachments throughout Zhob. The garrison of regular troops now consists of one native infantry regiment.

During the latter part of March 1890, a body of malcontents of the Darwesh Khel Wazirs attacked the Kajuri Kach post, which was held by friendly Mahsuds. The attack was beaten off, the raiders losing fourteen of their number killed. The affair was not considered serious and was subsequently satisfactorily settled.

Punitive expedition against the Khidarzai Shiranis. On the 22nd April 1890, Sir Robert Sandeman submitted proposals to Government for the punishment of the Khidarzai section of the Shirani tribe. This section, as already shown, had refused to come in during the previous January, and had accordingly been left out of the arrangements then entered into with the other tribes. Although numerically a small section, numbering not more than 250 or 300 fighting men, they had for many years adopted a defiant attitude towards the British Government. During the survey expedition to the Takht-i Suliman in 1883, they opposed the escort to the number of some 1,500 men at the *kotal* above the Pazai springs, but were routed with a loss of 15 killed and wounded. No settlement was, however, effected at that time, and they continued to behave in a contumacious manner. Besides firing on Colonel Jennings' party in the Kapip valley they were concerned in a raid at the end of March 1890, which led to the death of Saku, one of the principal Bargha Shirani Maliks and a faithful servant of the British Government.

On the 9th July 1890, Sir Robert Sandeman submitted a second letter to Government, in which he recommended that advantage should be taken of the collection of a force for the proposed settlement with the Khidarzais, to visit *en route* the northern Kakar country on the upper Kundar, and put an end to the feeling of uncertainty caused by the presence in that neighbourhood of the outlaw Dost Muhammad, and his son, and their following. Should a force not be sent to settle with the Khidarzais, Sir Robert Sandeman was of opinion that it was necessary for the peace of Zhob and the frontier generally, that the troops should be told off to expel Dost Muhammad and his following from the country under British protection. With this letter the Governor-General's Agent forwarded a memorandum, in which he proposed that the force should

assemble at Hindu Bagh in the Zhob valley at the beginning of October, and march in the direction of Dost Muhammad's headquarters. After having captured that outlaw, or expelled him from the Kakar country, the expedition was to march along the Kundar river to Domandi at the junction of the Kundar and Gomal streams, examining the country of the Zhob Kakars and the Mando Khel. From Domandi the column would proceed to Apozai, and thence to the Khidarzai Shirani country.

The Government sanctioned the expedition against the Khidarzai Shiranis, to be carried out by troops from Quetta as proposed by Sir Robert Sandeman. That officer was directed to arrange all details with Major-General Sir George White, commanding the Quetta district, to whom the conduct of the operations was entrusted, Sir Robert Sandeman accompanying the column as Chief Political Officer.

Punitive expedition against the Khidarzai Shiranis.

With regard to the Shiranis, the question of political control, whether this should be from Fort Sandeman or from Dera Ismail Khan, was reserved until the results of the expedition were known and the country had been thoroughly explored.

Arrangements were made for Mr. Bruce, the Commissioner of the Derajat, to join Sir Robert Sandeman in the Khidarzai country, so that all cases outstanding against that section of the tribe, whether connected with the Punjab or Zhob, might be satisfactorily settled, and the Government hoped that an agreement between the Baluchistan and Punjab officers might be effected relative to the boundary on this part of the border between the two jurisdictions.

In order to prevent any misleading rumours reaching the Amir, the objects of the expedition and the orders issued to our officers were explained to His Highness by the Viceroy, in a letter dated the 21st September.

At the end of August, orders were issued for the formation of the expeditionary force which was styled the "Zhob Field Force."

The Zhob Field Force.

CHAPTER X.

ZHOB AND SHIRANI AFFAIRS.

The Zhob Field Force. THE Zhob Field Force consisted of the following troops:—

No. 7 Mountain Battery, Royal Artillery.
2nd Battalion, King's Own Yorkshire Light Infantry.
[1] 18th Bengal Lancers (head-quarters and two squadrons).
No. 1 Company, Bombay Sappers and Miners.
[2] 29th Bombay Infantry (2nd Baluch Battalion).
[3] 30th Bombay Infantry (3rd Baluch Battalion).

Two sections, 23rd British Field Hospital, with two sections 24th and three sections 25th Native Field Hospitals, accompanied the force.

The British infantry battalion was ordered to move into the field 500 strong, and the native infantry battalions each 550 strong.

Concentration was to take place at Hindu Bagh by the 1st October.

The staff were as follows:—

Detail of Staffs.

Major-General Sir G. S. White, K.C.B., K.C.I.E., V.C.	Commanding the force.
Lieut.-Colonel P. D. Jeffreys ..	.. Assistant Adjutant General.
Captain A. H. Mason, R.E. ..	.. Deputy Assistant Quarter Master General for Intelligence.
Major J. F. Garwood, R.E. ..	.. Commanding Engineer.
.... ..	.. Assistant Superintendent, Army Signalling.
Deputy Surgeon-General S.A. Lithgow, M.D., C.B., D.S.O.	.. Principal Medical Officer.
Lieut.-Colonel J. R. Burlton-Bennett	.. Chief Commissariat Officer.
Lieut.-Colonel T. H. Holdich, R. E.	.. Survey Officer.

---

[1] 18th Tiwana Lancers.
[2] 129th D. C. O. Baluchis.
[3] 130th P. W. O. Baluchis.

The troops were equipped on Field Service scale.

One hundred thousand rounds of Martini-Henry rifle, and 10,000 rounds of carbine ammunition was held in reserve at Apozai.

Supplies.—Supplies for the whole force for 2½ months were collected. Depots were formed at Kazhe and at Apozai in the Zhob valley.

An extra allowance of five lbs. a man was allowed for warm kit on account of the severe cold expected.

First phase of the operations. The operations of the Zhob Field Force were naturally divided into two phases:—

1st.—The march from the Zhob valley into the valleys of the Kundar and Gomal rivers and thence to Apozai.[1]

2nd.—The operations against the Khidarzai and other sections of the Shirani tribe.

The troops which took part in the expedition were all stationed at Quetta, with the exception of the 18th Bengal Lancers and the 2nd Baluchis[2] at Loralai, and the 3rd Baluchis[3] at Hyderabad in Sind. The last named regiment was to be railed up so as to arrive at Khanai on the 28th September, and the regiments at Loralai were to march from that station and join the force in the Zhob valley.

The troops from Quetta were under orders to move on the 25th September, but owing to a sufficient number of camels not being forthcoming at the last moment, it was not until the 27th that they marched from Quetta.

On the 30th September the troops, as in the margin, with the field hospitals, were concentrated at Khanozai. On that date Major-General Sir George White assumed command of the force. Sir Robert Sandeman joined the expedition at Khanozai on the 30th. On the 1st October the force marched to Murgha (fifteen miles) and on the following day to Hindu Bagh in the Zhob valley (thirteen miles).

No. 7 Mountain Battery, Royal Artillery.
King's Own Yorkshire Light Infantry.
No. 1 Company, Bombay Sappers and Miners.
3rd Baluch Battalion.

The original plan proposed for the operations had been to try and cut off the retreat into Afghan territory of Dost Muhammad and his following, who were known to be on or near the Kundar.

---

[1] Now Fort Sandeman.
[2] Now 129th D. C. O. Baluchis.
[3] Now 130th P. W. O. Baluchis.

With this in view, Sir Robert Sandeman was to move by the most westerly route from upper Zhob to Tirwah, leaving the Rud valley near its head and skirting the Afghan frontier thence north—by Mian Khel Karez and Palezgir—to Tirwah. Meanwhile the main force under Sir George White was to advance on Thanishpa from the south, and the outlaws, finding themselves thus surrounded, would, it was believed, recognise the uselessness of resistance and submit. The Government of India, however, considering that any movement in the direction of Tirwah would be likely to raise suspicions in the mind of the Amir, directed that the operations should be limited to the country south of the Kundar river. These orders necessitated an alteration in the plan of campaign, rendering impossible the proposed turning movement, and making necessary a direct advance from Zhob.

Advance from the Zhob valley to Thanishpa in three columns.

With a view to learning as much geography as possible and extending our political influence as widely as opportunities would admit, it was decided that the march from the Zhob valley across the hills which form its northern boundry should be carried out in three columns, the objective being Thanishpa. No. 1 (head-quarters) Column under the personal command of Sir George White was to march by the Toi river route. No. 2 Column under the command of Colonel M. H. Nicolson, 3rd Baluch Battalion, and accompanied by Sir Robert Sandeman, was to move *viâ* Maidan Kach and Baraksia across the Khaisar valley on Thanishpa. No. 3 was a small column under the command of Captain A. H. Mason, Deputy Assistant Quarter Master General for Intelligence, with whom went Captain R. J. H. L. Mackenzie, R.E., of the Survey Department. This column was to cross the Dhana pass into the Rud valley and thence to gain the head of the Khaisar valley and march down it, rejoining head quarters at Thanishpa.

These three columns started on the 3rd October, 1890, and reached Thanishpa on the 10th. Dost Muhammad and his son Bangal Khan had, however, fled that morning, and, notwithstanding a vigorous pursuit by a detachment of the 18th Bengal Lancers under Lieutenant K. Chesney—accompanied by Captain I. MacIvor and Lieutenant C. Archer with a strong force of levies—made good their escape, abandoning a quantity of property which was captured by the pursuers. The force halted at Thanishpa from the

11th to 16th October to enable supplies to be brought up, and advantage was taken to come to an understanding with the Shahizai and other Jalazai sections inhabiting Thanishpa and its neighbourhood, and with the Maidanzai Kakars of Khaisar.

As it was reported that the onward march from Thanishpa presented great difficulties in the matter of supplies and that forage for horses and mules would have to be carried on camels, General White issued orders that all details not actually required were to be sent back to Apozai. A redistribution of the force into two columns was accordingly made, and the remainder of the troops under Lieut.-Colonel Morgan, R.A., with all spare stores, were ordered to march down the Toi and thence *viâ* the Zhob valley to Apozai, there to await further orders. Both the columns moved as light as possible.

Thanishpa to Apozai.

Head-quarters column.
No. 7 Mountain Battery, Royal Artillery—2 guns.
King's Own Yorkshire Light Infantry—400 rifles.
18th Bengal Lancers—1 troop.
No. 1 Company, Bombay Sappers and Miners—25 rifles.
2nd Baluch Battalion—400 rifles.

Colonel Nicolson's column.
18th Bengal Lancers—1 troop.
No. 1 Company Bombay Sappers and Miners—50 rifles.
3rd Baluch Battalion—400 rifles.

Colonel Nicolson's column moved from Nigange *viâ* the Chukan and Sharan routes to Gustoi War, crossing the Sharan or Narai kotal carrying nine days' supplies. The headquarters column marched to Nigange and thence down the Kundar valley: this column carried with it eight days' supplies.

The advance of both columns was uneventful and the junction at Gustoi was carried out. From Gustoi War the combined force marched to Husain Nika Ziarat.

From Husain Ziarat the force marched in two columns by separate routes to Apozai. Sir George White, taking with him a lightly equipped column, strength as in the margin, as an escort, marched *viâ* Domandi and the Gomal, while Colonel Nicolson with the remainder of the force, and accompanied by Sir Robert Sandeman, followed the direct route to Apozai. Each column carried four days' rations.

18th Bengal Lancers—20 lances.
2nd Baluch Battalion—330 rifles.
3rd Baluch Battalion—20 rifles.

On the 28th October the whole of the Zhob Field Force was concentrated at Apozai (Fort Sandeman).

The column under Lieut.-Colonel Morgan had arrived several days earlier from Kuria Wasta *viâ* the Zhob valley, and the escort of the 2nd Baluch Battalion, with Sub-Surveyor Asgar Ali, had arrived safely by the Shaighali route, the survey work having been satisfactorily carried out.

Throughout the march from Thanishpa onwards, the disposition of the people on both lines was friendly. The Chakan route led through country occupied by Mardanzais, Babars, and Mando Khel, who rendered all assistance in their power. Along the Kundar route, Lowanas, Zhamrianis, and Safis (a widely spread nomad tribe) were chiefly met with, and proved of much use in the collection of supplies. Indeed, a number of Safis attached themselves to both columns and drove a brisk trade in sheep and goats. On arrival at Gustoi War a considerable number of Suliman Khel flock-owners were found in the neighbourhood, as also near Domandi and Gul Kach and on the Gardao plain They furnished useful assistance in guides, supplies, etc., under the direction of their headman, Haidar Khan. Slight hostility was displayed on two or three occasions, but on the whole it is remarkable that the passage of so large a number of alien troops and followers with a considerable baggage train, over a route hitherto unexplored, and inhabited by wild and fanatical tribes, should have been accomplished with so little opposition.

On the 30th October a parade of the troops of the Zhob Field Force and the local garrison was held at Apozai, which was attended by Sir Robert Sandeman, the political staff, and many of the *maliks*, followed by a *darbar* at which Sir Robert distributed rewards to the chiefs of Zhob headed by Sardar Shingal Khan, who had heartily co-operated in our arrangements, and took the opportunity of congratulating the Sardars on the general good behaviour of the people of the valley since the establishment of the British protectorate.

On the whole it must be considered that the objects of the march were attained. It is to be regretted that Dost Muhammad and his son Bangal Khan were able to escape across the frontier. The very fact, however, of their flight was a heavy blow to their prestige, and it was hoped that the security taken from the northern Jallalzais and Mardanzais would be sufficient to ensure the active combination of the well-disposed among those tribes to

prevent the return of the outlaws. In addition to these results, a very large tract of hitherto unknown country was explored, including several of the best used caravan routes leading from India to Southern Afghanistan, and the limits of the Kakar country were determined with accuracy.

With the parade of troops and the darbar held at Apozai on the 30th October the first phase of the operations of the Zhob Field Force closed.

The second phase of the expedition comprised the operations against the Khidarzai and other sections of the Shirani tribe.

Second phase of the operations.

In his letter to Government, dated the 22nd April, 1890, Sir Robert Sandeman had proposed that two forces of equal strength, one from the Punjab and the other from Apozai, should be sent against the Khidarzais; the two to join hands in the Shirani country. The Lieutenant-Governor of the Punjab, however, considered that on account of the geographical position of the Khidarzais and the greater facilities for supplying the troops from the Punjab side, as well as for other reasons, the best plan of campaign would be for the main force to go from the Punjab, and a smaller column from the Apozai side. The Government of India, as has been seen, decided that the force should proceed from Quetta, and did not consider it necessary to send any troops from the Punjab. They directed that Mr. Bruce, the Commissioner of the Derajat, should join Sir Robert Sandeman in the Khidarzai country to facilitate a satisfactory and simultaneous settlement of all cases, both from the Punjab and Baluchistan, pending against the tribe. Subsequently, it was strongly urged both by Sir George White and the Punjab Government that a force should be sent in from the Punjab side; and it was finally decided that the troops, as in the margin, belonging to the Punjab Frontier Force, should be placed under the orders of Sir George White to act against the Shiranis from the east, based on the Derajat. This force was under command of Colonel A. G. Ross, C.B., 1st Sikh Infantry.[1]

1st Punjab Cavalry—1 troop
3rd Punjab Cavalry—1 Squadron.
No. 1 (Kohat) Mountain Battery—4 guns.
No. 7 (Bengal) Mountain Battery—2 guns.
Half battalion, 1st Sikh Infantry.
Half battalion, 2nd Sikh Infantry.
Half battalion, 2nd Punjab Infantry.
Total—1,651 of all ranks.

---

[1] 51st Sikhs.

As has already been mentioned no settlement had been come to with the Largha division of the Shiranis during Sir Robert Sandeman's tour through the Zhob valley in 1889-90, owing to the contumacious conduct of the Khidarzai section. After the termination of that expedition the Largha Máliks with the exception of the Khidarzai came into Dera Ismail Khan in February 1890, and a settlement was made with them on the condition that they should put pressure on the Khidarzais and force them to submit unconditionally within six months. If they failed to carry out this condition within that period the engagements would be considered cancelled.

At the time it was anticipated that these measures would succeed, but it soon became doubtful if the other sections of the Largha Shiranis would be able to carry out their part of the agreement. In June a deputation of most of the leading *maliks* of the Khidarzai section waited upon the Deputy Commissioner of Dera Ismail Khan at Sheikh Budin, but they were not accompanied by Murtaza Khan nor were they prepared to agree to the unconditional surrender of the refugees, four in number, accused of murder, who had obtained an asylum with them. The deputation was accordingly dismissed and the situation remained unchanged up to the time the force arrived at Apozai.

On the 26th October, Mr. Bruce, the Commissioner of the Derajat, had met Sir Robert Sandeman at Sapai (having come through the Gomal pass under a tribal escort) and had accompanied him to Apozai. From here an ultimatum (see Appendix B) was sent to Murtaza Khan and the other Khidarzai headmen, calling on them to make immediate submission. It may be mentioned that subsequent to the march of the expedition from Quetta two serious outrages had been committed within a short distance of Apozai. In one of these two sowars of the 12th Bengal Cavalry were murdered near Babar, and in the other three traders were robbed and wounded between Babar and Apozai. Both these outrages were eventually brought home to the Khidarzais, and to the refugees harboured by them. The only reply received to the ultimatum was a request from Murtaza Khan for a month's grace to consider its terms. Sir Robert Sandeman immediately informed General White that further delay was useless, and that it would be necessary to compel the Khidarzais to submit by force of arms.

Orders were accordingly issued for an advance into the Shirani country. The force was divided into two columns, one, under the personal command of Sir George White, was to march by Wala over the Maramazh range direct to the Khidarzai head-quarters of Nomar Kalan, while the other under the command of Colonel Nicolson was to proceed *viâ* the Chuhar Khel Dhana to Mogal Kot. At the same time Sir George White directed Colonel Ross to occupy Drazand, the largest village of the Largha Shiranis. This was done with the two-fold purpose of containing the other sections of the tribe in a military sense, and also of affording them the plea of *force majeure* against the tribal obligation of making common cause against the advance of the British.

Advance into the Shirani country.

A return of the strength of the Zhob Field Force previous to the advance into the Shirani country is given in Appendix B.

On the 30th October, a cavalry party under Captain Unwin 1st Punjab Cavalry, sent from Daraban, to reconnoitre the mouth of the Drazand Zam, was fired on by a Shirani picquet, which then withdrew to a *sangar* on the hill above. The enemy consisted of some twenty or thirty men from the Uba Khel village of Maidan. The cavalry were ordered to dismount and dislodge the enemy from their position, which they did, killing two and wounding three without any loss to themselves. Captain Unwin proceeded some way up the pass, meeting with no further opposition, and then returned to camp at Daraban. On the 1st November, Colonel Ross, accompanied by Mr. L. W. King, Deputy Commissioner of Dera Ismail Khan, as Political Officer, occupied Drazand with the troops, as in the margin, without opposition. The Uba Khel and Chuhar Khel *jirgas* had already come in, but the Hasan Khel steadily ignored all summonses to attend, and it was not until the 3rd November that their *jirga*—in consequence of a peremptory order, sent by Mr. King to attend at once on pain of being considered enemies—arrived in camp at Drazand. The ultimatum sent to the Khidarzais by Sir Robert Sandeman was read to all the *jirgas*, and a deputation from each of them was directed to proceed to the Khidarzai country, and

Affair at Drazand Zam.

3rd Punjab Cavalry—1 squadron.
No. 1 (Kohat) Mountain Battery—2 guns.
No. 7 (Bengal) Mountain Battery—2 guns.
Half battalion, 1st Sikh Infantry.
Half battalion, 2nd Sikh Infantry.

endeavour to compel the more important *maliks* to come in with the refugees. They do not appear, however, to have done much in this direction. On the 4th November Lieut.-Colonel A. H. Turner, commanding 2nd Punjab Infantry, occupied Domandi with the troops detailed in the margin. This is an important strategical position at the junction of the Khidarzai with the Chuhar Khel Dhana, and marked approximately the south-east angle of the theatre of operations, Drazand being at the north-east angle. Having established these two forces as "stops" at the eastern outlets of the Shirani country, the advance was continued from the west.

> 1st Punjab Cavalry—1 troop.
> No. 1 (Kohat) Mountain Battery—2 guns.
> Half battalion, 2nd Punjab Infantry.
> Domandi and Drazand occupied.

Nmar Kalan, the stronghold of the Khidarzai section, lies at the foot of, and between three and four thousand feet below, the Maramazh heights. These heights tower almost perpendicularly above Nmar Kalan, and cover it with a back wall most difficult to scale. From information received it appeared to Sir George White that the defiant attitude of the Khidarzais was based upon the idea that this higher approach to their capital was inaccessible to a British force, and that, consequently, they could retire unmolested with their flocks and herds to these heights and adjoining grazing grounds on the precipitous spurs of the Takht-i-Suliman before our advance from the easier or eastern line of approach. The General Officer Commanding determined therefore to march a small but picked force over the heights and descend upon Nmar Kalan, while Colonel Nicolson was making a practicable road through the Chuhar Khel Dhana, a very direct pass from Baluchistan to the Derajat, which had been closed for some years by landslips and large boulders blocking the river-bed at some of its narrowest parts.

> No. 7 Mountain Battery, Royal Artillery—2 guns.
> King's Own Yorkshire Light Infantry—2 companies.
> 18th Bengal Lancers—1 troop.
> Head-quarters No. 1 Company, Bombay Sappers and Miners.
> 3rd Baluch Battalion.

On the 31st October Colonel Nicolson's column, accompanied by Sir Robert Sandeman and Mr. Bruce marched from Apozai towards the Chuhar Khel Dhana. Four days rations were carried in regimental charge and six days in commissariat charge.

On the 31st Colonel Nicolson marched to Kapip Kach (8½ miles) on the left bank of the Siliaza nala, and the following day to Mani

Khwa (fifteen miles) crossing *en route* the easy Atsu Kotal (5,750') dividing the Ujasar plain from Spasta. On the 2nd November the march was continued to Sargasa Wasta (seven miles), a bad road for camels, and on the following day to Dhana Sar (sixteen and a half miles) where the stream enters the gorge, which at its entrance looks like a mere fissure in the hills. Colonel Nicolson and a small escort proceeded five miles down the Chuhar Khel Dhana to inspect the practicability of the route for transport animals. It was found that no road or track existed, the bed of the stream had to be followed, and it was necessary to climb over boulders and rocks. The stream, varying from six inches to more than two feet in depth, flows through this gorge with great velocity, and the pass gradually narrows to twenty yards and in some places to a few feet, with cliffs on either side rising perpendicularly to 2,000 feet. The Commanding Royal Engineer reported that it would be impossible to make a road through it passable for camels in less than four days. All available men of the King's Own Yorkshire Light Infantry and of the 3rd Baluch Battalion were accordingly placed at the disposal of the Commanding Royal Engineer for employment as working-parties on the road.

Meanwhile, Sir George White with the remainder of the force, carrying ten days rations, and accompanied by Captain MacIvor and Mr. Donald as Political Officers, had marched from Apozai to Kapip Kach on the 1st November; and the following day to Mani Khwa. From this camp a reconnoitring party was sent on to the Usha kotal, about seven miles, and it was reported that the road up to this point was practicable for camel transport. Nothing, however, was known of the road beyond, except from native reports.

At 1-15 A.M. on the 3rd, the General Officer Commanding marched with a flying column, strength as in the margin, from the camp at Mani Khwa, leaving the remainder of the column under Lieut.-Colonel Morgan, with the baggage to follow later. The progress at first was slow owing to the darkness. After passing the Usha kotal the road became very bad, and it was soon seen that it would be quite impracticable for laden camels. Orders were accordingly sent back to Lieut.-Colonel Morgan to proceed to Sargasa Wasta instead.

No. 7 Mountain Battery, Royal Artillery—2 guns.
King's Own Yorkshire Light Infantry—1 company.
18th Bengal Lancers—1 troop.
No. 1 Company, Bombay Sappers and Miners—40 rifles.
2nd Baluch Battalion—200 rifles.

of following the road taken by the General Officer Commanding. From Sargasa Wasta he was directed to send three days' supplies to meet the flying column at Wala. In the meantime that column had made slow progress owing to the difficulties of the road, which was barely passable for mules, and a halt of several hours had to be made two miles short of Wala, to enable the rear-guard to close up. The village of Wala was found deserted and here the troops bivouacked for the night. The rear-guard did not arrive until 6 P.M., having been nearly eighteen hours under arms, although the actual distance was not more than twelve miles.

At Wala information was received that the Khidarzais, aided by some members of other sections, intended to oppose the advance at the crest of the Maramazh range. Accordingly Sir George White advanced in fighting order from Wala early on the morning of the 4th November to attack this position and to reconnoitre or occupy Nmar Kalan as circumstances permitted.

Submission of the Khidarzai Shiranis.
Submission of the Khidarzais.

While the force was in full march on these heights, a deputation of Khidarzai Maliks headed by Baluch Khan, a man of importance in the tribe, met the column on the road and laying down their arms made their submission. They reported that Murtaza Khan had fled, and that no opposition would be offered. Taking these *maliks* with him as prisoners at large, the General Officer Commanding reconnoitred to the crest of Maramazh, height 8,310 feet. From here there is a magnificent view of the whole country to the east. On the north the view is shut in by the gigantic mass of rock forming the Takht-i-Suliman. Sheikh Budin and the Indus are seen in the distance, the latter winding like a silver thread along the whole front of the picture. Immediately below lay the Khidarzai country in panorama. From here heliographic communication was opened with Colonel Nicolson's column at Dhana Sar and with Colonel Ross at Drazand. This bird's eye view of the whole situation, and the heliographic communication established between the forces occupying the opposite corners of the Shirani country, brought home to the maliks very graphically the manner in which they were surrounded, and impressed them much. From the crest a party reconnoitred the path leading down to Nmar Kalan and reported it impracticable for laden mules. After inspecting the country the General returned to the bivouac at Wala.

On the 5th General White and staff with 130 men of the King's Own Yorkshire Light Infantry, under Major H. C. Symons, and 170 of the 2nd Baluch Battalion under Major O'Moore Creagh, v.c.,[1] moved to Ghawar Ghar (four miles) at the foot of Maramazh, preparatory to an advance to Nmar Kalan over the range on the following day. Major Richardson, 18th Bengal Lancers, was left at Wala with orders to take the remainder of the troops composing the flying column with all the animals back on the 6th to join Lieutenant-Colonel Morgan's column at Sargasa Wasta.

At 6 A.M. on the 6th the ascent of Maramazh was commenced.

Occupation of Nmar Kalan.

The men, besides their rifles and forty rounds of ammunition, carried their bedding, three days rations and their cooking pots. The ascent was 1,700 feet and very steep in places, and the rear-guard did not get up till 1-30 P.M. From the crest the descent to Nmar Kalan was about 3,600 feet, and the path extremely steep. Nmar Kalan was found deserted. The village consists of scattered hamlets, each owned by a *malik*, situated in a basin from which the water has no outlet and soaks into the ground. On three sides it is surrounded by lofty mountains which in parts are covered with oak trees. There is a good deal of cultivation and the soil is excellent. No opposition was met with throughout the day, but the march was very trying. The rear-guard did not reach Nmar Kalan until 10-45 P.M., having been nearly seventeen hours under arms, the actual distance not being more than six miles.

Nmar Kalan occupied.

Sir George White in his despatch says that none but willing men in high training could have accomplished such a march.

During the day a heliographic message was sent to Colonel Ross at Drazand, to move up the Khidarzai Dhana on the following day to meet the General.

Accordingly, on the evening of the 6th Colonel Ross, with the troops, as in the margin, marched from Drazand to China, situated on the right bank of the Shingao nala (Khidarzai Dhana), where the camp was pitched.

3rd Punjab Cavalry—20 sabres.
No. 1 (Kohat) Mountain Battery—2 guns.
2nd Sikh Infantry—280 rifles.

Early the following morning the march was continued up the bed of the Shingao to Karam, which was reached at 9 A.M.

---

[1] Now General Sir O'Moore Creagh, v.c.

Leaving the camp here Colonel Ross pushed on up the *nala*, and after passing the small village of Ambar the narrow part of the Khidarzai Dhana was entered, the cliffs on either side rising to a considerable height. Here a halt had to be a made to allow the men to construct a ramp up a huge rock which blocked the road. The advanced guard had just begun to move forward again when several shots were fired in rapid succession, and on turning a corner near the village of Khushbina a sepoy of the 2nd Sikh Infantry was shot dead. Firing then continued from both sides of the *nala*, but no further loss was suffered, and the advanced guard occupied the village of Khushbina without further opposition. This village was situated in a position of great natural strength, completely commanding the approach from the east. Here the column was met by Sir George White, who with Lieut.-Colonel Jeffreys, Assistant Adjutant General, and Mr. Donald, Political Officer, and an escort of sixty rifles, had come from Nmar Kalan. After a short conversation with Colonel Ross, General White returned to camp, taking with him seven Khidarzai Maliks who had surrendered after the skirmish above described. On approaching Nmar Kalan, Baluch Khan, the Khidarzai Malik, who was then in camp, made his escape. Men of the 2nd Baluch Battalion gave chase and fired, but he escaped into the hills. His companion Yarak Khan who ran away at the same time was, however, shot. In the morning Baluch Khan had stated positively that no opposition would be offered to the troops and it is probable that, hearing of the firing, he had anticipated evil consequences to himself. On the 10th November he gave himself up.

In the Khidarzai Dhana.

In accordance with the orders he had received from the General, Colonel Ross occupied Nishpa on the left bank of the Khidarzai Dhana opposite Khushbina, and held both those villages for the night, which passed quietly.

On the same day (7th November) a squadron of the 18th Bengal Lancers and 100 rifles of the 3rd Baluch Battalion proceeded to Mogal Kot through the Chuhar Khel Dhana from Dhana Sar. The cavalry received orders to reconnoitre and open up communication with Lieut.-Colonel Turner at Domandi, and the infantry were to assist in making the road from the Mogal Kot end of the pass.

On the morning of the 8th Major O'Moore Creagh, V.C., with 100 rifles, 2nd Baluch Battalion, marched from Nmar Kalan to Nishpa, where he relieved Colonel Ross. That officer, leaving behind fifty rifles, 2nd Sikh Infantry, with Major O'Moore Creagh, returned to his camp at Karam. The village of Khushbina was destroyed this day as a punishment for the opposition offered to Colonel Ross' advance.

On the same day Captain Mayne, taking with him fifty rifles of the 2nd Baluch Battalion, ascended the hills to the north-east of Nmar Kalan to try and capture some flocks belonging to the Khidarzais, which had been seen the previous day. His party was fired on but sustained no loss, and Captain Mayne brought back to camp 199 bullocks, sheep, and goats.

On this day the road through the Chuhar Khel Dhana was reported practicable for camels, and Sir Robert Sandeman, escorted by two guns, No. 7 Mountain Battery, Royal Artillery, two companies, King's Own Yorkshire Light Infantry, and 100 rifles, 3rd Baluch Battalion, marched from Dhana Sar to Mogal Kot. Here news was received of the firing on Colonel Ross's party at Khushbina on the previous day and of the flight of Baluch Khan. Sir Robert Sandeman accordingly on the following morning assembled in *darbar* the Shirani headmen, including all the Khidarzais in camp, and explained to them that as, after the Khidarzai headmen had come in and professed submission, they had treacherously and without excuse fired on the Government troops, it was no longer possible to place any confidence in their professions or to accept their submission as genuine. He was therefore compelled to place the Khidarzai Maliks, who according to universal tribal custom were responsible for their tribesmen's action, in confinement, which was accordingly done.

On the 9th the General, accompanied by Captain MacIvor, Political Officer, started *viâ* the Walwasta route for Mogal Kot to confer with Sir Robert Sandeman, taking with him the Khidarzai prisoners. The night was spent at Dhana War (nine miles), and the following morning the march was continued down the Chuhar Khel Dhana for five miles to Mogal Kot, which was reached at 9 A.M. About three and a half miles from Dhana War some petroleum springs were passed in the bed of the *nala*. The quality of the oil in these springs is pure, but the supply is scanty. After Sir George White had conferred with Sir Robert Sandeman as to future

movements, the latter, accompanied by an escort, marched to Parwara (eight miles) *en route* to Karam.

Colonel Nicolson with the remainder of his column arrived at Mogal Kot on the 10th from Dhana Sar. The first five miles of the road was still very difficult for camels. The column under Lieut.-Colonel Morgan moved up from Sargasa Wasta to Dhana Sar to take the place of Colonel Nicolson's column.

Colonel Ross, on this day, made a reconnaissance from Karam, visiting the villages of Torkhanai and Bohari. All the firearms that could be collected were brought away. The villages were almost deserted, but the people were beginning to return.

On the 11th the General and staff returned from Mogal Kot *via* Warghari (ten miles). Sir Robert Sandeman and Mr. Bruce on the same day arrived at Karam, and a *darbar* was held in the afternoon when the whole Shirani *jirga* was received. Colonel Nicolson's column marched this day from Mogal Kot to Parwara, and on the following day Lieut.-Colonel Turner moved from Domandi and occupied Mogal Kot with one troop, 1st Punjab Cavalry, two guns, No. 1 (Kohat) Mountain Battery, and a wing of the 2nd Punjab Infantry.

Colonel Nicolson's column halted at Parwara on the 12th to rest the camels, and marched to Karam on the 13th, relieving the troops under Colonel Ross which were under orders to return to Drazand.

In the meantime, Major Creagh at Nishpa had not been idle. With the detachment under his command he had scoured the slopes of the Takht and collected 80 cows, 14 donkeys, 62 goats, 114 sheep, and 20 *maunds* of Indian corn, which were handed over to the political authorities. Some of these on enquiry were found to belong to the Atal Khan Kahol and other friendly sections and were restored to the owners; those belonging to the Khidarzais were retained.

Ascent of the Takht-i-Suliman.

During the so-called Takht-i-Suliman expedition in 1883 our troops visited the western or Kaisa rghar ridge of the great mountain mass situated between the Gat and Khidarzai Dhana, but the eastern ridge, which culminates in the celebrated Takht-i-Suliman, was not visited. Sir George White, therefore, determined to march troops to the top of this range, and to ascend by its

precipitous eastern face, thus showing the people that even the rugged path up the face of the Takht, though impassable for mountain cattle and sheep, could be traversed by British troops. Accordingly on the 12th November General White, and fifty rifles, King's Own Yorkshire Light Infantry, under Captain Milton, marched from Nmar Kalan to Nishpa; thence taking Major Creagh, V.C., with fifty rifles, 2nd Baluch Battalion, and Mr. Donald, Political Officer, he started for the Takht. At sunset the Sultanzai village of Zindawar was reached. The distance from Nishpa was only six miles, but the road was very bad for mules, there being an ascent of 2,000 feet, and a descent of nearly 1,700 feet. The General bivouacked at Zindawar, the villagers being friendly. The baggage did not arrive before dark and had to remain out all night, the baggage guard with Captain Milton bivouacking on the road. The night was one of discomfort as there were six degrees of frost, and many of the men had not got their kits, nor could they obtain water to drink. At 8 A.M., on the 13th, the baggage arrived, and, after breakfast the whole party advanced to Tora Tizha (three miles). Here the mules were left behind and officers and men went on with their great-coat and blankets and one day's cooked rations. From Tora Tizha the path zigzagged for two miles up to the foot of the final ascent to the crest of the Takht, where the party bivouacked for the night near the Sighrai spring (7,400'). The ascent this day was 3,500 feet. The night spent at Sighrai was trying owing to the intense cold and the small amount of clothing it had been possible to carry. At 6 A.M. the ascent to the crest was commenced, and, after about $2\frac{1}{2}$ hours of steady climbing, the summit of the Manzalara kotal was reached. As it would have taken too long to go to the shrine, it was decided not to attempt it,[1] and after opening up heliographic communication with Daraban and Nmar Kalan, the force descended to Tora Tizha and bivouacked. The ascent to the crest of the Takht-i-Suliman was very difficulty in places, and here and there the men had to climb on their hands and knees. From the top of the Takht a grand view was obtained over the plains of India to the east, and to the west the high

---

[1] Captain MacIvor and Lieutenant McMahon visited the shrine at the end of June 1891. They ascended the range from the Pazai springs and bivouacked on the crest returning to the Pazai springs on the following day.

plateau of Maidan, covered with pine forest with the Kaisarghar range on the other side, was seen. In his despatch Sir George White says :—" The ascent of the Takht-i-Suliman was by far the most difficult operation, from a physical point of view, I have ever called upon soldiers to perform, and the fact that British soldiers and Baluch sepoys, fully accoutred, scaled these dangerous heights, will not be lost on the Shiranis." On the 15th November the General marched from Tora Tizha to Karam (sixteen miles) passing through the Sultanzai villages of Jat Aghbazai and Raghasar.

The descent from Tora Tizha to the Wagarai nala was steep, but practicable for mules. From there the road to Karam Hezai presented no difficulties. This route is much easier than that from Nishpa *viâ* Zindawar.

On the 14th November Captain MacIvor, Political Officer, with an escort of 150 rifles, 3rd Baluch Battalion, accompanied by Lieutenant Southey, Field Intelligence Officer, and Captain Mackenzie, Assistant Survey Officer, left Karam to explore the Khidarzai Dhana, and returned on the 16th, having visited Karim Kach. They reported the road easier than that over Maramazh to Nmar Kalan. In the meantime working parties were employed in improving the roads through the Shirani country, the important points of which, Karam, Drazand, Nishpa, Nmar Kalan, Moga Kot, and Dhana Sar were all occupied by British troops.

On the 17th November the cases against the Khidarzais and other Shiranis were brought up before a committee assembled at Karam, composed of Sir Robert Sandeman, Mr. Bruce, Captain MacIvor, and Lieutenant McMahon. The circumstances of each case were considered and orders passed for their settlement. The fine to be imposed upon the Largha Shiranis was fixed at Rs. 5,000, divided as follows :—Uba Khel (including the Khidarzai sub-section), Rs. 2,500, Hassan Khel, Rs. 1,500, Chuhar Khel, Rs. 1,000.

On the 18th Sir Robert Sandeman held a final *darbar* at Karam, at which he announced the results of the operations against the Khidarzais and also the terms imposed upon the Shirani tribe as a whole; *khilats* were at the same time bestowed on some of the headmen of Bargha and Zhob who had rendered good service during the expedition.

<small>Terms imposed on the Shirani tribe.</small>

The terms were briefly :—

1st.—That Murtaza Khan and the refugees, if in the Shirani country should be surrendered, or, in the event of their having left the country as had been reported, should not be permitted to return.

2nd.—A fine of Rs. 6,000 was imposed upon the tribe, including Rs. 1,000, inflicted on individuals for offences committed in Dera Ismail Khan and Zhob.

3rd.—The Khidarzai Maliks and other refractory members of the tribe who had surrendered or been taken prisoners to be detained as hostages until the terms had been fulfilled.

Termination of the operations. The objects for which the Zhob Field Force had been organized having thus been accomplished, corps were sent to their destinations, and their return marches were utilized to open out as many lines of communication as possible between the Derajat and Baluchistan.

As a result of the expedition and the knowledge that had been gained of the country, Government approved and confirmed the arrangement arrived at after Sir Robert Sandeman's expedition of 1889-90, in accordance with which the Bargha section of the tribe on the west of the Suliman range was placed under the control of the Agent to the Governor-General in Baluchistan, while the Larghawals, on the east of the range, were to continue to be managed by the Punjab Government.

The terms of the final settlement made with the Largha Shiranis were briefly as follows :—

(1) The Zao, Khidarzai, and Chuhar Khel passes to be kept open and the tribe to be responsible for the safety of caravans and travellers using these passes.

(2) British officers and other Government servants to be at liberty to travel in any part of the Shirani country. The tribe to be responsible for their safety.

(3) All arrangements with the tribe to be carried out through its headmen, and if Government orders should be disobeyed or disregarded, the Government to be at liberty to re-occupy the country.

(4) The taking of selected hostages for the future good faith of the tribe.

(5) The tribe to be responsible for the acts of its individual members.

(6) The restoration and redistribution of service, pay and allowances of the Larghawals.

(7) The establishment of levy posts at Mogal Kot, Nishpa Atal Khan (Kahol), Gandari Kach, Darazand, and Domandi.

Zhob affairs subsequent to 1890.

Since the Zhob campaign of 1890 there have been no military expeditions in Zhob, but the country remained for some time very unsettled owing to various causes. Dost Muhammad and Bangal Khan were still outlaws and liable to return at any time; the northern limits of Zhob were undefined, and this gave the Amir's officials opportunities to encroach, of which they fully availed themselves. The north-east of Zhob was continually harried by Wazirs, Suliman Khel and others.

1891.

In 1891, the first year after the settlement, the conduct of the tribes in the Agency was good. The Bargha Shiranis, Isots, Murgzans, Jafars, and Kharsins were called upon to pay revenue for the first time, and their conduct was exemplary. Very little crime occurred among these tribes and no outrage against any official or employé of Government. The Wazirs, however, constantly raided into Zhob and were responsible for forty-one reported cases of murder, cattle-lifting, etc. The celebrated outlaw Dost Muhammad visited Kabul and was well received by the Amir, who permitted him to return after giving him presents of some value.

1892.
Afghans in Zhob.

On the 31st January 1892, Saifulla Khan, Governor of Katawaz, and Munsur Khan, Governor of Mukur, with some 120 Afghan sowars and *khasadars*, arrived without warning at Gul Kach, having marched from Katawaz down the Gomal river. The two Governors quickly visited Wana, Spin, Girdao, and Siritoi; and then marched *viâ* the Kundar and Kandil route through Tirwah to Mukur and Kabul, taking with them as many of the headmen of the Suliman Khel, Wazir, and other tribes as they could induce to accompany them.

They left a small post at Gul Kach on the north of the Gomal river, subsequently relieved by about fifty *khasadars* under Yusuf Ali Khan, a brother of Munsur Khan.

In view of these proceedings it was decided to hasten the intended British occupation of Gul Kach on the south of the Gomal,

and about 100 of the Zhob Levy Corps were despatched and reached that post on the 15th of March. There was no friction with the Amir's men on the other side of the river : friendly visits were received, and returned.

Both Dost Muhammad and Bangal Khan met the Afghan officials and visited Gul Kach on their return from Kabul, and assisted the latter on their march up the Kandil.

The Amir also sent troops to Wano and Zarmelan on the extreme north-east edge of the district, during the early part of the year, and they remained there until September. Their presence in the neighbourhood, and the exaggerated rumours which spread about Zhob relative to the Amir's intentions towards the British Government, caused very unwholesome excitement in the minds of the tribes. This feeling was further increased by the movement of a small party of the Amir's men to Gustoi in the beginning of July. Sardar Gul Muhammad at the same time wrote to Major MacIvor, the Political Agent, stating that the people of Gustoi were the Amir's subjects, and requested him not to interfere with them. With the permission of the Agent to the Governor-General, Major MacIvor proceeded to take immediate measures to turn this party out of Gustoi, and, with that object, proceeded there on the 13th July with a small party of troops and levies. On his approach the Amir's men left Gustoi and retired to their own territory. This action had a salutary effect on the minds of the people, and the excitement began to calm down, ceasing altogther on the withdrawal of the Amir's troops from Wano and Zarmelan. While the excitement lasted, however, certain headmen of the district were injudicious enough to commit themselves by absconding to Kandahar. They returned the following year.

The Wazirs were again particularly active during 1892 in depredations in the Zhob district. The most serious of their offences were attacks on sentries and escorts between Mir Ali Khel, Khajuri Kach, and Gul Kach. All these raids were successful, and resulted in much loss of life, and of a certain number of rifles.

Dost Muhammad and Bangal Khan continued to give serious trouble. From their strongholds, trans-Kundar, their followers made repeated raids into Zhob and harassed not only Government subjects, the Nasirs and other Ghilzais in the neighbourhood.

It was evident that as long as these men were allowed to remain in Kakar territory, even though it were trans-Kundar, they would be able to terrify the neighbouring Kakar sections into allowing them a safe conduct through their limits, and assisting them in other ways; while it would be impossible for us to check their depredations. With the object of making another attempt to capture Bangal Khan and his father, and, failing that, to drive them out of Kakar limits, Major MacIvor with his full escort of regulars and levies visited trans-Kundar country in September. He failed to capture Bangal Khan, who fled across the Kakar border to a Ghilzai village a few miles within the Amir's territory. Dost Muhammad Khan, however, with two younger sons, came in and gave himself up to the Political Agent on the 20th September.

Notwithstanding the failure to capture Bangal Khan, Major MacIvor's mission had important political results. Bangal Khan and his gang were driven out of Kakar limits, and the Kakar sections, trans-Kundar, were encouraged by the visit of troops to their country to stand up against his depredations. Heavy securities were taken from them to prevent Bangal Khan's men from passing through their limits.

In addition to this, important results were obtained by our official recognition for the first time of the old long-standing Kakar boundary line between them and the Ghilzais.

The good effects of these arrangements were proved by the freedom enjoyed from depredations in Zhob and by the capture by the Mardanzais of the notorious outlaw Gola and four other *badmashes* of Bangal's gang in March 1893.

Sardar Shah Jahan died in the summer of 1892 and his death was soon followed by that of his son, Sardar Shingal Khan, under the most melancholy circumstances.

The opportunity of Sardar Dost Muhammad Khan's return was taken to settle the long-standing case of the murder of Sardar Shahmar Khan by Bangal Khan in 1885. The matter was placed before an influential and representative *jirga* at Fort Sandeman and settled on the 18th November 1892. The settlement gave satisfaction to both parties and was approved by Dinak, Shahmar's eldest son. To celebrate the close of this long-standing feud, the Political Agent gave the *jirga* and parties present a feast

of sheep on the evening of the day the settlement was arrived at. During the feast Dinak suddenly rose up, and with his father's sword, a weapon of well-known history, which only that day had been restored to him as part settlement of the case, struck Shingal two heavy blows nearly severing his arm. Sardar Shingal Khan died from the effects of his injuries on the 8th December. No sufficient reason could be attributed for such animosity on Dinak's part; and as he was known to be a youth of weak intellect, it was suspected that he had been the tool of some designing person. Suspicion fell upon Sardar Dost Muhammad Khan and Sultan Muhammad Pakhizai, who were placed before the Sibi *jirga* in February 1893. No actual proof was found of their instigation of the murder, but the *jirga* considered the grounds of suspicion so strong that they were ordered to be kept under surveillance at Quetta until further orders.

The tribes in the district were perfectly quiet during this year, but the Wazirs were as active as ever and committed no less than thirty-seven raids and other offences within the Zhob limits. The scene of most of these outrages was the Kajuri Kach-Mogal Kot road, which was rendered so unsafe that special measures had to be taken for the protection of travellers.

1893.

Bangal Khan was still living in the Amir's territory, but the capture of Gola and the four men mentioned above, no doubt produced a strong effect on his and his followers' minds. It showed them that the system of plunder by which they existed would not be tolerated any longer and that there was no hope of their being allowed to re-establish themselves in Kakar limits. On the other hand Bangal's position in Afghanistan was rapidly becoming untenable. He had received two orders from the Amir either to come to him or to leave his territory. He was thus compelled to choose between throwing himself on the mercy of the British Government or trying his fortune as an exile in Afghanistan. The death of Sardar Shingal in November 1892 and of Sardar Shahbaz Khan and Muhammad Nur in April and May, 1893, may have had some effect in determining Bangal's decision. For some time he hesitated, but finally recognised that his wisest course was unconditional submission. He crossed the Kand river, and, leaving his family within British territory, set out for Zhob, where he surrendered

himself with eighteen followers to the Political Agent at Hindu Bagh on the 24th June. His family and the remainder of his followers were brought in soon after.

There was no doubt that Bangal's offences rendered him liable to be severely dealt with, as indeed he himself admitted. There were, however, a number of extenuating circumstances. Although sharing in the booty obtained by his followers' depredations, on which, ever since his first false step, he may almost be said to have been dependent for subsistence, he had taken a personal part in very few of these outrages. Moreover, it was shown that he had never encouraged offences directly aimed at the British Government, and had discouraged *ghaza*[1] so far as was in his power, though unable to control at all times the more desperate members of his gang. Further, the evident good faith of his surrender and the openness of his behaviour afterwards tended to show the possibility and desirability of converting him, as had been done in the case of Shah Jahan, a much more determined opponent of the British Government, from an antagonist into a faithful and valuable servant. On these grounds it was decided to deal leniently with Bangal's past offences, while taking precautions to render him powerless for evil in future. On the 5th August 1893 the Agent to the Governor-General received Bangal's submission in *darbar* at Ziarat, and accorded him forgiveness for his past offences. Security to the amount of Rs. 10,000 was furnished by both Dost Muhammad and Bangal Khan for their future good behaviour, and non-interference in the affairs of the Jogizai family and the Zhob chieftainship. The Zhob Sardar, Muhammad Akbar Khan also furnished a similar security for the prevention of further acts of hostility between his own and Bangal's branches of the Jogizai family.

To provide for the maintenance of Dost Muhammad, Bangal Khan and the rest of his family, a re-distribution of the cash allowances and grain *jagir* granted to the Jogizai family was arranged with the concurrence of all concerned. Dost Muhammad, who was in confinement in Quetta, was released at the same time and allowed to reside there at liberty. Bangal Khan was ordered to reside with his family at Dirgi near Loralai.

---

[1] Murders dignified with the name of "fanatical outrages."

In January 1894, Bangal Khan and other Sardars were taken a tour round India, and visited among other places, Lahore, Calcutta, Bombay and Karachi. The tour was very successful and had a salutary effect on the minds of the chiefs.

It was during this year that the Baluch-Afghan Boundary Commission demarcated the boundary between Zhob and Afghanistan, from Domandi to Chaman.

Towards the end of the year, some trouble was caused by Malik Shahabuddin, the chief of the Khoedad Khel Suliman Khel, who appeared on the north bank of the Kundar river opposite Husain Nika with sixty sowars. In spite of the fact the Boundary Commission had fixed the waterway of Kundar as the boundary at this part, Shahabuddin still pretended ignorance of the settlement, and was inclined to maintain antequated and unfounded claims on Chachoba and Husain Nika and certain tracts of country south of the Kundar. Before the arrival of the Political Agent, Shahabuddin, however, had returned to his home.

Shiranis, 1895. The Shiranis, who had kept quiet since the Zhob Field Force invaded their country in 1890, now began to give trouble. It began with a quarrel between the Bargha and Largha Shiranis over a case of abduction.

The Largha Shiranis being under the Deputy Commissioner, Dera Ismail Khan, and the Bargha Shiranis under the Political Agent, Zhob, a great deal of delay occurred in settling this case owing to references having to be made from one district to the other. The *jirga* before which the case was sent were unable to agree.

In March 1895, the matter was again placed before a *jirga* at Mogal Kot in Largha. The majority of the *jirga* found that the abducted woman should be given back, and the case was submitted for the orders of the Government of India.

The long delay in settling the case wore out the patience of the Chuhar Khel and they began to despair of obtaining redress. Meanwhile they were exposed to the taunts of their neighbours and rivals reproaching them with having lost their woman and done nothing to vindicate their honour.

On the 6th June 1895, a small party of the Chuhar Khel surprised the camp of Lieutenant Hume, R.E., who was in charge

of the construction of the road. The camp-guard of six men of the Zhob Levy had three men killed, and lost all their rifles and ammunition.

The raiders then proceeded down the road towards Dhana Sar. Meeting Lieutenant Hume on the road, they killed him, and his horse, butler, and the camel he was riding. They continued doing further wanton damage. Pursuit parties from Fort Sandeman and Shingarh were quickly on their tracks. Captain McConaghey, the Political Agent, came up with the party on the 9th June between Loara and Dhana Sar. Shots were exchanged, a sepoy of the 40th Pathans was killed, and the leader of the robber gang, Shikari Khan, was wounded. The party escaped, however, to the Suliman Khel country, and eventually to Kandahar. Various fines were imposed on the Bargha Shirani tribes for proved complicity in this affair.

One of the murderers, of whom there were seven in all, was apprehended in 1897 and hanged.

From 1895 to 1897 the affairs in the Bargha-Largha Shirani country remained unsatisfactory. Nothing was done on the Punjab side towards controlling the Largha Shiranis, who openly defied all *jirga* decisions.

1898.

The Larghawals levied toll from all travellers and in many cases looted their property. On one occasion they stole the property of two British officers and a lady travelling through the pass accompanied by a guard of regular cavalry. They also carried off three of the Public Works Department sub-contractors employed on the road, but afterwards released them. Another band of fifty men seized and carried off another sub-contractor close to Dhana Sar. They were pursued by a detachment of troops and levies, and after some resistance the prisoner was released, but not until shots had been exchanged, in which one cooly, who was with the troops, was killed and one Shirani wounded; nineteen Shiranis were taken prisoners. Another party raided as far as Toi Sar in Musa Khel and broke into a house, ill-treated the owner and his wife and abducted the daughter.

There were certain petty disturbances between the Afghans and our subjects on the Khurasan border, but all were satisfactorily settled.

The Wazirs on the 25th May 1899, attacked a party of five Zhob Levy Corps sowars between Mir Ali Khel and Girdao. One sowar was killed, another wounded and their rifles with accoutrements were taken away by the raiders.

1899.

On the 20th January in the very early morning, Fazil and Shikari (who took a leading part in the Dhana outrage of 1895) and a third person, armed with swords, pistols, and rifles entered a house in Sam Khel near Hindu Bagh, where Duffadar Sobha Khan and Sowar Ghajjar of the Zhob Levy Corps had encamped with five horses. Taking advantage of their being asleep and unarmed the thieves secured them, and after divesting them of what they had, hamstrung two horses and rode off with the remaining three. The report of this reached Hindu Bagh at 4 A.M., when Ressaidar Diwana Khan, the commander of the Zhob Levy Corps post there, at once started off with a party in pursuit *viâ* Sam Khel, at the same time sending another party under a duffadar *viâ* Shamshobi. The Ressaidar caught up the raiders and secured one of them and one of the horses. The pursuit was continued, when Shikari was nearly caught, but he dismounted and took to the hills, leaving his horse behind. Owing to darkness and the deep snow, the rest escaped, but the horses and stolen property were recovered.

1900.

In December 1900, the Mahsud Wazir Blockade commenced and continued until March 1902. The Zhob section of the blockade is the only one with which this volume deals.

Mahsud Wazir blockade.

In November 1900, a detachment of the 6th Bombay Cavalry, a wing of the 24th Baluchistan Infantry, the 23rd Bombay Rifles, and the Zhob Levy Corps Cavalry and Infantry, were allotted for blockade duty under the command of Lieut.-Colonel R. I. Scallon, C.I.E., D.S.O., of the 23rd Bombay Rifles. The boundary of the Zhob district to be watched was roughly a line which starts from Gustoi to the south-west and follows the Kundar river up to its junction with the Gomal at Domandi. From this point the boundary continues along the Gomal to Toi Khula (where the Wana Toi joins the main stream), it then passes over the hills in a south-east direction to the Ghazamanda nala and thence across the

The Mahsud Waziri Blockade, Zhob Section.

Zhob river up to Kuchbina nala for about four miles, when it turns eastward into the Zao pass through the Suliman mountains, a distance of about fifty-five miles.

The troops were distributed with instructions to capture and hand over to the Political authorities any Mahsuds who might be discovered beyond the limits of their own district; to prevent any supplies of food or clothing from passing into the Mahsud country; to protect the persons and property both of the inhabitants of Zhob and of the *powindahs* and Nasirs who twice yearly pass along the Gumal valley to and from the Punjab; and for these purposes to co-operate with the troops and levies employed in Waziristan.

The Commissioner of the Derajat computed that during the *powindah* migration some 50,000 persons and 150,000 animals traverse the Gomal.

A large camping ground was selected on the left of the Gomal opposite Gul Kach, under the lee of an isolated hill which was occupied by a strong party of the 23rd Bombay Rifles. The *kafilas* were met as they crossed the Afghan border and conveyed by parties of the Zhob Levy Corps to the assigned camping-ground. Hence they were passed on in such numbers as could ensure no block taking place anywhere along the road to Khajuri Kach, escorted by parties of the 23rd Bombay Rifles as far as Toi Khula, when they were handed over to the Southern Waziristan Militia. Other parties using the Zhob valley were protected by detachments from Mogal Kot, Mir Ali Khel, Girdao, and Husain Nika.

The result of these arrangements was that the *powindahs* suffered no loss in person or property in Zhob or in the Gomal.

Several petty raids were attempted by the Wazirs, but as a rule the raiding parties which managed to enter Zhob returned with difficulty, and empty-handed.

The troops employed on this duty made many roads and tracks, the most important being a camel road from Mir Ali Khel in Zhob *viâ* Waziri Bagh to Gul Kach on the Gomal, twenty-three miles long and nine feet wide, which cost only Rs. 2,500, including explosives and tools.

The Blockade ended in March 1902, and was no sooner over than the Largha Shiranis again began to give trouble, by murdering

Arbab Farid Khan, Extra Assistant Commissioner, Punjab Shiranis. The murderer, Ahmad Khan, a Shirani of some local importance, escaped, notwithstanding the parties of troops that were out, both from Zhob and the Dera Ismail Khan side, searching for him and blocking the outlets. He appeared to have escaped to Afghanistan through Punjab territory east of the Takht-i-Suliman and *viâ* Waziristan. The result of this outbreak caused a good deal of inconvenience to Zhob, because the road through the Dhana, which is the main trade route between the Punjab and Zhob, was blocked for some time and rendered unsafe for travellers. At the same time a band of Shiranis, numbering about thirteen, shot the *bania* at the Dhana bungalow and burnt his shop, but the whole gang was shortly afterwards destroyed by a party of the 23rd Bombay Rifles.

From 1902 till 1906 affairs in Zhob were quiet. The Kakars througohut have given no trouble. In 1906, however, the Shiranis burnt the Political Agency house at Shingarh, as a demonstration against certain new forest rules regarding cutting of wood in their hills.

Several outrages have been committed in the Shirani country during the present year (1907) including the murder of a party of travellers and a road-contractor.

The whole of Zhob is administered by the British Government. The administration is in charge of a Political Agent who is directly subordinate to the Agent to the Governor-General in Baluchistan. His headquarters are at Fort Sandeman, and he is assisted by an Assistant Political Agent, an Extra Assistant Commissioner, Tahsildar, Naib Tahsildar, etc., all at Fort Sandeman; an Extra Assistant Commissioner, Tahsildar, Naib Tahsildar, etc., at Hindu Bagh; and a Tahsildar and Naib Tahsildar at Kala Saifulla. His authority is supported by a Native Infantry regiment at Fort Sandeman with detachments at Mani Khwa and Mir Ali Khel; and the Zhob Levy Corps, with head-quarters at Fort Sandeman and posts scattered at intervals all along the Afghan border. There are also detachments of regular troops at Kala Saifulla and Hindu Bagh.

Administration of Zhob.

Revenue is taken from all the tribes in the district and grazing taxes from the nomads in the summer months.

Each section and sub-section of the various tribes is directly under the control of the maliks or headmen, who are held responsible for the good behaviour of their followers. In return they receive allowances; but in addition to good behaviour they have to keep up certain numbers of country levies, mounted and footmen. It is through these *maliks* and their levies that the work of the district is carried on. The system is well suited to the needs of the country.

CHAPTER XI.

MAKRAN.

About the middle of the last century the whole of Makran, as well as Kharan and Mashkhel, was conquered by Nasir Khan the Great, of Kalat, and annexed to his dominions. He instituted a liberal system of government by which the administration was carried on jointly by a Naib, representing the Khan, and the local Gichki Sardar, between whom the revenues were divided in certain fixed shares.

History.

This arrangement seems to have worked satisfactorily until the Gichkis began to degenerate and the Naoshirwanis began to oust them by intrigues of every description.

The Noashirwanis who occupy Kharan are of pure Persian stock. Kharan stretches from the Jhalawan hills to the Persian border, a country of long sandy valleys with but little cultivation; its inhabitants a fighting, raiding, restless clan whose life was dependent on successful forays against the more settled countries of their neighbours.

Sprung from a bold and determined race, filled with the sense of their own importance, and possessed of a much higher order of intelligence than the other ruling races in Makran, the younger members of the Naoshirwanis, as they found their shares in the ancestral property insufficient for their wants, have endeavoured to carve out for themselves fortunes from the property of their less energetic neighbours. But they differ from the Arab conquerors of the country in that whereas the Arab converted the land from desert to oasis, the Naoshirwani reduces oases to deserts.

In 1888, led by Naoroz Khan, the Naoshirwanis raided Panjgur, and slew Mir Gajian, the Gichki Sardar, who was also

the Khan's *naib*. At this time Azad Khan was still head of the Naoshirwanis. Sandeman thus describes him:—

"In spite of his great age Azad Khan retains his mental faculties unimpaired. Bowed by age, he is unable to mount a horse without assistance, but, once in the saddle, his endurance is greater than that of many a younger man. Possessed of unflinching resolution, impatient of wrong, generous to reward, stern and relentless in punishment, Sardar Azad Khan has above all things enjoyed a reputation for unswerving honesty. He is never known to depart from his word once given, and has a sincere contempt for chicanery or falsehood."

Azad Khan.

Sandeman visited the country in 1884. Disputes between the Naoshirwanis and the Khan of Kat were adjusted, and before his death three years later, at the age of 101, the veteran chief had shown his friendship for the British Government by rendering valuable assistance in the matter of transport to the Russo-Afghan Boundary Commission. He had also arranged, in co-operation with our officers, for the protection of trade routes.

Sandeman's visit, 1884.

The Khan of Kalat, owing to his dislike of the Naoshirwanis, was displeased with the settlement; he wished rather to establish his own power in an absolute form in Panjgur; therefore in order to get the Naoshirwanis into trouble he countenanced disturbances.

Result of settlement.

Muhammad Hasan, Gichki, of Sami claimed the sardarship of Panjgur. He was aided by the Noshirwanis under Baluch Khan, and was enabled to keep the whole countryside in a distracted condition, causing damage to the resources of Panjgur, estimated at several lakhs, and reducing the unfortunate people to the extremity of wretchedness.

In 1890-91 Sir Robert Sandeman again visited Panjgur, which was in a state of almost complete anarchy. Peace was introduced by the occupation of Panjgur by British Indian troops, but after their withdrawal in 1893, complaints were received of the misbehaviour of Muhammad Ali, the Khan's *naib*, and in 1896 he was replaced by Kaoda Muhammad Khan, an influential and capable Baluch headman.

Second visit.

MAKRAN.

Affairs in Kej.

The state of Kej was somewhat less disturbed, owing chiefly to the high character of the Gichki Sardar, Bhai Khan, and his influence with the tribes. But as the Sardar grew feeble with age the Khan's Naoshirwani Naib, Mir Shahdad, raised feuds in order to increase his power and lessen that of the Gichkis, great destruction of property and loss of life ensued, and the ruling power was brought into contempt.

The attempt to manage the Rinds of Mand through the Naib and Sardar of Kej was also far from successful. They looted the caravans carrying the Persian trade, and it was impossible to exact from them any reparation for the damage caused by their raids.

Mir Shahdad was replaced shortly afterwards by Abdul Karim, Gichki. In revenge for his supersession in the naibship, Mir Shahdad attacked and severely wounded a British officer, and then fled the country.

The Gichki Sardars.

So low had our influence in those parts sunk that, in 1890, Sher Muhammad, a nephew of Sardar Bhai Khan, openly defied the British Agent, and fired upon his camp from the stronghold of Nasirabad in Kej.

Nasirabad had been held by one Mehrab Khan, who was expelled by Sher Muhammad. The two men were relations and disputed the right of ownership. In 1891, Sir Robert Sandeman decided in favour of Mehrab Khan, but required him to pay Sher Muhammad Rs. 100 per annum compensation.

In 1893 the latter forced Mehrab Khan to sell the fort to him for Rs. 1,300 or about a quarter of its value.

The Khan visits Makran, 1896.

In 1896 the Khan of Kalat made a tour in the Makran country, accompanied by Lieutenant E. LeMesurier, Officiating Political Agent in Kalat, and by Mir Yakub Khan, eldest son of Sardar Sir Naoroz Khan[1] and by several leading men of the Sarawan and Jalawan tribes.

The principal incidents of the tour were :—

(a) The surrender of the Nag fort in Kolwa by the sons of Baluch Khan, Naoshirwani.

(b) The surrender of the Nasirabad fort near Kej by Sher Muhammad, Gichki.

---

[1] Who succeeded Azad Khan as head of the Naoshirwanis in 1887.

(c) The arrangements initiated for the future administration, under the Khan's orders of the districts of Kej (including Bolida, Kolwa, and Panjgur).

At Nasirabad a *jirga* was assembled and, on their finding, Sher Muhammad was confirmed in possession of the fort on a payment of Rs. 100 per annum to Mir Mehrab Khan.

The Khan's troops are introduced into Makran.

Having regard to Sher Muhammad's turbulence in the past, the Nasirabad fort was garrisoned by seventy-five Kalat sepoys, Panjgur also was garrisoned by twenty-five of the Khan's troops, and the Nag fort was held by twenty levies. The Nazim was provided with an escort of twenty levy camel sowars.

Afterwards Baluch Khan's grandson, Muhammad Umar Khan, was made Naib of Kolwa, and was living with Baluch Khan at Hor Kalat, in 1898.

Thus tranquility was introduced into this wretched country.

The seeds of rebellion remain.

Yet in Panjgur, Kej and Kolwa the elements of disturbance still remained. In Panjgur the fear of Naoshirwani aggression, in Kej also Naoshirwani intrigue, and smouldering feuds and animosities amongst the Gichkis, and in Kolwa the notorious freebooter Baluch Khan left in power to oppress and to rebel; and moreover the universal dislike of a Muhammadan people to a Hindu Nazim,[1] were sparks to be fanned by the first breath of opportunity into a conflagration.

It would indeed appear, from a study of after events, that this pacification of the country resulted in gradually combining all the ruling Sardars in common cause against the paramount power, thus putting a temporary end to internal feuds. The troubles in northern Baluchistan, and the outbreak in Persian Makran, where Mr. Graves of the Telegraph Department was murdered, caused a certain amount of unrest throughout the country.

Nazim Diwan Udho Das.

Baluch Khan, Mehrab Khan Gichki, and a large number of other Sardars of Kej all attributed their own discontent and rebellion to the appointment of, and alleged oppression and tyranny of Diwan Udho Das. It may be here stated that in the final settlement an enquiry was held into these allegations, and the Kej *moti-*

---
[1] Diwan Udho Das.

bars signed a paper saying they had no cause for complaint against Udho Das, and no complaints against him were substantiated. Nevertheless, this probably was the cause of the outbreak.

On the 6th January 1898, Mehrab Khan, Gichki, attacked the Nazim Diwan Udho Das, looted his treasury and took him prisoner; but on the representation of his elder brother he was set at liberty and shut up in Kalatuk, in Kej, under protection of Abdul Karim, Naib of Kej. Mehrab Khan then sent a messenger to Baluch Khan, telling him what he had done. It appears probable that the country at this time was in a state of unusual internal quiescence, and that no outbreak was suspected, because four officers of the Survey Department, with a large unarmed following of lascars, etc., and a very small escort of local levies, were sent to undertake survey operations in the Kolwa and Kej valleys.

Events that led to the expedition of 1898.

On the 9th January at daybreak the camp of Captain Burn, R.E., at Murghi Hor village was attacked and looted; six lascars and ten Punjabis were slaughtered in cold blood. The fifteen men, local escort—under the command of Rustam Khan, brother of Mehrab Khan, Gichki—offered no resistance. Amongst other things Rs. 15,000 and some thirty-five rifles were stolen. Captain Burn, who was sleeping out of camp on a hill about three miles away, was informed of the raid by one of his men who escaped from the camp. He at once started off on foot twenty-five miles to Balor. Here he sent off messengers to warn Lieutenant Turner, R.E., and Messrs. Hickie and Prunty who were engaged on survey work at various places between forty and ninety miles away. Burn then obtained a camel and proceeded to Urmara whence he telegraphed the circumstances to the Officer Commanding Sind District, on the 11th January.

Captain Burn's Camp attacked.

This attack really arose from no feeling of hostility towards the surveyors. It was merely the first act in a campaign of resistance against the paramount power, and a demonstration of determined lawlessness. The answer was prompt. A small force was despatched from Karachi under Colonel Mayne.

Within two hours of the receipt of the telegram from Captain Burn, 250 men of the 30th Baluchis with 3 British officers, 1 Medical Officer and 400 rounds per rifle, all under the command of Colonel Mayne, were despatched from Karachi on board the tug *Richmond Crawford*, which towed behind it a native craft carrying followers, baggage, and one month's rations. On the evening of the 9th January, 100 rifles, 21st Bombay Infantry, under Lieutenant Creagh had left Bombay for Charbar, and 50 under Lieutenant Waller for Jask to protect the telegraph officers at those places.

<small>Despatch of troops to Makran.</small>

In the meantime Sardar Muhammad Hassan of Sami was escorting Messrs. Hickie and Prunty in safety to Urmara, arriving there on the 18th instant, and Sardar Mir Dura Khan, cousin of Mehrab Khan, brought in Lieutenant Turner on the 15th; Ghulam Jan of Balor also assisted him. Muhammad Umar, Naib of Kolwa, hurried him away, being anxious to get rid of him, probably in order that he himself might not be implicated and lose his Naibship. He asserted that Baluch Khan was going to attack at once, and that he himself must return to defend Nag fort against his grandfather's attack. When Lieutenant Turner had gone this Naib looted his belongings.

<small>Loyalty of Sardars.</small>

On arrival at Urmara, Colonel Mayne found that the landing for troops by local *bunder*-boats was easy; horses could be landed in *bunder*-boats which were careened over and the animals forced over-board into four feet of water. The water-supply at Urmara was found to be sufficient for 500 men, but brackish. No supplies or food were available nearer than Kej valley; firewood was scanty, and only twenty-four camels in poor condition could be hired for transport purposes. He therefore decided to leave fifty men at Urmara and to move the remainder of his force to Basol, twenty miles north, covering the Pasni and Balor roads, where good water is abundant and firewood and camel grazing plentiful.

<small>Arrival at Urmara.</small>

Orders were issued for the concentration of a force at Karachi consisting of 250 men, 30th Baluchis; half a squadron, 6th Bombay Cavalry, and a section of No. 4 Hazara Mountain Battery. Two months' supplies were also collected there. The

<small>Concentration of troops at Karachi.</small>

Lieutenant-General Commanding the Forces, Bombay, was directed to settle all further arrangements, dispositions, operations, and despatch of troops to Makran, in direct communication with the Agent to the Governor-General in Baluchistan.

It was reported that at Pasni no supplies, and probably no transport, would be procurable whilst the country was in a state of disturbance; but that at Gwadur plenty of supplies and 100 to 200 camels might be collected in a week or ten days. Also that plenty of supplies of all kinds, and fodder, were procurable in the Kej valley.

On the 16th January 150 men of the 30th Balchuis were sent to Pasni, also warm clothing for the troops already at Urmara. On the 19th January, Colonel Mayne, having collected 190 weakly camels and 65 donkeys, left Urmara to march along the line of telegraph, repairing it as he went, to Pasni, a 100-mile march, which was found difficult owing to scanty water and heat and deaths amongst the camels.

On the 25th January the position and strength of the Makran force were as follows:—At Pasni, 400 rifles, 30th Baluchis, 2 guns, No. 4 Hazara Mountain Battery, and 88 transport mules, under Lieut.-Colonel Mayne, 30th Baluchis. There were also at Karachi, to leave for Pasni on the 27th in I. M. S. *Canning*, $\frac{1}{2}$ squadron, 6th Cavalry,[1] eighty rifles, 30th Baluchis, one British officer, one Native officer and twelve men, Bombay Sappers and Miners, "C" and "D" Sections, No. 42 Native Field Hospital and twelve transport mules.

The orders issued in connection with the operations in the Kej valley were, "Force now under Lieut.-Colonel Mayne at Pasni will push on at once *viâ* Turbat to relieve Khan of Kalat's Nazim, who is shut up in Kalatak fort, and to restore his authority. Force leaving Karachi on 27th instant in *Canning* for Pasni will join Lieut.-Colonel Mayne's force as soon as possible, except the eighty rifles which are intended to afford protection to telegraph working parties at Urmara, Pasni and Gwadar."

A messenger who left Turbat on the morning of the 22nd January reported, on the 25th, through Mir Dura Khan to the Political Agent, Kalat, who was at Pasni, that Baluch Khan and

---

[1] Jacob's Horse.

Mir Rustam Khan joined Mehrab Khan, Gichki, at Turbat on the 17th January, and that they had closed all roads to Turbat. That they had been joined there by Mir Murad and Mir Shukhrullah, Gichkis of Tump; by Mir Ashraf of Mand, the most powerful Rind chief; by Mehrab Khan and Mohim Khan, brother Naoshirwanis from Bolida; also by the Kulanch Sardars Mobarik and Haji Murad. Sher Muhammad, Gichki, was also reported to be strengthening the Nasirabad fort. The enemy were reported to number about 2,000 men armed chiefly in country fashion.

At this time Panjgur seemed quiet. Baluch Khan made it known that he would oppose the troops *en route* to Turbat. No fighting had taken place at Kalatak, though the rebels were threatening to fight Abdul Karim if he protected the Nazim any longer. The Nazim, however, appeared to be quite safe for the present in Kalatak fort.

Pasni chosen as base of operations. Pasni was chosen as the base of operations because the route thence to Mehrab Khan's fort at Turbat is the shortest, and lies over undulating country; also because it is the nearest point from which to support troops in the Kej valley near Sami. Sir Robert Sandeman always recommended it as a port of embarkation, and officers who were with him report that the beach is sandy and shelving, and that sixty horses were embarked there without difficulty. On the 26th January the guns and 159 of the 30th Baluchis were despatched five miles inland, on account of the difficulty of procuring sufficient water and grazing at Pasni, which were to be had in abundance higher up the Shadi river.

The march from Pasni. On the 27th January Colonel Mayne left Pasni at 6 A.M., joining the guns at 8 A.M. The whole force then proceeded fifteen miles from Pasni up the Shadi Kor valley. Owing to difficulties in transport, and the feebleness of such camels as were obtained, due to the recent famine and drought, the force would have been unable to move unless baggage had been reduced to a minimum. Consequently, tents were not carried, and the troops moved on a kit allowance of twelve pounds per man.

The heat by day was great, and there was no shade in the sandy desert. Low rolling hills broke the monotony of stretches of sand,

and pools of fresh water in the otherwise dry river-bed enabled the column to slake their thirst at intervals; while the mimosa and tamarisk shrub relieved the hunger of the camels.

Report said that Mehrab Khan and Baluch Khan with 1,200 men were coming to attack the column, probably at night. Consequently on the nights of the 29th and 30th all were alert, and the officers fully accoutred slept with their men. On January 31st the column set out at 7 A.M. for Turbat. At 7-30 A.M. the advanced guard sighted the enemy.

On this day the road lay for the first four miles from camp, at Basol Kor, over a level plain, then for 7 miles through a long and very narrow defile finally debouching into a broad open stony plain, stretching four miles to Turbat.

Action of Gokh-Prusht. The Baluch Sardars fortunately elected to hold the mouth of the defile, and took up a position half a mile long on some steep hills commanding the entrance. The enemy exposed almost their whole position at a distance of about 4,000 yards, by appearing on the tops of the ridges; their strength was estimated at about 1,500. When the advanced guard arrived within 900 yards of the enemy the latter fired with their breech loaders, of which they had a fair number. At 8-30 A.M., the guns and infantry opened fire from a hill on the left of the road. Captain Jacob was sent with fifty men to occupy a high hill on enemy's left, and Captain Southey with twenty-five men was presently directed to turn their right.

As the turning movement developed, the guns took up an advanced position from which an oblique fire was brought to bear with such telling effect that the enemy's right was broken and rolled back on their centre. At this time, 9 A.M., fifty sabres of the 6th Cavalry, under Lieutenant Naylor, appeared on the scene. This detachment had arrived at Pasni two days after the column had left, and had followed by double marches. Hearing the sound of the guns from their camp about seven miles in rear of Basol Kor, Lieutenant Naylor had pressed on. Lieut.-Colonel Mayne despatched the cavalry to assist in turning the enemy's right with dismounted fire. As the flank attacks developed, enfilading the enemy and commanding his line of retreat, the remainder of the infantry advanced to attack the entrance

of the defile. The guns firing on this portion with great precision caused considerable loss: they were then brought up alongside the firing line, and opened with case at 300 yards. The enemy broke and fled in great disorder, leaving their dead on the ground. A number of camels and horses fell into our hands.

All seemed over, when, suddenly, a band of *ghazis* headed by Baluch Khan himself rushed out from behind a rock where they had been concealed. Flinging away their rifles they drew their swords, and, with cries of "Allah!" "Allah!" charged straight at Captain Jacob and his men. They were all shot down, some getting within twenty paces. So near did they come that Captain Jacob himself shot Baluch Khan with his revolver.

The attack, which lasted two hours, was completely successful. From 200 to 250 of the enemy were dead on the field, amongst them Sardars Baluch Khan, Naoshirwani of Kolwa, Mehrab Khan, Naoshirwani of Bolida, Shakhrullah Khan, Gichki of Tump, Haiatan Khan, Rind of Wakhai, Gul Muhammad Khan, Naoshirwani of Bolida, and other minor chiefs.

Our casualties were:—

	Killed.	Wounded.
6th Cavalry (Jacob's Horse)	1	1
No. 4 Hazara Mountain Battery	1	1
30th Baluchis	2	10

This ended the engagement of Gokh-Prusht, which may be translated "the breaking of the bullock's back." The extract from the *Gazette of India* will be found in Appendix I.

The force at once advanced on Turbat and six shells were fired into the fort to put an end to the garrison's long range firing. Mehrab Khan Gichki refused the terms offered, and determined to face a siege.

On February 1st and 2nd the troops were given a rest pending the arrival of Lieutenant Bovet with detachment of Bombay Sappers and Miners with guncotton, etc., to blow up the fort.

Demolition of Turbat and Charbuk forts.

He arrived at 6 P.M., having marched forty miles in thirteen hours. Next morning, 3rd February, it was discovered that Mehrab Khan and his garrison had fled in the night, evading the patrols.

About noon the same day information was received that he had fled to Charbuk about thirty miles away, and taken refuge with Sher Muhammad. About 5 P.M. the cavalry started to surround the place. They were followed, at 8 P.M., by forty-six infantry mounted on ponies and camels, and later on at 10 P.M., the remainder started. The cavalry arrived about midnight and surrounded the fort, the mounted infantry being only about four hours behind them, and at 10 A.M., the guns and main body arrived, having marched all night except for a halt of one hour. Sher Muhammad agreed to surrender the forts, the great towers of which were blown down by Lieutenant Bovet in the afternoon.

At the commencement of the rising Sher Muhammad did not openly side either with the Nazim or with the rebels. The humiliation to which he was subjected was a cause of great joy to the ryots of his village, who lived in terror of him, but, so long as he had a fort, were compelled to obey his behests. Neither Mehrab Khan, nor any of his wives, or property were found in the fort.

The whole force now reassembled at Turbat, awaiting the arrival of supplies of food, forage, tents, kits, etc., from Pasni. The villagers were much pleased to have troops in their vicinity, as they found a ready market for their produce; and supplies were plentiful.

On the 16th February the heavy baggage arrived, and on the

<small>Expedition to Bolida. Demolition of Chib and Khushk forts.</small>

17th a column of 2 guns, Hazara Mountain Battery, 150 rifles, and the detachment of Sappers and Miners was despatched, under command of Major Evan, to the Bolida valley, where the inhabitants were anxious to please, and supplies plentiful. The forts of Chib and Khushk were demolished. They belonged to Mehrab Khan, Naoshirwani, who was killed at Gokh-Prusht. Bolida is 1,000 feet higher than Kej and the climate more temperate. The march was forty miles; in the second march a wonderful *tangi*, the Garok gorge, is traversed, about six miles in length with good clear water flowing the whole way. It is in places only four feet wide and the precipices on either side rise to a height of several hundred feet.

The Bir fort in the Bolida valley was occupied. This fort is perched on a rocky promontory overhanging the left bank of the Ghish Kor. The houses of the village are built into the rock.

Expedition of Mand.

The column left the Bolida valley on the 21st February and marched to Kalatak. On the 24th February, Lieut.-Colonel Mayne proceeded with 100 rifles to Mand, picking up Major Evan's detachment at Kalatak *en route*. Lieutenant Knox, Political Agent, interviewed the various headmen and Chiefs of Mand, who signed an *ikrarnama* in which they acknowledged themselves to be the Khan's subjects and that remission of revenue would be a favour. They returned to Turbat on March the 8th, 1898.

Difficulties of transport.

The chief difficulty the Makran expedition had to encounter was the want of proper transport. The three previous years had been almost rainless, and the camel-grazing had deteriorated in consequence. The camels, cattle and flocks were all thin and mangy; and there were few camels able to carry a load of more than four maunds; the majority could not carry more than three. A considerable number died during the various marches, although the strain was not excessive.

Arrangements were made to return all Government transport with the cavalry, guns, and 100 rifles with 1 British officer, as an escort to the Political Agent, to Quetta *viâ* Kalat, the remainder of the force with all surplus stores and details to march back to Urmara and return by steamer to Karachi.

The Darbar.

Before leaving Turbat Lieutenant Knox, the Political Agent, held a Darbar which was attended by headmen of Kej and Makran generally. He rewarded with *khilats* those who had been loyal, and addressed the assembly, inviting them to submit petitions against any recent bad government, and promising to return in six months and give petitioners their rights; he also warned all Baluchis that they were expected to assist Government officials in securing peace. He inflicted on rebels fines amounting to about half a lakh of rupees, and was assured that the fines would be realised within three years. The justice of the punishment was generally acknowledged by the guilty. These fines were inflicted and everything was done on behalf of the Khan of Kalat.

The last of the rebels.

At this time Shah Nawaz Khan, son of the late Baluch Khan, having looted twenty-two Martini-Henry rifles of French manufacture from three Pathans who were arrested by Captain Tighe at Urmara, was plotting

a raid on Bolida. He had with him only fifty rifles; it was therefore decided to leave sixty rifles of the 30th Baluchis at Tump under Subadar Ahmad Khan.

Return of the Expedition. These arrangements having been made, the Quetta column, under command of Captain Jacob, consisting of ninety rifles of the 30th Bombay Infantry, the detachment of Bombay Sappers and Miners, the two guns of the Hazara Mountain Battery and the half squadron, 6th Bombay Cavalry, started for Quetta on the 12th March 1898. The remainder of the force followed next day, marching *via* Sharak, Sami, Sohrabih Bet, Ragiwara, Kil Kaur; here the Quetta column branched off to Kolwa; the remainder proceeded by Marestan, Balor, Garm-i-Bent, Dedari Sunt, Draj Bent, Basul Kor, Kandelag to Urmara. Here the baggage was carried in *tonis* to *baggalows* which were towed to the I. M. S *Canning*, on the 29th March 1898.

The Quetta column having blown up the forts of Sharak, Nag, Ser, and Hor Kalat, arrived at Kalat on the 7th and 9th April 1898.

The Tump Detachment. The Tump Detachment was detained in Makran for some time by the Naib of Kej, who feared that he might be attacked by Mehrab Khan Gichki, who had escaped into Persia, and by Shah Nawaz, Naoshirwani. However, the Naib of Kej concluded a treaty with these men, by which they agreed to return to their respective places, presumably Pishin and Kharan, and on the 31st May the Tump detachment marched, arriving in Karachi on the 18th June 1898. The troops of the Khan of Kalat were left to police the country.

With regard to this expedition Colonel Holdich says:—

A small force was despatched under Colonel Mayne, which for the remarkably prompt and effective manner in which (making light of really formidable difficulties) it settled the dispute and dealt out even-handed justice to the leaders of the attack on the survey camp, deserved far more credit than many a frontier expedition which has made more noise in the world.

Pardon to rebel Sardars. In January 1899, a pardon was granted to Mir Mehrab Khan, Gichki, Mir Shah Nawaz, Naoshirwani, and Mir Isa Khan, Naoshirwani, for the part they had taken in the rebellion. Kaoda Muhammad Khan,

late Naib of Panjgur, and Muhammad Umar Khan, Baluch Khan's grandson, who were among the refugees, were also induced to return and make their submission.

After the recall of the troops it was decided to inaugurate in Makran the Brahui form of government. Diwan Udho Das was therefore recalled, and Sardar Mir Mehrulla Khan, Raisani, took over the new administration at the end of the year 1898.

Subsequent history of Makran.

The first act of Mir Mehrulla Khan was to make terms with the refugees of the late rebellion. He placed most of the power in Makran in the hands of Mir Mehrab Khan, Gichki, and recommended Muhammad Umar Khan, Baluch Khan's grandson, to be made Naib of Mashkai, which is the upper part of the Kolwa valley. On the other hand the principal Naoshirwanis of Kolwa and Bolida signed an agreement that they would not acquire fresh landed property in Kej-Makran without the consent of the Khan's representative. The repentant Sardars all signed agreements to remain faithful to the Government, and to create no more disturbances or sedition in the country. Appendix II gives a translation of the bonds signed by them.

It will be remembered that Mir Mehrulla Khan, on taking over the Nazimship, went out of his way to treat Muhammad Umar Khan, Naoshirwani, well. He recommended him for a Naibship, and though apparently this recommendation was not carried out, he gave him an allowance of Rs. 50 a month, with the service of two sowars at Rs. 40 a month more, or Rs. 90 in all.

Muhammad Umar Khan.

For a year or more all went well, but in April 1900, in direct opposition to the Nazim's wishes, Mir Muhammad Umar, Naoshirwani, married one of Sher Muhammad, Gichki's daughters. He then, for a time, took up his abode at Nasirabad, where he joined Sher Muhammad in his unlawful proceedings, and assumed towards the people of the surrounding country the position of an official or chief over them. He was therefore sent back to Kolwa by the Nazim.

In July 1900, Sher Muhammad was killed,[1] and Muhammad Umar with his brother Muhammad Ali and his cousins Naoshir-

---

[1] By Mehrab Khan acting under the orders of the Nazim.

wan and Dur Muhammad (sons of Shahbaz Khan, the fourth son of Baluch Khan) fled *viâ* Bolida to Kuhak in Persia.

He apparently misconceived his position, and imagined that it was incumbent on him, as a son-in-law, to avenge Sher Muhammad; or else he thought that by giving trouble to the authorities he might win his way to favour and preferment. It is not impossible that, putting a wrong construction on the leniency shown to the rebels concerned in the 1898 rising, and noting in particular the greatly increased power and influence lately acquired by Mir Mehrab Khan, Gichki, the only surviving leader of the rising, Muhammad Umar may have entertained some such idea.

At the same time he had a dispute pending with Mir Shahnawaz Khan, the eldest son of Baluch Khan. It also appears that, in accordance with traditional Naoshirwani procedure, he now lays claim to Nasirabad fort and lands. Judging, moreover, from the promptitude with which the Persian tribes, inhabiting a long stretch of country extending from Irafshan to Sarhad, joined forces with Muhammad Umar, it appears more than probable that some preconcerted arrangement had been made for this rising, and that the reported intention of Sher Muhammad to fly to the hills and there commit further mischief was something more than idle rumour.

Having fled to Persian territory Muhammad Umar collected a following of Persian tribesmen, and embarked on a course of border depredations.

Border depredations.

These culminated in December 1900, in the attack on and plunder of the large village of Kantdar in the Dasht district which forms a part of, and lies to the south of, Kej. He had with him over 600 men, and carried off property to the estimated value of Rs. 71,583. In the defence of their village ten of the Kantdar people were killed, and eight wounded. The Nazim of Makran, who had collected a force of 1,500 Makran tribesmen, went in pursuit of Muhammad Umar, and had one or two encounters with him, the results being inconclusive, as Muhammad Umar would not hold his ground. The Nazim meantime had been in communication with Ali Hasham Khan, the Sartip of Bampur, and it had been arranged that the Nazim with his force should join the Sartip at Dizak, and co-operate with him there in effecting the capture of Muhammad

Umar and the punishment of such Persian subjects as had taken part with him in his raids. As the situation demanded the presence in Makran of a British officer, Captain H. L. Showers, Political Agent, Kalat, was despatched accompanied by five Baluch Sardars with twelve mounted followers, and an escort of two British officers (Lieutenants W. O. Grant and A. B. Merriman) and 200 men, 1st Baluchis[1] and a Duffadar and 9 men of the Sind Horse.

Tour of the Political Agent, 1901.

The whole party sailed from Karachi on the 13th January and reached Gwadur next day. At Gwadur they were met by Mir Mehrulla Khan, the Nazim, Mir Mehrab, Gichki, and other Kej Sardars. The Nazim had been on the point of starting for Dizak, but, on receiving the news of the intended tour of the Political Agent, he dismissed his *lashkar* and went to Gwadur. Baggage and horses took nine hours to unload. Camel transport was procured from Turbat through the Nazim, who can at short notice have 1,000 camels available and ready for troops at Gwadur. The hire of a camel was eight annas a day.

It was reported that Muhammad Umar was residing in the local fort with his friend Mir Azam Khan, the chief of the Irafshan district. But the Sartip requested the Political Agent to meet him at Dizak. Accordingly he left Tump on the 14th February and marched by the Nihing and Shahri Kor route. The first 33 miles in our territory, the remaining one 130 in Persia. The country passed through included the Persian districts of Irafshan, Bampusht, Sib and Dizak.

Irafshan and Bampusht are mountainous regions with few villages and a scanty population. The inhabitants joined to a man in the Kantdar raid, and fearful of consequences they invariably fled at the approach of the party. The fairly large village of Hong was found completely deserted. The march through this country has had an excellent effect. The *purdah* has been lifted from it, and the confidence of the people in the security of their mountain fastnesses has been rudely shaken. At the same time it is necessary to recognise that the pursuit and capture of

Irafshan and Bampusht.

---

[1] Now 127th Baluchis.

a small band of fugitives, in such a tract, would be a matter of much difficulty, and could only be accomplished if undertaken by at least half a dozen small and very mobile parties of, say, thirty men each. The local Persian officials are manifestly powerless to help us. Their control over the tribes is of the weakest; and if they succeed in recovering from time to time some portion of the revenue, they do not bother their heads about much else. Thus the region forms a veritable Alsatia for the border outlaw, and if the peace of Kalati Makran is not to be continually disturbed by absconding malcontents, some means must be employed to deprive the neighbourhood of the security it affords. The country round Sib and Dizak is much more open. The local chiefs too, like Sardar Ghulam Rasul of Sib and Sardar Abdullah Khan of Dizak, are men of respectability and importance, who, if made responsible, should be able to exclude unauthorised persons from finding refuge in their country. Sardar Abdullah Khan is nominally the chief of all the Persian districts, from Jalk to Irafshan, that border on Makran. But the Bampusht, Irafshan, Magas, and Kuhak people are practically independent of him.

Sibi and Dizak.

The Political Agent and his party arrived at Dizak on the 27th February, and found the Sartip endeavouring to subdue three forts, *viz.*, Surjo and Shastun held by Mir Ali Muhammad and his brother Mir Bairam Khan, and Bakshan held by their confederate Ghulam Muhammad. The three forts between them could muster some 300 fighting men, and the defenders were in possession of sixteen B. L. rifles, several M. L. rifles and smooth bores of obsolete military pattern, and a large number of matchlocks. Surjo and Shastun are half a mile apart. Bakshan stands by itself a mile and a half away. Round about each fort there is a village, in which the inhabitants of the neighbouring date-groves had fortified themselves, and were making common cause with the rebel Sardars.

Ali Muhammad and Bairam are Baranzais, a small tribe of Afghan origin. They are connected by marriage with the Naoshirwanis, and though not as powerful as Sardars Abdullah Khan and Ghulam Rasul, they hold a position of some importance in Persian Makran. They have a younger brother, named Muhammad Amin, who with several of their men took part in the Kantdar

raid, and received a share of the plunder. It was also ascertained that the property plundered from a Panjgur *kafila* in November 1900 had been brought to Surjo, and there divided, the three brothers receiving a share.

Thus the subjugation of these men was certainly a matter of importance, and one in which we were interested. But it was very soon apparent that the Sartip's promises of a full settlement of all our claims were, to say the least of it, a little premature. In the first place his force was too weak to effect the reduction of the forts. He had with him two guns, one an obsolete and useless muzzle-loader, the other a B. L. piece of small calibre, and about 240 so-called regular troops. To these were added an unorganized and practically useless rabble of tribesmen furnished by Sardar Abdullah Khan. This force had been before Surjo forty days and had effected nothing. It was indeed far more *kilaband* than were Ali Muhammad and Bairam Khan. The latter moved about as they liked, collecting supplies and keeping up free communication between the three forts. The Sartip's men, on the other hand, were all huddled together among the walls of an old ruined village half a mile from Surjo. Nearer the forts they had constructed some advanced posts, from behind the walls of which they kept up a desultory and harmless cannon and small-arm fire. Secondly it was practically certain that Muhammad Umar had neither been recently, nor was now, with Bairam Khan; and thirdly, Bairam Khan, however important, was only one of several leaders who had assisted Muhammad Umar, and if his subjugation was a matter of so much difficulty to the Sartip, there would be small hope of his bringing the others to account, and making them disgorge their share of plunder within any reasonable time. Had the Sartip been strong and able to subdue Bairam Khan, it may be assumed that other chiefs, like those of Irafshan and Magas, would either have joined him at Dizak or made some attempt to meet the claims for the Kantdar raid. But none of them were present at Dizak, and the Sartip had no power to command their attendance. Emboldened by Bairam Khan's success, they had shut themselves up in their forts, and nothing but a siege would bring them to submission.

For the credit of our good name on the border it was impossible to depart again from Dizak leaving Bairam Khan unsubdued. Accordingly after reconnoitring the forts, and visiting the Sartip's outposts, additional posts were established, which would have the effect of confining Bairam Khan more closely to his forts, and of preventing communication between one fort and another. At the same time the troops began the construction of scaling ladders, as, having no guns, it was only by assault that the forts could be taken.

But before letting our men take an active part in the proceedings, the Political Agent deemed it advisable to hear what Bairam Khan had to say, and with the Sartip's consent he opened communications with him. Negotiations continued for two or three days, but on the fourth day Ali Muhammad, Bairam Khan's elder brother, came under guarantee for his safe return, to make his *salaam*. This was followed by a long discussion, and finally the terms of a thoroughly satisfactory settlement were arranged, a result for which great credit is due to Mir Mehrulla Khan and other Sardars. The main terms are, (1) that Bairam Khan and Ali Muhammad would never again shelter or assist Muhammad Umar, or any other person absconding from Makran; (2) that they were to take oath on the *Koran* as to the nature and extent of the property carried off by Muhammad Amin and their men, engaging at the same time to restore at once such articles as were now in Dizak, and to make good the remainder within three months, it being in the possession of various adherents scattered about the district. When the Sartip came into camp, and Ali Muhammad made his submission, it was also agreed, verbally, that Bakshan fort should be handed over to the Sartip, a rider to the compact being that if Ghulam Muhammad, the owner of Bakshan, refused to abide by the arrangement, Ali Muhammad and Bairam Khan were to stand aloof while the Sartip took forcible possession of the place. All this the Sartip fully agreed to.

Next day Bairam Khan came to make his *salaam*. So fearful were the two brothers of treachery, although the distrust was not of us, that nothing would induce them both to leave their fort at the same time. However, Bairam Khan was at once taken

over to the Sartip, to whom he made full submission and was granted in return a written pardon.

The negotiations at Surjo were not concluded until the 10th March, and, with a 480-mile march to Quetta, it was necessary to return, leaving the chief offenders still at large. The Political Agent, however, proposed to meet the Sartip again earlier in the cold season at Sarbaz, where Sardar Husain Khan lives, whence Irafshan, Magas, and other places, occupied by those concerned in the offences, are within easy striking distance.

Makran, 1901.

Regarding the internal state of affairs in Makran, the Political Agent found that the Nazim's administration had, on the whole, been satisfactory. The various chiefs were, outwardly at least, loyal to the Nazim's administration, and prepared to assist him.

The crisis manufactured by Muhammad Umar was of course important for Mir Mehrulla Khan, being the first of any moment he had encountered in the two years of his administration.

The present administration has to face certain dangers. Mir Mehrulla is both feared and respected, but the feature of his administration is the prominent place occupied by Mir Mehrab, Gichki. His influence is not confined to Kej proper, but extends to Tump and Mand, and in a lesser degree to Kolwa, Bolida and Panjgur. He is a *persona grata* with Sardar Husain Khan of Sarbaz and is closely related by marriage to Sardar Ghulam Rasul of Sib. He is thirty-three years of age.

The second cause for apprehension lies in the inevitable exclusion from a share in the administration of other men of importance like Mir Abdul Karim, late Naib of Kej, and Khan Bahadur Muhammad Husain Khan of Sami; Mir Shaikh Umar, the Gichki Sardar, too, is of course dissatisfied at the final triumph of his younger brother, and feels keenly the stoppage of his share, Rs. 2,260 a year, of the telegraph subsidy, which was suddenly transferred from him to Mehrab Khan in 1899.

Another danger is, that three forts are still in the hands of their owners, and are a temptation to set the Nazim's authority at defiance. Again there is a dispute pending between Sardar Shaikh Umar and Mir Mehrab Khan as to the division of the Gichki Sardari rights. The younger brothers Sarfaraz Khan and

Rustam Khan are supported by Mehrab Khan in their claim for a share of the Gichkigari, or dues for maintenance.

Mir Rustam Khan, who commanded Captain Burn's levy escort in 1898, is of a restless and uncertain disposition. At Kolwa, Mir Muhammad Akbar, Naoshirwani, a younger son of Mir Baluch Khan, is Naib, and is doing good work.

Mir Shah Nawaz Khan, who also lives in Kolwa, and who may be considered the chief of the Kolwa branch of the Naoshirwanis, is thoroughly with the Nazim, and is also warmly attached to his younger brother Muhammad Akbar.

At Tump the old Gichki Sardar, Mir Murad Khan, is well meaning but without power or influence. There is in Tump, which includes Nasirabad, no man of particular prominence. A good many Rinds from Mand have acquired possessions in Mand Revenue is collected from them with some difficulty.

The Mand Rinds are now well behaved and contented, except as regards some complaints against their Pishin neighbours. The two leading and most useful men in Mand, now, are Mirs Ashraf and Nur Muhammad, Rinds. They get each Rs. 50 a month from the Nazim's administration.

The present head of the Bolida branch of the Naoshirwanis is Isa Khan, the son of Mehrab Khan who was killed at Ghokh Prusht. He is a well disposed and very promising youth of twenty years of age. He lives with Mir Sarfaraz Khan, a brother of Baluch Khan, a straightforward and respectable man.

Kaoda Muhammad Khan died in 1900, and the Gichki Sardars Mir Abdulla Khan and Muhammad Ali are now fast friends and allies. These two Sardars have two *vakils* whom they use to give trouble, and the *vakils* are disposed to slight the authority of the Nazim's Naib Mir Wahid Bakhsh, Raisani, late a Risaldar in the Kalat State Camel Corps, and a smart, intelligent and energetic man. Abdulla Khan, who is twenty years old, takes little or no interest in the affairs of his chiefship.

At Kharan, Sir Naoroz Khan, showed the Political Agent over his fort. This stronghold, though often assailed, has never succumbed to an enemy, and its reputation for strength is unrivalled among the forts of Baluchistan.

On the 23rd April 1901 the Nazim had a successful encounter with Muhammad Umar and killed eight of his followers. He met

him at Zamran, and Muhammad Umar and the remainder of his following fled into Persian territory.

In August the Nazim reported that Muhammad Umar's men raided Dasht (Panjgur), and in October information was received that a caravan of twenty camels laden with merchandise had been looted by the same party on the road between Kolwa and Panjguri Dasht.

Operations in Makran, 1901-1902.

The Persian Government readily consented to a proposal that the British and Persian forces should act in co-operation on the border during the cold weather of 1901-02.

To this end Captain (now local Lieut.-Colonel) Showers proceeded, in November 1901, with an escort as detailed in the margin, under the command of Major Tighe, D.S.O., 27th Baluchis.

Infantry	..	..	300
Cavalry	..	..	50
Sappers	..	..	20
Mountain guns	..	2

In the meantime, unaware of the intended tour of the Political Officer, Muhammad Umar Khan, early in November, again planned the invasion of Makran. He himself went north to meet Jhiand Khan, the Damani Chief, who had been one of his principal Persian supporters in his attack on Kuntdar, and from whom he hoped to collect additional recruits for his gang, while his brother, Muhammad Ali Khan, made a sudden raid into Kej and occupied the fort of Nodiz. The fort was at once invested by the Nazim and his local forces, and when Colonel Yate, Agent to the Governor-General in Baluchistan, who had proceeded by sea to Makran to meet Colonel Showers, arrived in Turbat, he found that the Nodiz fort had been besieged by the Nazim for 53 days with a force of 985 men, but that Mehrulla Khan had failed to make any impression on the occupants, and despaired of taking the fort without the aid of guns. In these circumstances, the Nazim appealed to Colonel Yate for assistance, and on the arrival of Colonel Showers and his escort a few days later, it was decided to give him the help he needed.

On the 18th December, 1901, Major Tighe moved his camp to within two miles of Nodiz Fort. With him were:—

Capture of Nodiz fort.

250 Rifles, 27th Baluch Light Infantry under Captain Hulseberg.
20 Sappers and Miners under Lieutenant Corry, R.E.

Colonel Showers, Political Agent, also accompanied him.

Captain G. E. Stewart, I.M.S., 27th Baluch Light Infantry was Medical Officer to the force.

On that day at 7 P.M. the Scinde Horse detachment under Lieutenant Maunsell arrived, accompanied by Lieutenant Orton, Intelligence Officer : this detachment had marched sixty-five miles in thirty-six hours.

On the 20th at 9 A.M., the two guns, Murree Mountain Battery, under Lieutenant E. G. Hart, R.A., with the escort of fifty rifles, 27th Baluchis, arrived : they had marched fifty-nine miles between 7 A.M. on the 18th and 9 A.M. on the 20th December. Major Tighe gave these last troops a rest of one hour and a half and then marched into action.

The following is an extract of Major Tighe's orders for the attack on this fort :—

*　　*　　*　　*　　*　　*

EXTRACT OF ORDERS.

Nodiz, 20th December, 1901.

The orders for the attack are as under :—

(i) A guard of forty rifles, 27th Baluchis, will be detailed to guard the camp. Particular attention should be paid to the *karez*[1] west of the camp.

(ii) The Nazim's levies will occupy their present *sangars*[2] round the fort and on no account leave them.

(iii) The guns, with an escort of ten rifles, 27th Baluchis, will take up a position to the south-east of Nodiz fort. Their objectives will be—

　1st—The loopholed tops of the west flank towers.

　2nd—The top of the main tower.

(iv) When the tops of the west flank towers have been demolished, the commander of the guns will sound his "Battery call." This will be the signal that the gun fire has been turned from the west flank towers to the main tower.

(v) The Infantry will be disposed as under—

　(a) *Storming party.*—Forty rifles, 27th Baluchis, under Lieutenant Grant ; Sappers and Miners under Lieutenant Corry, R.E.

---

[1] Underground water channels.
[2] Stone breastworks.

Supports.—Fifty rifles, 27th Baluchis, all under Captain Hulseberg, 27th Baluchis.

Reserve.—Eighty rifles, 27th Baluchis, at the disposal of the Officer Commanding.

This will form the main infantry attack, which will be directed on the south-west bastion of the fort through the date groves.

(b) Fifty rifles, 27th Baluchis, under Lieutenant Orton will push their way to the east side of the fort and occupy the mosque which is outside the fort, and take up a position there to prevent the escape of the enemy.

(vi) The cavalry will take up a position in rear of the guns, ready for pursuit.

(vii) The Hospital and reserve ammunition will be stationed with the reserve.

(viii) The Officer Commanding will be with the supports.

The various parties were timed to leave camp so as to arrive at their respective positions round the fort simultaneously. The direction of the attack was kept secret until the last moment.

The guns opened fire at 11-20 A.M., from a position 600 yards from the fort. The position was within rifle range of the fort, but no other could be found whence the battlements of the south-west flanking defences could be properly shelled.

The guns came under rifle fire directly they appeared in sight, but the enemy's fire was high, and the surrounding scrub afforded shelter from view. The pack animals were protected in a dry watercourse.

As soon as the guns opened fire, Lieutenants Grant and Corry with their parties advanced rapidly through the date groves to the south-west of the fort, and coming under fire " trickled " up to a *karez* and some cotton fields within 200 yards of the walls. Here they found good cover, and opened fire on the loop holes. Only two casualties occurred in this advance. Meanwhile Lieutenant Orton had also moved up to within short range of the fort on the eastern side.

Lieutenant Hart continued to fire on the flank defences, and demolished all the loopholed battlements on the towers. The walls were not fired on, being too thick to be affected by small shells. He then gave the pre-arranged signal; and concentrated his guns on to the main tower.

The enemy, who had deserted the loopholes when shelled, now returned and reopened fire from them. However, the assaulting party had now crept close up to the walls, and Lieutenant Corry, R.E., was ordered to breach the wall of the fort with gun cotton. He advanced with a mining party, Lieutenant Grant covering the loopholes with rapid fire. Finding, however, that the wall near the southwest tower had been sufficiently breached, Lieutenant Corry sent back information. The guns ceased firing, the "charge" was sounded, and the storming party of Baluchis and Sappers and Miners, headed by Lieutenants Grant and Corry, dashed tough the breach, Colonel Showers accompanying them. The storming party was met by a furious fusilade from the "keep" as it entered the breach. Lieutenant Grant was the first to fall, shot through the neck.[1] Several men were killed and wounded, and Lieutenant Corry was shot through the shoulder. The garrison then dashed out of the keep, sword in hand. A fierce *mêlée* ensued in the enclosed space, during which Lieutenant Corry had his hand almost cut off while defending himself against several assailants. Fortunately reinforcements were at hand. Captain Hulseberg, at the head of the supports, was quickly on the scene and drove the swordsmen back to cover.

The guns were advanced to effect a more practicable breach and the reserves were sent in. The enemy then fled from all but the western redoubt, and surrendered to Lieutenant Orton. The western redoubt still held out. It was shelled and the top blown in. The "cease fire" was then sounded and the troops with Captain Hulseberg swarmed in to the assault. Seeing the futility of further resistance, however, the garrison threw down their arms and surrendered.

It was then 1-30 P.M., the action having lasted a little more than two hours. Our losses were four killed and eight severely wounded, including the two officers mentioned above; there were also several men slightly wounded. The enemy had fourteen killed and thirteen wounded. Among the killed were Muhammad Ali (the leader of the gang), and Murad Khan, the owner of the fort. Muhammad Ali's brother and cousin—Dur Muhammad and Bahadur Khan—were both wounded. The rest of the garrison, sixty-three in

---

[1] His wound, though serious, did not prevent his proceeding with the force in its subsequent marches.

number, were taken prisoners. They were subsequently tried by a tribal conference (*jirga*) and sentenced to various terms of imprisonment.

Of the sixty-three prisoners taken, thirty were Persian subjects, residents of Sib and Dizak; the remainder were mostly outlaws from Makran. Some twenty-five Martinis and ten Sniders were taken, and a considerable number of cartridges, apparently obtained from Maskat, besides twelve muzzle-loading rifles and numerous *jezails*.

After the affair at Nodiz, the Political Agent proceeded with his escort to meet the Sartip of Bampur on the Persian border.

Up to the present time there is nothing more to relate of military nature regarding Makran. The Khan's troops having been proved unfit to keep order in the country, a corps has been formed called the Makran Levy Corps commanded by the Assistant Political Agent. The strength of this force is 137 Cavalry and 203 Infantry.

Makran Levy Corps.

The head-quarters of the corps is at Panjgur (180 men) and there are detachments at Diz, Parom, Mand, Suntzar, and Jiwani. The corps was raised by Captain McConaghey in 1904, and is now commanded by Mr. T. O. Hughes. The expenses of this corps are borne by Imperial funds.

BIBLIOGRAPHY.

Blue Books—
Military Operations in Afghanistan	1843
Scinde Administration	1848
Baluchistan 1, 2, and 3	1876
Southern Afghanistan	1878-80
Reorganisation of the Western and North-Western Frontier of India.	1878

Official Publications—
Imperial Gazetteer, Baluchistan	1903
Gazetteer of Dera Ghazi Khan	1897
Gazetteer of North-West Frontier.	
Gazetteer of North-West Baluchistan.	
Census Report, Punjab	1881
Census Report, Punjab	1901

Census Report, Baluchistan .. .. .. 1901.
Gazetteer of the Province of Sind.
Administration Reports, Sind.
Administration Reports, Baluchistan.
Second Afghan War.
Zhob Valley Expedition.
Zhob Field Force.
Zhob Military Report 1906
Makran Expedition 1901
Makran Military Report 1901
Notes on Dera Ghazi Khan Tribes (Bruce).
Derajat Military Report.
Notes on Makran (Holdich).
Kalat. A memoir. (Tate.)
Thal Chotiali and Harnai. (Duke.)
Central Asia, Part III.
Macgregor's Gazetteers.

Non-Official—

Rough Notes, 1838-39	Outram.
James Outram	Goldsmid.
Memorials of Afghanistan	Stocqueler.
Afghanistan, 1839	Hough.
Afghan War	Kaye.
Service in Baluchistan, 1840-42	Stacy.
Travels in Baluchistan, 1810	Pottinger.
Diary of a march through Sind and Afghanistan, 1839-40	Revd. Allan.
History of British India	Murray.
History of British India	Thornton.
Invasions of India from Central Asia.	
Administration of Sind	Sir W. Napier.
Views and Opinions	John Jacob
Records of the Sind Horse	John Jacob.
General John Jacob	Shand.
Sir Robert Sandeman	Thornton.
The Forward Policy and its Results	Bruce.
Indian Frontier Policy	Adye.
Indian Border-land	Holdich.
Baluch Race	Dames.

PART II.

THE FIRST AFGHAN WAR.

THE FIRST AFGHAN WAR.

CHAPTER XII.

AFGHANISTAN.—THE COUNTRY AND PEOPLE.

AT the time of the first Afghan War the frontiers of Afghanistan, which lay between the Indus and the Oxus, were Geographical position. not clearly defined as they are in our day. The great powers moving forward from the east and north-west, which have since closed in on the north also, had not then impinged on the Kingdom of Kabul. The frontiers of British India were still remote, and between them and the present borderland lay an independent Punjab ruled by Ranjit Singh; and the country of the Amirs of Sind. On the north stretched the unknown regions of the Pamirs, while on the north-west the advanced guard of Cossacks had not yet appeared within many marches of the Afghan border, where the country was occupied by independent or semi-independent tribes. Persian territory lay, as now, upon the west, and Afghan dominion extended into Baluchistan.

It will thus be understood that the political and geographical limits of the Afghanistan of seventy years ago cannot be defined. The country, although a few Europeans had visited it, was practically a *terra incognita*, lying on either side far from the borders of western civilization. A land of rocks and stones, bounded on the north and east by great mountain ranges, and on the south and south-west by vast sandy deserts, it possessed but little attraction to the traveller; whilst its people, as wild and inhospitable as their country, were no less forbidding.

But the want of physical attractions in Afghanistan has ever been compensated for by the political importance of its geographical situation on the frontiers between the Western world and the rich Empire of Hindustan.

Mountains. Afghanistan has been well described as "consisting of a star of valleys radiating round the stupendous peak of the Koh-i-Baba, and everywhere surrounded by mountains of a rugged and difficult nature." The whole country is traversed from east to west by the Hindu Kush, a range stretching from the Pamirs, and taking north-west of Kabul the name of Koh-i-Baba. Westward again the great mountain barrier splits into three ranges—the Band-i-Turkistan, Band-i-Baba, and Band-i-Baian.

The north-eastern section of the Hindu Kush, rising to a height of 28,000 feet in its loftiest peaks, presents a formidable barrier. From the north of Kabul, where it is crossed by several passes—the most important the Khawak and Chahardar, 10,560 and 13,900 feet in height respectively—it is practically impassable, until the range is turned in the direction of Herat.

The Koh-i-Baba, which is lower, is traversed by the pass of Hajigak, connecting Kabul and Bamian.

Rivers. The principal rivers of Afghanistan are the Kabul, Helmund, Hari-rud, Logar, Murghab, and Arghandab, while the Oxus now forms a portion of the northern boundary. The Murghab, a mountain stream, rises at the junction of the Band-i-Baba and the Band-i-Turkistan, flows past Bala-Murghab and ends in a lake in the desert north of Merv.

The Hari-rud, rising where the Koh-i-Baba divides, runs west to Herat. Thence flowing north-west to the Perso-Afghan border, it turns north to Zulfikar, and ultimately dividing into two branches is lost in the Tejend swamp. The valley of Herat is irrigated by canals drawn from this river, which is generally fordable.

The Helmund rises in the south-eastern slopes of the Koh-i-Baba, 30 miles west of Kabul, and flows through Hazarajat to Girishk; it then runs through Registan, and is finally lost in the famous Hamun of Sistan, a province which is rendered fertile by its waters.

The Kabul river rises west of the city, then flows through the Tangi Gharu gorge, and after being joined by the Panjshir, which comes down from Ghorband, takes a south-easterly direction. Above Jalalabad it is joined by the Surkhab from the south, and a few miles farther on by the Kunar from the north, the united streams

being nearly a mile in breadth. Passing Dakka and Lalpura, some 40 miles below Jalalabad, the river tends northwards and flowing rapidly through a narrow gorge in the Mohmand hills, enters the Peshawar Valley near Michni, and joins the Indus at Attock. It is generally unfordable below Kabul.

A country varying from snow-clad mountains to fertile and well-watered valleys and sandy and arid deserts, naturally possesses a great diversity of climate. Kabul itself, with an elevation of 5,900 feet, possesses a bracing climate which would be more salubrious were it not for the absolute disregard of sanitation that is to be observed in all Afghan cities. Kandahar (3,342′), Herat (3,062′) and Haibak in (3,511′) can all be unpleasantly hot during two months in midsummer, but on the whole possess a better climate than is to be obtained in the plains of India. In winter snow often lies for two or three months in Kabul. Near Jalalabad (1,850′) and along the Kabul river valley below Jalalabad, the heat is extremely trying during the summer months. The monsoon, which brings relief from the extreme heat to India, has little effect west of the Suliman range, so that the heat in the low-lying valleys is aggravated by frequent dust-storms and only alleviated by occasional thunder-storms.

Afghanistan may be properly divided into its eastern and western regions; the former having the towns of Kabul and Ghazni and the great valley of the Kabul river; the latter containing Kandahar and Herat.

The city of Kabul, 5,900 feet above the level of the sea, lies in a triangular gorge formed by two ranges of high and steep hills which encompass it on three sides. It is approached from the west by a restricted entrance traversed by the Kabul river and the road from Ghazni. On the southern side there is only a narrow path between the city wall and the base of the hills, which are steep, bare and rocky, crowned by a wall with round towers at intervals. This wall is carried along the hills and across the narrow entrance which lies between them. At the period of this narrative the city extended about a mile from east to west, and about half a mile from north to south. It was surrounded by a mud wall. On the summit of a rocky eminence east of the town and separated from it by a

ditch, stood the Bala Hissar, having on its slopes the royal palace and gardens, with an extensive *bazar*, the whole surrounded by a wall and ditch. The chief *bazars* in the city run east and west. The largest *bazar* consisted of a broad street of two-storied houses with flat roofs which extended between their tops. This street had several small squares, with alleys leading into the adjoining streets. The rest of the city was formed of narrow and irregular streets with houses of sunburnt bricks. The population was computed by Burnes at 60,000.

The Kabul river runs close under the northern wall; it is a small brook from August to October, but swollen to large dimensions at times by the melting of the snow in the mountains where it takes its rise.

East of Kabul the country is more open; the road to Peshawar running nearly due east between the two ranges of hills, which form a broad valley. The valley runs east for 25 miles, when it meets a chain of rugged hills crossed by a difficult path over the Lata Band Pass. The valley is about 10 miles broad, but at a short distance from the town a low rocky and barren ridge runs for about 3 miles east and west, dividing it into two nearly equal portions.

On the northern side of the valley the Kabul river runs through fertile country, and leaves the valley, after being joined by the Logar, 5 miles east of the city, passing out through a gorge in the Lata Band. The tracts on the banks of the Logar on the south side are low, marshy and fertile. But the centre of the valley, traversed by the rocky range, is dry and barren. To the west of Kabul lies a broad plain, entered by a narrow pass through the hills, and forming a spacious amphitheatre about 8 miles broad and 12 long. From this plain, which is highly cultivated and fertile, watered by streams from the Kabul river, the hills rise in a succession of ascending heights to the summits of the Hindu Kush. The river, having trees, villages, and forts upon its banks, runs through this plain. The surrounding country is fertile and productive of grain and fruit.

From Kabul to India the main road then ran due east down
The Kabul-Peshawar road. the Kabul valley for 10 miles; it then turned southwards between lofty and barren

hills, through a narrow defile only a few yards in breadth; this pass, the Khurd Kabul, rises to a height of 7,500 feet above sea-level. Ten miles beyond the pass rise the Tezin hills (8,200 feet), whence there is a descent of 1,800 feet into the valley of Tezin. Twenty-two miles beyond this valley, the road entered the Jagdalak Pass. From Jagdalak to Gandamak the road passed through a broad and barren waste encompassed by inaccessible mountains, and passing over rocky ridges and through narrow defiles.

Gandamak, 4,600 feet above the sea, forms an oasis in this desert and cultivation begins again in the valley of Fatehabad, 18 miles from Gandamak. After another 17 miles, the last five over a level and inhabited country, the road reached Jalalabad, distant 105 miles from Kabul and 91 miles from Peshawar, standing in the centre of a plain extending about 22 miles from east to west, and with a breadth of ten or twelve miles. Here the river is broad, clear, and rapid, with numerous villages on its highly-cultivated banks. Jalalabad was at the period of this history a town of some 300 or 400 houses, surrounded by an irregular mud-wall, and by gardens, buildings and ruins, with a population of about 2,000.

From Jalalabad the road ran 42 miles to Dakka across a hilly tract between two ranges of mountains which are barren and stony, and slope from north to south. The Kabul river here runs along the northern edge of the plain, flowing frequently through narrow passages in the rocks. About 44 miles from Jalalabad, high hills rise between the Safed Koh and the secondary ranges of the Himalayas, blocking the valley of the Kabul for 30 miles. The river runs through narrow gorges, while the road penetrated the high hills by the Landi Khana defile, where it entered the Khaibar pass.

The following description of the celebrated pass was written by an officer who traversed it from west to east in 1840:—Landi Khana, 8½ miles. We traversed for some two miles a stony plain, and then entered the mouth of the Khaibar Pass. Just before emerging among the hills the Safed Koh became again visible, but was soon shut out from view. The defile into which we entered was by no means narrow (never less than fifty yards in breadth), and the hills neither steep nor difficult, but at nearly every point accessible by infantry. After

The Khaibar Pass.

about two miles of defile, the passage widened considerably at about six hundred yards, and here in the centre we passed an isolated eminence, on the summit of which we passed a small fort or breast-work constructed of loose stones, and garrisoned by a company of *Jazailchis*. After this the pass narrowed again. We ascended considerably, but the road was by no means difficult, though everywhere stony. Stunted trees and bushes throughout the defile. Encamped on uneven ground close to the foot of the ghaut, leading over the summit of the pass, some cultivated land rising in terraces to the summit of the hills to the south, and some rude fortifications, now dilapidated, are to be seen on the same side of the defile. Looking back, the summits of many mountains visible to the north-west the most distant partially covered with snow. We travelled towards the south-east to-day.

From Landi Khana the road led up the side of the hill to the left, passing round two shoulders. The ascent not steep, but the road wound in and out, occasioned by various fissures, or water channels, in the face of the mountain. After rounding the second shoulder we descended gently into the bed of the stream, which was previously too confined and rocky to allow of guns passing. The was the case again occasionally, necessitating the road to pass, over parts of the hill, the ascents on these occasions, though short and not very steep, difficult on account of awkward bends occurring at the very foot. Most of the carriages had to be unlimbered on this account at three of the ascents. After about four miles we reached the summit of the pass; the hills seceded right and left and we entered on a broad extensive tableland, sloping gently towards the east, well-cultivated and sprinkled with forts, hills on all sides, but not very lofty, also a few insulated eminences. The plain sometimes stretched miles across, and here and there valleys branching off to the right and left. After about five miles the valley narrowed, and the descent became more sensible; and as we approached Ali Masjid we entered into a narrow defile, enclosed by precipitous rocks; this, however, only continued for about half a mile, when we passed close under the fort of Ali Masjid, and encamped about a mile lower down the glen. Distance marched to-day, 14 miles.

The Khaibar hills, and the defile through which we passed, are tolerably well wooded, but the trees are stunted, indeed, scarcely

anything more than bushes. On the open land, at the most elevated part of the pass, there are many forts, and much cultivation also in the valleys branching off on either side; but the forts are the worst I have met with. They have only one tower each, and that very weak. The fort of Ali Masjid is better built and designed, but its strength consists in its situation, it being on the summit of a lofty hill, insulated and difficult of access to the south-west of the road. The mosque is in the valley below. Immediately after passing Ali Masjid, the hills decrease in altitude and steepness. Our direction of march tortuous to-day, but generally south-east.

16. Jamrud, 7 miles. From our last ground we ascended the hill-side on our left by a steep, tortuous road; there was another road to the left, but we did not know of it, exceedingly easy, so we pulled the guns up the ascent; after which we proceeded for some distance over undulating ground, an elevated table-land, and passed over one narrow defile by a well-built bridge. We then descended into the bed of a stream by a good road cut in the side of the hill. The remainder of the march lay through low hills, until we debouched into the plain near Jamrud.

Kabul to Ghazni. The road from Kabul to Ghazni runs for six or seven miles through a highly cultivated tract until it ascends the high ground on leaving the Kabul valley. There is then a descent of three miles to Arghandi. It is then hilly and difficult along the ridge of the Maidan valley for twenty miles to Maidan, four miles beyond which the Kabul river is crossed. From Shekhabad it descends to the valley of the Logar, and passes through a defile, emerging in the vicinity of Haidar Khel. The last fourteen miles to Ghazni there is a steady ascent for three miles at first to the Sherdahan, a formidable pass at an elevation of 9,000 feet. The road then descends to a plateau which stretches to Ghazni. In winter the pass is blocked with snow and impassable.

Ghazni. The town of Ghazni lies some 7,800 feet above sea-level and ninety miles south-west of Kabul on the road to Kandahar, from which it is distant 222 miles. It is built upon an isolated ridge, with the citadel in the centre on the highest point. The outer wall winds round the hill with a circuit of about a mile and a quarter. The houses,

which were loop-holed, had flat roofs. The streets are narrow. The citadel contained the houses of the *sardars*. The town is commanded by a low hill near its north-western angle. The town contained at this period some 3,500 mud houses. The surrounding country is fertile.

From Ghazni to Kandahar is a distance of 222 miles, Kala-i-Ghazni being reached after a gradual descent of 138 miles, as the road approaches Kandahar, after traversing the narrow Tarnak defile, the valley expands to a width of some thirty miles. The open portions of the valley are populous and well-cultivated, the hills rising from the banks of the Tarnak, being undulating and barren.

Ghazni to Kandahar.

The town of Kandahar is separated from the Tarnak river by the Tarkani range of hills, and is surrounded on three sides by lofty and rocky mountains, which rise abruptly from the plain. The open side leads to the city from the valley of the Tarnak. The plain of Kandahar is fertile and well cultivated, watered by numerous canals from the Arghandab, a tributary of the Helmund. A few miles to the east, however, is a bare and sterile desert.

Kandahar.

The town is situated on the north side of an extensive plain, about two miles from the Baba Wali mountain. It is surrounded by a wall, thirty feet in height, having numerous bastions, in the form of a quadrilateral 1,600 by 2,000 yards in extent. The four principal *bazars* lead from a gateway which opens nearly in the centre of each side, and meet in a large market place in the centre. The rest of the town is traversed by narrow lanes between lofty houses. It is noteworthy that the present town was founded by Nadir Shah, when he besieged old Kandahar in 1738.

Herat lies 400 miles north-west of Kandahar, and 500 miles by the direct road from Kabul. Known as the "Gate of India," from its being the main route of invading armies, it possesses more strategical importance than, perhaps, any other point in Asia. From Kandahar it is reached by way of Girisk, Farah, and Sabzawar; the first named being a fort commanding the passage of the Helmund.

Herat.

Herat lies in an expanse of fertile plain, and all the great roads leading on India converge within the limits of its territory.

By this way alone could a well-equipped modern army make its way to the frontiers of India. Both the nature and resources of the country are such as to favour the success of an invader. All the materials necessary for the organisation of a great army are to be found in the neighbourhood of Herat. The extraordinary fertility of the plain has entitled it to be called the "Granary of Central Asia." Its mines supply lead, iron, and sulphur; the surface of the country is laden with saltpetre; and upon the possession of such a country would depend, in great measure, the success of operations for the invasion of India.

The city of Herat in 1837 stood within solid earthen walls, surrounded by a wet ditch. The four sides were each about a mile in length, facing towards the points of the compass. The town sloped from its most elevated quarter in the north-east to the south-west. The real defences of the place were two covered ways on the exterior slope of the embankments, one within and the other without the ditch. The lower one was on a level with the surrounding country, its parapet partly covered by a mound of earth on the counter-scarp, the accumulations from the cleansings on the ditch.

On the northern side the citadel overlooked the city. Built entirely of masonry, with lofty ramparts and numerous towers it was a place of considerable strength; but its defences were in a state of disrepair, and crumbling into decay, when news was received of the approach of the Persian invading army in 1837.

The interior of the city was divided into four nearly equal divisions by two streets which crossed each other at right angles in the centre. The inhabitants numbered about 45,000, the majority Shiah Muhammadans.

This wild and inhospitable country is naturally inhabited by a hardy and warlike people. It is not necessary here to describe the general character of the Afghans or Pathans, which has been sufficiently set forth in the Introduction to this series, while it is also displayed in the events recorded in this narrative.

The people.

Only about half the various races inhabiting the country are true Afghans or Pathans. The people have no common bond, save that to be found at times in common subjection to a strong ruler. Even in religion they are divided into the Sunni and Shiah sects.

The Duranis, who have been the ruling race for the last 160 years, number about 1,200,000; and it should be noted that of two of the principal figures of this history, Shah Shuja was a Saddozai and Dost Muhammad a Barakzai of this tribe.

The Duranis are divided into sections:—

(a) Barakzai live round Kandahar and have a colony at Herat, inhabit the most fertile parts of Afghanistan and hold the chief appointments.

(b) Achakzai—Kandahar and Quetta.

(c) Popalzai. The best known branch is the Saddozai, they inhabit the hills north of Kandahar and have a colony in Derajat which supplies recruits to the 15th Bengal Lancers.

(d) Alikozai, a small scattered tribe.

(e) Nurzai, in the valley between Quetta and Kandahar; also at Girishk, Sabzawar, and Herat.

(f) Ishakzai, on the banks of the Helmund as far as Sistan and near Girishk.

(g) Alizai, Zamindwar, north of Girishk.

(h) Khugianis on the skirts of the Safed Koh.

(i) The Mohmands, partly in Afghanistan, partly in British territory. Their country is enclosed by the Kunar, Kabul, and Swat rivers.

There are eight principal clans of **Ghilzais**. They are essentially a nomadic people. Their boundaries are Kabul and the Laghman valley on the north to Kalat-i-Ghilzai and Zhob on the south; the Paghman and Sanglakh ranges on the west, to the Kabul province. They are also found in Herat. Their numbers are 1,000,000.

Other Pathan tribes—

(a) Shinwaris, Jalalabad Valley.

(b) Jadrans, south of Khost.

(c) Jajir, between the Paiwar Kotal and the Shuturgardan and Northern Khost.

(d) Mangals, Upper Kurram Valley.

(e) Khostwal, Khost.

(f) Wazirs, Upper Tochi. They are all Darwesh Khel.

(g) Makbils.

(h) Chamkannis.

(i) Tanis.

(j) Kakars.

(k) Barechis, connected with the Duranis. West of Quetta and south-east of the Registan.

Non-Afghan tribes.

The Hazaras—of Tartar origin. They inhabit the country north of the Kandahar-Ghazni road and their northern boundaries stretch from Daulat Yar to Haibak. They speak Persian and are Shias; their trade is that of shepherds, and, having great powers of endurance, they make excellent labourers and furnish the material for the 106th Pioneers. They number about 500,000.

The Tajiks (or Parsiwans) are of Arab descent. They speak Persian and are mostly Sunnis. They are scattered throughout Afghanistan and number 1,500,000.

The Uzbaks are of Turkoman origin and are chiefly found in Badakhshan and Afghan Turkistan. They are principally zamindars. They number 750,000.

The Kazilbashis are of Persian origin and are settled at Kabul. They mostly speak Persian and are Shiahs. They are well educated and make good soldiers. They are well-disposed to the British, and number 100,000.

The Chahar Aimak—Nomad tribes.

(1) Jamshedis. Inhabit the country north of Herat. Are Sunnis, speak Persian, and are a pastoral people. Numbers 20,000.

(2) Firozkohis. Sunnis; language Persian. Numbers 50,000.

(3) Taimanis. Inhabit the Upper Farah Rud Valley. Shepherds and cultivators; Sunnis; speak Persian; numbers 160,000.

(4) Taimuris. Of Arab descent. Inhabit the Perso-Afghan frontier. Numbers 150,000.

There are in addition the Brahuis, on the Helmund and in Registan, and the Balochis, inhabiting the Helmund Valley and Afghan Sistan. Kafiristan is peopled by an aboriginal tribe, the Kafirs, of whom little is known.

Early History.

The history of the various dynasties which have ruled over Afghanistan is largely the history of the invaders of Hindustan; for the existing frontier of British India has never presented a serious obstacle to invading hordes, and the natural frontier of India would appear to be on the Hindu Kush. In the dawn of history we find the country from Kabul to the Hydaspes (Jhelum) under one ruler, a *satrap* of

Darins; so that the army of Alexander the Great, having conquered the region which is now Afghanistan, met with no opposition on the direct route through the Khaibar Pass.[1]

It is foreign to this work to enter into a description of the dynasties of Mahmud of Ghazni, Muhammad Ghori, the Mughals, who overran the whole of Central Asia and the Ghilzais. They are ancient history.[2] It is, however, interesting to note that in 977 A.D., Sabaktagin of Ghazni invaded India by way of the Khaibar Pass while his successor, Mahmud, made many invasions between the years 1001 and 1024, by way of the Khaibar, the Gomal, and the Tochi Valleys.

Invaders of India.

After a contest with Ghazni, the house of Ghor prevailed, and established their rule in Afghanistan; and Muhammad Ghori invaded India more than once. These invaders were followed by Taimur, the descendant of Changiz Khan, who established Mughal rule in Afghanistan, and by Babar, the founder of the Mughal Empire in India.

In 1737 Nadir Shah of Persia conquered Kandahar and Kabul on his way to India. He was murdered on his return to Persia in 1747. He had in his army a contingent of Abdalis under Ahmad, a Saddozai Chief. The Abdalis seized the treasure of the dead Shah, and marched to Kandahar, where Ahmad was proclaimed Shah, and established the Durani Empire.

The Durani Empire.

Like his predecessors, Ahmad Shah invaded Hindustan, entering by the Khaibar with 12,000 men in 1748, and coming again through the Bolan on two occasions in 1756 and 1758. His son, Taimur, married a daughter of the Emperor of Delhi, who brought the Punjab as her dowry. Ahmad Shah died in 1773, and was succeeded by Taimur, on whose death the five provinces of Kabul, Kandahar, Herat, Peshawar, and Kashmir were held by five of his sons; and a struggle for the supreme succession ensued.

The Barakzais now come on the scene. Their most powerful Chief, Sirdar Painda Khan, supported Zaman and proclaimed him Shah. Rebellions followed, and after one of these Ranjit Singh

---

[1] While Alexander entered the Punjab by way of Swat and Bajaur, his Lieutenant ephæstion marched through the Khaibar Pass, accompanied by Taxiles, King of the country between Kabul and the Jhelum.

[2] See *The History of Afghanistan* by Colonel G. B. Malleson, C.S.I.

was appointed Governor of the Sikhs in the Punjab. Later, Painda Khan was put to death by Zaman Shah; and his son, Fateh Khan, fled for refuge to Mahmud, brother of the Shah, and assisted the latter to defeat Zaman and proclaim himself King of Kabul.

In 1803 Shuja-ul-Mulk imprisoned his brother, Mahmud, assumed the sovereignty, and appointed Fateh Khan his Wazir.

Both French and Russian influence were early active in Persia, with a view to encroachments into Afghanistan on the road to India. Already when in Egypt in 1799 we find Napoleon Bonaparte contemplating the invasion of India and corresponding with Tipu Sultan, the inveterate enemy of the British in Mysore. At this time Bonaparte wrote to the Directory—"Mistress of Egypt, France will by and by be the Mistress of India." A mission was then sent under Captain (afterwards Sir John) Malcolm to counteract French influence in Persia. Again in January 1805, when preparing for the invasion of England, Napoleon proposed to attack the East Indies with the Brest squadron and 30,000 men; and in 1807 he concluded a treaty with the Shah, under the terms of which " France promised to drive Russia from Georgia, and to supply Persia with artillery; in return the Shah was to break with England, confiscate British property, instigate the peoples of Afghanistan to rebellion (*sic*), set on foot an army to invade India, and in case the French should also despatch a land force against India, he was to give them a free passage along a line of march to be subsequently laid out, together with means of sustenance."

Western designs on Afghanistan and India.

The favourite project of the invasion of India was discussed by Napoleon with Alexander of Russia at Tilsit, where it was suggested that an expedition to Egypt should sail from Corfu, while the united armies of Russia, France, and Austria were to march on India.

It will thus be understood that the designs of European powers to wrest the Empire of Hindustan from the grasp of the British by means of an invasion from the north-west, date back to the earlier times of our hold on India. And it was inevitable that not only Persia but Afghanistan should in course of time come within our political purview.

---

1 Sloane's *Life of Napoleon Bonaparte*.

The British first had dealings with the Afghans in 1808-09, when Elphinstone was sent to establish friendly relations with Shah Shuja.[1] Shortly after this Shah Shuja deprived Fateh Khan of his offices, and the latter with his brother, Dost Muhammad, raised a force of Barakzais, defeated Shah Shuja, who fled to Ludhiana, and replaced Mahmud on the throne. Fateh Khan now became the virtual ruler, but the jealousy of the King's son compassed his downfall; he was first blinded and afterwards put to death.

The Barakzais then rebelled, and Dost Muhammad defeated Mahmud and established himself at Kabul. Meanwhile Peshawar and Kashmir had fallen into the hands of the Sikhs, with whom Dost Muhammad was at war when this history opens.

In 1834 Shah Shuja left his asylum at Ludhiana and entered Afghanistan with an army by way of the Bolan Pass. Dost Muhammad defeated him at Kandahar; and consolidated his power at that place, and at Kabul, Ghazni and Jalalabad.

---

[1] The treaty concluded with the Shah by Mountstuart Elphinstone was to counteract the designs of the French and Persians, who had entered into a compact to invade the dominions of the King of the Duranis.

CHAPTER XIII.

BURNES MISSION TO KABUL.

IN the autumn of 1835 Lord Auckland was appointed Governor-General of India; the Whig Government, which had just been returned to power, having cancelled the appointment of Lord Heytesbury. The new appointment occasioned some surprise. India was in a state of profound tranquility, and the work demanded of the new Governor-General promised to be of a tranquil order. Nor did the early days of his Government disappoint popular expectation; although he probably did not disregard the menaces of Persia nor the intrigues of Russia. The reports of the British Minister at the Persian Court were, however, probably read with a vague interest, but the prospects of a British Army being encamped before the capital of Afghanistan were certainly little anticipated. It was necessary, however, to collect information about the countries lying between the Indian frontier and the eastern boundaries of the Russian Empire, and the conclusion arrived at from the study was that although Russia might not be advancing she was at any rate urging Persia in an easterly direction.

In the spring of 1836 Dost Muhammad wrote a letter of congratulation to Lord Auckland, in which the following prophetic words occurred "I hope that your lordship will consider me and my country as your own." In his reply the Governor-General alluded to the possibility of a commercial mission to Kabul, and reminded the Amir that it was not the British Government's policy to interfere with the affairs of independent States.

The project of a commercial mission had been before suggested, and Lord Auckland probably thought that information not of a commercial character might be obtained at the same time, for the aspect of trans-frontier affairs caused him some uneasiness.

Lord Wellesley[1] had been disturbed by the thought of Afghan invasion, and much had been learnt concerning the countries between the Indus and Oxus. Before the close of the eighteenth century Forster had travelled *viâ* Kabul, Kandahar, and Herat to the Caspian. Elphinstone, although he had seen little of Afghanistan, had written a standard work on the history and geography of the Durani empire. Moorcroft under the aegis of Sir Charles Metcalfe, but with no encouragement from Government, had spent the last six years of his life in exploring Ladakh, Kashmir, Afghanistan, Balkh, and Bokhara. In 1828 Stirling returned from furlough *viâ* Afghanistan and, so little did the Government appreciate his efforts, he was penalised for overstaying his leave of absence. No interest whatever was taken in Trans-Indus affairs.

<small>Travels in Afghanistan.</small>

Conolly, however, met with a kinder fate when he returned to India *viâ* Persia and Kandahar. The delay in the publication of the results of his journey, however, deprived him of the credit which was his due. In 1830 Alexander Burnes traversed Sind *viâ* the Indus and visited Lahore, where Shuja-ul-Mulk expressed his longing to see an Englishman at Kabul, and the road between India and Europe opened. At Simla he succeeded in firing Lord William Bentinck with some of his own enthusiasm and obtained his countenance to a journey to England *viâ* Central Asia. He was hospitably received at Kabul by Dost Muhammad, of whom he formed a very favourable opinion. He visited Meshed, Tehran, Isfahan, and Shiraz, making the acquaintance of the Shah, and reported the result of his travels to the Governor-General before proceeding to England. While at home he urged upon the Court of Directors the desirability of a commercial mission to Kabul, but it was feared that politics would soon intrude themselves and that difficulties would arise, and his proposal was negatived. On his return to India, however, the Government of India decided to despatch him on a commercial mission to Afghanistan, and at the close of 1836 he, with his party, set out " to work out the policy of opening the River Indus to commerce." Visiting Haidarabad, Bahawalpur, and Dera Ghazi Khan, the

<small>Despatch of the Mission.</small>

---

[1] Governor-General from 1798 to 1805.

mission reached Peshawar, and passing safely through the Khaibar Pass reached Kabul on the 20th September 1837. Their reception was all that could have been desired, and on the following day Dost Muhammad formally received the mission. In spite of the name by which it was designated, the Commercial Mission at once developed into a political one. Two days later a long conversation took place, the war with the Sikhs furnishing the chief topic. At subsequent interviews the Amir frankly placed politics in the fore front, and a correspondence then commenced between Burnes and Mr. Macnaghten, the Foreign Secretary.

Kandahar at this time was bent on a Persian alliance, and had sent presents to the Shah and the Russian embassy; this was largely due to the belief that the Kabul Chief was entering into an arrangement with the British to their exclusion. Burnes stated his belief that but for the timely arrival of the mission the Russians and Persians would have had agents at Kabul. Burnes now wrote to Mr. Macnaghten that the British position at Kabul was most satisfactory, and alluded to the substantial offers of Russia, Persia, Bokhara and other States, to all or any of which the Kabul Chief preferred the sympathy and friendly offices of the British. Before he entered Afghanistan, Burnes had written to the British Minister in Persia to use his utmost endeavours to stop the intercourse of the Kandahar Chiefs Pur Dil Khan and Kohan Dil Khan, with the Russian Mission. Earlier he had warned Kohan Dil Khan of the displeasure of the British Government if he continued his intrigues; the latter promised compliance with his wishes, and Lieutenant Leech, with full instructions, was sent to Kandahar; Burnes hoping thereby to keep the Persians in check and, at any rate, obtain early information which would enable him to act promptly. He was severely censured by Government for exceeding his instructions, and informed that, were it not through the fear of weakening his position, the promises he had made would have been cancelled. Lord Auckland subsequently confessed that Burnes had acted in the best way possible. The Kandahar Chiefs now embraced the Persian alliance and entered into a formal treaty with the Shah under a Russian guarantee.

Kandahar politics.

Friendly disposition of Amir.

On the 19th December a Russian officer, named Viktevitch, arrived at Kabul, to act as agent for the Russian Government. An account of his reception was at once reported by Burnes to the Indian Government. On the arrival of this fresh mission the Amir sought Burnes' advice, offering to dismiss the Russian forthwith, should that course commend itself to him. Burnes was, however, for some time doubtful as to his real character and the value of his credentials. A month later he reported that he had as yet no further information to shake his *bonâ fides* and that Viktevitch's reception had been the reverse of encouraging. Dost Muhammad still preferred help from England than from any other State; his hopes were shortly rudely shattered. Burnes, tied by his instructions, was unable to hold out any prospect of the mediation of the British Government between the Amir and Ranjit Singh. He recommended Dost Muhammad to waive all claim to Peshawar and to be content with such arrangements as could be made by his brother, Sultan Muhammad, with Ranjit Singh. The Amir protested that he would rather Peshawar should remain in the hands of the Sikhs. In March, Burnes was forced to repeat his inability to help. The British Government called upon Dost Muhammad to abstain from connecting himself with any other State, and in return promised to restrain Ranjit Singh from attacking him; more they would not offer.

A few days later Jabbar Khan, brother of the Amir, again appeared before Burnes with the Amir's demands, *viz.*, protection from Persia; the surrender by Ranjit Singh of Peshawar, and several other proposals. Burnes replied that he could accede to none of these propositions, and wrote a letter requesting permission to depart. In spite of what had taken place, the Amir invited Burnes to a further conference at the Bala Hissar, but though the meeting ended amicably it produced no results.

On the 21st March the Amir wrote a friendly letter to Lord Auckland as a last despairing effort, but it failed in its object. Other meetings with Burnes took place, but he had no hope of bringing matters to a favourable issue. British policy had now done its work; one of the Kandahar Sardars arrived at Kabul to

win over the Amir to the Persian alliance, and Viktevitch was sent for and paraded through the streets. Burnes left Kabul on the 26th April, Viktevitch soon afterwards left for Herat, having promised all Dust Muhammad wanted, money to the Barakzai Chiefs, and the propitiation of Ranjit Singh, to whom he had already made overtures. British influence, however, was at this time strong at Lahore. Mackeson managed the business of counteracting Russia's designs with skill, and won a promise from the Maharaja to have nothing to do with her agent. The knowledge of these advances, however, made Government specially desirous of conciliating the Maharaja.

Departure of British and Russian Missions from Kabul.

Russian promises now began to carry everything before them. The Russian Ambassador wrote to the Sardars that Muhammad Shah had promised to restore Herat and that he himself would also obtain for them Ghorian. This letter did not bring an equal amount of satisfaction to the Amir. The Russian alliance was unpopular at Kabul, and the dissolution of the friendship with the British was deplored. The Persian army was rushing on failure and other tidings came to alarm him. The Russian game was nearly played out and the resentment of the British was about to break forth. He saw that the Russo-Persian alliance was built upon a foundation of sand, and that a British subaltern within the walls of Herat was setting his new friends at defiance.

Russian ascendancy.

It is now necessary to describe briefly the events which at this period were taking place at Herat. A son of Yar Muhammad Khan, the Wazir, was governor of the city; as his salary was insignificant he supplemented it by plunder and the sale of the inhabitants into slavery. This tyranny incited the people against their Afghan masters, and many looked forward to emancipation at the hands of the Persian King.

The Siege of Herat.

Such was the last remnant of the old Afghan monarchy in the hands of Shah Kamran; his government was one only in name and he himself was weak and broken down by a life of debauchery. His Wazir, Yar Muhammad, was an even less attractive personality. Although courageous he was absolutely unscrupulous, and bore the unenviable reputation of being the worst man in Central Asia.

In the summer of 1837 rumours of the movements of the royal army were astir in the city. The King and his Wazir were campaigning in Sistan, where the attempted reduction of the fortress of Juwain had crippled their military resources, for which they soon had cause to lament. After events showed that the cavalry, thus frittered away, would have sufficed to prevent the Persian Army from leaving its own frontier.

News of the projected return of the army speedily reached Herat. Orders for the collection of grain and the repair of the defences were daily coming in. The reasons were clear. An Ambassador had been sent to Muhammad Shah to solicit his assistance in the recovery of Kandahar and Kabul; the reply was couched in no vague terms. The Persian monarch claimed both principalities for himself, and, as the first step in the operations to make good his claim, intended to take possession of Herat. It was said that the Shah-in-Shah proposed to the Amir his submission as the price of assistance in a religious war against the Sikhs. Herat was to be reduced and Kamran deprived of his titles; coins were to be struck in the name of the Persian King, and a Persian force was to garrison the city. Shah Kamran indignantly rejected these terms.

The greatest excitement now prevailed in Herat. The Shiahs hailed the coming of the Persian monarch with enthusiasm, and predicted the success of the enterprise, while the Sunnis were firm in their intention to resist the invader to the last drop of their blood.

On the 17th September the King returned to Herat. Among the many who went out to witness his entrance was Eldred Pottinger, a Lieutenant of the Bombay Artillery, who had reached Herat from Kabul a month before. He had been travelling unofficially to gather information concerning Afghanistan. Although very slightly acquainted with the Persian language, and ignorant of Muhammadan ritual, he had passed on his way almost unquestioned. When challenged on the score of his apparent ignorance he allayed suspicion by quoting Indian usage.

He sent a message to the Wazir offering to meet him, and, to his surprise, Yar Muhammad at once consented to receive him. A few days later he was received by the King. He was all

eagerness to share in the coming struggle, convinced that his duty to his country demanded all his energies in the arrest of a movement which not only threatened the independence of Herat, but the stability of the British Empire in the East.

An order was now issued that all grain and forage should be brought from the surrounding villages into the city; and that the villagers themselves should live within its walls. On intelligence reaching Herat at the close of October that the Persian army had arrived at Turbat, further orders were given for the entire destruction of all remaining supplies, and the soldiers were let loose upon the country to give effect to the decree. While these measures kept the grain, firewood, and forage from falling into the enemy's hands, it had the undesired effect of destroying the little discipline which the soldiers possessed. Henceforth it was impossible to control them.

It was ascertained that the Persians were advancing in three bodies, the advanced party, some 10,000 men, being under the command of Alayah Khan, better known as the Asaf-ud-Daulah. Their movement in compact bodies nonplussed the Afghans, who could make but few captures, and who ascribed their formations to fear.

Promises of a hard winter, a prediction cruelly falsified, buoyed up the hopes of the Heratis. It had also been expected that the invaders, as on a previous occasion, would content themselves with masking Ghorian, reputed even stronger than Herat. It was, however, besieged, and its fall announced on the 15th November. Yar Muhammad attributed its capitulation to the cowardice or treachery of his brother, Sher Muhammad Khan; but, at the time of its surrender, Colonel Stoddart pronounced it to be untenable. Arrangements for the defence of Herat were now carried on with redoubled energy. No one was permitted to leave the city, and the people from the surrounding country crowded in. Excitement and alarm were general. Many suspected of infidelity were imprisoned and their property was confiscated. The Shiah Mullas were arrested and confined lest they should foster disaffection. Work upon the fortifications went on incessantly, and troopers scoured the country to cut off stragglers. Still the Persian army advanced, and on the 22nd November the advanced guard took

up a position to the north-west of the city. The Afghans charged the Persian cavalry with success, but the infantry beat them off. The Persian field guns opened, and were replied to from the city. Afghan horsemen, dismounting, and taking advantage of cover, fired upon the Persian gunners, but were driven back by the enemy's skirmishers. The contest had now fairly commenced.

The following day, the 23rd November, the siege commenced,

Siege of Herat.

one of the most remarkable in history, alike from its protracted nature, the gallantry of the chief actors, and the magnitude of the political results. The Persians established themselves to the west of the city, and although the Afghans disputed every inch of ground they were driven within the walls. Two facts were to be deduced from the preliminary operations. First that little reliance could be placed upon the strength of the defences ; secondly, that the war would be carried on with hatred and inhumanity to supply deficiencies of science and courage. The Heratis bent their attention to the strengthening of their defences, while the Persians entrenched themselves and threw up batteries. The rockets struck terror into the hearts of the besieged, though the practice was too wild to be efficacious. In this way the siege continued throughout the months of November and December, without any success to the Persians, and the besieged gathered new courage. Three of the five gates were kept open, and the communications with the surrounding country preserved ; the cattle were sent out to graze, and firewood and other necessaries brought into the city. Nightly sallies were made by the garrison with much loss and destruction to the besiegers. The prisoners captured by either force were barbarously maltreated. A breach having been effected an assault was attempted, but driven back with loss, among the slain being a deserter from Herat, named Muhammad Sharif, who was much dreaded, and whose death brought delight to Kamran, who looked upon it as a fatal blow to the Persian hopes of success.

The siege operations continued with but little access of vigour, albeit the garrison was prone to exaggerate the danger. On the 18th January Yar Muhammad arranged that Pottinger should proceed as an envoy to the Persian camp, and the following day

he was conducted to the residence of the Shah. The message he was commissioned to carry was, that on condition that the Persians raised the siege, Herat would be given up, when, with Persian assistance, he should have regained his kingdom. Kamran decided that, before his message was despatched, an important blow should be struck. The projected night attack, however, proved a failure, and policy dictated that Pottinger's departure should be delayed. On the 26th January it was determined that the cavalry and infantry should sally out and bring the Persians to action. At first the Afghan charge was successful, the Persians evacuated their posts, and after a protracted struggle the besieged were left in possession of the field.

On the 8th February Pottinger left for the Persian camp with an escort; this, however, he sent back and proceeded with a single attendant. He was taken to the Russian General Samson's quarters, and received with much courtesy and sent in safety to the Persian camp, where he was graciously received by the Wazir who granted him permission to deliver the Government of India's letter to Colonel Stoddart.

He then proceeded to deliver Kamran's message to the Shah, who denounced the Afghan as a treacherous liar and declared that he would not rest satisfied until a Persian garrison was in the citadel of Herat. On the 10th February Pottinger returned to the city. The siege now continued without intermission, the Persians having twice, during February, sent an emissary to state that if the Afghans would acknowledge the Shah's sovereignty, operations should cease The negotiations produced no result. The siege continued to the distress of the garrison, who were suffering from the inclement weather and want of food. On the 8th March the Persians gained possession of a fortified post 300 yards from the north-east angle of the fort. Towards the end of March the Asaf-ud-Daula offered to be the mediator for a suspension of hostilities, but the subsequent negotiations proved fruitless. On the 6th April Mr. M'Neill, the British Minister at the Persian Court, arrived in the Shah's camp, but met with a cold reception; but his tact gradually smoothed down the irritation at first engendered. The Russian Minister, Count Simonich, was, however, on his way from Teheran, and Mr. M'Neill felt that his approach might prove fatal to his

success. On the 13th April he had an audience with the Shah and pointed out that his proceedings in Afghanistan were a violation of the treaty between Great Britain and Persia, and that the former would be justified in taking measures to compel the withdrawal of the Persian army from Herat. The Shah protested that he never meditated anything injurious to the interests of Great Britain and consented to accept the mediation of the British mission.

The 18th April was one of the most memorable days of the siege. The Persian batteries redoubled their activity, and by evening two of the breaches were practicable. The Afghans made a counter-attack, but were repulsed by the Persians. It was now announced that an Englishman sought admittance, but the statement was received with incredulity. On the following morning Major Todd, an officer of the Bengal Artillery, made his appearance. He announced that the Persian sovereign was willing to accept the mediation of the British Government. He was received with courtesy by Shah Kamran, and returned to the Persian camp with assurances of Kamran's desire to accept the mediation.

Hostilities were not, however, suspended, and that evening the aspect of affairs was more warlike than ever. On the 21st April Mr. M'Neill arrived to negotiate, and the Shah professed himself willing to agree to any terms proposed by that officer. On the 23rd April, however, Major Todd brought the information that Muhammad Shah had changed his mind, and refused to submit to arbitration. The siege recommenced, Count Simonich, who had arrived on the 21st April, freely assisting with advice and money. The Heratis now began to consider the expediency of throwing themselves into the arms of Russia, and it was proposed to send an envoy to the Russian Ambassador, acknowledging the dependence of Herat upon his country. News of the energetic course pursued by Mr. M'Neill threatening British hostilities if Herat should fall into Persian hands, however, altered the complexion of affairs, and the idea of a Russian alliance was abandoned. Pottinger did his best to counteract Russian influence, by expressing the conviction that Britain would come to the help of Herat, but was embarrassed by injunctions from Mr. M'Neill that he was on no account to commit the British Government to any line of policy.

Arrival of Simonich.

Exasperated by this announcement, the chiefs broke out into violent reproaches against Pottinger, M'Neill, and the whole British nation, and began to discuss the advantages of a Russian alliance. Pottinger exercised great tact, and on his promising to make a further representation to Mr. M'Neill the chiefs resolved to await the results of the reference.

The influence of Mr. M'Neill at the Persian Court was, however, rapidly declining, and the Russians were correspondingly exalted. On the 7th June the British mission left the Persian camp and the British-Persian alliance ended.

The Herat garrison had meanwhile been undergoing much suffering, and the Persians, under Russian direction, continued to prosecute the siege with increased vigour, and the lines of investment were drawn closer. Two ineffectual assaults were made, and a third followed on the 24th June. The defenders were off their guard, when suddenly a heavy fire betrayed the intentions of the besiegers. Simultaneous assaults were made at five points; four of these were repulsed; the fifth, and more determined one, was at first successful, and it was only the indomitable courage and masterfulness of Pottinger which saved the situation and Herat. Both sides were equally dispirited and a week of inaction supervened. The siege began to assume the character of a blockade in July, and the besiegers were comparatively inactive.

But in the meantime, far from Herat, events were taking place which were to affect the issue of the contest. Lord Auckland determined to despatch an expedition to the Persian Gulf, to be employed with a view to maintain British interests in Persia. The demonstration terrified the Persians, and Mr. M'Neill seized the opportunity to make another effort to secure the withdrawal of the Persian army and re-establish British ascendancy at the Persian Court. Colonel Stoddart was despatched to the Shah with a message that the occupation of Herat, or any part of Afghanistan, would be viewed in the light of a hostile demonstration against England. Muhammad Shah promised to comply with the demands. The Russian envoy was in the meantime persuading Kamran to come out of Herat, and make his obeisance to the Shah-in-Shah, as a preliminary to the with

British action.

Russian intrigues.

drawal of the Persian army; with the idea of giving a colour of victory to the latter's retirement, and to enable Russia to claim a diplomatic success.

The struggle was now nearly at an end, though the movements in the Persian camp were imperfectly known in Herat. In September, however, there was no longer any doubt that the Persians were breaking up their camp.[1] Before the 9th, the Persian army had commenced its retrograde march to Tehran. Pottinger afterwards expressed the deliberate opinion that Herat might have been taken by assault within twenty-four hours of Muhammad Shah's appearance before its walls, had his troops been efficiently commanded.

Something must now be said about the intrigues of Russia. There is no doubt that she egged on Muhammad Shah to undertake the expedition against Herat, and that Russian officers aided in the siege operations. She thereby placed herself in direct antagonism to Great Britain. English advice was systematically opposed by the Russian Ambassador. When called upon for an explanation Russia replied that if Simonich had really acted as alleged, he had exceeded his instructions. Russia, however, had been playing a successful and safe game. However the expedition terminated, she would carry an important point. Had Herat fallen, Kandahar and Kabul would have made their submission, and Russian influence would have impinged upon India. If England interfered to save Herat, on the other hand, she was compromised with Persia as a nation.

Whilst the Persians were laying siege to Herat, under the aegis of Russia, the English in India, on account of these movements across the border, were turning their attention to the safeguarding of their own frontier. The danger was believed to be great and imminent. The Native States on our own borders were evincing symptoms of unrest. From Nepal and Burma came threatenings of invasion; even our own provinces were in a state of disquiet. To the Mussalmans the movement beyond the Afghan Frontier presaged a Muhammadan invasion, and rumour had it that the Company's Raj was almost at an end.

The policy of the Indian Government.

---

[1] The British expedition to Karrak, described in Vol. VI, was an important factor in causing the Persians to raise the seige of Herat.

Ignorance magnified the danger. That Herat would fall appeared certain, and it was believed that Muhammad Shah would not remain content with this success; Kandahar and Kabul would follow suit, and Persia, with her ally, Russia, would secure Afghanistan as a base for future operations.

To secure the independence of Afghanistan was plainly the policy of the British Government. Before the advance upon Herat, their Minister at Tehran had advocated the expediency of a counteracting movement in the country between Persia and India, and had written to Burnes, setting forth the advantages of subsidising the Amir, and placing both Kandahar and Herat under his rule. He suggested that a British loan would be sufficient to effect this purpose, and that as a condition Afghan foreign policy should be directed through the British Agent. In the Kandahar Sardars he had no faith.

Captain Wade, however, who was conversant with the politics of Central Asia, was strongly opposed to the consolidation of Afghanistan under Dost Muhammad. He advocated the preservation of the different Governments as they stood, and the use of our influence in keeping the peace.

So far as Herat was concerned, Kamran was playing the game which best suited British interests; it was acting as a barrier against Russo-Persian invasion, and fighting single-handed the first battle of resistance at the gates of Afghanistan.

Mr. M'Neill's project for the consolidation of the Afghan empire found little favour with Indian statesmen, but many were of opinion that, by means of small offers of assistance, the *de facto* rulers of Afghanistan would co-operate in resisting invasion from the west Captain Burnes, however, had no power to offer this assistance. He was tied hand and foot, and was impotent to treat with Dost Muhammad. He could make demands, but could offer no *quid pro quo*. The Amir, although obviously desirous of a British alliance could obtain not even the glimmer of a guarantee, and was at last naturally compelled to turn his eyes in another direction. Russia came forward with tangible offers of money and assistance, and the Amir had no course but to accept the situation.

To re-establish Sultan Muhammad at Peshawar would have paved the way for the march of Ranjit Singh's army to Kabul;

it was better to have a single enemy in the person of the Maharaja. Sultan Muhammad had by his treachery lost Peshawar, and, as he was unable to hold his own, better arrangements should be aimed at to preserve the integrity of the frontier. So reasoned Dost Muhammad. Primarily he desired Peshawar on his own account; failing this, a tenancy, conjointly with Sultan Muhammad, in vassalage to Ranjit Singh. It is probable that had the British Government come forward with something more substantial than sympathy, the Amir would have proved a faithful ally.

It was, however, decreed that Dost Muhammad should be a hostile Chief; and British policy soon made him one. Had Burnes been permitted to follow his own convictions, the Kandahar Sardars, with the Kabul Amir, would have interposed as an effective barrier to Persian invasion, backed by Russian intrigue. The policy actually pursued created the difficulties which led to the First Afghan War.

Lord Auckland was essentially a man of peace, but he saw the necessity of establishing British influence in Afghanistan as a barrier to invasion. He had abandoned all desire to propitiate Dost Muhammad and the Barakzai Chiefs, and his thoughts turned to Shah Shuja,[1] who had made so many fruitless efforts to seat himself on the Durani throne. His idea was confined to an expedition by Shah Shuja and Ranjit Singh, accompanied by a British agent, subsidised by the British Government and assisted by British officers.

Of the three alternative schemes for the defence of the frontier, that of adopting the Indus as our boundary, and leaving Afghanistan to its fate, was abandoned without consideration, as playing directly into the hands of Persia and Russia. The second scheme, the attempt to save Afghanistan by succouring the existing chiefs at Kandahar and Kabul, would only strengthen their hands against the Sikhs. The third was the Shah Shuja-Ranjit Singh alliance above referred to.

Macnaghten was sent to Lahore to sound Ranjit Singh on the subject of the proposed confederation.

Macnaghten's Mission to Lahore.

The only mention of the employment of British troops till now had been the demonstration of a Division

---

[1] It must be borne in mind that Shah Shuja was a Sadiozai. The Barakzai Chiefs were brothers of Dost Muhammad.

at Shikarpur. The mission was received by the Maharaja on the 31st May, the proposal was unfolded, and it was explained that the alternatives were to act independently or in concert with the British Government. Ranjit immediately elected for the latter. He was enthusiastic at the suggestion of the English joining in the tripartite treaty with himself and Shah Shuja. Macnaghten thereupon explained the Governor-General's views—that the Shah should advance by the Kandahar route and the Sikhs move upon Kabul *via* the Khaibar, while the British Government sent a force down the Indus to repel any threat of aggression in that direction. Ranjit Singh declined to have anything to say to an independent expedition on his own account.

It now remained to settle the details, and so little was it contemplated that a British force should take part in the expedition, that Ranjit Singh, who was by no means confident of success, asked if in the event of a reverse the British Government was prepared to support them. Although Macnaghten replied in the affirmative, Ranjit Singh evidently wished that British troops should play a more prominent part in the expedition. The treaty was, however, prepared and formally signed by the Maharaja on the 26th June. Briefly the contents were as follows:—

1. Shuja-ul-Mulk disclaimed all title to the Maharaja's possessions on either bank of the Indus.

The Tripartite Treaty.

2. None of the people beyond the Khaibar should trespass on the eastern side.

3. No one to cross from the left to the right bank of the Sutlej, without a passport from the Maharaja, and similarly no one should be allowed to cross the Indus.

4. Shikarpur and the Trans-Indus territory to be the subject of arbitration between the British Government and the Maharaja.

5. Details of the annual tribute to be paid by the Shah to the Maharaja when re-possessed of Kabul and Kandahar.

6. The etiquette to be observed.

7. Free passage to merchants of either country.

8. Tokens of friendship to be sent annually by the Maharaja to the Shah.

9. Facilities to be granted to traders.

10. Prohibition of the slaughter of kine when the two armies shall be assembled together.

11. The division of spoil.

12. A constant exchange of missions.
13. Mutual aid.
14. The friends or enemies of one party to be the friends or enemies of all.
15. Relinquishment by the Shah of arrears of tribute from the Amirs of Sind.
16. Subsidy to be paid by Shah Shuja to the Maharaja.
17. The ruler of Herat to be left in possession of his territories.
18. The Afghans to negotiate with foreign powers through the British and Sikh Government.

This treaty was sent to Lord Auckland for signature, but he declined to sign it until approved and signed by Shah Shuja.

When the news of the British designs reached his ears, Shah Shuja already saw himself *en route* for the Bala Hissar, but he was suspicious of both the British and Sikhs. After considerable discussion the terms were agreed to, and the treaty signed, and he was all eagerness to commence operations without delay.

Meanwhile Lord Auckland's advisers had urged that the expedition, as arranged, must prove a disastrous failure, and strongly advocated the employment of a British force. Burnes' opinion was now invited, and he advised that the case of Dost Muhammad should be reconsidered, and that Government should act with and not against him. However, if Dost Muhammed was to be counteracted, the restoration of Shah Shuja was more feasible than the establishment of Sikh influence at Kabul.

Captain Wade, although he did not entertain a favourable opinion of Dost Muhammad, insisted that the wisest policy was to support the existing rulers.

The Simla Council discussed the several projects; whether the first scheme were feasible, or whether a few regiments of British troops would suffice to escort the Shah's army. Neither of these plans was followed.

Sir Henry Fane, the Commander-in-Chief, is believed to have disapproved of interference in Afghan affairs, but argued that if interference was settled upon, it should be done in such a manner as to command success.

By nature inclined towards moderate measures, Lord Auckland yielded to the judgment of others, and the order for assembling the army on the frontier, early in the cold weather, to march upon Kandahar

Military preparations.

was issued. The proposed expedition was the one topic of conversation; many officers gave up staff appointments to join the force, and at the worst season of the year corps were set in motion for Karnal from stations as remote as Benares.

The strength of the force warned for service was one brigade of artillery, a cavalry brigade, and five brigades of infantry. The Divisions were to be commanded by Sir Willoughby Cotton and Major-General Duncan.

The regiments selected were [1]:—

Her Majesty's 16th Lancers.
Her Majesty's 13th Infantry.
Her Majesty's 3rd Buffs.
The Company's Bengal European Regiment.
2 Regiments of Native Light Cavalry.
2 Troops of Horse Artillery.
3 Companies of Foot Artillery.
Some Sappers and Miners.
2nd
5th
16th
27th
28th
31st
35th   Regiments, Bengal Native Infantry.
37th
42nd
43rd
48th
53rd

While the Bengal Army was assembling on the northern frontier under the personal command of Sir Henry Fane, the following force was being collected in Bombay under Sir John Keane, with Major-General Thackwell as Cavalry Commander, Colonel Stevenson, Commanding Artillery, and Major-General Willshire, the Infantry.

Cavalry Brigade (including Her Majesty's 4th Dragoons).
Artillery Brigade.
Her Majesty's 2nd Queen's ⎫
Her Majesty's 17th Foot   ⎬ Infantry Brigade.
1 Native Infantry Regiment ⎭

---

[1] For details of the force, see Appendix I.

A third force, to be led by Shah Shuja, was being raised for service across the Indus in the Company's territories, commanded by the Company's officers, and paid by the Company. This had originally figured as the principal force, but now the disciplined troops of the Indian Army were to bear the brunt of the campaign. Recruiting for the Shah's force progressed rapidly; he himself watching its growth with pride, and fearful lest the assumption of control by the British officers should deprive him of the *éclat* of independence. Captain Wade had a difficult position to fill in managing Shah Shuja; the transition from pensioner at Ludhiana to an independent chief, a maker of treaties, a commander of armies, had been very rapid, and he was desirous of spurring forward on his new enterprise.

Political arrangements.

The political management of the campaign now commanded Lord Auckland's attention. Captain Wade was selected to accompany the Sikh troops through the Khaibar. The name of Burnes naturally occurred to the Governor-General as the fittest person to guide Shah Shuja. He appreciated his talents but mistrusted his discretion, so he finally fixed upon Mr. Macnaghten for the appointment, and he was duly gazetted as "Envoy and Minister on the part of the Government of India at the Court of Shah Shuja-ul-Mulk." Burnes was to be employed under him as "Envoy to the Chief of Kalat and other States." It was believed that when Shah Shuja had been seated on his throne, the former would return to India, leaving Burnes at Kabul; and this reconciled the latter to his present subordinate post. He was sent forward to smooth the way for the progress of the Shah through Sind, whilst Macnaghten remained at Simla to assist in the preparation of the manifesto, which was to declare the grounds upon which the British Government had determined to destroy the power of the Barakzai Sardars, and to restore Shuja-ul-Mulk to the throne of his ancestors.

The manifesto provoked much criticism and found very few supporters. Had the relief of Herat been the object of the expedition, it would have been generally approved. It was not, however, clear that because Muhammad Shah made war upon Herat, England was justified in making war upon Dost Muhammad. In the summer of 1838 there was an undoubted *causa belli*, but it was

largely traceable to our policy in connection with the Barakzai Sardars.

The most experienced Indian politicians foretold disaster to the expedition at the outset; among them were the Duke of Wellington (Lord Wellesley) Sir Charles Metcalfe, Mr. Edmonstone, Mount-Stuart Elphinstone, Sir Henry Willock, and Mr. Tucker. The Duke of Wellington prophesied that our difficulties would commence where military success ended; and that to settle a government in Afghanistan would mean a perennial march into that country. Sir Charles Metcalfe stated that to cross the Indus and meddle with the countries beyond was the surest way of bringing Russia down upon us. Elphinstone, while not doubtful of military success, anticipated that it was a hopeless task to attempt to keep our nominee on his throne. The Court of Directors were strongly opposed to the war.

In spite of the raising of the siege of Herat the Governor-General, on the 8th November, published an order that the expedition would not be abandoned.

CHAPTER XIV.

OCCUPATION OF AFGHANISTAN.

THE army intended for the occupation of Afghanistan assem-
bled at Ferozepore at the end of November. The Governor-General arrived on the 27th. The concentration had been effected with rapidity.[1] On the 29th the first meeting between Lord Auckland and Ranjit Singh took place. On the day following the Governor-General returned the visit. Next followed manœuvres by the British and Sikh forces. Ranjit Singh returned to Lahore, followed by Lord Auckland, and the British troops prepared to cross the frontier. There was now, however, no Persian Army at Herat, aided by a Russian force in the back-ground, so the force had been reduced in strength, and the enthusiasm of the troops had waned. Sir Henry Fane selected the most efficient of the troops for the expedition. The Bengal Army consisted of one Division under Sir Willoughby Cotton. Sir John Keane, coming round from Bombay with his Division, was eventually to take the chief command.

Assembling of the Army of the Indus.

The Bengal Army at Ferozepore numbered 9,500 men of all arms. The force for the service of Shah Shuja was passing through, and was composed of two regiments of cavalry and four of infantry, with a troop of Horse Artillery—6,000 men in all—and was to cross the frontier on the 2nd December. On the 10th the Bengal Division was to leave Ferozepore.

The invading army's line of march ran in a south-westerly direction, through Bahawalpur, and crossed the Sind Frontier near Sabzalkot, to the banks of the Indus, which was to be crossed at Sukkur. Thence in a north-westerly direction *viâ* Shikarpur, Bhag, and Dadar, to the Bolan Pass, and, passing that, to Quetta and *viâ* the Khojak to Kandahar. This roundabout route was dictated by political considerations

Line of march.

---

[1] No worse season could, however, have been chosen for the movement of troops.

Twenty-five thousand rupees had been fixed as the ransom money to be paid by the Amirs of Sind for Shikarpur. Pottinger considered the demand unjust, and he represented this to the Government of India. He was informed in reply that circumstances alter cases, and that the paragraph in the existing treaty, prohibiting the use of the Indus for the carriage of military stores, must be ignored at the present time. The Khan of Bahawalpur and the Sind Amirs were ordered to facilitate the passage of the troops by the collection of supplies and transport, at their peril.

Sir Alexander Burnes was sent to treat with the Sind Amirs, and to obtain the temporary cession of the island at Bhakkar. The Amirs of Khairpur stipulated that the forts on either bank should remain untouched.

The Talpur Amirs now began to feel alarm, for the British Government, besides assisting Shah Shuja to regain his throne, had encouraged him to assert old claims, had announced the intention of stationing a subsidiary force in Sind for which the Amirs were to pay; and of treating Sind and Baluchistan as if they were principalities of India. The Amirs felt their helplessness in the face of the Government's determination, and apparently abandoned all thought of resistance.

The Bengal Army moved parallel with the river, availing itself of the waterway. The force consisted of 9,500 men, 38,000 camp followers, 30,000 camels. When the army entered Bahawalpur all seemed favourable to the expedition. The country was open, the road, 280 miles in length, had been previously prepared for the march, and was in good order, and supplies were plentiful.

Desertion among the camp followers was now, however, rife, the cattle were falling sick and dying by the wayside, and it was soon evident that the questions of transport and supply would prove formidable.

On the 29th the capital of Bahwal Khan's country was reached and on the 14th January, 1839, the Army of the Indus entered Sind territory near Sabzalkot. Sir Alexander Burnes had joined the British camp on the preceding day; his report of the feelings of the people of Sind was not encouraging, and it shortly-

appeared probable that some of the Talpur princes would give trouble. The Haidarabad Amirs had insulted Colonel Pottinger, and were collecting troops for the defence of their capital. Sir John Keane had landed at Vikkur at the end of November, and thence had proceeded to Tatta. He had no carriage, and the Sind rulers were rather inclined to oppose than to assist him. He, therefore, remained inactive until the 24th December. Opportunely a certain amount of carriage arriving from Kach, the column then commenced its march into Sind, and proceeding along the right bank of the Indus to Tarrak, there waited the result of the negotiations at Haidarabad.

Shah Shuja with his contingent had preceded the Bengal column, and crossing the Indus during the third week in January, encamped at Shikarpur, where he was joined by the British envoy.

Cotton was to have crossed the Indus at Rohri opposite Bhakkar, but some delay took place in connection with the cession of the fortress, and it was not until the 29th of January that the British flag waved from its ramparts.

The military authorities now determined that the bulk of the Bengal column should proceed down the

Bad intelligence.

left bank of the Indus to co-operate with Sir John Keane against Haidarabad. The two columns were entirely ignorant of each other's operations[1] in the absence of an Intelligence Department, a want which continued to be felt until the close of the war. Mr. Macnaghten did not approve of this diversion, believing that it involved the sacrifice of the legitimate objects of the campaign; he therefore took upon himself the responsibility of preventing the march. The military and political authorities were brought into a state of undisguised antagonism. The Amirs, however, consented to the terms of the treaty, and the necessity for the advance on Haidarabad was obviated.

---

[1] Stacy, page 142. "After pointing out the difficulties attending the procuring an dconveying supplies between Quetta and Kandahar since the affair at Haikalzai which dispelled the illusion that we could obtain supplies in the Pishin valley, I observed that that affair, however unfortunate, had not been wholly without use, in showing how imperfect were our means of information. The existence of a fortified position, which, it appeared, the enemy had been employed upon for the preceding two months was utterly unknown to us, nor should we have learned that similar works had been prepared in the Khojak but for our advance on Haikalzai: our ignorance of this intrenched position proved no less our want of common information beyond our picquets, than the unanimity of the people around us."

The Bombay troops which had halted opposite Haidarabad now heard of the arrival of the Reserve at Karachi, which surrendered after a show of resistance.

Surrender of Karachi.

On the 20th February Sir Willoughby Cotton arrived at Shikarpur, where he had a stormy discussion with the Envoy, each considering that the other was trenching upon his province. That evening, however, despatches were received from the Governor-General, read and discussed, and that night the General and the Envoy parted good friends.

Arrival at Shikarpur.

On the 23rd Cotton again put his force in motion, but, owing to the insufficiency of carriage, Shah Shuja's contingent remained halted at Shikarpur.

The difficulties of the march now began. Between Sukkur and Shikarpur the camels had dropped dead by scores; but there was a worse tract of country in advance. The distance to Dadar from Shikarpur is 146 miles, and it was accomplished by the Bengal column in sixteen painful marches. Water and forage were very scarce; numbers of camels died,[1] and, further on, the Baluchi robbers carried them off with appalling dexterity. On the 10th of March the column reached Dadar at the mouth of the Bolan Pass.[2] Major Leech, who had been endeavouring to collect supplies,[3] had signally

Bolan Pass.

---

[1] Hough, Appendix 79. The total loss of public camels in the Bengal Column of the Army of the Indus in 14 months was 20,000.

Hough, page 9. There must have been from 25,000 to 30,000 camels with the army, and so early as December it was found necessary to allow them to quit camp some hours before the troops, as they fell off in condition, owing to their arriving late in camp and being unable early enough to get forage or to graze.

[2] Havelock, Vol. I, 274. "The patience with which for three months and a half the native soldiers and mustered followers of the Bengal force bore their privations, when their ration was reduced to a full moiety, and in truth did not suffice to satisfy the cravings of hunger, ought ever to be remembered to their credit by the Government which they were serving."

[3] Outram, page 61. 9th April. "Marched with the Artillery Brigade eleven and a half miles into the pass along the bed of the Bolan river, the channel of which is the only road; a stream of clear water from thirty to forty feet broad, and from one to three in depth, crossing the road six times. During the floods the stream, which is in some places confined between perpendicular precipices, within a channel sixty or eighty feet wide, would preclude the possibility of escape to an army caught in the torrent. The mountains on every side are the most abrupt, sterile, and inhospitable I ever beheld—not a blade of vegetation of any kind being found, save in the bed of the stream, where there is some coarse grass on which horses and camels pick a scanty subsistence. The mountains are as repulsive in appearance as they are barren in reality, being everywhere of a dull and uniform brown colour."

failed; and the prospects of the force, with only one month's supply in hand, were anything but encouraging. Cotton determined to push on at once, and resumed his march on the 16th. Burnes, aided by the Baluchi authorities, who had preceded the column, secured its safe passage. The baggage animals were, however, dying in numbers and the horses of the artillery were much distressed.[1] The Baluchi free booters cut off stragglers and carried off baggage and cattle. The road through the pass, which is sixty miles in length, was execrable, and it took six days to effect the passage.

On emerging, however, the clear, crisp climate braced the European frame and the prospect delighted the eye. On the 26th March Quetta was reached, and here, with starvation staring him in the face, Cotton was to await further orders. The prospect was perplexing. To stand still or to move forward appeared equally impossible. To push on to Kandahar on very reduced rations would leave him on arrival with only a few days' supply in hand; to remain halted would only aggravate the evil. The supplies available in the Quetta district would only suffice for a few days. He, therefore, despatched his Adjutant-General to Sir John Keane for orders, while Burnes proceeded to Kalat to work upon the fears or cupidity of Mehrab Khan and the troops were placed upon a reduced scale of rations. The sufferings of the whole force were rapidly aggravated.[2]

Burnes was courteously received by Mehrab Khan, who, however, prophesied evil for the expedition, complained of the devastation caused by the march of the troops, and hoped that his claims

Burnes' Mission to Kalat.

---

[1] Outram, page 77. "It is a fact now fully proved, and admitted by all parties that the Arab and Persian horses stand their work and privations infinitely better than stud and country-breds; the latter, although younger, stronger and in far better condition at starting, have invariably been the first to give in, while they seldom rallied afterwards. A few Cape horses lately imported to the Bombay Army have also proved themselves superior to our stud-breds."

Hough, page 96. Afghan horses eat green forage in great quantities and seldom get any grain. The Turkomans prefer dry food—barley flour made into balls with the fat of the *dhumba* sheep.

[2] Atkinson, 179. "The sick being still numerous it became of consequence to provide against the chance of having more to carry, when the army was ordered to move, than our existing means, extensive as they were, could supply. With this view I drew the attention of the Commander-in-Chief to the expediency of employing camels, each furnished with a pair of *Kajawahs*, or panniers, a mode of conveyance common throughout Upper Asia, and always used in travelling for the females of a family. * * * These resources being most ample, and sufficient for about five hundred patients not the smallest inconvenience attended our forward movement to Ghazni."

would command attention, and that he would be relieved of the mastery of the Saddozai Kings. He spoke freely of our British policy in Central Asia, and complained that while he might have allied himself with Persia and Russia, he had safeguarded the force in their passage through the Bolan and yet remained unrewarded.

Burnes had brought with him a draft treaty. As a condition of peaceable negotiation it stipulated for a visit to Shah Shuja in his camp, to which Mehrab Khan took exception, and pleaded sickness. To secure the acknowledgment of the supremacy of Shah Shuja, the Government agreed to pay Mehrab Khan one and a half lakhs of rupees annually; in return he was to collect and protect supplies. Mehrab Khan affixed his seal, but none the less disliked the bargain. He, however, promised to collect what provisions he could from the already poverty-stricken country.

In the meantime the Shah's Contingent and the Bombay Division were making their way through Sind, much hampered by want of transport. More and more sensible, after every march, of the miserable country and the difficulties which beset the expedition, Macnaghten was anxious to push on, but Sir John Keane recommended a halt while the possibilities of supply in the Bolan were being investigated. On the 4th April he met Sir Willoughby Cotton, who had ridden out from Quetta, and the tidings he received were of the gloomiest. On the 6th April Sir John Keane assumed command of the Army at Quetta, and determined to push on to Kandahar.

The Shah's and Bombay Columns.

On the 7th April the army resumed its march; and on the 9th was at Haikalzai. The army of the Indus surmounted the Khojak Pass in safety, the Shah leading the way, joined by many of the chiefs and people of Western Afghanistan. Macnaghten received intelligence that Kohan-dil-Khan and his brothers had fled from Kandahar, that there was no union among the Barakzai brothers, and that if a stand were to be made it would probably be nearer the northern capital. The Shah, therefore, pushed on. The Afghans had begun to discover that the supply of British gold was unfailing and, as Macnaghten had prophesied, their cupidity would not be proof against it. The Envoy now opened the treasure-chest ungrudgingly, which in the end caused the ruin of his policy.

Flight of the Kandahar Sardars.

On the 25th April, Shah Shuja-ul-Mulk re-entered Kandahar and was received with a mixture of curiosity and enthusiasm. The future appeared to be unclouded, and it seemed that Dost Muhammad would imitate his brother's example and fly. The 8th May was fixed for the public recognition of the restored sovereign. Both the British columns had now arrived and marched past before the reinstated monarch. Popular enthusiasm had, however, abated, and the affair was a painful failure. The Durani tribes were spiritless, and they viewed with apprehension the arrival of the British army. They pressed upon the Shah their claims for the restoration of old privileges, which it was plain the King could not recognize. He had established himself at Kandahar, the brothers had fled into Persia where they remained as guests of Muhammad Shah, until the withdrawal of the British from Afghanistan. Dost Muhammad was, however, still dominant at Kabul. The Shah, therefore, was obliged to conciliate the Duranis, and granted much but not all they asked. The latter were prepared to welcome the grandson of Ahmad Shah as the enemy of the Barakzai Sardars; but they regarded the movement for restoration in the light of a foreign invasion.

Arrival at Kandahar.

The halt of the Army of the Indus at Kandahar was long and weary. Provisions were scarce, and it was necessary to await the ripening of the crops. The city itself disappointed expectation, although its surroundings were pleasant to the eye, but there was little to break the monotony, and when, on the 9th May, a brigade under Colonel Sale was despatched to Girishk, seventy-five miles west of Kandahar, in pursuit of the fugitive Sardars, there were few officers who did not long to accompany it. The short campaign was, however, inglorious, and Sale returned to Kandahar on finding that the princes had fled. But Dost Muhammad was mustering his fighting men in the north to defend his capital. Misunderstanding the causes of the halt at Kandahar, Dost Muhammad thought that a movement upon Herat was contemplated, and that operations against Kabul would be deferred to the following year. He, therefore, turned his attention to the defence of the eastern line of road. It had been arranged that Prince Timur, the eldest son of Shah Shuja, should advance upon Kabul *viâ* Jalalabad and Jagdalak; his force was now advancing, and Dost Muhammad

sent some of his best fighting men against it, under his favourite son Akbar Khan. Macnaghten had, however, no intention of moving upon Herat, so long as the desired results might be attained by less costly and hazardous means. Muhammad Shah was unlikely to re-invest Herat, so it was determined to send only a few engineer and artillery officers to improve the defences at the expense of a few lakhs of rupees.

In September, 1838, Muhammad Shah turned his face towards his own capital, and Eldred Pottinger, joined by Stoddart, began to repair the ravages caused by the protracted siege. The Wazir, however, did not approve of their measures; they had played their part, and he desired no interference with his methods of oppression. Within two months of the conclusion of the siege they were insultingly ordered to withdraw from Herat territory. Stoddart[1] proceeded to Bokhara, but Pottinger remained and the hostile temper of the Wazir became more apparent. News of Shah Shuja's advance had reached Herat, and Yar Muhammad began to intrigue with the Persian court and the Kandahar Sardars; and endeavoured to form a confederacy for the expulsion of the Shah and his allies from Afghanistan. The Persian Court would not commit itself, and there was no prospect of organized opposition. Yar Muhammad, therefore, sent a friendly mission to the British camp and congratulations to the Shah. Macnaghten now determined to attempt to negotiate a friendly treaty with Shah Kamran, and Major Todd was despatched on the errand, accompanied by James Abbott and Richmond Shakespear of the Bengal Artillery, and Sanders of the Engineers.

Herat after the siege

The force, which had remained halted at Kandahar from the 25th April to the 27th June, recommenced its march a few days after the departure of the mission. During their stay the harvest had ripened and the transport animals had recovered their strength. Sickness,[2] however, had broken out among the troops, due largely to the excessive heat under canvas, and fever, dysentery, and

---

[1] Colonel Stoddart was despatched to Bokhara to try and obtain the liberation of ussian prisoners. He was confined by the Amir and executed in June 1842.

[2] Havelock, II, 33. The Bombay troops continued healthy, but sickness amongst the European soldiers from Bengal had increased to a fearful degree.

jaundice claimed many victims; money was scarce, and Macnaghten was unable to negotiate a loan. The Afghans regarded the intrusion of the British with hatred, and stragglers were assassinated. The Ghilzais were disinclined to the Saddozai yoke and rejected all overtures. The supplies had now come into camp, although the absence of transport would probably render its carriage on the march to Kabul difficult; 20,000 maunds of grain were available, but through fear of the vengeance of Dost Muhammad, the camel-drivers refused to proceed; it was therefore stored at Kandahar. However, on the 27th of June, the British Army resumed its march and reached Ghazni on the 21st of July.

The disunion of the Barakzai brothers lost Afghanistan to the Sardars. The fall of Kandahar did not astonish Dost Muhammad. Had he and the Kandahar Sardars banded themselves together and proclaimed a religious war, and by their example encouraged Mehrab Khan of Kalat to oppose our passage through the Bolan and Khojak Passes, they might have given a check to our famine-stricken army, from which it would not soon have recovered. Dost Muhammad now beheld his countrymen either flying from or bowing down before the invaders, with feelings of bitterness and mortification. He was not confident of being able to offer effectual resistance, and the dual advance upon Kabul compelled him to divide his forces. Nearer home Kohistan was in rebellion, and the Kizilbashis were opposed to him. His national defences were crumbling before his eyes. He could only place reliance upon his sons. Akbar Khan had been sent to oppose the Sikhs; Haidar Khan commanded at Ghazni, and Afzal Khan with some cavalry was in the neighbourhood of that fortress, with orders to operate upon the flanks of the British army as it traversed the open country. The Amir himself awaited events at the capital. His information as to our movements appears to have been very imperfect. Our plan of campaign was at first supposed to be a march upon Herat; now the masking of Ghazni and a move against the capital.

His plan, formed upon this idea, was to allow the British force to march some distance beyond Ghazni, when Afzal Khan and Haidar Khan would fall upon its rear, while he himself opposed it in front.

The strength of Ghazni was the boast of the Afghans, while Sir John Keane underrated its defences, and, leaving his siege guns at Kandahar advanced without them. His resolution promised disaster. The fortress lies 230 miles from Kandahar and 90 from Kabul. The country to be passed through offered no obstacles to the advance of an army, being open and level. As a city it was of less importance than either Kandahar or Kabul, but its strength had long been famous, and the 9 and 6-pounder guns accompanying the force would prove powerless against it.

Capture of Ghazni.

Haidar Khan watched the approach of the British Column from the fortifications. External defence had been but ill-provided for, a few parties only being stationed in the surrounding villages and gardens, and these were soon dislodged.[1] The morning was spent in skirmishing, the range of the enemy's guns were tried, and the engineers reconnoitred the fort. It was determined to camp on the Kabul side, whence Dost Muhammad was reported to be advancing, and to cut off his communications with the fort. The pitching of the camp presented an opportunity to Afzal Khan of which he did not avail himself.

At daybreak on the 22nd of July, Sir John Keane with Cotton and the engineers reconnoitred the fortress, which he had determined to carry by assault. The King, in the absence of siege guns had recommended that it should be left alone, and the advance on Kabul continued. However, though it might be impossible to break the walls, it was practicable to blow in one of the gates. This was the Kabul one, which alone had not been built up. For this information Sir John Keane was indebted to Abdul Rashid Khan, a nephew of Dost Muhammad, who had deserted the Barakzais, and whose reports proved of the utmost value.

Keane now issued orders for the assault, which was to take place at daybreak on the following morning.[2] On this day the

---

[1] Judging from my limited military experience, I am of opinion that the opposition offered by the Afghans was highly creditable. *Outram,* page 93.

[2] Kennedy, II, 46. "On the evening before the storm my duty led me to prepare the field hospitals, etc., and to arrange for the expected casualties. On visiting the hospital tents of Her Majesty's 2nd and 17th Regiments I was surprised to find them cleared of sick! The gallant fellows had all but risen in mutiny upon their Surgeons, and insisted on joining with their comrades! None remained in hospital but the hopelessly bed-ridden, who literally could not crawl; and even of these, a portion, who could just stand and walk, were dressed, and made to look like soldiers, to take the hospital guard: no effective man could be kept away!"

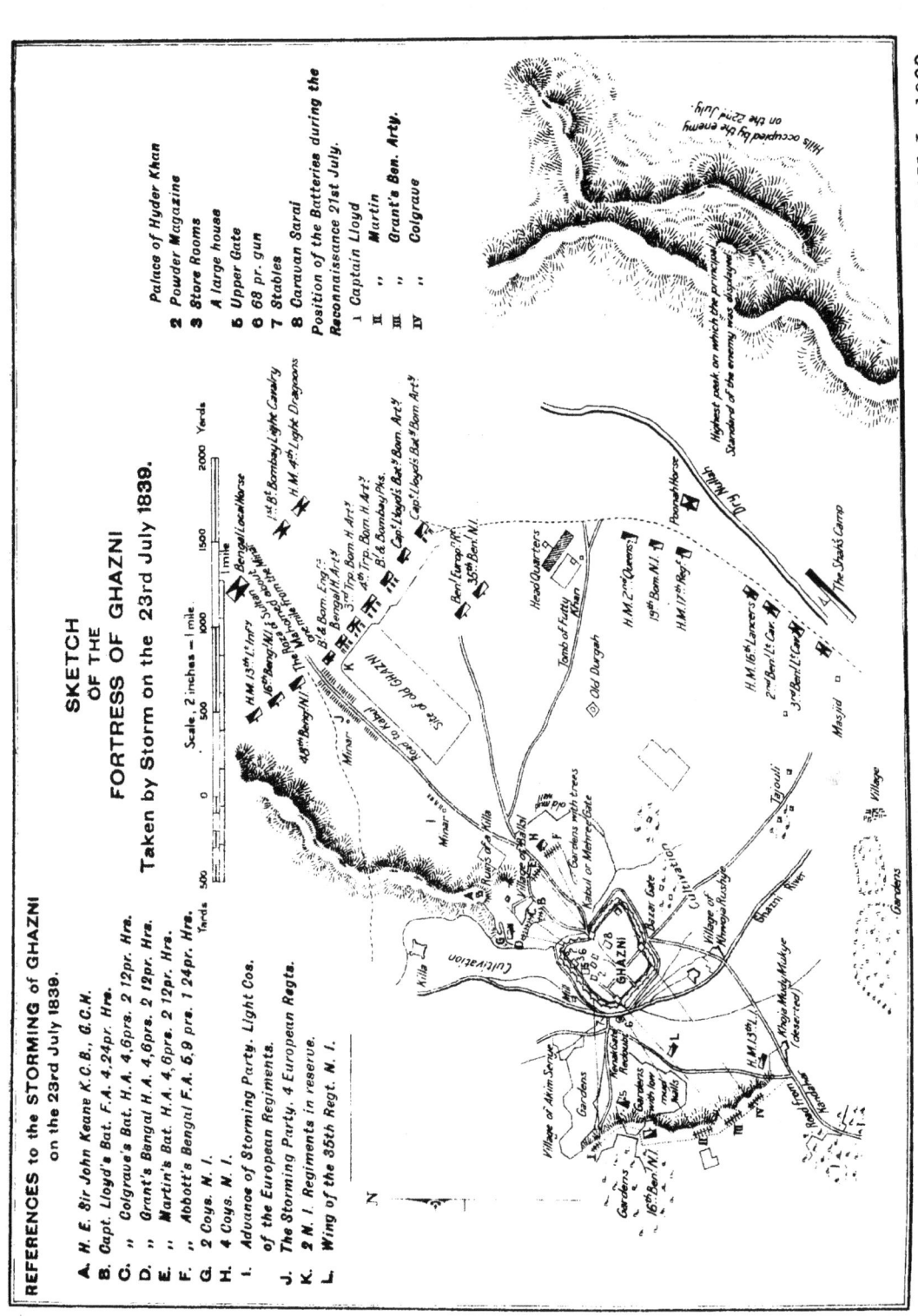

SKETCH OF THE FORTRESS OF GHAZNI
Taken by Storm on the 23rd July 1839.

REFERENCES to the STORMING of GHAZNI on the 23rd July 1839.

- A. H. E. Sir John Keane K.C.B., G.C.H.
- B. Capt. Lloyd's Bat. F.A. 4.24pr. Hrs.
- C. " Colgrave's Bat. H.A. 4.6prs. 2 12pr. Hrs.
- D. " Grant's Bengal H.A. 4.6prs. 2 12pr. Hrs.
- E. " Martin's Bat. H.A. 4.6prs. 2 12pr. Hrs.
- F. " Abbott's Bengal F.A. 5,9 prs. 1 24pr. Hrs.
- G. 2 Coys. N. I.
- H. 4 Coys. N. I.
- I. Advance of Storming Party. Light Cos. of the European Regiments.
- J. The Storming Party. 4 European Regts.
- K. 2 N. I. Regiments in reserve.
- L. Wing of the 35th Regt. N. I.

1. Palace of Hyder Khan
2. Powder Magazine
3. Store Rooms
4. A large house
5. Upper Gate
6. 68 pr. gun
7. Stables
8. Caravan Sarai

Position of the Batteries during the Reconnaissance 21st July.

- I   Captain Lloyd
- II " Martin
- III " Grant's Ben. Arty.
- IV " Colgrave

J. B. Topo. Dy. No. 7.2293.
Bxd. C. J. A. May 1908.

No. 4.451-I. 1908.

character of the fanatics, named *Ghazis*, was to be first disclosed. A party of these men was assembled near Ghazni; and had determined to rid the country of a King restored to power on the shoulders of infidels. Their rush was checked by a gallant charge of the Shah's horse, led by Peter Nicholson, and Outram following them to the heights, whither they had been driven captured fifty prisoners who were shortly afterwards massacred by the King's orders.

A gusty night had heralded a gusty morning when Keane, inwardly bewailing the absence of his heavy guns, planted his light artillery on the heights opposite the citadel, and posted his musketeers in the gardens near the city walls. All was quiet within the fortress as the engineers carried their powder-bags to the gates. The advance was under Colonel Dennie of the 13th Light Infantry, and the main column under Sale. At 3 A.M. all was ready for the assault.

Keane now ordered his field guns to open fire as a demonstration, which was responded to by the enemy. Blue lights on the walls illuminated the fortress. The enemy, misled by the cannonade, concentrated their attention upon the guns, while the British engineers were engaged in piling their powder-bags at the Kabul gate. Their work was quickly effected, though the noise of the wind dulled the report of the explosion, and heavy masses of masonry and timbers collapsed in ruin and confusion.

The bugles sounded the advance; Dennie with his stormers rushed forward through the aperture, and the leading soldiers were soon within the fortress. Sale pushed on to support the advanced party, but was informed by an engineer officer that the passage was choked, and that Dennie had been unable to force an entrance.

Sale thereupon sounded the retreat and the column halted in doubt and anxiety, to be shortly cheered by the sound of the "advance." A report had been received that Dennie had after all made good his entrance. The enemy had, however, profited by the check, and a resolute opposition was met with at the gateway. Afghans crowded at the gate, some for purposes of defence, others to escape from the hail of bullets which Dennie's party was showering upon them. There was a sturdy conflict and Sale

himself was cut down and with difficulty regained his feet. Colonel Croker's support now pushed forward, followed by the reserve, and the capture of Ghazni was complete.

There remained, however, much hard fighting within the walls, and the Afghans rushed upon the stormers, to meet their death by bullet or bayonet. There was dreadful confusion and carnage, many wounded being burned to death by the blazing timbers. Some were bayonetted on the ground, others were hunted and shot down with curses upon their lips. The British soldier was, as ever, merciful in the hour of victory and never failed to give quarter.

When resistance was over, the Commander-in-Chief and the Envoy entered the captured fortress, bringing Shah Shuja with them; Haidar Khan's *zenana* was located in a building under the protection of Munshi Mohan Lal. Haidar Khan was discovered in a house near the Kandahar gate, and threw himself upon the mercy of his captors; he was placed in the charge of Sir Alexander Burnes and conducted to Shah Shuja, who received him with courtesy and, declaring his forgiveness, told him to go in peace.

Ghazni was handed over to Shah Shuja. Its capture had been effected with a loss of 17 killed and 165 wounded.[1] Of the garrison, 500 were buried by the besiegers, many more are supposed ve been killed outside the walls by the British cavalry, and 1,600 prisoners, with a large number of horses and arms, were captured by the British force.[2]

---

[1] "The European portion of our force has now for five days marched without the aid of their spirit ration, the commissariat stores of rum having at length been completely exhausted. The sudden withdrawal of this species of stimulant is certainly a trial to the human constitution at a period when unwonted labour and exertion, the want of a good vegetable diet and wholesome farinaceous food, and of pure water, form a combination of circumstances peculiarly unfavourable to a healthy state of the digestive organs. But I am fully persuaded that when the soldier has by a few weeks' use become habituated to the change, his physical powers will gain strength, whilst his discipline improves, under this system of constrained abstinence, and the troops will enjoy an immunity from disease which will delight those who are interested in their welfare."—*Havelock, II, 52.*

[2] Referring to the wounded—"All the sword-cuts, which were very numerous, and many of them very deep, united in the most satisfactory manner, which we decidedly attributed to the men having been without rum for the previous six weeks."—*Atkinson, 209.*

The booty found in Ghazni was great, but perhaps the most valuable portion of it came into the hands of the commissariat in the shape of horses and other beasts of burthen. The cavalry and artillery, which had become well nigh inefficient, received, in consequence, a considerable remount; and the commissariat, as well as individuals, experienced much relief in the supply of fresh baggage animals, which they were thus enabled to purchase.—*Gleig, page 41.*

The fall of Ghazni struck terror into the heart of Dost Muhammad and his sons. Afzal Khan, when he saw the British colours flying from the citadel, fled to Kabul, abandoning all his elephants and camp equipage. His father refused to receive him.

Dost Muhammad's opposition.

The news of the fall of Ghazni reached the Amir in twenty-four hours; he assembled his chiefs and, complaining of the defection of some of his subjects, declared his conviction that, without the aid of treachery, the fortress would not have fallen.

He begged all waverers to leave him at once, but all professed their fidelity. A council of war was held, and Jabbar Khan was despatched to the British camp to treat with the alies. Mohan Lal went out to meet him some miles beyond the camp, and Burnes received him at the picquets; a tent was pitched for him near the Envoy's, and he was well received by the British Mission, and courteously by Shah Shuja. He tendered the Amir's submission, but claimed on behalf of the brother of Fateh Khan the hereditary office of Wazir. The claim was rejected, and an asylum in the British dominions offered in its stead. Jabbar Khan plainly said that, even had his cause been far more hopeless, Dost Muhammad would rather fling himself upon the British bayonets, and returned to Kabul.

Dost Muhammad now marched out to dispute the progress of the invaders, and drew up his troops at Arghandeh; it was not upon this ground that he had determined to give battle; but at Maidan upon the Kabul river. The action was, however, never fought. At Arghandeh treachery manifested itself; the Kizilbashes were fast deserting the Dost's standard; Haji Khan Kakar had long gone over to the enemy, and scarcely one true man remained in his ranks. The Amir made a last appeal to his followers, but in vain. He then dismissed all who were inclined to purchase safety by tendering allegiance to the Shah, and with a small handful of followers, leaving his guns in position, turned his horse's head towards the Hindu Kush. This event occurred on the 2nd of August, and the news reached the British

army on the following day. The pursuit of the Amir was at once undertaken, but a traitor was in the camp in the person of Haji Khan Kakar; he had once been Governor of Bamian, and knew the country through which the Amir had taken flight; so appeared to be the very man to lead the expedition. He had for some time been in treasonable correspondence with Dost Muhammad and, under various pretences, delayed the column as much as possible. When Outram seemed almost to have the quarry in his grasp his guide thwarted him.

On the 9th of August, Bamian was reached, where the Haji declared that the fugitive would halt; he was, however, thirty miles in advance. Further pursuit was hopeless, the cavalry was exhausted and the game was up. Outram reported Haji Khan Kakar's behaviour on his return; evidence of treason was readily forthcoming, and he was sent as a state prisoner to Chunar.

On the 7th of August Shah Shuja entered Kabul, after an exile of thirty years. There was no popular enthusiasm, and the voice of welcome was still. The objects of the Simla manifesto had been seemingly accomplished, and the originators of the British policy were filled with exultation. Now that Shah Shuja was restored to his throne he was still dissatisfied, finding how much his kingdom had been curtailed. It was, however, larger than he could govern.

Arrival at Kabul.

The British Government had fulfilled its undertaking, and the time had arrived for the withdrawal of the army; but it was obvious that the measure was at present premature; the experiment of leaving Shah Shuja to himself was not to be lightly tried. Both parties would have been pleased at the withdrawal of the troops, but the reception of the restored Amir was not sufficiently enthusiastic to inspire confidence.

Military problems.

The Governor-General considered that half a dozen regiments would suffice to keep Shah Shuja on his throne; and issued orders for the withdrawal of the Bombay army *viâ* the Bolan, and part of the Bengal Army *viâ* the Khaibar. Posts were to be

established at Kabul, Kandahar, Ghazni, Quetta, Jalalabad and Ali Masjid. Sir John Keane had accurately anticipated these orders. Sale with a brigade was to remain in Afghanistan. Sir John Keane was to accompany the Bengal force, and General Willshire the Bombay troops.

On the 3rd of September, prince Timur arrived at Kabul, skilfully pioneered by Wade. At Ali Masjid the force had met with a show of resistance, but the place was captured on the 26th of July. It was in a large measure due to Wade's force that Keane's army had met with such slight opposition. Through his diplomacy the Kohistanis had been induced to rise against the Amir, but the whole affair was an illustration of the lukewarmness of our Sikh allies.

Arrival of prince Timur.

September passed pleasantly[1] and the officers were happy in the belief that they were to turn their backs upon Afghanistan for ever. On the 18th the Bombay column commenced its return march. On the 2nd of October an order arrived for the main part of the Bengal force to remain in Afghanistan, under Sir Wiloughby Cotton; only a small portion was to return with Sir John Keane.

---

[1] "Wherever Englishmen go, they sooner or later introduce among the people whom they visit a taste for manly sports. Horse racing and cricket were both got up in the vicinity of Kabul ; and in both the chiefs and people soon learned to take a lively interest. Shah Shuja himself gave a valuable sword to be run for, which Major Daly, of the 4th Light Dragoons, had the good fortune to win ; and so infectious became the habit that several of the native gentry entered their horses, with what success no record seems to have been preserved. The game of cricket was not, however, so congenial to the taste of the Afghans. Being great gamblers in their own way, they looked on with astonishment at the bowling, batting, and fagging out of the English players ; but it does not appear that they were ever tempted to lay aside their flowing robes and huge turbans and enter the field as competitors. On the other hand, our countrymen attended them to their mains of cocks, quails, and other fighting animals, and, betting freely, lost or won their rupees in the best possible humour. In like manner our people indulged them from time to time in trials of strength and feats of agility on which they much pride themselves and to their own exceeding delight, though very much to the astonishment of their new friends, they in every instance threw the most noted of the Kabul wrestlers. The result of this frankness was to create among the Afghans a good deal of personal liking for their conquerors."—*Gleig*, page 60.

"The 13th Light Infantry could boast of a very ingenious individual among its officers. Mr. Sinclair possessed a great mechanical genius, which he now applied to the construction of a boat, which he succeeded in rendering comp'ete in all respects during the interval of the rains. Carriages being provided it was conveyed with its oars, mats, and sails to the lake, and there launched. Now there had never been seen in Afghanistan before that moment such a thing as a boat of any description."—*Gleig*, page 72.

The garrison of Afghanistan.

The garrison of Afghanistan was to be distributed as under:—

At Kabul—
　His Majesty's 13th Light Infantry.
　3 guns, No. 6 Light Field Battery.
　35th Native Infantry.

At Jalalabad—
　48th Native Infantry, 4th Brigade.
　Detachment, Sappers and Miners.
　2nd Cavalry and a *risala* of Skinner's Horse.

At Ghazni—
　16th Native Infantry.
　A *risala* of Skinner's Horse, some of Shah Shuja's troops.

At Kandahar—
　42nd Native Infantry.
　43rd　　"　　"
　4th Company, 2nd Battalion, Artillery.
　A *risala* of the 4th Local Horse.
　Details of Shah Shuja's troops.

To prevent the return of Dost Muhammad a detachment the Shah's troops with some artillery was sent to Bamian.

The problem of housing the troops was no easy one. The winter was approaching, and they could not remain camped on the plain; they were therefore located in the Bala Hissar, which stood on a hill overlooking the city, the houses of which were flat-roofed, and the streets narrow and tortuous. The most important feature was the great *bazar*.

On the 18th of October the Bombay force, and on the 15th that for Bengal, set out on their march.[1]

Departure of the troops.

Macnaghten was to accompany the Shah who wished to escape the rigour of the winter, to Jalalabad.

---

[1] *Gleig*, page 75. The men's arms were for the most part of an inferior description. Old flint and steel muskets had become, through much use, so imperfect in their hands that numbers were in the habit of missing fire continually, and the best and most serviceable in the whole brigade was just as likely to carry its ball wide of the mark as in a straight line towards it. Sir Robert Sale, who knew the importance and value of effective weapons, stated these facts at head-quarters. He reminded the authorities that there were in store four thousand muskets, constructed on the detonating principle, perfectly new, and never likely, at least with the present force to be sullied by using, but he begged permission to arm his regiment from that heap * * * * but General Elphinstone would not listen to the proposal.

while Burnes remained at Kabul. The state of affairs, both at Kabul and Kandahar, was unsatisfactory; and unpopular and unscrupulous Afghan agents were already acting in a very different manner from those of the British. Macnaghten does not appear to have noticed the sowing of the seed of sedition, and have no forebodings of evil.

However, in the west, the Ghilzais were demonstrating their unruly nature, and in the east the Khaibar was bristling with hostile tribes.

The outlook.

They rose against the detachments which Wade had left between Peshawar and Jalalabad; Ali Masjid was attacked, and a battalion of Najibs, encamped near the fort, was cut up. The appearance of Sir John Keane quieted the tribes for a time, but when he had quitted the pass they harassed the detachments sent to the relief of Ali Masjid; and a force under Colonel Wheeler was sent from Jalalabad to overawe them. His baggage was attacked, but his operations were for a time successful. Not until Macnaghten conciliated them with bribes did they sink into temporary quiescence.

Sir John Keane and General Willshire returned to India and the Army of the Indus was broken up.

Honours for the campaign.

Lord Auckland was created an Earl; Sir John Keane a Baron; Mr. Macnaghten a Baronet; Colonel Wade was knighted, and a shower of lesser distinctions descended upon the subordinate officers.

The King and the Envoy spent the winter at Jalalabad, and there was something like a lull in Afghanistan. Macnaghten investigated the state of internal affairs, and found them unsatisfactory. Help from India was asked for, but our foreign relations distracted the thoughts of the Government.

Contemporary politics.

The Russian question was now forcing itself into notice, and a Russian force was reported to be on the eve of departure from Orenburg into Central Asia, with a view to threaten the State of Khiva, which had been throwing obstacles in the way of Russian commerce. It was believed, however, that Russia had other objects in view; and that if the British Army had not occupied Afghanistan, the

Russian designs.

Czar's manifesto detailing the objects of the expedition to Khiva would have remained unissued. The expedition was the one subject of discussion in the winter of 1839-1840; matters nearer home, however, troubled Macnaghten. At Herat, Yar Muhammad was playing a game of treachery; in Central Asia, a British Envoy was groaning under the tyranny of the Amir of Bokhara. At Kandahar the Duranis were chafing under the exactions of unpopular revenue officials. The Kohistanis were already sighing for the return of Dost Muhammad. Mehrab Khan's country was breaking out into rebellion against our newly established authority, and the Sikhs were intriguing against us.

Shah Shuja was averse from granting an asylum to Dost Muhammad's family, in spite of the recommendations of Macnaghten, and would not contribute a rupee towards their support.

The court remained at Jalalabad until the third week in April. It was now certain that a Russian Army was advancing upon Khiva. Dost Muhammad's adherents were inciting the Usbegs against us. The petty chiefs were in a state of doubtful vassalage, and the despatch of a strong brigade to Bamian was strongly advocated by the Envoy. As the month advanced Macnaghten began to think that the Russian expedition was a greater danger than he had believed.

On the 13th of March news was received of the failure of the Russian expedition, and one source of disquietude was removed. During the spring and summer, however, two subjects engaged the Envoy's attention. One was the conduct of the Sikhs; the other the state of affairs at Herat. Since the death of Ranjit Singh the Envoy was convinced that decisive measures alone would bring our allies to regard the terms of the treaty. They had rendered no effectual aid to Prince Timur; were making light of the obligation to maintain a force on the frontier, and were engaged in treasonable correspondence with our enemies in Afghanistan; and they were harbouring the rebel Ghilzai Chiefs at the frontier stations. A question had, moreover, arisen concerning the passage of our troops and convoys through the Lahore dominions. Without this it would be impossible to maintain our force in Afghanistan.

Macnaghten's anxieties.

The authorities at Calcutta began to think that a war with the Sikhs was not an improbable event.

Meanwhile the British Government were lavishing treasure upon Herat, while the chief minister was insulting the British officers and intriguing with the Persian Court. He was playing off one Government against the other. He hated the interference of the British officers, but bore with them for the sake of the money which they brought him. Macnaghten recommended the annexation of Herat to Shah Shuja's dominions, but Lord Auckland was disinclined to embrace the proposal; so, instead of an army, further supplies of money were sent, and Yar Muhammad continued his intrigues. Sir Jasper Nicolls,[1] who had been averse to the Afghan expedition, viewed with suspicion any proposal to despatch yet more troops from India; and Lord Auckland received in consequence no warlike promptings from the military side. Nevertheless the burden of Macnaghten's letters still remained the same: nothing could be done until Yar Muhammad and the Sikhs had been chastised, and Herat and Peshawar re-annexed to the Durani Empire.

In the meantime in the dominions of Shah Shuja everything was amiss. Macnaghten was unwilling to admit that the people were in a disturbed condition, but awkward evidence to the contrary was periodically forthcoming. The Ghilzais were again in rebellion and their chiefs had returned from Peshawar, probably with Sikh gold. In April our communications between Kabul and Kandahar were cut. General Nott, who was in command at the latter place, underestimated the strength of the rebels, and sent out a detachment of 200 horse to clear the road. Reinforcements were found to be necessary and on the 7th of May Captain Anderson marched with a regiment of foot, 4 guns, and 300 horsemen and came up with the first detachment near the Tarnak river. The Ghilzais were eight miles distant, and, as his cattle were exhausted, Anderson halted and opened negotiations. The enemy replied that they would fight, and

Internal affairs of Afghanistan.

Expedition against the Ghilzais.

---

[1] Commander-in-Chief in India.

Anderson prepared to attack them. Sending his cavalry to the flanks he marched with his infantry and guns on the 16th, and found the enemy occupying some hills on his front. Twice the enemy charged; the first attack was repelled by the guns, and the second by the bayonets of the infantry. Anderson had sent back the greater part of his cavalry, having heard news of the enemy's retirement; nevertheless his victory was complete, and the enemy fled to their mountain fastnesses, while Anderson reformed his troops and occupied a position near Olan Robat. The enmity of the Ghilzais was, however, only increased by these operations.

Meanwhile affairs had not been progressing favourably in Baluchistan; but an account of the troubles there will be found in the part dealing with that country, and will not be alluded to here.

Baluchistan.

Colonel Dennie was now about to march with the 35th Native Infantry to reinforce the Bamian detachment, and take command of all the troops upon the northern frontier.

CHAPTER XV.

MILITARY OPERATIONS.

THE small force which had been sent to Bamian, in the autumn of 1839, was, in the coming spring, released from inactivity. Jabbar Khan was with Dost Muhammad at Khulm. Early in June a party was sent out, under Captain Garbett, ostensibly to reconnoitre the passes to the north. It was also believed that the movement would decide Jabbar Khan to seek the hospitality of the British. He came into Bamian, and the fortress of Bajgah being found deserted, one of the Shah's regiments was sent to garrison it. The post was found to be unsuitable, and the temper of the surrounding tribes hostile. Captain Hay, the only officer present, fell sick, and on the 2nd of August Lieutenant Golding, with two companies, arrived to reinforce him. The chief received his party with a show of friendliness, but on its return to Bajgah it was fired upon. Two companies of Gurkhas coming up rescued them, and the force returned to Bajgah. The tidings of this disaster reached Kabul and the Envoy's anxiety was increased. In the middle of August sedition reared its head in the vicinity of the capital, and it was made evident that Sikh intrigue was at work for the restoration of Dost Muhammad. He, with his sons Afzal Khan and Akbar Khan, had tasted the bitterness of confinement at Bokhara. Once the former narrowly escaped being murdered. Their condition was somewhat bettered through the intervention of the Shah of Persia, and availing themselves of the greater freedom allowed them, they effected their escape, and the ex-Amir was received with open arms by the Wali of Khulm. He soon found himself at the head of a considerable force. The Usbegs flocked to him, and he determined to strike a vigorous blow for the recovery of his kingdom. Early in September he advanced upon Bamian with about 7,000 men.

In September the Envoy wrote that Turkistan was in arms against us, and that Haibak had fallen to the Dost.

On the 30th August the Usbegs had attacked Bajgah and, Codrington's Gurkhas, aided by Rattray's Afghan Horse, had driven them back; but the post was no longer tenable, and the garrison retired to Saighan.[1] This post, also, was too weak to hold against a

Attack on Bajgah.

---

[1] One of the greatest errors committed by the British authorities in Afghanistan was the splitting up of the disposable forces into small detachments.

In this connection and with regard to affairs in general, the following extract from a letter published in the *East India Army Magazine* for 1853 is interesting and instructive:—

"During my residence in Kabul I had opportunities of seeing many papers and letters connected with the earlier occurrences of the British occupation, and I am persuaded that had the advice of Brigadier Roberts, who then commanded the Shah's force, been followed, the later disasters would never have taken place; but Sir W. Macnaghten was so wedded to his own opinion, and so little aware of the true nature of the people he had to deal with, that whilst he rejected all advice that militated against his own fixed notions and preconceived ideas, at the same time he either irritated the Afghans by his arbitrary conduct, or alienated them by his coldness. Even in the summer of 1840 Sir William showed how little he was able to understand the nature of the opposition he might be called upon to encounter, when he quarrelled with Captain Hay about the unfortunate affair at Bajgah, though in the opinion of those best able to judge, Captain Hay did all in his power to prevent the lamentable retreat that then occurred, by making a full report of the state of Bajgah, and the impossibility of defending it. I know Brigadier Roberts deemed it of such importance, that he went at night to Sir William to beg that the troops might be recalled before the people of the country could have time to assemble. Sir William, however, would not listen to him, but said that Dr. Lord had ordered the troops to advance, and there they should remain until the Doctor reached Kabul. Immediately this happened, I believe the Brigadier wrote officially to the Envoy, pointing out what was likely to occur, but still the detached column was not recalled, and was eventually forced to retreat from the advanced posts of Saighan and Bajgah, a proceeding most prejudicial to our interests. Lieutenant Sturt of the Engineers had previously pronounced those places untenable, but to no purpose, and the fault was most unjustly visited upon Hay, who was deprived of his regiment shortly afterwards.

"Both Brigadier Roberts and General Nott saw the true state of affairs, and did all they could for the preservation of the country, but it was the wish of the Envoy to remove both, and he succeeded with the former, who was most anxious to remain. It is well known that Brigadier Roberts strongly protested against the site and plan of the cantonments, and pointed out that they were on too extended a scale, besides being commanded and having a river between them and the Bala Hissar.

"I can well remember that he recommended that forts should be built in echelon for wings or regiments, which, with mere parapet walls, could be defended by few men, and that the Bala Hissar should be put in a state of defence, with guns mounted and troops quartered in it. But those were truly times when wisdom cried aloud in the streets, and no man regarded her. It was I think at this period that the Brigadier had store-rooms erected in the Bala Hissar in which the commissariat stored grain sufficient for the supply of the Shah's force for some months, and removed the treasure from the house of Sir A. Burnes in the city to the Bala Hissar; yet it is a matter of history that soon after the Brigadier's return to the provinces the treasure was again removed to its insecure position in the heart of the city; and fell into the hands of the Afghans, on the breaking out of the rebellion, whilst the Envoy was left without a rupee . . . . there is little doubt that had the advice of such men as Nott and Roberts been followed from the first, the retreat, with its disasters and dishonour, would never have occurred, and the British might still have been in possession of Kabul."

considerable force, and they fell back upon Bamian. A recently raised regiment of Afghan infantry, under Salah Muhammad, deserted, and a number joined the enemy.

Day by day the cloud over Kabul grew darker; an open enemy was in the field, and the Sikhs were pushing their intrigues to the very gates of the Bala Hissar. Macnaghten wrote to the Governor-General, describing the state of affairs, and quoted a note from Cotton, in which he said there was now no Afghan army, and that unless the Bengal troops were strengthened the country could not be held. He himself reiterated his oft-expressed opinion that another brigade should be sent.

The 18th September was the turning-point of our fortunes in Afghanistan. On the 14th reinforcements under Dennie, had reached Bamian. His first measure was to disarm the Afghan corps; he then began to think of marching to Saighan to meet the Amir's advancing troops, but the enemy were nearer than he anticipated. On the 17th he received information that bodies of cavalry were entering the valley six miles from Bamian, and on the following morning they attacked a friendly village. On the 18th a detachment was ordered out to drive the enemy from the valley; the force consisted of 2 horse artillery guns, 2 companies, 35th Native Infantry, 2 companies of Gurkhas, and 400 Afghan Horse, supported shortly afterwards by Dennie himself, with 2 more companies each of the 35th and Gurkhas. Instead of an advanced guard he found an army in front of him. He, however, never hesitated, and Mackenzie's guns opened fire. The Usbegs fell back, followed by the guns. They fled, pursued by the cavalry, who cut down numbers, and dispersed the remainder in all directions. Dost Muhammad himself owed his life to the fleetness of his horse. The intelligence caused the spirits of the British Resident at Kabul to rise at once. Never was victory so much needed and never did one promise so many results. Handsome terms were offered to Mir Muhammad Beg, the Wali of Khulm, which detached him from his alliance with Dost Muhammad. The fight at Bamian showed him the futility of resistance. The country south of Saighan was ceded to Shah Shuja, that to the north to the Wali.

Engagement with Dost Muhammad at Bamian.

These favourable results were, however, only local, and Dost Muhammad re-appeared in Kohistan, where disaffection was rife. Sir Robert Sale was ordered to take the field, accompanied by Burnes. On the 29th September Sale invested the enemy's position at Tutam Darra, at the entrance of the Ghorband Pass, and met with very slight resistance.

On the 3rd October Sale attacked Julgah, a very strong position.

Attack on Julgah.

The guns were light and the ladders short, while the enemy offered a determined resistance. The storming party of the 13th Light Infantry made an ineffectual attempt to effect a lodgment; but their gallantry was in vain and the column was withdrawn. The enemy, however, withdrew, and the works were destroyed.

During October Dost Muhammad was flitting from place to place with no settled plan of action. On the 11th October he was at Ghorband,

Anxiety at Kabul.

some fifty miles from Kabul, and Macnaghten grew very anxious. The prospects of a siege of Kabul were anticipated by the political chiefs; guns were mounted on the citadel to overawe the town; the guards were increased; the Bamian detachment was ordered to return to the capital. Shah Shuja placed an intercepted letter in Macnaghten's hands, addressed to Sultan Muhammad, proposing that, with his aid and that of the Sikhs, Shah Zeman should be placed on the throne. The letter bore the seal of the old blind king himself, and the envoy wrote to the Governor-General recommending that no mercy should be shown to the Dost.

The force under Sir Robert Sale pursued the Amir into the Nijrao country; on the 18th October they were encamped at Kardarah, and on the 20th were meditating an attack on the place. On the 21st it was discovered that the enemy had left their exceedingly strong position without an effort to defend it.

On the 27th October Dost Muhammad moved towards the capital. News of his approach having reached the British camp at Bagh Alam on the 29th, the troops moved out

Encounter with the Dost at Parwandarah.

to meet him. The two following days were occupied in reconnoitring and surveying the surrounding country, and on the 1st November the force encamped before Mir Musjidi's fort.

Here it was ascertained that they were in the neighbourhood of the enemy, and preparations for battle were begun. On the 2nd November the force came in sight of the enemy posted in the valley of Parwandarah. The Nijrao hills were bristling with the armed population of a hostile country. Dost Muhammad was unprepared to fight on this day, but an unexpected movement precipitated the collision. On the first appearance of the British he began to evacuate his positions, and, at Dr. Lord's[1] suggestion, the British cavalry moved forward to outflank the Afghan Horse. The Afghans were on the hills skirting one side of the pass, the British troops were on the opposite side. When he saw the cavalry advance, Dost Muhammad relinquished all idea of retreat. He himself led his cavalry to the attack. The English officers, who led our cavalry, covered themselves with glory, but the native troopers fled like sheep. The Afghans charged right up to the British position. Lieutenants Broadfoot and Crispin were cut to pieces; Lord was stabbed to death, and Captains Fraser and Ponsonby were severely wounded. Flaunting their national standard in front of our columns, the Afghans stood for some time masters of the field, and withdrew from the scene of battle when the infantry came up. Burnes wrote to Macnaghten that there was no alternative but for the force to fall back upon Kabul, and begged him to concentrate all our troops there. Dost Muhammad, on the other hand, in the very hour of victory, felt that it was hopeless to contend against the British. He knew that his success would lead them to redouble their exertions, and entertained no bright visions of the future; however, he had fought a good fight and might now retire from the contest without a blot upon his name.

The British neither knew his thoughts nor whither he had gone. On the day following his victory he was before the walls of Kabul, attended by a single horseman. He told the Envoy he had come to claim his protection, and offered his sword, which was returned. He wrote to his sons and counselled them to follow his example. A few days later his eldest son, Afzal Khan, came into camp. Dost Muhammad remained ten days in the camp,

Surrender of Dost Muhammad.

---
[1] Dr. Percival Lord, a medical officer of rare accomplishments accompanied as political officer, the force sent to Bamian.

but Shah Shuja refused to see him. On the 12th of November 1840, escorted by the Company's European regiment, joined by the 48th Native Infantry at Jalalabad, he commenced his journey towards India. Macnaghten wrote that he hoped the Dost would be treated with liberality. The Shah had no claim upon us, whereas we had deprived Dost Muhammad of his kingdom, in support of our policy, of which he was the victim. Lord Auckland received the deposed Prince with becoming hospitality and respect, and allotted him a pension of two lakhs of rupees.

The remainder of November was peaceful. Macnaghten now strongly recommended the stationing of a subsidiary force in the Punjab and the cession of the districts to the west of the Indus.

Risings of the Duranis and Ghilzais.

The court proceeded to their winter quarters at Jalalabad, where the Envoy found Cotton anxious to depart, and Macgregor, the Political Agent, regarded as a father by the district chiefs. Very little leisure was, however, granted to Macnaghten. The Ghilzais and Kohistanis had already risen against the Shah, and now the Duranis were in revolt. They had looked for much from the restoration of the Shah Shuja, but were disappointed; his imperfect liberality irritated them.

In Zamindawar to the north-west of Kandahar, symptoms of disquiet began to evince themselves at the end of 1840. Affairs at Kandahar were at this time under the superintendence of an able officer, Major Rawlinson, who had superseded Leech. Major-General Nott, a capable officer of rather irritable temperament, commanded the troops. Such were the men upon whom, at the beginning of 1841, devolved the duty of facing the Durani outbreak. Nott's task was the easier of the two; to defeat the enemy in the field. The Zamindawar insurgents had beaten a party of the Shah's horse, and a detachment, under Captain Farrington, was sent against them. On the 3rd of January they came up with the Durani Horse, some 1,500 strong, who showed a bold front, but the fire of Hawkins' guns soon shook them and the infantry completed their dispersal.

The British officials at Kandahar.

Rawlinson, on the other hand, had to ascertain the causes of the Duranis' dissatisfaction; but his views were at variance with

Macnaghten's. The latter did not believe in any general discontent, or that the presence of strangers was hateful to the people, and still less that the King who himself was said to be desirous of seeing the last of the white faces was unpopular. He suspected that the disaffection of the Duranis had been engineered by Yar Muhammad, and proofs were shortly forthcoming to substantiate his theory. The Wazir had long been accommodating his demands to every change in the political barometer. The disaster of Major Clibborn, the fall of Kalat, and Dost Muhammad's progress in the Hindu Khush, encouraged him to raise his demands. At one time he contemplated a descent upon Kandahar, but Dost Muhammad's surrender led him to change his mind. The Zamindawar outbreak caused the project to be revived, and he fomented the spirit of revolt, at the same time asking for pecuniary assistance from Persia, the expulsion of the mission from Herat being the price offered; and urged an united attack upon Kandahar while communications between Herat and Kabul were blocked by the snow.

Todd determined to retalitae, and suspended the payment of his allowance. Yar Muhammad, however, believed that his mission to Mashad had been favourably received; that the Duranis were ripe for rebellion; and that the British Government would forbear and yet forbear. He, therefore, increased his demands. Todd replied that he would require some guarantee that the concessions, if made, should not be thrown away; and proposed the location of a British garrison at Herat. Yar Muhammad agreed to a force being cantoned in the valley on the payment of two lakhs of rupees, without, however, the slightest intention of fulfilling his part of the contract. Todd demanded that his son should be sent to Girishk to await Government's reply and escort the British force should the measure be approved. Yar Muhammad refused, and demanded either the payment of the money, or the withdrawal of the mission. The British Agent, therefore, turned his back upon Herat, a proceeding of which Lord Auckland disapproved, and Todd was relegated to regimental duty.

In one sense the Herat mission had failed, but some of Todd's measures were successful; he had despatched, with advantage, Abbott and Shakespear to Khiva, substantial benefits

The withdrawal of the mission from Herat.

had accrued to the people of Herat, still remembered with gratitude; the behaviour of the mission had raised the character of the British nation. His departure, however, was inopportune, as a settlement with Persia was on the point of being arrived at, and Lord Auckland never forgave the diplomatic failure. Todd, however, was ignorant of this fact or would undoubtedly have remained at Herat.

On receiving intelligence of Todd's departure, Macnaghten meditated a demonstration in the direction of Herat, beating up the rebels on the Helmund and crushing Akhtar Khan on the way to the western frontier; and wrote to Rawlinson to prepare for the siege of Herat. Against an armed interference with Herat, however, Lord Auckland had always set his face; believing that it was necessary first that we should establish ourselves in Afghanistan. Macnaghten's opinion was exactly the opposite. His instructions, however, were imperative.

It was manifest at Kandahar that the aggressive designs of Yar Muhammad, who contemplated the seizure of Girishk, and the hostility of the Duranis in the western districts rendered immediate operations necessary. A force was, therefore, sent to the Zamindawar country to beat up Akhtar Khan's quarters, or intercept his advance. The political conduct of the expedition was entrusted to Elliot, Rawlinson's assistant, and he did his duty well. It was not our policy to fight but to obtain Akhtar Khan's submission and, as his force was insignificant, it was expected that he would come to terms. The hope was justified by the event, and at an interview a conditional pardon was granted, some concessions made, and a dress of honour conferred upon him. The most important condition was the disbandment of his followers, and the hope was entertained that the country would be tranquillised without further shedding of blood. Rawlinson was not so optimistic, and foresaw only a temporary cessation of hostilities, and still considered that, when opportunity should serve, the rights of Her Majesty's Government should be asserted in a strong and dignified manner.

Akhtar Khan.

The Ghilzais, also, were in the spring and summer of 1841 in revolt against Shah Shuja and his allies. Lieutenant Lynch, of the Bombay Army, was in political charge of Kalat-i-Ghilzai.

The Ghilzais.

He attributed the restlessness of the tribes to the fact that the families of some of their chiefs, who, after the operations of 1839 had fled to the Sikh frontier, had, at the instigation of the British Envoy, been cast into captivity. However this may have been, the rebuilding by the English, in the spring of 1841, of the fortress of Kalat-i-Ghilzai, between Kandahar and Kabul, with the idea of posting a strong garrison there to overawe the tribes, was the proximate source of irritation. The proceeding was viewed with jealousy by the Ghilzais; and those in the neighbourhood assumed an insolent and defiant attitude.

Action near Kalat-i-Ghilzai.

About two miles away was a fort bristling with armed men, and these grossly insulted Lynch as he was riding past. To discourage such acts of aggression the troops at Kalat-i-Ghilzai were summoned to attack the fort. Aided by Captain Sanders of the Engineers, Captain Macan, who commanded one of the regiments of Shah Shuja's force, led his Hindustanis against the stronghold, and captured it after a brave resistance. The chief and many of his followers were slain, and the irritation of the Ghilzais was greater than before.

It was a gallant exploit but a great misfortune, condemned alike at Kabul and Calcutta. Lynch was removed from office, although, when the circumstances became more fully known, Burnes took a more lenient view of the matter. It was expected that the whole country would rise against Macan's detachment, so reinforcements were called for from Kandahar. Nott was unwilling to expose his troops during the hot weather, but the political necessity was great, Macan was in danger, and troops could not be spared from Kabul.

Colonel Wymer, therefore, with 400 of the 38th Native Infantry, 4 horse artillery guns, and some of Christie's Horse, took the field in May. The Ghilzais, eager for the fray, moved down to meet the troops and on the 19th gave them battle. Night was coming no as they neared Wymer's camp at Assiya-i-Ilmi. They came on gallantly, but were met with a heavy fire from Hawkins' guns, which created much havoc. The Ghilzais now divided into three columns to fall upon the front and flanks, and charged sword in hand. Wymer was hampered by his extensive convoy, and

Wymer's action at Assiya-i-Ilmi.

his movements being thereby crippled he was compelled to assume the defensive, but the grape from the guns and the steady musketry of the sepoys drove them back again and again. For five hours the fight continued, and then the Ghilzais gave way, leaving many dead on the field, and during the night the moving lights showed that many more, both of killed and wounded, were being carried off to their camp.

At this period the proceedings of Akhtar Khan[1] and the Duranis were again exciting the apprehensions of the Envoy. The Chief had tendered his allegiance to the King; the hated revenue officers had been removed; Usman Khan had succeeded the old minister; and Macnaghten was contemplating other reforms; but their disaffection was more deeply rooted. The whole system of Government was offensive and the presence of the British hateful.

May found Akhtar Khan, our implacable enemy, collecting his forces, and the Duranis were again to be corrected. At the end of June the Khan with 3,000 men was still before Girishk and it was necessary to strike a blow.

Woodburn, who commanded one of the Shah's regiments, was sent against him with the 5th Infantry, two detachments of Afghan Horse, and some of the Shah's Horse Artillery. On the 3rd of July he found 6,000 of the enemy, formed in six divisions, on the other side of the Helmund. The fords in the vicinity were reported impassable. At 4 P.M. the enemy struck their camp and began the passage of the river. The Duranis made a spirited attack, but Woodburn's infantry, supported by Cooper's guns, damped their ardour. The Afghan Horse did not distinguish themselves.

Akhtar Khan's fight on the Helmund.

It was a busy night. The enemy far outnumbered Woodburn, but the steady gallantry of his troops achieved the success they deserved. Before daybreak the enemy had withdrawn. A pursuit was out of the question, as the cavalry was unreliable, and the whole country up in arms. Woodburn, therefore, wrote for reinforcements and pushed on to Girishk, whence he reported the rebellion to be more extensive than had been supposed, and that the rebels at Kandahar and the Helmund were equally disaffected.

---

[1] Akhtar Khan was a son of Dost Muhammad.

August found the Envoy still sanguine and cheerful, but Rawlinson took a more serious view of the situation. More chastisement was, however, necessary for the Duranis. Small detachments had gained small victories, but the enemy's strength was not broken. Akram Khan had now joined Akhtar Khan, inspired with the same bitter hatred.

A force under Captain Griffin, who had been sent to reinforce Woodburn, strong in cavalry, was sent out against them. His troops consisted of 800 sabres, 350 bayonets, and four 6-pounders.

Another action with Akhtar Akhtar Khan.

On the 17th August he came up with the enemy. The Afghan Horse had not won the confidence of their British officers, and it was a moment of some anxiety. Here, however, they were associated with some of the King's regular cavalry and may have felt the danger of detection. Whatever the cause, they did not shrink from the encounter. The enemy were strongly posted in a succession of walled gardens and small forts, whence they opened a heavy fusillade; but the fire of our guns and musketry drove them from the enclosures, and the cavalry, led by Prince Safdar Jang, charging with terrific effect, routed the Duranis.

The Ghilzais, too, had received another check. Early in August, Colonel Chambers had taken against them part of the 5th Light Cavalry, the 16th and 43rd Native Infantry, and some Irregular Horse. He came up with the enemy on the 5th, and the cavalry immediately scattered them in disastrous flight.

Chamber's expedition against the Ghilzais.

Macnaghten's confidence now rose higher, and the only circumstance which caused him any disquietude was the fact that Akhtar Khan, Dost Muhammad's favourite son, was hovering about Khulm. He was, however, at this very time arranging for the despatch from Kandahar of a large force to the Tarin and Derawat country, to break up the rebellion there. By the end of the first week in September the force was ready for its difficult march. It was in good condition, well equipped, and took a month's supplies. It was composed of the 2nd and 38th Native Infantry, a regiment of the Shah's Cavalry, two of the Shah's Horse Artillery Guns, a company of European Artillery with two 18-pounders, and a

Expedition to Tarin and Derawat.

detachment of Sappers. It was commanded by Colonel Wymer, much to the disgust of Nott who had been ordered not to leave Kandahar. These restrictions were now, however, removed, and he followed the force. Elliot went in political charge. Although every effort had been made to obtain reliable information, the want of local knowledge was severely felt, and the difficulties met with were greater than had been anticipated. Nott joined the column on the 23rd September, and it entered the Derawat country. Dismayed by this formidable display of force, many of the principal Durani Chiefs came into camp early in October, and professed their willingness to proceed to Kabul and make their submission to the Shah.

Akram Khan, however, refused to submit, and it was determined to capture him. One of his own countrymen undertook to betray him; and although his good faith was doubted, Elliot grasped at the proposal, and obtained the permission of the General to send a regiment of Irregular Cavalry, under John Conolly, to beat him up. A rapid march brought them to a small fort, where the chief was preparing to take to the hills. Within 36 hours he was a prisoner in Nott's camp, and was eventually blown from a gun at Kandahar by Prince Timur's orders. Before the end of October, Nott was back at Kandahar with the greater part of his force, and Lieutenant Crawford had been despatched to Kabul with the Durani Chiefs who had tendered their submission. There were now prospects of tranquillity in Western Afghanistan, for the Ghilzai and Durani confederacies had been crushed, and the facility with which we had moved our regular troops and heavy guns about the difficult country had produced a good moral effect upon the people, who had heretofore only known us by report.

Capture of Akram Khan.

The King was in the Bala Hissar in September 1841, discontented and complaining that he had no authority, but that it had been usurped by his allies. He watched with satisfaction the growth of their difficulties, hoping it would hasten their departure. His health was also failing, and he was nervous and irritable.

Situation at Kabul.

Macnaghten had just been appointed Governor of Bombay, and was looking forward to a speedy departure.

PLAN OF BRITISH CANTONMENT AT KABUL
AND ENVIRONS

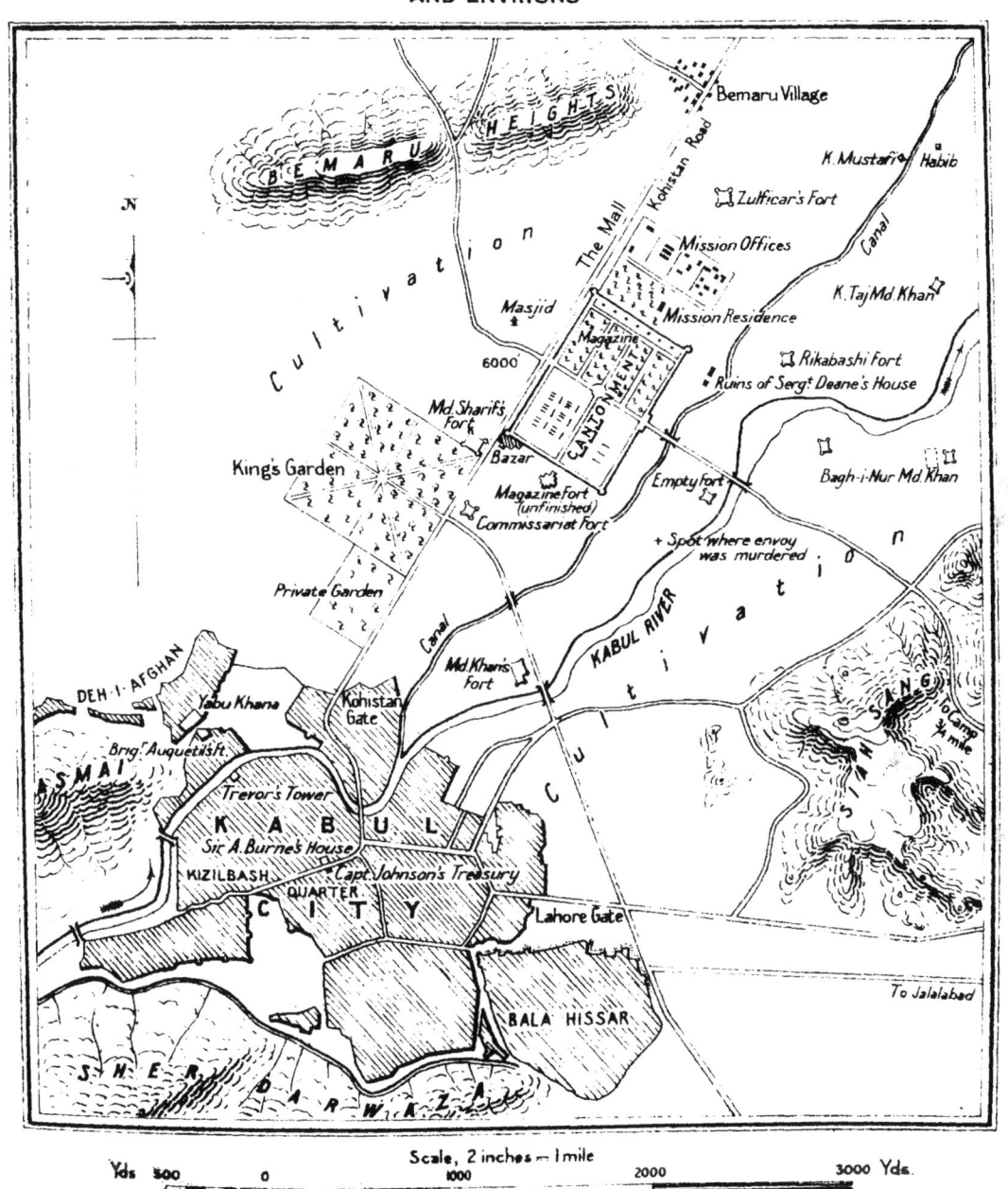

Topographical detail from modern Surveys, other detail from a Sketch by Lieut Vincent Eyre. R.A

No. 4.450-L. 1908.

Burnes was also at Kabul, in a nondescript situation; Macnaghten disagreed with his views, and treated them with contemptuous dissent; however in a few weeks Burnes' ambition would be gratified, and he would be supreme at Kabul.

General Elphinstone[1] was in command of the troops, a situation for which his physical disabilities and ignorance of India ill-fitted him. Sir Jasper Nicolls would have placed Nott in command, but he was not a *persona grata*. Next in rank to Elphinstone were Sir Robert Sale and Brigadier Shelton, both officers of long Indian experience. The Shah's troops were commanded by Brigadier Anquetil, who succeeded Roberts, who had been removed because, divining the danger more clearly, his opinions clashed with those of Macnaghten.[2]

The cantonment.

The main body of the British troops were in the new cantonments. These had been built in the preceding year, and were situated on low ground, open to the Kohistan road. They were nearly one mile in extent, with contemptible defences. Near by was the mission house, surrounded by buildings belonging to the officers and retainers of the mission; and the defences were very weak. The whole were commanded from all sides, and surrounded by villages, forts, and gardens, which would give cover to an enemy. The supplies were stored in a small fort beyond the cantonments, and the communication between the two places was commanded by an empty fort and a walled garden.

The engineers had urged upon the Envoy that the troops should be located in the Bala Hissar; which was, however, afterwards

---

[1] Vincent Eyre, page 29.

"I might add that, during the siege, no one exposed his person more fearlessly or frequently to the enemy's fire than General Elphinstone; his gallantry was never doubted."

Vincent Eyre, page 46.

"Let me here, however, pay a just tribute to the memory of two of his staff officers now, alas! no more. Few men have ever combined all the excellent qualities which constitute the good soldier and the good man more remarkably than did Major Thain of Her Majesty's 21st Fusiliers, Aide-de-Camp to General Elphinstone, while of Captain Paton, Deputy Quarter Master General, it may be safely affirmed, that in solid practical sense and genuineness of heart he was never surpassed. Would that all, to whom the General was in the habit of deferring, had been equally wise to counsel and prompt to execute with the two above-named gallant men!"

[2] See note on page 112. Divided counsels, friction between the civil and military power, and the want of a proper adjustment of the functions of each, were, in this case, as they have been before and since, a fruitful cause of disaster.—*Editor*.

given up for the accommodation of the Shah's harem. Sturt, who succeeded Durand as engineer, had recommended that the Bala Hissar should be re-occupied and placed in a state of defence. Roberts objected to the cantonment plan, but the Envoy was firm and put aside all objections.

The English quickly accommodated themselves to the new conditions. Lady Sale, Lady Macnaghten, and other English women took up their abode in the cantonments; and games and entertainments were the order of the day. Politically Macnaghten considered that all was well. The Duranis were subdued; the Ghilzai Chiefs were at Kabul, apparently contented. It is true that Pottinger's reports from Kohistan and Nijrao were not too favourable; but Macnaghten made light of them. A small expedition was indeed to proceed to Zao to reduce some turbulent tribes, but as even ladies were talking of joining it, this could not be looked upon as a very serious effort. No opposition was met with, and the forts were destroyed; but the result was said by Pottinger to be likely to be unfavourable to us. The Kohistanis exaggerated our difficulties. During the early part of October they remained quiet, but Pottinger reported the brewing of an extensive conspiracy. Neither Macnaghten nor Burnes, however, could perceive any grounds for suspicion. The Eastern Ghilzais were also breaking out into revolt, and Pottinger was of opinion that the two were leagued with the Duranis.

The political aspect.

The expenses of the occupation had been draining the revenues of India to the extent of over one million sterling per annum. The Board of Control recommended the abandonment of the country and a frank confession of failure; nor did the surrender of Dost Muhammad alter their views. Lord Auckland, however, decided in favour of continued occupation.

Great Britain was on the eve of a change of ministry, and the Conservatives had always been hostile to the policy of the expedition. Macnaghten's opinion was strong for the continued support of the Shah; and, fearing the abandonment of this policy, he determined to practise a system of economy; and, dangerous though he knew the measure to be, commenced by reducing the subsidies paid to the chiefs. These held secret meetings, and bound them-

selves by oaths to support one another in their attempts to recover what they had lost, or to subvert the system whence these proceedings had arisen. The Eastern Ghilzais were the first to throw off the mask. They quitted Kabul; occupied the passes on the road to Jalalabad; plundered a valuable *kafila*; and cut off our communications with India.

Hamza Khan, the Governor of the Ghilzais, who was at the bottom of the whole conspiracy, was sent by the Shah to recall them to their allegiance, and to quell the disturbance which he himself had fathered. Macnaghten at first made light of the matter, but in a few days changed his opinion, urging Macgregor to return to accompany the proposed expedition; but wrote to Rawlinson that he expected the rebellion would be easily quelled.

Sale's brigade, which was returning to the provinces, was to stifle the insurrection *en route* to Jalalabad. Macnaghten, to strengthen the force, with a view to the operations against the Ghilzais, wrote to Trevor, who, pending Macgregor's arrival, was negotiating with the enemy, that he believed the force would consist of two 8-inch mortars, two 9-pounders, Abbott's battery, the 5th Cavalry and Sappers and Miners with Her Majesty's 13th Light Infantry, 35th and 37th Native Infantry.

Affair at Butkhak.

On the 9th October Colonel Monteith marched from Kabul with the 35th Native Infantry, a squadron of the 5th Cavalry, two of Abbott's guns and Broadfoot's Sappers and Miners. That night his camp was attacked at Butkhak, the first march on the Jalalabad road. On the 10th, therefore, Sale received orders to march at once with the 13th Light Infantry, and on the following day he started to clear the passes. On the 12th he entered the Khurd-Kabul defile.[1]

Affair in the Khurd-Kabul.

The enemy occupied the heights in considerable force, and opened a galling fire upon the advancing column. Sale was wounded at the first

---

[1] Lady Sale, page 11. The Khurd-Kabul is a narrow defile, enclosed by high and rugged rocks; it is said that the number of the enemy did not exceed 60 men, but they possessed considerable advantage over our troops in their knowledge of the country and in the positions they took up; for until they commenced firing, not a man was known to be there. They were concealed behind rocks and stones, and by a stone breast-work that they had hastily thrown up, behind which, on our troops entering the pass, [they laid in wait, and appeared to pick off the officers in particular.

onset, and the command devolved upon Dennie. The 13th Light Infantry, largely composed of young soldiers, ascended the almost precipitous heights with great gallantry, rivalled and equalled in steadiness by the sepoys of the 35th. The pass was cleared, and the 13th returned to Butkhak, leaving Monteith, with the 35th and other details, encamped in the valley. Macgregor, who had reached Kabul on the 11th of October, at once joined the camp. Macnaghten believed that the outbreak was purely local, but Pottinger clearly saw that a storm was brewing. As October advanced the attitude of the Kohistanis and Nijrawis became more threatening. Pottinger demanded hostages from the Kohistani Chiefs, and to this the Envoy consented with reluctance. Mir Musjidi, the Nijrac Chief, had now openly raised the standard of revolt, and his people were gathering round it.

In the meantime Monteith in his isolated post was subjected to frequent night attacks. Aided by the treachery of the Afghan horsemen the rebels were admitted within the lines. An officer and several sepoys were killed, and a number of camels carried off. Monteith reported this treachery, but Macnaghten resented his suspicions. Sale, however, now reinforced him with two regiments of infantry, more guns, and more sabres, and, after a brief halt, due to want of carriage, the force moved on to Tezin, where it halted for some days,[1] while Macgregor negotiated with the enemy. The Ghilzais demanded that their former salaries should be restored, and that they should not be held responsible for robberies committed beyond their boundaries. Macgregor consented, and the affair appeared to have been settled.[2]

March to Gandamak. Macgregor soon learned the value of his treaty. From Tezin to Gandamak the Ghilzai agents were in our camp; but there was some hard fighting for the brigade. The enemy mustered in force and attacked the column, and the chiefs confessed their inability to

---

[1] Gleig, page 95. The same caution which had marked the whole of Sir Robert Sale's proceedings from the outset was manifested in the arrangement of his Camp in the valley of Tezin. Strong piquets were planted on every side, and not they alone, but the advanced sentries, were ordered to construct *sangars* for their own protection.

[2] The principle may here be enunciated that in Asiatic warfare no terms should be made with an unbeaten enemy. It will be illustrated again in the course of this narrative.—*Editor.*

control the tribes. The baggage-encumbered column found great difficulty in forcing their way, but Jagdallak was gained with little opposition. During the next march, however, the heights were crowded with armed men, and from every coign of vantage a heavy fire was poured in. Sale threw out flanking parties,[1] and the skirmishers dislodged the enemy from the hill sides; and Captain Wilkinson, pushing through the defile, found that the passage was clear. The march was resumed, but the enemy were not yet done with. They fell upon the rear-guard and created terrible disorder. The officers soon restored the young soldiers' confidence, however, and Broadfoot, Backhouse, and Rennick rallied and re-animated them. Our loss was heavy; more than 100 men were killed or wounded; Captain Wyndham of the 35th being among the slain.[2]

Sale halted at Gandamak. Macnaghten, when he heard of the losses, expressed the belief that it was the enemy's last effort, and wrote to congratulate Rawlinson on the tranquil appearance of affairs at Kandahar. On this very day he had decided to leave Kabul, and did not doubt but that his emancipation was close at hand.

---

[1] *Gleig*, page 105. The usual distribution of the force into advance, main body, and rear-guard, was of course made; and the companies allotted for the latter service being ordered upon piquet at sunset were in their places and ready to cover the march of the baggage after the column had moved on. Protection, however, was required this day for the column itself, as well as for the baggage, and flanking parties were in consequence thrown out to clear the nearest hills.

[2] Wyndham, who was lame, dismounted from his horse to help a wounded soldier, and being unable to keep up, was killed when the rear-guard broke before the Ghilzai charge.

CHAPTER XVI.

THE OUTBREAK OF INSURRECTION.

NOVEMBER dawned brightly and the Envoy and Burnes were, from different causes, looking forward to the former's departure; and both were confident for the future. Others, however, viewed the gathering portents in a different light. Captain Colin Mackenzie had told Macnaghten at the end of October that Akhtar Khan had arrived at Bamian from Bokhara and meant mischief; but the Envoy disbelieved the news. John Conolly also warned him of a meditated rising in the city. The Munshi Mohan Lal, who had returned from Sale's Camp, declared his opinion that a conspiracy was brewing and that, if not promptly crushed, it would become too strong to be easily suppressed. Burnes promised to act on Macnaghten's departure, and to raise the allowances of the Ghilzais and Kohistanis to their former amounts. On the 1st of November, the Munshi reiterated his warning. On that very evening the hostile chiefs held a meeting to plan the overthrow of the British. It took place at the house of Sardar Khan, Alakozai. Foremost among the chiefs was Abdulla Khan, who was writhing under an insult received from Burnes. It was determined to attack the latter's house on the morrow.

Day had scarcely dawned when rumours of a disturbance in the city reached the cantonment. Conolly conveyed the intelligence to Macnaghten, who received it with composure. Now a note came from Burnes, who, while speaking slightingly of the disturbance, asked for military support. The Envoy proceeded to the General's

Storm warnings.

Murder of Burnes.

quarters; but before assistance was sent Burnes had been cut to pieces.[1]

The houses of the latter and Captain Johnson were contiguous. The latter had spent the previous night in cantonments. With Burnes were his brother Charles and Lieutenant William Broadfoot. Before daylight on that fateful morning a friendly Afghan sought admittance to warn Burnes of his danger; but his words were received incredulously. Usman Khan, the Wazir, now came with the same intelligence, and there was no longer room for scepticism. The excited populace was assembling beneath the windows, and the Englishman turned to face the fury of the mob. He sent to the Envoy for support, and messengers to Abdulla Khan, assuring him, that if he would restrain the crowd, every effort would be made to adjust all grievances. In vain Burnes, with the other two officers beside him, harangued the crowd, some of whom were thirsting for blood; others greedy for plunder. His address was of no avail.

Broadfoot was the first to fall, shot in the chest. The crowd had now become a multitude. A party set fire to Burnes' stables, and forced their way into the garden, calling him to come down. He offered large sums of money in exchange for life; but they repeated their demand. Charles Burnes and some *chuprassis* were now firing on the mob, when a Kashmiri Musalman, who had entered the house, swore that he would convey Burnes and his brother to the Kizilbash Fort; but disguised as a native, he no sooner stepped into the garden than he was denounced by his guide, and the brothers were cut to pieces. The crowd wreaked vengeance, murdering and plundering to their heart's content.

---

[1] *Troops in Kabul on the date of Burnes' murder.*
1st Troop, 1st Brigade, Bengal Horse Artillery.
A battery of Artillery, Shah Shuja's Force.
Detachment, Bengal Sappers and Miners.
Detachment of Sappers, Shah Shuja's Force (3 companies).
Two squadrons, 5th Bengal Light Cavalry.
One *risala*, 1st Irregular Cavalry.
One *risala*, 4th Irregular Cavalry.
2nd Regiment of Cavalry, Shah Shuja's Force.
Her Majesty's 44th Foot.
5th Bengal Native Infantry.
54th Bengal Native Infantry.
The Envoy's Body-Guard.
6th Infantry Regiment, Shah Shuja's Force.
On 3rd November, in addition, 37th Bengal Native Infantry.

The only movement to crush the insurrection at its birth was set on foot by Shah Shuja, who had been looking down on the disturbance from the Bala Hissar. He sent out a regiment of Hindustanis, with Fateh Jang and the Wazir, but it was soon dispersed.

Military measures.

In the meantime Brigadier Shelton, with some infantry and artillery, arrived at the Bala Hissar, in time to cover the retreat; but on that day nothing else was done. Shah Shuja sank into a state of dejection, and Elphinstone vacillated. The Afghans themselves admitted that, had steps been taken in time, the insurrection would have been at once put down.

Shelton, in his narrative, says that much valuable time was wasted at the outset. His report is as follows:—"On the morning of the 2nd November I passed under the city wall about seven o'clock, when the cavalry grass-cutters, who were in the habit of going through the town for their grass, told me that the city gate was shut, and they could not get in. All was quiet at this time, and I rode home, thinking some robbery might have taken place, and that the gate might have been shut to prevent the escape of the thieves. About 8 or 9 o'clock various reports were in circulation, and between nine and ten I got a note from General Elphinstone, reporting a disturbance in the city, and desiring me to prepare to march into the Bala Hissar, with three companies, 54th Native Infantry, the Shah's 6th Infantry, and four guns, all I had in camp (the remainder of my brigade having been called into cantonments). I soon after got another, telling me not to go, as the King objected to it. I replied to this note that, if there was an insurrection in the city, it was not a moment for indecision, and recommended him at once to decide upon what measures he would adopt. The answer to this was, to march immediately into the Bala Hissar, where I would receive other instructions from the Envoy's Military Secretary, whom I should find there. Just as I was marching off, a note came from the latter person to halt for further orders. I then sent in the engineer officer to see the cause; but he was cut down by an Afghan, in dismounting from his horse, just outside the square, where His Majesty was sitting. Soon after this the Secretary himself came with orders to proceed.

then marched in, when the King asked me, as well as I could understand, "who sent me, and what I came there for." He was not allowed to operate upon the disturbed city, and could only cover the retreat of the Shah's Hindustanis. Shelton was not, therefore, to blame, but neither the Envoy nor the General appears to have recognized the necessity for prompt measures. The wishes of the Shah seem to have been the preponderating influence.

Next morning all was bustle in the cantonment. Intelligence had been brought that a large body of men, thought to be enemies, were marching over the Siah Sang hills. It proved to be the 37th Native Infantry who had been sent for on the previous day.

The rebellion spreads.

A movement was made upon the city at about 3 P.M. By this time the enemy had much increased in numbers, joined by the neighbouring villagers. The road between the cantonment and the city was alive with them. The party, under Major Swayne, consisted of one company, Her Majesty's 44th, two companies, 5th Native Infantry, and two Horse Artillery guns. Such a force could do nothing, and was fortunately able to withdraw in good time. By some misunderstanding no troops had been detailed to co-operate from the Bala Hissar; and even had they been sent they would have been cut to pieces. The Envoy had withdrawn to the cantonment and an attempt was made to put the place into a state of defence. Every available gun was placed in position; but there was an insufficiency of artillery. Macnaghten wrote to Macgregor to recall Sale's force, and to Kandahar to stop the troops which were returning to India, and send them to his relief. Neither of these orders was carried out.

Next day the subaltern's guard of eighty men over the commissariat stores was threatened; and another fort nearer the cantonments was in the enemy's possession. The proposal to garrison it had been disapproved by Macnaghten. The King's Gardens were swarming with insurgents. The communications between the cantonment and the fort were thus cut, and the enemy besieging the latter began to mine the walls. Lieutenant-Warren reported his position, and two companies of the 44th were sent to reinforce him. However, the enemy attacked them

in strength, killing Captains Swayne and Robinson and wounding other officers; and the companies were compelled to retire. A second party, consisting mostly of cavalry, was sent out, with even more disastrous results.

It now became known to the Commissariat officers that the General contemplated the abandonment of the fort, with all our grain and hospital stores. Captain Boyd at once went to the General, and prayed him to alter his decision and reinforce the guard. He agreed; no reinforcement being sent, another appeal was made. The General, however, was talked over by other officers, and wavered in his decision. Another urgent letter came from Warren, and the General promised to send reinforcements after midnight. The march, however, was postponed until the following morning; but the guard had abandoned the post, and returned to cantonments. Nor was this our only loss. Shah Shuja's supplies were stored on the outskirts of the city; they consisted of 8,000 maunds of *atta*. Captain Mackenzie was in charge of the fort, which was attacked on the morning of the 2nd November by the armed population of Deh-Afghan. The garrison defended the post throughout the day. Water and ammunition were scarce. They were hampered by baggage, women and children. Reinforcements were in vain called for. A demonstration from the cantonments would have saved them. On the 3rd November at midday the enemy got possession of Trevor's house, and it soon became certain that not for much longer could Mackenzie hold his post. At last, after a difficult and dangerous march, abandoning their post, the detachment fought their way to the cantonments.

The abandonment of the stores not only threatened the British force with starvation, but this evidence of our weakness encouraged the waverers among the enemy, who now openly declared against us. By noon thousands had assembled to share in the booty, and the troops clamoured to be led against the Afghans. Lieutenant Eyre[1] urged the General to permit him to lead a party for the capture of Muhammad Sharif's fort; and he reluctantly agreed to send out 50 of Her Majesty's 44th and 200 native

---

[1] Afterwards Sir Vincent Eyre.

infantry. The party under Major Swayne, instead of acting promptly, wavered; the opportunity was lost and the General ordered a withdrawal. The sepoys of the 37th were enraged and disappointed at being held back, and the confidence of the enemy increased.

It soon became clear that the insurrection was no mere local outburst; and our outposts were exposed to imminent danger. At Kah Darra, Lieutenant Maule, of the Bengal Artillery, with his Adjutant and Sergeant Major, had been cut to pieces by the men of his own Kohistani Regiment; and intelligence now arrived that the Gurkha Regiment at Charikar, in the Kohistan, where Eldred Pottinger was Political Agent, was threatened with annihilation. Captain Codrington, the Commandant, and other officers had been killed; and water was becoming very scarce. The General suggested that a bribe be offered to buy off the Kohistan Chiefs.

The outposts.

On the 6th of November a success attended our efforts. A party of the 37th Native Infantry, under Major Griffiths, was sent against Muhammad Sharif's fort, which was captured with *éclat*. The garrison fled to the hills, whence they were driven by Anderson's horse. The rest of the day was spent in skirmishing, but there was no cohesion; the several branches of the service acting independently. Had a general action been undertaken the British force, in their then temper, could have overcome five times the number.

Capture of Muhammad Sharif's fort.

The Commissariat officers, Captains Boyd and Johnson, began to exert themselves to collect supplies from the surrounding villages; and were more successful than could have been anticipated. The villagers sold their grain at fairly reasonable rates and, although the troops were placed upon half rations, there was no immediate danger of starvation.

Ammunition was, however, now running short, in the General's opinion; though in reality there was an ample supply in store. The Envoy feared that any military measures under a weak commander were hopeless, and began to tempt the cupidity of the chiefs. Mohan Lal, who was residing in Kabul, was the agent he employed; and his first attempt

Political developments.

was to bribe the Ghilzais. Two lakhs of rupees were mentioned but before the bargain was completed the Envoy withdrew his offer. which naturally offended the Ghilzais. On the 7th November, Macnaghten wrote to Mohan Lal to offer bribes to Khan Sharin Khan, and Muhammad Kumayi, and to assure them that the rebels would be beaten in the long run. He counselled the encouragement of Muhammad Yar Khan, Amin-ullah's rival; and altogether guaranteed 5,00,000 of rupees.

News now reached Kabul that Muhammad Akbar Khan, Dost Muhammad's second son, had arrived at Bamian from Turkistan. Mohan Lal suggested the advisability of attempting to bribe him, but Macnaghten thought it useless, and had more hopes from the Kizilbash chief and others on the spot; but stipulated that not more than half a lakh should be distributed until some return should have been obtained for the money. The time had, however, passed when the mere distribution of money could avail.

The insurrection had now been raging for a week, and the enemy had increased in numbers and daring. The British troops were disheartened, and the General began to write about negotiation.

Shelton comes into cantonment. General Elphinstone's health had now completely broken down, and Macnaghten advised the recall of Shelton from the Bala Hissar. Taking only one of the Shah's regiments and a single gun with him, the Brigadier reached the cantonment on the 9th November in broad daylight without interruption. Although he was not popular with either officers or men, he was held to possess sturdy qualities and never to shrink from a fight; he was accordingly hailed by the garrison as a deliverer. He at once inspected the defences, and saw what a large force was required. The men were spiritless, and the outlook was far from promising. It was evident that he and the General could never pull together, and, through the absence of a right understanding between them, nearly all their enterprises were unsuccessful.

The Envoy was now anxiously looking for the return of Sale's brigade from Gandamak, not expecting that they would meet with serious difficulties. But no assistance was to come from that quarter; the force was moving in another direction.

On the 10th of November the enemy mustered in force on the heights commanding the cantonment, with shouts of defiance. They posted themselves in several small forts near the walls, and harassed the soldiers on the works. On the urgent representation of the Envoy, a party was to be sent to capture the Rika Bashi fort, and Shelton with two Horse Artillery guns, one mountain gun, Walker's Horse, Her Majesty's 44th Foot, the 37th Native Infantry[1] and the Shah's 6th Regiment, some 2,000 men, were held in readiness. The General, however, thought the expedition too dangerous, and it was abandoned, to the Brigadier's disgust. The scruples of the General were now overruled, but the enemy had profited by the delay and the result of the movement was a doubtful success. The fort was indeed taken on that day, but in a disastrous and calamitous manner. It was determined to blow in the gate, and Captain Bellew, the Assistant Quartermaster-General, undertook the work. It was, however, incompletely done and the storming party could with difficulty force their way through the narrow opening. After heavy losses a few managed to effect an entrance; this was enough for the enemy, who immediately evacuated the fort. The storming party was now charged by the Afghan Horse, and Europeans and natives turned and fled. Shelton with much difficulty succeeded in rallying them, but again they gave way before the Afghan cavalry, to be once again brought back by Shelton. The heavy guns from cantonments were now playing upon the horsemen and the Brigadier led his men to the capture of the fort. In the meantime the garrison, finding how few of their assailants had gained an entrance, returned with new courage. The Englishmen had endeavoured to shut the gate, securing the chain with a bayonet; but the enemy forced the obstacle and rushed in. When the storming party entered they found Colonel Mackerell fearfully wounded; he died shortly after he had been conveyed to the Cantonment. Lieutenant Bird and two sepoys of the 37th Native Infantry had barricaded a stable, and were found uninjured with thirty of the enemy lying dead around them.

Affair at the Rika Bashi fort.

---

[1] The conduct of the 37th is highly spoken of. They drove the enemy (who had got on top of a bastion) with their bayonets clean over the side, where they were received on the bayonets of the 44th.—*Lady Sale, page 90.*

On the fall of this fort others were abandoned by the enemy, who were threatened by Shelton in the position they had taken up on the Siah Sang hills; but there was no attempt to bring on a general action. Had there been a reserve and a stronger body of horse, the infantry would have been more confident and greater results would probably have been obtained. The capture of the fort, however, was not without its effect. Supplies were obtained and a retreat averted. The Afghans quieted down for a time, and negotiations with the Ghilzais were resumed. The Envoy, through his agent Mohan Lal, redoubled his efforts to set the chiefs by the ears; and rewards were offered for the apprehension of Amin-ullah Khan and the other rebel Durani chiefs. He followed this dubious course as there appeared to be so little to hope for from the military commanders; but had there been any prospect of successful honest fighting, he would have preferred that alternative. Capitulation stared him in the face; a disgrace of all others which he was intent upon averting.

On the 13th November the enemy, in great strength, occupied the Bemaru hills. The question of dislodging them was the subject of much discussion between the Envoy and the Generals: finally, the former had his way, and a force under Shelton was ordered out for service. It was composed of—

Fight on the Bemaru hills.

2 squadrons, 5th Light Cavalry (Colonel Chambers),
1 squadron, Shah's Horse (Lieutenant LeGeyt),
1 troop, Skinner's Horse (Lieutenant Walker),
6 companies, Her Majesty's 44th (Major Scott),
6 „ 37th Native Infantry (Major Griffith),
4 „ Shah's 6th Infantry (Captain Hopkins),
1 Horse Artillery and 1 Mountain Gun (Lieutenant Eyre), escorted by a company of the Shah's 6th Infantry under Captain Marshall.

It was nearly 4 P.M. before the troops were ready to take the field. They marched rapidly, in three columns by different routes, to the foot of the hills. The guns were delayed; and our musketry was wild even at the closest range. Emboldened by the absence of loss the Afghan horse charged down with irresistible force upon the British bayonets, and for a while all was panic and confusion, while the enemy charged through and through the ranks and entirely

routed them. They soon, however, rallied behind the reserve, and under cover of the guns again advanced to the attack; and Anderson's Horse drove the enemy up the slopes. The infantry following carried the heights, and the enemy, abandoning their guns, fled along the ridge. Night was closing in, but it was deemed imperative to remove the abandoned guns. The Shah's 6th Infantry easily withdrew one, but the other gun could not be removed. It was therefore spiked, and Shelton's force returned to their quarters at 8 o'clock, hampered by the enemy who were, however, beaten off by Mackenzie's *jezailchis*. Many on both sides had fallen in the action of the afternoon.[1]

For some days the enemy remained comparatively inactive. The Envoy sent repeated letters for the return of Sale's brigade, and gave Macgregor very gloomy reports of the situation at Kabul.

On the 15th of November, Pottinger and Lieutenant Haughton came in wounded from Charikar, and reported that, after a gallant resistance, the Gurkhas had been cut to pieces. They gave the following account of the affair.

The disaster at Charikar.

Before the end of October the Kohistanis and Nijrawis were in open revolt; and, on the 1st of November, Mir Masjidi with a strong force took up a position at Ak Sarai, cutting off communications with Kabul. Pottinger was living at Lughmani, two miles from Charikar, where the Gurkhas occupied semi-fortified barracks. Reconnoitring parties were sent out to ascertain the exact disposition of the enemy. Encumbered with baggage, women and children, it appeared impossible to move the Gurkhas from Charikar, and Pottinger, sending for help to Kabul, began to strengthen the defences. Many Kohistani and Nijrawi chiefs protested their friendship, but their refusal to co-operate for the suppression of the insurrection belied their professions. On the morning of the 3rd the insurgents round the Residency increased in numbers. At noon the more powerful chiefs were accorded an interview. Mischief was, however, brewing; 'Rattray was shot down and Pottinger escaped into the castle, where he was soon invested. Haughton now moved down to the relief, and Codrington, making

---

[1] "The Afghans have many advantages over our troops: one consists in dropping their men fresh for combat; each horseman takes a foot soldier up behind him, and drops him when he has arrived at the spot he is required to fire from."—*Lady Sale, page 64.*

a sortie, united with his force. The enemy were driven from the garden with loss. As evening was closing in, Codrington, leaving a detachment, returned to his barracks. On the following day he came back with four companies to relieve Pottinger's guard and bring more ammunition. The column, however, met with a check, and was compelled to fall back with Lieutenant Salisbury mortally wounded. Many of the Gurkhas fell in the retreat. Seeing little prospect of relief, and having only a few rounds left, Pottinger determined after nightfall to move to Charikar.

Disguising his intentions by collecting grain during the day, he mustered his Hindustanis outside the gate, upon the pretext of making a sortie, and, avoiding the main road, marched to barracks.

On the morning of the 5th November numbers of the enemy assembled round the barracks, and closely invested them. Pottinger took charge of the guns; and, moving out to support the skirmishers, was wounded in the leg. The Gurkhas were driven from the huts; Codrington was mortally wounded, and the Adjutant, Haughton, assumed the command. The enemy were driven back from the gardens, but the Afghans renewed the attack again and again; the Gurkhas, however, held their ground until night put an end to the conflict. The unequal contest was continued on the following days. Three hundred yards from the barracks was a castle which commanded them, and which it was found necessary to occupy with a garrison of fifty men, but, through the treachery of the regimental *Munshi*, it was induced to surrender. The garrison had now been reduced to half their original strength; water was scarce; the enemy had increased in numbers and fury; to shut themselves up in the barracks was to die of thirst; to attempt to fight their way out meant to be cut to pieces.

On the 8th the enemy offered terms; the condition being that they should become Muhammadans. On the 10th half a wine glass of water was served out. On the 11th there was not sufficient to go round.

At night they stole out to obtain a few drops from a neighbouring spring, but the enemy discovered the practice and shot them down. Every attempt to obtain water failed; the men leaving the ranks in the madness of their thirst, and all discipline being at an end, they were shot down by the enemy. A Gurkha

havildar related that the officers gave their men some sheep, and they sucked the raw flesh to extract some moisture from the stomachs of the slaughtered animals. It was difficult to load the muskets, fouled by constant use; the men's lips became swollen and bloody, and their tongues clave to the palate. All hope was now at an end. Two hundred men with thirty rounds apiece alone remained; and many were dying of thirst. Pottinger and Haughton determined on a rapid and unencumbered march to Kabul. Accordingly on the evening of the 13th Charikar was evacuated. Pottinger led the advance. Haughton had been wounded by a sabre and could hardly sit his horse; Grant (a medical officer) spiked the guns and led out the main body, whilst ensign Rose brought up the rear. The force soon became a disorderly rabble, and it was impossible to lead them to the capital. Pottinger and Haughton, exhausted by the pain of their wounds, their services being no longer of avail, pushed on with a single sepoy and two followers. The road was unknown, and they had no guide. They reached, however, the neighbourhood of Kabul, where their dangers increased. Missing their way they found themselves among the enemy's sentinels and made for Deh-Afghan; but being challenged by the sentries, were obliged to enter the city, through which they eventually made their way to the cantonments. The remainder of the column was cut up; Grant being killed within three miles of the cantonment.[1]

Macnaghten now learned that Sale's brigade had marched for Jalalabad; he, however, wrote to Macgregor in the hope of recalling it. He soon heard from the latter that it was impossible; he then asked Macgregor to apply to Mackeson for Sikh assistance.

The military authorities now represented to the Envoy the futility of further resistance, but he still hoped on. On the 18th November he wrote to the General recommending holding out, and representing

<small>Macnaghten's recommendation.</small>

---

[1] It was providential that Major Pottinger had, from his habits as a traveller through unknown and difficult regions, accustomed himself to ascertain and remember the bearings of the most conspicuous landmarks of the countries he traversed; it was, therefore, comparatively easy for him to pave the way over the steep and rugged peaks.—*Vincent Eyre, page* 84. *Greenwood, page* 202.

that there was plenty of wood and water, and giving his opinion that the position was impregnable. A retreat to Jalalabad would entail the sacrifice of valuable Government property and of the Shah; the troops would find no shelter there and perhaps no provisions; few of the camp followers would survive the march. He suggested a retreat to the Bala Hissar as a possible alternative, but with serious drawbacks. He thought it possible that help might come from Kandahar, when the cold weather caused the enemy to disperse, and ended up by saying that if provisions could be obtained he would not entertain a thought of relinquishing the cantonment.

There had been many discussions as to the advisability of withdrawing to the Bala Hissar. It had been recommended by Sturt and others soon after the first outbreak. The General had formed no opinion on the subject and the Brigadier was opposed to it. It would appear, however, to have been the soundest course to adopt. Shah Shuja had been watching events with profound anxiety and alarm. Danger threatened him, real or imaginary, on every side; and the small garrison of the Bala Hissar, under Major Ewart, only consisted of the 54th Native Infantry, part of a Horse Artillery troop under Captain Nicoll, and some details of irregular troops.

At the end of November the enemy had reappeared on the Bemaru hills, and began to raid the villages which had supplied our Commissariat officers with grain. On the 22nd a weak detachment under Major Swayne had been sent against them without result; and a council of war was held. Shelton recommended a simultaneous attack upon the hills and the village, but was overruled. At daybreak on the 23rd the force enumerated below took possession of the hill.

Second fight on the Bemaru hills.

5 companies, Her Majesty's 44th (Captain Leighton).
6 companies, 5th Native Infantry (Lieut.-Colonel Oliver).
6 companies, 37th Native Infantry (Captain Kershaw).
1 squadron, 5th Cavalry (Captain Bott).
1 squadron, Irregular Horse (Lieutenant Walker).
100 of Anderson's Horse.
1 Horse Artillery gun.
100 Sappers (Lieutenant Laing, 27th Native Infantry).

The solitary gun was placed to command an enclosure in the village, where many of the enemy were collected. These sprang up under the salute of a shower of grape, and, firing a volley from their *jezails*, sought the shelter of buildings and thence kept up an ineffective fire. As day dawned it was seen that the enemy were abandoning the village, and it was determined to carry it by assault. Major Swayne made a vain attempt and was recalled.

The movements of the British troops had been seen from the city, and soon large bodies of the enemy moved across the plain. The fire from the enemy's hill, separated by a narrow gorge from that upon which our own troops were posted, soon became galling. Leaving five companies at the extremity of the hill above the village, Shelton took the remainder of his force, with the gun, across the gorge to a position near the brow of that hill, upon which most of the enemy were assembling. Here he formed his infantry into two squares, with the cavalry massed in rear. The solitary gun for a time told with great effect upon the Afghans; but from repeated rapid firing soon became unserviceable. The enemy now poured a destructive fire into the squares, the bullets from which did not reach them,[1] the advantage therefore being altogether with the Afghans.

Between the British troops and the brow of the hill there was some rising ground, which hid the enemy's movements from Shelton. Those in the cantonments, however, could see a party of Afghans climbing up the hillside from the gorge and rushing up

---

[1] It is astonishing at what an enormous distance the fire from their long heavy rifles is effective. Our men were continually struck by the Afghan bullets, when we could reach the enemy with nothing under a six-pounder. Our muskets were useless when playing at long bowls. The fact is our muskets are about as bad specimens of firearms as can be manufactured. The triggers are so stiff that pulling them completely destroys any aim the soldier may take; and, when the machine does go off, the recoil is almost enough to knock a man backwards. Again the ball is so much smaller than the bore of the barrel that accuracy in its flight, at any considerable distance, is impossible. The clumsy flint locks also are constantly missing fire.

"Errors—
(1) Taking only a single gun.
(2) Failure to gain advantage of the enemy's panic.
(3) Not utilising Sappers to build a *sangar*.
(4) Forming squares against distant fire.
(5) Cavalry hemmed in by infantry.
(6) Delay in retreating until troops exhausted."
Vincent Eyre, page 113.

on our infantry. The troops turned and fled. Shelton in the thickest of the fire vainly called upon his men to charge. The officers stood up like brave men and hurled stones upon the enemy. Captain Mackintosh and Lieutenant Laing and Captains Mackenzie, Troup, and Leighton were killed. Nothing could infuse courage into our panic-stricken troops. The cavalry, when called upon to charge, refused to follow their officers. The artillerymen stood to their gun and were cut down. The field piece was lost, and the disheartened regiments fled. Shelton, however, sounding the "halt" stopped them, and they again faced the enemy; and the *Ghazis* taking the horses and limber, but abandoning the gun, fled in their turn. The enemy's cavalry on the plain had been thrown into confusion by the fall of their leader, Abdulla Khan, and they fled towards the city. In spite of the representations of Macnaghten, who with Elphinstone was watching from the cantonment, no pursuit was made. Now was Shelton's opportunity to withdraw; but the moment passed. The enemy returned to the attack with fresh recruits, and a second gun which had been sent out fired on them with effect. The Afghans' musketry, however, again got the upper hand of ours; the artillerymen were falling fast, and Shelton withdrew the gun to a safer position. Emboldened by this the enemy redoubled their efforts, and again the British troops began to waver.

A party of the enemy, headed by a band of furious *Ghazis*, again crawled up the hill, and the last spark of courage that remained to the British troops was extinguished. Shelton turned to give some orders, and the front rank gave way; in a moment the whole force was flying down the slopes of the hill. The Afghan horse, seizing their opportunity, dashed upon them, and all was confusion. The artillerymen made a desperate effort to save their gun, but in vain. Fortunately the enemy did not pursue, and the disorganized mass gained the cantonment. All was now chaos, and fighting was to be no more thought of; the enemy destroying the bridge over the Kabul river at their leisure.[1]

---

[1] *Vincent Eyre, page* 66. "Our infantry soldiers, both European and native, might have taken a salutary lesson from the Afghans in the use of their fire-arms; the latter invariably taking steady deliberate aim, and seldom throwing away a single shot; whereas our men seemed to fire entirely at random, without any aim at all."

Only two courses now remained open; and the political and military chiefs began to take counsel. The question of concentration in the Bala Hissar was negatived by the military, and the envoy began to consider about negotiating. Elphinstone strongly recommended this course. On the 25th of November, Macnaghten sent to meet at the bridge the chiefs—Sultan Muhammad Khan, Barakzai, and Mirza Ahmed Ali, Kazilbash.

Captains Lawrence and Trevor went out to interview them, and the conference lasted two hours. Sultan Muhammad Khan's tone was insolent and his terms impossible and the party proceeded to Macnaghten in cantonments.

The discussion was long and animated; Muhammad insisting that as conquerors the Afghans should dictate the terms. These were that the British should surrender at discretion, as prisoners of war, and give up their arms, ammunition, and treasure. The terms were resolutely rejected. "We shall meet then on the field of battle," said Sultan Muhammad. "At all events we shall meet at the day of judgment," replied Macnaghten. And so the conference ended. Thus ended the first attempt to secure, by negotiation, the safety of our discomfited troops. While this movement was in progress a strange sight might have been seen on the ramparts of the British cantonment. Over the low walls the European soldiers were conversing with their Afghan enemies. The Afghans, armed to the teeth, came clustering round; many of our soldiers went out unarmed amongst them, and were to be seen familiarly shaking hands with those whom the day before they had met on the field of battle. The Afghans were giving vegetables to the men of the 44th Regiment, and declaring that everything had been amicably settled between the two contending armies.

Akbar Khan's return. The advent of Muhammad Akbar Khan had for some time been expected. During October he was at Bamian, watching the progress of events. His presence undoubtedly encouraged the Afghans, though there is no proof that he played an active part in the early days of the insurrection. His appearance at the capital was hailed with delight by the insurgents. The British, on the other hand, did not fear that his presence would add to their embarrassments, the fact that so many of his family were prisoners in our hand

being considered a guarantee for his behaviour. Akbar Khan did not at once assume the direction of affairs; Muhammad Ziman Khan, a humane and honourable man, a cousin of Dost Muhammad, having already been proclaimed King. His nephew, Usman Khan, of whom Macnaghten entertained a high opinion, was deputed to negotiate with the British Minister. The negotiations dragged on, and the supplies of the Army were dwindling; this appeared to Akbar Khan his strongest weapon, and he threatened with death any who should assist the British with provisions. The Envoy was, however, as hopeful as the General was pessimistic. The former, through the medium of Mohan Lal, was attempting to secure the assistance of the hostile tribes by bribery, knowing the avaricious nature of the Afghan. This would have been a comparatively simple matter had all been unanimous, but one tribe bid against another and the difficulties of the situation were only increased.

On the first of December supplies for barely eight days remained in store. The camp followers were receiving only half a pound of barley per diem, and the cattle were without provender, and had to be fed up on twigs and the bark of trees. Both Elphinstone and Johnson represented the seriousness of the situation; and the latter urged the necessity of an early retreat to Jalalabad; but Macnaghten still temporised. Both the General and the Envoy knew that the troops were not to be trusted, but the Envoy, jealous of his country's honour, was loth to throw away the chance that a turn of the wheel of fortune might bring. On the 5th of December the enemy completed the destruction of the bridge over the Kabul river. The river was now fordable, but it was a disgrace that the enemy should have been enabled to destroy it in the face of 5,000 troops. A small number of the enemy, too, on the 6th of December, climbed the walls of Muhammad Sharif's fort,[1] and the garrison abandoned it at once, and no effort was made to re-capture

Distress in the garrison.

Abandonment of Muhammad Sharif's fort.

---

[1] *Lady Sale, page 77.* "I often hear the Afghans designated as cowards: they are a fine manly looking set, and I can only suppose it varies from the British idea among civilized people that assassination is a cowardly act. The Afghan never scruple to use their long knives for that purpose, *ergo* they are cowards; but they show no cowardice in standing as they do against guns without using any themselves, and in escalading and taking forts which we cannot retake."

it. The troops were becoming daily more and more demoralized.[1] The Envoy and the General were now in constant correspondence as to the best way to preserve the army and British honour. The former counselled a withdrawal to the Bala Hissar, declaring a retreat to Jalalabad without terms to be impracticable. He also suggested that provisions might be obtained by means of night attacks; but the General would have none of it.

On the 8th of December Macnaghten wrote to the General asking him if it was his opinion that a retreat upon the most favourable terms was the best and only policy to pursue. The General replied that he considered this the only thing to be done; and this view was concurred in by Brigadiers Shelton and Anquetil and Colonel Chambers. In spite of this the Envoy sought an interview and persuaded Elphinstone to make one more attempt to obtain supplies, and it was determined to send a party the next morning, with Captain Johnson, to the village of Khoja Riwash, four miles from cantonments, where it was believed that a considerable quantity of grain was stored. Preparations were to be made for a start at 2 A.M. Eventually the enterprise was abandoned.

Cheering intelligence now arrived from Jalalabad. Sale's little garrison had sallied out and defeated the enemy; and the Envoy hoped that the example would stimulate the efforts of the military at Kabul; but his hopes were soon dissipated. The General only saw another reason for entering into terms with the enemy. The hope of reinforcements from Kandahar was rapidly waning, Maclaren's brigade having met with insuperable difficulties. On the 11th one day's food remained for the fighting troops, and the followers were starving. Food could not be purchased, as the villagers would not sell; nor could it be obtained by force, for the soldiers would not fight. Macnaghten had done his best but now despaired of military success. Nothing remained but negotiation or death by starvation; so he drew the rough draft of a treaty, and met the Afghan Chiefs in conference. The meeting took place on the banks of the river,

News from Jalalabad.

Discussion of the treaty.

---

[1] *Lady Sale, page* 116. It is more than shocking, it is shameful, to hear the way the officers go on croaking before the men is sufficient to dispirit them, and prevent their fighting for us."

about one mile from cantonments. Captains Lawrence, Trevor, and Mackenzie, with a few troopers, accompanied the Envoy. The Chiefs of all the principal tribes in the country were present. The proposed treaty, in brief, was as follows :—

(1) The Kabul force to retire to India viâ Peshawar.

(2) The Sardars to safeguard the journey and provide provisions and carriage.

(3) The Jalalabad garrison to retire to Peshawar as soon as the Envoy should be satisfied that their progress would be uninterrupted.

(4) The Ghazni garrison also to withdraw.

(5) The Kandahar troops to march as soon as arrangements could be made and the season should permit.

(6) The restoration of Dost Muhammad's property.

(7) The property of British officers to be sent to India so soon as opportunity offered.

(8) Shah Shuja to remain in Afghanistan with a pension of one lakh of rupees or to accompany the force to India.

(9) Should the Shah accompany the British, such of his family as could not accompany him to remain in the Bala Hissar.

(11) When Dost Muhammad should return, Shah Shuja's family to proceed to India.

(12) Four British officers to be left as hostages for the fulfilment of the above conditions.

(13) Influential chiefs to accompany the column.

(14) Afghanistan to treat with foreign powers through the British Government.

(15) Should the Afghans desire it, a British Resident to be posted to Kabul.

(16) No one to be molested for the part he took in the war.

(17) From date of signing, provisions to be supplied on payment.

(18) British troops which cannot leave with the returning column to be well treated.

The conference lasted two hours ; the terms of the treaty were discussed with comparative calmness and moderation, and the main points agreed to by the Chiefs. It was resolved that the British troops should evacuate their cantonments within three days, and that the Chiefs should send in provisions for their use. Captain Trevor accompanied the Khans to the city " as a hostage for the sincerity of the Envoy."

The Envoy justified his conduct in the following words: "The whole country, as far as we could learn, had risen in rebellion; our communications on all sides were cut off; almost every public officer, whether paid by ourselves or His Majesty, had declared for the new governor, and by far the greater number even of His Majesty's domestic servants had deserted him. We had been fighting forty days against very superior numbers, under most disadvantageous circumstances, with a deplorable loss of valuable lives; in a day or two we must have perished from hunger, to say nothing of the advanced season of the year and the extreme cold, from the effects of which our native troops were suffering severely. I had been repeatedly apprised by the military authorities that nothing could be done with our troops; and I regret to add that desertions to the enemy were becoming of frequent occurrence among our troops. The terms I secured were the best obtainable, and the destruction of 15,000 human beings would little have benefited our country, whilst the Government would have been almost compelled to avenge our fate at whatever cost. We shall part with the Afghans as friends, and I feel satisfied than any government which may be established hereafter will always be disposed to cultivate a good understanding with us. A retreat without terms would have been impracticable.

It is true that, by entering into terms, we are prevented from undertaking the conquest of the entire country—a measure which, from my knowledge of the views of Government, I feel convinced would never be resorted to, even were the means at hand. But such a project, in the present state of our Indian finances, and the requisition for troops in various quarters, I knew could not be entertained."

Orders were sent for the evacuation of the Bala Hissar, and it was advertised that the retreat would commence in two days. The chiefs withheld the promised supplies, but small quantities of grain were procured from the Bala Hissar. New arms and accoutrements were obtained by the soldiers from the stores, and the camp-followers were supplied with ammunition.

<small>Evacuation of the Bala Hissar.</small>
The Bala Hissar was evacuated by the British troops on the 13th of December; Akbar Khan having promised a safe passage to cantonments. The packing and loading of 1,600 maunds of wheat occupied twenty-four hours of precious time, and the force was compelled

to withdraw before all had been loaded up. It was 6 o'clock, dark and bitterly cold, when the force began to march slowly out of the Bala Hissar. It was now whispered that a trap had been laid for the destruction of the force. Scarcely had it cleared the gate when a rush was made to enter the Bala Hissar. The gates were immediately closed, and the King's troops on the walls commenced an indiscriminate fire upon friend and foe. The Siah Sang Hills were bristling with armed tribesmen, and Akbar Khan stated that the force must halt till the morrow. The miseries of the night were succeeded by the perils of the dawn. The force was only 600 strong, and the enemy mustered in his thousands on the road. Happily Akbar Khan was true to his word. The rear-guard was attacked, but the chief himself intervened, and at 10 o'clock cantonments were reached. The British authorities called upon the chiefs to send in the provisions which they had promised; the atter demanded the cession of the forts in the vicinity of the cantonments; this was agreed to. Provisions commenced to come in slowly, but no carriage was supplied. Outrages were committed under ˙e noses of the guards, but not a shot was fired upon the plunderers. Nothing in fact was to be done to hurt the feelings of " our new allies." Both parties were anxious to postpone the day of departure, and each suspected the good faith of the other. Macnaghten still hoped for the arrival of Maclaren's brigade from Kandahar; not knowing that it had retraced its steps.

Snow began to fall on the 18th of December, and the force looked upon this new peril with dismay. The 22nd was now fixed upon as the day of departure, and orders were sent for the evacuation of Ghazni, Kandahar, and Jalalabad. Money was paid to the chiefs for cattle which were never received; and it was believed that Muhammad Khan was employing the funds so obtained for our destruction. Macnaghten now heard of the retreat of Maclaren's brigade, and relinquished all hope of beating the enemy in the field. Diplomacy alone remained. While treating with the Barakzais, offers were also being made to the Ghilzais and Kizilbashis. Meanwhile the demands of the Sardars were increasing. They called upon us to deliver up our arms

Preparations to leave Kabul.

and ammunition, and to surrender the married families as hostages, for the fulfilment of the conditions of the treaty. Shelton was demanded as a hostage, but the proposal was declined. On the 21st of December Lieutenants Conolly and Airey were handed over. On the following day Lieutenant Eyre, the Commissary of Ordnance, was ordered to conduct Zaman Khan over the magazine and allow him to take what he fancied. The Envoy sent his carriage and horses as a present to Akbar Khan. He began to despair of the Ghilzais, and to doubt the wisdom of his policy. On the 22nd Akbar Khan sent Captain Skinner with a string of fresh proposals. It was suggested that on the following day Akbar Khan and the Ghilzais should unite with the British troops outside cantonments, attack Mahmud Khan's fort, and seize Aminullah Khan; and finally an offer of the latter's head was made for a consideration. Macnaghten scornfully rejected the offer. Other proposals were that the English should remain in Afghanistan until the spring and then withdraw as if of their own free will. Shah Shuja was to remain as King with Akbar Khan as his Wazir. The price, an annuity of four lakhs and a bonus of thirty lakhs for Akbar Khan.

The Envoy accepted these proposals and the delegates returned to the city. The next day Macnaghten was restless and excited, and sent for the General to acquaint him with the proposals. The latter was startled, and asked the Envoy if he did not suspect treachery; and in spite of his assurances recommended him to consider before he committed himself to such a perilous course. His warnings fell upon deaf ears. On his return to his quarters he wrote a letter, again pointing out the dangers; but it never reached its destination.

At noon Macnaghten, Lawrence, Trevor, Mackenzie, and a few horsemen set out on their ill-omened expedition. Shelton was otherwise employed and was unable to attend them. The troops were not ready, and Macnaghten bitterly complained of the military arrangements. Mackenzie was sent back for an Arab horse which Akbar Khan had coveted, and Lawrence was ordered to hold himself in readiness to communicate with the King. Suspicious appearances roused the apprehensions of all except the Envoy. Midway between Mahmud Khan's fort and the bridge, about 600 yards from the cantonment, were some small hillocks, on which

Murder of Macnaghten.

jhools had been spread by some of Akbar Khan's servants. The party dismounted and sat down, and the business of the conference opened. Akbar Khan asked the Envoy if he was prepared to carry out the proposals of the previous evening; Macnaghten assented. Afghans were now gathering round, and Lawrence and Mackenzie suggested that the intruders should be removed. Akbar Khan, however, said that their presence was of no consequence. Scarcely were the words uttered when the Envoy and his companions were violently seized from behind. There was a scene of terrible confusion. The officers of the staff were dragged away, and each compelled to mount a horse ridden by an Afghan Chief. Soon they were running the gauntlet through a crowd of *Ghazis*, who struck at them as they passed. Trevor slipped from his seat and was cut to pieces; Lawrence and Mackenzie, more fortunate, reached Mahmud Khan's fort alive. Meanwhile the Envoy was struggling on the ground with Akbar Khan. Exasperated by the resistance of his victim the latter drew a pistol and shot Macnaghten through the body, which was hacked in pieces by the knives of fanatics.

The capitulation. No attempt was made to avenge the Envoy's death which was not generally known until the next day; but the on-lookers must have been aware that some violence had been committed. General Elphinstone ordered that the safety of the Envoy should be announced to the troops. The day had been one of intense anxiety. The Afghans in the cantonment had been evicted, and a lull supervened. As the evening advanced, however, the confusion in the city was such that the troops manned the cantonment works in anticipation of coming danger. The *Ghazis* had expected that the troops would avenge the Envoy's death; but no such idea was entertained. A letter from Captain Lawrence on the 24th of December confirmed the rumour of the murder; and stated that the chiefs wished to continue negotiations, on the lines of the treaty initiated by Macnaghten. Major Pottinger was selected as the fittest person to deal with the situation. In the evening he met the four senior military officers. A letter had been received from the principal chiefs, with a memorandum of their terms for the safe conduct of the army to Peshawar.

The main features were the immediate evacuation of Ghazni, Kandahar, Kabul, and Jalalabad; the restoration of Dost Muhammad; and that Shah Shuja should be allowed to follow the bent of his own inclinations. A certain number of English gentlemen were to be left as hostages, and Afghan Chiefs, by their presence, were to guarantee the safe passage of the troops to the frontier. Large sums of money were of course, in addition, to change hands. Had Pottinger received the least encouragement from the military chiefs he would have rejected the terms; but, under the circumstances, the treaty was agreed to. Needless to say, the Afghans very shortly made further demands.

On the 26th of December encouraging letters were received from Macgregor at Jalalabad, and from Mackeson at Peshawar, announcing that reinforcements were on their way from India, and urging the authorities to hold out to the last. Again, Pottinger urged resistance, but the Council of War would not hear of it, and diplomatic intercourse with the enemy was renewed. On the 27th of December fourteen lakhs of rupees were signed away. All but six field pieces were to be given up to the Afghans. The soldiers chafed under the indignity, but the chiefs could not bring themselves to risk a renewal of the conflict, by openly refusing to accede to the demand. Pottinger determined to procrastinate and gave up the Shah's guns in pairs on successive days. From day to day guns, wagons, small arms and ammunition were surrendered. The hostages were given up; and Captains Walsh and Drummond with Lieutenants Warburton and Webb were sent to join Conolly and Airey. They were all well treated by the chiefs. The officers would not allow their wives to fall into such treacherous hands, though the Afghan were particularly anxious to obtain them also as hostages. On the 29th the sick and wounded were sent into the city, in charge of Drs. Berwick and Campbell. On the 1st of January, 1842, the ratified treaty was sent in, bearing the seals of eighteen Afghan Sardars. There were other causes of humiliation. The *Ghazis* were insulting our people at their very gates, and bearding them at the muzzles of their guns. They drove off the purchased cattle and ill-treated their attendants; and the British authorities ordered that the *Ghazis* should not be molested.

The Afghans had triumphed so long with impunity that they now believed the English sunk into hopeless cowardice, and as patient of insult and injury as a herd of broken-spirited slaves. Rumours of the dangers threatening the retreat were received from the city, and that treachery menaced our wretched force. Mohan Lal sent repeated warnings that the chiefs were not to be trusted, and that the troops would be attacked so soon as they quitted cantonments. Other warning notes of a still more ominous character were sounded at this time. Worse than all, the snow had been falling heavily and winter had set in with great severity. All preparations for the march had been made. The officers had collected such of their property as they could carry with them, and destroyed the remainder. On the evening of the 5th of January the engineers received orders to cut passages through the walls to facilitate the egress of the troops; and on the following day the British force commenced its ill-fated retreat.

CHAPTER XVII.

THE RETREAT FROM KABUL.

While Elphinstone was ensnared at Kabul, Sale was holding out manfully at Jalalabad. Whether he should have returned to Kabul or maintained his ground at Gandamak is a problem inviting discussion. Probably the presence of the brigade would have saved Kabul; but General Sale did not consider that he could reach it. He would have been obliged to leave 300 sick under a guard which he could not trust; he had insufficient transport; and was short of ammunition. At Gandamak he could not command a day's provisions or water; and would have been hemmed in by hostile tribes which could either have burnt Jalalabad or, holding it, have left no alternative but a retreat to Peshawar. On the 10th of November news of the outbreak at Kabul had been received, and a requisition for Sale's brigade. The military objections above enumerated, written by Sale five months subsequently, were not then existent in their entirety. The irregulars were not then known to be treasonable, nor the surrounding country hostile. Food was procurable, and the valley of Gandamak fertile. The prospects were encouraging; provisions were coming in and the Ghilzai Chiefs making their submission. Mir Afzal Khan, however, possessed a fort two miles from the camp and was beginning to molest us. It had been suggested that the fort should be taken, but Sale would not agree to this course. However, Havelock resumed his arguments and was partially successful, to the delight of Broadfoot and Backhouse. Not, however, until 5 P.M., were orders issued for the attack. The enemy fled and some of the Shah's troops under Captain Gerard were installed as garrison. The spirits of the troops rose and the enemy were awakened from their belief that Sale was afraid to attack them.

A council of war was now held; the majority decided against the proposed relief of Elphinstone's force, and it was determined

that the Brigade should throw itself into Jalalabad. The proposal for the retention of Gandamak found no favour.

On the 11th of November the force commenced its march, with as little baggage as possible, most of the transport animals having been looted when out grazing. The property left at Gandamak was entrusted to the care of the Shah's Irregulars; and, as soon as Sale's brigade left, the cantonment was attacked, the Janbaz, true to their character, deserting to the enemy, the property was looted, the cantonment burnt to the ground, and the surrounding country rose in open revolt.

The march to Jalalabad was accomplished without any serious difficulty. On the morning of the 12th, however, the tribes attacked the rear-guard and attempted to carry off the baggage. A running skirmish for a distance of some miles brought out the fine qualities of our troops, their admirable discipline and steadiness under fire, and the rapidity of their movements. The depredators were dispersed, and the remainder of the march was undisturbed. Dennie skilfully drew the enemy into his toils, and exacted heavy retribution. Placing the cavalry in ambush, the infantry attacked; then simulated a retreat; when the enemy, making a headlong pursuit, were drawn into open ground where the cavalry charged and cut them up, until their right arms were weary from the blows which they struck. The Afghans, thinking that the brigade was making the best of its way to India, fled as it unexpectedly entered Jalalabad, which was occupied without a shot being fired. The town, however, was soon surrounded by rebels, who threatened death to the infidels if they did not at once quit it. The place lacked effective defences, and the troops were almost as much exposed as they would have been in the open. Guards were posted at the gates and an inlying piquet told off; the remainder lay down to rest, with their officers beside them, and Sale summoned the Commanders to a Council of War.

Rear-guard action.

It was debated whether it would be expedient to abandon the town, the extent of which rendered it difficult to defend, and to withdraw to the Bala Hissar, which was surrounded by a wall, and offered sufficient accommodation for the brigade, or to hold the former,

Plan of defence.

Dennie and others considered that the abandonment of the town would be interpreted as a confession of weakness, and it was decided to continue to hold it. Its defences now called for earnest attention.

The perimeter was upwards of 2,300 yards, the trace was vicious; it had only a few hundred yards of parapet two feet high, the population was disaffected, and there was ample cover for an enemy in the shape of ruined forts, mosques, and gardens within thirty yards of the walls. Captain Broadfoot and other officers inspected the existing works with difficulty. On the north side the wall rose to a great height towards the town, but sloped to the exterior, where heaps of rubbish made it everywhere accessible. The surrounding ruins were occupied by the enemy, and the posts held by the troops were untenable. Had the enemy attacked, the fight would have developed into a street combat.

The engineers, aided with a will by the troops in garrison, at once set to work. Wood and iron had to be collected, for there were no supplies of either. The former was obtained from ruined houses, and the latter from the surrounding country. Difficulties were made to be overcome, and there were no such things as impossibilities at Jalalabad.[1] Before, however, the work could be put in hand, it was necessary to give the enemy a taste of our quality.

First fight at Jalalabad. The 16th of November was fixed for the purpose. Monteith of the 35th Bengal Infantry was to give the enemy battle with a force of 1,100 men. At early dawn he ascended one of the most commanding edifices in the city, and examined the ground and the enemy's depositions.

Some 5,000 of the latter were gathered on the hill-sides and in enclosures on the plain; they appeared to have little discipline, but were sturdy and well-armed. Monteith, having concluded his inspection, placed himself at the head of his men. The little force was well-composed and well-commanded. The guns not taken, covered the advance from the ramparts. What the

---

[1] *Gleig, page* 144. In Jalalabad a more important field of usefulness was afforded to him. (Major Sinclair, see *ante*.) There was not a mill in the place, and hence the corn which the foragers brought in, however acceptable it might be to the horses, could not by the men of the garrison be converted into bread. Major Sinclair took the matter up, and in due time produced as many hand mills as sufficed to grind from day to day the quantity of flour that was required * * * * cakes baked upon the coals, or cooked over heated stones, now took the place of parched corn, and the change was felt by all to whom it applied as a serious improvement in their physical condition.

artillery commenced, the infantry followed up, and the cavalry completed. The enemy were beaten at all points. The faithless Janbaz now met the 5th Cavalry in fair fight, and were remorselessly hewn down. In a short time the panic-stricken Afghans fled, pursued and cut down by the British horsemen. The bugles sounded the recall, and the force, flushed with success, returned to the city. The Afghans for many a day remained quietly in their homes.

Broadfoot now proceeded with the work of defence. Abbott got his guns into position, and made up ammunition, as best he could, from the materials at hand. Macgregor, bringing his political influence to bear, busied himself with obtaining supplies; with such good effect that sufficient for one month were soon in hand. Although the men were on half rations they worked with a will.

Not again till the 1st of December was the mettle of Sale's men tried in the field. For some days before the enemy had been hovering round and threatening the garrison, who, chary of their ammunition, did not reply to the Afghan fire. On this day, however, their numbers increased and they became more menacing, and Sale could no longer neglect their attentions. Dennie was chosen to command on this occasion, and sallied out at midday with his men against the besiegers. Two guns of Abbott's battery poured grape upon the discomfited mass. They, who had hitherto been so bold and defiant, were charged by the cavalry, who drove them across the plain into the river, whilst the infantry pursued them up the hillsides, and fell upon them with the bayonet. Without the loss of a single man Dennie dispersed the investing force.[1]

Second engagement.

News of the Kabul disaster. The defences now began to grow rapidly. The men were in good health, good spirits and in an admirable state of discipline. But the worst rumours were coming in from Kabul. The defenders of Jalalabad could not understand how it was that Elphinstone's force was meet-

---

[1] *Gleig*, page 123. Meanwhile the infantry, passing through the Kabul gate, advanced towards the hills. They were thronged with defenders, who kept up a heavy, but not very effective, fire; and among them was a piper who ceased not to play on his most unmusical instrument, regardless of the shower of balls that whizzed past him. As a matter of course, the piper became the subject of many a rude joke among the men of the 13th. They laughed while they took deliberate aim at him, showing, however, this much of respect to his acknowledged bravery, that in honour of him they forthwith denominated the heights "The Piper's Hill. * * *". The piper escaped unhurt.

ing with such disastrous defeats. The want of provisions could hardly account for it; for they themselves had been in similar straits. The defences at Kabul, too, were superior to those they had found at Jalalabad. They themselves had managed to create fortifications and collect provisions; and the Kabul garrison out-numbered them by nearly four to one.

Midway through December rumours reached them that the Kabul force had capitulated; they could not believe their ears. Sale and Macgregor knew how things had been mismanaged, but kept their information to themselves. The news of Macnaghten's murder brought fresh consternation. It seemed hardly credible, but a letter from Pottinger soon confirmed their worst fears. Elphinstone's retreat was discussed, and they could hardly conceal from themselves the probability of his fate. In spite of all this there was no Thersites at Jalalabad, and the men continued their work as cheerfully as before.

The first week of January passed; days of anxiety to Sale and Macgregor. No good news came to them from Kabul, and on the 8th of January a letter from Pottinger, written in French, told them that the position of the British force at Kabul was becoming more and more perilous; that the late Envoy's treaty was still being negotiated; but that the delay on the part of the Afghans in supplying carriage and provisions was delaying the march; and that it was more than probable that the force would be obliged to fight its way to Jalalabad. In conclusion Pottinger spoke of orders for the evacuation of Jalalabad that had been despatched by Macnaghten, but urged Macgregor to stand fast until the receipt of further orders from Kabul.

Proposals for evacuation.

On the following day these further orders arrived. Macgregor laid the letter before Sale, and a Council of War was held. There appear to have been few doubts and misgivings, and each asked the other whether they should further degrade their country's honour by abandoning their post, and flinging themselves into the snares of the enemy; for few doubted that a bait had been laid for their destruction. Macgregor knew that Akbar Khan had issued a proclamation to the chiefs, calling upon them to annihilate the English while on the march; he was all for the retention of the

post; and the military chiefs were of the same temper. Sale and Macgregor, therefore, wrote to Pottinger and Elphinstone as follows:—

Jalalabad, January 9th, 1842.

Sirs,

We have the honour to acknowledge the receipt of your letter of the 29th ultimo, which you therein state was to be delivered to us by Abdul Ghafur Khan, appointed governor of this place by the existing powers at Kabul. That communication was not delivered to us by him, but by a messenger of his; and though dated 29th of December, 1841, has only this moment reached us. I have, at the same time, positive information that Muhammad Akbar Khan has sent a proclamation to all the chiefs in the neighbourhood, urging them to raise their followers for the purpose of intercepting and destroying the forces now at Jalalabad. Under these circumstances we have deemed it our duty to await a further communication from you, which we desire may point out the security which may be given for our safe march to Peshawar.

We have the honour to be, &c.,

R. SALE, *Major-General*,

G. H. MACGREGOR,
Political Agent.

In explanation of the above letter Macgregor subsequently stated that he had good information of the intentions of Akbar Khan; and that the retention of Jalalabad would, in the circumstances, have proved of inestimable advantage to the retreating force; should it succeed in reaching that place a stand might be made, pending the receipt of re-inforcements for the recapture of Kabul. By the time the letter reached Jalalabad the Kabul force would already have been three days on the march, and their fate sealed; the rendition of Jalalabad would have entailed the destruction of the garrison, and increased the difficulty of re-establishing British authority in the country; a course which national honour and the safety of India alike rendered of paramount necesssity.

General Sale stated that, in the absence of instructions from India, he apprehended that he was at liberty to consider himself bound by the treaty or not as he thought best, a treaty which was forced, moreover, knife at throat; that he had provisions sufficient to last until reinforcements should arrive from Peshawar, and that he proposed to hold on until ordered by Government to withdraw. He stated that the Afghans respected his strength, and that he would have compromised the safety of the Kabul force had he evacuated Jalalabad before it arrived.

A season of suspense and anxiety followed the receipt of Pottinger's letter; but the arrival of money from Mackeson, through the agency of Torabaz Khan, the legal chief of Lalpura, which was badly wanted, raised their spirits. The defence, too, had proceeded apace, and by the middle of January the parapet was nowhere less than six feet high. The gates were repaired and strengthened by buttresses, and roads were made where most needed. The scarcity of ammunition alone rendered the garrison apprehensive on their own account; but every day made them more anxious concerning the fate of their countrymen.

Progress of the defences.

At last, on the 13th of January, when the garrison were busy on the works, a sentry looking towards Kabul saw a solitary white-faced horseman struggling on towards the fort. The ramparts were lined with officers looking out, with throbbing hearts, through unsteady telescopes. Clinging round the neck of his wretched pony rode an Englishman. A shudder ran through the garrison as they watched the messenger of death.

Dr. Brydon's arrival.

Colonel Dennie had predicted that only one man would bring the news of the destruction of the remainder, and now he exclaimed: "Did I not say so—here comes the messenger." A party of cavalry was sent out to succour him and brought him in wounded, exhausted, half dead. The messenger was Dr. Brydon[1]; and he now reported

---

[1] *Greenwood*, page 252. Dr. Brydon himself owed his life to the generosity of a native of Hindustan. His horse had been shot under him, and at the time of the utter disorganization of the force, he was making the best of his way on foot along the road, when he was accosted by an old Subadar who was bleeding by the side of the path, but with one hand holding the bridle of his horse which stood beside him. "Sahib," said this noble fellow, "my hour has come: I am wounded to death and can ride no longer. You, however, still have a chance, take my horse which is now useless to me, and God send you may get into Jalalabad in safety."

his belief that he was the sole survivor of an army of some sixteen thousand men.

Dr. Brydon's story has few parallels in history. A British army of 4,000 fighting men, with 12,000 followers, had disappeared in the course of a few days. Some had perished in the snow; others had fallen victims to a savage enemy; a few had been carried into captivity.

The retreat from Kabul.

On the 6th January 1842 General Elphinstone's army, after sixty-five days' humiliation, evacuated their position. It was a clear, frosty morning when they marched out; the cold was intense, and the snow lying thick upon the ground. It was 8 o'clock before the baggage was ready to move. At 9-30 A.M. the advanced guard, consisting of the 44th, 4th Irregular Horse, Skinner's Horse, two 6-pounder guns, Sappers and Miners, Mountain train and the late Envoy's escort, moved out of cantonment with the English ladies and children.

The main body included the 5th and 37th Native Infantry; the latter in charge of the treasure, Anderson's Horse, the Shah's 6th Regiment and two six-pounder Horse Artillery guns.

The rearguard was composed of the 54th Native Infantry, 5th Cavalry, and the remaining two Horse Artillery guns.

It had been agreed that the chiefs should supply a strong Afghan escort; but the army commenced its march without it, and Nawab Ziman Khan, whose good faith was beyond suspicion, warned Pottinger of the danger of leaving without it. But it was now too late to stand still. The mission premises had already fallen into the enemy's hands; and it was considered imprudent to recover it by force. Ziman Khan admitted the potency of Pottinger's arguments and promised to do his best to protect the retreating force. He fulfilled his promises, so far as was possible, but lacked the power to control the lawlessness of the people. Everything seemed to favour delay where expedition was of the first importance. Shelton's MS. contains the following passage: "I knew nothing of the arrangements for the retreat till they were published the evening before. The order was for the baggage to assemble at 8 A.M. At that hour I went to Elphinstone's quarters, to beg that he would let the

carriages of the gun-wagons go out that were to form a foot bridge for the infantry over the Kabul river, about 300 yards from the cantonments, and got offended for my trouble. He was just sitting down to breakfast. They did not go out till between nine and ten, and having to be dragged through a canal caused further delay, so that the bridge was not completed for the advanced guard till past twelve." The river was, however, fordable at many places. Had the army crossed before noon, and pushed on to Khurd-Kabul, it might have been saved; but the delays sealed the fate of the unhappy force. Colin Mackenzie urged the General either to expedite the advance, or to recall the force to expel the intruding Afghans. A reluctant assent was wrung from the General, and Mackenzie galloped back to communicate the orders to Shelton. The advanced guard moved out with some order and steadiness, but the rush of camp followers soon threw all into confusion. It was vain to endeavour to control this mass of lawless and suffering humanity.

The main body, under Shelton, with innumerable transport animals, was moving out of cantonments during the greater part of the day. The rear-guard manned the walls, and looked down upon a scene of indescribable confusion. The enemy began to turn their attention to plunder, and cutting down the hapless camp followers carried off whatever they could seize. At the bridge there was a fearful crush, and a babel of noises, above which rose the savage yells of the *Ghazis*. The rear-guard did not move out until 6 P.M. and the Afghans poured in to plunder. All the buildings were soon in a blaze; and the British army scattered between Kabul and Bigrami looked through the frosty night at the great conflagration which lit up the country for miles round. The rear-guard did not reach its camping ground until 2 A.M., having been under arms since 8 o'clock in the morning, and having been savagely attacked on leaving cantonments; fifty being slain and their guns lost. They had now only accomplished five or six miles of their journey, and had seen enough to fill them with forebodings of their fate. The road was strewn with wretches smitten by the cold; even the sepoys were sinking down and quietly awaiting death. The night was one of suffering and horror; all was chaos; the regiments encamping anywhere. Soldiers, camp followers, horses, camels, and

Vol. III.

baggage ponies were mixed up in confusion. The weary wretches lay down to sleep; some never rose again, and some were crippled for life by the biting frost. Pottinger had recommended that the old horse *jhools* should be cut into strips to form leg bandages for the men, but his advice was not heeded.

Morning dawned; and without orders or any attempt at restraint the camp-followers and baggage struggled on ahead, many of the sepoys going with them. Discipline was fast disappearing and regiments were dwindling to the merest skeletons. The enemy pressed on the rear, capturing guns and baggage and cutting up all in their way. The soldiers, weary, feeble and frost-bitten, could make no stand against the fierce charges of the Afghan horsemen. It seemed as if the rear-guard would be speedily cut off. All thoughts of effectual resistance were at an end; there was nothing now to be hoped for, but from the forbearance of the Afghan Chiefs.

Ziman Khan wrote to Pottinger urging that the force should halt, and promising to send supplies of food and fuel, and to disperse the fanatic bands, which were hovering on the flanks. The General consented to the halt; but Shelton was eager for an advance. He pressed his recommendations upon Elphinstone but without effect; and the doomed army halted at But-khak.

Akbar Khan now rode up with 600 horsemen. Captain Skinner was despatched with a flag of truce to communicate with him, and brought back a friendly message, reproaching the British for their hasty movement on the previous morning, and stating that he had come to protect them from the *Ghazis*. His instructions were to demand other hostages, as security for the evacuation of Jalalabad; until that had been effected the force was to halt, being supplied with all it required. The army, therefore, spent another night of inactivity and suffering in the snow. The confusion far exceeded that of the preceding night. There was no shelter, firewood, nor food. The sepoys burnt their caps and accoutrements to obtain a little warmth; then all huddled together and lay down to sleep. Next morning the paramount desire to escape death held possession of that wretched multitude; and a crowd of soldiers and camp-followers began to push to the front at an early hour. Skinner again went out to meet Akbar Khan. It was proposed that the army should halt where it was, or push

on to Tazin; there to await news of the evacuation of Jalalabad. The Sardar declared himself willing to receive three hostages—Major Pottinger, Captain Lawrence, and a third to be selected by the former. Colin Mackenzie was named.

The force now set out for Tazin; before it lay the formidable pass of Khurd-Kabul. For five miles it runs between precipitous mountain ranges so narrow that the sun rarely penetrates it. Down the centre dashed a mountain torrent, now partly frozen, which the force had to cross and re-cross eight and twenty times. All was confusion. In vain did Akbar Khan issue his orders; in vain did his adherents attempt to control the hordes of *Ghazis*. The wretched fugitives fell an easy prey to the Ghilzai marksmen, who shot them down from the hill-sides. Baggage and ammunition were abandoned; and even the firelocks were taken from the sepoys' hands. On leaving Kabul each sepoy had 40 rounds of ammunition; there were 60 camel loads per regiment and 100 spare loads. On January, the 8th, three camel loads remained.

In the Khurd-Kabul Pass 3,000 men are said to have perished by the fire of the enemy and Afghan knives. In the midst of this carnage rode English ladies, trying to keep their children in sight in the confusion and bewilderment of the march. Many European officers perished in the pass; among them Captain Paton, the Assistant Adjutant-General, and Lieutenant Sturt of the Engineers, who had exerted himself with unfailing activity, and had invariably sided with those who advocated the more manly and courageous course; his wife was the daughter of Sir Robert Sale. Another night in the snow, now deeper, succeeded. The same suffering, the same death, the same starvation marked it. At early morn there was another rush of camp-followers and sepoys to the front; but the march was countermanded by the General. This course was recommended by Akbar Khan, who promised a supply of provisions and his protection. There was an unanimous opinion against the delay, but nothing would move Elphinstone from his purpose. The native troops began to think of deserting to the enemy. The General had paraded the wreck of his regiments to repel an anticipated attack; and Captain Grant explained to them that Akbar Khan had threatened instant death to any who deserted to him. The contagion was, however, fast spreading; and nothing

could stop the progress of the disease. The Shah's 2nd Cavalry had gone over nearly to a man.[1]

Major Pottinger was now in communication with Akbar Khan; Captain Skinner acting as the vehicle of communication between him and Army Head-quarters. The Sardar proposed that the English ladies should be placed under his charge for conveyance to Peshawar. Pottinger, remembering that Akbar Khan's families were prisoners in British hands, and believing he was sincere in his anxiety for the safety of the women and children, sanctioned the proposal; and Skinner was sent to obtain the General's consent. Elphinstone agreed to the arrangement, and Lady Sale, Lady Macnaghten, and the other widows and wives of the British officers, with the married men, conducted by an escort of Afghan Horse, placed themselves under the protection of Akbar Khan. The men joined the party with Elphinstone's sanction; though it is improbable that either Akbar Khan or Pottinger contemplated this extension of the invitation.

The remnant of the force resumed its march on the 10th of January, in the same miserable state of confusion as before. The sepoys threw down their arms and mixed with the camp-followers, frost-bitten, paralysed, and panic-struck; the Afghans, watching their opportunity, came down with their long knives and slaughtered them like sheep. The dead and dying choked the defile, and there was soon not a sepoy left. All the baggage had been looted; and fifty horse artillerymen, 250 of the 44th, and 150 cavalry troopers now composed the entire force.

Hovering on the flanks, Akbar Khan watched the butchery which was going on below, and declared that he was powerless to restrain the Ghilzais. He proposed that the remainder of the force should throw down their arms and rely upon his protection; but Elphinstone declined. The wreck of the British force made its way down the steep descents of the Haft Kotal into a narrow defile, choked with the bodies of camp-followers who had preceded

---

[1] *Vincent Eyre,* page 212. These men had hitherto behaved remarkably well notwithstanding the numerous efforts which had been made to retract them from their duty; and, if their fealty at last gave way to the instinct of self-preservation, be it remembered in their favour that it was not until the position of the force, of which they formed a part, had become altogether desperate beyond the reach of cure.

it. The enemy opened a destructive fire upon their rear, commanded by Shelton, who, with a handful of Europeans, repulsed their attacks; though they were obliged carefully to husband their ammunition. The gallantry of these few men was for a time the salvation of the whole. After another futile attempt at negotiation it was determined, at Shelton's suggestion, to make a desperate effort to reach Jagdalak by a rapid night march. Despair had given the enfeebled soldiers renewed strength; and when the order was given, having spiked their remaining gun, they moved off quietly, hoping that, under cover of darkness, they might shake off their incubus of camp-followers. As soon as they began to move, however, the tentacles closed round them again and paralysed the movements of the force

The night was bright and frosty; and for some miles they proceeded unmolested. At Seh-Baba, however, the enemy again opened fire upon their rear, and the camp-followers rushed to the front only to struggle back again when firing was heard at the head of the column. They overwhelmed the handful of soldiers who were still able and willing to show a bold front, blocked the road, and presented a splendid target to the enemy. Soon after day-break the advance reached Kata-Sang, and they were still ten miles from Jagdalak. Halting till the rear-guard closed up they then pushed on; but it was now too late; the enemy were crowning the heights, and there remained no hope of escape. Shelton with the rear-guard faced the overwhelming crowd of Afghans with a courage worthy of British soldiers; and fought his way to Jagdalak, contesting every inch of the ground. At last they reached the spot where the advance had halted behind some ruined walls on a height by the road side Scarcely any of the advance now remained, and some twenty British officers formed line and showed a front. The enemy who had followed the rear-guard increased in numbers and crowned the heights commanding the position of their victims. The British, now withdrawn from the excitement of the actual conflict, began to suffer the agonies of hunger and thirst. The snow which they devoured only increased their torments, and they could not approach the stream hard by without being struck down by the fire of the enemy. Behind the walls they tried to snatch a hasty meal; three bullocks had been found among the camp-followers and these were

hastily killed and devoured raw. The respite was of brief duration. A party of horse appeared, said to be commanded by Akbar Khan. Skinner went to remonstrate with him against the continued attacks; but he had scarcely set out ere the firing was resumed. Volley after volley poured upon the men, who had lain down, and they and the camp-followers were compelled to quit the enclosure in which they had bivouacked. A handful of the 44th made a gallant rush and cleared the ground in front of them. Thinking that the whole force would follow, the Afghans fled in dismay. But the little party was soon recalled, and the whole sought the refuge of the ruins; when the enemy returned and continued their fire.

That night and the following day the force remained halted at Jagdalak, while Akbar Khan communicated with the British Chiefs. He entertained them kindly and gave them a much-needed meal. The Sardar promised to send provisions for the famished troops, but insisted on the retention of the General, Shelton, and Johnson as hostages for the evacuation of Jalalabad. The conference was resumed next day; and the English officers implored the Sardar to save the remnants of the force; he promised to do his best, but the tribes were uncontrollable. They loudly declared that they only wanted the blood of the Englishmen, and in vain Akbar Khan tried to dissuade them. In vain he urged that his family were the prisoners of the British Government; vain was the offer of large sums of money for a safe conduct to Jalalabad. Johnson, who understood their language, gathered that their one desire was for blood. Two lakhs of rupees were offered for a safeguard to Jalalabad; and at length a grudging consent was given. Hardly was the bargain concluded when heavy firing was heard in the direction of the bivouac. At about 8 P.M. the remainder of the force, now numbering barely 200, prepared to resume their march. The rabble again hampered the fighting men, and the Afghans again resumed their butchery. The soldiers turned and bayoneted the plunderers, and fought their way bravely on. They struggled through the Jagdalak Pass, when they were suddenly brought up by a barricade erected across it. The soldiers, in spite of the camp-followers, fought with desperate valour; but the Afghans, who had been waiting for this moment, were soon at work with

their knives and *jazails*. The massacre was terrible to contemplate. Officers, soldiers, and camp-followers were stricken down at the foot of the barricade. A few managed to struggle through it; but all hope was at an end. The British army had ceased to exist.[1]

Twelve British officers fell at the barrier; among them Brigadier Anquetil and Captain Nichol of the Horse Artillery. The artillery had borne themselves as gallantly as the best of English soldiers in any place and at any period of history; and the enemy looked upon them with mingled admiration and awe. A few struggled on towards Gandamak; and at daybreak twenty officers and forty-five European soldiers were assembled there. The enemy were mustering round them, and not more than two rounds of ammunition per man remained. They refused to surrender and decided to sell their lives dearly. With the exception of Captain Souter of the 44th, who had wrapped the regimental colour round his waist, and a few privates, who were taken prisoners, all were killed.

A few, however, had pushed on from Surkhab, between Jagdalak and Gandamak, in advance of the column. One by one they fell by the way until the number was reduced to six. Captains Bellew, Collyer and Hopkins, Lieutenant Bird and Drs. Harpur and Brydon reached Fatehabad, sixteen miles from Jalalabad, alive. As above related, Brydon was the only one to reach his destination.[2]

---

[1] This formidable defile is about two miles long, exceedingly narrow, and closed in by lofty precipitous heights. The road has a considerable slope upwards, and, on nearing the summit, further progress was found to be obstructed by two strong barriers formed of branches of the prickly holly-oak, stretching completely across the defile.—*Vincent Eyre, page 22-I.*

[2] This has always been the popularly-accepted version up-to-date. Recent correspondence, however, published in the Journal of the Royal Artillery for November, 1906, shows that at least two other Europeans (Sergeant-Major Lisant, 37th Native Infantry, and Mr. Barnes, a merchant), and a good number of natives, managed to reach Jalalabad alive during the month of January 1842.

CHAPTER XVIII.

THE AVENGING ARMY.

LORD AUCKLAND was on the horns of a dilemma when tidings
Efforts at retrieval. of the disaster reached him. He had long ago repented of the policy which had embroiled us with the Afghans, and the Court of Directors had ever been opposed to it. The Conservatives, too, had now come into office; and they were opposed to the policy which had been pursued. Lord Ellenborough had been nominated Governor-General; and Lord Auckland had fondly hoped to lay aside the reins of government during a period of profound peace. He began to despond, and steadfastly set his face against any measures of military re-establishment. When on the 25th of November he received letters from Mr. Clerk and Captain Mackeson, confirming the news of the disaster, he wrote to Sir Jasper Nicolls deprecating any idea of reconquest. The Commander-in-Chief had been consistently opposed to the scheme of Afghan invasion. He had displayed much political sagacity, and gave as his opinion at this juncture that it would be impossible to keep an adequate force in Afghanistan, without unduly weakening the garrison of India. There was, however, something more than the restoration of the Saddozai dynasty to be accomplished. The supremacy of Britain in Central Asia was at stake.

In opposition to the opinions of the Governor-General and the Commander-in-Chief, there were those nearer the scene of action in whose judgment a course of energetic procedure was demanded.

Mr. Robertson, the Lieutenant-Governor of the North-West Provinces, and Mr. George Clerk, the Agent on the North-West Frontier, recognized the necessity of pushing on troops to Peshawar with the utmost despatch. On the 16th of November the latter wrote to Colonel Wild, Commanding at Ferozepore, and to Colonel Rich at Ludhiana, urging them to send on the 30th, 53rd, 60th, and 64th Native Regiments to Peshawar. Having expedited the

movements of these regiments, Mr. Clerk wrote to General Boyd at Sirhind for the despatch of another brigade. He informed the Court of Lahore of the intended march of the regiments; asking for boats to transport them across the Sutlej, and requesting that 5,000 of the best Sikh troops under Kunwar Partab Singh might be ordered to march from Chach Hazara. Mackeson had already applied to the Sikh authorities at Peshawar for 6,000 men to march on Jalalabad; but General Avitabile had replied that he needed all his troops for the protection of Sikh territory. Lord Auckland was strongly opposed to the advance of the second brigade, representing that the single brigade with artillery would be sufficient to force the Khaibar. Even this brigade, however, never went to Peshawar. The Native Infantry crossed the Punjab with Wild, and some Artillery went with them; but there were no guns. It was hoped that the Sikhs would provide these. The Sikh artillerymen were, however, disinclined to hand them over to the British and their value was doubtful. Wild declined to push on without guns; and the force halted at Peshawar. On the 3rd of January, however, four rickety guns were handed over, and the limbers breaking at once, they had to be replaced. The camel men were deserting; the Afridi Maliks had not yet been bribed into submission by Mackeson, and the loyalty of the Sikhs was doubtful. The sepoys were at first eager to advance, but the Sikhs tampered with their loyalty and played upon their bears.

Active preparations for the despatch of reinforcements to Peshawar were going on in the North-West Provinces. Lord Auckland did not wish to interfere with Mr. Clerk, although he disapproved of sending a second brigade. The 9th Foot was ordered to be in readiness, and the 26th Native Infantry, some Irregular Horse, two 9-pounders, and a howitzer were to accompany it. The 10th Cavalry were subsequently added; and on the 4th of January the brigade, consisting of 3,000 fighting men, crossed the Sutlej.

The despatch of reinforcements.

It was now necessary to select a Commander for the whole force; and finally the choice rested upon General George Pollock, Commanding at Agra. He had entered the Indian Army as a Lieutenant of Artillery in 1803, and had a distinguished record of service. He was unassuming and averse from personal display,

but was sagacious and firm; equable and temperate. Possibly a more suitable man could not have been chosen. On the 22nd o January the Commander-in-Chief met Mr. Clerk at Tanesar, near Karnal. Sir Jasper Nicolls considered that the troops remaining in Afghanistan should retire beyond the Indus. Mr. Clerk was all for a forward movement.

He argued that the safety and honour of the nation demanded the retention of Jalalabad; and that, when reinforced, the garrison, with that of Kandahar, should first chastise the Afghans and then withdraw with dignity and honour from the country. Mr. Clerk persuaded the Chief to order the 6th and 55th Native Infantry to hold themselves in readiness to proceed to Peshawar. He, however, resisted the demand for a detachment of British Dragoons; and the question was referred to Calcutta. Government had now received intelligence of the massacre of Elphinstone's army, and replied that it was necessary that a commanding force should assemble at Peshawar; that it was important that it should be effective in cavalry and artillery, and that at all events two squadrons of Dragoons should be pushed on. The 1st Regiment of Native Cavalry and a troop of Horse Artillery were subsequently added to the third brigade.

On the 10th of February the Governor-General in Council wrote to the Commander-in-Chief instructing him to inform General Pollock that the main inducement for maintaining a post at Jalalabad having passed away, he should, unless favourable conditions appeared, confine himself to the withdrawal of the garrison and concentrate at Peshawar.

Brigadier Wild's position at Peshawar was not a very hopeful one. His difficulties were formidable and his means slender. His four Native Infantry Regiments contained a large number of young soldiers whom the Sikhs had done their best to discourage. He had only one troop of Irregular Horse and four indifferent pieces of artillery. Ammunition was scarce and carriage was beginning to fail altogether; the camel-owners refusing to proceed further than Peshawar. The intelligence from Afghanistan was most dispiriting. Sale and Macgregor were urging the immediate advance of the brigade and Avitabile was warning the Brigadier of the danger of entering the Khaibar with his present force. There appeared to be a very

Brigadier Wild at Peshawar.

faint possibility of the co-operation of the Sikhs, who were on the verge of mutiny. The negotiations with the Afridis were not proceeding favourably; and there appeared to be every prospect of heavy opposition in the pass.

He did not, however, remain long in doubt and inactivity. The fortress of Ali Masjid lies five miles within the Khaibar Pass and twenty-five miles from Peshawar. It consisted of two small forts connected by an insignificant wall and standing upon a rock, commanded on the south and west by two lofty hills; it was important that this "Key of the Khaibar" should be held by British troops or their allies. It was at this time held by Yusufzais, who had gallantly resisted the attacks of the Afridis. There was now, however, every chance of its falling into the enemy's hands; and it was resolved to push forward half the brigade and seize and garrison the post.

Accordingly, on the 15th of January, Colonel Moseley, with the 53rd and 64th Native Infantry, accompanied by Mackeson, started at night and reached their destination the next morning. Captain Mackeson now discovered to his dismay that instead of 350 bullocks only fifty or sixty were with the rear-guard. The two regiments were therefore without provisions. The only hope of extrication from this dilemma lay in the advance of the two other regiments, with the Sikh guns and Sikh allies. Reinforcements, however, did not come, and Wild was frustrated in his attempts to throw supplies into Ali Masjid. He had intended to move forward on the 19th of January; but the Sikh troops mutinied to a man. At 7 o'clock the 30th and 60th Native Infantry, with the Sikh guns, commenced their march; but the enemy met them with the fire of their *jazails*. The sepoys wavered, stood still, and fired aimlessly. The officers moved forward, but the regiments did not follow them. In vain the Brigadier and his staff called upon them to advance; but they only huddled together in confusion. The Sikh guns broke down one after another, and the sepoys lost all heart. Lawrence exerted himself to save the guns, but the men would not help him; and one was finally abandoned. There was nothing for it but to fall back. The Brigadier and several officers were wounded, and the loss among the sepoys was severe. The column retreated to Jamrud, and Ali Masjid remained unrelieved.

Ali Masjid.

It is not easy to explain how this disaster happened. Exaggerated reports of the enemy's strength had been in circulation, and the men were unnerved by the rumours. The news from Kabul, and still more the lies disseminated by the Sikhs, had alarmed them. But the opposition was not strenuous and troops in good heart would easily have beaten it back. The men, however, had never evinced a keenness to advance; the defection of the Sikhs and the breakdown of the guns had still further damped their ardour; the battle was lost before it had been fought.

The regiments at Ali Masjid were now in a parlous condition; there was a lamentable scarcity of provisions; the water seemed to disagree with them; there was neither bedding nor tents; and ever on the alert in a trying climate under depressing conditions the health and spirits of the men were breaking down. The hospital soon became crowded and there was no promise of relief. On the 23rd of January, therefore, Colonel Moseley determined to evacuate the fort and cut his way through to Jamrud.

Mackeson saw clearly that anything was better than the abandonment of the post. A small party might hold it and could be fed. Captain Burt, of the 64th, offered to hold it; but none of his men would volunteer. Captain Thomas next volunteered to remain with 150 Yusufzais; but the latter's fidelity broke down, and on the 24th the fort was abandoned to the Afridis.

The communications between the two detachments had been cut off, and up to the evening of the 22nd they had failed to reestablish them. On the 23rd the two regiments under Colonel Tulloch, with the two serviceable guns, moved forward to line the pass and cover the retirement of Moseley's regiments; but, seeing no signs of the column, they returned to camp, moving out again next morning. Moseley was making the best of his way to Jamrud, and the sepoys doing their duty well the regiments made good the passage. Two officers were killed, some baggage was lost, and some of the sick and wounded abandoned;[1] but when the four regiments

---

[1] *Greenwood, page* 161. During the retreat from Ali Masjid a young officer of the 64th was disabled by a wound and fell behind. Calling out to a sepoy, who was passing, the latter shot one Afridi and bayoneted another. He then expressed his regret that he could not carry the officer out of the pass, but that as he had a few rounds left he would remain with him and they could, at any rate, die together.

were once more assembled at Jamrud a general feeling of relief was experienced, and congratulations were exchanged that it had been no worse. There was now nothing for it but to await the arrival of General Pollock with reinforcements from the Punjab. It was obvious that with neither cavalry nor guns the relief of Jalalabad was out of the question. Artillery was the first, second, and last great need; and it is astonishing that its provision had not demanded more serious attention. Had guns accompanied the force to Ali Masjid, events would in all probability have turned out very differently. In the first instance expedition was of the first importance; and to wait for artillery would have caused very considerable delay. Mackeson, Lawrence, and Clerk had all pressed upon Sir Jasper Nicolls the expediency of forwarding some guns; but the fact of the matter is that the regiments had crossed the Sutlej before the Commander-in-Chief heard anything of the move; it is plain, therefore, that no odium attaches to any one for not forwarding guns with Wild's Brigade. Mr. Clerk had written to General Boyd on the 27th of November. "Though I have not yet heard that any artillery is ordered up to the frontier, I would beg leave to recommend, in anticipation of the speedy arrival of reinforcements so necessary on the Sutlej, that artillery should move forward from hence. I shall transmit a copy of this letter to Lieutenant-Colonel Wild, in case he may think proper to halt one of the regiments under his command, until the arrival of such artillery as you consider can best be spared from Ludhiana or Ferozepore; but the latter is, I believe, from want of horses, incapable of moving; and this leaves an insufficiency for the due protection of the border, during an unsettled state of parties at Lahore." He asked Captain Alexander, with his guns, to move on in anticipation of sanction; but a few days afterwards Sir Jasper Nicolls prohibited the despatch of the Horse Artillery, and half a battery of Foot Artillery proceeded with M'Caskill's brigade, which did not reach Peshawar till February. Meanwhile Wild had been beaten in the Khaibar, and Ali Masjid had fallen to the Afridis.

Sickness attacked Wild's troops during their enforced halt at Peshawar; the men crowded into the hospitals, and a mutinous

spirit was engendered. Many, under the influence of the Sikh soldiers, deserted ; and others declared that nothing would induce them to face the Khaibar again. Pollock heard of the state of affairs at Peshawar, as he was advancing through the Punjab ; and he was moreover compelled to take notice of the unguarded language used by officers of the regiments. When he arrived at his destination he found nearly 2,000 men in hospital, so, even with the new brigade which quickly followed him, he was not much better off in point of numbers than Wild had been in the first instance.

A good deal had to be done before the Khaibar could be forced and Jalalabad relieved. The General visited the hospitals, endeavoured to trace the source of the sickness, and tried to put fresh spirit into the patients. There was much to be done outside the hospitals also. The soldierly qualities of the troops were at a very low ebb. Four of the five regiments openly refused to advance. An officer of the 26th Native Infantry which came up with M'Caskill's Brigade wrote : " In less than 48 hours after our arrival, active emissaries, particularly from the 53rd and 60th Regiments, were in our camp, using every effort to induce our men to desert, and to refuse to enter the Khaibar ; and had actually gone the length of sending Brahmans with the Ganga Jul to swear them in not to advance ; and did not desist until orders were given to seize the first man caught in the lines under suspicious circumstances. This information was several times communicated to me by old sepoys and non-commissioned officers, and the fact of the attempts made to seduce the men from their allegiance is too well known to the officers of the 26th to admit of a moment's doubt."

It was a difficult task which Pollock had before him ; but with tact and sagacity he set to work to re-animate and re-assure the troops. He taught them to recognize in him a father, and one, moreover, who would never call upon them for an effort which he was not prepared to make himself. The soldiers soon learnt to place in him a child-like faith ; and when the hour of trial came they were not found wanting.

The force remained inactive at Peshawar during February and March. Sale and Macgregor called for an early advance, but it was Pollock's duty to wait. The sepoys were gradually

recovering their health and spirits; reinforcements with British Dragoons and Horse Artillery were coming up; and a hurried advance without fresh troops would be only too likely to entail disaster. Surely Pollock's position was one which demanded resolution and strength of mind.

On hearing Dr. Brydon's account of the disaster to Elphinstone's force, horsemen were sent from Jalalabad to search the surrounding country and to bring in the bodies of any dead that should be found. There were faint hopes, too, that some survivors might be rescued, and every effort was made to attract the attention of such, should there be any. Bugles were sounded at night from the walls to guide the footsteps of any wanderer. No success met these efforts, however, for the few who had escaped the massacre were captives, and it was questionable, in the light of experience of the savage nature of the Afghans, if their lot was the more happy one.

The defence of Jalalabad.

Work is ever the best salve of sorrow; and plenty of the former lay ready to their hand. It was anticipated that, when satiated with plunder, the Afghan hordes would come down upon the garrison, eager to repeat their devilish orgie. It was rumoured that the Sardar was collecting an army at Lughman; it behoved them therefore to be prepared. Thanks to Broadfoot's exertions, the defences were fast becoming really formidable; and the garrison was confident that nothing but a failure of provisions or ammunition would enable the position to be captured. The fighting men being insufficient in number to man the defences, Sale embodied the camp-followers, and freed his effective troops for service beyond the walls. Large supplies of firewood and grass were brought in by the foraging parties in view of a speedy investment, and 200 of Ferris' Jazailchi Regiments, who were believed to be untrustworthy, were expelled.

The younger spirits heard of Wild's failure undismayed; they had expected little from it. The probable delay in Pollock's advance was a more serious question. But as it was only now January, and they were confident of being able to hold out till May, the relieving force had three clear months in which to effect their object. The soberer minds, however, began to debate whether Government really concerned themselves about their

salvation; all that they had heard of Lord Auckland's views led them to suppose that they were to be abandoned to their fate. In the meantime, in addition to the Sardar's army, it was reported that Shah Shuja, possibly under compulsion, was intent on expelling the garrison of Ghazni also. Macgregor received a letter from the Shah on the 21st of January, reproaching us with not having acted upon his advice, and stating that money was now what he wanted, not men. A further letter called attention to our stipulation to leave the country; and inquired when Jalalabad would be evacuated.

Both Sale and Macgregor were much perplexed. The crisis was not less serious than the responsibility. The retention of Jalalabad was evidently of no service to their countrymen in Afghanistan, for the Kabul force had been destroyed, and the line of retreat for the remaining garrisons lay through Sind. The Shah himself had freed them from the duty of personal service, and the safety of the prisoners would probably be more certain should the force withdraw, which it was also more than probable would aid the Calcutta policy. Sale convened a council of war on the 26th of January. Those present, in addition to himself and Macgregor, were: Colonel Dennie, commanding the 13th Light Infantry; Colonel Monteith, commanding the 35th; Colonel Oldfield, commanding the Cavalry; Captain Abbott, the Company's Artillery; Captain Backhouse, the Shah's Artillery; and Captain George Broadfoot, Sappers and Miners. Macgregor, having explained the circumstances which had brought them together and having read all the documents bearing upon the question, expressed his opinion that there was little hope of relief; and that they must rely upon themselves. Were the other members of the same mind as himself and Sale, *viz.*, that it was their duty to treat with the Shah for the evacuation of the country? The terms upon which the garrison would consent to the evacuation were as follows:—Four hostages to be given as a proof of their sincerity; that the King should send a force to conduct them to Peshawar, to be commanded by one of his sons; that carriage and supplies should be supplied to the garrison for the march; Akbar Khan and his force to be withdrawn before the troops

quitted Jalalabad; and that Afghan hostages should accompany the British force to Peshawar, there to be exchanged for our own hostages and prisoners; the Afghan hostages were specified by name.

An excited debate followed; popular opinion veered towards self-preservation, irrespective of the interests of Government. Broadfoot was strongly against capitulation, and threw the paper of terms upon the ground. He pointed out to his comrades that a new Governor-General was on the point of arriving, and that the Duke of Wellington was in power at home. His very violence handicapped his cause. He was, however, so far successful that he obtained an adjournment of the council. When they met again the next day it was obvious that the majority was in favour of capitulation. Broadfoot persisted in his line of argument; and produced in its support the written criticism of Henry Havelock. He then took the sense of the meeting, as to the propriety of any negotiation at all; and then, one by one, he argued the several items of the proposed treaty. All but two, however, were against him. Finally, the terms were carried, with the exception of the question of hostages, and the phraseology being slightly altered, the letter was prepared for transmission to the Shah. When his answer was received another Council of War was held; and, after warm discussion, was again adjourned. The result was a letter more or less on the lines suggested by Broadfoot and Backhouse, but it was not a renewal of the negotiation. It happily left them free to act as they considered best; for the very next day news was received that their relief was to be attempted. It was now plainly their duty to hold out till the last; and there was no longer any talk of withdrawal.

On this date, the 13th of February, the garrison was in good heart and the fortifications were growing rapidly. In spite of opposition Broadfoot had taken with him from Kabul a good supply of working tools; and had subsequently submitted an indent for others. The wisdom of his policy now appeared. A great calamity befell the garrison on the 19th of February. The men were working with a will at the fortifications, which were now very different from those which Sale found on his arrival; and it seemed as if sthe defences were on the point of completion,

a time when they would be most needed. Every day an attack by Akbar Khan was expected. Suddenly an earthquake shook down all the parapets upon which so much labour had been expended. The Kabul gate, with its adjoining bastions and part of a new bastion which flanked it, were thrown down; and several large breaches were made in the curtain. Thus, in a moment, the result of three months' labour was in a great measure destroyed. The garrison, by no means dismayed, at once set to work to repair the damage; and before night the breaches had been filled up. By the end of a month the defences were re-established, and the enemy, seeing that no traces of the damage remained, attributed the result to witchcraft; for they thought that Jalalabad was the only place which had escaped the earthquake. If Akbar Khan had known how the defences had been weakened, he acted with strange supineness in not seizing the opportunity to attack. The garrison had fully made up their minds to an encounter.

The earthquake.

Sale published the Government of India's manifesto, anent the relief, in orders; and the hearts of the defenders leaped with hope and exultation; they actually rather regretted that the Barakzais showed no inclination to give them battle. The Afghans, indeed, appear to have entertained a marked respect for Sale's soldiers; and one cannot help speculating on the results had a similar enterprizing spirit pervaded the Kabul garrison. Akbar Khan, considering discretion to be the better part of valour, decided upon a blockade. His troops were moved nearer and nearer to the walls, in the hopes that starvation would destroy the indomitable spirit of the garrison. The foraging parties and the grasscutters' escorts were freely attacked; but not until the 11th of March was there any skirmishing worthy of record. It was then reported that the enemy intended to resort to mining. *Sangars* had been thrown up on the previous evening, from which the enemy began to fire briskly. It was plain that mischief was brewing, so Sale, keeping the artillery at their guns on the ramparts, sent out Dennie with a strong party of cavalry and infantry and two hundred of Broadfoot's Sappers. Akbar Khan at first seemed inclined to give battle; but the guns drove the enemy back as fast

The blockade.

as they advanced, and the skirmishers rapidly destroyed their *sangars*. The mine was found to be a fable and the recall was sounded. The enemy emboldened fell upon the retreating column, but on its facing about turned and fled. The carnage was all among the enemy, but unfortunately Broadfoot was wounded.

The remainder of the month passed quietly; but provisions had become scarce, ammunition was running short, and forage for the horses could not be obtained. The relieving force was anxiously looked for, and Sale and Macgregor were justified in their applications for its expedition.

Pollock was, however, much handicapped. The cavalry was delayed, taking five days to cross the Ravi—the Hindus at one time did not hesitate to refuse to go forward, and were evidently suffering from a severe attack of nerves. He, however, wrote to Sale hoping to be with him by about the 7th; the date being dependent upon the fall of Ali Masjid. The dragoons reached his camp on the 30th, and on the following day the forward movement began.

General Pollock's difficulties were largely accentuated by the reluctance of our Sikh allies to face the Khaibar. Lawrence was of opinion that the fact of Mehtab Singh having admitted Afridis to his camp was sufficient justification for the dismissal of him and his troops with disgrace. But Gulab Singh was bringing with him a different class of men; and his influence over the hill levies was so great that it was hoped that a new order of things would soon be established in Pollock's camp. These hopes were, however, soon dissipated. Gulab Singh was not able to put his heart into the work before him. He had neither confidence in his troops nor any inducement to exert himself. The bribe of Jalalabad was thought of, but as quickly dismissed; and Mr. Clerk proceeded to Amritsar to use his influence with the Sikh Court. As a result of his mission the Maharaja sent orders to Gulab Singh to co-operate to the best of his ability; but it was plain that fear of an open rupture with the British Government was the leading thought which guided him. The Sikh soldiers at Peshawar now settled down and made up their minds to penetrate the Khaibar Pass.

Lawrence and Pollock had exercised their powers of persuasion with the best results; and the arrival of more European troops increased the confidence of the Khalsa, who, when the hour of trial came, rendered more effective service than the British officers had dared to expect.

On the 31st of March Pollock pitched his camp at Jamrud in the expectation of an advance on the following morning. The camel-drivers were, however, deserting; and Gulab Singh had not come up; while the rain was descending in floods. To move forward at such a time was impossible. In spite of Pollock's efforts the proportion of baggage was enormous; and desertions among the camel-drivers had rendered the carriage, even for the ammunition, insufficient. The 33rd Regiment could not come up from Peshawar for want of transport; and another day's halt was imperative. The sepoys of Wild's brigade were deserting; and the purchase of a passage through the Khaibar from the Afridi Maliks had not been effected. The halt, however, was not without its advantages; as it gave the Sikhs leisure to prepare themselves for co-operation in the combined movement.

Arrival at Jumrud.

Arrangements for the march. The details of the march were now published and carefully studied by the Commanding Officers.

Brigadier Wild was detailed to command the advanced guard and M'Caskill the rearguard. The Grenadier Company of Her Majesty's 9th Regiment, one company of the 26th Native Infantry, three companies of the 30th Native Infantry, and two companies of the 33rd Native Infantry, the whole under Major Barnewell of the 9th, were to head the column. These were to be followed by the Sappers and Miners, nine pieces of artillery, and two squadrons of the 3rd Dragoons. Then were to come the treasure and ammunition camels, followed by a squadron of the 1st Native Cavalry. Next the commissariat stores, escorted by two companies of the 53rd Native Infantry, with a squadron of the 1st cavalry. After them the baggage and camp-followers escorted by a *risala* of Irregular Horse, and a squadron of the 1st Native Cavalry, with more ammunition, litters, and camel panniers for the sick.

The rearguard was to consist of two foot-artillery guns, the 10th Light Cavalry, two *risalas* of Irregular Horse, two

squadrons, 3rd Dragoons, two Horse Artillery guns, three companies of the 60th Native Infantry, one company, 6th Native Infantry, and one company of Her Majesty's 9th Foot.

Two other columns were told off to crown the heights. That on the right comprised two companies of the 9th Foot, four companies, 26th Native Infantry, with four hundred *Jazailchis*: all under Colonel Taylor of the 9th Foot.

Seven companies of the 30th Native Infantry, under Major Payne; three companies, 60th Native Infantry, under Captain Riddle; four companies, 64th Native Infantry, under Major Anderson, with some details of Broadfoot's Sappers, and one and a half companies of the 9th Foot: all under Major Davis of the 9th Foot.

The left column consisted of two companies, Her Majesty's 9th Foot; four companies, 26th Native Infantry, and 200 *Jazailchis*, under Major Huish, 26th Native Infantry; seven companies, 53rd Native Infantry, under Major Hoggan; three companies of the 60th Native Infantry under Captain Napleton; and four and a half companies, 64th Native Infantry, and one and a half companies, 9th Foot, under Colonel Moseley of the 64th.

The flanking columns were to advance in detachments of two companies at 500 yards interval.

Pollock marched his force to Jamrud, and on the 4th of April he issued further orders for the following morning, personally ascertaining from the commanding officers that they understood them, and assuring himself of the temper of the men, which had vastly improved.

<small>Action in the Khaibar.</small>

At 3 A.M. on the 5th of April the force marched without noise; and the flanking columns quietly crowned the heights which were occupied by the enemy, who, taken by surprise at this novel manœuvre, were not aware of the advance until the flankers had made considerable progress; when the light revealed the opposing bodies to one another the struggle commenced. A formidable barrier of stones and trees had been built across the mouth of the pass. As soon as the flankers had cleared the hills this was easily removed. Nothing could have been better than the General's arrangements, and his orders were carried out with intelligence. The left column soon effectually performed its part

of the programme. The nature of the ground on the right was more difficult, but Taylor circumvented the base of the mountain and found a practicable ascent. The British troops fought admirably under the novel conditions, and everywhere the Khaibaris were seen flying across the hills. When the flankers had turned the enemy's position the main column began its advance into the pass. The remaining difficulties were chiefly in connection with the long line of transport. Besides the supplies for his own force Pollock was conveying food and ammunition for Sale; the advance was, therefore, necessarily slow; but it was skilfully conducted. The greater part of the day, which was intensely hot, was occupied in reaching Ali Masjid. The sepoys had fairly won back their reputation, and Pollock wrote of the day's work as follows:— " The Sepoys behaved nobly. They merely required a trial in which they should find they were not sacrificed. There were, however, many desertions before we advanced. Now they are in the highest spirits, and have a thorough contempt for the enemy. This is a great point gained. * * * * The Sikhs are encamped near us, and are much more respectful and civil since our operations of yesterday."

Ferris' *Jazailchis* garrisoned Ali Masjid, which had been evacuated in the morning; and a part of Pollock's force, with the head-quarters, bivouacked close by. Parties crowned the heights throughout the night, which was bitterly cold; and the enemy, who were hovering round, indulged in a good deal of sniping. During the day they lost about one thousand killed and wounded. The Sikhs, who it had been arranged should occupy the pass until the 5th of June, had moved forward by the Shadi-Bagiari Pass; as Pollock distrusted them too much to have them near his own troops. That they were untrustworthy is proved by the sequel; for, bargaining with the Afridis to keep open the pass for a fixed time, thereby giving away valuable information, they, early in May quitted Ali Masjid and returned to Jamrud, unloading some of our transport animals and placing upon them their own property The Sikhs acted under instructions from their own authorities; but, although four of our regiments were in the neighbourhood, gave no notice of their intention.

Occupation of Ali Masjid.

In the meantime Pollock had reached Jalalabad. He wrote to a friend as follows:—"We found the fort strong; the garrison healthy; and except for wine and beer better off than we are. They were, of course, delighted to see us. We gave three cheers as we passed the colours; and the band of each regiment played as it came up. It was a sight worth seeing. All appeared happy."

Arrival at Jalalabad.

Welcome, indeed, was the arrival of Pollock to Sale's force, which had been shut up for five months. The two Generals had much to relate of each other's doings. On the 1st of April the garrison had made a sortie and captured 500 sheep and goats, which were divided among the troops. The 25th Native Infantry declined to accept their share, requesting that it might be given to the Europeans, who stood more in need of it. Thenceforward a close friendship sprang up between them and the 13th Light Infantry.

On the 5th of April Macgregor's spies brought tidings from Akbar Khan's camp that Pollock had been defeated in the pass with heavy loss; and on the 6th the Sardar's guns fired a salute in honour of the reputed victory. Other rumours spoke of a fresh revolution at Kabul, and that the Sardar was about to break up his camp and proceed to the capital. In any event the moment appeared to have arrived when a blow should be struck; and a council of war was assembled, which, contrary to tradition,[1] decided to fight on the following morning. Havelock persuaded Sale to take this course. The force was divided into three columns; Her Majesty's 13th, five hundred strong, under Dennie, in the centre; the left column was under Lieutenant-Colonel Monteith; and the right under Havelock. These were to be supported by the Light Field Battery and the whole of the small force of cavalry. They left the western gate at daybreak, and found Akbar Khan on the *qui vive*, his right rested on a fort and his left on the Kabul river; his force numbered six thousand. Dennie was ordered to attack a small fort some hundred yards to the right, which was strongly occupied.

Action at Jalalabad.

---

[1] It was Clive who said "a Council of War never fights;" and he related that the only occasion on which he called such a council was prior to the battle of Plassey, when, however, he did not abide by their decision.

The attack penetrated the outer wall, but found itself exposed to a heavy fire from the keep. Here the gallant Dennie received his death wound. While the force was thus divided the Afghan Horse came down upon Havelock's small column of less than four hundred men, and Sale recalled the 13th at his suggestion. A general attack was now made upon the Sardar's camp with an impetuosity worthy of the garrison. The action is thus described by the General:—" The artillery advanced at the gallop, and directed a heavy fire upon the Afghan centre, whilst two of the columns of infantry penetrated the line near the same point, and the third forced back its left from its support on the river, into the stream of which some of his horse and foot were driven. The Afghans made repeated attempts to check our advance by a smart fire of musketry, by throwing forward heavy bodies of horse, which twice threatened the detachments of foot under Captain Havelock, and by opening upon us three guns from a battery screened by a garden wall, and said to have been served under the personal superintendence of the Sardar. But in a short time they were dislodged from every point in their position, their cannon taken, and their camp involved in a general conflagration. The battle was over; and the enemy in full retreat in the direction of Lughman by about 7 A.M. We have made ourselves masters of two cavalry standards, re-captured four guns lost by the Kabul and Gandamak forces, the restoration of which, to our Government, is matter of much honest exultation among our troops; seized and destroyed a great quantity of material and ordnance stores, and burnt the whole of the enemy's tents. In short, the defeat of Muhammad Akbar in open field, by the troops whom he had boasted of blockading, has been complete and signal." The loss on the British side was ten killed and three officers and about fifty men wounded.

The news of the victories of Sale and Pollock were received with joy throughout India. Lord Ellenborough wrote in enthusiastic terms; and in a proclamation issued at Benares dubbed the former's force " The illustrious Garrison." Sale now ceased to command at Jalalabad, and Macgregor no longer exercised political functions. In Pollock and Nott had been invested the supreme authority. Macgregor became aide-de-camp to the former, and Shakespear was his Military Secretary; and their Chief turned

the experience of both to account. Lord Ellenborough, however, had ordained that there should be no more " Politicals." The Governor-General did well in trusting Pollock and Nott; but there was something to be said upon the other side also. These officers had ever a difficult task to perform; and, although Nott was very bitter on the subject, the services of Pottinger, Macgregor, H. Lawrence, Mackeson, Broadfoot, Outram and others cannot be lost sight of.

CHAPTER XIX.
KANDAHAR.

The last days of Shah Shuja.

THE rumour had spread throughout India that the Kabul insurrection was directed against the English and the King, but, since the departure of the former, the King had been regarded as the supreme authority. His power was, however, merely nominal. The chiefs recognized in him a suitable puppet to act as a buffer between them and the vengeance of the British nation. Coins were struck in the name of Nawab Ziman Khan who, however, cheerfully reverted to the position of Wazir. There was, in spite of outward show, no real union between the King and the chiefs. He and the Barakzais were mutually distrustful of each other. Aminullah Khan held the balance between them, and was, in everything but name, the true ruling power. Funds were, as ever, the great difficulty; and no one would move without pay, which was not forthcoming; so Akbar Khan looked in vain for reinforcements. All parties were jealous of each other and of the Sardar's rising star. The elder chiefs spoke of raising an army to obstruct the march of the relieving force through the Khaibar; but the want of money prevented the execution of the design. The Shah, while speaking of embarking on a *jihad* himself, assured the British authorities that he was heart and soul with them; and clamoured for money.

In the meantime Muhammad Ziman Khan treated the British prisoners with the greatest kindness and consideration. Ever faithful, he resolved to defend them at all risks, and never wavered for an instant. There was no one more patriotic; but he never entertained hatred for the British, nor would he stain his name with the foul crimes which were so prevalent elsewhere. He abhorred the actions of his fellow-countrymen, and did all he could to atone for their cruelty. No father could have been kinder to his own children

The British prisoners.

than he to his captives. There was need, however, for more than mere kindness, at a time when feeling ran so high. He raised an army of his own for their protection, and spent his money freely with that object. He raised 1,000 footmen armed with English bayonets, a thousand horse, and as many *Jazailchis*. He refused, moreover, to yield up the English guns to the Shah.

The King mistrusted him, and there was no love lost between them. At last the Shah bribed his followers to desert, and they went over to the Bala Hissar. This event threw Kabul into a ferment; the shops were closed and the people began to arm. The Nawab demanded the restoration of his troops; but the King only yielded a conditional assent; the terms being the rendition of the prisoners. The Nawab refused, and the hostages nearly forfeited their lives. Conolly's suspicions as to the fidelity of Shah Shuja were now strengthened.

It now appeared as if Kabul was to become the scene of internecine strife. The Shah never ventured beyond the Bala Hissar. The chiefs were all mustering retainers, and the Nawab and the King were casting aspersions upon one another. The Popalzai leaders clustered round the monarch; but he was neither popular nor powerful. He had money, but held it close, and his parsimony was abused. He called upon the British to supply him with funds to further their cause; but they turned a deaf ear.

His days were, however, numbered; the excitement in Kabul was increasing, and the enmity of the chiefs grew more bitter. His inconsistency estranged both the English and his own countrymen; and by either road he was rushing upon his destruction. The chiefs at length called upon him to lead them to Jalalabad, and he yielded a reluctant consent, and advertised his departure for the 31st of March. Dissension and want of money, however, postponed the undertaking. Akbar Khan in vain called for re-inforcements, and inveighed against the dissensions which prevented them from making common cause against the English.

After a few days the King again consented to set out, but his suspicion of the Barakzais, which was not without foundation, was not easily allayed. Impartial critics prophesied his death at their hands. The

Death of Shah Shuja.

Nawab sent his wife to assure him by an oath on the Koran of their fidelity; and, fortified by this assurance, he moved out of the Bala Hissar on the 4th of April, only to return before nightfall. On the 5th he proceeded towards his camp on the Siah-Sang, accompanied by a small party of Hindustanis. But the Nawab's son had laid an ambush for him; and on their way the party was fired upon and the King killed, and his body was stripped and thrown into a ditch. The news quickly spread, and caused great consternation. The King's second son, Fateh Jang, fled to the Bala Hissar, but found the gates closed against him. He was, however, restored to the palace by Muhammad Khan, who held the Bala Hissar with Aminullah, and proclaimed King. The old Nawab viewed the murder with horror and swore never to see his son again.

The fidelity, or otherwise, of the Shah will ever be shrouded in obscurity. He defended himself against the aspersions cast upon him in a series of letters to the British authorities; but in the circumstances they failed to carry conviction. His main object appears to have been to extract money, without which he professed himself powerless. Over twenty lakhs were, however, found in his possession after his death.

Shah Shuja.

An atmosphere of doubt and suspicion must always have surrounded him. A forged and inflammatory document, which was used by the chiefs in his name, was proved not to be genuine, and it is unlikely he would have allowed such evidence of his guilt to become available. He would undoubtedly have rejoiced to be freed from the English alliance, and possibly, therefore, viewed the progress of events with satisfaction; but he was not proved to have taken an active part in them. It was his policy to run with the hare and hunt with the hounds; he knew, however, that his political existence depended upon the will of the British Government; but he was wholly unprepared for the defeat of his allies. Mackeson was of opinion that he engineered the Kabul insurrection; Macgregor in the main agreed with him. Rawlinson thought that he was well-inclined to us. Mackenzie credited Shah Shuja with friendliness for Macnaghten and an equal amount of hatred for Burnes, and considered that, although he was aware of the plot in the first instance, he subsequently exerted his influence

to subdue the insurrection. Conolly, who was probably in the best position to judge, at first thought that the Shah was favourable to us; but gradually his faith was shaken and he eventually formed the belief that he was implicated in the insurrection. As the Afghan proverb has it, he was like grain between two millstones.

To sum up, it is fairly evident that Shah Shuja was faithful neither to his allies nor to his own countrymen. He was a poor creature, with few good qualities, placed in a very difficult position. He soon tired of being a puppet, and longed to be a King; or to return to his peaceful captivity at Ludhiana. All men suspected and none loved him. Shah Shuja was not a hero, nor did he play a heroic part. He was picked up from the dust of Ludhiana for the convenience of the British Government, and it is not surprising, perhaps, that he considered his own convenience as well as theirs. He could hardly be expected to develop all at once from a figure-head into a powerful reigning monarch.

Affairs at Kandahar. The troops at Kandahar consisted of Her Majesty's 40th Regiment; the 2nd, 16th, 38th, 42nd and 43rd Bengal Native Infantry; Captain Blood's battery of Bombay Artillery; the Shah's Horse Artillery, under Captain Anderson; some regiments of the Shah's infantry; and detachments of the Shah's and Skinner's Horse. The country appeared tranquil; and, to diminish the strength of the brigade, the 16th, 42nd, and 43rd Regiments commenced their return march to India on the 7th of November; but that evening startling news reached Kandahar.

Massacre at Saiyidabad. A detachment of 130 men, under Captain Woodburn, was proceeding from Kandahar to Kabul when they were attacked near Ghazni by a party of Afghans. Woodburn fought his way to the fort of Saiyidabad, occupied by a man of the postal department, supposed to be friendly. But the fort, which he defended for a day and a night, gave no protection; ammunition fell short, and tidings came of the Kabul insurrection. The Chief now admitted parties of Afghans into the towers of his harem, which overlooked the courtyard in which the sepoys were quartered, and a massacre took place. Many were killed on the spot; others threw themselves over the walls and were cut up. Woodburn

with a few men defended himself in a tower for several hours; but the enemy burnt them out and killed them almost to a man.

Maclaren's Brigade. Rawlinson at once recommended the halt of Maclaren's brigade, and it returned to Kandahar. A week passed in doubt and anxiety. Letters came from Macnaghten and Elphinstone, reporting the insurrection and calling for Maclaren's brigade. Endorsements by Palmer at Ghazni and by Leech at Kalat-i-Ghilzai gave warning of the coming storm. On the 17th of November the three regiments, with a troop of Horse Artillery, commenced their march northward. Rawlinson, fearing that some evil might arise from the presence of Safdar Jang, persuaded him to follow Maclaren's brigade with Captain Hart's *Janbaz* regiment. Rawlinson was glad to be quit of both parties, whose fidelity he doubted.

During November Kandahar remained tranquil; but it was obvious that the tide of insurrection was setting towards the west. The road to the capital was infested by the insurgents. Crawford had been attacked near Ghazni, and lost the Durani prisoners whom he was escorting to Kabul, together with a number of his horses and men.

On the 8th of December Maclaren's force returned to Kandahar; the reasons for this retrograde movement are not clear, for it appears that the force might have reached Kabul. The relief of Ghazni alone would have been a gain. Nott never wished them, however, to leave Kandahar; and possibly Maclaren, knowing this, took the first excusable opportunity to return. Had the real state of affairs at Kabul been understood, there is little doubt, but that the effort to reach that place would have been a more determined one.

Disquiet soon manifested itself at Kandahar. Muhammad Attar Khan had been sent from Kabul expressly to foment it. Major Rawlinson soon perceived the necessity of suppressing the disorder; at first by the exercise of tact.

Concentration at Kandahar. With this object he withdrew all detachments and concentrated them at Kandahar, leaving only a small party of *Janbaz* at Tezin. He next exerted himself to cause a Durani movement in our favour, binding the chiefs by a sacred bond ratified by the priesthood. The chiefs were sent to the eastern

frontier to raise the tribes against the Barakzais and Ghilzais, while the British remained at Kandahar as spectators, hoping that the contest would resolve itself into a trial of strength between the Sadozais and Barakzais. Rawlinson's objects were, however, only partially attained, although he succeeded in gaining time. When the Dr..nis heard that Shah Shuja was also our enemy, they .,nged their tune, and fell away from us, though they d not at once profess open hostility. The new year came in with a crowd of fresh embarrassments. Safdar Jang had returned to Kandahar, declaring that he could not trust the *Janbaz*. The latter, who accompanied him, soon threw off all disguise and openly sided against us. They were to have com-

Mutiny of *Janbaz*.

menced their march to Girishk on the 27th of December; 400 in all under Lieutenants Golding and Wilson with Lieutenant Pattinson in political charge. The object of the move was to escort treasure, and, at the same time, to rid Kandahar of their presence. Owing to unforeseen difficulties the march was postponed, to the surprise of the men, who had intended to mutiny and desert when on the march. They now decided to do so at once; and proceeding to their officers' tents attacked them, and when they thought they had accomplished their purpose mounted their horses and fled, Pattinson was only stunned and, though wounded in seven places, mounted a horse and escaped, only to die in the following March. Golding fled on foot towards the cantonments, but was cut down by the *Janbaz*. A party of the Shah's Horse and a detachment of Wilson's *Janbaz*, who had remained true, sent in pursuit, caught up the fugitives twelve miles from Kandahar, and dispersed them after a hand to hand struggle; thirty of the enemy were killed, more wounded, and the remainder fled to Attar Muhammad's camp. Two days later Safdar Jang fled and joined Attar Muhammad. The Sardar had fixed his head-quarters at Delhi, 40 miles from Kandahar, and Rawlinson was eager to attack him early in January, perceiving the expediency of crushing the insurrection in the bud, as fresh adherents were daily going over to the enemy. Nott, however, was unwilling to divide his force by sending a brigade to Delhi. The former took a political and the latter a military view of the situation. Nott argued

that to detach a brigade, far from support, at such a season of the year, would result in the destruction of his men in the field, and the exposure of the city to attack. He wrote to Rawlinson: " I have no right to interfere with the affairs of the Government of this country, and I never do; but in reference to that part of your note where you speak of political influence, I will candidly tell you that these are not the times for mere ceremony, and that under present circumstances, and at a distance of 2,000 miles from the seat of the Supreme Government, I throw responsibility to the winds, and tell you that, in my opinion, you have not had for some time past, nor have you at present, one particle of political influence in this country."

However, the point in dispute was soon settled; for the enemy quietly moved down the valley of the Arghandab, and on the 12th of January established themselves on the river, five miles west of Kandahar.

General Nott now promptly moved out to attack them. Taking five and a half regiments of infantry, the Shah's 1st Cavalry, a party of Skinner's Horse and sixteen guns, a force weak only in the mounted branch, after a march of four hours over a very difficult country, he came in sight of the rebel army, from fifteen to twenty thousand men, drawn up in a strong position on the banks of the Arghandab. The British troops crossed the river and at once advanced to the attack in column of battalions, flanked by the artillery and cavalry. At the end of twenty minutes, during which our guns and musketry, telling with deadly effect upon the dense masses of the enemy, were answered by a wild and ineffective fire, the rebel army was in full flight. The Ghilzais fled in one direction, the *Janbaz* in another, and the villagers returned to their own homes. Attar Muhammad attempted to make a stand; but our troops moving forward carried the village of Kala-Chak by storm, killing all within the walls. Line was then re-formed; and Attar Muhammad prepared to meet a second attack, but the cavalry charging, the enemy fled in dismay.

Action of the Arghandab.

The Durani Chiefs were not in time to take part in the action, and only arrived to see their countrymen in flight. Safdar Jang, Attar Muhammad, and the other rebel chiefs sought an asylum in

Vol. III.

the Durani camp; and our quondam friends became our open enemies. From the 20th of January until the end of February the Duranis remained encamped in the neighbourhood of Kandahar. The winter was severe, and Nott was unwilling to expose his troops; while the enemy appeared to be equally disinclined for action. During this mutual truce the occupations and feelings of the two forces were very different. Nott's force, conscious of their strength, were neither despondent nor anxious, officers and men fell back into the ordinary routine of cantonment life, and indulged in steeplechases and other amusements. The enemy, however, were in a continued state of restlessness. Mirza Ahmad saw the danger of allowing the Durani Chiefs to dwell too much on the embarrassments of the situation, and kept them both from a premature engagement with the British and from breaking out into internal dissensions. He alone could have played the part so well.

Situation at Kandahar.

However, the garrison was by no means without anxieties. Provisions were scarce, and fodder scarcer. The horses were becoming unserviceable from lack of food; the sheep were so thin as to be hardly worth killing. It was bitterly cold, and fuel was so scanty that even the sick had to do without fires; there were patients in the hospitals, but no medicines. Above all, money was becoming very scarce. The arrival of a convoy from the southward was looked for with an anxiety which can only be imagined.

While the hopes of the garrison were directed towards the south, their thoughts and fears turned to the north. On the 21st of February the order came for the evacuation of Kandahar and Kalat-i-Ghilzai. Rawlinson, while recognizing the genuineness of the document, which was a copy of the original, did not for a moment consider himself bound by it. Still the change in Kabul affairs placed him in a peculiar position. Shah Shuja was now the recognized sovereign; and it could not be said that British troops were any longer necessary. The Durani Chiefs also grasped the situation, and resorted to argument instead of force, to expel the British from Kandahar. A letter was received from the Durani camp on the 23rd of February. In it Safdar Jang and the chiefs

Orders for evacuation.

represented that the British had played their part, and had no longer any excuse for remaining. Two alternatives lay before them; either they could retire unmolested to Quetta or remain to share the fate of the Kabul garrison. Mirza Ahmad, in a private letter, begged Rawlinson to retire before the Durani nation should rise *en masse*. A letter from Shah Shuja to Prince Timur, which arrived at this time, was, perhaps, the most important incident. The purport of it was that the contest had now resolved itself into one between the Prophet's followers and the unbelievers. That he himself had been unanimously recognized as King, and that he wished to be kept informed of all Kandahar proceedings. Timur protested that the document was a forgery, while Rawlinson well knew that it was genuine. He and the General now took counsel as to what reply should be dispatched. Both decided to maintain their position at all risks. Their answer to the Duranis pointed out that there was every reason to believe that Shah Shuja was acting under compulsion, and desired the support of the British, who would not, therefore, retire before a final explanation had been entered upon with him. The position at Kandahar was explained to be by no means on all fours with that at Kabul; that the British had no hankerings after Afghanistan, but could not move until more specific instructions should be received. A postscript was added, stating that later information had been received, which proved that the estimate formed of Shah Shuja's position was a true one, and that an avenging force was on the march from India.

Rawlinson exerted himself successfully to detach different tribes from the rebel cause. In spite, however, of this and other favourable indications, both the military and political Chiefs considered it desirable to strike a blow for the suppression of the insurrection and their own security. So Nott determined to attack the enemy, and Rawlinson to expel the Afghans from the city. The latter justified this, at the first sight, harsh measure in the following passage from his Journal:—" March 1.—The General has now made up his mind to take the field; and, after considering the case fully, I have determined that the Afghans must be turned out of the city. It is not as if the present affair were a mere transient disturbance. We are engaged in a regular national war,

and Outram does not anticipate that we shall be able to take the field in sufficient force to put down all opposition before next winter. We must, therefore, look forward to a protracted struggle at Kandahar all through the summer, and the security of the city appears to me, under such circumstances, indispensable." A letter from the Government of India spoke of the continued occupation of Kandahar as conducive to the interests of the State. Nott and Rawlinson had, therefore, anticipated Government's wishes. A census was made of the inhabitants, and retaining some merchants, mechanics, and priests, the remainder, consisting of about 1,000 families, were expelled without opposition. The property which they were unable to carry with them was safeguarded, and all grain taken over and paid for by the commissariat.

Action near Kandahar.

Nott took the field on the 7th of March with the 40th Queen's, 16th, 38th, 42nd, and 43rd Native Infantry, a wing of one of the Shah's regiments, the whole of the available cavalry and sixteen guns, leaving in the city a garrison of the 2nd Native Infantry and two and a half of the Shah's regiments of foot. Most of the gates were barricaded, and the place was considered secure against any possible assault by the Duranis.

The enemy in the vicinity of Kandahar retired before Nott's advance; and he crossed the Tarnak and advanced upon the Arghandab in pursuit, but they fought shy of the guns and bayonets, their dislike of the former being enhanced by the shells fired into their dense masses. On the 9th, however, the enemy seemed inclined to make a stand, and opened fire from a range of hills, upon which their infantry were posted. The light companies of the Queen's regiment and 16th Native Infantry were sent to storm the hills on the right, and the Grenadiers of the 40th those on the left; and the enemy was soon driven off. The cavalry[1] were now seen drawn up in front of our columns, their right resting upon high ground and their left on a fort built upon a high scarped mound. Hoping to draw them on the guns remained silent; but

---

[1] *Hough, page* 134. The Kandahar horse of the present day is far inferior to that so well known in the history on former Indian warfare; the horses we saw were small and indifferent.

they were planning another game. The enemy retired before the advancing battalion, spreading a report that they intended to make a night attack upon Nott's camp, re-crossed the river, and doubled back upon Kandahar. This stratagem was attributable to Mirza Ahmad. On the morning of the 10th it was seen that a number of footmen had taken possession of old Kandahar, and appeared intent upon an attack on the city. This information was at once transmitted to Nott. The scouts brought news, moreover, that the Durani army was to concentrate before Kandahar during the day, and make a night attack. During the day the enemy increased in numbers; and at sunset Safdar Jang and Mirza Ahmad arrived and posted themselves in the cantonments. The night was dark and the garrison could not trace the movements of the enemy; there were no blue lights, or other means of illuminating the ground beyond the defences. At 8 o'clock the Ghazis commenced the attack, setting fire to faggots, which they had previously deposited at the Herat gate, which burned like tinder, and showed up the crowd of Afghans. The resistance was as steady as the attack was desperate. A gun poured grape and the guard kept up a heavy fire upon the besiegers. The Ghazis, however, encouraged by the success of their first move, pressed on with desperate resolution, tearing down the burning planks with their hands and, intoxicated with *bhang*, rushing upon their death. Major Lane, who commanded the garrison, and who was ably seconded by Rawlinson, brought the gun down from the bastion, and planted it in the gateway, another was brought from the citadel, and the infantry was reinforced at the point of assault, while the *bhisties* were engaged in extinguishing the flames, and commissariat grain bags were piled against the burning gate. At nine o'clock the gate fell and the Ghazis surmounted the grain bags, many falling dead or wounded beneath the fire of the defenders. During three hours the Ghazis made assault after assault, but at midnight drew off in despair of effecting an entrance. Simultaneously attacks were made upon the Shikarpur and Kabul gates, but the brushwood would not ignite, and the garrison were on the alert. When the attacks had failed Mirza Ahmad called a council of war. The attackers, irritated beyond measure at their failure, laid the blame at his door; and were with difficulty restrained from

laying violent hands on him. The Ghazis are said to have lost 600 during the four hours' fighting, and were busy until daybreak in carrying off their dead. Had Kandahar fallen the consequences might have proved serious ; for the force in the field had no tents and little ammunition, and it would have proved no easy matter to recapture the city. The General was obviously outmanœuvred ; but he fully believed the garrison he had left sufficient for the defence. He appears, however, to have been very badly supplied with information.

Nott re-entered Kandahar on the 12th of March. The repulse had given a decided set-back to the rebel plans, brought disunion in its train, and caused the Ghazis to denounce their chiefs. The *rayats* resumed their peaceful avocations, and Rawlinson exerted himself to reassure the public mind, and to restore the peace and prosperity of the surrounding villages.

The Duranis, however, soon recovered and by the third week in March were on the move. On the 24th they were near Kala-Chak, where they had met with their former reverse, and the Parsiwan *Janbaz* attempted to open negotiations, agreeing to go to Kabul if the expense of their march should be defrayed. Nott told Rawlinson he would not only not give them a rupee, but would exterminate them if he could come up with them.

On the 25th Colonel Wymer was sent out with three regiments of infantry, a troop of Horse Artillery, and 400 mounted men to clear the country on the Kandahar side of the Arghandab of the Durani Horse which were then threatening our position, and to protect the animals sent out to graze. The Duranis advanced to the attack which Wymer prepared to meet, at the same time informing the General of his situation. The Hindustani Cavalry were driven back by the Duranis who bravely charged our squares. The guns and musketry, however, soon checked them and the affair resolved itself into a series of skirmishes. Nott, in the meantime, hearing the firing, moved out in support. He found our infantry formed in a hollow square protecting the camels ; the Horse Artillery were playing upon the enemy's cavalry, which was thus kept at a distance. Under cover of this fire Lieutenant Chamberlain, at the head of a small party, charged them, but was driven back, and re-formed behind the infantry. As

the reinforcements approached, the enemy retired, unmolested owing to the paucity of our cavalry. Nott wished to attack the Durani camp, which had been left standing, but it was difficult to move the guns down to the banks of the river, which was practically unfordable. Leaving Wymer in position, he, therefore, withdrew to Kandahar.

On the 26th Nott again moved out with his brigade, but the enemy had struck their camp during the night, and the Durani Horse moved off and dispersed as soon as day broke. The General, therefore, withdrew, Wymer remained out to protect the cattle, and Rawlinson stayed in the valley, attempting to restore the confidence of the villagers, who were loud in their complaints of the depredations of the Ghazis.

The disunion in the Durani camp broke out anew; each chief abused the others, and all Mirza Ahmad. Reassuring tidings began to come to them from north and south, and the news of the capitulation of Ghazni served to re-animate them. It had held out for some weeks in the face of an overwhelming force, but had fallen before the receipt of orders for its evacuation from Kabul.

The fortress, captured with so much difficulty, was now in the hands of the enemy, who had appeared before it on the 20th of November; on which day snow began to fall. Hearing of the advance of Maclaren, the investing force drew off, but soon re-assembled. The garrison was now completely surrounded. The city, indeed, was in their possession; but they could not stir beyond it. The inhabitants undermined the walls and admitted the enemy. The city was no longer tenable, and the garrison withdrew to the citadel. Winter set in and the sepoys, kept on the *qui vive*, sank beneath the paralysing cold. Men bred on the plains of India were obliged to break the ice before they could allay their thirst. Only a *seer* of wood was available for each man to cook his meal and obtain warmth. All were on half rations of an extremely poor quality, and numbers were taken to hospital severely frost-bitten. The Afghans fired when any showed their heads, and this state of affairs continued until the middle of January. Then the news from Kabul caused some suspension of hostilities. It was under-

stood that a treaty had been effected, and that Shamshuddin Khan would shortly arrive as Governor. About the middle of February he came and summoned Palmer to surrender. The English officer, unwilling to submit to this demand, and yet hopeless of being able to make an effective resistance, temporised until the beginning of March. At last the patience of the chiefs was exhausted, and they threatened a resumption of hostilities, if the citadel were not instantly surrendered. On the 6th of March Palmer, under the promise of a safe conduct to Peshawar, marched out with his men. The British troops had hardly taken up the quarters assigned to them when the Afghan Chiefs threw off the mask. The next day when the troops were at their meal the Ghazis rushed with fury upon the lines. Three terrible days followed. House after house was attacked by the infuriated enemy, and fire, famine, and slaughter worked together for the destruction of the unhappy men. At last only two houses, crowded to suffocation, remained. The guns of the citadel, which none of the garrison had been able to work, sent shells crashing through the walls; and the Afghans only seemed to defer the final massacre to accentuate the misery of the sufferers. Shamshuddin Khan had, however, begun to relent, and was prepared to admit his victims to terms. The remnants of the garrison eventually surrendered on a promise of a safe conduct to Kabul. The sepoys, who had resolved to take their way to Peshawar at all costs, wandered about the fields, helpless and bewildered. Many were cut down or made prisoners, and a season of intense suffering now commenced for all the survivors alike.

John Nicholson was at Ghazni when the enemy entered, and drove them thrice beyond the walls at the point of the bayonet before he would comply with the order that his company should lay down their arms. He at length obeyed and gave up his sword with tears, to accompany his comrades to an almost hopeless imprisonment.

CHAPTER XX.

POLLOCK'S ADVANCE.

MEANWHILE Kalat-i-Ghilzai was bravely holding out. The fortress stands upon a barren eminence, some eighty miles from Kandahar, and is one of the most dreary and exposed spots in Afghanistan. The garrison consisted of the Shah's 3rd Infantry Regiment, 40 European Artillerymen, some Sappers and Miners, and 250 of the 43rd Regiment, under the command of Captain J. H. Craigie, of the Shah's service. For months the cold was a worse foe than the enemy. The barracks were unfinished, and had neither doors nor windows; and fuel was scarce. There was plenty of grain, but it could not be ground owing to the hostility of the surrounding country, and it was two months before serviceable hand-mills were constructed. The Europeans often lived for days upon bread and water, but there was no grumbling. During the winter the enemy were inactive; but with the spring came the renewal of hostilities. The garrison employed themselves in strengthening the defences while the enemy, ever growing more numerous, drew the cordon closer. By degrees they made trenches, to the fire from which the defenders could not give an effective reply. Craigie and his men never thought of surrender, and thankfully took their few opportunities of getting in a shot.[1]

The question of withdrawal from Kandahar.

At this time news reached Nott of the failure of General England to get through from Quetta with the much needed supplies, and of the unfortunate action of Haikalzai. (Part I of this volume.)

Failure of England's column.

Brigadier England reached Quetta on the 16th of March. The next day he wrote to Lieutenant Hammersley, Political Agent at that place, proposing to move to Haikalzai on the 24th, and there to await

England's column.

---

[1] The sword, in my opinion, is not the weapon for a trooper in Asia; had our men been armed with lances, they would have killed many more and suffered less.—*Stacy, page* 152.

intelligence from the north of the Khojak Pass. On the following day he wrote to say that he intended to halt in the Pishin Valley unless Nott's regiments had arrived at the Khojak. There were not wanting those who prophesied disaster between Quetta and the Khojak.

On the 26th of March the Brigadier moved on the Pishin Valley, with five companies of Her Majesty's 41st Regiment, six companies Bombay Native Infantry, a troop, 3rd Bombay Cavalry, fifty Poona Horse, and four Horse Artillery guns. On the 28th the force arrived at the entrance of a defile which leads to the village of Haikalzai, where England intended to await the arrival of the remainder of the brigade. It was evident that no reinforcements were to be expected from Nott, although Rewlinson had strongly advocated their despatch. Wymer's brigade was out to the south of Kandahar, it was believed with the object of holding out a helping hand to England's column; however, it was withdrawn, and the enemy interpreted this move as a confession that the opening up of communications with the troops below was hopeless. It would have been well had England, in these circumstances, awaited the arrival of reinforcements from the south; for he now found himself in an absolutely strange country without any idea as to the movements of the enemy. Colonel Stacy, who was in political charge, had warned the General that he might expect to meet with opposition at Haikalzai; but it was not until England was close upon them that he became aware of the enemy's presence. Muhammad Sadiq had determined to oppose our advance and had posted his troops behind *sangars* on the heights.

The British force halted and England rode forward to reconnoitre. In about a quarter of an hour the order was given to advance. The Horse Artillery opened fire on the hills to the left, and the light battalion, under Major Apthorp, was ordered to storm those on the right. The battery performed its part admirably, but the infantry were disastrously repulsed. Major Apthorp was wounded, Captain May, of the 41st shot, and nearly twenty-five per cent. of the force were either killed or wounded. The enemy fought with much gallantry, and many were shot, or bayoneted on the hill.

In spite of their failure the men soon rallied and asked to be again led forward. Stacy volunteered to carry the position with 100 men, and three times repeated the offer, but the General had fully made up his mind to retreat, believing that at least a brigade with mortars was requisite to carry the heights. He sent to Nott for reinforcements, and fell back to Quetta.

It would appear that England believed the defences to be stronger than the facts warranted. Lieutenant Evans, of the 41st, who had seen them, reported that there were no breastworks, but merely a four-foot ditch filled with brushwood. The strength of the enemy also appears to have been overestimated. The General reported that they were one hundred times as numerous as had been expected; while in effect there were little more than one thousand all told.

The Duranis were dispirited by their want of success in the neighbourhood of Kandahar, and were only too pleased to accede to Muhammad Sadiq's request for help, seeing an opportunity for revenging themselves for their defeats. However, there was no need for their assistance, as England had been driven back before they arrived. It was as well that they were not needed for, Afghan-like, they fell out by the way, and only a small portion of their force continued the march.

England, in contrast to Nott, seems to have had little faith in the value of his native troops. Anent this Outram writes: "If he is ever heard to libel our sepoys in that manner, surely it will be noticed by our officers." It would appear that England should either have waited for reinforcements at Quetta, considering his known views of the insufficiency of his force, or have made strenuous efforts to force the pass; half measures were worse than useless.

Nott was more than annoyed at this failure, and still more disgusted that England declined to redeem it by a strong forward movement. He was crying out for cavalry, ammunition, stores, medicines, and money, and they seemed as far off as ever. Had he had these, especially the former, he would already have been on his way to Kabul. So far from England dreaming of putting his force again in motion he wrote to Nott that "whenever it so happens that you retire bodily in this direction, and

that I am informed of it, I feel assured that I shall be able to make an advantageous diversion in your favour."

This was too much for the fiery Nott, who at once wrote a letter, saying that he had well considered England's position, that he knew the country well, and that he was determined to uphold English honour; and finally that he must have the supplies from Quetta. He concluded:—"I am well aware that war cannot be made without loss; but yet, perhaps, the British troops can oppose Asiatic armies without defeat."

There was no resisting this appeal and England's brigade now prepared to move. This decision took the troops by surprise, no forward move having entered into the calculations of the garrison; indeed the officers had been buying houses and settling down to the routine of cantonment life.

Exactly one month after his previous failure England was again before Haikalzai. The enemy were posted on precisely the same ground as before, and probably expected an equally easy success: but this was not to be. The British troops were told off into three parties, one, under Major Simmons, to storm the hills to the left; another, under Captain Woodburn to attack the hill on the right, the scene of the former disaster; and a third, under Major Browne, in reserve. As before, Leslie's guns opened the fight; then the infantry advanced with loud cheers. There was no mistaking who were to be the winners this time; the enemy broke and fled, pursued by Delamain's Cavalry, and Haikalzai was captured.

Co-operation of Wymer. On the morning of the 30th the column entered the Khojak, and, in spite of Colonel Stacy's representations that all the laurels would fall to the Kandahar troops, who were entering from the other side, General England halted them. Wymer meanwhile crowned the heights and opened the way for the Bombay Force.

The united Brigades entered the city on the 10th of May, to find that the enemy had broken up and dispersed. The Durani Chiefs, although disunited, were not inactive; but their objects were hard to determine. Spring heralded a more cheerful state of affairs than had existed since the outbreak of the insurrection. The chiefs were scattered, some wounded and dying, others eager to come to terms. Mirza Ahmad and Safdar Jang contemplated a withdrawal across

the frontier, and the latter communicated to the British Agent his desire to return to our camp. The Kabul *Janbaz* had deserted, and the village headmen offered to follow suit, on a guarantee of immunity from depredation by our troops. The relief of Jalalabad by Pollock, and his determination to march upon Kabul, was the signal for a royal salute; and as the English barometer rose that of the Afghans correspondingly fell.

With Mirza Ahmad and Attar Muhammad still restless, there was no prospect of permanent peace. The former was raising money in the name of the Government, and employing it for carrying on the war. Nott, therefore, proposed the issue of a proclamation warning the people not to pay the taxes; but he went beyond this, and wished that a reward should be offered for the apprehension of the two chieftains. A lengthy argument as to the propriety of the latter measure ensued between Rawlinson and Nott; and in the end the former prevailed. The ex-chief of Kandahar, Kohan-dil Khan, who had all this time been quietly living in Persia, now began to intrigue for the recovery of his lost dominions. The anxiety thus caused was, however, short-lived, as the Persian Government was understood to have agreed to restrain him from crossing the frontier. Now, however, the heaviest blow of all, from the supreme Government itself, was to fall.

Pollock and Nott were both eager to advance. Their position was favourable for the maintenance of a bold front, and to overawe the surrounding country. The public placed complete confidence in the two Generals and their forces were in high spirits. Everybody looked forward to a speedy re-establishment of the national honour. The Governor-General, however, viewed matters in a different light. Lord Ellenborough landed at Calcutta on the 28th of February, with the situation at his fingers' ends, and was only ignorant of his predecessor's plans for the extrication of Indian affairs from their state of entanglement. The reader will remember that those plans were dictated by the policy of withdrawal. Everyone was waiting to see whether the new Governor-General would approve of these measures.

<small>Government policy.</small>

His first document of importance was a letter to the Commander-in-Chief, which contained an able review of the position.

He recognised that we owed nothing further to Shah Shuja, and that purely military considerations would dictate our future policy. Of first importance was the security of the troops and the last act should be a blow at the Afghans, which would prove that the British nation was not weak and pusillanimous as they supposed; but fully capable of exacting retribution for Afghan treachery and Afghan barbarity. This was the policy of Clerk and Robertson, of Pollock and Nott; and the policy which the public of British India was prepared to back. Lord Ellenborough's opinion, however, soon underwent a change. During his journey to Benares he heard of England's defeat at Haikalzai, and he was now all for evacuation.

Sir Jasper Nicolls was only too glad to comply with the order to withdraw; and informed Pollock that only three conditions would permit him to delay : 1stly, that the safety of the captives should not be endangered ; 2ndly, that a lightly equipped force should be sent for their rescue ; 3rdly, that should the Afghans attempt an attack, which appeared improbable, he might strike such a blow as to cause them to remember him.

At the end of April the Chief Secretary wrote that should Pollock have advanced upon Kabul, he was not to understand that Government's view had changed as regards the withdrawal. The General replied in the following terms:—He opines that his instructions leave him a measure of discretion in the matter of a short delay, which has been caused by a paucity of cattle; that the state of affairs at Kabul is such that a precipitate retreat would compromise our reputation; that a retirement, before the release of the captives had been accomplished, would be construed as a panic; that the season is unfavourable for a retreat; and that the health of his troops need cause no anxiety; he regrets that Nott should have been ordered to retire, as a combined advance upon Kabul would meet with undoubted success. In the meantime he will procure cattle if possible to carry out his orders; whether they be for a forward or retrograde movement.

By this time the announcement of the Governor-General's intention to withdraw the troops had reached Kandahar, Nott had his own opinion as to the wisdom of this measure, but placed obedience, to orders above all other considerations, and expressed his

readiness to comply with his instructions. The following extract from Rawlinson's correspondence will, however, show that it was gall and wormwood to all concerned: "The peremptory order to retire has come upon us like a thunder-clap. No one at Kandahar is aware of such an order having been received, except the General and myself, and we must preserve a profound secrecy as long as possible. The withdrawal of the garrison from Kalat-i-Ghilzai and the destruction of the fortifications at that place must, I fancy, however, expose our policy and our situation will then be one of considerable embarrassment.

Rawlinson's views.

General Nott intends, I believe, to order all the carriage at Quetta to be sent on to Kandahar. * * * *
It must be our object to collect carriage, on the pretext of an advance on Kabul; but how long the secret can be kept it is impossible to say. When our intended retirement is once known, we must expect to have the whole country up in arms, and to obtain no cattle except such as we can violently lay hands on. * * * * * *
Should the Barakzais triumph at Kabul, and should we no longer oppose the return of Kohan-dil, he will be the most likely chief to succeed; but the natural consequence of his return, and of our determined non-interference with the affairs in this quarter, will be of course to render Persian influence paramount at Herat and Kandahar; and with the prospect of a Russian fleet at Astarabad, and a Persian army at Merv it is by no means impossible that the designs which threatened us in 1838 may at last be directly accomplished. Strong measures of intimidation, both against Russia and Persia, will be our best protection."

A brigade, consisting of the 2nd, 16th, and 38th Native Infantry, under Colonel Wymer, was sent off on the 19th of May to withdraw the garrison and destroy the defences of Kalat-i-Ghilzai. With them went Her Majesty's 40th Regiment, Leslie's troop of Horse Artillery, four guns of Blood's battery, the Bombay Cavalry details, and the Shah's 1st Regiment of Horse, together with a few of Haldane's troopers, some details of Bengal Artillery, and Madras Sappers.

Thus at the end of May Pollock was holding on at Jalalabad, hoping for orders to march on Kabul, and rejoicing that want of transport presented him with an excuse for not immediately withdrawing.

Pollock at Jalalabad.

Nott, much against his will, was preparing to obey the Governor-General's injunctions, while the latter was exhorting them both to keep his intentions secret—no easy matter when copies of official correspondence were supplied to many individuals in different places. The plans for the future were soon the subject of common gossip; and bets were actually made as to the probable date of withdrawal. Pollock did his best to mystify, and went the length of having a camp marked out in the Kabul direction, while he instituted enquiries about supplies for a forward movement. On the 1st of June the Governor-General intimated that since circumstances pointed to the impossibility of the troops being withdrawn before October, it would be as well to lure the enemy into a situation in which an effective blow might be struck.

This was a pleasant surprise to Pollock. He had, in accordance with his instructions, collected a considerable amount of carriage, which would be available for a movement on Kabul; and eagerly looked forward to the autumn to provide the opportunity. Meanwhile he occupied his leisure in doing his best for the relief of the captives. Akbar Khan endeavoured to obtain good terms for himself; but Pollock wrote to Government that his peculiar position disqualified him from being placed upon the same footing as other chiefs, and received the following reply: "It is not consistent with the honour of the British Government to enter into any terms for the making of a provision for so great a criminal. We might engage to spare his life if he were to fall into our hands, because it would be difficult so to bring him to trial as to protect the Government from a colourable charge of violently prosecuting an unworthy revenge; but no more than this can be done, and this only, if he should promptly do all he can to repair the crimes he has committed." The negotiations had no result, but Mackenzie, who acted as intermediary, was the bearer of much valuable information, and gave Pollock many important documents. The General had wished for information as to the causes and progress of the insurrection at Kabul; and obtained much which threw light on the dark points of recent history.

A Civil War broke out at Kabul on the death of Shah Shuja.

<small>Affairs at Kabul.</small> Fateh Jang, his second son, was proclaimed King. He was of infamous character, and

rather deficient in intellect; but was reputed to be friendly to the English, and was hated and feared by the Barakzais. Aminullah Khan, however, knowing where the treasure lay, sided with the Prince; and by his influence balanced affairs. Fateh Jang had no love for his position, but was astute enough to see which way the wind blew, and anticipated the speedy re-establishment of British supremacy. He, therefore, wrote to Macgregor at Jalalabad protesting his loyalty to the English, and begging for advice.

The Barakzais proclaimed Ziman Khan King, and defied the Sadozai power; and soon the two parties broke out into open hostilities. Aminullah Khan was the first to draw the sword, and on the 1st of May general fighting began in the city. The following day, to dishearten the Barakzais, Aminullah Khan seized the chief Mullah. The effect, however, of this was the opposite of what he had expected. Nearly all the neutrals, joined by the Kohistanis, rose to avenge the insult. The Mullah was released, but popular feeling still ran high; Aminullah Khan's house was burnt, and he threw himself into the Bala Hissar. The Prince made a show of welcoming him; but secretly proposed to hand him over to the British if Pollock should march upon Kabul.

The contest now increased in violence; the guns in the Bala Hissar opened upon the city; and many of the inhabitants fled. There were 5,000 men in the citadel, amply provisioned. The Prince had plenty of money, which he distributed freely among his followers; while the Barakzais were very badly off in this respect.

Akbar Khan did not regard these proceedings at the capital with unconcern. He only awaited the return of his mission from Jalalabad to proceed to the scene of strife himself; and on the 3rd of May, taking Pottinger and Troop with him, he set out.

Arrived there he encouraged the belief that he had been in

Akbar Khan captures the Bala Hissar.

treaty with General Pollock, who, it was rumoured, recognized his authority; thus enhancing his own importance, and creating division among the followers of Fateh Jang. Many of the neutrals joined him, and the Kizilbashis promised him their support. There was a good deal of fighting which favoured the Barakzais. The works round the Bala Hissar were soon carried, partly by

treachery; but Pottinger stated that the fighting was beneath contempt. Fateh Jang, fearful that the Bala Hissar would fall, wrote to Jalalabad urging the necessity of a speedy advance, and Mohan Lal seconded his efforts, representing that the Barakzai position would be much strengthened should they obtain the treasure, which would fall into their hands if they captured the citadel.

On the 12th of May three holy men presented themselves with overtures of peace from the Sardar. Fateh Jang sent for several Korans, covered with seals, and asked if they thought that after the experience which these books attested he could be expected to rely upon Afghan oaths. The Saiyids were dismissed, after a fruitless visit, and now Muhammad Shah Khan was sent to try his fortune. The proposals he had to make were that Fateh Jang should be acknowledged as King and Akbar Khan be appointed State Minister, with Aminullah Khan as his deputy. The two latter were then to raise an army and march against the English, but the King was to accompany them. A war with the Barakzais was to follow; and the King was to be free to go where he liked, taking his father's family with him. With this alluring prospect before him he was the more anxious for the British advance. Nevertheless in the circumstances of the case he felt bound to accede to the demands. Muhammad Ziman Khan was not at all pleased that these arrangements should have been made without consulting him.

The Nawab now attacked the Bala Hissar, but was repulsed with heavy loss. The Barakzais resumed the siege with renewed vigour, believing that it was only held for the English; but the weak garrison successfully held out. An attempt was made to mine the walls, but the art of engineering was not a strong point with the Barakzais; and the explosion caused considerable loss to the besiegers and had no effect upon the fortifications.

Next day, however, heavy guns were brought into action against the citadel, and the defenders lost heart. The garrison deserted the Prince who had no alternative but to surrender the fortress. Akbar Khan pronounced himself to be the servant of the Sadozais, simulated extreme humility, and attempted to patch up his quarrel with Muhammad Ziman Khan. But the difficulties only increased. The Nawab declared that he was King, that Akbar

Khan was at liberty to be Commander-in-Chief, but that the office of Wazir was reserved for Usman Khan. The Sardar was now gaining over the Kohistanis to his side, in view of the coming conflict. The Kizilbashis, on the other hand, proclaimed their intention of joining the British. The Nawab, seeing that all hope of reconciliation was past, prayed for the speedy advance of the British; so that he and Akbar Khan might fly before the dreaded civil war should break out.

Nor was Akbar behindhand in his efforts to avert strife. On the 21st of June, however, the two factions came into collision. The battle lasted for some hours, and Ziman Khan was defeated. The Prince was enthroned on the 29th of June, but all the power was vested in the Sardar. He longed to get the British captives into his hands, and importuned Mir Haji, in whose charge they were, to send them to the Bala Hissar. The latter was very avaricious, and, for a bribe of four thousand rupees, handed them over, and the Munshi Mohan Lal was seized and tortured.

The summer passed; and still Pollock and Nott were at Jalalabad and Kandahar. No one knew whether the Governor-General intended an advance or a retirement. Public opinion was loud in its demands for the redemption of our honour. Pollock, Nott, Robertson, Clerk, Rawlinson, Outram, Macgregor, Mackeson and others were unanimous for a forward movement and however much Lord Ellenborough might affect to despise public opinion, he was bound to be influenced by the views of such men as these. From England, too, he learned that a retrograde movement would find no favour either with the Government or the people. He accordingly instigated Pollock and Nott to advance as a prelude to retirement. He had maintained that the true policy of Government was to bring back the armies to India, and that the re-establishment of our reputation in Afghanistan was immaterial, but public opinion made it necessary to push further into Afghanistan. To enable both games to be played he wrote letters to Pollock and Nott, stating that, although his opinions had undergone no change, it was possible that Nott might feel disposed to retire from Kandahar *viâ* Ghazni, Kabul, and Jalalabad; and, that to lend him a helping hand, it might be advisable for Pollock to advance to Kabul.

The advance from Jalalabad.

The great obstacle to a retirement or to an advance had been the scarcity of carriage. But during the summer the authorities in Upper India had been making strenuous efforts to procure a supply. Lord Ellenborough had been giving the matter his attention; but more than anyone Mr. Robertson, the Lieutenant-Governor of the North-West Provinces, had been unremitting in his exertions. He does not appear to have obtained full credit for his work, but General Pollock never lost an opportunity of thanking him for his assistance. There was, therefore, before the end of June, a sufficiency of cattle at Pollock's disposal; and he reported that he was in a position to make a demonstration in the neighbourhood of Jalalabad. The Governor-General fell in with the proposal; but warned him that his resolution to withdraw was as strong as ever.

Transport.

On the same date, the 4th of July, two letters were sent to Nott with a copy of Pollock's instructions, giving him a free choice as to his line of withdrawal—Quetta and Sukkur, or the more northerly route, whichever he preferred; he, too, was ever to keep in mind that any movement was preparatory to withdrawal.

Their instructions appeared to throw all responsibility upon the Generals, but they were the very men for the situation; and unlikely to be fettered in their actions by fear.

Pollock expressed his opinions thus:—"If I have not lived long enough to judge of the propriety of an act for which I alone am responsible, the sooner I resign the Command as unfit the better. I assure you that I feel the full benefit of being unshackled and allowed to judge for myself."

The Generals had now obtained all they wanted. They fully trusted their troops, and transport was either available or in course of supply. It was only necessary that their operations should be combined, and that the blow at Kabul should be struck in unison. To establish communication between Jalalabad and Kandahar was no easy matter. Five messengers were despatched at intervals to Nott's camp, but not until the middle of August did Pollock hear of his intention to march upon Kabul. Akbar Khan himself was employed as an unwitting means of communication. Troup took him a letter with a request that it might be

forwarded to Nott. A few unimportant lines were written in ink, and a great deal of important matter in rice-water which could be brought out by the application of iodine. Pollock had feared that Nott might already have commenced his retirement by the southern route; but all doubts were now set at rest.

Meanwhile, at Jalalabad, Pollock had been making demonstrations against some hostile tribes, and negotiating for the release of the British prisoners. He sent Monteith into the Shinwari Valley, the tribes of which had possessed themselves of some of the plundered property and one of our guns. These they were to disgorge, of their own free will, or, failing that, at the point of the bayonet. Monteith descended into the valley in the middle of June, with a mixed European and Indian brigade and a proportion of guns. The troops were all keenness; and the sight of some of the plundered property at Ali Bughan maddened them past control. Monteith and Macgregor were obliged to interfere when they began to fire the houses and plunder the inhabitants.

Actions in the Shinwari Valley.

The report of these proceedings soon spread throughout the surrounding country, and the villagers began to fly with their property, but regained confidence and returned to their homes on Macgregor explaining the real designs of Government. It soon became evident, however, that the object of the expedition would not be effected by peaceful means alone. The gun and property had to be recovered, and it was known that the chiefs at Gulai were in possession of a portion. It had also been ascertained that the gun was at Deh-Sarrak; so it was determined that the brigade should move against those places. Gulai was the first to receive attention. It was a flourishing settlement, and the inhabitants had only had time to carry away a portion of their grain. Monteith pitched his camp on some rising ground near the village, and demanded the restitution of the plundered property. Evasive answers being returned the village was destroyed. Of all their property the Afghans probably value their trees the most; and as the heaviest penalty which could be inflicted they were destroyed by "ringing." The work of destruction continued for several days and

as the gun was given up and the value of about half the property and a good number of supplies having been appropriated, the brigade's object appeared to have been attained. But the Shinwaris, always refractory, had not been thoroughly coerced, and a severer lesson was considered necessary. Monteith, therefore, marched through their valley, burning the forts and shooting the tribesmen down in their places of refuge. At one time thirty-five forts were in flames simultaneously. At Mazina the tribes made a show of resistance, but it availed nothing against Her Majesty's 31st Regiment and their Indian comrades. On the 26th of July the work of the brigade was accomplished, and on the 3rd of August they were back at Jalalabad. Since the 7th of June the force had subsisted on the country, and the cattle having improved with good fodder, the expedition was entirely satisfactory.

In the meantime Pollock was engaged in negotiations for the relief of the prisoners; and matters appeared to be progressing satisfactorily.

The prisoners.

He sent a verbal message to Akbar Khan, demanding all the guns and trophies in the enemy's possession; but the Sardar was not satisfied with this, and consulted Pottinger and Troup. They advised him to send the prisoners to Jalalabad, as a proof of his sincerity, pointing out that if there was any delay the army would commence its march upon Kabul. Akbar Khan demanded a written promise of withdrawal as the condition of their release, and threatened, in the event of an advance, to distribute the prisoners throughout Turkistan.

Pollock did not attach any value to these threats, and was still less inclined to promise to withdraw. He had already moved a brigade to Fatehabad, two marches in front of his old position, under Sale, who had described it as a good place for a fight. Pollock would, therefore, only promise not to advance further for a certain number of days. The General, eager to push his battalions into the heart of the country, saw that the negotiations could not be brought to a successful conclusion. He now only awaited news of the movements of the Kandahar force, and was not left long in doubt; for in the middle of August he received the following letter from Nott:—

"Kandahar, July 27th, 1842.

My dear General,—You will have received a copy of a letter from the Governor-General under date the 4th instant, to my address, giving me the option of retiring a part of my force to India *viâ* Kabul and Jalalabad. I have determined to take that route, and will write to you fully on the subject as soon as I have arranged for carriage and supplies.

Yours truly,
W. NOTT."

On the 20th of August, Pollock set out from Jalalabad, the advanced guard, with the General, reaching Sultanpur on its way to Gandamak. Here he intended to assemble the following troops, in all about 8,000 men, to accompany him to Kabul:—

3rd Dragoons; 1st Native Cavalry; a squadron of the 5th and 10th Native Cavalry; 600 of the 3rd Irregular Cavalry; Her Majesty's 31st Regiment; 33rd Native Infantry; the whole of Sir Robert Sale's and Colonel Tulloch's Brigades; 17 guns, a company of Sappers and Miners; and a regiment of Bildars under Mr. Mackeson.[1] On the 23rd Pollock, with the advance, reached Gandamak. Two

Action near Gandamak.

miles from this place is the village of Mamu Khel, where a strong body of tribesmen were in position; and determining to dislodge them, Broadfoot's Sappers and a squadron of Dragoons were ordered up from Sale's camp. Next morning as the brigade advanced the enemy retired. Pollock divided his force into two columns, each headed by a wing of the 9th Foot, and entered the village, which the enemy had abandoned, as also Kuchli Khel. They, however, rallied, and took up a position on the heights near the latter village; whence they opened fire on our forces. Colonel Taylor attacked them on one side and Broad-

---

[1] *Greenwood, page* 158. Before the war Mackeson was employed on a survey of the Khaibar and captured Ali Masjid by a *coup de main*, and with a few tribesmen in English pay held it against the Khaibaris. The garrison was hard put to it for water over which the besiegers kept a vigilant watch. Mackeson's fertile imagination hit upon a plan of obtaining supplies. The Afghans are very keen upon getting possession of the bodies of their dead. Mackeson, therefore, brought in the bodies whenever he repulsed an attack, and fixed the price of redemption at two *massaks* of water per corpse.

foot, with his Sappers, on the other, and carried the heights; when the enemy dispersed and the villages were burned. Our losses in this after were seven killed and about fifty wounded. This attack being merely a diversion, Pollock returned to Gandamak to assemble his force, and make sure of his supplies.

The army was all eagerness for the advance; and in their keenness prepared to march as light as possible, sending back all superfluous baggage. The General was anxiously waiting for a reply from Nott, to whom he had sent ten messengers, but it was not until midnight of the 6th of September that it arrived. Supplies were coming in freely, and the troops were living upon the fat of the land. The neighbouring chiefs were coming in and making their submission; and it was evident that the news of the projected advance had struck terror into the hearts of the Afghans.

On the 1st of September, Fateh Jang, in miserable plight, rode into camp and was kindly received and suitably accommodated. His existence at Kabul had not been a happy one. He had been only a puppet in the hands of Akbar Khan, who did with him what he would. He determined therefore to seek British hospitality; and with some difficulty escaped.

On the 7th of September, General Pollock with Sir Robert Sale and the 1st Division commenced their march, leaving two squadrons, two guns, and eight companies to garrison Gandamak. The 2nd Division, under General M'Caskill, marched the following day. A party of the Sikh Contingent, under Captain Lawrence, accompanied this division; the remainder occupied positions at Nimlah and Gandamak.

When the Jagdalak Pass was reached on the 8th of September, the hills which commanded the road were found to be occupied by the enemy. The guns made excellent practice; but the Ghilzais held their ground. The infantry were, therefore, launched to the attack. On one side Broadfoot led his Sappers; on the other, Taylor led the 9th Foot against the enemy in position, horse and foot, behind a ruined fort; Wilkinson pushed up in the centre against the key of the position with the 13th. It was plain that the British were not to be denied, as they pushed on with impetu-

Action of the Jagdalak Pass.

ous gallantry. The best of the Ghilzai tribes were their opponents, but they had to deal with different men under new leaders. They became panic-stricken and fled before the bayonets,[1] pursued by the Dragoons; and only escaped annihilation owing to the unsuitability of the ground for cavalry. All was not yet over, for a considerable body had retired to an apparently inaccessible height, where they planted their standards and bid defiance to the troops. Broadfoot and Wilkinson again advanced under cover of the guns; the rush was arduous, but the troops were equal to it. The Ghilzais watched their progress with astonishment and dismay, then lowered their standards and finally fled in confusion. The victory, which was complete, was mainly achieved by the old Jalalabad garrison, Sale himself, ever in the thickest of the fight, being wounded.

The 2nd Division arrived at Surkhab at about 3 P.M. without opposition. At this hour the 1st Division rear-guard had not left its camping-ground. Many Afghans crowned the heights, but except for a little sniping at night gave no trouble. The next morning the force moved to Jagdalak. General M'Caskill was too ill to sit a horse and the command devolved upon Brigadier Monteith. The route was very difficult, eight miles of it through a formidable pass, and the Ghilzais kept up a running fight the whole way. At the mouth of the pass is a small plateau, and as the rear-guard was having hard work, and it was getting late, the Brigadier determined to halt here. The baggage followed the advanced guard into the pass and two *sangars* on the right and left of the road were occupied to assist the rear-guard while the baggage was moving into camp. Swarms of Ghilzais followed the rear-guard, firing continuously. Frequent counter-attacks were made which sent the enemy flying, but as soon as the pursuit was discontinued, they returned to the attack. It was two hours before the baggage was in, followed by the rear-guard which had suffered severely. The march was now resumed and half way through the pass a number of Ghilzais, who had again collected on the heights, fired a volley and dropped

[1] *Greenwood*, page 215. There is no weapon like the bayonet in the hands of a British soldier. The Afghans would stand like swarms against firing, but th sight of the bristling line of cold steel they could not endure. The bayonet has decided numerous conflicts in all quarters of the globe, and, I doubt not, will decide many more.

several men. A furious action followed, but the Afghans soon had enough and subsequently contented themselves with a few long shots. Next morning the march was continued towards Kuttasang, the enemy firing upon the column from the heights; but, with the exception of a few attacks on the baggage, which were easily repulsed, the enemy attempted nothing during this march. Next morning orders arrived from General Pollock that the division was to make a double march and join him at Tezin. This was difficult and fatiguing. The artillery horses were exhausted and the men had to drag the guns. The enemy disputed every inch of ground, and made several attacks on the baggage; and camp was not reached until long after dark; the force quite knocked up, and minus over one hundred transport animals destroyed with their loads on account of their exhaustion. Here was found a pile of 1,500 dead bodies of Elphinstone's sepoys and camp-followers, who had been stripped by the enemy and left to die in the snow.[1] Nothing was gained by this forced march as the division was so exhausted that the whole force was obliged to halt for a day; moreover a great quantity of stores had been lost. On the 12th of September it was evident that the enemy was close at hand, and that a great struggle was approaching. Akbar Khan, true to his word, had sent the bulk of the prisoners to the Hindu Kush, and was preparing to meet our army.

On the 13th the two forces met on ground particularly favourable to the Afghans. The valley of Tezin is commanded by lofty hills which were crowned by *Jazailchis*; in fact the camp was surrounded by them. There was evidently a day of hard work before the troops, but they were a splendid body in fine condition and ready for anything. All arms were to have their opportunity; the plain for the cavalry, the hills for the infantry, and the guns everywhere.

Action of Tezin.

---

[1] *Greenwood, page* 176. There is a ferocity about the Afghans which they seem to imbibe with their mother's milk. In storming one of the heights a colour sergeant was killed, and from some cause or other his body was left where it fell. A soldier of the same corps happening to pass by the same spot some time after, saw a Khaibari boy apparently about six years of age with a large knife which his puny arm had scarcely sufficient strength to wield, engaged in an attempt to hack off the head of the dead sergeant. The young urchin was so completely absorbed in his savage task, that he heeded not the near approach of the soldier, who coolly took him upon his bayonet and threw him over the cliff.

Fortunately the baggage acted as a bait and drew the enemy's horsemen into the valley. The Dragoon's opportunity was at hand, and a squadron, led by Unett, was let loose upon them. A brilliant charge dispersed the enemy, who fled, pursued by our cavalry who cut up many.

The infantry gallantly climbed the heights, and the Afghans as gallantly advanced to meet them. The 13th Light Infantry took the hills to the right, and the 9th Foot and 31st those on the left, and as they ascended a hail of bullets rained upon them from the *jazails*. At the top the men fixed bayonets and charged; down went the Afghan marksmen and, awed by their comrades' fall, the remainder fled. The fighting was, however, not yet over. All through the day the skirmish on the hills continued. The Afghans, firing from cover, avoided coming to close quarters. The sepoys vied with their European comrades in gallantry, Broadfoot's Sappers, especially, driving the stalwart Afghans before them. Desperate efforts were made to prevent the British from clearing the heights of the Haft Kotal, but loud cheers announced the attainment of their object.

The Afghans had brought the best of their troops to a field, peculiarly suited to their tactics. They could, however, offer no effectual resistance to Pollock's force, and were fairly beaten on their own ground by their own tactics. The scenes that met the sight of the soldiers on the march may have maddened them, but the temper of the men was such that they needed no such stimulus to their efforts.[1]

Akbar Khan recognized that the game was up, and taking Captain Bygrave with him fled to the Ghorband Valley. The warriors hurried homewards by the mountain paths, seeking safety from the avenging army; whilst Pollock resumed his march and encamped on the Kabul race-course on the 15th of September.

---

[1] *Greenwood, page* 221. A dragoon had his horse shot under him while riding at a chief. He quickly disengaged himself, slew his opponent, and mounting his horse continued the charge with his comrades.

The Risaldar of Tait's Horse also performed a gallant action. Finding a large ravine intervening between his men and the enemy, being well mounted, he leapt his horse over the obstruction, cut through the enemy, and back again, killing five and again taking the leap, rejoined his men. He was rewarded with the Order of British India.

CHAPTER XXI.

FINAL OPERATIONS.

The advance from Kandahar.

WHILE Pollock's force was marching Nott was moving towards the same goal from the west. But before recording his progress the circumstances preceding the evacuation of Kandahar must be recounted.

Defence of Kalat-i-Ghilzai.

On the 19th of May, Wymer's forces started for the relief of Kalat-i-Ghilzai. The enemy, hearing of his coming, decided to make a desperate assault on the place. They, therefore, prepared ladders and practised escalading. In the early morning of the 21st of May they advanced in two columns of 2,000 strong each. Placing their ladders they gallantly mounted to the assault. Three times they were repulsed by Craigie and his men; the heavy showers of shot and grape did not, however, turn them from their purpose, and they advanced again and again to be bayoneted on the walls. The struggle had lasted upwards of an hour before they abandoned the assault, with a loss of nearly five hundred, while the defenders escaped scatheless. On Colonel Wymer's arrival nothing remained to be done but the withdrawal of the garrison. Before his return, however, the Duranis had again been beaten in the field.

Actions near Kandahar.

Early on the morning of the 29th of May the enemy began to appear in the neighbourhood of Kandahar, and carried off some baggage cattle. The General believed that they were only reconnoitring the position and were not intent on giving battle. Under this impression he sent out Colonel Stracy with two regiments and four guns to brush them away. The *Ghazis*, believing he was retiring, pushed forward, and occupying some heights west of the cantonments opened fire. Nott now sent out Her Majesty's 41st and eight guns, and at 1 P.M. mounted his horse and, accompanied by

Rawlinson, rode out to take command. Covered by the fire of the guns the light companies were ordered to take the heights; and the work was rapidly done. Chamberlain's Horse swept round the hills and cut the enemy up with heavy slaughter. Rawlinson, with the Parsiwan Horse, and supported by Tait, proceeded to the right to clear the hillocks. The ground was difficult, and the enemy made for the mouth of the Baba-Wali Pass. Rawlinson followed in hot pursuit; but, attracted by a party of the enemy's horse, missed the outlet and nearly captured Muhammad Attar himself. The rout was nearly complete, and would have been more so, had not the movements of our troops been so slow.

On the following day Stracy went out with a brigade, and Rawlinson took the Parsiwan Horse to the banks of the river; but the enemy's cavalry were disinclined for more fighting and crossed to the other side. Safdar Jang surrendered on the 19th of June.

The first three weeks of July passed away, and Nott was preparing for his retirement from Afghanistan. At the end of June a convoy of camels arrived from Quetta, and sufficient carriage and provisions were now in hand. The Governor-General's letter reached him at this time and he replied that he had decided to withdraw a portion of his army *viâ* Ghazni and Kabul.

The Kandahar force was now to be divided. General England was to take part *viâ* Quetta and Sukkur, and the remainder were to move with Nott. England was to take the heavy guns and six pieces of the Shah's Artillery, the Bombay Infantry, two companies of Bengal Artillery, three regiments of the late Shah's force, and some Irregular Cavalry. Nott's route was not yet made public. Some even thought he would march *viâ* Dera Ismail Khan. Before starting, however, the question of the disposal of the Prince had to be decided. Timur wished to accompany the force; but this was vetoed by the Governor-General, nor was he to be permitted to remain at Kandahar. It was decided to send him to India *viâ* Sind, a determination which was by no means agreeable to the Prince.

On the 7th of August the British force quietly evacuated Kandahar, without any demonstration of ill-will on the part of the inhabitants, Safdar Jang being left in possession. The following day was

Evacuation of Kandahar.

spent in completing the commissariat arrangements, and on the 9th the columns started on their several ways; England by no means pleased that he was not to take an European regiment. The march as far as Mukkur, 160 miles from Kandahar, was uneventful, and was completed by the 27th of August. Now, however, it seemed as if active work was in store for the troops. Some days previously Shamshuddin Khan had moved out from Ghazni, with 500 horse and two guns, to collect revenue. When he heard of the British advance he prepared to contest it, and commenced to raise the country with a view to making a stand at the source of the Tarnak, where was the most formidable position between Kandahar and Kabul. The force had hardly left Mukkur on the 28th before the enemy came down upon the rear-guard. The cavalry was ordered out, and only the presence of a ravine saved the Afghans from destruction. Without further molestation the force reached its halting-place. Shamshuddin Khan was known to be somewhere in the neighbourhood, but the thick haze screened his movements. The camels were sent out to graze and the grass-cutters in quest of forage; at 11 A.M. a report came in that the latter were being cut up. Delamain at once took out all his cavalry, but found the alarm to be false. However, he proceeded to reconnoitre three miles from camp, and came up with a party of the enemy's footmen, some twenty of whom the troopers cut down. Delamain followed the remainder, and, turning the shoulder of a range of hills, found the heights occupied by the enemy in considerable strength, and fell back on their opening fire upon him. While retreating, a body of the enemy's horse, about 150 strong, showed themselves on the ridge of a hill, flaunting a white standard. Delamain at once determined to attack. A squadron of the 3rd Bombay Cavalry charged up the hill, but they were taken in flank by a heavy fire from the *Jazailchis*, and the enemy's horse charged down upon them with tremendous effect. Captains Reeves and Bury and Lieutenant Mackenzie were shot or cut down, and the troops, seeing their officers fall, turned and fled down the hill; their companions at the foot caught the contagion, and the whole were soon in disastrous flight, and were not easily rallied. Two officers were

Cavalry action.

killed and three wounded, and fifty-six troopers were either killed or disabled.

Exaggerated stories of the disaster had spread through the camp; and twice Nott sent out instructions for the troops to return. At last it was reported that the enemy was about 7,000 strong and that Delamain's position was precarious. Nott, therefore, moved out with his army, but, when he arrived, he found that the enemy had gone off. There were, however, some fortified villages in the vicinity, from which shots were said to have been fired. The inhabitants begged for mercy which was granted. A company of the 40th Foot, which had been sent to search the houses for plunder, was, however, fired upon, and a terrible retribution was exacted. Meanwhile the cavalry were collecting their dead. On the 30th the division engaged the enemy with better success. Shamshuddin Khan had taken post on the hills to the right of the camp, and it was believed that an attack was intended. On

Action near Ghoyen. the morrow Nott marched to Ghoyen, the Afghans moving parallel to him, and again taking up a position on the hills with the object of waiting for reinforcements. Near the camping-ground the enemy held a fort which Nott determined to attack; but as the troops were weary, he postponed the operation for a few hours. At 3 P.M. the General went out with the 40th Foot, the 16th and 38th Native Infantry, all the cavalry details, Anderson's Horse Artillery, and four other guns. The ground between the camp and the fort was difficult, and some time elapsed before the guns could be brought within range, and when they did open fire it was with so little effect that the chiefs persuaded Shamshuddin to move to the attack at once. Sending his horsemen to outflank the British, he moved down with the main body of his infantry and guns. The latter, posted on the nearest height, opened a rapid and well-aimed fire on the British columns, but, on account of the height from which they were fired, the shot did not ricochet and was comparatively harmless. Nott now relinquished his attack on the fort, and moved in column to the right, flanked by Anderson's guns and Christie's Horse, upon the enemy's main body. The Afghans crowned the other flank, while keeping up a heavy fire. Nott thereupon changed front to the left, deployed, threw out skirmishers

and advanced in line, supported by the guns. As the troops came to the charge their opponents turned and fled. One of their guns broke down, and was captured, and Christie sabred the drivers and carried off the other. Shamshuddin's camp equipage and stores were found scattered over the plain; he himself fled to Ghazni, and the tribes dispersed to their homes.

Nott resumed his march on the 1st of September; and on the 5th reached Ghazni, where the day was spent in desultory fighting. Shamshuddin, who had been reinforced from Kabul by Sultan Jan, occupied some heights to the north-east of the fortress. The gardens, ravines and water-courses were filled with *Jazailchis;* and the city seemed to be swarming with men. Before camping Nott determined to clear the heights. The troops went up in splendid style and drove the enemy before them, until every point was gained. Two infantry regiments with two guns were left to occupy the heights, and the remainder of the force was withdrawn to camp. The site was, however, found to be within range of the big Ghazni gun, "Zabbar Jang"; and, after fourteen shots had fallen into it, the camp was moved to the village of Roza, two miles off. An active and spirited enemy might have seized this favourable opportunity, but a little cavalry skirmishing was all that occurred.

Action at Ghazni.

Sanders now began to make his arrangements for the siege: not that it was believed that there would be a vigorous defence The tribes, who had been summoned with that object, began to lose heart, and Shamshuddin, on the plea of the necessity of forage for his horses, could not be induced to come inside the walls. During the night the would-be defenders quietly quitted the fortress, and took to the hills; and Shamshuddin, seeing that all was over, fled with a few followers to Kabul.

The engineers worked steadily throughout the night; but the stillness within the walls aroused their suspicions. At early dawn a small party went down to reconnoitre, and seeing that the city was apparently abandoned, sent intelligence to the party on the hill, and the 16th Regiment was sent down to occupy it. A few Hindus and some sepoys of the 27th were the only occupants, Colonel Palmer and the other British officers having been taken to Kabul. The British flag soon floated from the highest tower, and a salute

was fired with Shamshuddin's artillery. The General rode out to inspect the place and make arrangements for its destruction. He found the city a mass of ruins. The citadel was in good repair, however, and those who inspected it wondered why Palmer had given it up. The guns were burst and the fortifications blown up, and the town and citadel were fired; and throughout the night the flames lit up the sky.

The engineer officers sounded the well in the citadel and found fifty-one feet of water in it. The bottom being below the river level it could not be drained and the well might have been secured by constructing a covered way and protecting it with guns.

In accordance with the orders of the Governor-General, the gates of the Sultan Mahmud's tomb, said to be those of the Temple of Somnath,[1] were removed by a party of English soldiers. Rawlinson was of opinion that the gates were not what they were represented to be, but that it fitted in with the interests of the Mullahs to assume that they were. He did not think either that the Afghans cared about their removal and that a little religious excitement was all that need be feared.

Somnath gate.

On the 12th Nott was before Saiyidabad, where Woodburn and his men had been massacred. The fort was destroyed and another burnt by the camp-followers. It was Rawlinson's opinion that these half-measures were not good policy, and only exasperated the Afghans without intimidating them. The enemy crowned the hills, and on the 14th Nott attacked them. The Afghans had thrown up breastworks at the gorge of the hills stretching towards Maidan. Nott, however, hastened on the fight and carried the heights, but did not occupy them. Rawlinson writes in this connection: "The attack upon the heights and their subsequent abandonment might have led to unpleasant consequences, had not the news of Akbar's defeat arrived just in time to prevent Shamshuddin from availing himself of this advantage." The enemy, however, moved off to Arghandeh, a few miles nearer the capital. On the following day the work at the pass was found to have been abandoned, but the tribes harassed the

Action at Saiyidabad.

---

[1] These gates were carried off by Mahmud of Ghazni when he sacked Somnath during his invasion of India in 1024 A. D.

force throughout the march; the breakdown of one of the guns handicapping our movements. The artillery did excellent work, the infantry fought with their usual gallantry, and the cavalry made the most of their opportunities. The Maidanis now craved the General's protection, but Nott was relentless. By the evening twenty-six of their forts were in flames. On the 16th Arghandeh was passed, and on the 19th the force halted a few miles from the city, which they found already in the possession of the British.

The day after his arrival Pollock prepared to take formal possession of the Bala Hissar; and a mixed force was detailed for the ceremony. Pollock and Macgregor thought it proper that some sort of rule should exist while the British remained at Kabul, so Prince Fateh Jang headed the procession. In the palace the ceremony of appointing officers of State was gone through, and the British officers then left the King with his ministers, and went about their own work. The British colours were planted upon the highest point of the Bala Hissar, under a salute from the guns and to the accompaniment of the National Anthem. In case Fateh Jang should be under the impression that he was still to be under the aegis of the British Government, Macgregor was sent to explain the situation. He was clearly told that neither men, money, nor arms were to be expected; and that he had better do his best on his own account.

Pollock was now anxious as to the fate of the British prisoners. Immediately on his arrival Sir Richmond Shakespear, with 600 Kizilbash Horse, had set out to overtake them and their escort. Sultan Jan was said to be on the move to cut off the party. It was advisable, therefore, that a substantial backing should be given to the enterprise. Nott rather ungraciously declined to have anything to do with the rescue; so Pollock detailed Sale, with a brigade of the Jalalabad garrison, to carry out the duty. Meanwhile, however, the prisoners had accomplished their own libertion.

The minister had been anxious to pay his respects to Nott but had been refused an audience. The latter believed that Lord Ellenborough desired that no Afghan Government should be recognized; and acted on that supposition. As Pollock had different views, it followed that suspicion was entertained as to the sincerity

of our proceedings. Nott, however, was not in the humour to be courteous to anyone. In his opinion the army ought even now to have been *en route* for Jalalabad, and he was sore that Pollock had not supplies ready for the march. Had he been in command he would have burnt the Bala Hissar and destroyed the city.

He declared that it would be necessary for him to make military requisitions, to rescue his troops from starvation; and denounced Fateh Jang and his new ministers as enemies. Pollock was, however, inclined to discriminate between friend and foe. While supplies were accumulating he favoured the striking of another blow at the hostile chiefs. Aminullah Khan was reported to be in Kohistan gathering up the remnants of the Barakzai force. It was anticipated that he would interfere with the British on their march to India, and that it was therefore expedient to break up his force, and punish that part of the country which had supplied the bulk of the insurgents. A force, taken from the two divisions under M'Caskill, was, therefore, despatched to scatter the enemy collected at Istalif, and to destroy the place. It was, moreover, thought not unlikealy that, dreading retribution, Aminullah Khan might give up Muhammad Akbar Khan, if he could get him into his keeping. The Sardar had sent his family into Turkistan, and was watching the progress of events in the Ghorband Pass, ready to follow his belongings on a threat of pursuit.

The hostile chiefs were now at the end of their tether, and' with Aminullah Khan, were anxious to conciliate the British. Akbar Khan, with a similar object in view, sent in his last prisoner, Captain Bygrave.

Already Fateh Jang was beginning to acknowledge his inability to stand alone. The English would not help him, and he had made eternal enemies of the Barakzais by the destruction of their property. Ziman Khan, who had so faithfully protected the hostages, was one of the sufferers. Usman Khan and Jabbar Khan also shared his fate. The Prince thought thus to prevent an alliance between his followers and the Barakzais, and, anxiously watching the result of the Kohistan expedition, deferred his final decision until its return.

With the valuable aid of Havelock, M'Caskill, making a rapid march, took the enemy at Istalif by surprise.

Action at Istalif.

The town is built in terraces on two ridges of the spur of the Hindu Kush, which bounds the Kohistan Valley on the west. The Afghans were so confident of their security that they had made practically no military dispositions. From intelligence received, M'Caskill determined to assault the right face of the city. Early on the 29th of September the force was in motion, and the enemy, believing that the columns were in retreat, opened a sharp fire. Growing more and more bold the Afghans pressed closely upon the covering party, and Broadfoot's Sappers soon found themselves in collision with a large body of the enemy, posted in a walled garden. The Sappers pushed the Afghans up the slopes in the direction of the city. Havelock and Mayne now pointed out the necessity for supporting Broadfoot's men; and M'Caskill gave the order to advance upon the city. The 9th Foot and 26th Native Infantry, each striving to outdo the other, raced across the intervening space; whilst the 41st, 42nd, and 43rd Bengal Infantry stormed the village and vineyard to the left. The Afghans fled, and were pursued up the slopes. It was no longer a case of defence but the salvation of their women and property. Aminullah Khan was the first to run; and as the troops entered the town, the hill beyond was seen to be covered with laden baggage cattle and streams of women, seeking a place of safety. Much booty was taken and the town partially burned; and M'Caskill proceeding to the hills without opposition, destroyed Charikar, the scene of the Gurkhas' gallant defence, and some other fortified places, and returned to Kabul on the 7th of October.

It was now time to think of withdrawing, for already Pollock had transgressed the limits of his orders; there still remained, however, work to be done. Willing to spare the city and Bala Hissar for the sake of a friendly government, Pollock had sent Shakespear to interview Khan Shirin Khan and the other chiefs of the Persian party. They proposed that Prince Shahpur should be set up in place of his brother. A general meeting of the chiefs was held in Kabul, which unanimously upheld this recommendation. The Prince, a high spirited youth, accepted the crown, and a

declaration to that effect was sent to Pollock's camp. The latter resolutely refused the chief's request for men and money; and the question of leaving a mark of our displeasure now remained to be settled. At the chief's earnest entreaty Pollock agreed to spare the Bala Hissar, and determined to destroy the great *bazar*, as the place where the remains of the Envoy had been exposed to public ridicule. The order for its destruction was given to the engineers, and a detachment under Colonel Richmond was told off to protect the town and its inhabitants from injury. Abbott did not find the pulling down of the massive buildings an easy task; and gun-powder had to be used.

On the 11th of October orders were issued for the commence-
The return march. ment of the return march on the following day. Fateh Jang, Ziman Shah, and the family of the late Shah Shuja were to accompany the troops to India, under the charge of Captain George Lawrence. The British colours were lowered, the regiment was withdrawn from the Bala Hissar, and the force prepared to march.

On the following morning the two divisions commenced their journey. Pollock took with him what trophies he could, but had not carriage for all the guns, of which he took forty-four and a large quantity of ordnance stores. He also took a large number of Indians, crippled by wound or frost; the remnants of Elphinstone's army. As the force was leaving Kabul, the salute was heard in honour of the succession of Prince Shahpur, whose reign was very brief, as he was dethroned before the force reached India.

The news of the victories of Pollock and Nott, and of the
Effect of the victories. release of the prisoners, was received with enthusiasm in India. To Lord Ellenborough the results were a source of boundless satisfaction.

Hindustan was quieting down, and there promised to be a period of undisturbed repose. The Native States, which had been wavering in their loyalty, were now recalled to their senses by our successes. Lord Ellenborough proclaimed that Dost Muhammad was only "believed to be hostile to British interests," and that it had been decided to leave the Afghans to themselves, and recognize any government which they might form. After such a

proclamation the retention of Dost Muhammad in captivity was out of the question. He, therefore, returned to Afghanistan.

The Governor-General busied himself at Ferozepore in arranging for the reception of the victorious troops. Pollock had brought his army with but little loss through the passes, and was now marching through the Punjab. There had been some apprehension that the tribes would interfere with the retirement, but so completely had their strength been broken that the Afghans made no combined effort to annoy the British columns. Pollock indeed wrote that he had not seen an enemy; but M'Caskill and Nott with the centre and rear divisions were not quite so fortunate. From Kabul to Jalalabad, however, all was practically plain sailing, except for some desultory night attacks on the baggage.

Nott reported to General Pollock that his rear-guard was attacked on the 14th of October by large bodies of the enemy in the Haft Kotal's Pass, and that he had sent 200 sepoys, a wing of Her Majesty's 40th Regiment, and two companies of Her Majesty's 41st to help Captain Leeson of the 42nd Native Infantry, who commanded the rear-guard. He reported that the sepoys defeated and dispersed the enemy, and that Captain Leeson spoke highly of the conduct of his men. He added that the British portion of the force behaved with their usual gallantry.

Action of the Haft Kotal.

The retirement of M'Caskill's Division is described by Lieutenant Greenwood. A good deal of confusion was caused at the start through the baggage getting ahead of the column and jamming in a narrow road, with a morass on either side; and a delay of several hours was the consequence. Sale's Division crowned the heights of the Khurd-Kabul while the main column passed through. In the Tezin Pass the enemy, taking advantage of the darkness, attacked the baggage, but were repulsed with heavy loss after a sharp fight.

M'Caskill's Division.

The force halted at Jalalabad for some days, as Pollock had determined to destroy the defences. It had been proposed to hand the place over to the Sikhs; but the work of destruction was completed before the orders of Government were received.

Pollock now pushed on for Peshawar. The Afridis offered to

sell the passage of the Khaibar, but Mackeson answered that it would be taken *gratis*. The First Division passed through with only the loss of a few privates. M'Caskill, however, did not take the precaution to crown the heights, and the Afridis attacked the rear-guard, under their old enemy, Brigadier Wild. Two officers were killed and two guns abandoned. Had M'Caskill and Nott taken the same precautions as Pollock, it is more than probable that the enemy would never have appeared. General Pollock, to ensure that no plunder should fall into their hands, had ordered that when a camel broke down it was to be shot and its load destroyed. Ali Masjid fort was pulled down and the force soon reached Peshawar. The march through the Punjab was uneventful, but sickness broke out and, owing to the shortage of carriage, it was difficult to provide transport.

A final extract from Rawlinson's journal will be of interest:—

<small>Rawlinson's review of Afghan affairs.</small> "A messenger arrived to-day from Kabul with two letters from the Kizilbash party, inviting the Nizam-ud-Daulah to return, as Ghulam Muhammad Khan had already given offence by endeavouring to reestablish an exclusive Durani influence round the puppet King. At present Khan Shirin is, so far as real power is concerned, paramount, and he seems determined to carry things with a high hand, having given out that if Shahpur lends himself to Durani intrigue he will force him to abdicate in favour of another Prince. A strong Kizilbash detachment has at the same time been sent to Ghazni under Muhammad Husain Khan to occupy that place, and in conjunction with the Hazaras to hold in check any possible movement of Ghilzais or Duranis from the westward. Prince Haidar, with another party of the Ghulam Khana, has gone to Bamian, and expects to secure the passes during the winter agianst the return of the Barakzais. Muhammad Akbar's force, which remained for some time at Khinjan, is said to have completely dispersed, the Sardar himself, with Aminullah, having gone to Tashkurghan, and the men having all returned to their homes at Kabul. Nawab Ziman Khan, Jabbar Khan, Usman Khan, and Mir Haji are said to be at Khulm. The people of Kabul have nearly all returned to the city, and are busy re-opening their houses against the winter. Many of the Kohistan Chiefs have also

paid their respects to Shahpur, and Aminullah was expected shortly to return. Muhammad Akbar either really fears for his own personal safety, now that a party with which accommodation is impossible has come into power, or he thinks it better policy to allow dissension to fructify in the capital before he makes his re-appearance on the scene. The Duranis are in a large minority at Kabul, and must necessarily give way before the Ghulam Khana, if Khan Shirin acts with any energy. I look to Kandahar as their natural and necessary retreat, and no doubt at that place Sadozai royalty, supported by their influence, will continue to glimmer on, until Persia turns her attention to her eastern frontier, and pushes forward the Barakzai Sardars to play a game for her. The Kizilbashis, at the same time, cannot expect to hold their ground at Kabul for any length of time."

Shahpur's reign soon came to an end. Akbar Khan descended upon Kabul and carried all before him; and the boy-king fled to Peshawar. Dost Muhammad meanwhile was on his way to his old principality.

On the 17th of December Sir Robert Sale crossed the Sutlej at the head of his Jalalabad men, and the Governor-General went to meet him.

Arrival at Ferozepore.

Pollock and Nott crossed the Sutlej on the 19th and 23rd respectively.

Bibliography.

(1) History of the war in Afghanistan—J. W. Kaye, F.R.S.

(2) Army of the Indus—Major W. Hough.

(3) Narrative of Services in Baluchistan and Afghanistan—Colonel L. R. Stacy, C.B.

(4) Narrative of the Campaign of the Army of the Indus—R. H. Kennedy, M.D.

(5) Narrative of the Late Victorious Campaign in Afghanistan under General Pollock—Lieutenant Greenwood.

(6) The Expedition into Afghanistan—James Atkinson.

(7) Rough Notes of the Campaign in Sind and Afghanistan—Captain James Outram.

(8) Narrative of the War in Afghanistan—Captain Henry Havelock.

(9) Sale's Brigade in Afghanistan—Reverend G. R. Gleig, M.A.

(10) Journal of the Disasters in Afghanistan—Lady Sale.

(11) History of Afghanistan—Malleson.

APPENDIX I.

THE BENGAL AND BOMBAY ARMIES.

The Bengal Force.

First Infantry Division.—Major-General Sir Willoughby Cotton, G.C.B K.C.B.

First Brigade.

Colonel Sale, C.B. of Her Majesty's 13th Light Infantry.
- Her Majesty's 13th Light Infantry (Somersetshire Light Infantry).
- 16th Native Infantry (disbanded, 1857).
- 48th Native Infantry (mutinied, 1857).

Second Brigade.

Colonel Nott of the 42nd Native Infantry.
- 42nd Native Infantry (5th Light Infantry).
- 31st Native Infantry (2nd Q. O. Rajput L. I.).
- 43rd Native Infantry (6th Jat Light Infantry).

Third Brigade.

Colonel Dennis of Her Majesty's 3rd Buffs.
- 27th Native Infantry (disbanded, 1857).
- Her Majesty 3rd Buffs (East Kent Regiment).
- 2nd Native Infantry (disbanded, 1859).
- One Company of Sappers.

Second Infantry Division.—Major-General Duncan.

Fourth Brigade.

Lieutenant-Colonel Roberts of the Bengal European Regiment.
- Bengal European Regiment (Royal Munster Fusiliers).
- 35th Native Infantry (disbanded 1857).
- 37th Native Infantry (mutinied 1857).

Fifth Brigade.

Lieutenant-Colonel Worsley of the 28th Native Infantry.

    5th Native Infantry (mutinied, 1857).
    28th Native Infantry (mutinied, 1857).
    53rd Native Infantry (mutinied, 1857).
    One Company of Sappers.

Cavalry Brigade.

Colonel Arnold of Her Majesty's 16th Lancers.

    Her Majesty's 16th Lancers.
    2nd Regiment Light Cavalry.
    3rd Regiment Light Cavalry.
    4th Local Horse.
    Part of 1st Local Horse (Skinner's).

Artillery.

Lieutenant-Colonel Graham, of the Bengal Horse Artillery.

    2nd troop, 2nd Brigade, Horse Artillery.
    3rd troop, 2nd Brigade, Horse Artillery.
    3rd Company, 2nd Battalion.
    4th Company, 2nd Battalion.
    2nd Company, 6th Battalion.

N.B.—Of the Bengal Infantry only the First, Second and Fourth Brigades crossed the Indus. Of the Artillery, two troops of Horse Artillery had a battery of 9-pounders.

The whole was formed into one Division under Sir Willoughby Cotton.

THE BOMBAY FORCE.

Lieutenant-General Sir John Keane.

First Infantry Brigade.

Colonel Willshire of Her Majesty's 2nd Regiment (The Queen's).

    19th Native Infantry (119th Infantry).
    Her Majesty's 17th Regiment (Leicestershire Regiment).

Second Brigade.

Colonel Gordon of 1st Native Infantry (101st Grenadiers).

    2nd Native Infantry (102nd Grenadiers).
    5th Native Infantry (105th Light Infantry).

Cavalry.

Lieutenant-Colonel Scott,—4th Light Dragoons.
    2 squadrons, Her Majesty's 4th Light Dragoons (4th Hussars).
    1st Regiment, Light Cavalry (31st Lancers).

Artillery.

Colonel Stevenson,—2 troops, Horse Artillery.
    2 troops, Foot Artillery.

APPENDIX II.

Composition of the Force which returned from Kabul.

First Division.

4 guns, 3rd troop; 1st Brigade, Horse Artillery (now 58th Battery Royal Field Artillery).

No. 6 Light Field Battery (manned by 2nd Company, 6th Battalion—afterwards 7th Battalion, mutinied at Nasirabad in 1857).

2 18-pounders and details, European Artillery.

Mountain Train.

Her Majesty's 3rd Light Dragoons (now 3rd King's Own Hussars).

4 Risalas, 3rd Irregular Cavalry (partially mutinied at Saugor, 1857; disbanded 1861).

1 Squadron, First Light Cavalry (mutinied at Mhow, 1857).

Her Majesty's 9th Foot (now 1st Battalion, the Norfolk Regiment).

Her Majesty's 13th Light Infantry (now 1st Battalion, the Somersetshire Light Infantry).

26th Native Infantry (disarmed at Mian Mir, afterwards mutinied, and was destroyed at Ajnala, 1857).

35th Light Infantry (disbanded, 1859).

5th Company, Sappers and Miners (now 1st Prince of Wales' Own Sappers and Miners).

Broadfoot's Sappers (became 9th and 8th Companies, Bengal Sappers and Miners).

Second Division.

2 guns, 3rd Troop; 2nd Brigade, Horse Artillery (became 2nd Company 2nd Depôt Division, Royal Artillery).

Captain Blood's Battery of 9-pounders (became 3rd Company, First Battalion, Bombay Artillery, now 30th Field Battery, Royal Field Artillery).

2 Squadrons First Light Cavalry (mutinied at Mhow in 1857).

Her Majesty's 31st Foot (now 1st Battalion, East Surrey Regiment)

2nd Regiment, Native Infantry (disarmed at Barrackpur, 1857).

16th Regiment, Native Infantry (disarmed at Mian Mir, 1857; disbanded, 1859).

Wing, 33rd Native Infantry (now 4th Prince Albert Victor's Own Rajputs).

Wing, 60th Native Infantry (mutinied at Rohtak, 1857).

General Notts' Force.

One Troop, Bombay Horse Artillery (afterwards First Troop, Bomby Horse Artillery; now "N" Battery, Royal Horse Artillery).

One troop, Horse Artillery, Shah Shuja's Force (afterwards 5th Troop, 1st Brigade, Bengal Horse Artillery converted into a European Battery, 862; now "T" Battery, Royal Horse Artillery).

Detachment, Foot Artillery.

3rd Bombay Light Cavalry (now 33rd Light Cavalry).

Detachment, First Irregular Horse (Haldanes') (now Skinner's Horse,

Christie's Horse (became 9th Irregular Cavalry; disbanded, 1861).

Detachment, Sappers and Miners (now First Prince of Wales' Own Sappers and Miners).

Detachment, Madras Sappers and Miners (now Queen's Own Sappers and Miners).

Her Majesty's 40th Foot (now 1st Battalion, South Lancashire Regiment).

38th Native Infantry (mutinied at Delhi, 1857).

3rd Shah Shuja's Infantry (now 12th Pioneers).

Her Majesty's 41st Foot (now First Battalion, The Welsh Regiment.)

42nd Native Infantry (now 5th Light Infantry).

43rd Native Infantry (now 6th Jat Light Infantry).

APPENDIX III.

Captain Broadfoot to Major-General Sir Robert Sale.

Note on the Defensive Works in Jalalabad.

Jalalabad, 16th April 1842.

'Sir,

On the 12th of November, the Major-General Commanding having resolved to occupy Jalalabad, directed me with a committee of officers to examine and report on the works of the place.

The committee reported unanimously that they were then not defensible against a vigorous assault.

As will be seen by the accompanying plan* the town is an irregular quadrilateral, having half of the western side salient, and the southern side broken by a deep re-entering angle. It was surrounded on every side with gardens and houses, enclosed fields, mosques, and ruined forts, affording strong cover to an enemy; these were everywhere close to the walls, and in many places connected with them. Beyond these on three sides (north, east, and west), at from 400 to 500 yards, run the ruins of the wall of the ancient city, on which the sand has accumulated so as to form a line of two heights, giving cover to the largest bodies of men. Opposite the south-west angle a range of heights, composed of bare gneiss rocks, commences at 330 yards from the works and extends about 400 yards from north-north-east to south-south-west; these completely overlook the town, and from the vicious tracing of the works, enfilade some of the longest curtains; parallel to the north side, at 170 yards, runs a steep bank 20 feet high; it extends a considerable way to the west and several miles to the east, affording a secure and unseen approach to any number of men; it is, probably, an old bank of the river. From it numerous ravines run up towards the walls, affording the enemy a covered passage into the buildings and enclosures adjoining the works.

Two very solid walls, 300 yards apart, run from the place to this bank, thus enclosing on three sides a space probably occupied originally by the Mogul Emperor's palace, but found by us to contain a large mosque and numerous gardens and houses occupied by *fakirs*; one of the gates of the town opens into it, and it was traversed by a water-course, about 10 feet

* Not traceable?

wide, which entered the town by a tunnel under the rampart, large enough to admit several men abreast. A similar tunnel allowed it to pass out of the town on the eastern side. The walls of the town extended about 2,000 yards, without reckoning the bastions, of which there were 33.

The works were of earth, and in the usual style of the country, *viz.*, a high thin rampart, but in a state of ruin, without parapets and without ditch, covered way, or outworks of any kind.

The bastions were full, but in some places lower than the adjoining curtains, very confined, without parapets, and sloping downwards from the gorge to the salient, so that the terrepleine was completely exposed.

There were four gates and a postern, all of the usual vicious native construction, and, except that on the northern side, in a ruinous state.

To give some idea of the state of the works, I may mention that of the Committee sent to inspect them on the 13th of November, not one, except myself, succeeded in making the circuit.

Large gaps cut off the communication, or insecure footing compelled the officers to descend among the adjoining enclosures, from which it was difficult to find the way; while on the south side the ramparts were so embedded in houses and surmounted by them, that its course could only be traced by laboriously threading the lanes of the native town.

On the north side the wall rose to a very great height towards the town, but sloped down to the interior in a heap of ruins, almost everywhere accessible while, at the foot, were houses and gardens so strongly occupied by the enemy that during the night of the 13th of November our troops were unable to maintain their posts, and, with the exception of the gateway, a line of 400 yards on the northern face was without a man in the works.

Had the enemy then attacked us we must have been reduced to a street combat.

On the following morning (14th November), the Major-General ordered a sortie in force, which drove the enemy from his positions with such loss that it was some time before he ventured near enough to disturb our works which were now as vigorously prosecuted as our scanty supply of tools and the difficulty of procuring materials allowed.

We had only the tools as per margin,* brought from Kabul with the Sappers for the operations expected in the Tazin Valley, and we were without wood or iron. Wood was obtained from the ruins of the cantonment and from houses demolished in the town. Iron was collected in small quantities from the neighbourhood, but it was that of the country, good in quality, but imperfectly melted, and requiring about ten

*330 Pickaxes.
390 Shovels.
Other tools in proportion; many tools have been made there.

times as much labour and time as English iron. By the persevering labour of the troops, however, much was done, and when the enemy next attacked us (1st December) ramparts had been made and the guns mounted on the bastions for which they were destined, the water-course and other passages through the walls blocked up, the foot of the scarps cleared from rubbish, and parapets built in all the bastions and many of the curtains, while much of the external cover was destroyed.

On the 1st of December the enemy were again routed, and the works proceeded with little or no interruption.

By the middle of January (the commencement of the rainy season) a parapet, nowhere less than 6 feet high, with a banquette, as wide as the nature of the rampart allowed, was completed entirely round the place. The gates were repaired and strengthened by buttresses; two of them were retrenched and a ditch carried round the north-west angle, while some of the most dangerous ravines were laid open to our fire, and roads were opened into the low ground on the north side.

By the middle of February the ditch was carried round the place, with as good a covered way as the size of the ditch and supply of earth allowed; while the mosques, forts, gardens, and cover of every description, had been destroyed for several hundred yards round the place.

At this time Muhammad Akbar Khan moved into the valley in order to attack the place, but they were unable to effect more than a distant investment; they frequently occupied the rocks on the south-west, but the parapets and the traverses rendered their fire harmless.

On the 19th of February an earthquake, which nearly destroyed the town, threw down the greater part of our parapets, the Kabul gate with the two adjoining bastions, the north-west bastion, and a part of the new bastion which flanked it. Three other bastions were also nearly destroyed, while several large breaches were made in the curtains; one on the Peshawar side, eighty feet long, was quite practicable, the ditch being filled in and the ascent easy. Thus, in one moment, the labours of three months were, in a great measure, destroyed.

No time, however, was lost; the shocks had scarcely ceased when the whole garrison was told off into working parties, and before night the breaches were scarped, the rubbish below cleared away, and the ditches before them dug out; while the great one, on the Peshawar side, was surrounded by a good gabion parapet.

A parapet was erected on the remains of the north-west bastion, with an embrasure allowing the guns to flank the approach of the ruined Kabul gate; the parapet of the new bastion was restored so as to give a flanking fire to the north-west bastion, while the ruined gate was rendered inaccessible by

a trench in front of it, and in every bastion round the place a temporary parapet was raised.

From the following day all troops off duty were continually at work, and such were their energy and perseverance that by the end of the month the parapets were entirely restored, the Kabul gate again serviceable, the bastions either restored or the curtain filled in when restoration was practicable, and every battery re-established.

The trenches have been built up, with the rampart doubled in thickness, and the whole of the gates retrenched.

It is not easy to give an adequate idea of the extent of the labour performed by the troops.

The parapets, banquettes, etc., are built of the ruins of the buildings thrown down cemented with clay mixed with straw and bound together, when requisite, by bond timbers; of this masonry about 104,500 cubic feet had been built before the earthquake, and since then (including new works) about 103,900 cubic feet have been erected, making in all above 208,000 cubic feet of masonry. But the material had to be procured from a distance by the laborious process of demolition; and the ruinous wall had to be scarped, cleared at the base, and prepared for the work.

The quantity of walls of forts, mosques, gardens, etc., destroyed were considerably more than double that of the walls of the place, and the excavation from the ditch exceeds 860,000 cubic feet.

In addition to this the troops had to build barracks for themselves and guard rooms round the works, each corps undertook its own barracks, while the construction of the guard-rooms was superintended by Captain Moorhouse, Quarter-master of brigade, and Lieutenant and Quarter-master Sinclair, of Her Majesty's 13th Light Infantry, whose assistance on this point left me more leisure for the defensive works.

To Lieutenant Sinclair also we owe the mill used by the Commissariat. Long furnished materials and workmen; the credit of the whole contrivance and construction is due solely to Lieutenant Sincliar, G.B.

The working parties, in emergencies, consisted of all men off duty, often assisted by the guards when the works were near their posts. On ordinary occasions they consisted of all the Sappers and Miners, about 200 men of Her Majesty's 13th Light Infantry, 130 of the 35th Native Infantry, a party of Artillerymen of Captain Abbott's battery, and all the men off duty in Captain Backhouse's Mountain Train, and the detachment of the 6th Infantry; Shah Shuja's Force, doing duty with the Mountain Train detachments; also camp-followers were employed in bringing materials, etc.

Nothing could exceed the cheerful energy of every officer and man in these labours.

The Sappers and Miners worked from daybreak to sunset (with 2½ hours for meals), and, when occasion required, at night. Their conduct was such as to leave me nothing to desire, and it has been honoured with the Major-General's recorded approbation.

*   *   *   *   *   *   *

The other troops having very severe garrison duty, laboured for a short period, yet seldom less than 6 hours a day.

It will be seen that the largest parties were furnished by Her Majesty's 13th Light Infantry, and I know not how adequately to express my sense of the services of this admirable body of men; though having little more than every other night in bed, they laboured for months, day after day, officers and men, with a cheerfulness and energy not to be surpassed. To enumerate all, whose zeal and energy were conspicuous, would almost require me to go over the list of the officers and to mention even many of the valuable non-commissioned officers.

*   *   *   *   *   *   *

The 35th Native Infantry were much employed in destroying the forts and other covers around the place; and it is due to Captain Seaton to mention his great activity, and the skill with which, by directing the watercourses used for irrigation, on the most massive ruins, he effected a quantity of demolition which, with our short supply of gunpowder, would have otherwise been impracticable.

With the exception of a few of the larger bastions, the whole of the batteries were prepared by the Artillery themselves, under the superintendence of their own officers. Besides this a party of Captain Abbott's artillerymen was always ready to assist in the works generally. *   *   *   *
Captain Backhouse, with his own men, and a detachment of the 6th Infantry, Shah Shuja's Force, not only prepared the parapets and embrasures for his own guns, and repaired the damage done to them by the earthquake, but he undertook and completed several of the most useful and laborious operations; he executed, among others, a large and widely-breaching series of ravines, giving cover to many hundred men, within pistol shot of a very weak part of the works, which was filled up; or entirely laid open to fire, and that with a number of men, which without his untiring zeal and personal exertion would have been inadequate.

*   *   *   *   *   *   *

I have, etc.,

GEORGE BROADFOOT.

53 I. B.

CRONOLOGICAL TABLE OF EVENTS.

1835.—Lord Auckland appointed Governor-General of India.
1836.—The Burnes Mission starts for Kabul.
1837.—The Mission reaches Kabul on the 20th of September.
    Viktevitch arrives at Kabul on the 19th of December.
    Eldred Pottinger arrives at Herat in August.
    Ghorian falls before the Persian Army in November.
    Commencement of the siege of Herat on the 23rd of November.
1838.—Perso-Afghan alliance proposed on the 21st of March.
    Burnes leaves Kabul on the 26th of April.
    Treaty signed by Ranjit Singh on the 26th of June.
    Siege of Herat raised on the 9th of September.
    November.—Army for invasion of Afghanistan assembles at Ferozepur.
    Burnes sent to treat with the Baluchi Princes.
    December.—The expedition starts.
1839.—*14th January.*—The Army of the Indus enters Sind.
    21st January.—Shah Shuja's Contingent at Shikarpur.
    29th January.—Cession of Bakkar.
    20th February.—Cotton reaches Shikarpur.
    23rd February.—Force leaves Shikarpur.
    10th March.—Arrival at Dadar.
    26th March.—Arrival at Quetta.
    March.—Burnes Mission to Mehrab Khan.
    6th April.—Sir John Keane assumes command.
    7th April.—March resumed.
    9th April.—Arrival at Haikalzai.
    25th April.—Arrival at Kandahar.
    27th June.—March resumed.
    21st July.—Arrival at Ghazni.
    22nd July.—Attack by Ghazis.
    23rd July.—Fall of Ghazni.
    2nd August.—Flight of Dost Muhammad.
    7th August.—Arrival at Kabul.
    3rd September.—Prince Timur reaches Kabul.

2nd October.—Orders received for the greater part of Bengal Division to remain in Afghanistan.

15th October.—Bengal troops begin return march to India.

18th October.—Bombay troops begin return march to India.

1840.—*13th March.*—News reaches Kabul of the failure of the Russian Expedition to Khiva.

7th May.—Anderson's expedition against the Ghilzais.

17th May.—Anderson's action against the Ghilzais.

June.—Disaster at Bajgah.

August.—Dost Muhammad escapes from Bokhara.

30th August.—Attack on Bajgah.

September.—Rising in Turkistan.

14th September.—Dennis reinforces Bamian.

18th September—Defeat of Usbegs near Bamian.

3rd October.—Sale attacks Julga.

11th October.—Dost Muhammad reaches Ghorband.

11th October.—Withdrawal of Bamian detachment.

2nd November.—Action at Parwan Dara.

2nd November.—Surrender of Dost Muhammad.

12th November.—Dost Muhammad leaves for India.

November.—The court moves to Jalalabad for the winter.

1841.—*3rd January.*—Farrington's action near Kandahar.

January.—Todd's Mission leaves Herat.

7th April.—Action near Kalat-i-Ghilzai.

May—Wymer's action at Assiya-i-Ilmi.

3rd July.—Action on the Helmund.

5th August.—Chambers' Expedition against the Ghilzais.

17th August.—Action at Girishk.

September.—Expedition to Tarin and Derawat.

September.—Capture of Akram Khan.

October.—Nott returns to Kandahar.

9th October.—Attack on Monteith's camp at Butkhak.

12th October.—Affair of Khurd-Kabul.—March to Gandamak.

2nd November.—Murder of Burnes.

2nd November.—Shelton arrives at the Bala Hissar.

3rd November.—Arrival of 37th Native Infantry at Kabul.

3rd November.—Macnaghten writes to recall Sale's force and the troops returning to India.

3rd November.—Abandonment of Mackenzie's post.

CHRONOLOGICAL TABLE OF EVENTS.

4th November.—Fort containing commissariat stores abandoned.
6th November.—Capture of Muhammad Sharif's fort.
6th November.—Action by Anderson's Horse.
7th November.—Return of Akbar Khan to Bamian.
9th November.—Shelton returns to Cantonments.
10th November.—Affair of Rikab Bashi's fort.
10th November.—News of Kabul outbreak reaches Sale.
11th November.—March to Jalalabad from Gandamak commenced.
12th November.—Rearguard action.
12th November.—Arrival at Jalalabad.
13th November.—First fight on the Bemaru Hills.
15th November.—Arrival of Pottinger after the Charikar disaster.
16th November.—First action at Jalalabad.
18th November.—Macnaghten recommends holding out.
23rd November.—Second fight on the Bemaru Hills.
25th November.—Macnaghten interviews the Chiefs.
November.—Massacre at Ghazni.
November.—Capitulation of Ghazni.
1st December.—Second action at Jalalabad.
6th December.—Abandonment of Muhammad Sharif's fort.
8th December.—Macnaghten consults Elphinstone on question of retreat.
8th December.—Discussion of treaty.
8th December.—Return to Kandahar of Maclaren's Brigade.
13th December.—Evacuation of Bala Hissar.
22nd December.—Orders issued for the evacuation of Ghazni, Kandahar, and Jalalabad.
23rd December.—Murder of Macnaghten.
26th December.—Encouraging letters from Jalalabad.
27th December.—Mutiny of *Janbaz* at Kandahar.
1842.—*1st January.*—Treaty ratified.
4th January.—First Brigade of the Relief Force crosses the Sutlej.
6th January.—Retreat from Kabul commences.
7th January.—Skinner proceeds to Akbar Khan with flag of truce.
8th January.—Sale receives letter from Pottinger.
8th January.—Kabul Force marches to Tazin.
9th January.—Orders received at Jalalabad for the evacuation.—The reply.
12th January—Action of Arghandab.

12*th January.*—The end of the Kabul Force.
13*th January.*—Arrival of Brydon at Jalalabad.
26*th January.*—Sale convenes council of war.
10*th February.*—Governor-General issues order prescribing object of Relief Force.
13*th February.*—Earthquake at Jalalabad.
19*th February.*—Disaster at Ali Masjid.
21*st February.*—Order for evacuation reaches Kandahar.
23*rd February.*—Evacuation of Ali Masjid.
7*th March.*—Action near Kandahar.
10*th March.*—Attack on Kandahar.
25*th March.*—Wymer's action near Kandahar.
28*th March.*—England's defeat at Haikalzai.
31*st March.*—Pollock reaches Jamrud.
1*st April.*—Death of Shah Shuja.
5*th April.*—Action in the Khaibar.
7*th April.*—Action at Jalalabad.
30*th April.*—Passage of the Khojak.
May.—Pollock at Jalalabad.
May.—Relief of Kalat-i-Ghilzai.
May.—Akbar Khan captures the Bala Hissar.
29*th May.*—Action near Kandahar.
June.—Operations in Shinwari Valley.
7*th August.*—Evacuation of Kandahar.
20*th August.*—Pollock sets out from Jalalabad.
20*th August.*—Action near Gandamak.
28*th August.*—Cavalry action near Mukur.
30*th August.*—Action near Ghoyen.
5*th September.*—Action at Ghazni.
8*th September.*—Action in Jagdalak Pass.
12*th September.*—Action at Sayidabad.
September.—Progress of M'Caskill's Division.
13*th September.*—Action at Tazin.
15*th September.*—Pollock arrives at Kabul.
19*th September.*—Nott arrives at Kabul.
29*th September.*—Action at Istalif.
12*th October.*—The force leaves Kabul.
14*th October.*—Action of Haft Kotal.
17*th December.*—Arrival at Ferozepur.

[THE END OF VOL. III.]

GENERAL MAP
TO ILLUSTRATE VOLUME III of FRONTIER and OVERSEAS EXPEDITIONS

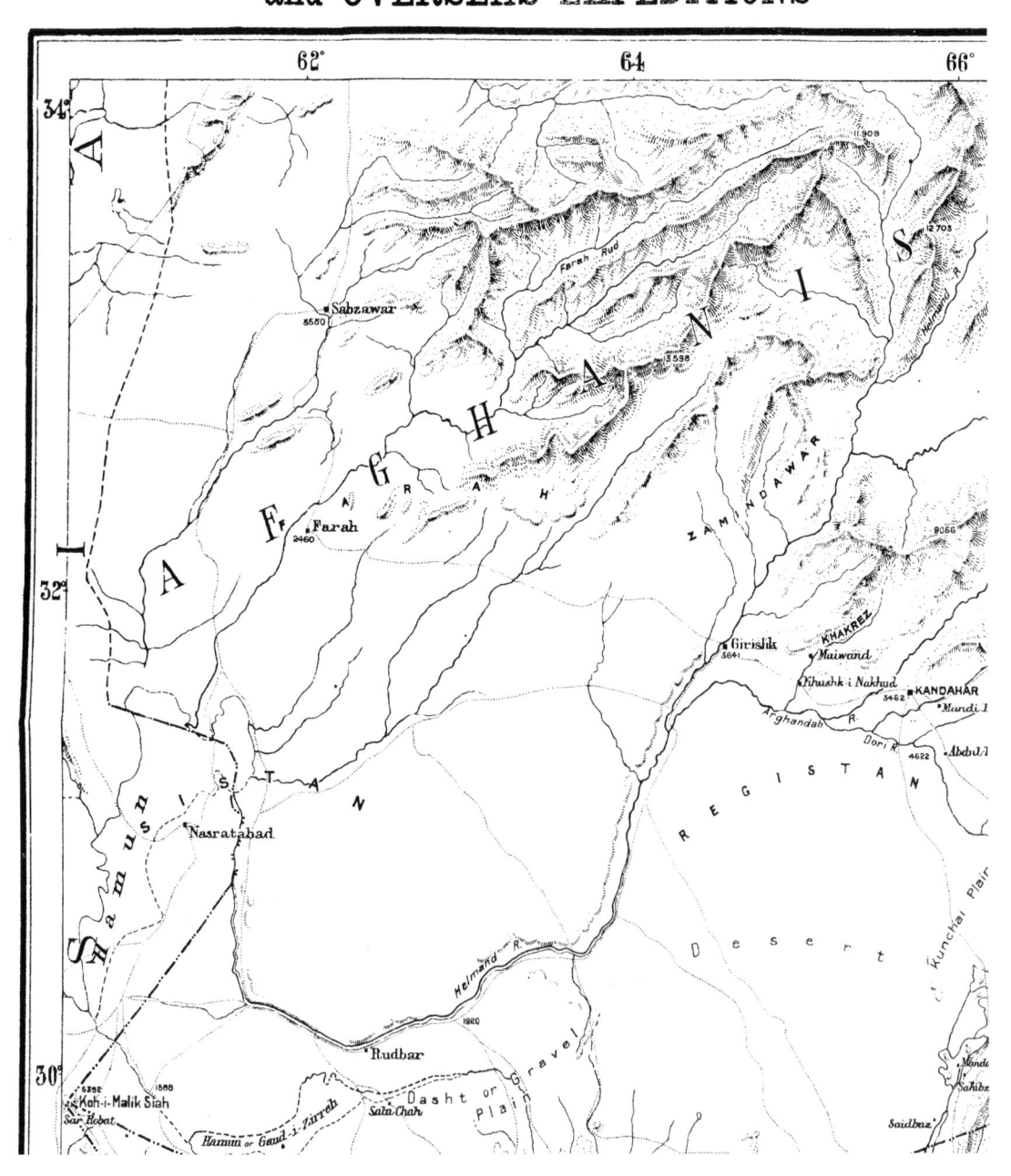

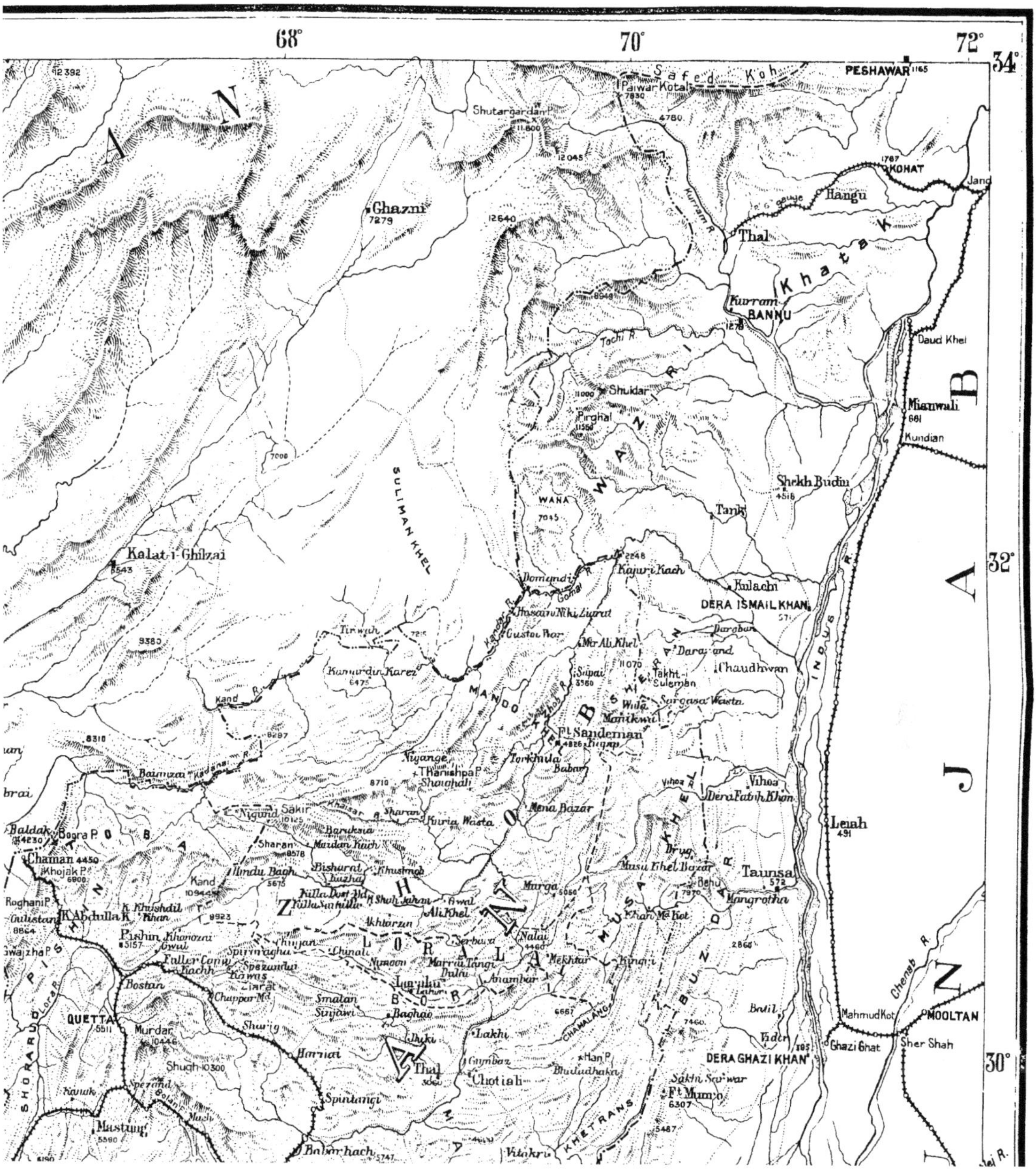

68°
70°
72°
34°
32°
30°
Safed Koh
PESHAWAR 1165
Paiwar Kotal
Shutargardan P.
KOHAT
Jand
Hangu
Ghazni
7279
Thal
Kurram R.
Khatak
Kurram
BANNU
Daud Khel
Tochi R.
Shuidar
Pirghal
Mianwali
Kundian
SULIMAN KHEL
WANA
Shekh Budin
Tank
Kalat-i-Ghilzai
Domandi
Gomal R.
Kulachi
DERA ISMAIL KHAN
Kajuri Kach
Kand R.
Kanurdin Karez
Mir Ali Khel
Takht-i-Suleman
Chaudhwan
Daraban
INDUS R.
Ft. Sandeman
Niyange
Baimzai
Dera Fatih Khan
Vihoa
Mena Bazar
Kuria Wasta
Leiah
Baldak
Bogra P.
Chaman 4450
Khojak P.
Hindu Bagh
Bisharat
Musa Khel Bazar
Taunsa
Mangrotha
Gulistan
K. Abdulla
Pishin
Murga
Killa Saifulla
Ali Khel
Akhtarzan
Nalai
Mekhtar
Roghani P.
Bostan
Chapper Md.
Smalan
Baghao
QUETTA 5511
Murdar
Shugh 10300
Harnai
Thal
Chotiali
Lakhi
Han P.
Bhududhaka
Chenab R.
Mahmud Kot
MOOLTAN
Ghazi Ghat
Sher Shah
DERA GHAZI KHAN
Ft. Munro
Spintangi
Mastung
Bibar Kach
KHETRANS
MUSA KHEL
BOZDAR
ZHOB
LORALAI
AFGHAN
WAZIRI
SHERANI
PUNJAB
BORI
PISHIN
SHORARUD

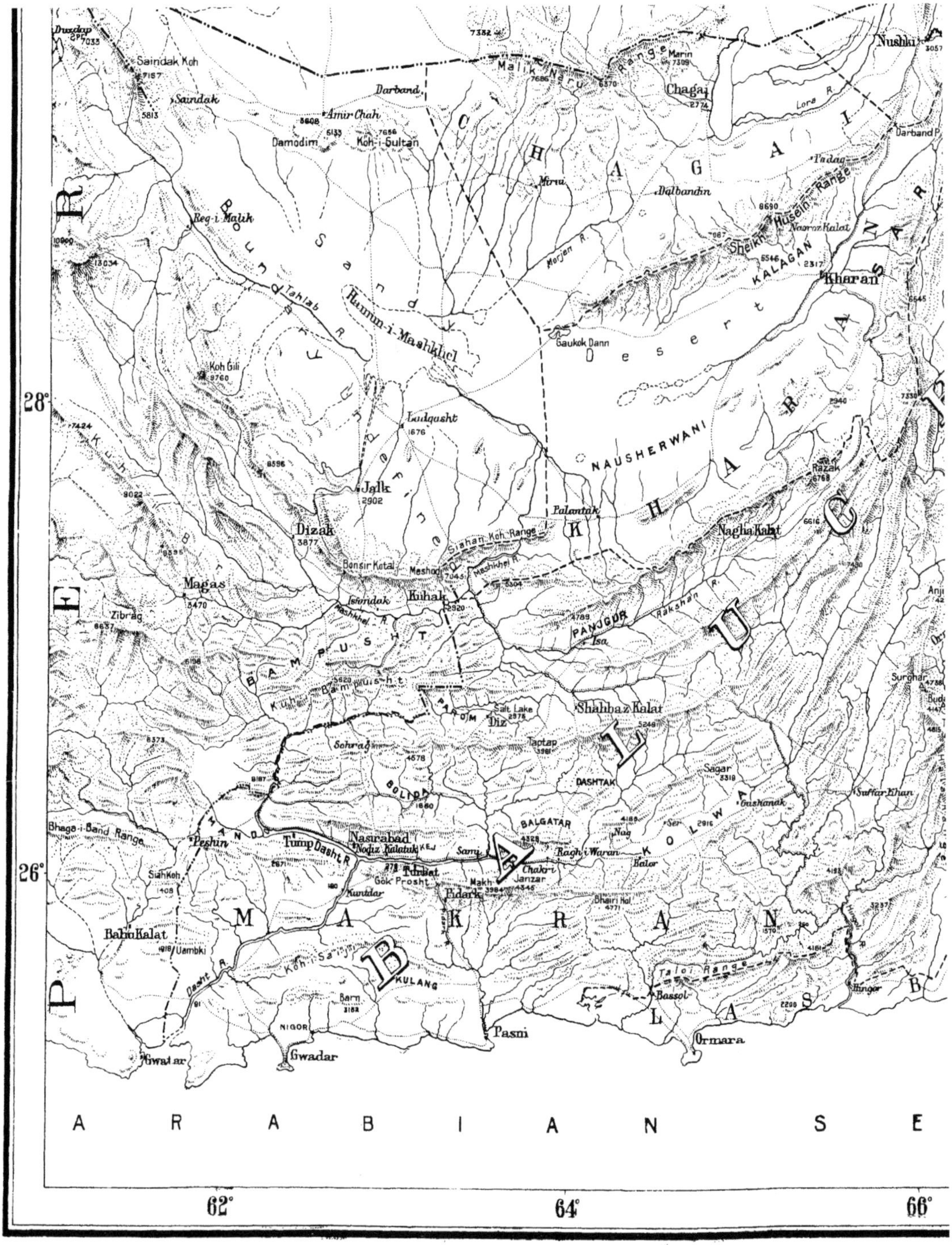

I. B. Topo. Dy. No. 7,306.
Exd. C. J. A. June 1908.

Scale 1 Inch = 32 Miles.

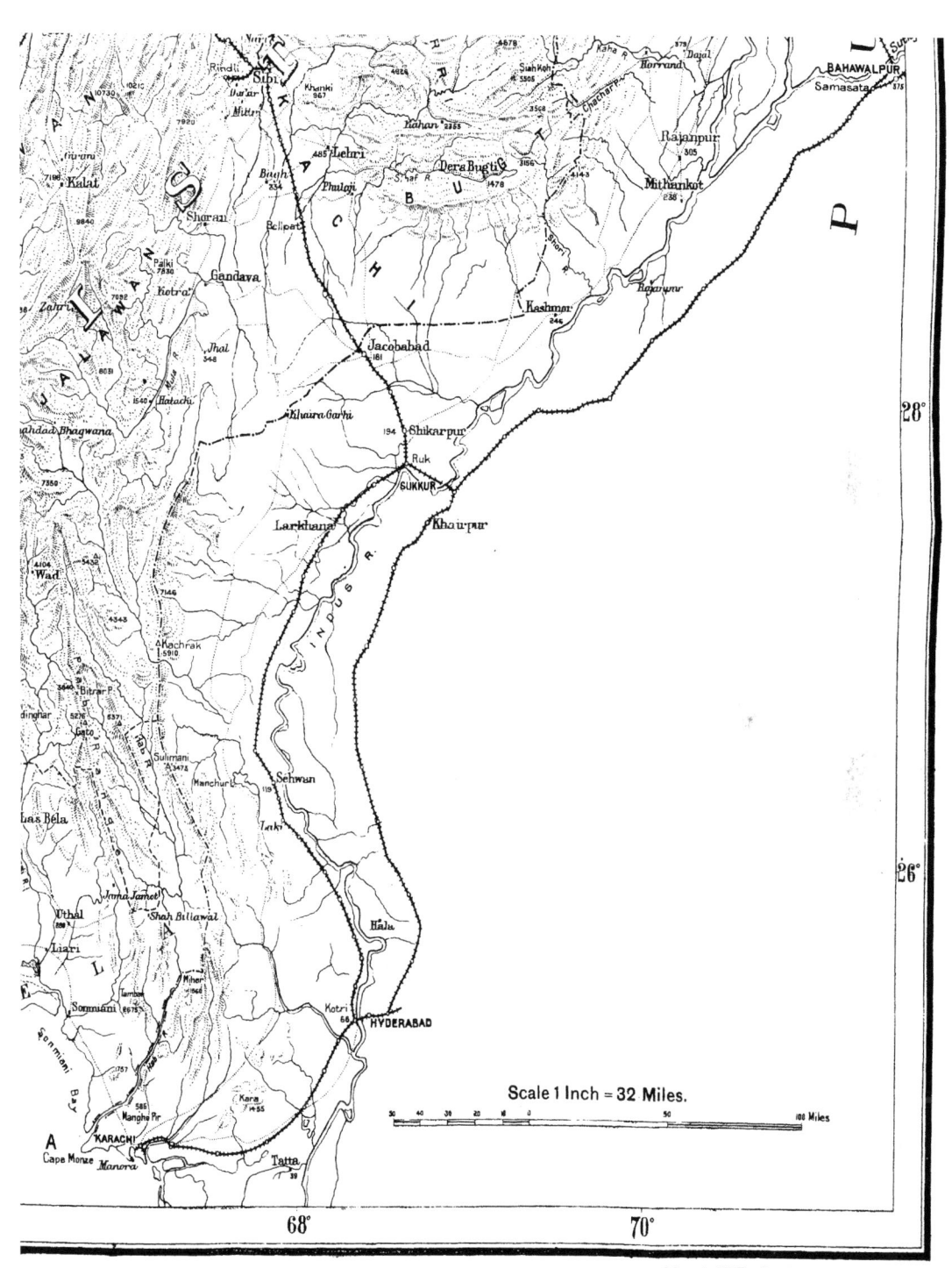

No. 4,457.,-I., 1908.

MAP
OF
MARRI COUNTRY
TO ILLUSTRATE THE MOVEMENTS
OF THE
EXPEDITIONARY FORCE
UNDER
BRIGADIER-GENERAL C. M. MacGREGOR, C.B., C.S.I., C.I.E.,
October & November 1880

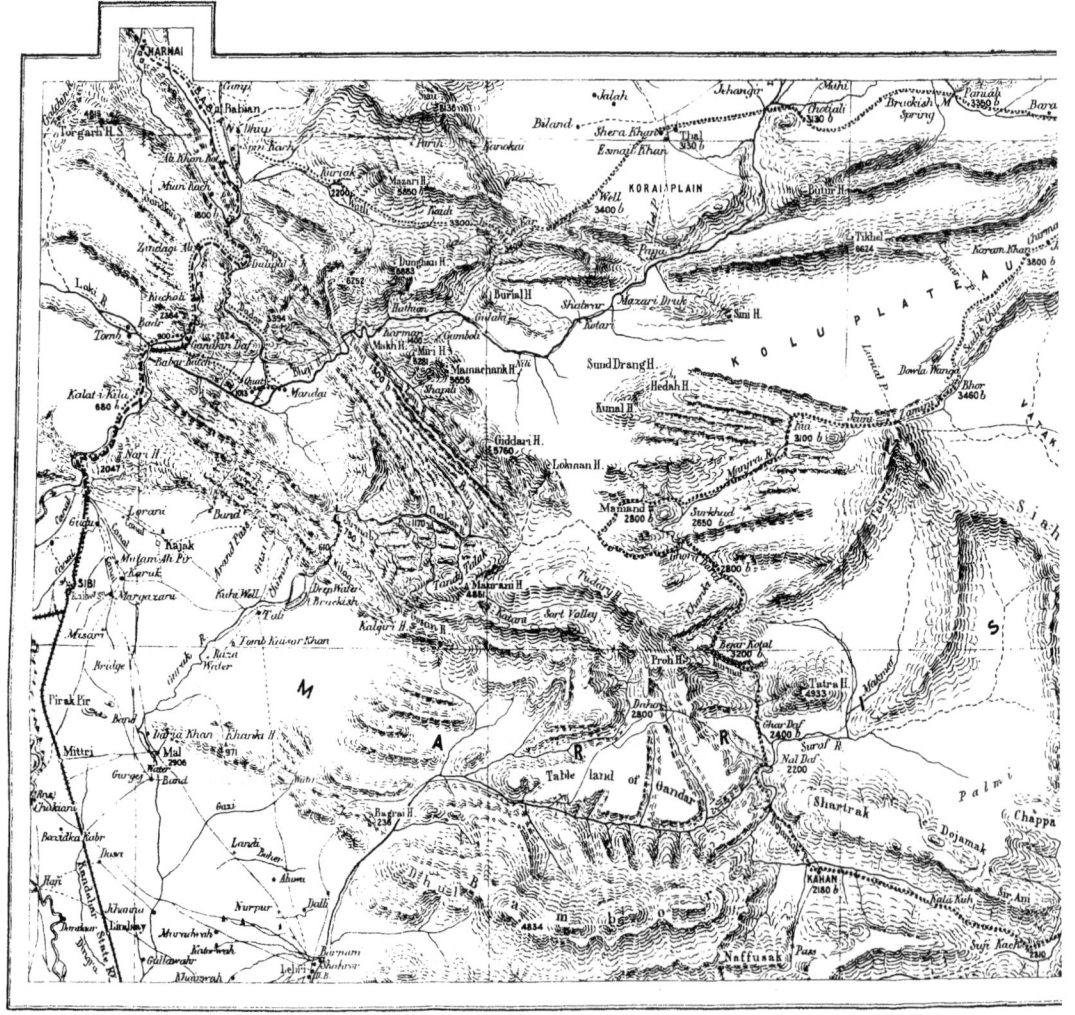

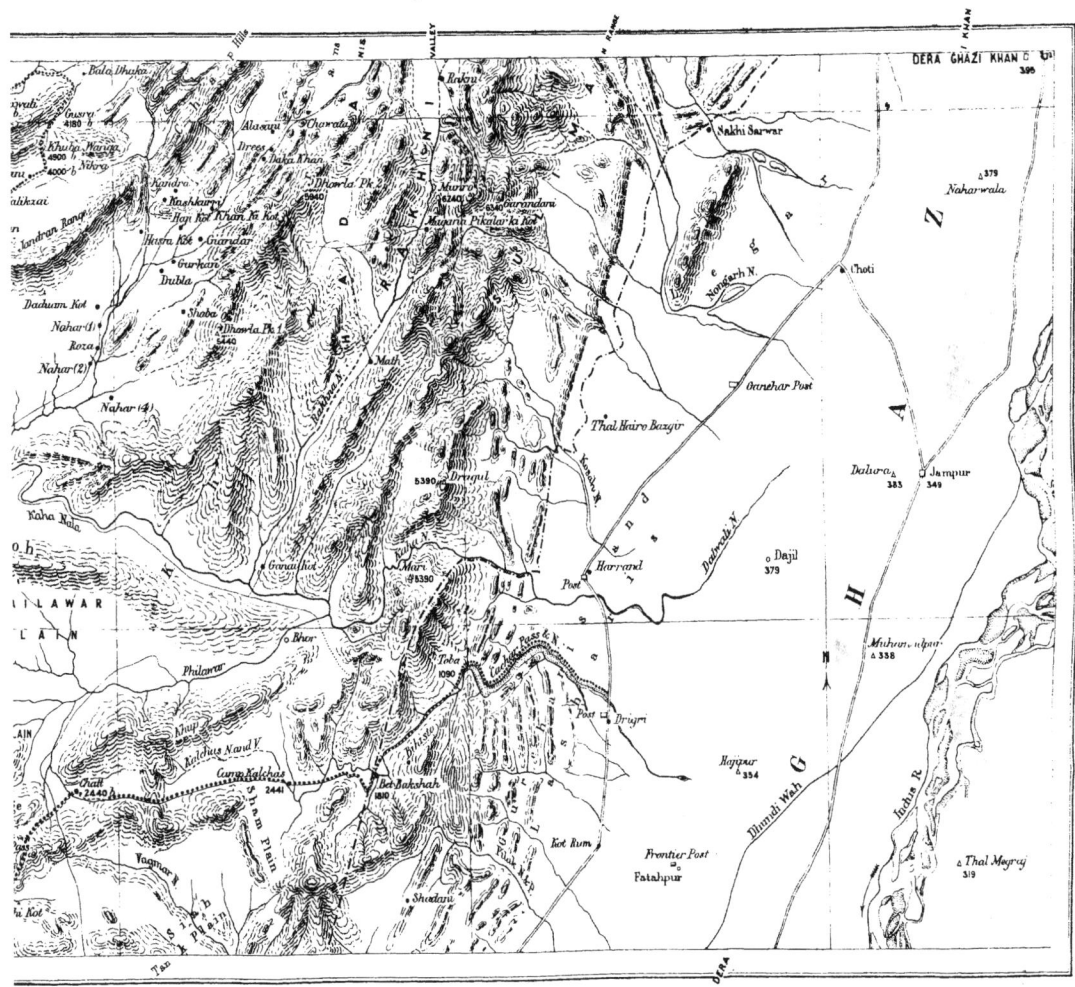

No. 4.429-I., 1908.

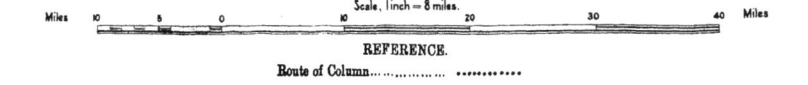

Scale, 1 inch = 8 miles.

REFERENCE.

Route of Column .... ••••••••••

EXPLANATORY SKETCH

Of the forcing of the KHAN BAND, held by the Bozdar Tribe against a force under BRIGADIER-GENERAL. N. CHAMBERLAIN, C. B., on the 7th March 1857.

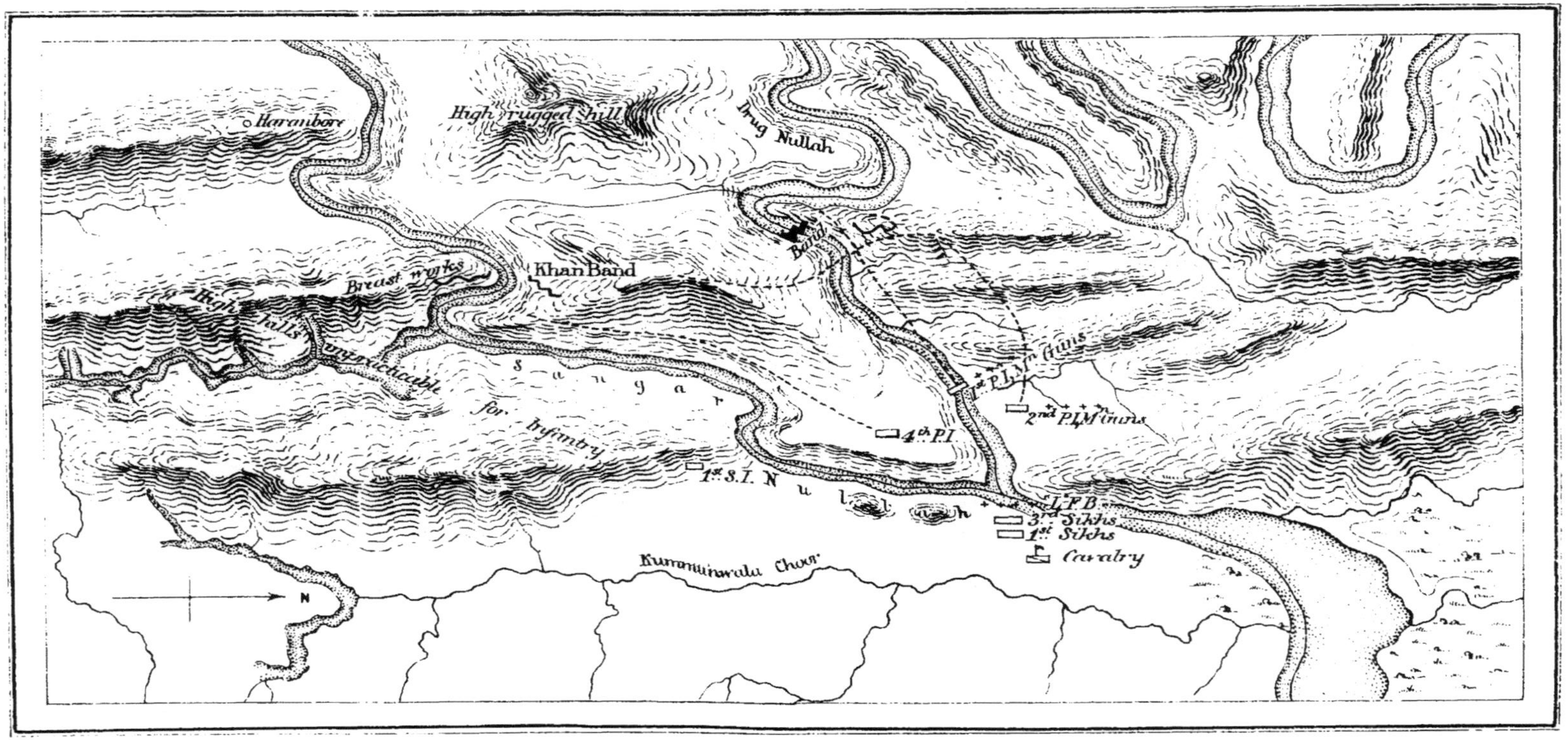

Scale 1 inch = 1 mile.

Yards 1000 0 1000 2000 3000 4000 5000 6000 Yards

I. B. Topo. Dy No. 7.274.
Exd. C. J. A. April 1908.

No. 4.430-I., 1908.

REFERENCES.

British Forces ... ... + + + +
Bozdars ,, ...
Routes taken by British Forces ... ... - - - - - - -

POCKET MAP No. II.
PART OF THE
SHIRANI COUNTRY

To illustrate the operations of the force under BRIGADIER-GENERAL HODGSON in 1853; the route followed by the SURVEY EXPEDITION to the TAKHT-I-SULIMAN in 1883, and THE ZHOB FIELD FORCE under SIR GEORGE WHITE in 1890.

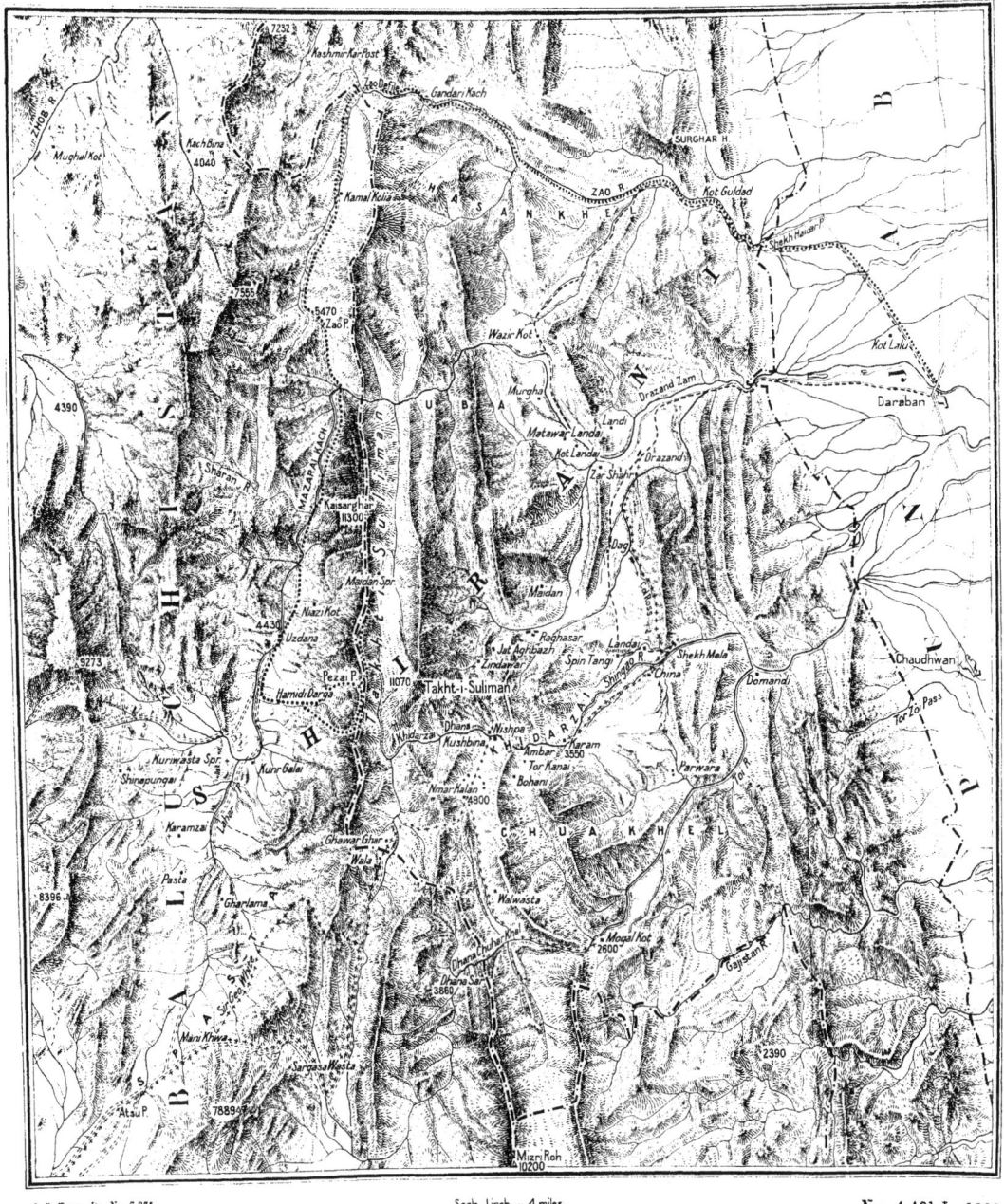

Scale. 1 inch = 4 miles.

REFERENCES.
Route of Expedition 1853 — — — — —
 " " " 1883 •••••••••••
 " " " 1890 + + + + + + +

No. 4.431-I., 1908.

Made in the USA
Monee, IL
12 August 2022